DROGHEDA: ITS PLACE IN IRELAND'S

DROGHEDA:

Its Place in Ireland's History

Ted Greene

First published in 2006 by
Ted Greene, Smithstown, Julianstown, Co. Meath.
Telephone number: 041-982 9067
www.arrowtours.ie

British Library Cataloguing in Publication Data is available

Printed and bound in Ireland by ColourBooks Ltd.

ISBN No: 0-9554518-0-9
978-0-9554518-0-5

Dust Jacket Montage:
Originations by Jimmy Weldon
From a concept by the Author.
Central photograph by Tony Murphy

SPONSORSHIP

In addition to the many willing hearts who have helped in bringing this work to fruition, there are several institutions and private individuals who have made a financial contribution. Its publication at a price level attractive to the average reader would not have been possible without funding from them.

Mention must be made ot Arrow Tours, whose facilities and general disposition were endlessly avail of. Also, on learning of the book's imminent publication, a member of a prominent Drogheda family, Eugene Kierans, President of the Drogheda Chamber of Commerce, expressed a wish to be associated with it, and offered an unsolicited and generous donation towards the printing costs.

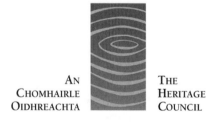

AN
CHOMHAIRLE
OIDHREACHTA

THE
HERITAGE
COUNCIL

This publication has received support from the Heritage
Council under the 2006 Publication Grant Scheme.

Ulster Bank
let's do things differently

DEDICATION

To the memory of my Parents,
Edward and Kathleen Greene
Who loved so well their native town.

Table of Contents

ACKNOWLEDGEMENTS

Researching the material for this work entailed delving into many existing history books and making contact with a great many people, and I hasten to acknowledge with unstinted thanks the assistance which they so kindly put my way. The goodwill with which the wealth of information was volunteered was in itself a great encouragement to me. Indeed, the wholeheartedness of the many interviewees has made my work 'a labour of delight' and has helped to establish new and genuine bonds of friendship.

First and foremost, the book owes much to historians of the past who have prepared the groundwork for this book. Secondly, one of its sections focuses on what I have termed 'living history', that is, recollections provided by some of Drogheda's oldest citizens – their input forms the backbone of one complete section of the book; these are word-pictures and experiences relating to the early part of the century that is now behind us. Their powers of recall are to be envied, and their depiction of scenes from their childhood enlighten and enrich us all. Notwithstanding their advanced years – some of them were nonagenarians and one was a sprightly centenarian – their memories were crystal clear and their description of scenes and events in Drogheda in olden days was remarkably vivid. Some of these veterans have not lived to see the completion of this book, having since gone to their eternal reward, and Drogheda is poorer without them. *Ar dheis Dé go raibh a anam.*

In the pursuit of historical information and the verification of facts I have enlisted the aid of friends and strangers alike. Those names that immediately come to mind include Liam Conlon; Jim Corcoran; Sheila Crehan; Paddy Cluskey; Ray Dempsey; Terry and Donal Fairclough; Dermot Foley; Jim Glennon, TD; E and J Hewson; Brendan Kerr; Dermot Kierans; Peter Leech; Brendan Matthews; Sr. Dominic McCarthy RSM; Malachy McCloskey; Sr. Colette McCloskey PBVM; John McCullen; Pat McDaid; Noel McVey; Anne-Marie Moroney; Anthony Murphy; Pat O'Mahony; Michael Reid; Tom Reilly, Seamus Roe; Noel Ross; Jackie Tallan; Jim Walsh, Balbriggan; Sr. Olivia DC; Ormonde Waters, and not forgetting Paula, Josie and Leo. Leo, though by no means an academician, has helped to keep the book's progress on schedule whenever my energy or enthusiasm was flagging with an occasional 'How is the book getting on'? I owe each a special debt, and if I have omitted the name of a contributor or two through a faulty memory I sincerely beg their indulgence.

I sought and obtained the expertise of a few professionals and skilled amateurs who, one again, gave freely and generously of their know-how and their time in shaping the fullness of the book. Drs. Matt and Geraldine Stout are to be envied in their Bohemian approach to life and for their in-depth knowledge of the subjects in which they specialise, archaeology and Irish history, and which they so freely impart – their enthusiasm in quite infectious. Dr. David Godden has proof-read the work, and his appreciation of the English language and its subtle nuances are reflected in many of these pages. If errors still appear, it is because of some last-minute additions to the text which bypassed his scrutiny. Who better to edit the completed work than someone who has behind him a lifetime's experience in journalism and editorship, and, as an added bonus, is a Droghedean with a keen knowledge of the town and its storied past; these desirable qualities exist in the person of Paul Murphy.

In the matter of photography, I am indebted to Tony Murphy and David Godden for several pictures. Jimmy Weldon has put his vast library of photographs, old and new, at my disposal; a selection of them is included here plus some fresh material which he willingly prepared. He makes light of every favour that is asked of him, and his middle name ought to be 'No Problem'. His wizardry is particularly evident in the book's dustcover.

The Old Drogheda Society has granted me the use of their archives. The material on Ballykinlar Prison Camp is by courtesy of the Fairclough family – Harry Fairclough, of course, was a founder member of the Society as well as being an enforced guest at Ballykinlar during the War of Independence. The benefits of the half-dozen books published by the Boyne Valley Honey Co. have been put at my disposal through the auspices of Malachy McCloskey. Others have facilitated me by granting me access to their valuable libraries of rare books and their private collections of historical artefacts and works of art. They wish to remain anonymous, but my gratitude is no less ardent.

I have availed of the services of several institutions and business houses. I wish to thank, for their help and courtesy, the management and staff of the Central Statistics Office, the County Louth Library, the Drogheda Borough Council, the Dundalk Museum, the Louth County Archives, the Heritage Service, the House of Lords Record Office, the Military Archives, the National Archives, the National Library of Ireland, the National Museum, the Office Public Works, the Old Drogheda Society, the Dept. of the Environment, Heritage and Local Government, the Drogheda Independent and the Drogheda Leader.

Today's generation is conversant with the Computer and is fully aware of its true worth in the performance of myriads of office tasks. In this regard I have been handicapped, being a relative newcomer to its capabilities, and finding a strangeness in grappling with its infinite functions. Here the helpful little team of Caoimhe Mulroy, Christine Mulroy and David Graham of 'Once Upon Design' have come to my rescue. Truly heroic has been Jim Walsh whose computer skills were always to hand. Ever courteous, ever obliging, ever patient, he has shepherded me through the labyrinth of its countless pathways in the furtherance of my objective and in the quest of excellence. His back-up is his dear wife Phil who has sustained us both, when burning the midnight oil, with coffee and home-made apple tart. I also owe the presentation of the several graphs, tables and some maps that appear within these pages to his adroitness. Indeed, the ultimate completion of this book to due in no small measure to Jim's outstanding skills at the Computer.

TO ONE AND ALL I BID A HEARTFELT THANKS.

INTRODUCTION

The Drogheda of today is a vibrant, thriving town, and, with its satellite villages, it is Ireland's largest. Its freely elected representatives are examples, as Abraham Lincoln might have phrased it, of 'government of the people, by the people, for the people'. It sounds almost trite to make that point today, but anyone who takes such circumstances for granted is overlooking a lengthy period of Ireland's past that was fraught with deprivation and suffering on a massive scale, and by the long and arduous struggle that was involved in attaining sovereignty and nationhood.

The Battle of Kinsale (1603) broke the back of Ireland's resistance to the English presence, but hopes rose again when the Gaelic clans combined with the Old English, giving rise to the Confederation of Kilkenny – it was formed near Beamore Cross, Drogheda and ratified a week later at Tara. It was crucial for the resurgent forces to capture Drogheda, following which Dublin would be at their mercy. The protracted Siege of the town (1641/42) failed, and this was a serious setback to the Confederate plans. Indeed, from the moment the Siege was lifted the destiny of Ireland slid downwards into a deep and dark abyss. A few years later (1649) Cromwell demonstrated how effectively a town could be taken, and thereafter Ireland was racked by torment that was to last for almost 3 centuries.

Cromwell was a remarkably successful leader – his unwelcome appearance in Ireland in 1649/50 paralysed its people with fear. His brief visit had the effect of a bolt of lightning, and its rumbling after-effects are still being felt today. What the Anglo-Normans had failed to achieve in the course of 450 years – the submission of the entire island – this man accomplished in nine months. His storming of Drogheda together with King William of Orange's victory in the Battle of the Boyne which occurred only 41 years later, had a profound and permanent effect on Ireland's subsequent history, precipitating the majority of the populace into a dark age of discrimination and marginalisation. These two events were elemental factors in shaping the fate of the nation and the subsequent destiny of its people, and Drogheda played a pivotal part in them.

It is true that the relating of major events such as the visits by Cromwell and William of Orange lose impact unless they are presented in their proper context. The *background* always provides added value when recounting them because this enables us to visualise the scenes in their conjoined perspective. The proximity to Drogheda of the actual battle-ground of the Battle of the Boyne, for example, tends to obscure the fact – at least for locals – that that battle was just one episode in a pan-European war in which the Boyne played only a momentary but crucial part. That battle was not a simple case of King James confronting King William over the English Crown. Much more than that, it was King Louis XIV of France, the splendid 'Sun King', versus most of the states of Europe. *Even the Pope took a lively interest in the affair and sided with the Protestant King William!* The luckless James was being used merely as a cat's-paw in a European struggle, and the Catholic/Irish dimension was incidental to the main plot.

Likewise, when a dejected Red Hugh O'Neill passed through Drogheda, having just signed the Treaty of Mellifont, it formed part of a much wider picture in which Kinsale was the focal point. In the period leading up to the Battle of Kinsale

England's grip on Ireland had become very tenuous and was all but relinquished. It was another of those crucial moments when Ireland's destiny hung in the balance.

Such events in our history, insofar as they relate to Drogheda, are recounted in these pages, and at the same time the relevant *background* is also furnished, rendering the episodes more complete. In piecing together these and other events in Drogheda's storied past my original objective grew far beyond its modest intentions until it embraced, not only the momentous events of the 1600s and other crucial occurrences such as the Great Famine, but also the very origins of the town itself and its later development. Indeed, the major challenge has been to contain so many events within the confines of one single volume.

*   *   *   *   *

This book is essentially a synthesis of studies undertaken by learned authors of the past who have researched well their subject-matter, and in addition some primary sources have been consulted. In that way the major events of Ireland's history, insofar as they affect Drogheda (and vice versa), have been drawn together into a single book. It is hoped they will give the non-specialist an overview of the part played by Drogheda in Ireland's mercurial past.

PART 1

THE FIRST FOUR THOUSAND YEARS

Chapter One

The 'Cradle' in which Drogheda was Born

THE EARLY RESIDENTS: The valley of the River Boyne has been the scene of human activity from the time that prehistoric communities first stepped upon the shores of Ireland. Its fertile hinterland has induced them to settle down there, to clear the forests and the undergrowth and then to cultivate the land and to coax the bountiful fruits of nature from the generous soil. Traces of early human habitation are still constantly coming to light, and these finds tell us that from earliest times the general region of south Louth and Meath was the 'cradle' in which the early arrivals obtained sustenance, resulting in an inevitable growth in their numbers and strength. In the fullness of time the region has given rise to the thriving town of Drogheda. In a manner of speaking, the Boyne's course is the town's jugular vein, and its tributaries and broad hinterland constitute its arteries and its sinews, giving it nourishment and strength.

How did the town of Drogheda come into being? What were the components that gave rise to its foundation and growth? Why is it sited in the particular place that it occupies? Little Topsy might answer these searching questions on the town's origins with the disarming reply that 'It just growed'. But there is much more to it than that. To deal fully with these matters it is necessary to step back in time many millennia. The component parts from which the town sprung encompass a wide geographical area and extend along a broad band of the river Boyne, and were some thousands of years in the making. It is necessary for us to recount these because they were essential elements in Drogheda's birth and subsequent development.

So in tracing the town's origins and inevitable blossoming into full flower, we must of necessity follow the river's lazy course as it wanders over the green, lush pastures and the rich, arable lands that make up the valley of the Boyne and the overall region that embraces south Louth and Meath. The Elizabethan poet Spenser referred to it as 'the pleasant Boyne'. The exact source of the river is in Offaly, at a little spring or 'holy well' called Trinity Well near the village of Carbury, and almost on the very border with County Kildare. In pre-Christian times the well was known as 'Segais' and is bound up with mythology. Boann, the wife of Nechtain, the King of Leinster broke its spell by walking around it. The waters rose up and blinded her in one eye, whereupon she fled towards the sea. The waters followed her, forming the course of the river which today bears her name. It is on its middle and lower course that we will now focus our attention, because it is to that region in particular that the early residents were drawn, and it was there that they concentrated their activities, establishing their family clusters and nucleated settlements.

From Trim to the sandy seashore at Baltray and Mornington the gently flowing river wends its way past history and pre-history almost at every bend. In the heartland of Meath and a short distance from the river basin is located Tara, and it behoves us to refer to it as *Royal* Tara because there we ponder over the tantalising scraps of evidence that indicate the site of Ireland's kingly residence, where the high kings received tribute from subordinate Celtic chiefs. The territories of these lesser kings set the boundaries which, in the fullness of time, became the counties of *Lughbhaidhe* and *Midhe*. Further downstream we gaze with a mixture of puzzlement and awe at the mysteries in stone left by Neolithic Man in a much earlier era.

Later, when the Anglo-Normans arrived, King Henry II very soon supplanted the existing kingships with his own powerful overlords, Bertram de Verdon in Louth and Hugh de Lacy in Meath. These chiefs subdivided their territories among lesser vassals who most certainly were content with their lot; and de Lacy made a shrewd decision when he built his own prestigious castle by the very banks of the Boyne at Trim. The river's course was his main avenue leading to the estuary from whence he could make the short sea crossing to his country of origin. In a later era the region's tranquillity was shattered by angry, belching cannon when two kings disputed England's crown on its green, grassy slopes. However, that was about five thousand years from where our story begins.

Relics of the Past: Today, having stepped across the threshold of time into the third millennium AD, it is a rewarding experience for the enquiring mind to inspect the monuments of the remote past at Brú na Bóinne. The focal point of the entire site has been moved across the river close to the storied village of Donore where an Interpretative Centre and a partial reconstruction of the Newgrange chamber serve the visitor and the student of pre-history with a wealth of information. This arrangement was a compromise, and was necessary because of the detrimental effect of the throngs of sightseers to the ancient structures which are now Ireland's premier tourist attraction. This is in contrast to former times when visitors to Newgrange were few and infrequent; the tumulus had been in a state of neglect and was indifferently referred to by the locals as 'the caves'. Cattle grazed on its grassy roof which was crowned with a few stately oaks. This author recalls being taken there as a child in the nineteen-thirties when, in crossing the field to the tumulus, one had to be vigilant to avoid stepping on the many cowpats. A greater hazard for a barelegged boy was the forest of tall, inhospitable nettles that guarded the entrance to the chamber. This in itself was evidence of the infrequency of visitors and of the general neglect. Nowadays Newgrange is receiving the attention it deserves, drawing close on 200,000 visitors annually and they arrive from every corner of the globe – all eager to learn more about Ireland's remote past. It is one of the world's most important archaeological landscapes, and has been designated a World Heritage Site by UNESCO.

Newgrange:
as it appeared prior to the work carried out by archaeologists.

Our thirst for knowledge has been whetted, and we want to know more about the early arrivals to our shore. It would certainly be an injustice to the Stone Age People if we were to accept the passage-graves as being their sole achievement. Their creations have suffered through the damage wrought by the ignorance of their successors of recent centuries. Apart from that they have withstood the weathering by the elements, and are in a remarkably good state of preservation. We should not study them in isolation, but we should endeavour to peer through the mists of time and visualise the lifestyle of those who built them. What we see today is enough to tell us that they were a sophisticated society. Everything on display at the Interpretative Centre points to an advanced, civilised people who possessed a high degree of intelligence. Articles found at Newgrange include arrowheads and other hunting weapons, scrapers and other domestic tools, although other finds such as precious personal ornaments, gold rings, bracelets, coins and pottery came later.

Those who peopled the landscape were domesticated farmers who lived in small communities. They led a pastoral existence, living in farmsteads. Bones and other such clues found scattered throughout the area tell us that they herded cattle, sheep, pigs and goats, and in addition to farm animals, they kept a dog or two; they also grew corn. They supplemented their fare by hunting so that an occasional rump of venison or wild boar provided variety to their diet. All land was held in common, there being no individual ownership of property, and the people were grouped into natural family clans.

The massive tumuli which we see today could not have been built by a people who were either impoverished or indolent – this is clear from the prodigious amount of endeavour that was invested in their construction. The work demanded creativity, initiative and energy on an enormous scale in overcoming the challenges of that era, using such limited tools as were at their disposal. The Bronze Age had not yet arrived, but nonetheless Neolithic Man succeeded in making life an agreeable and relatively comfortable experience.

The region, by inference, was well populated. '...when the great tombs were being built, a population of some 4,000 people based on 'urban' dwellings were carrying out large scale farming in the Boyne valley.'[1] All this had an influence on the surrounding countryside, the virgin forests and scrubland being selectively cleared as the population grew. The heavily forested wilderness adjoining the river was shorn of trees to create clearings for grazing livestock, cultivating crops and accommodating small communities for the performance of their daily routine.

It was no accident that a bountiful river flowed right beside them – it teemed with salmon. The absence of roads and the dense wilderness meant that the river Boyne was the all-important highway that took people upstream and down to the open sea. In particular, this gently flowing river was a godsend for transporting the massive boulders and other construction materials to the building site at Brú na Bóinne. (The site in more recent times is referred to as 'The Bend of the Boyne', which is a more meaningful title, especially to foreign visitors and those who have no knowledge of Irish. 'Brú' or 'Bruagh' is a palace, a word that does not describe the function of these edifices). The river was navigable for about 30 km. from its mouth, and as they wended their way upstream these early inhabitants passed through one particular area, where at a time in the distant future the town we know as Drogheda was destined to stand.

Some answers are sought: where did these people at the Bend of the Boyne come from? Opinions vary, some favour North-West France where there are stone structures similar to those in Ireland; but the eminent professor Frank Mitchell, who lived locally, opted for Britain from whose western hilltops Ireland could be seen on a clear day; and it presented the advantage of a short sea crossing. They did not come in one great invading force, but more likely they arrived in small family groupings. At what point of the coast did they step ashore? Much of the periphery of the island consists of uninviting hills, mountains and indifferent terrain, but there is a significant section along the east coast stretching from the Mournes to Wicklow which is covered, not with bogland or unfriendly, sterile mountains, but with rich alluvial soil which, with the application of human endeavour, would yield bountiful rewards. This was indeed an enticing landfall for those in search of a new life. The Boyne beckoned.

The region was well stocked with salmon and eels; wild pigs and deer were aplenty along with other creatures that roamed the woodlands. Work on building the Passage Tombs did not commence immediately. The evidence indicates a lengthy period of continuous habitation long before the tumuli were built.

The site was well chosen, the fruitful alluvial soil presenting an important balance between tillage and grazing. The riparian alder trees fringed the river, while oak, elm, ash, hazel and birch otherwise dominated the landscape. The domestic livestock which the newcomers brought with them made them largely self sufficient, and they tilled the soil and planted the precious seed-corn which they also brought with them. A hierarchical system probably existed and they honoured their chiefs in death, and thus in the course of time they set about constructing their 'cathedrals' wherein the priests performed their mysterious rites and ritual burials. Even if most other traces of their existence has disappeared, at least they have left these Passage Graves for us to marvel at – structures which have defied the ravages that five millennia of time can inflict.

They also represent a monumental pile of mysteries that remain a challenge for modern man to ponder over, enigmas in search of insoluble answers. The area contains in excess of 600 stones decorated with abstract art[2] – twice as many as exist at all other Neolithic sites put together, including those in Continental Europe.

What was the significance of the circles, lozenges, zig-zags and other geometric figures that were painstakingly etched on the boulders? Such figures were common among other prehistoric societies. (Strikingly similar designs were inscribed, coincidentally, by early Indians on rocks in the Arizona Desert and also by Aboriginals in the Australian outback). They were much more than casual graffiti or decorations. Perhaps they have some astronomical significance? But it is beyond our wildest expectation that another Rosetta Stone will be found to provide the key to unravelling this intriguing puzzle.

What is certain is that a considerable amount of surplus wealth (in whatever form, but mostly cattle) must have been at hand to sustain such protracted and *non-productive* labour. This in itself is demonstrative evidence of the margin they created between survival conditions and comfortable living standards. It is estimated that the construction of the Newgrange tumulus absorbed the efforts of a sizeable army of men over a period of about forty years – thus covering several life-spans. The total weight of the stones and boulders used is estimated at 200,000 tonnes. Sadly, at one stage in the not too distant past the site was used as a convenient quarry, and untold cartloads of stones were removed to pave local roadways. Other important features have disappeared without trace.

When we peer through the mists of time we see a sophisticated and closely-knit people. The mean temperature which they experienced was several degrees higher than is ours today, and thus they enjoyed a warmer climate. The spin-off was that vegetation had an extended growing season, (say) about eleven months of the year, and livestock thrived in consequence on fresh grass – a real bonus for the farmer. We are entitled to conclude that the populace enjoyed a relatively comfortable lifestyle enabling them accumulate such surplus funds that were utilised in sustaining the teams engaged in the construction work – funds which would yield no tangible return, but only spiritual satisfaction. The creation of Newgrange was a colossal achievement by any standard: –

- A well-regulated, **structured society with a central authority** must have existed to enable prehistoric man undertake these awesome projects.
- Since the life span of the people was little more than 35 years at that time, their civilisation was not of short duration but was continuous, and **flowered over an extended period of time.**
- The construction work, which took perhaps 40 years to complete, called for clear thinking and for **forward planning**, the over-all scheme being handed on for completion to the generations that followed.
- Knowledge of the existence of suitable building material in distant regions is indicative of reliable and regular **lines of communication.** Some of the materials used came from nearby Clogherhead (the evidence of their work is still to be seen on the rocky Head), while far away Wicklow and the Mourne Mountains were the probable sources of the snow-white quartz and in particular the enormous granite boulders. The selecting of suitable building material from such distant places tell us that the builders were in constant touch with those areas and with the people who occupied them – all without the use of cell-phones!
- Mathematical skills and the **expertise of "professionals",** viz. architects and engineers were employed. The drainage experts did their work well because Newgrange's roof still admits no rainwater. The existence of allied megalithic structures in Malta, Brittany and elsewhere lead us to conclude that expertise was brought here from the continent. This infers that there were close and constant lines of communication with mainland Europe.
- When suitable boulders were selected, there remained the mammoth task of transporting them, some weighing up to five tons. The tools of the Iron Age were still a long way off. All was achieved by **muscle, sweat, ingenuity and the co-ordination** of a dedicated society.
- The accumulated evidence of so much activity clustered around "the Bend of the Boyne" indicates that the general region supported **a dense population,** and people converged on the area from afar.

- A crucial **division of labour** was necessary to allow the gangs of workers leave their abodes and set off for the Mourne Mountains, select boulders suitable to their needs, man-handle them many miles to the shore, prepare rafts to transport them along the coast and then ferry them up the course of the Boyne to their final destination. (Would a dedicated work-gang deliver half a dozen of these colossal boulders in a single season?). Newgrange has 500 and Knowth 1,500 such boulders. While the men were away, it was vital to arrange that others stay back to till the fields, milk the cows, tend the livestock as well as look after the young and the elderly.

- These people were obviously not living from hand to mouth – they lived well. Their living conditions enabled them to **accumulate surplus resources** for launching and completing this ambitious civic project.

- A necessary evil was **a system of raising the taxes** required to fund the project – yes, they were probably harassed by civil servants and income tax inspectors, just like today!

- In particular, we marvel at their **in-depth knowledge of astronomy** that enabled the position of the completed edifice to be predetermined with such exactitude that a shaft of sunlight would penetrate the passageway and illuminate the central chamber precisely as the sun peeped over the horizon at its perigee.

NEWGRANGE: The entrance in olden times

There is nothing in creation more inflexible or incorruptible than a sunbeam. So no guesswork was permitted in predetermining the route of the shaft of light at it entered the central chamber. Until recent times archaeologists had regarded as an irrelevance the aperture over the entrance (although tradition had hinted otherwise). But in 1967 its significance was confirmed. It is, in fact, a roof-box or "fanlight", and this emphasises the ingenuity and skills of its creators. It meant that on the occasion when the ribbon was being cut at the 'official opening ceremony' five thousand years ago the entire work had been completed with such exactitude that, precisely at the winter solstice, the morning shaft of golden sunlight passed through the 'fanlight' at the entrance, and shot along the 19m. passageway to be captured with pin-point accuracy in the inky blackness of the central chamber. It was spot on! Surely it was an occasion for the champagne corks to pop at the inaugural ceremony – provided, of course, that the occasion was not spoiled by an overcast sky!

It was, however, a triumphal moment in Time, when Nature's glory was corralled by Man, fallible as he is. Fallible, yes, but Mankind was always imbued with an indomitable spirit of endeavour, that same spirit which in a much later time resulted in such crowning achievements as the Theory of Relativity and putting a man on the Moon. The complex structures at the Bend of the Boyne are a manifestation of his unending quest for knowledge – they represent 'one giant leap for Mankind' – preludes to inventing the computer and splitting the atom. The many comforts of every-day living that we enjoy in the 21st Century are indirect bonuses arising from Stone Age Man gazing at the firmament and asking *'WHY?'*

In the matter of durability, Newgrange has the distinction of being the oldest roofed building in the world. Follow that!

Archaeologists today at the Bend of the Boyne spend endless hours in piecing together the clues to the social life and living conditions of our predecessors – they have been at work there, on and off, for several centuries. Their methodical, pains-taking and delicate work still continues to bear fruit and new evidence regularly comes to light. It also enables the experts to deduce more and more information on their habits and their way of life.

A particularly fruitful source of information was presented (c. 2000) when the Drogheda Bypass (the M1 Motorway) was under construction. This work entailed cutting a broad, deep ribbon into the terrain – it is 17km in length from the River Nanny to Monasterboice, encircling Drogheda. A veritable repository of ancient artifacts came to light, indicating a concentrated presence of prehistoric settlements throughout the whole area. Habitation sites, timber circles and cooking pits containing cremated bones, flints and sundry pottery shards were found, making it an Aladdin's Cave for the archaeologists. These revelations repeat the message that the entire region of the Boyne valley abounds with evidence of sustained prehistoric occupation[3] and prompt us to reappraise upwards the extent and the concentration of activity throughout the area.

The information wheedled from the soil so far by architects is truly astonishing, and the discoveries are unending. Continued probing has established that there exists a synchronised alignment between the edifices at all three locations at the Bend of the Boyne – Newgrange, Dowth and Knowth. It has now been established that Dowth is aligned to the position of the *setting* sun at the winter solstice. The passageway is considerably shorter, being only 3m., but the phenomenon here, if anything, is more spectacular because the beam of light is larger and remains longer than that at Newgrange. If weather conditions at the winter solstice did not allow Stone Age Man to observe the miracle of the dawn at Newgrange, then Dowth was able to oblige with a sundown performance! Professor Herity stated that this is 'of world shattering significance, if true'. He needn't have doubted it, because *it is true!* Anne-Marie Moroney has studied the phenomenon at length, has taken photos of it and she tells us in her publication *Dowth: Winter Sunsets* that

> *'The two passage tombs Newgrange and Dowth share the special solar event making the end of one year the promise of a new beginning. Dowth South receives the beams of the evening sun for about two hours before nightfall. ... The beam of the sun is so strong that the whole chamber is lit up'*[4].

We pause in astonishment that '… the astronomy of Newgrange can no longer be discussed realistically without taking into account that it is part of the intricate system which includes Dowth and Knowth. …[These structures are] not riddles or follies but living testimony to the indomitable spirit of a Stone Age people, who built, not only for themselves, but for future generations.'[5]

We are presented with the realisation that the whole region that encompasses the Boyne valley, strewn as it is with souterrains, ring forts, graves, and objects of antiquity of one kind or another, sustained in those far off times a sophisticated population of considerable density. This is evident from the 20 further sites that are dotted around the area which await excavation. 'The valley must have presented a magnificent site, a thriving, bustling centre such as the island had never previously known. Today the remains survive as reminders of a great civilisation, sadly long silenced'.

Were these people our forefathers? It is an unlikely possibility that we carry any of their genes – they probably became extinct in the course of several thousands of years. What they did for us was to tame the landscape and render the area habitable for the people that followed. They made the Boyne valley a focal point and a suitable home for the intrepid adventurers of later periods.

As with all other ancient civilisations, this one that inhabited the Boyne valley eventually underwent changes from external forces. This happened about 2000 BC. The cause we do not know. Did newcomers to Ireland kill them off in combat? Or perhaps the indigenous people succumbed to some contagion carried in by the newcomers? (Consider the devastating effect on the native American population when the white man arrived and introduced, however unintentionally, a series of Old World diseases against which the Indians had no natural defence). Research tells us that the long-term climate turned very wet from about 2,000 BC, and this would have had an adverse effect on tillage and general farming conditions, causing hardship and bringing about a population decline.

A pall of oblivion descended, in the course of which the existing civilisation gradually faded away, leaving us with a profusion of unanswered questions. The massive stones remain silent, and yield up their secrets all too slowly. Thus we are left to ponder over the era of obscurity that followed, an era which was to continue for a further two thousand years. We know that 'the beaker people' (so called because of the quantities of beaker shards found at their sites) later occupied the area, and it is possible that the two sets of people lived side by side. Later still another race of people arrived – we call them the Celts.

THE CELTS: The Celts had come from central Europe and the upper basin of the Danube in a slow, peripatetic migration along the lands adjoining the Mediterranean Sea. They were quite primitive and barbaric, and were more adept at tearing down the habitations of other tribes that they encountered on their wanderings rather than constructing ones of their own. By about 500 BC they had reached Ireland. Whether they assimilated the existing peoples or exterminated them we do not know. They were bellicose by nature, and we know that in Gaul they were a constant thorn in the side of the Roman armies whom they regularly encountered in the course of the empire's expansion.

They evidently found Ireland suitable to their needs, for they settled down to make it their permanent home, and there they were left undisturbed by outside intrusion for over a thousand years. This enabled them engage in cattle raids, skirmishes and internecine wars to their hearts' content. They were individualistic by nature rather than gregarious, so that there was little in the nature of a central governmental structure to bind them and regulate their lives. Crucially, they lacked unity, a shortcoming that would in the course of time militate against their progeny when facing in succession the Vikings, the Normans and the English.

The Celts placed great value on education and oral tradition; they fostered druids, poets, harpists, story-tellers and historians, but all of their knowledge was passed down orally from generation to generation. They were a fun loving people, at times hospitable and generous, and had an artistic flair, as the surviving artefacts and pieces of personal ornamentation clearly show. They were fond of music, dancing and song, traits that have been handed down to their descendants of the twenty-first century. They were also superstitious and credulous, but these latter traits somehow went astray in the transmission of their genes prior to the present day – their more pragmatic descendants no longer believe in leprechauns and fairies!

The various Celtic sects occupied lands ranging from Turkey and Greece to Iberia, Brittany and Cornwall. The particular branch which is now the subject of our discourse was the only one in the effusion of time to establish a distinct sovereign state, and it was that race of people who were the progenitors of the Irish nation.

A Well-populated Region: The mist of prehistory that enveloped the great Passage Graves and their people did not begin to dissipate until the dawn of the Christian era. It was Saint Patrick and his followers who would later set the Celts on the course of enlightenment. Tara in time became the hub of activity and the seat of the high kings; Cormac Mac Art founded three colleges there, and in those flourishing times the Tailtean Games were a feature. Today there is little trace of the structures that existed in that era. Such factors would have had an influence on the demographics of the Meath area, giving rise to a multitude of scattered habitations, nucleated settlements and other civic structures such as ring forts and roadways. We know that at that time five roads radiated from Tara, although they were impermanent and their construction lacked the skills such as were employed on the Roman roads of Britain. During the 1990s and into the new millennium a government-funded programme has enabled a team of archaeologists to explore the whole Tara complex. They have identified ten new sites in the area.

All these discoveries again indicate a thriving, populous community. They mark a significant advance in our knowledge of settlement patterns, showing just how populated the general landscape was throughout earlier millennia. Their habitations often took the form of collective ring forts or *raths*, and even if we find but little visible evidence of these today, we have clues of their location in the names of local townlands, e.g. Beg*rath*, Cruice*rath,* the Hill of *Rath*, *Rath*mullen, *Rath*kenny, Town*rath* – there are dozens of them.

THE ROMANS: When Julius Caesar completed his conquest of Gaul he then set his sights on Britannia. He led expeditions there in 55 and 54 BC – the rest is history. According to Shakespeare, Brutus criticised Caesar of being ambitious, but evidently he was not that ambitious as to make the short sea crossing over to the green and misty isle further to the west.

His writings tell us of his many bloody encounters with the Celts in the course of the Gallic wars and of his difficulty in subduing them. Experience told him that they were quarrelsome among themselves as well as with others. He was not alone with these impressions of the Celts; the Greek geographer Strabo thought that Ireland was where 'the limits of the known world should be placed' and that it was the extreme cold that made the people so savage.[6] Perhaps he was right! He added, "The whole race is madly fond of war". Right again! Thankfully, Caesar's memoirs, which were the bane of every Latin scholar's studies up until Vatican II, have now been consigned to the dusty attic. Only once in his writings does Julius Caesar mention Ireland – he states that it was *'INHABITED BY A FIERCE AND WARLIKE PEOPLE'*. Good Heavens! Surely they are not *that* bad! Anyway, he dismisses the island and its people with those few disparaging words.

Both Britannia and Hibernia remained in the era of prehistory up to the time of Caesar's arrival. With his approach to the white cliffs of Dover (which prompted him to use the name 'Alba', being Latin for 'white') the destinies of the two islands diverged. Britain came under the influence of Imperial Rome – but Ireland did not. It is Ireland's great loss that the Romans, even with their conflicting traits of sophisticated domesticity and brutal forms of entertainment and punishment, did not extend their Empire to encompass Hibernia. Ireland was destined to remain pre-literate for another 400 years until the arrival of Christianity.

The priceless legacies of learning, an advanced civic structure and *Lex Romana* were introduced to the Britons by the Romans. No longer was the populace depending solely on word of mouth when trading and negotiating contracts. A fundamental Roman precept which had universal application was that *Ignoratio legis non excusat* (Ignorance of the law is no excuse) so that every citizen knew where he stood in his dealings with others. He was now able to conduct business, to agree contracts and to settle disputes without resorting to the sword and shedding blood.

They also introduced a fresh gene strain, genes of proven quality. Wherever they went, the Romans brought profound changes to the peoples they conquered, replacing chaos with order. With conquest came the Latin language and literacy; they replaced ignorance with their progressive brand of civilisation, albeit in a heavy-handed and often cruel manner. As Frank Mitchell put it: "The keystone of their empire was order, order in law, order in

10

language, order in thought."[7] Order is a quality in which the Celts, the precursors of the Irish people, was often found wanting. Let us here indulge for a few moments in further comparisons:

The attribute of civic order is still evident in the Britain of today, whereas the Irish are more fun loving, individualistic and, it has to be said, often wayward, feckless and disunited. These traits would frequently recoil on them in the centuries ahead especially in their endeavours to throw off the foreign yoke. Those who peopled Ireland at the time of the Roman Empire were not a 'nation' in any sense of the word. They were simply a loose collection of disparate tribes of 'wandering Celts', complete with little more than their herds of livestock and some crude tools. Cattle rustling and inter-tribal warfare was their wont. Their wealth was mainly in the form of cattle, assets that are conveniently mobile, obviating the need for wheeled vehicles and therefore roadways. Of towns and cities there were none. The Roman influence would have brought the benefits of communal life and social discipline together with a set of laws under which all could live regulated lives in relative harmony.

A transformation took place in Britain during the four hundred years of Roman occupation. The newcomers brought with them those attributes that had enabled them extend the boundaries of their empire until it encompassed much of the known world. In particular, they introduced a code of civic laws – *Lex Romana*. This was the bedrock that promoted civic order.

They founded Londinium on the Thames, which was destined in the course of time to become the capital of another vast empire. They established a host of other towns that still thrive today – Chester, Dorchester, Gloucester, Lincoln, Manchester, York, and many more. This growth of urban communities transformed rude, uncultured peasants into law-abiding citizens. They mutually benefited from pooled knowledge and resources, and they were able to pursue their daily routine without molestation. They reciprocated with a commitment of fealty to the community of which they formed part.

Fairs and markets sprang up, and commerce was greatly facilitated by the introduction of coinage. This stimulated trade, bringing prosperity and wealth in its wake. Living conditions improved; the exchange of ideas promoted knowledge and education – even the common Roman foot soldiers could read and write. Civic amenities such as public buildings, roads, bridges, amphitheatres and public baths were constructed.

A network of inter-linking roads (some survive today) bound the inhabitants of these towns together, promoting commerce and inter-communication. This constituted an environment suitable for planting the seeds from which a greater nation would one day blossom. This cohesive civic structure was kept in place by the well-disciplined Roman Legions, an army that was geared at all times, not only to quell internal strife, but also to repel any threat from without. The fusion in later times of the native tongues with the Romantic French introduced by the Normans was the foundation of that language which is spoken today in places ranging from Drogheda to New York and Sydney and Hong Kong and Cape Town.

The town of Chester was one of the important Roman centres, and it still abounds with evidence of Roman occupation, including an amphitheatre sited next to the town's present day main street. The short sea crossing via Holyhead made commercial traffic with Ireland feasible. There is evidence that they established settlements along Ireland's east coast e.g. on Lambay Island. At Loughshinney, an hour's sailing south of the Boyne, there are traces of a Roman colony covering 40 acres and this may have contained up to 5,000 inhabitants.

In any event it would seem that the inclement weather encountered in the tentative Roman settlements was not what they were accustomed to back home in sunny Italia, so they dubbed the country *'Hibernia'*, and decamped without further ado. Students of the classics will know that *'Hibernia'* is Latin for *'Winter'*. (Alternatively, the name may have derived from a visitor named Heberus who arrived in a much earlier era, while others speculate that the name originates in the Spanish river Hiberus, from whence the Hibernians came.[8]

A Loss to The Celts: Thus, Ireland was denied all the advances in civilisation that a Roman occupation would have introduced. This crucially placed Ireland four hundred years behind

Britannia in matters of social advancement and of a civic infrastructure – no towns or villages, no durable homes, no paved roads, no municipal buildings, no public baths or amphitheatres. Nor was there a medium of exchange, a factor which would have facilitated trade and commerce. (Even in later times when the Vikings were using coinage in Dublin, it did not quickly catch on with the indigenous people). Above all, no literacy and no *Lex Romana*.

Instead, the Celts were still floundering in the backwater of pre-history, enveloped by the swirling mist of ignorance. They were indulging in desultory, uncoordinated tribal warfare, still engaging in rustling cattle from their neighbours. It meant, too, a lack of unity and cohesiveness – essential requirements when repelling an invader in the event of that danger reaching the shores of the land they had made their permanent home. The concept of nationhood was a long, long way off.

Trading and commerce did occur between the neighbouring islands, and such contacts would have pointed the way towards a better life-style. Whatever the extent of Roman penetration of the Boyne may have been, the Roman influence was nonetheless informal and impermanent. Later, the Irish took advantage of the Empire's decline, and raids on Roman Britain for plunder and slaves became a feature. One particular captive who was set to work as a shepherd made his escape, but he subsequently returned of his own volition, and tradition tells us that his crusade took him up the Boyne to Slane. The changes that followed that particular event were the origin of Ireland's most splendid period, and the person in question is honoured at Ireland's national saint.

Roman coins (about 25 in all, showing a variety of dates ranging over a time span of 300 years) and other artefacts of Roman origin have been found at Newgrange. These are presumed to be votive offerings to the gods. Does that mean that the intrepid Romans ventured up the Boyne? They almost certainly did. And does it mean that they passed through Drogheda? We will discuss this possibility further on. Additional evidence of their presence in the locality has been found at Lambay Island, Bettystown and at the Hill of Tara.

An Eroding Coast-line: The intrepid Romans might well have encountered difficulty in negotiating the sand bars at the Boyne estuary – it lacked the man-made channel that exists today to facilitate navigation. The mouth itself was somewhat further out to sea than presently, coastal erosion being responsible for the retreat of the land. Indeed, the inexorable action of the sea has brought changes elsewhere along the coast. At the mouth of the next river south of the Boyne – the Nanny – there stands a solitary, picturesque cottage, resplendent in its white-washed coat. It is located on the south side of the river mouth, perched at the very verge of the strand, and is in imminent danger of being claimed by the waves. A local man tells us that his father played football in fields to the *east* of that cottage, in grassy fields that are now lost forever to the encroaching sea.[9]

A few miles further south, at the next river mouth, which is the Delvin River, stands another isolated home beside the beach; piles of rocks and stones are in place as barricades in a valiant attempt to repel the hungry sea. Near the water's edge at low tide lies a collection of about a dozen extraneous boulders, half buried in the sand. They are conspicuously out of context among the seashells, the seaweed and the sand. Geologically, they are not native to this area. How did they get there? They are the scattered remains of a structure painstakingly built by Neolithic Man – clear evidence that he hunted, gathered, and held ritualistic ceremonies right there, an area which today the sea claims as its own exclusive domain. The question arises as to how far inland was this site when originally selected by prehistoric man, because it is unlikely that the structure was initially sited at the water's edge; or putting it another way, to what extent has the sea made inroads on the coast during the past 5,000 years of man's occupation?

Prehistoric Remains
on the coast at the Mouth of the Delvin River, near Gormanston

In 1991 some school children were playing on the beach at Hampton Court, Balbriggan when they observed prehistoric artwork on a large boulder. The OPW arrived on the scene and had it lifted – it weighed 2½ tons – to a more convenient site. Having coaxed the encrusted barnacles from its surface, several sets of circles, lozenges and a double arc presented themselves. The stone had been at the bottom of a 20m high cliff, and it would seem that it was the last remnant of another prehistoric structure that had been demolished through coastal erosion. This stone is presently on view at Ardgillan House, near Balbriggan. Other such vestiges of early man's activities are located close to this eastern coastline and await the patient, methodical trowel of the archaeologist. Finds of this nature are further evidence that the area along this section of the coast was well populated by mankind 5,000 years ago.

Greek and Egyptian mariners must also have found their way to Ireland. Ptolemy the astronomer and geographer of the second century AD, published his *Geography*, which depicts Ireland and the Boyne, giving the river the name *'Buvinda'*.

If, in fact, the Romans did make their way up the Boyne, intending to stop off at *Pontana* (Latin for 'the Bridge of the Ford') to partake of a meal in a local hostelry, they were too early by about a thousand years, because Drogheda as a settled community did not exist. To left and right the rolling slopes of the Boyne valley were still covered in forest and scrub, interspersed with occasional clearings where the native Celtic people grazed their livestock, but nothing existed that we could remotely describe as a town, or even a village. The small family groupings built enclosures or stockades for protection from wolves and other predators – and that included other marauding tribes.

Eight kilometres upstream from *Pontana* a big surprise awaited the Romans. Some of them may previously have gazed in wonderment at Egypt's ancient pyramids in the course of their conquests, but they would now learn with no little astonishment that, in the matter of edifices for the dead, those at the banks of the Boyne predated the Egyptian ones by five hundred or perhaps a thousand years. Hibernia's great Passage Tombs at the Bend of the Boyne were already ancient buildings when the Egyptians were rafting their weighty monoliths down the Nile for the construction of the pyramids.

Indeed, something similar can be said of Stonehenge – Newgrange predates it by an even greater time-gap. It has not been established definitively whether or not slave labour was employed in any of those mammoth undertakings, but slavery was certainly a way of life throughout that era. Some Egyptologists hold that the work on the pyramids was accomplished by a dedicated citizenry – the same may possibly have applied to Newgrange.

Reconnoitring the Drogheda Area: Mudflats fringed the river, and thus it was shallower and wider than at present; today the mudflats or slob-lands are still in evidence at Queensboro' and Baltray and bordering the Mornington Road. Donor's Green (built on land reclaimed from the river *circa* 1860 and named after the Harbour Engineer) and the quays were constructed along the shoreline to confine the course of the river into a much narrower and deeper channel, scouring it and facilitating the passage of ships to their berths at the quayside.

Approaching the town from Donor's Green today we come to the roadway which we call the North Strand – the word '*Strand*' used in this context reminds us that in medieval times the waters of the Boyne lapped the shore or strand which is today's North Strand. (Similarly, the Liffey which enters Dublin Bay today passes through a much narrower channel than formerly and, by the same token, the fashionable Strand, not far from Trafalgar Square in London's West End, which today presents a bustling scene of shoppers, cars and red double-deckers, was washed by a much broader Thames when the Romans founded Londinium).

The reclaimed foreshore by the Boyne was put to use in the construction of extensive flour mills, coal yards, cattle stockades and warehouses that now occupy the Mall, Merchants Quay and Steampacket Quay.

Likewise, the opposite (southern) shore was reclaimed to provide additional quayside facilities and accommodation for housing and industrial use. This was a gradual process, accomplished over the centuries. Eastwards from the point opposite Constitution Hill the Ordnance Survey Map shows that the riverside was lined with mud-flats in 1835. People traversing the roadway that runs parallel to the south bank of the river seemingly had difficulty picking their way along the swampy terrain since they named it the '*Marsh* Road'. These mud-flats were filled in immediately after 1835, and the Topographical Dictionary by Samuel Lewis reveals in 1837 that 'a very extensive mill for spinning flax has recently been erected by a company of proprietors...'[10] An entry in the Drogheda Corporation's official records in 1784 states: -

> '*that the sum of £61.8.4 being the amount of the estimate laid before the Assembly by Mr. Thomas Matthews for completing and making the road without [i.e. outside] Blind Gate from the* **Strand** *Well [viz. at the junction of Constitution Hill and Bachelor's Lane] to Green Hills be paid by the Treasurer when the work is done'.*[11]

Interestingly, a gap still remained in the extended quay wall between the Cairnes Brewery property and that of the Irish Oil and Cake Mills, (now forming part of the Scotch Hall complex) at a point directly opposite Constitution Hill. Here the primeval shore remained untouched until recent times, and the housewives living at the Marsh Road and Scotch Hall – that is, the *original* Scotch Hall which comprised a series of abject tenements – were wont to pick their way across the muddy foreshore with their baskets of clothes for laundering at the riverside, just as their ancestors had been doing from early times – the flowing tide of the Boyne continued to be their only 'running water', and little boys paddled in it in their bare feet. The author recalls such scenes up until the mid 1940s.

The recovered ground space on the south bank has been utilised over the years to accommodate a wide variety of industrial enterprises ranging from ship building, a foundry, a gas works, chemical manures, edible and technical oils, brewing, and linen processing, and also to printing, footwear and margarine manufacturing. A combination of rationalisation and external competition saw the gradual demise of each of these industries. Developers have responded to the sophisticated demands of the shopper in the twenty-first century and have transformed this area beyond all recognition. The year 2005 saw the creation of a shopping complex, a high-rise hotel, a car park and other such facilities that would cause the townspeople of yesteryear to gasp in disbelief. A discordant note is sounded here: these fundamental alterations in the town's character and commercial structure are geared in their entirety towards <u>spending</u> money rather than <u>creating</u> it, and a long stretch of priceless wharfage – the scene of intense commercial activity in Drogheda's industrial past – is no more.

Traffic from Greenhills to Drogheda
The river shore was the roadway prior to the condstruction of Donor's Green

Continuing from the North Strand in the direction of Shop Street, we pass along Bachelor's Lane and Bessexwell's Lane. It seems that these thoroughfares run along what was formerly the continuing river shoreline in pre-Norman times. This assertion is supported by the fact that the steep laneway leading to it from Laurence Street – the High Lane – was formerly known as Keyser's Lane. The curious word 'keyser' means 'ship wharf', and lo! the building at the bottom of the lane (west side) was a custom house, strategically placed for keeping a watchful eye for smuggled cargo arriving on vessels moored along the quays.

Proceeding past present day Bachelor's Lane, we can visualise herdsmen with their livestock in prehistoric times wending their way along the river's northern shoreline. In that way they created a beaten pathway or 'boreen' adjoining the lapping water, without realising that one day in the far distant future the density of traffic would increase greatly, that dwellings would arise along the route, later giving way to scenes of bustling humanity and thriving shops, and that the thoroughfare would in time be known as West Street. Thus the Romans, had they sailed along the course of the river, would have seen mud-flats extending close to where the Tholsel and Saint Peter's Church now stand, and where curlews and herons were foraging for frogs and worms.

Digging Up the Past: In preparing the foundations for the present Augustinian Church in Shop Street ('the Low Lane') Fr. Doyle, whose formidable task it was to oversee the construction of the church and then raise the wherewithal to pay for it, noted in his diary in 1860:

> *"In boring the different parts of our site, we found that there were about ten feet on average of 'made' ground below the level of Shop Street; in some places four or five feet more. ... On*

yesterday the workmen found a gold 'tibia' or ornament, and on the instant sold it for six shillings. I had some difficulty in getting it back. It is of the purest gold and weighs five pennyweights. The place where it was found must have been near the ancient course of the river; foundations of houses built hundreds of years ago were over it. I have forwarded it to Dr. Wilde of Dublin for his opinion ... He stated that the brooch is most ancient ... Fr. Meehan of the Royal Academy called on me today about a portion of an old Irish harp that was found on digging a well in the garden adjoining the new church. It must be a couple of thousand of years old, yet it is as sound as the day it was made. There is an inscription on it, but no one understands the characters. "[12]

Another item unearthed was 'a portion of chain armour' – such as was worn by the Crusaders. (We know that some of Strongbow's followers had campaigned as Crusaders in the Holy Land). These unexpected 'finds' were sent to the Royal Irish Academy, and are of great interest even to the casual historian. However, the reference to the ten feet of 'made' ground is what gains our attention now – it tells the archaeologist that in times past the inhabitants of the town (the beaver-like Normans) had transported that soil load by load for the purpose of filling in the foreshore of the river. In that way the river channel was greatly narrowed; this facilitated the bridge-builders to span the river with a much shorter bridge than would otherwise have been necessary; it accelerated the flow of the current thereby scouring the river bed, and in addition it provided quay walls and a safe anchorage for vessels.

And what about the gold 'tibia' that was mentioned as one of the finds? What was its origin? How old is it? What skilled hands fashioned it? What other such items lie hidden? These are tantalising questions that may never be answered. On front of the new Garda Barracks near West Gate a slip-road named Fr. Connolly Way was constructed about 1996 running along the edge of the river; it commences at the point opposite Barlow House at West Gate and leads via a ramp to the riverside, Dominic's Bridge and Wellington Quay. When the foundation work for the roadway was in progress, the author witnessed a JCB unearthing a huge disc-shaped stone with a central hole. It had a diameter of about six feet and weighed several tons. It was a millstone. Redundant, it had been dumped there as part of the in-fill for the 'made' ground at the time the quays were being constructed. What other relics of Drogheda's past lie buried under our feet? The archaeologists avail of all opportunities in their search for clues on Drogheda's past, keeping a watchful eye whenever old buildings are replaced and the ground disturbed. Foundations of the old town wall were unearthed in the car park close to St. Dominic's Bridge in the course of archaeological probing conducted in 2006.

Chapter Two

St. Patrick Comes to Drogheda

By the time the Roman Empire had adopted the Christian religion under Constantine the Great, the Roman influence did eventually reach Ireland. It arrived in a fortuitous way – in the person of a former slave named Patrick. Initially kidnapped from Britain, he was brought to Ireland from whence he later escaped. It was destined that he would return, this time under his own volition and with a definitional mission – he was bringing the message of Christianity to a pagan people.

Tradition has it that his second coming was in 432 AD and that his port of entry was the River Boyne, stepping off at Inver Colpa – today's Colpe, at Mornington. Traces of ancient boats found here point to this being the site of a dock or a landing stage in bygone times. The story of the Pascal Fire and the ensuing events that took place at nearby Slane and Tara, and the apocryphal tale of the Shamrock need not be retold here. Suffice it to say that when Saint Patrick introduced Christianity it was readily adopted throughout the land – the first land to accept Christianity without the shedding of blood or the creating of martyrs. Martyrdom would come later.

A golden age of learning and deep piety spread across Ireland in the wake of Saint Patrick's evangelism. Religious communities sprang up throughout the land, not only in readily accessible locations such as Monasterboice and Clonmacnoise, but also in remote, inaccessible sanctuaries ranging from Tory Island off the coast of Donegal to Skellig Michael off Kerry's windswept coast. There the monks, in their sparse little beehive huts, withstood the privations and rigours of Atlantic winters and self imposed solitude; they spent their time in contemplation and penance. One particular monk, Saint Kevin, sought out an austere and lonely cave on the side of a steep mountainside in Wicklow.

We know that Saint Patrick did stop off in the 'Drogheda' area. He could not have been impressed by the few scattered stockades and primitive, flimsy huts that dotted the landscape – it certainly did not constitute a village. At Cloughpatrick (*'Patrick's Stone'*), a short distance from the top of Mell on the Collon road, he is reputed to have baptised some locals at a well (now closed up) called St. Patrick's Well. Perhaps he prayed at this point for the courage to continue the work of spreading the message of Love. It would seem that he knelt to pray there, because the large boulder by the side of the road at a labourer's cottage still carries the deep impression of his knees where he knelt – if you wish to believe it. (Either he was big and very heavy, or the rest of us are very credulous!).

D'Alton, in his *History of Drogheda*, tells us that during Saint Patrick's stay in the area he baptised many of the locals at the holy well that still bears his name at Patrickswell Lane, off West Street, and he established a society of monks there; and postulants came there to receive the message of Christ. It is on record that both Saint Columba, the Apostle of the Picts, and Saint Killian were among its members. These saints would later assume the role of missionaries and, as we shall see, carry the Gospel to foreign parts at a crucial time of Europe's need.

The conversion of the people was more than simply from paganism to Christianity and from druids to monks. Significantly, it was also from illiteracy to learning, from dark ignorance to scholarship. The gap left by the Romans in the spread of civilisation was now filled – it took 400 years, and the natives were quick to respond. Monasteries and other such establishments sprang up; the monks were avid students and they learned to speak and write

Greek, Latin and a smattering of Hebrew, and spent their time studying, praying and teaching. Students and pilgrims came from afar to the monasteries in the pursuit of knowledge.

An important monastery was in Clonard, near Trim. Its functions included teaching, and every branch of knowledge then known was taught there. It was, in effect, a university and we are told that at one time it served as many as 3,000 students under Saint Finnen of Clonard; he died there in 549. Many pupils came from Britain and from the Continent to study there.[1] Such activities focused attention on the area and gave an added importance to the general region. They contributed to the basic structure of the wide hinterland from which the town of Drogheda would one day arise.

Likewise, County Louth contained its share of religious houses. The land belonging to a church was called 'termon land', a description that is perpetuated in the picturesque village we know as Termonfeckin. But while the Irish people were receiving the Word of God and were uplifted through engaging in studies, dark clouds were gathering over mainland Europe. The Roman army was recalled from Britain to help repel the barbarian hordes that had broken through the eastern borders of their empire. These were the Vandals, Alans, Goths and Sueves, and they swarmed across civilised Europe, taking delight in ransacking the towns and pillaging everything that was of value. The final humiliation was the capitulation of Rome – the Eternal City – which was sacked by Alaric, king of the Visigoths, in 410 AD.

When the Roman Empire finally fell apart and darkness descended upon the existing civilisation, the light of learning still burned brightly in that green island that lay off Europe's western seaboard. At that critical moment in history, many Irish monks took up the challenge and left their native shore on crusades to rekindle the flame that had been extinguished by the barbarians. Saint Brendan the Navigator sailed westwards with his followers and discovered the New World. Saints Columcille, Aidan, Columbanus and a host of other Irish monks bravely and selflessly carried the torch to England, Scotland and the European mainland. Monasteries were founded in Iona (novices came there in their hundreds for spiritual nourishment, later to depart and establish other monasteries), Lindisfarne, Annegray, Fontaines, Luxeuil, Bobbio, Saint Gall and many more. The indefatigable Columbanus is said to have founded literally dozens of monasteries in France, Germany, Switzerland and Italy.[2]

'Drogheda' played its full part in this missionary work. Columba was a member of the religious community at Saint Mary's Abbey – the 'Old Abbey' of today. The famous Irish manuscript 'the Book of Durrow', which is preserved in Trinity College, Dublin, is attributed to Columba's own hand. Having completed his studies, he left the abbey and founded several monasteries throughout Ireland, including Lambay, Swords, Durrow and Kells. Two local churches are named in his honour, St. Columba's in Colpe and St. Columba's in Mornington. Two local holy wells bear his name, Shallon and Minnistown.

He then turned his attention to Scotland and set off with twelve companions to convert the Picts. That race of people was particularly truculent and unruly – even the Romans were unable to handle them, and had resorted to building Hadrian's Wall to keep them at bay. But Saint Columba, or Columcille ('Dove of the Church') as he was also called, accepted the challenge. The inhabitants of Scotland and the Hebrides yielded to his gentle persuasion and his teachings, earning him the appellation 'Apostle of the Picts'. But it is the monastery at Iona that brought him most fame. After a lifetime of dedication in spreading the word of God, he died kneeling before the altar in Iona in the year 597. He was in his seventy-sixth year, and was buried within the monastery which he founded. Saint Killian, who, like Saint Columba, had also served as a novitiate in Drogheda, was known as 'the Apostle of Franconia'. He was martyred in 689.[3]

And in that wondrous, strange manner the earlier events of history were now reversed. The message of the Christian religion and its accompanying civilisation had been brought by Patrick, the captive slave from Roman Britain, to the shores of pagan Ireland and up the River Boyne. There it was embraced and nurtured. When Europe, pillaged by the barbarians, was enveloped by the Dark Ages, the kindly Christian ethos was now being restored. It was being restored – through a querulous quirk of fate – by the same 'fierce and warlike people' who emanated from that insignificant island which the Romans deemed unworthy of colonising. No wonder that Ireland earned the epithet "The Island of Saints and Scholars".

THE BRIDGE BUILDERS: Crossing the River Boyne was a challenge to traders and other travellers traversing the land. From earliest times a ford would have existed for crossing the river. No doubt a few enterprising fellows provided the facility of a ferry service in the knowledge that the river was tidal, and thus the ford could be used only when the tides allowed it. Others set up stalls and booths for the sale of sustenance to those who were preparing to cross. The supply of and demand for these services, however rudimentary they might be, would inevitably have given rise to a hostelry, a few scattered huts and other habitation at that section of the river bank, but even if viewed collectively, they would hardly be termed a village.

St. Mary's Abbey, Mary St. in 1792
The Carmelites built it in 1300, Henry VIII closed it in 1541,
Cromwell bombarded it in 1649, the elements devoured most of what remained.

The concentration of traffic increased in the course of time, creating a bottleneck or a 'traffic jam' of sorts at the jetty – it was becoming a focal point. The need for a bridge became more pressing. Given that there was no regulated social structure or 'local government' to handle such matters, the need was left unfulfilled until the monks stepped in to accommodate the need.

We have seen that Saint Killian, who died in 747, sojourned in the monastery near Patrickswell Lane. He had been known as 'Killian of Drogheda'. This piece of information is significant because it contains a clue – it is perhaps the earliest mention of the name 'Drogheda' – the Bridge of the Ford,[4] and it implies that **a bridge and a ford were already in place by 747 AD.** However, we must not presume that the location of the bridge was anywhere within the precincts of present day Drogheda – it was in all probability a few miles further upstream.

Religious congregations of their nature were closely-knit and unified communities. These were qualities that were vital in the establishment and promotion of civic societies, but they were absent outside the monastery walls. As we shall see, the energies of the monks were focused on commercial activities as well as on spiritual ones, and it is they who were best fitted to undertake the construction of a bridge.

The original crossing point along this stretch of the Boyne may well have been a short distance upstream from present day Drogheda – at Oldbridge. Indeed, our forefathers could not have presented us with a more obvious clue as to its location than applying the name that described the structure that stood there, which was an _old bridge_. At that point the river was fordable (a fact which King William was to exploit in 1690). It was also adjacent to the monks at Mellifont (they arrived in 1142) whose intensive commercial activities encompassed both sides of the river. It should be noted that they were at times referred to as 'the abbots of Mellifont and <u>Drogheda</u>', the word 'Drogheda' in that context referring to the general locality of the bridge/ford which we surmise was west (upriver) of the position where today's town stands.

The High Cross at Monasterboice

Undoubtedly the first bridge was a ramshackle affair, and certainly not of stone – but at least it was a **bridg**e – and it was adjacent to the existing **ford**. No prize was offered for having given the place the obvious title 'the bridge of the ford' or 'the ford by the bridge', the Celtic or Gaelic version of which was '*droichead átha'*. (Indeed, the name is something of an enigma; 'the bridge <u>at</u> the ford' would seem to have been a more correct description).

The grange at 'Drochatatha' as mentioned by the monks is identified with *vetera ponte*, or 'old bridge', and there is a subsequent reference to 'the *novus pons* de Drochatatha', the latter being 'the new bridge' which was sited further downstream – at present day Drogheda.[5]

A question arises: What prompted the bridge builders to select a different site when a new bridge was in the offing? Answer: Pragmatism! A broad river presented a more difficult challenge to the engineers. The river valley is appreciably narrower at the steep slope we now call Millmount. Also, the subsoil allows firmer foundations, as opposed to the earlier site which is boggy. Thus, a bridge at this point required a shorter span, and we speculate that this was the deciding factor in selecting the new site. (The bridge that now spans the Boyne at Oldbridge as part of the M1 Motorway was completed in 2003. It is all of 385m. in length and is known to engineers as an A-symmetric cable stayed bridge.).

It should be particularly noted that *there is nothing to indicate that any substantial settlement existed at this location prior to the arrival of the Normans*. Nonetheless, this is the womb from which in the fullness of time an infant town named *Droichead Átha* would emerge. As time progressed, this place-name *Droichead Átha* was elided and Anglicised into a variety of pronunciations and spellings. This is not surprising, since there were no directories or dictionaries to consult or to provide guidelines – the first proper English dictionary did not appear until 1755. Nor were there definitive spellings or pronunciations of words. (In ancient documents it is possible to find a word spelt in several different ways in the same paragraph, or even in the same sentence). Words were usually spelled phonetically, and thus the accent of the individual writer was an influencing factor.

Various old documents show a plethora of spellings such as 'Droghdogh', 'Drokeda', 'Droghade', 'Drougheda' and 'Drodag', and we must bear in mind that in those far off times the written word was rare, and only the privileged few could read or write. In 1671 they were still struggling with the Anglicisation of the word *'Droichead Átha'*, and Saint Oliver Plunkett, who was very familiar with the town, having lived and worked in it, used the spelling 'Dreat' in a letter to Rome in that year. It was also known as 'Treoit' and 'Tredagh'. It is interesting to note that the phonetic pronunciation 'Drokeda' (using three syllables) is still used today in parts of Northern Ireland. It is uncertain when the definitive and undisputed spelling became **'DROGHEDA',** but it is amusing to find a spelling of 'Drodaugh' (phonetically *'Drawda'*) as far back as 1441, which is the exact pronunciation used by locals today!

Local Christian Art: We have seen that Christianity brought with it a great wave of religious fervour from which sprang an abundance of monasteries and nunneries. Therein was fostered the pursuit of knowledge, and what followed was a flowering of culture and learning, and this continued for five glorious centuries.

A unique feature of many monasteries was the Round Tower, constructed during the ninth and tenth centuries. Their function was to provide an escape from the depredations of the prowling Vikings, of whom we will have something to say below. Rumours that these *banditti* were in the offing would cause panic, and the monks would quickly gather their precious manuscripts, gold chalices and other regalia and scurry aloft via a retractable ladder. These towers, of course, conveyed an unintended message, their very eminence making them conspicuous and therefore proclaiming to the world the existence of booty in the vicinity. Locally, the towers at both Donaghmore and Monasterboice (which had been a renowned seat of learning) received unwelcome attention from the Vikings. Slane's early round tower was burned in 950, and Monasterboice's in 1097 'with its books and treasures'.

The Irish monasteries of the early Middle Ages have left us with another noteworthy and distinctive feature. These are the High Crosses, of which Counties Louth and Meath contain more than a fair share. There are three centres in Louth (Monasterboice, Dromiskin and Termonfeckin) and five in Meath (Slane, Killary, Kells, Colpe and Duleek). An important example is the massive Muiredach's Cross at Monasterboice which stands at the lordly height of 5.20 m. (fifteen feet) A collage of Biblical scenes is depicted thereon. Near to the round tower is the Tall or West Cross – it has the distinction of being Ireland's tallest cross, being a stately 7 m. (twenty two feet) in height.

Two old Celtic Crosses have come to light in the Drogheda area in recent times. In 1981 a small cross-head of sandstone was unearthed at Colpe. It is unlikely that it fractured without human agency. In that case we ask what hands broke it? This is the route taken by Cromwell's Puritan soldiers when hauling their cannon into Drogheda in 1649, and the inference provides us with a speculative conclusion. It is preserved in the local church of the Church of Ireland. A similar one was discovered at Fennor, Slane in 1990 and can be seen in the Catholic Church in Slane.[6] Who know what other relics of the past await discovery!

The type of stone that the monks selected for fashioning into high crosses was occasionally sandstone, a material that is easy to work and yields more readily than granite or limestone to the stonecutter's chisel. The downside is that it more quickly succumbs to the agents of denudation – frost and the other weathering elements. A recent culprit, arising from man's activities, is acid rain. Lord Killanin made this suggestion: "Unfortunately, many of the crosses are made of sandstone, and I believe that they should not be left out in the open to weather in the Irish climate, as it is now possible to recreate accurate models or reproductions...". And so say all of us.

The scribes, goldsmith, silversmith and other craftsmen continued to create masterpieces up to the Middle Ages, and we marvel at the workmanship in the examples that still survive. The National Museum abounds with gold Croziers, Crosses, Chalices, Shrines and other priceless examples of supreme artistic achievement. Skills were not confined to the visual arts; the Annals of the Four Masters record the death of 'the chief poet of Ireland, the Bard of the Boyne', which occurred in 921.

It is fitting that we pay homage to the craftsmanship applied in the creation of the illustrated manuscripts, of which the Book of Kells is but one example. The widely travelled Giraldus Cambrensis, who visited many parts of Ireland, was dumbstruck when his eyes met the illustrations in the Book of Kells. His conclusion was that no mortal could have produced such perfection, and that it was therefore "the work of an angel". Other such Irish manuscripts are treasured in museums scattered across Europe – England, France, Switzerland, Germany, Sweden, Italy and even Russia. How many other valuable treasures graced the Irish religious settlements and are now lost forever to mankind we will never know. What is certain is that the monastic tranquillity was unceremoniously interrupted. The sanctuaries were plundered and ransacked, and countless works of art carried away as booty. The Vikings had arrived.

Chapter Three

The Vikings

A truly remarkable people, the Vikings were endowed with exceptional ability, and as seafarers they were unrivalled. They sailed out of Scandinavia (Norway, Sweden, Jutland and other parts of the Baltic coast) in their fleets of longboats as traders and pirates a full thousand years before Britannia began to rule the waves. Western Europe was in a state of terror while they were on the rampage between the 8th and the 12th centuries. Their peregrinations were one of the most remarkable expansions in history, taking them to such far-flung places as Gibraltar and the Mediterranean Sea, and by penetrating and passing southwards from Scandinavia through

The Vikings were greatly feared wherever they went

the vast Russian landmass they arrived at the Black Sea; they also reached Iceland, Greenland and Vinland (modern Newfoundland). Some settled in Normandy, and from there they reappeared later in history as the Normans, invading England under William the Conqueror and then Ireland under Strongbow. Let us now focus our attention on their impact on Ireland's eastern seaboard, including the region where Drogheda now stands.

These fearsome warriors found easy pickings among the religious communities. They pillaged as they went, starting with the coastal areas, and as they grew bolder and greedier they also penetrated inland in search of loot; Viking hoards of silver and Middle Eastern coins have been found at Lough Owel in Westmeath.

The reputation of Saint Kevin, hermit and holy man, had aroused such fervour throughout the land that he was enticed to come down from the tiny hermit's cave on the cliff face which he had made his home in an isolated valley in the wilderness of Wicklow and move to the valley floor of Glendalough where thousands flocked to kneel at his feet and join him in prayer so that a church was built together with cells for the clerics and other adherents who had come as eager students, and their presence gave rise to further activity in constructing accommodation to house the burgeoning community, not forgetting the work of creating a series of High Crosses and a lofty Round Tower, all cradled in the picturesque and utterly peaceful and idyllic setting of the green valley with its two lakes, giving the region the role of a quasi university city, and then along came the Vikings who burned the place to the ground!

In point of fact, Glendalough was ransacked and torched no fewer than nine times by the Vikings.[1] We will never know the full extent of the destruction that these marauders wreaked. They treated the abbeys as repositories for portable booty, ransacking them, burning the precious manuscripts and relics, wrecking altars, laying their pagan paws on precious gold chalices and other sacred booty, murdering monks and taking others of them into slavery, and finally making off with choice maidens kicking and screaming for release – "nasty Viking monk-bashers" as one writer light-heartedly put it.

Those times were certainly terrifying for the unfortunates whom they encountered, mainly because their victims were uncoordinated and ill-prepared to defend themselves. We know they were uninvited guests at the monasteries in the Louth/Meath area on many occasions. Monasterboice, eight kilometres northwest of Drogheda was occupied by them for a while until ousted by Domhnall, King of Tara, in 968.[2] The monasteries at Duleek, Slane and Donaghmore among others also experienced their depredations. They plundered the abbey at Duleek in the year 830, and for good measure they returned on at least four subsequent occasions. Today, some of the museums of Norway display prizes robbed from the monasteries of Ireland.

The Annals of the Four Masters record that a battle took place at Raholland, Beamore in 850 AD in which 300 lives were lost. Folklore stories recall how 'one of the last battles between the native Irish and the Vikings took place in the moat field at Tullog in the year 1053 AD.'[3] Tullog, a village long disappeared, was located near Stamullen.

For the record, the native Irish chieftains themselves did not regard the Fifth, Sixth and Seventh Commandments which Moses handed down, as an impediment to murder, rape and plunder. Records show that up to the year 810, of more than a hundred raids on monasteries, three quarters were perpetrated by Irish chiefs,[4] pillaging the communities and murdering the hapless inmates – more 'nasty monk-bashers'!

Some of the captives found themselves as slaves in Iceland, a land that the Vikings had discovered and colonised. Indeed, Icelanders today regard the Irish people as their 'cousins', as evidenced by the high percentage of the population having the features of the Irish rather than the Nordic blond type. One of their offshore islands is still called Westman Island, acknowledging the link with their Irish origins – 'Westmen' was the name given by the Vikings to Irishmen.

Viking Settlements: Their first Irish settlement or longphort (shipping port) is said to have been at Linn Duachaill in 831 AD, about 20km. north of the Boyne estuary along the County Louth coast. The name of that settlement was later changed to Annagassan. From there they made forays inland as far as Clonmacnoise. They also established a camp at Carlingford (= the Fjord of Carling) a short distance further north. They did not have everything their own way, for in 869 they suffered a severe defeat outside 'Drogheda' at Killineer at the hands of Connor, king of Connaught.

Whatever attracted them to sleepy little Annagassan we know not. To start with, the Glyde/Dee River on which this village is located is no Rhine or Danube, and it was deficient in facilities for berthing their longboats. They settled there for a while, but later sailed southwards until they reached the Liffey. The particular settlement they founded at that point was destined to flower into that city which we know today as Dublin. We should be thankful that they shook the dust of Annagassan off their boots; the exhilaration of a day's shopping in Grafton Street would greatly diminish at the prospect of Grafton Street being located in the middle of Annagassan!

Excavations at Wood Quay, Dublin, have provided archaeologists with endless scope in their pursuit of knowledge of the past, digging up bones and old domestic artefacts such as combs and pottery and other bits and pieces discarded during the Viking occupation – literally tens of thousands of items were unearthed. A find that initiated a degree of puzzlement – which later became the cause of subdued arousal – was the unearthing of a compressed mass of small wads of grass – lots and lots of small wads of grass. What was their purpose, they wondered. The solving of the riddle sent them into a tizzy of excitement. However, we will spare the reader's delicate sensitivity by simply explaining that the age of toilet paper had not yet arrived!

Dr. Harbison in his book *'Treasures of the Boyne Valley'* proffers an interesting speculation concerning the Viking's choice of a site for a settlement, namely that, if they had sailed up the Boyne instead of the Liffey, Drogheda might well be the capital of Ireland today. So be it. At least that fortuitous decision has spared Drogheda all those small wads of grass!

In fact an early expedition of Vikings did sail up the Boyne – this was in 830 AD. No doubt their reputation preceded them, and the poor unfortunates who lived in the locality must have been struck with absolute terror at the sight of the approaching sails. (Apart from sails, some of their vessels were propelled by oars, and rowed by 40 to 80 men – many, no doubt, being Irish slaves). King Turgesius (or Thorgils) was their leader, and he was the most renowned of all the Danes. "He quickly subjected the whole island to himself in many varied conflicts and fierce wars ... and from him sustained great evils. He journeyed through the whole country and strengthened it with strong forts and suitable places."[5] Three times within one month he sacked Armagh, and had established posts at Dublin, Limerick, Dundalk and Carlingford.

He returned to the Boyne again in 837 AD with a mighty fleet of sixty ships and established a base at Millmount. This lofty site overlooked the monastery at 'the Old Abbey', which lay across the river; his men plundered and torched it, murdering the 260 unfortunates who sought shelter therein, and then they set off on a rampage, plundering 'churches, forts and dwellings.'[6] Knowth, Dowth and Oldbridge also claimed their attention, and no doubt they went away on each occasion well laden with booty.

 In 917 the Danes paid a return visit to the Millmount area, murdering the abbot Indrech Indracta, and again in 950 they ransacked Slane and devastated the countryside, giving free rein to those pursuits in which they excelled – plunder, destruction, rape and murder. In 1032 the Danish chief Sitric landed at Colpe and soon came into conflict with the inhabitants in the battle of Mornington, killing 300 men. (With such a vile reputation it is questionable whether the Danes should have been allowed into the European Union!).

Resistance: No concerted effort was made by the Irish chieftains to challenge these marauders. But individual chiefs put up a resistance, including King Malachi of Meath who put a stop to the gallop of Turgesius when he had him drowned in Lough Owel in Westmeath. Giraldus Cambrensis has another version of this event, stating that:

> *" ... the Irish people immediately had recourse once again to its accustomed practices in the evil art of deceit. Turgesius happened at the time to be very much enamoured of the daughter of the King of Meath. The king hid his hatred in his heart, and granting the girl to Turgesius, promised to send her to him with fifteen beautiful maidens to a certain island in Meath, in [Lough Owel]. Turgesius was delighted and went to the rendezvous on the appointed day with fifteen nobles of his people. They encountered on the island decked out in girls' clothes to practice their deceit, fifteen young men, shaven of their beards, full of spirit, and especially picked for the job. They carried knives carried on their persons, and with these they killed Turgesius and their companions in the midst of their embraces".[7]*

Thereafter the Danes suffered further defeats. Later, Malachi II, also known as Malachi the Great, inflicted a most crushing defeat on them at Tara, when vast numbers of them were slain. One of the coveted trophies he acquired on that occasion was alluded to in Thomas Moore's rousing song 'O'Donnell Abu': -

> *'When Malachi wore the collar of gold*
> *Which he won from the proud invader'.*

Malachi was not yet finished with these intruders. He and his Meathmen played a key role when Brian Boru was bidding them farewell at the Battle of Clontarf. Malachi's contingent stood back until the crucial moment. When the Norsemen were wavering, his men, seizing the moment, rushed forward and cut off their retreat and annihilated them, and thus the victory of the Irish forces was total. This was the last great battle between Christianity and heathenism. It is ironic that all the turbulence that was to bedevil Ireland in future history would be between Christians and Christians.

We have seen that the Boyne river had a much wider, if shallower, channel in former times – the same applies to the Liffey. Dublin Bay extended southwards to Merrion Square and northwards to present day Annesley Bridge, the North Strand and Gardiner Street, with the area of Clontarf covering a more westward location. Tradition tells us that the point where King Brian Boru's tent was pitched during the battle was at present day Mountjoy Square, and it was there in his tent and kneeling in prayer that his life was extinguished by the fleeing chief Broder. This was in the year 1014, one of the few dates in Irish history that every young scholar can readily recall – perhaps because it happens to be one of the few decisive battles that favoured the native Irish.

Although many artefacts of Hiberno-Norse origin have come to light in the urban settlements at Dublin and other towns along the eastern seaboard, no such evidence has been found at Drogheda. Indeed, of the various Viking ports along the east coast, Drogheda has the distinction of retaining its Gaelic name – presumably the Viking occupations were too intermittent and so did not make a sufficient impact on the neighbourhood to leave the permanent imprint of a place name. Besides, the local chieftains made things very hot for these cut-throats, and saw to it by continual harassment that they would eventually release their hold on the area. To have named the town 'Turgesius-ford' in honour of the Danish king sounds improbable, and does not sit well. Generations of usage, and without a trace of Viking influence, have presented us with the name 'Drogheda'!

If Brian Boru Had Lost at Clontarf: We exult in the final defeat and banishment of the Vikings. But by that time they had ceased to be raiders and had settled down in a string of civilised communities, mainly along the East coast. On reflection, it might not have been such a setback had they stayed, because the native Irish were very backward in many ways and would have benefited by integrating with them, and we have made reference above to

Ireland's loss of not having been settled by the Romans. The Vikings have nonetheless left landmarks that, unquestionably, have been to Ireland's benefit. They were the first to establish identifiable and permanent urbanisation. Many of their settlements – not surprisingly they were all coastal ones – have survived the passage of time and have developed into thriving towns such as Wexford, Waterford, Arklow and Dublin on the east coast, and Cork and Limerick in the south. Today this handful of towns contains two-thirds of the Republic's population.

Surprisingly, Drogheda is not on this list. Most of those place-names, to which we can add Annagassan, Carlingford and Lambay have Viking roots. The very names 'Ireland' and 'Leinster' are likewise of Viking origin. They established settlements in north County Dublin – in Fingal. This name (*Fionn Gaill* or fair haired foreigners) reveals to us that the Norsemen populated that region. The Viking name *stadr* (= homestead) is the root of several local place-names e.g. Stabannon, Stameen, Stamullen, Stadalt, a clue that tells us that the Vikings were settled farmers throughout the area, and presumably interbred with the indigenous population. The prefixes Sta and Ste are common throughout Scandinavia and refer to homesteads. The name of the island of Holmpatrick (off the Skerries coast) is derived from *holm* (= island), another Viking prefix. They also left the Gaelic language with several other words: their navigational prowess introduced us to *bád* = boat, *ancaire* = anchor, *dorú* = fishing-line, *stiúir* = rudder, and helped to advance the local knowledge in fishing and shipping. It is surprising that the Celts, surrounded by water as they were, had not their own terms for these sea-faring and fishing pursuits. It points to a lack of industry, initiative and enterprise. Half a millennium later the Irish were importing herrings when they could have been inundating Europe with fish from the bountiful harvest that existed on all sides. The result is that today continental fishing fleets tend to regard the seas around Ireland as their own 'traditional' fishing grounds. By stimulating a greater kinship with the sea, the Celts could have become synonymous with seamanship and maritime skills; those roles have been taken over notably by the Greeks, some of whom are among today's great shipping magnates.

The word '*fuinneóg*' (= window) is of Norse origin. What word had the Celts previously been using? We know that 700 and 800 years later the Irish were occupying single-roomed cabins that had neither chimney nor window.

The Vikings used sets of folding bronze scales – instruments applied in the assessing of weights of commodities and in striking commercial bargains. They introduced coinage and have added other words to the Irish vocabulary e.g. *pinginn* = penny, *schilling* = shilling, *margadh* = market, words which indicate their propensity for commercial activity; the concept of markets began in Viking Dublin. This also suggests that the native people were not advanced in matters of trade and commerce, and were slow to recognise the advantages of coinage as a medium of exchange.

Had the native people worked in unison with the Vikings/Norsemen and taken more readily to the type of weaponry they were using, (such as the lethal iron swords and axes that have been found in their graves) they would have been better equipped to tackle the next wave of invaders. This occurred 156 years after Clontarf, and the valley of the Boyne had to wait until then before the newcomers, theNormans, looked at the region and recognised that it was an ideal location for the establishment of a community to be known as ***Droichead Átha.***

Chapter Four

The Cistercians

Mellifont: The Cistercians' first Irish Monastery
They had a profound influence on the Irish way of life.

The 'Island of Saints and Scholars' recovered in God's own good time from the predations of the Vikings, although it must be said that many benefits had accrued from their coming. The next leap forward came in 1142 when the Cistercian monks arrived from France. They sailed up the Boyne, passed 'Drogheda' and reached Oldbridge where the little tributary, the Mattock, joins the main river, and a short distance from there they settled in an idyllic vale to which they gave the delightfully pleasant name 'Mellifont' or 'Fountain of Honey'.

Saint Malachy, who had been to their monastery at Clairvaux and met St. Bernard, was greatly impressed by the purity and asceticism of the Cistercian way of life. 'Our food is scanty, our garments rough; our drink is from the stream and our sleep often upon our book'. (One brother took up residence in the hollow of an old oak tree!). Malachy was responsible for bringing them to Ireland. Later on, their community at Mellifont grew to 140 members.[1] They brought with them enlightenment and the latest techniques in farm husbandry, and they were to exercise a powerful and lasting influence on the surrounding countryside and its people. It was their wont to establish abbeys in terrain that was poor and impoverished, and then to enrich it by sheer dint of muscle and sweat.

The chapter house, cloisters, refectory, lavabo and church were fully in place within 15 years. According to tradition, a subterranean passage connects Mellifont with the Old Abbey in Drogheda and with Monasterboice, but this possibility is discounted today. For a considerable time the monks maintained a close link with the parent establishment at Clairvaux.

The native inhabitants were greatly attracted to the Cistercian ethos, and they flocked to Mellifont. There were said to have been 300 lay brothers there within a short time, but this may be an exaggeration.[2] Five daughter houses were founded within a matter of only four years, and the total number eventually reached about 40, including a Scottish daughter house in the Mull of Kintyre.

They introduced a whole new world of know-how and a much better life style to a backward and introverted people. As an offshore island on the continental shelf, Ireland was disadvantaged in several ways, being quite isolated from the European mainstream. It suffered in consequence from cultural inbreeding, and was deficient in the matter of social intercourse, a condition that tended to accentuate its insularity. A bright new light was now being shed on a people who were living in a twilight zone through a dearth of communication with the outside world.

Architecture: A new concept of monastic architecture appeared; the new buildings were large and impressive, employing ornate stonework, and the stamp of systematic planning was very evident in the layout of the buildings. By contrast, there had previously been little semblance of regulatory pre-planning in Irish buildings – they tended to be scattered haphazardly in the monastic enclosures, and the materials used were, for the most part, of impermanent clay and wattle or timber.

Doorway of the Chapter House. It was cannibalised in the late 1700s

In the construction of Mellifont Abbey the monks were not satisfied by using any materials that happened to be nearby, but went to great lengths in seeking out the most suitable materials. To illustrate their uncompromising efforts to attain excellence, they used local slate and stone for the rubble walling of their buildings, but for selected sections they tastefully used sandstone from further afield. Much of the selected materials required to be shipped from abroad to Ireland and hauled up the Boyne to the building site; limestone was imported from both the Dundry quarries near Bristol and from Caen in Normandy.[3] Evidently a bi-lateral trading arrangement existed with Bristol which became extensive, for in the twelfth century a street in Bristol was called 'Irish Street'.[4]

The consecration of the abbey in 1157 was performed with pomp and circumstance in the presence of the High King of Ireland, several lesser kings and seventeen bishops. Donations included most of the initial land endowment, also 'seven score cows and three score ounces of gold', a gold chalice and altar cloths.[5] There were many other generous donations, an indication that the people at large embraced the new arrivals and were over-awed by the innovations and splendour that they created. This appreciation of the presence of the Cistercians was a prerequisite if the native Irish way of life were to advance, and they would benefit by following their example. Within the precincts of Mellifont they were admiring one of the most important and magnificent monastic edifices ever erected in Ireland.

The Cistercian Influence: The Irish were very successful at dairy farming, as proven by the 45,000 traces of ring forts that still dot the Irish countryside. As to other farming practices, these were deplorably primitive; there had been a predilection to rearing livestock rather than tilling the land – it was less arduous! Whatever tillage took place was accomplished by attaching makeshift wooden ploughs to the tails of oxen. The newcomers were self sufficient, producing all their own crops and foodstuffs. They introduced up-to-date farming methods and intensive cultivation. They demonstrated that additional fruits could be wheedled from the soil through crop rotation and the application of labour in a more knowledgeable way. Barren land became productive.

Religious practices had degenerated and were in urgent need of reform, and under the Cistercian influence that golden era of learning received a refreshing boost to continue flowering. A Synod was held in Drogheda at the 'Old Abbey' in 1152 where Cardinal Paparo distributed the four Archiepiscopal palls at Armagh, Dublin, Cashel and Tuam. After 1322 only persons of English descent were allowed within the abbey, a proviso that was

29

'introduced by the enemies of the human race', and was a portent of future racial divisiveness that bedevilled Ireland thereafter.

Much of the vast expanse of land which they acquired was undeveloped, and included moorland, marshland and wasteland and they applied their expertise and energies in draining, manuring and cultivating the soil. Their territories covered parts of both present day counties Louth and Meath, and included locations as far away as Ballymascanlan, north of Dundalk, and familiar local townlands such as Townley Hall, Newtown Stalaban, Mell and 'Drogheda'. Preparing the land for cultivation called for a considerable amount of labour. Initially they performed the work themselves, but in time they engaged outside help, a policy that would have sustained many families that were scattered in and around their territory.

This drew people to the area, a factor which contributed to a population increase among the nucleated settlements. We must bear this in mind when visualising the gradual growth in the infrastructure of the region, and it had a direct bearing on the ultimate establishment of a much larger settlement, namely the town of *Droichead Átha*. We will see that several other religious orders came to the area in the years following the arrival of the Anglo-Normans. All of these institutions contributed to the dissemination of general knowledge within the native population and, in particular, they shed light in the matter of land management. They were major contributors to the region's socio-economic development which is the lifeblood of any community.

The lands owned by the Cistercians included a number of out-farms known as 'granges', a word which describes an outlying farm belonging to a religious community. The average size of a grange was 700 acres, and as early as 1185 they held no fewer than fourteen of these, including Sheepgrange, Grangegeeth and Littlegrange. A new grange acquired by them which lay along the banks of the Boyne, and where some curious pagan buildings existed, received the pedestrian name of 'New Grange'.

They were the dominant force in the land, and in later times, under the influence of the Normans, the abbot was also a Lord of Parliament and a Justice of the Peace, and as such he became increasingly prominent in public affairs.[6] We will continue to encounter the name 'Mellifont' time and again throughout the pages of local history under a variety of contexts, inferring that its influence was certainly great and extended well beyond the abbey itself into regional and national affairs. The monks' activities covered not alone spiritual matters, but also impinged on civic and commercial matters. This had long lasting consequences for the inhabitants in the adjacent territories, setting the scene for one region in particular that would develop in time into a great, thriving community – the town of Drogheda.

> "The Cistercians were claiming that the site of the church of Saint Mary at Drogheda was originally the site of a chapel held by the Cistercians at Mellifont. This chapel, they claimed, was located on their own abbey lands and had been built for the sake of the parishioners of Mellifont dwelling at a distance from the parish church, that is, the abbey church.
>
> "Not only the members of the community, monks and lay brothers were subject to the abbot's authority, but all the hired labourers, the serfs and the tenants were also his subjects even in temporal matters: for the medieval abbot was also a feudal lord and the landlord of an extensive domain. ... The abbot of Mellifont was lord of **a domain amounting to fifty thousand acres** which was populated by tenants and vassals of various degrees as well as serfs ... [He held] the power of life and death over his secular subjects of which the manorial pillory and gallows were a grim reminder".[7]

This illustrates that the impact of the Cistercian community on the local populace was profound. *In short, they revolutionised the way of life that then existed, and their presence was a prime factor in the ultimate establishment and growth of the town of Drogheda.*

They had not long settled down at Mellifont – only a short thirty years – when the Normans arrived. A friendly relationship was established from the outset, although a rivalry later developed with monks who emanated from England. King Henry II confirmed in 1178 their title to the lands held by them, and indeed augmented it with lands that the invaders had seized from the native Irish. King Henry III granted them in 1227 the right to hold a fair every

Coracles made from hides were still being used on the Boyne in the early 1900s.

Tuesday in Collon – a lucrative concession. Fairs were important building-blocks in the creation of the commercial structure of the region. In later times the monks exercised their position as landlords, leasing some of their land rather than working it directly.

Commercialism had entered the scene, and while this helped to stimulate a sense of business acumen among the lay community, it tended to erode the asceticism which had been the *raison d'etre* of the monks. Another privilege was granted to them 26 years later whereby they and their successors were absolved from paying tolls and other such dues on all their goods being bought or sold for their own use in markets throughout the king's dominions. These concessions were of considerable value and indicate that the monks were heavily engaged in commercial enterprises – the enormous extent of their lands certainly gave scope for this. They exported great quantities of corn and other farm produce to England. They also constructed several mills, the waterwheels of which were powered by the waters of the Boyne. Another source of income was fishing rights. At the time of the dissolution of the monasteries they had 16 fishing coracles or skin-boats at Oldbridge. This was the distinctive type of vessel that was still in use in that stretch of the Boyne up to the early part of the twentieth century.

In his treatise on pre-Norman settlements, T.B. Barry tells us: "Most scholars of the Early Christian Church in Ireland would now probably agree that by the eleventh century the most successful monasteries had outgrown their original purely religious functions, and this was possibly an accidental result of the eighth century *Cele De* movement which sought to separate the religious core of the monastery from the lay accretions that grew up around it.[8]

The Abbot was a man of influence and often held down another job; he was closely involved in secular affairs and was not necessarily an ordained priest. It can be seen that the confraternity comprising of the abbot, the monks and the lay brothers had assumed the role of a 'local government' and was as dominant as the landlord system that later replaced it. The monks were also hard-headed businessmen.

On the other hand, they had the obligation of maintaining the roads and bridges. The commercial activities in which they were engaged involved the constant haulage of farm produce, and it was in their own interest to improve the infrastructure of the area by constructing roads and bridges. No doubt other religious houses stimulated trade in the same way and contributed to the overall commonwealth of the region.

An ecclesiastical settlement was sited at Duleek dating back probably to the fifth century, and a grange from the monastery at Llanthony was established there in the twelfth century, attracting a self-supporting settlement from which today's village of Duleek sprung. The Cistercians also had a presence there. Wealthy Anglo-Norman families in medieval times erected wayside crosses to commemorate departed relatives, asking passers-by to pray for their souls. A few of these are in the Duleek area, one dating from the reign of Elizabeth I:

THIS CROSS WAS BUILDED BY JENET DOWDALL WIFE TO WILLIAM BATHE OF ATHCARNE, JUSTICE OF HER MAJESTIES COURT OF COMMON PLEES FOR HIM AND HER 1601. HE DECEASED THE 15 OF OC 1599 BURIED IN THE CHURCH OF DULEEK WHOSE SOULES I PRAY GOD TAKE TO HIS MERCIE.

Within only twenty years of their arrival at Mellifont, eleven more Cistercian abbeys were established throughout Ireland, and the final figure was almost forty. So evenly were they scattered throughout the island as to suggest a degree of pre-planning. One was Bective Abbey located further upstream by the banks of the Boyne. Their presence impacted on the populace at large, introducing the local citizenry to an enhanced welfare that operated in parallel with the religious communities. They may not have realised that the social and economic advancement of which they formed part had a root cause – the overall prosperity being created was the result of colonies of people working in unison towards a common goal. Like the honey in a beehive which bees accumulate, wealth was being created and was being shared by all. A progressive, unified society begets its own welfare.

The hoard found at Sheephouse

In that way the dynamic force of the Cistercians dispelled the pre-existing introspection and insularity, and continued to make a desirable impact on the land, on the economy and on the people, a happy state of affairs that continued for centuries. Then came a sudden halt. We will later discuss the reason, but suffice to say that the abbeys were vacated, only to become derelict and ivy-clad ruins, and about half of these still remain as silent memorials of a glorious bygone age. Today they are objects of admiration and awe, and some are well worth a visit, notably those at Boyle, Jerpoint, Baltinglass, Bective, and of course the Mother House at Mellifont.

A huge quantity of floor tiles have been found at the Mellifont site, together with about 1,600 carved stones. Some restoration work has been undertaken, including a section of the Romanesque cloister arcade, giving the visitor a glimpse of the architectural splendour of the past.

The proprietor of Sheephouse Quarry tells us that a hoard of liturgical artefacts was found by a workman, Jack Farrell, in the quarry in 1899. They consist of an elaborately designed cross, a candlestick and a bell. They are thought to have been secreted there by the monks of Mellifont, which is only 3km away, and the items are now in the National Museum.[9] Excavations in 1953-54 yielded a small silver chalice and a paten.

Henry VIII was the person who unceremoniously put an end to it all when he passed legislation placing all church property in his hands. By that time the Cistercian vigour was in decline throughout Ireland, but Mellifont still had a community of 21 – it was the wealthiest, after St. Mary's in Dublin, of all their abbeys. They were taken over piecemeal by the king's men, that of Mellifont taking place on 23rd July 1539. It then became the property of the Moore family, from which **the Earls of Drogheda** arose, a subject that will receive our attention.

It was ordained that the impartial pendulum of Fate would in the course of time swing all the way back from whence it had come. In 1938 a group of monks made its way from Mount Melleray in Co. Waterford to re-establish a monastery at New Mellifont – only 3km from the site where the original Irish Cistercian monastery was founded 800 years earlier. Today they occupy the former property in Collon of Speaker Foster. The Fosters had acquired it from the Moore family, and the Moores had sequestered it from the Cistercians.

*   *   *   *

This brings us to a seminal point in our exposition. We have seen that a group of early arrivals to Ireland selected the valley of the Boyne in which to settle. They cleared the terrain of virgin forests to make way for the cultivation of the land. Later the Celts took over, and they continued to adapt the land to their requirements. The Romans barely gave Ireland a passing glance. Had they settled down, they would have changed everything. Everything was changed several centuries later with the arrival of Saint Patrick.

Looking back, we see that the Boyne valley region had been frequented by several disparate races of people from time to time, starting with Neolithic Man, and later by the Celts, and (superficially) the Romans. These early arrivals made a contribution in one way or another to the environment. They helped in clearing the wilderness of the dense undergrowth, and in presenting the more recent arrivals with wide, open spaces of well-drained agricultural land that was suitable both for grazing and tillage. In that way they adapted Mother Nature to their needs.

Apart from constructing the passage graves and taming the environs, they left but little visible impact on the topography in the form of permanent civic structures such as housing, villages, roads, bridges, etc. (The latecomers – the Vikings and then the Cistercians – introduced a more concentrated form of communal living, to which the native population were merely on the periphery – they were little more than onlookers). The region hosted a population which, whatever its numbers, was pastoral and agricultural; it had been semi-nomadic and was at best living in small family farmsteads or ring forts. Their efforts throughout the hinterland of the Boyne valley were a preparation for a thriving town that would one day blossom into full flower in the region. But there was as yet little evidence of a cohesive, permanent settlement in that particular area on which our attention is focused. The concept of social integration and village life was as yet absent from the Gaelic ethos. In other words the town of Drogheda was, as yet, unborn.

However, with the coming of Christianity there arose an abundance of monastic establishments throughout the area, such as at Ardbraccan, Bective, Colpe, Clonard, 'Drogheda', Duleek, Kells, Mellifont, Monasterboice, Mornington, Slane, Termonfeckin, etc. These were at or near the Boyne valley. Undoubtedly, there were webs of inter-communicating links between them, and these provided a makeshift civic infrastructure that also served the general community. Their influence and authority on the populace and on the civic development grew with the centuries, especially after the arrival of the Cistercians.

Few traces of the early churches and monastic buildings, being made from timber or wattle and daub (mud), have survived. With the passage of time they have simply melted into the terrain from whence they came, leaving little or no trace. What is surprising is the fact that the early monks, so meticulous in matters of art, showed such lack of initiative and know-how in the construction of their buildings. The church of Saint Cianan at Duleek (which the Vikings vandalised in 1027) is specifically mentioned in the Book of Armagh as being built of stone, inferring that stonework as a building material was quite exceptional in that period. The very name 'Duleek' means 'house of stone'. It seems that prior to the eighth century, churches were, for the most part, timber structures.[10]

It was around these monasteries that people tended to cluster; there were many reasons for this, not least of which was the prospect of employment by the monks. Moreover, the communal monastic lifestyle was seen to be successful and served as a model for those in the outside world to follow. We can pass over the Vikings' visit to the area because they left no enduring marks on the local landscape. They had selected the Liffey in preference to the Boyne for the construction of a major community centre. When Brian Boru finally saw them off, the influence of the monasteries on the populace – both temporal and spiritual – continued to grow.

It has been necessary so far within these pages to use inverted commas whenever we encounter the name 'Drogheda' because all references up to this point of our discourse have been to *the general area, or to the site now occupied by the town, but not to the town as such,* since we are discussing a green valley where there was little or no concentrated habitation. However, the essential requirements for the founding of a town were falling into place. The inverted commas that accompany the name 'Drogheda' disappear forever with the arrival of another race of people. This occurred in the year 1169 AD when the Anglo-Normans arrived.

They were different. They changed the landscape and they changed the way of life of all who inhabited the landscape. More than that, they changed the course of Irish history, and it was they – and nobody else – who put the town of Drogheda on the map.

PART 2

THE BIRTH OF DROGHEDA

It took our predecessors 4,000 years of preparation to establish an environment that was conducive to the founding of a town. When the time was right, along came the Anglo-Normans, versatile, creative, adaptable and quick to recognise that the prerequisites were in place for the founding of a new and lasting settlement along the banks of the Boyne. It would provide them with the necessities of life and a bit more. We will see that Drogheda's growth to maturity was surprisingly rapid, and that the town played an important part in Ireland's overall development – these were the glory days of Drogheda.

It is hardly an exaggeration to say that Drogheda was central to Ireland's destiny in the period that followed, when two uninvited – but important – visitors arrived in the town. They were Oliver Cromwell and then William of Orange, characters who influenced Ireland's fate immeasurably during the 250 years that followed their arrival.

Chapter Five

The Founding of Drogheda and Its Early Growth

THE NORMANS: Up to this point, the various peoples who from time to time occupied the land did not seriously interfere with the environment. That is to say, they accepted the existing surroundings as they found them and made few modifications to the topography (the tumuli excepted). They coalesced with the landscape they had chosen as their home. The Normans, on the other hand, were creative, assertive and dynamic, and they rapidly insinuated their dominance everywhere they went.

They made a permanent imprint not only on the land, but also on the lives of the people who occupied it. They were the descendants of the Norsemen who had settled in Normandy a few centuries earlier and had become Christianised. The blood of the Vikings ran through their veins; they were adventurous, industrious, vigorous and innovative; they were also military minded, and above all they were disciplined. They operated in unison and in a common cause, and these traits were to bring them success at every turn.

They proved their military superiority when they invaded England from their base in Normandy. Straight away they tackled the unfortunate King Harold and defeated him, piercing his eye in battle with an arrow, according to legend – 1066 and all that. They were pro-active, impacting the environment with their presence wherever they went. It is astonishing to observe that within the brief period of 20 years they had constructed 5,000 fortified castles throughout the length and breadth of England. This work involved quarrying a greater volume of stones than used by the Egyptians when they were building the pyramids. Their trademark of discipline and efficiency is manifest in that mammoth achievement known to history as the Domesday Book, a comprehensive survey of property and land that embraced the whole of England; it had been prepared for taxation purposes. No accomplishment as ambitious as that had ever before been produced anywhere in the world up to that time. This gives us an insight into their character and their capabilities as organisers.

These are the people who invaded Ireland – and we pause in wonderment that this momentous event occurred a mere century after their arrival in England. They were a formidable foe, not to be trifled with. To repel such a talented adversary any defenders would need to be exceptionally well prepared. But there was no effective centralised governing authority within Ireland to challenge them; on the contrary there was disunity, with the various chieftains constantly squabbling among themselves.

THE NORMAN INVASION: The immediate cause of the invasion was the chagrin of Dermot McMurrough, king of Leinster. He was a rough, tough individual, cruel and treacherous, and his whole career was one of violence; all in all, he was a bad egg. The Annals of the Four Masters record that he visited Brú na Bóinne in 1170, plundering and setting fire to Dowth. The Norman historian Giraldus Cambrensis wrote of him that he was 'one who preferred to be feared rather than to be loved, who was obnoxious to his own people and an object of hatred to strangers. His hand was against every man, and every man's hand against him'. At that time the constant struggles among the Irish chieftains were in full spate, with each one trying to dominate the other, and McMurrough was always near the top of the pile.

He had invaded Breffni (Cavan/Longford) and he made away with Dervorgilla, the wife of Tiernan O'Rourke, prince of Breffni. O'Rourke appealed for help to Turlough

O'Connor, the High King, who in 1153 marched with an army composed of the men of both Breffni and Meath against McMurrough, forcing him to restore Dervorgilla together with her rich dowry. We are told that she spent the rest of her days in Mellifont Abbey doing penance and performing works of charity. (The suspicion remains that her kidnapping by Dermot McMurrough might better be described as an elopement – they had been in correspondence with each other! Anyway, she paid in full for her indiscretion because her spell of penance was a lengthy one – she was 85 when she died). Here we perceive a pointer that Mellifont was already occupying a dominant place in the minds and lives of the Irish people – it had been established a mere eleven years at this time but was already making its presence felt. The ruins of the monastery that we see today, impressive as they are, tell us but little of its former importance and of its influence on the surrounding countryside and on its people.

Smarting from the indignity of having to return both the lady and the loot, Dermot McMurrough sought the aid of King Henry II of England, offering to hold his kingdom of Leinster under the sovereignty of the English king, and to acknowledge him as his lord and master. It was an offer that the king could not refuse, and in May 1169 a mail-clad contingent landed at Bannow Strand under Maurice Prendergast and Robert FitzStephen.

The native Irish went barefoot into battle

The following year Richard de Clare, better known as Strongbow, arrived with a force of 3,000, many of whom were clad in chain armour. Wexford, Waterford and the other Hiberno-Norse strongholds fell one by one to superior military strength. When Dublin was captured, McMurrough, to fulfil a promise, gave the hand of his daughter Aoife in marriage to Strongbow who was a widower. By the same token, Strongbow also became the heir-in-succession to the kingdom of Leinster. This was in contravention of the old Brehon laws whereby the king's sons were empowered to elect a successor. Here we encounter the first break with Gaelic tradition, and by such a facile means did Leinster fall into the lap of the Normans, and thereby did the destiny of Ireland eventually take an irreversible turn.

Let it be said that it was only a matter of time before an invasion force would arrive. It was inevitable that it would happen sooner or later because of Ireland's proximity to the Normans, and conquest was in their blood. Colonisation came easy to them, as was their predilection for law and order – we have seen how effectively they brought the Anglo-Saxons to heel.

It is known that William the Conqueror himself had cast his covetous eye on Ireland. His successor King Henry II had been in discussion with the Pope as far back as 1155 concerning its acquisition. The Church in Ireland had become undisciplined and morally lax. Many aspects of Church life were in need of correction. (We must bear in mind that the rule of celibacy was only at that time being introduced into the Church). King Henry II had been granted 'hereditary possession of Ireland' by a papal bull issued by Pope Adrian IV. His claim to fame is that he was the only Englishman ever to have been elected Pope. He has a lot to answer for, one might be prompted to remark, in the light of subsequent events in Ireland. But in fact the Pope was acting in the firm conviction that this would be for the betterment of the Christian religion and for the general good of the Irish people. The Papal Bull, which was named *'Laudabiliter'*, was aimed at 'rooting out vice' and it directed King Henry:

> *" ... to extend the bounds of the church, to proclaim to a rude and untaught people the truth of the Christian faith, and to root out nurseries of vice from the fields of the Lord ... So we ... are pleased and willing ... that you shall enter that island and do therein what tends to the honour of God and the salvation of the people."[1]*

Henry II granted the province of Meath to de Lacy

Shortly after the initial invasion took place Henry II himself arrived. He was worried at the success of Strongbow and he foresaw the possibility of this ambitious adventurer setting up a rival Norman dynasty, and he deemed it necessary to clip his wings. He granted the Lordship of Meath to Hugh de Lacy, whose name we shall encounter again within the pages of this book, and Uriel (Louth) to Bertram de Verdon, who had experience as a Crusader in the Holy Land. These allocations of territories were intended as a counterbalance, and Strongbow was thereby kept in check. The Kingdom of Meath at this time was very extensive, stretching from the east coast at Bettystown all the way westward to the Shannon and incorporating Westmeath and parts of Offaly and Longford in addition to present day Meath. Indeed, there were five provinces at the time, Meath constituting the fifth one; Louth at that time formed part of Ulster.

One of the endless internecine wars between Irish chieftains had been in progress at that time in Meath; on this particular occasion it was a war of succession brought about by the death of Murrough O'Melaghlin in 1153, the outcome of which was that Donnell O'Rourke and Rory O'Connor were victors and they partitioned Meath between themselves. This factionalism eased the way for de Lacy, because O'Rourke, who became the new king of Eastmeath, supinely submitted to him without a fight. The king's grant to de Lacy stated that he was to hold the territory "as Murrough O'Melaghlin or any other before or after him best held it". The power attaching to the grant was known as a 'liberty', meaning that the king was delegating a portion of his royal prerogative to de Lacy. It can thus be seen that he was all-powerful – virtually a king – in his new domain which covered most of present day north Leinster, and reached into Cavan.

The native Irish were held in distain by the clean-shaven, business-like newcomers who were wont to pull the beards of the indigenous chieftains – this may be interpreted as an unconscious display of superiority. The Irish wore clothes of wool, which took the form of long cloaks reaching to the knees, and the colour was the natural grey or black. They did not wear armour, and they were sometimes barefooted going into battle. They rode their horses bareback and without stirrups. Some Irish clans supported the invaders who relentlessly swept forward, while the local chiefs continued to bicker among themselves. This characteristic of disunity, coupled with the treachery of informers, was to plague Irish resistance to foreign domination right into modern times, frustrating the selfless sacrifices of the true patriots.

De Lacy quickly asserted himself in the land he had just taken over. The Anglo-Norman penchant for order and discipline is evident from the organised manner in which they divided the land into shires or counties. They accepted, more or less, the existing boundaries of the native kingdoms and sub-kingdoms and then set to work in adapting them to their own requirements.

SYSTEMATIC COLONISATION: To consolidate his conquest, de Lacy straight away implemented a policy of systematic colonisation. This method he employed throughout his territory, and it brought him success with surprising ease. Through the policy of infeudation he apportioned Eastmeath among ten major barons, (retaining large portions for himself). These barons further subdivided their expansive holdings into manors – thus there were three strata in all. In that way de Lacy was able to build up a well-structured, functional system of administration.

Some of the resulting settlements which he created have survived into today's market towns and villages. The major ones were the walled boroughs of Ardee, Trim, Kells, Navan and Athboy – all of which are still the principal towns of Meath – and, of course, Drogheda.

The intermediate stratum contained seven smaller, unwalled settlements which had names that are still familiar to us today, viz. Slane, Nobber, Dunshaughlin, Dunboyne, Duleek, Skryne (or Skreen) and Ratoath.

These settlements have not only survived into the twenty-first Century but have grown into self-contained communities in their own right – Skryne excepted. They were sited at strategic locations, and were already monastic centres. In addition, many manorial villages sprung up throughout Meath, but most have since disappeared underneath the sod. Finally, mottes (or fortifications) were constructed, and these were mainly at river crossings, around which further settlements grew up. The mottes created stable conditions for everyone engaged in the pursuit of farming and marketing, and the element of security for the settlers was a major influence in the region's growth and prosperity.

The fringes of the overall area now occupied by the Normans, which would later be known as the Pale, were constantly exposed to attack by the Irish, but within the Pale itself a mixed farming economy was established and continued to expand. Little is known of roads in Ireland in medieval times, but it may be taken that they were primitive, being little more than beaten tracks. (It has been suggested that the Irish word 'bóthar' (= 'road') is derived from the word 'bó' (= 'cow'), but it is readily conceded that the tracks left by the random meanderings of a cow are not the answer to the requirements either of a medieval courier or one of today's busy commercial travellers! Paved, purpose-built roads were conspicuously absent. The excavation of ancient burial sites in Britain and elsewhere have turned up *wheeled* vehicles and chariots, but not in Ireland.

The construction of mottes was an effective means by which the Normans were able to protect their conquered territories from the hostile Irish. These mottes sprang up like mushrooms wherever they went. A motte was a substantial earthen mound surrounded by a fosse or ditch. On the summit of the motte was erected a timber tower surrounded by a protective wooden palisade. Locally, they were set up at Duleek, Skryne, Navan, Knowth, Slane and Drogheda. This military control was essential to the colonisation and progressive settlement of Louth/Meath, affording the essential element of security for the inhabitants.

The next requirement was a place of worship, and every community had one. Early references to alehouses are hard to find – the 'local pub' seems to have been an innovation introduced by the native Irish. It is hardly necessary to point out that the origin of the words *shebeen* and *poiteen* is neither Latin, Norse nor Saxon! And the word 'whiskey' is derived from *uisge beatha*. Being gregarious by nature, the newcomers were particularly adept at founding townships, knowing well the clear advantages that communal living offered – they had already founded many bustling towns throughout England. A community thrives on unity, to coin a phrase.

Occasionally mottes were built on top of existing ring-forts. (It was only in 1908 that it was established that the mottes were Norman structures – prior to then they were attributed to the Vikings/Danes). Sometimes an outermost wall – called a bailey – was added. The territories granted to de Verdon (in Louth) and de Lacy (in Meath) had a greater concentration of mottes than anywhere else in Ireland – there were about thirty of them distributed within de Verdon's territory and in the much more expansive territory of de Lacy there were about one hundred. This suggests that the Louth/Meath area had an early concentration of Normans and supported a greater population than most other parts of Ireland. Settlements tended to develop around these mottes, and carpenters, masons and other craftsmen were encouraged to come over from Britain and settle, and in that way the Norman influence was affirmed. Later, the mottes or mottes-and-baileys were replaced by stout, sturdy castles – castles that were constructed of stone to effectively withstand both hostile assaults and the ravages of the elements. The colonists were here to stay.

Although the newcomers were settling down and being consolidated into thriving communities, one factor was missing, namely a major trading post or central marketplace where the goods being produced could be sold or exchanged, and where surplus produce could be taken for export. The infrastructure was now in place and the requisite disparate parts were present for this to occur; all that was required was some leader with entrepreneurial ability to unify the component parts. Such a man was at hand – his name was Hugh de Lacy.

HUGH DE LACY – A Pen-picture: De Lacy was certainly an important personage, judging by the large slice of territory that was apportioned to him by the king. He was also appointed Justiciar of Dublin. (The post of 'Justiciar' was at later times variously known as Chief Governor, *Custos*, King's Lieutenant, Lord Deputy, Chief Justice, Lord Lieutenant, and later again as Viceroy). In effect he was the king's representative and was the highest authority in the land. Between de Verdon and de Lacy, they both possessed some of the most fertile lands in Ireland.

For the location of his own residence, de Lacy selected an area by the banks of 'the pleasant Boyne' where a religious community and a handful of peasants were already formed into a community – in the course of time it would burgeon out into the town of Trim. The complexity and extent of his castle – it was later extended by his son Walter – was a clarion call to the world; it proclaimed that de Lacy was a powerful man. The castle, complete with protective outer walls and turrets, was built for prestige purposes rather than as a fortification, and at the time it vied with the best in Europe. Even today (partly restored) it is a very impressive sight. Nonetheless he took no chances, for some of the walls were 3½ m. (11ft.) thick. The ravages of time and the local community had not succeeded fully in destroying it, and the recent restoration efforts by the Board of Works are most commendable. A visit to the site is an instructive and rewarding experience and is highly advocated; indeed, a fine should be imposed on anyone purporting to be a student of local history who fails to visit it!

De Lacy's people came from Normandy, and he was blessed with those qualities that produce good leadership. He was firm and resolute, vigilant and farsighted, and was also benign and sensitive towards his underlings. He was energetic, intelligent, diplomatic and was also an excellent administrator, assets that helped him in his thirsting ambitions of acquiring honours and renown. In appearance he was dark, with small, deep-set eyes, a flat nose, a scarred cheek, a short neck and a hairy sinewy body.[2]

An envisionment of de Lacy's castle at Trim in its heyday

Following the Norman invasion, King Henry allotted him the expansive province of Meath which at that time extended to the Shannon and also included most of Offaly and Longford. Straight away he subdivided his territory, making grants of land among his barons, and he consolidating his territory with many castles, the more local ones being at Slane, Duleek, Delvin, Kells and Drogheda. He also founded monasteries at Duleek and Colpe. His ability as an organiser was accomplished by applying a tight rein to those under his control, and this policy was helped by restoring appropriated lands to the local peasants on the understanding that they would comply with the laws of the new régime. This was the perfect recipe for a sustained and peaceful co-existence.

His commitments took him away from Ireland in 1174. Indeed, given the facilities for travel and the vicissitudes of sea journeys during those times, one must admire his energies. His peregrinations are akin to those of a modern high-pressured business executive, for we find him in Canterbury in 1172, Caen in Normandy in 1173, in both Ireland and Rouen during 1174, Northampton in 1175 and Shrewsbury and Winchester in 1176. Between these journeys he was establishing mottes and castles throughout his new domain – more than 60 of these were constructed by him and his son Walter throughout the greater Meath area.

He initially 'fortified a house at Trim, and threw a fosse around it, and then enclosed it with a herisson [or stockaded rampart]',before departing for Normandy. While he was away, the Irish 'threw down the motte and levelled it even with the ground, but first of all they put the house to flames'. The castle that later replaced it was of stone, and was one of the finest in the whole of Europe. Today's remnants, partly restored by the OPW as stated, are still a very impressive sight and a delight to examine.

King Henry appointed him Justiciar, or Chief Governor of Ireland. In 1180 he married Rose, Rory O'Connor's daughter, a step that was taken without King Henry's sanction. Likewise, Strongbow had married Aoife (or Eve), the daughter of Dermot McMurrough. The king was suspicious of these moves, surmising that these powerful lords were aiming to set up a separate kingdom. Thereupon he stripped de Lacy of his offices, but restored them a year later. His subsequent campaigns took him not only to Connaught against the native Irish but also to Languedoc in France against the Albigenses. He touched base occasionally at his original castle in Wales.

He also found time to focus his attention on a green valley down-stream from his castle at Trim. He was seeking a suitable location where his followers could settle down. It was close to the mouth of the Boyne and a convenient departure point leading to their motherland. Thus came into existence the Town of Drogheda.

Hugh de Lacy had an untimely end. He was in the process of building a castle at Durrow when he met his death in an unexpected way. He had chosen a site that was within the precincts of the monastery founded by St. Columcille, and the local chieftain, known as 'An Sionnach' ('The Fox'), deemed this to be a sacrilegious act. Resenting it, he instructed a follower to kill him. The assassin bore the enigmatic name Gilla gan Inathair O'Meyey ('the Lad without Bowels'); he set out for Durrow with an axe secreted beneath his long cloak, and he withdrew it at the opportune moment, namely when de Lacy was making a tour of inspection of the construction work. His head came off with a single blow and rolled into a ditch. The assassin then made a speedy exit back to his master. This incident occurred in the year 1186.

His body was at first interred at Durrow, but later translocated to Bective Abbey. The head was sent to Dublin for burial at the instigation of the Pope. The populace, including the native Irish, grieved at his passing – he had been revered as their king. Indeed, as Lord of Meath and as the king's Viceroy or Chief Governor he was the King's Deputy.

It can be seen that Hugh de Lacy was a remarkably talented man. He was endowed with rare qualities, enabling him to supplant the former Irish way of life – such as it was – with a better, more organised system. Unlike the earlier intruders, the Vikings and those that followed in a later age, namely the New English, he is associated neither with massacres or wanton destruction. No pillaging took place, no abbeys were demolished, no inhabitants were butchered. As a Christian, he worked closely with the Cistercians and the other religious houses. He himself founded new churches and abbeys. Supplanting the old native ways could not have been an easy task, but he won the confidence of the natives and then absorbed them, backward as they were, without undue acrimony. He ruled his province with justice and the result was peace and prosperity. It can be said that his premature death was a serious setback to the development of Ireland.

Why has he, as the founder of Drogheda, been given so little recognition at local level? The town hosts no statue to his memory. No street, nor public building, nor business enterprise carries his name. It is a feature of the Irish mentality to look askance at most things English, and this is not surprising, given their treatment of the Irish people over the centuries. But de Lacy was not English – his people sprung from Normandy, and they were Vikings who had settled down. A sure sign of the maturing Irish mind was the naming of a foot-bridge in his honour at Scotch Hall in 2005.

His successors intermarried with the de Verdons of Louth. They and the other great Norman families that had accompanied him to Ireland, such as the Fitzgeralds, integrated and became part and parcel of the Irish people eventually becoming 'more Irish than the Irish themselves'. The sorrow and sufferings of the Penal Days and the deprivation that followed in later centuries were not of their doing. Indeed, they fought side by side with the native Irish to expel the more recent English, and they experienced confiscations, evictions and beheadings in the same way as did the indigenous people.

THE BIRTH OF DROGHEDA: Hugh de Lacy cast an experienced eye on a region that was further downstream from his residence at Trim; it was in a lush, green, river valley and was conveniently close to the sea. A seaport could be developed there to receive shipping, and its location presented a close link with his homeland which was a mere four or five hours away with a fair wind. Spanning the river was a bridge – this was the *new* bridge – that bridge which was a few miles downstream from Oldbridge (referred to in an earlier chapter).

The overall region contained communities of monks, their satellite granges and dependent workers and sundry scattered homesteads. Apart from that and a few booths and hovels, de Lacy was looking at 'a green field site'. He concluded that 'the place had potential', to use a phrase commonly used by today's property developers. Moreover, he knew that the land he was viewing had great natural fertility and was capable of sustaining a community in comfort. It had a desirable balance of grazing and arable land throughout the region.

His soldiers were mercenaries – soldiers of fortune – and as yet had received no pay for their services other than promises. What motivated them was the prospect of the spoils of war, and they had now completed their task. So this was pay back time. He deemed this location in the peaceful valley of the Boyne to be ideal in which his men could settle down, establish their roots, and raise families. So they put aside their longbows and spears and instead took up spades and scythes and they set to work.

We can see that something in the nature of an embryonic town was evolving – like a foetus stirring in the womb. Delivering the newly born town was a skill in which the Anglo-Normans were very adept – they had established them by the dozen in their homeland. They tackled the project with a will, sweeping away whatever old wooden shacks that stood about indifferently, erecting new sturdy houses and municipal buildings with a degree of refinement that amazed the onlookers, constructing paved streets – not in a haphazard manner, but streets that were set at right-angles to one another, and to a pre-designed layout. They land-filled the foreshore of the sluggish river to create a swifter current; this plus a fall of 2.1 metres between the town's bridge and the bar ensured an effective scouring action. Quays were constructed for the safe berthing of vessels and the discharging of cargoes.

The River Boyne, which was navigable as far as Trim (40km. upstream), was the main thoroughfare for traffic between de Lacy's new castle and the open sea, so that in the course of time farm produce of every description found its way downstream, giving the port a distinctive mercantile importance – it was at first no more than a trading post, but was becoming the focal point and the commercial centre for the entire region.

Just as the main river itself was the catchment area for a series of tributaries, it was likewise the catchment area for a wide variety of farm produce and livestock, all finding their way to the central marketplace. We can see that a symbiotic relationship was developing – this trading post was ideally located as the outlet for the surplus produce of Meath and Louth, and thus it was destined in the course of later centuries to become one of the principal ports of medieval Ireland, even eclipsing Dublin. The exported cargoes were mainly skins, hides and wool, and in the 1400s cargos of fish and particularly salmon were being exported to Bristol, Liverpool and Chester, with linen becoming pre-eminent in succeeding centuries. In 1558 exports from Drogheda yielded £8,700 compared with Dublin's total of £5,400. Between 1565 and 1598 linen yarn left Drogheda for Liverpool in 135 sailings.

The vessels returned with pottery, kitchenware, floor tiles and iron – we know this because these durable items have left their traces and still lie uncorrupted in the soil until they occasionally surrender to the archaeologist's trowel. We ponder at what other items were imported that have left no trace. The written records tell us that great quantities of wines were imported; we are not surprised that business was brisk when we discover that the price was 8 pence (€0.04) a gallon!

Archaeologists working in 1981 at the site that abuts the north-west corner of Saint Mary's Bridge at Shop Street have exposed an alignment of wooden posts which suggest that they may have formed part of a wharf, and dendrochronological analysis of the timber revealed dates of about the year 1200. This points to the berthing of vessels very soon after the town's founding. Limited as the archaeological probing had been, 5,000 small items came to light, including many medieval shards of pottery that originated in Bristol (Ham Green), also Chester and as far away as Bordeaux (Saintonge). Here we should note that Bordeaux and many other ports of France were under Anglo-Norman rule at that time. Similar finds which have come to light at Trim Castle no doubt found their way there from distant ports having entered the estuary at Baltray/Mornington and then been hauled slowly up the course of the Boyne.

Shipbuilding seems to have been an important industry throughout the centuries, and continued up to the mid 1800s. What is surprising is the fact that it commenced so soon after the town's founding. As early as 1222 King John 'ordered a galley to be constructed in the town of Drogheda'.

The diet of the townspeople is revealed from animal bones found at the site; they were mainly of sheep, with lesser quantities of cattle and pig bones plus a few bones of wild animals. A curious fact was the dearth of items relating to the 1400s and 1500s which may indicate a contraction of the population consequent to the Black Death (to be discussed later) and its aftermath. Finds of post-medieval pottery, floor tiles, clay pipes, etc. in the upper layers of soil all point to a subsequent recovery in trade and in the town's fortunes.

The initial bridge spanning the river at Droichead Átha was undoubtedly a crude, impermanent one, since it was made of hurdles resting on piles. Bridge building was another forte of the Normans, and here once again their penchant for orderly planning became evident, because they called in their experts and set about constructing a new and sturdier bridge – a permanent bridge of stone. This was set in place as early as the year 1204 – several years before Dublin got its first bridge. It is evident that these industrious people were building, not only for immediate needs, but also with an eye to the future. The town of Droichead Átha was beginning to take shape.

King John came to Ireland in 1210 and, true to form, he set about defining the boundary lines for the first twelve of the 32 counties that we have today. These were Dublin, Kildare, Meath, Uriel (Louth), Carlow, Kilkenny, Wexford, Waterford, Cork, Kerry, Limerick, and Tipperary. (Meath was sub-divided during the reign of Henry VIII to create the separate county of Westmeath; Longford also came into being at that time). He visited both Mellifont and Drogheda in August of that year, and is said to have held a parliament in the priory of St. John the Baptist. He ordained that English laws be applied in Ireland, and thus Norman authority was enforced on the indigenous population, although the ancient Brehon Laws still continued to operate in regions not under Norman control.

A granite boulder, suitably inscribed, stands in the forecourt of St. Peter's Church in West St.

The whole concept of land ownership and land usage was reshaped under the new régime, a régime which would soon be extended to regulate the territories owned by the various religious houses, organising them into dioceses and parishes. Churches were endowed, and staffed by clergy brought over from England and Wales. Also, artisans and craftsmen could practice their trades only if they belonged to a guild; and in true Norman fashion membership was restricted to those who were 'of English name and blood, of honest conversation, and also a free citizen.'[3] They were enticed over from England and given plots, each with an allotted, specified frontage inside Droichead Átha itself. In addition, three acres outside the town were parcelled out to each; citizenship and other privileges such as existed in England and Wales were also conferred on them.

These benign living conditions were conducive to the promotion of trade, and this was greatly facilitated by the introduction of coinage. Commerce was certain to bring prosperity under these circumstances, and being based on a market-oriented economy, continued to expand. Here we see in action the methodical, organisational skills that were the hallmark of the Normans. The result was a confident and contented community. In that way we are presented with a brand new town, a town that was conceived by the Normans, built by the Normans and – be not mistaken – it was to be *occupied exclusively by the Normans.*

We have seen that one of the first steps that they took in consolidating their hold on any new territory was the building of castles, and Drogheda was no exception. D'Alton tells us:

'On this principle, immediately after the invasion, two castles were erected here, the Castle of Drogheda, properly so styled, and the Castle of Blackagh or Ulnagh, as it is otherwise called in some ancient documents, both situated at the Meath side of the Boyne. It may be reasonably presumed that these were erected by Hugh de Lacy, the first Palatine of Meath, and who, by such erection of castles along the marches [or border areas], best secured the settlement of English rule within the district called the Pale ... In Newcomen's map the castle of Drogheda is distinctly marked as near the bridge, at the south side of the town, and it appears to have been the fortress designed in the corporate seal; not a trace, however, even of the foundations of this, or of the castle of Blackagh now remains to suggest their precise site; and during the lapse of centuries nothing worthy of historical notice is recorded in connection of either'.[4]

The charm of the Irish fair sex cast its spell on the newcomers, and there were several marriages in high places between the two cultures. A shrewd move on de Lacy's part was to marry in 1180 Rose, a daughter of Rory O'Connor, former High King of Ireland and recognised by Henry II as King of Connaught. This would open doors for him, and help to consolidate his objective of conquest and permanent settlement. It enabled him construct over

60 mottes throughout his territory. His eventful life ended abruptly, as we have seen, by being murdered in 1186. **He is the man who is acknowledged as being THE FOUNDER OF THE TOWN OF DROGHEDA.**

Drogheda has the distinction of being the first *new* town in Ireland that followed the Norman invasion. (The pre-existing towns were of Viking origin.) Such towns as Clonmel, Galway, Roscommon, Sligo, Tralee, etc. came decades or centuries later. Other new towns, none of which were in the east, were not allowed to survive, but were ransacked and obliterated by the 'wild Irish'. The settlement that blossomed into the town of Drogheda occurred a few years prior to 1186, and the formal date of its founding is fixed as being 1194 – the date of the first Charter. The Eight-Hundredth Anniversary of this event was marked by the issuing in 1994 of a special commemorative postage stamp – a rare distinction conferred by the postal authorities (See colour plate). In addition, a one-and-a-half-tonne boulder of best Wicklow granite and suitably inscribed has been placed on the forecourt of Saint Peter's R.C. church in West Street.

The text of the Charter is in Latin and the translation states:

GRANT OF URBAN LIBERTIES (THE LAW OF BRETEUIL) TO DROGHEDA BY WALTER DE LACY, EARL OF MEATH, 1194:

Walter de Lacy, Earl of Meath, to all his men and friends, French, English and Irish, greetings. Know that I have given, granted and by this present charter confirmed to all my burgesses of Drogheda dwelling on that side of the bridge which is next to our castle of Drogheda, that is, the southern side, the town and the burgages assigned to them formerly by lawful consideration and oaths of lawful knights and burgesses, namely, so that each burgage assigned to them should have fifty feet of front and three acres in the (common) field. I have granted also to them the river of Boyne from the sea to the bridge of Trim, free of all obstacles and the impediments of any weir, pool, or fishery so that with other boats and merchandise they may (freely) go and return there.

Further, I have granted to them the free Law of Breteuil even as such (liberies) are most freely and fully held in the land of the King of England. And all the above-said town, burgages and three acres, and the free law of Breteuil aforesaid I have given, granted and by this present charter confirmed to my said burgesses and their heirs after them, to have and to hold in heritage in free burgage of me and my heirs, rendering yearly for each burgage 12d. namely 6d. at Easter and 6d. at Michaelmas, for all service. Wherefore I will and firmly enjoin that the aforesaid burgesses and their heirs shall have and hold in heritage the abovesaid town, burgages and the three acres, well and in peace, freely and quietly, peaceably and honorably, fully and entirely, in wood and plain, in meadows and pastures, in ways and paths, with all the free liberties and customs appertaining to the free law of Breteuil.

'The Law of Breteuil' is a reference to a series of privileges that had been initially conferred on the town of Breteuil in Normandy; they were considered an ideal set of citizen rights and were later applied in many towns of England and France.

45

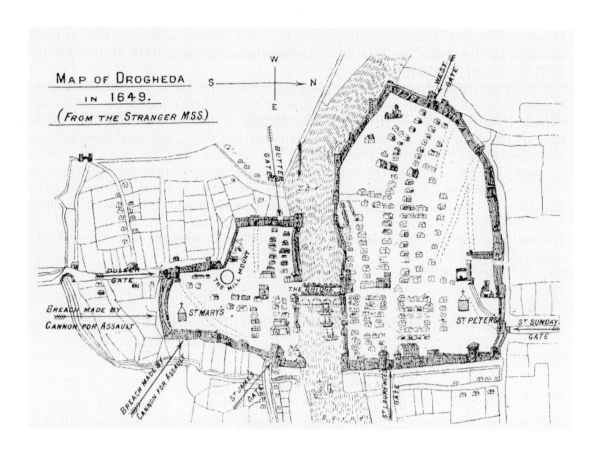

NEWCOMEN'S MAP OF 1649
The layout of the streets has changed but little into modern times.

The Twin Towns: In fact *two separate towns* had been established. They had separate identities, one each side of the river and facing each other. Each had its own parish – this was necessary since the Boyne River was the line of demarcation between the Armagh and the Meath Dioceses. A separate Corporation governed each, although both towns were under the jurisdiction of de Lacy. They were to remain as two distinct towns for more than 200 years in the course of which a keen rivalry existed between them; at times they were at loggerheads, causing bloodshed and loss of life on both sides.

'Drogheda-in-Louth' and 'Drogheda-in-Meath' are quaint, if not awkward, names for these twin towns to carry. In fact they were known respectively as *'Ponte Ferrari'* and *'Villa Ipsa de Ponte'*. Thus, the south side was not designated with a proper name, but was referred to in an oblique way that translates as *'the Town at the Bridge'*. Here we have a description that has been echoed by subsequent generations. It amuses us to observe that, by an eccentric and subconscious quirk, today's inhabitants continue to colloquially refer to it as 'the Far Side' (of the river). Some things never change!

Evidence of the importance attached to the town is clear from the fact that, in confirming de Lacy's lordship of Meath, King Henry III nonetheless in 1220 retained the town of Drogheda and its castle *as his own property.*

Defensive earthen barriers were thrown up, encircling both towns. These were later replaced by stout stone walls with towers called toenails, features that identify Drogheda as a truly medieval town. Seven gates were originally constructed to control access to the town and to collect tolls – a lucrative and vital source of revenue for the administrators. Those on

46

the south side were St. James Gate (also called Dublin Gate), St. John's Gate and Duleek Gate. On the north side the four original gates were St. Laurence Gate, St. Sunday's Gate, West Gate and St. Catherine's, which was located at Constitution Hill. Fair Gate was added in the eighteenth century to ease congestion of fair days. In addition there were several flanking towers and 'blind gates'. Towards the end of the 1770s the gates and walls were in a dilapidated condition which provided the opportunity, of which the authorities were fully aware, for smuggling to take place at night time by avoiding the gates. Thus they were dismantled piecemeal, and in 1795 the stones and materials of Sunday's Gate were sold by public auction and 'The Purchaser to be allowed one month to carry off the materials'. The so-called 'Butter Gate' was not, in fact, a gate but a buttress, and should more properly be referred to as 'Buttress Gate'. It survived until 1958 when it was torn down, being deemed to be unsafe.

The walls were constructed primarily as a partition to separate the town Burgesses (i.e. people who were freemen or privileged citizens of the borough – these men had voting rights) from the indigenous peasants living outside; the latter were obliged to pay a toll at the town gates on goods being brought in for sale. The walls' defensive function was of secondary consideration. The indigenous people were not treated as citizens. *Herein lies the root cause of the dissension and the turmoil that was to afflict Drogheda (and Ireland) until recent times.*

The newcomers were regarding Drogheda (and Ireland) as their very own possession. As to their attitude towards the indigenous inhabitants, they considered themselves superior, and they were applying the policy of 'Apartheid' eight hundred years before that term was given currency. They were making a statement from the very start – it was not their intention to integrate with the native Irish, or to share their newly found community with them. This meant that henceforth two distinct races were occupying one island – a recipe for perpetual strife. Any hope of later integration vanished with the Reformation, when the two races could be clearly identified by opting for two differing brands of Christianity, giving permanence to divisiveness and dissention. Sadly, the repercussions are all too evident today in Northern Ireland.

Burgesses (i.e. registered citizens) who brought materials into Drogheda for use in the course of their trades were exempt from tax. Hawkers and indigenous peasants entering the town to sell their produce were obliged to pay a toll thereon. The earliest extant records (which relate to the 1600s) form a very comprehensive list of merchantable goods, ranging from livestock to iron implements and chattels of every description, including such obscure items as 'dogstone' and 'sheirlings' (whatever they are!). The list set out the toll payable on each item. For example:

ffor Every live Beefe	one penny
ffor Every carcassoe of Beefe	one penny
ffor Every Hide	½ penny
ffor Every Horse worth 40s or above	two pence
ffor Every Lambe or Kid	one farthing
ffor Every Hog, Goat or Swine	one farthing
ffor Every Barrell of Beere	one penny
ffor Every cwt. Of tobacco or sneezing	one penny
ffor Every Millstone	6 pence
ffor Every dowsen payre of Brouges	one penny

The town walls remained intact until the late 1700s, but by then vegetation had taken over the summit of Laurence Gate.

Included in the list are spices and other produce from exotic, far-away lands, such as ginger, cloves, pepper, 'Allmonds' and 'ffigs'. Such snippets of information indicate that the inhabitants were enjoying in those far off days a surprising degree of sophistication and a high standard of living. Arriving from afar, these luxury items would have been very costly.

The town gates were closed and locked each night. The Minute Book of the Drogheda Corporation in 1656 states that

> 'the keeper of the gate's keys of this towne ... be given a payment of 2/- [€0.13] per week ... provided he be dilligent in opening and shutting the said gates earley in the morning and late in the eveninge for the benefitt and advauntage of strangers and Travellers.'[5]

Chapter Six

The Town's Development

If we want to get a glimpse of the native Irish as seen through the eyes of the Normans, we must take a look at the writings of Giraldus Cambrensis (c.1146 – 1223). We are fortunate to have the impressions of Ireland and its people as set down in writing by an outsider at the time of the arrival of the Normans. They enable us to 'see ourselves as others see us'.

Eight hundred years later we are able to study these impressions, even though they are not without certain blemishes, and sometimes open to question. Giraldus Cambrensis (or Gerald of Wales) was a cleric and an erudite scholar and was educated at the University of Paris; he had the command of eight languages. He was a member of one of the leading Norman families (the Fitzgeralds) involved in the invasion of Ireland and was also one of the most influential and colourful British churchmen of the twelfth century. Born in Wales, he travelled extensively and visited Ireland on four occasions, remaining for a duration of several years on one of these trips.

His treatise, the 'History and Topography of Ireland', is therefore of great value to us since it is based on first-hand knowledge, and it gives us quite a unique insight into the Ireland of the Middle Ages and the native Irish people. We will look at some of his observations, but be prepared, dear reader, because they are not in the least bit flattering.

We know that he travelled through Meath and this presupposes that he was acquainted with Hugh de Lacy. It is almost certain that he walked the streets of Drogheda since he was also companion and counsellor to Bertram de Verdon, the baron who was allotted Uriel (Louth) by King Henry. He tells us that Ireland was "about one short day's sailing from Wales"[1] and that "the island is rich in pastures and meadows, honey and milk",[2] and in this regard he may well have had Louth and Meath in mind.

But he must have been displeased with some of the dealings he had with the locals, because he expresses his disenchantment with those he encountered in the bluntest terms. His observations are generally taken to be quite accurate on such matters as the religious practices and the morals of the Irish, even if today his descriptions raise eyebrows – and perhaps our hackles as well. As regards the general behaviour of the Irish and their dealings with others he is very scathing indeed:

"This is a filthy people, wallowing in vice. Of all the peoples [he having been to France and Rome] it is the least instructed in the rudiments of the Faith ... there are many even still who are not baptised ... They do not yet pay tithes or first fruits or contract marriages. They do not avoid incest. They do not attend God's church with due reverence ... they always practice treachery. When they give their word to anyone, they do not keep it. They do not blush or fear to violate every day the bond of their pledge and oath given to others. ... You must be more afraid of their wile than their war; their friendship than their fire; their honey than their hemlock; their shrewdness than their soldiery; their betrayals than their battle lines; their specious friendship than their enmity despised. For this is their principle: 'Who asks of an enemy whether he employs guile or virtue?' These are their characteristics: they are neither strong in war, nor reliable in peace".[3]

Sketch of the Town Walls, showing supporting arches.
The splayed loop-holes facilitated the discharging of arrows and other missiles.

To fund the construction of the walls and towers, a murage charter was granted in 1234 (to be followed by several others), 'murage' being a tax levied for the purpose of constructing a town wall. Periodic subsidies were voted to Drogheda for the upkeep and extension of the walls; these walls averaged 7 m. in height, and their thickness at the base was 1½m. to 2m. They measured about 2.2 km (1½ miles) in total circumference and encompassed an area of about 45 hectares (113 acres) – much larer than the the area of the walled city of Dublin.

It was deemed prudent to incorporate the mound of Millmount within the town walls since this elevated point presented a commanding view of the surrounding countryside, and thereby provided a timely warning of an approaching enemy from either land or sea. Provision was made within the walls for later expansion of housing. Within fifty years of the town's foundation the street layout, houses, shops and churches were in place, and the entire creation was snugly surrounded by protective town walls. They were still in place in the late 1700s, following which they were taken down piecemeal. A few small sections still remain today, namely at Laurence Gate, at St. Mary's churchyard (Mary St.) and at West Gate. Butter Gate stood until 1958, leaving the intact Laurence Gate as a rare relic of the town's medieval past – and it is truly an imposing and magnificent structure.

What is remarkable is the speed with which the town's development took place. The population growth and the attendant civic infrastructure were evolving hand in hand at a fast pace. Artisans from England and Wales were still encouraged to come over and settle down, to apply their skills at construction and to help in the development of markets. Bradley tells us that:

> '...the Anglo-Norman colonisation of Ireland between 1170 and 1220 must have occurred on a massive scale, particularly in the urban areas ... the town [of Drogheda] did not develop organically, rather that a decision was taken to found a town at this point in time ... The remarkable point about Drogheda is that so much of it was established within the generation

from c.1186 – c.1215 ... The selection of a new site in preference to the old one, the establishment of new parishes, the early grant of privileges, the rapid development of the site, all indicate that Drogheda was a planted town'.[4]

Demographers have speculated that the population in 1345 may possibly have been as high as 6,600.[5] Bearing in mind the high infant mortality rate, the primitive knowledge of medicines and the general life expectancy at that era, such growth is truly astonishing.

The lush farmland that extended on each side of the Boyne, the earlier groundwork undertaken by the industrious Cistercians, the provision of markets and fairs, the access to foreign markets through the all-important sea port, these were major contributors to this phenomenal urban growth. Drogheda was rapidly becoming the commercial centre and hub of a broad agricultural hinterland. The scattered religious communities and family groupings that had already been in place throughout Louth and Meath contributed to the overall commercial activity and development.

Fairs and Markets: As early as 1205 – merely 30 years from the time of their first arrival – the newcomers had proved their creative ability and commercial aptitude in realistic ways. The English monarch King John visited Drogheda in 1210 and directed that a fair of 8 days duration be held each year in Drogheda on the Feast of Saint John the Baptist, and in 1229 Henry III granted further charters to Drogheda (Louth side).

Not to be outdone, Drogheda (Meath side) in 1247 obtained similar charters, including the right to hold a market and a fair of 6 days duration once a year. An annual fair on the vigil of the Feast of the Assumption was also established and this was of seven days duration, and a weekly market every Wednesday. Other fairs were granted later in the century.[6]

Some years later Drogheda (Louth side) was given the right to hold an annual fair of 15 days. To oversee the workings of fairs and markets, a market mayor, who had authority on both sides of the Boyne, was appointed in 1375.[7] The town was becoming the hub for the sale of livestock and farm produce from the surrounding countryside. The limit of a working horse's journey was approximately 10/12 miles in a day, and it may be taken that that radius was a governing factor for many fairs and other commercial activities. Others, of course, came from further afield and they overnighted in hostelries on the way. Commerce was developing and the local merchants were accumulating wealth. In the course of later centuries further charters were granted, attracting buyers and sellers from far and wide, and all contributing to the success of Drogheda as a prime market town.

Why all these fairs and markets, one is prompted to ask. We are tracing the growth of a town that is based on a pastoral and agricultural society, and the establishing of these institutions was an important factor in the promotion of any town's vitality; these were the conduits through which farm and dairy produce, handicrafts and other goods were bought and sold – markets constituted the pulsating heart of the town's commercial life, facilitating trade and commerce to the benefit of both producer and consumer. They were also a social occasion, where gossip was exchanged as well as goods – a spin-off that is easily overlooked in the present age of the radio, television and mobile phones. In today's world the emphasis is on convenience, and open market places have largely been superseded by covered shopping malls, supermarkets and hypermarkets, but although they are part and parcel of modern living, that evolutionary step took another eight hundred years to reach us.

Such charters to hold fairs and markets were very lucrative to the grantee because they conferred on him the right to impose tolls on the vendors. In return the grantee was obliged to provide a suitable venue for the market and also to regulate other attendant facilities which today we take totally for granted, such as policing the mart, imposing law and order, regulating weights and measures, providing an acceptable medium of exchange – coinage, furnishing pens and stalls for livestock, etc. These were accomplishments in which the Anglo-Normans excelled.

The ability to promote commercial transactions is one of the characteristics that gave the Anglo-Normans a clear advantage not only over the native Irish but also over the many other races with whom they were to come in contact in later centuries. Conquest was invariably followed by exploitation in the pursuit of profit wherever they went; merchants, import/export agents and retail shopkeepers always followed in the wake of colonisation. In a later age that supreme military genius Napoleon Bonaparte would disparagingly refer to England as being 'a nation of shopkeepers'. But he spoke too soon – the same 'shopkeepers' would later cause his downfall at Waterloo.

The Streets Pattern: The layout of the medieval streets has changed only marginally through the centuries. The crossroads at the present site of the Tholsel (which was also known as the Market House or Guildhall) was the hub of the infant town's activities, and it was there that markets were held. On 'the Far Side' there was another Tholsel to administer the affairs of Drogheda (south side), the second one being in James St. and known as the Castle of Comfort, and the Bull Ring was the marketplace.

The original Tholsels were no doubt constructed shortly after Drogheda itself was founded, and were timber buildings. Following the unification of the twin towns, it seems that the northern Tholsel assumed the dual role; it was sited exactly where the present structure stands. The Corporation Minute Book of 1656 tells us

> "... that Thomas Dixon, Alderman, John Towers, Joseph Wherloe and John Oxford, gent. or any three of them be impowered to make inquiry where any ould walls and matterrial stones may bee conveniently had for and towards the finisheing and buildinge of the Thollsell of the Towne, and that they get workmen for the pullinge down and carryinge away of the same for the use and purpose aforesaid".[8]

This building served the civic authorities for about a hundred years. About 1770 it was pulled down and replaced by a stone structure, and this is the building that we see today. For the next 130 years it was the home of the Court of Law and the Town Council Chambers. *West* Street, *East* Street (now Laurence Street) and Great *North* Street (later Pillory Street, now Peter Street) tell us that here was the central point of the town, and that business and commerce pivoted around that junction, with Bothe Street (later called Booth St., and now Shop Street) leading to the town's only bridge. And central point it has remained to this day.

Likewise, the basic street pattern remains intact. The townspeople of present day Drogheda, in their daily pursuit of working, playing and shopping, still tread the self same streets that were laid down by the Anglo-Normans eight hundred years ago. However, it is understandable that the central cross-roads (at the Tholsel) is no longer the ideal site for a market-place.

The main and most destructive change in the street pattern occurred in the 1970s when a new dual carriageway tore the heart out of the old south side of the town centre, virtually erasing John St., the Bull Ring and the north side of James St. In former times the Bull Ring had been the central marketplace on the south side. The medieval character of Dyer St. disappeared with the setting back of the shop fronts on the north side of the street during the 1990s.

James Street was the road that fringed the south bank of the river. Mary Street, formerly called *New* Street, is of much more recent origin. The Drogheda Railway Station, which was constructed in the 1840s, was linked with the town by laying down a new thoroughfare that was called the *New* Dublin Road.

The authorities were not sufficiently sophisticated to introduce a budget on Budget Day. Nonetheless they had their own effective means of raising medieval taxes or tolls. Funds were needed to defray administration expenses for the upkeep of roads, bridges, etc., and to meet the cost of a standing army, and we have seen that a tax was levied on most articles entering the town. **Passage** was a toll levied for clearing and maintaining passes and roadways; **Pontage** was for the maintenance and repair of bridges; **Murrage** was a tax for the construction and upkeep of a town wall; **Lastage** was a duty on goods sold by weight; **Stallage** applied to the right to erect a stall in a market place. Collectively, these medieval charges were called **'TOLLS',** which were levied in the Toll Seat or Toll-seld, giving us the word 'Tholsel'. However, the truck drivers and motorists of today who are required to dip into their pockets at the Toll Booth on the M1 Motorway would no doubt dispute the description given here of a toll as being a *'medieval'* tax !

BUTTRESS GATE
(better known as Butter Gate)

THE RELIGIOUS ORDERS: Because of the dissension that arose in subsequent centuries on the thorny issue of religion, and the bloodshed that would later be spilled in that cause, we need to remind ourselves that at this point in history the newcomers were of the same religion as the native Irish – both were Christian. Indeed, the religious houses were given encouragement and support, both monetary and otherwise, by the Anglo-Normans. In time the Norman monks took over the role of appointing clergy so that senior positions were invariably given to Norman stock. The Cistercians at Bective Abbey, for example, came from England, and they forbade any Irish-born person to enter their buildings. In that way the Norman influence grew inexorably stronger.

A system of tithes was instituted whereby one-tenth of all the fruits of the land went to the church. But money, which we are told is the root of all evil, caused dissension on at least one occasion between the bishop and the Cistercian monks. Pope Gregory IX was obliged to intervene. He set up two commissions to hear the dispute that arose, and the place chosen where they should sit to settle the argument was Drogheda. The monks won their case, but in a judgement of Solomon, they were obliged to pay 20 pounds of silver to the bishop, and in addition a butt of wine was to be given in the event of the monks being tardy in delivering the money.[9]

Having the Cistercians and the many other religious establishments in their midst, one would assume that the local populace was well catered for in spiritual matters. Others seemed to think otherwise, so several of the Mendicant Orders (monks who embrace poverty and depend on alms for sustenance) came to Drogheda in quick succession. They were welcomed by the Normans and were facilitated by being donated lands for the construction of their churches and abbeys: –

- Dominicans (c.1224)
- Franciscans (c.1240)
- Augustinians (1295)
- Carmelites (c.1300)

But before the arrival of these religious orders, the **Hospital of St. Mary de Urso** was set up. The genuine Christian ethos of the Normans is evident in the fact that they had

53

founded this hospital for the care of the sick and the poor so soon after their arrival in Ireland. It was founded by Ursus de Swemele and his wife Christiana in 1206 on the north bank of the Boyne (a site now occupied by the Garda Barracks) and it had connections with the Augustinians and the Observantines. The site is next to the ruins known locally as 'the Old Abbey' and in earlier times was a monastery founded after a visit by Saint Patrick; it was sacked several times by the Danes. Its closure came with the Dissolution of the Monasteries (1543). The Annals of the Four Masters and the Annals of Ulster make frequent reference to it. Also, several other Orders of Hospitallers arrived in Louth hot on the heels of the invaders; they cared for the sick and wounded of the army; the Knights Templars settled in Kilsaran and in Templetown in north Louth on funds provided by Matilda de Lacy who was a daughter of Hugh de Lacy.[10]

The Dominicans: The great Dominican Priory was founded by the Norman settler Louis de Netter Ville, Archbishop of Armagh in 1224 and it was known as Saint Mary Magdalene's. Its location was next to the town wall at Sunday's Gate, which is the highest point in the town. Some writers presume that the name borne by the gate, Saint Sunday's, was to honour a 'Saint Sunday', but no person of that name is known, and it is in any event improbable that a person was named after a day of the week. (Even the character Man Friday in *Robinson Crusoe* is fictional!). More than likely, it comes from the Irish *Geata Naomh Dominic*, since the abbey adjoined the gate. It is suggested that the confusion arose from the similarity between the Irish word for Sunday (De Domhnac) and Dominic. A similar error may have occurred in Cork in the translation of 'Sunday's Well', which in fact is more properly 'Dominic's Well'.

Excavations conducted at this site have uncovered artefacts such as richly glazed floor tiles, leading us to conclude that the monastery was a place of opulence, and enjoyed considerable prestige. King Richard II and his retinue sojourned there in 1394 when, on the 16th March of that year he received the submission of the chiefs of Ulster including the O'Neills, the O'Donnells and the O'Hanlons. The English novelist William Thackeray, who inspected the remains of the monastery in 1842, refers to a lively description of that event in an old manuscript at the British Museum. It describes, he wrote,

> *'these yellow mantled warriors riding down to the King, splendid in his forked beard, peaked shoes, and long, dangling scalloped sleeves down to the ground. They flung their skenes or daggers at his feet, and knelt to him, and were wonder-stricken by the richness of his tents and the garments of his knights and ladies'.*

Contemporary woodcut depicting King Richard II at St. Magdalene's Priory, Drogheda accepting the submission of the Ulster chieftains

To one of the friars of this monastery goes the credit of uniting the two parts of the town in 1412 (see below). The monastery later fell on hard times, but by an Act of Parliament held there in 1468 an annuity was voted to bolster its finances. Several other sessions of Parliament were held there.

The Franciscans: The disciples of Saint Francis reached Drogheda in about 1240. The Verdon family, barons of County Louth, were major benefactors. An example of the good relationship that existed is that King Henry III provided a grant to them for the purchase of habits for the community.

> *"The royal alms became a regular feature in supporting the Drogheda Franciscans. It was sometimes paid in kind, such as in 1324 when they received 16 crannocs and 13 pecks of oats, or in coin, for example in 1366 when they received 73 shillings and 4 pence ... the Franciscans were right beside the river, so close that boats could come alongside parts of the building and smaller craft or currachs could actually pass under a section of the friary to unload at the stores and workshops within the cloister area".*[11]

In 1347 Drogheda was devastated by the Black Death. The Franciscan Friary lost 25 of its members to it. This gives us an indication of the numerical strength of the community – it was one of the biggest in Ireland. Some of them were English and there had always been a preponderance of Anglo-Irish or English stock among the friars, especially in the selection of the provincial of the Order.[12] Some idea of the prestige attaching to this friary can be gleaned from the fact that King Richard II, when on a visit to Drogheda in 1394/5, stayed with the Franciscans for eighteen days in January 1395. Today there is neither English nor Irish stock in their monastery at the 'High Lane', to give it its colloquial name. Alas, after 750 years of selfless service to the people of Drogheda, the few remaining monks, stooped and grey, closed their church door for the last time and departed in 2001. It reverted to the people of Drogheda and, following refurbishment, it now serves as the proud Low Lane Art Gallery.

The Augustinians built their church in Booth Street (Shop Street) – this was in 1295 – and today's church stands on the same site. Caring for the souls of the people was not their only task. They made their monastery a place of education for the young of all classes. Some were skilled in medicine and in the treatment of fevers. They taught music, art and painting to the sons of the nobility. They kept an open house for travellers and pilgrims, and they also supplied the poor with the necessities of life.[13]

The Carmelites: their church was located at the top of Mary Street, next to the town wall, overlooking the Dale. Sir Henry Tichburne, who defended Drogheda during the siege of 1641 lies buried in the adjoining cemetery (1667). A remnant of the old town wall with arched buttresses is still to be seen here. This location was in the direct line of fire from Cromwell's cannon in 1649; the guns were positioned a short distance away on the opposite side of the defile known as the Dale and they pummelled the wall at that point until they succeeded in making a breach wide enough to gain entry.

Several other friaries existed within the town. The Priory of Saint Laurence stood next to the Cord Cemetery. Saint Benet's Chapel was in Dyer Street, where a Parliament was held in 1467. Saint John the Baptist Priory was in John Street – King John is said to have held a Parliament there in 1210. Saint Saviour's Chapel stood at the end of Shop Street next to the bridge (west side). The Hospital of Saint James was at the east end of James Street outside the town wall.

An early example of the Norman insinuation on the native religious protocol was when King Edward I (1272-1307) issued an order that no Irishman was to be appointed an archbishop. The reason? 'Because they always preach against the king' – a trait that has persisted for some considerable time afterwards! In consequence only 'men of English blood or birth' were to be chosen'.[14]

Much more work remains to be done by archaeologists if we are to elicit further information on the town's past. The surrounding countryside was home to how many other abbeys? How did the monks live? What impact did they have on the people and on the general area? Much information can be adduced by patient work, money and time, but the work will not be easy. Lands adjoining these old monasteries that were closed in the Reformation have since come under the plough; and it has been customary to bury the dead of later generations within the deserted, roofless church property. Archaeological surveys of medieval churches are awaited in at least twenty-three of these in County Louth alone, and a further thirty or forty in County Meath.[15]

It must not be assumed that everything ran smoothly in the regimented world created by the Normans. The following record indicates that matters could get out of hand – it is reminiscent of the lawlessness we see in films about the Wild West:

"On 27th April 1313 a number of men were charged in Drogheda for having supported Robert Verdon in his war with having plundered the town of Collon of 200 cows, oxen and afers, 300 sheep, and other goods to the value of 20 marks. On the same day Henry de Rede and William Frende were charged with having by night robbed the town of Collon of 4 afers worth 10 marks, seven score cows and heifers worth £20, 20 oxen worth 10 marks, 300 sheep worth £9, 100 lambs worth 30, 2 pigs worth half a mark, a chalice worth 20 shillings, and divers other vessels, utensils and vestments worth 100 shillings, and brought all the said goods and beasts with them to the castle of Crewmartin".[16]

Vessel crossing the bar at Mornington

THE BRUCE CAMPAIGN: Edward Bruce arrived in Ireland with an army of 6,000 in 1315. Many Irish flocked to his side, and he was offered the Crown of Ireland in the hope that he would accomplish for Ireland what his brother Robert had done for Scotland in driving out the English. The coronation ceremony took place at Faughart, north of Dundalk. His policy was to destroy everything in his pathway, and this he accomplished with great cruelty and reckless loss of life. He stormed and torched Dundalk. Marching onwards to Ardee he burned the church and all who had sought refuge there. Next, he moved into Meath and routed an army of 15,000 at Kells, and then torched the town He failed in his efforts to take Drogheda. Dublin likewise refused him entry, and he was defeated in battle at Ratoath. The final battle took place at Faughart where he was opposed by Sir John Bermingham. Here his army was not only defeated, but he himself was killed, with his body hacked to pieces. The limbs were hung up to view in various parts of the Pale. Bermingham, in a gruesome display of exultation, had the head salted and taken in a box to England where it was presented to King Edward II while a banquet was in progress. The king was 'right blyth' with this trophy and was so overjoyed that he elevated the donor, creating him Earl of Louth and giving him the manor at Ardee.

So much destruction and death was caused in the Bruce campaign (which extended into all four provinces) that vast numbers of people lost everything, and the economy of the entire country collapsed. Drogheda fared better than most towns, some of which lay in ruins, and crops had been destroyed throughout the land, causing famine and pestilence from which it took several generations to recover.

The Culprit:
The Black Rat carried the Plague from the Continent to Drogheda

THE BLACK DEATH (1348-1350): Mention was made above of the great bubonic plague known as the Black Death. It swept across Europe, decimating the population as it travelled from town to town. It was transmitted by fleas, parasites that were carried on black rats. By the time the plague had run its course, a quarter of Europe's population lay dead. The seas surrounding Ireland offered no protection to its inhabitants, for rats have the convenient but crafty habit of hitching lifts on ships, and by that means of transport the plague inevitably reached Europe's offshore western island.

At that time Drogheda vied with New Ross in being Ireland's busiest port. The docking facilities were at the North Quay and the South Quay, next to the town's only bridge. The schooners sailed up the Boyne to the quays at the very centre of the town where there was so much congestion that they were often moored three or four abreast. (Even up to the early twentieth century it is said that it was possible to cross the river by walking from ship to ship). It was through the port of Drogheda that the dreaded Black Death was introduced into Ireland (with Dalkey and Howth being the two other suspected points of entry – these were out-ports of Dublin because of silting on the Liffey). This occurred in the winter of 1348/49.

The plague quickly spread to Dublin and then to the rest of Ireland. The archbishop of Armagh, Richard FitzRalph, who was a well-known preacher, exhorted the people of Drogheda in a sermon on the Feast of the Annunciation in 1349 at the Carmelite Monastery at the top of Mary Street to pray for deliverance. Their prayers were ineffectual. The ravages of the plague were reported by Friar Clyn of Kilkenny who stated that the cities of Dublin and Drogheda were almost completely depopulated within a few weeks; and in Kilkenny 'there was hardly a house in which only one had died, but as a rule man and wife with their children and all the family went the common way of death.'[17] The friar's detailed narrative ends abruptly, and this tells its own sad tale.

Excavation work carried out by Sweetman at the Shop Street site, now occupied by Wogans furniture store, suggests that the 'hiatus in the activity at the quayside might be the result of depopulation and contraction of the occupied area due to the Black Death.'[18] It is generally agreed that the Black Death claimed between a quarter and a third of Europe's population in the course of a few years. It was most virulent wherever rats tended to frequent, namely in towns rather than rural areas. Thus it may be taken that Drogheda, which was 'almost completely depopulated' lost perhaps one-third of its inhabitants.

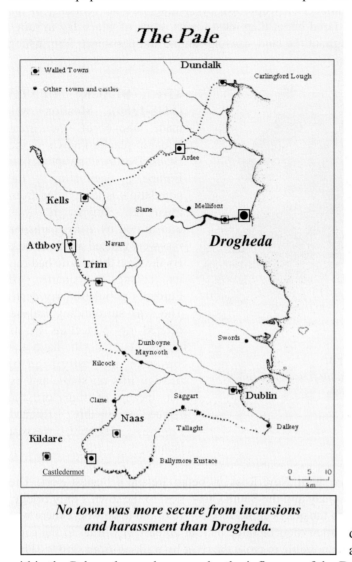

The Pale

Walled Towns
Other towns and castles

Dundalk
Carlingford Lough
Ardee
Kells
Slane
Mellifont
Athboy
Navan
Trim
Drogheda
Dunboyne
Maynooth
Swords
Kilcock
Clane
Saggart
Dublin
Naas
Tallaght
Dalkey
Kildare
Ballymore Eustace
Castledermot

0   5   10
km

No town was more secure from incursions and harassment than Drogheda.

THE PALE: The Normans had the entire country conquered (nominally) by 1235, but with their forces being over-extended, some parts were difficult to hold, especially Ulster, Connaught and west Munster. During the Wars of the Roses (1455-85) England had other matters on her mind, and control over these areas waned considerably until only a section of Leinster covering all of County Louth and a portion of counties Dublin, Meath and Kildare were firmly under the jurisdiction of the Crown of England. The Pale's contraction was at a critically severe point during this era, but Drogheda always remained a Norman town within the Pale and was always under the influence of the Dublin Parliament.

The River Fane, 7km. south of Dundalk, marked the northern boundary, although Dundalk itself was a peripheral town of the Pale, as were Ardee and Athboy.[19] The construction of an actual pale or line of demarcation was commissioned by several Acts of Parliament held in Drogheda (1488/1494); it was a boundary line to indicate the Pale's perimeter and consisted of an earthen 'double ditch of six feet high above the ground'. It was not a continuous ring-fence or boundary, but rather a demarcation that was thrown up in the proximity of towns and other areas of population. It stretched, with gaps, from Dundalk to Dalkey, and embraced Ardee, Kells, Trim and Naas near its outer limits. The word 'Pale' was in common use at that time, and was applied also to the small English enclave at Calais.

The Tower House at Termonfeckin

The defensive line was secured at Drogheda by a small standing force in 1437 under the command of Sir Laurence Taaf and Richard Bellew.[20] A glance at the map shows that Drogheda was located snugly in the middle of the Pale and, with the protection of the Irish Sea at her back, the need for military protection would hardly seem necessary since incursions were few; no other town was further from its perimeter.

Continual efforts were being made by the native Irish to regain their lands; they constantly harassed the Anglo-Normans whose holdings were never out of danger. Other towns suffered from continual harassment, pillage and bloodshed, and much of Munster was laid waste by the Normans in their efforts to suppress the rebellious Irish. Dundalk suffered, and Carlow was burned twice. All this time the inhabitants of Drogheda continued to go about their business of attending markets, buying, selling, importing and exporting, and growing prosperous in the process.

A source of great annoyance during this era was the constant incursions being made from outside the Pale by the native Irish and along the coast by the Scots. To combat their pillaging Dublin joined forces with Drogheda, and in recompense King Henry VI granted a remission of rent because of the efforts made in combating 'the king's enemies'. The Mayor of Drogheda at the head of 500 archers and 200 men armed with pole-axes took part in an engagement at Malpas Bridge. They defeated the forces of O'Reilly and his confederates who had entered County Louth, ravaging the area. In return for his valiant deeds the mayor was allowed to have a sword of state borne before him.

The Bruce Campaign had created widespread chaos and this loosened the grip of the settlers. The Irish took advantage of the situation by ousting them in many areas. The coastal towns of County Wicklow were attacked by the O'Tooles and the O'Byrnes, the Midlands were raided by the O'Mores, and Dundalk was besieged by the O'Hanlons. Indeed, at one stage the Pale had contracted to include little more than Drogheda and Dublin, although Drogheda did not suffer greatly from these destructive incursions. On the contrary, the vessels that sailed up the Boyne were laden with the produce of other lands, and the merchant princes of Drogheda flourished by catering for the needs of the peripheral areas.

The perilous circumstances in which the settlers (later to be known as the Old English) lived resulted in a most distinctive feature of the Irish countryside, the tower houses. The government advocated that each of the landlords construct one of these on his estate, and as an inducement they provided a subsidy of £10 to the gentry of County Louth. Later this offer was extended to County Meath and the other parts within the Pale. The dimensions of the tower houses were specified as "in length 20 feet, in breadth 16 feet, in height 40 feet". North Louth, as we have seen, was vulnerable to attacks from the Gaelic people outside, so Parliament took further measures to fortify this region. The peasants were compelled under penalty to 'labour with their spades and shovels.[21] for eight days in each of three years at specified sites, and 'freeholders and husbandmen having carts' were obliged to assist in transporting the building material. Local examples of tower houses can be seen at Dardistown, Dowth, Ballygarth and Termonfeckin.

THE *FIRST* 'BATTLE OF THE BOYNE': As mentioned above, the two distinct towns of Drogheda were constantly squabbling with each other. For generations there was bitterness between them, and they were often at daggers' drawn. The rivalry and jealousies sometimes erupted into serious violence, causing loss of life. It was a curious situation, which from today's perspective, defies logic – it resembles a dispute between Siamese twins! The main reason revolved around markets, commerce and trading conditions. The Louth side had imposed tariffs on imported merchandise, and thus all vessels arriving at the port found it more advantageous to discharge their cargoes on the Meath side. In consequence, the traders who conducted business in the marketplace at Millmount and the Bull Ring enjoyed monopoly conditions and the price gap presented them with greater volumes of trading and higher profits. This bred resentment.

> *"Hence arose jealousies, animosities and contentions that put the inhabitants of both places in arms against each other. In their contests blood was often shed and many lives lost, especially on one occasion when the bridge became the scene of a sanguinary engagement between the conflicting parties."[22]*

Here we have two opposing factions engaged in conflict at the banks of Boyne several centuries before King James faced King William in combat across the same waters. Happily, the first occasion produced a satisfactory outcome for both sides, unlike that of 1690, because a permanent peace was brokered. All credit for this happy event goes to a friar from the local Dominican Friary, Fr. Philip Bennet OP and Master of Divinity, who assumed the role of peacemaker.

Reconciliation: He brought the two sides together in the Collegiate Church of St. Peter to hear his sermon. It was the feast of Corpus Christi and, quoting from the Bible, he said: "Behold how good and pleasant it is for brethren to dwell together in unity. Will ye be united in the Body of Christ?" "We will!", came the ready response. Alderman William Symcock answered in the name of all. Then they all shook hands, and 'they were profusely entertained in the refectory of this convent.'[23] Whether it was the exhortations of the reverend father or the generous libations that were dispensed is hard to say from today's standpoint, but the upshot was that a joint petition was signed by the Archbishop of Armagh and sent with one Robert Ball to King Henry VI in London. Ball, whose family name is still retained in the town, returned to Drogheda on 15th. December of the same year with the Charter. It was dated 1st. November 1412 and stated that both towns would henceforth constitute one single county, distinct from those of Meath and Louth, and to be known henceforth as **the Town of the County of Drogheda**. This arrangement stood until 1899 when the town was merged with County Louth under the provisions of the Local Government Act (1898). The newly incorporated town of 1412 would in future be presided over by a single mayor, and the first one was William Symcock. He was a benefactor to the town and is said 'to have honorably governed the town to the content of them all'. He died in 1420.

This auspicious event in the town's history was celebrated annually for centuries thereafter. It took the form of a burlesque, and it was performed every Shrove Tuesday in an atmosphere of gaiety. The Dublin Penny Journal of 1832 described the scene:

> *The 'Mayor of Flea Lane' (an obscure suburban lane behind Millmount) crossing the bridge, enters the northern part of the town, mounted on an ass, in mock procession, attended by his sheriffs, bailiffs and other officers, all fantastically dressed with straw, and each bearing the insignia of his dignity, together with several ragamuffins disguised in petticoats and masks, and armed with blown bladders tied on poles, who clear the way, and enforce the passengers and lookers-on to treat 'his worship with proper respect; the cavalcade is proceeded by a bough, or garland, and music; in this way they parade the principal streets of the town, levying contributions: at the same time another party enters the town by Laurence's-gate, consisting of 'the mayor of the chord' and his followers who are generally dressed in cast-soldiers' clothes, perambulate the town in another direction until evening, or they conceive they have enough collected, when they meet, and after a mock encounter between the 'bladder*

60

men' to the great amusement of children and idlers, they all adjourn to the 'chord field', outside Laurence's gate, and spend the evening in mirth and jollity!

This lively description was recorded in 1832 by a contemporary reporter. A native of Drogheda recalled that this custom was still being observed up to the 1890s, although he was unaware of its significance.[24]

Cause Célebre: We are entitled to enquire why this custom was allowed to lapse. Nowadays we seem to celebrate just about any event at the drop of a hat. Here we are presented with a ready-made Day of Celebration – a red letter day exclusive to the people of Drogheda – to commemorate a great occasion when the hatchet was buried forever and revelry replaced rivalry. Surely it is an occasion truly worthy of celebrating. By a strange coincidence, the date of the Charter – the First Day of November – became significant in a more recent age of Drogheda's history. A momentous reconciliation occurred once more on 1st November, but exactly 430 years later. This was in 1842 when Drogheda's governing elite were obliged to make way, by the operation of universal suffrage, for the town's first Catholic Mayor, an event that was also celebrated on a grand scale.

What about the man who was primarily responsible for splicing the two towns into one happy family – the great peacemaker, Father Bennet? Surely he is worthy of positive recognition. Today's heavily burdened rate payers would undoubtedly grumble at the erection of a great statue in bronze, but a more acceptable gesture would be to name a street or a terrace of houses in his honour. After all, we have *William* Street to mark the occasion of King William's victory a short distance further up the Boyne, and *Wellington* Quay to commemorate the Duke of Wellington's victory at Waterloo – both of these were occasions of suffering and bloodshed. Even that arch-criminal Oliver Cromwell is commemorated – in fact he gets <u>two</u> place-names *(Cromwell's Mount* and *Cromwell's Lane)* whereas Fr. Bennet, who brought unity and peace to the town, is today completely ignored!

Fr. Bennet was the man who was responsible for introducing harmony, substituting co-operation for competition between the two communities. Perhaps the Mayor and Borough Council of Drogheda will give consideration to marking the Unification of Drogheda in some appropriate manner now that its Six Hundredth Anniversary is nigh – it occurs in 2012. Let the joy-bells peal and the fireworks sparkle on that historic occasion!

Silver Coin (enlarged) minted in Drogheda

DROGHEDA'S MINT AND COINAGE: During the fifteenth century Drogheda was empowered to mint coins. The location of the premises is thought to have been at Millmount, which had the advantage of offering security, being under the close eye of the military. Coins were first minted there in 1467, consisting of double and single groats as well as pennies. The obverse side showed a stylised head of Edward IV, and the reverse side depicted a large sun emitting 24 rays and a rose at the centre; surrounding this were the words ' *VILLA DE DROGHEDA'*. The groat was a silver coin with a value of four pennies. Other issues of coins during the reign of Edward IV were in 1470, 1475 and 1478. The last coinage produced were a groat and a penny – these were issued during the reign of Richard III (he who was 'determined to prove a villain' and murdered the Princes in the Tower); the reverse side contained the words *'VILLA DROGHEDA'*. These coins remained in circulation throughout the realm for two hundred years.

DROGHEDA – SEAT OF THE IRISH PARLIAMENT: Unlike today, parliaments were not held on a regular basis – they were very infrequent affairs, often several years apart. The town was selected as the seat of Parliament on at least six occasions, and laws were passed there. Lord Gormanston held a parliament in Drogheda in 1493. The law that was enacted seems to have been *ultra vires* and riled the king, for it precipitated an event which was to have long term effects, detrimental to Ireland – Poyning's Law.

Of all the laws passed in Ireland, the one that had the most crucial and far reaching effects on its inhabitants was the *STATUTES OF DROGHEDA,* more popularly called **POYNING'S LAW**. Within his short tenure (1494/5) as Lord Deputy of Ireland, Sir Edward Poyning succeeded in having enacted the all-important law to which his name is attached. In the War of the Roses the Fitzgeralds of Kildare (who were very powerful and had held the chief offices of state, including that of Lord Deputy) were showing distinct signs of disloyalty to Henry VII who was a Lancastrian. Their sympathies lay with the House of York, and when the impostor Lambert Simnel came to Ireland they received him with open arms and actually crowned him king as Edward VI. Another pretender was Perkin Warbeck; his patron was given Irish citizenship and the right to customs dues at both Drogheda and Dublin ports. Here was evidence that loyalty of the Old English was suspect. Poyning set out to clip their wings.

He convened a parliament in Drogheda in November 1494. By the terms of this enactment the approval of the King of England would henceforth be required before the Irish Parliament could meet, and in future all parliamentary business required the approval of the King's Deputy and Council in Ireland and by the King and his Council in England. This drastically curtailed the powers of the Irish Parliament, and in that way administration within Ireland came under the firm thumb of London, and the country was henceforth legislatively dependent on England.

In effect, the affairs of the people were to be managed 'by remote control' and by a régime that was not attuned to the needs and circumstances of the people. This became a major grievance especially to those living outside the Pale. The law remained in force for a lengthy 300 years until it was repealed in 1782 mainly through the exertions of Henry Grattan. The era of Grattan's Parliament was short-lived and was replaced by the disastrous Act of Union.

A source of great annoyance during this era was the constant incursions being made from outside the Pale and along the coast by the Scots. To combat their pillaging Dublin joined forces with Drogheda, and in recompense King Henry VI granted a remissio9n of rent because of the efforts made combating 'the king's enemies'. The Mayor of Drogheda at the head of 500 archers and 200 men armed with pole-axes took part in an engagement at Malpas Bridge. They defeated the forces of O'Reilly and his confederates who had entered County Louth, ravaging the area. In return for his valiant deeds the mayor was allowed to have a sword of state borne before him.

A UNIVERSITY FOR DROGHEDA: the Franciscan monastery was located close to the north bank of the river, between Bachelor's Lane and the Mall, and stretched from the town's east wall to Mayoralty Street. It was very extensive and included a high tower of cut stone and an orchard. We have seen above that 25 of the monks died in the plague (1347) – this is an indication of its size. The building had facilities deemed suitable to host King Richard II and his retinue; he honoured the monastery with his presence for 18 days in 1394 and held council there.

At this period the archbishop of Armagh moved his residence from Armagh city to Termonfeckin. This brought him within the Pale and closer to the centre of his jurisdiction. On the accession of Edward IV (1471) it was pointed out that there was no university in Ireland and that Dublin, through lack of funds, had declined to establish one there. Drogheda was deemed to be a suitable venue by virtue of the high standing of the School of Theology located there, and also because Drogheda was close to the seat of the Primate of Ireland. An Act was accordingly passed whereby

" ... it is therefore ordained, established, and granted, by authority of Parliament that there be a university established in the town of Drogheda, in which may be made bachelors, masters and doctors, in all sciences and facultiesm as they are made in the University Of Oxford: and that they may also have, occupy and enjoy all manners of Liberties, privileges, laws, and laudable customs, which the

said University Of Oxford hath occupied and enjoyed, so that it be not prejudicial to mayor, sheriffs, nor commonality of the said town of Drogheda."

This rare offer made to Drogheda was not taken up – the proposed seat may have been at St. Magdalene's Friary. The commitment was an onerous one and perhaps, like Dublin, it had insufficient funds to finance so ambitious a project, and it wasn't until 120 years later (1591) that Queen Elizabeth founded Trinity College, Dublin.

DROGHEDA – THE ECCLESIASTICAL SEAT: Aside from the town's political status, it was also the choice of residence for the Primates of Armagh, both Catholic and Protestant. Palace Street is so named because this was the site of the bishop's palace. Saint Oliver Plunkett thought highly of Drogheda, operated a school there and used it as the centre of his administration for many years. The Catholic Primate resided in Drogheda until 1835 when the move was made to Armagh.

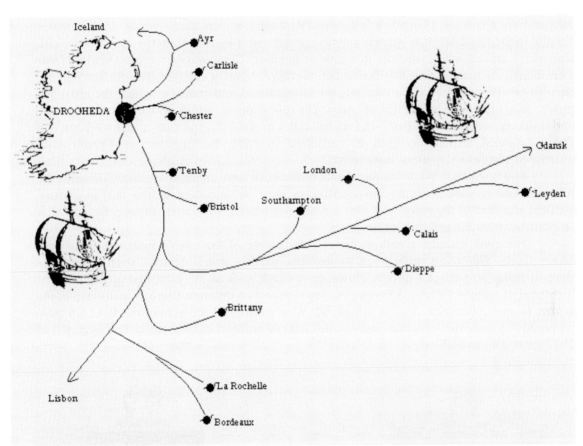

TRADE AND COMMERCE: Under the influence of the Anglo-Normans, who were as clear-thinking in formulating plans as they were single-minded in implementing them, the infant town grew in size and importance as well as in prosperity. It had the appearance on an English town, with a law-abiding citizenry conducting their trade and commerce in a peaceful, orderly fashion. The town was a hub for marketing livestock and the farm produce of the bountiful plains of Meath, Louth and the Midlands. The port of Drogheda was a key factor in the town's growth and wealth, and it vied with New Ross as being the busiest in Ireland.

A visitor to Drogheda during that period must have been impressed when he wrote that it was 'the greatest towne that tetherto I have seen in thys country.'[25] Holinshed (c.1570) says: 'Drogheda, accounted the best town in Ireland, and truly not far behind some of their cities; the one moiety is in Meath, the other planted on the further side of the water, lieth in Ulster. There runneth a blind prophecy on this town, that [New-]Ross was, Dublin is, Drogheda shall be, the best of the three.'[26]

Assuredly, traffic across the Irish Sea to 'the motherland' was of prime importance; but there was also traffic with France, Spain, Portugal as well as with such improbable places as Gdansk in Poland, and Iceland. Livestock, hides, grain and other agricultural produce were

the main exports. The returning vessels from France and Spain carried wine and other continental produce. In this regard Drogheda acted as an important entrepot warehouse, distributing wines to towns as far inland as Roscommon and Kilkenny and to ports as far south as Youghal, and even to Chester in England. Indeed, trade with Chester was quite considerable, and there are records showing wine and herrings being discharged there from Drogheda vessels. Trade with Bristol was also a feature, as was trade with la Rochelle in France. Such traffic, both internal and foreign, amply attest to Drogheda's commercial status.

THE TOWN CREST: The Corporation seal includes the Star and Crescent, which symbol is derived from the arms of King John, and thus there may be some connection with the Near East and the Crusades. (King John's brother, Richard I, known as *Coeur de Lion,* defeated Saladin in the Crusades. It is alternatively suggested that it derived from the flag of a Turkish ship which arrived with foodstuffs in a time of famine). The motto on the crest reads: *"Deus Praesidium, Mercatura Decus".* Translated, we have: '*God is our Safeguard; Merchandise our Glory'.* This serves well to illustrate the strength and importance to which the town had grown as a mercantile centre for shippers. On reflection, it would be hard to find a more craftily contrived each-way bet! The motto seeks to weld the spiritual to the temporal – a finely balanced artifice designed to reconcile suppliant homage to our Creator with unabashed, shameless, godless materialism!

And it worked! While the merchants of the town were engaged in earthly pursuits, the religious orders were applying the Christian virtues by attending to the laity's spiritual welfare, and each of the orders was also serving as a school, a hospital, a model farm as well as a sanctuary for the sick and infirm.

The crest includes a sailing vessel – indicative of the town's intensive trade with foreign ports. We raise a smile when we examine the flag that is depicted over the vessel's stern. It bears St. George's ensign. However, a closer look at the crest that appears on the letterhead of today's Drogheda Borough Council reveals a different flag – it is lily white, *the ensign is omitted!* What does this signify? Who authorised the alteration? It is not now proposed to pursue this particular issue – the changed political circumstances that occurred in 1922 speak for themselves!

A Town of Great Distinction: The esteem in which the town was held by the Administrators in Dublin is evident, as indicated above, from the fact that it was deemed suitable as a university city on the lines of Oxford, also that a mint was located there. Furthermore, until the reign of Charles II the chief governors of Ireland occasionally resided in Drogheda.

Confirmation of this pre-eminent position is manifest in the observance of a time-honoured custom described in D'Alton's *History of Drogheda*:

> *"It is indeed within the memory of some of its oldest residents that ... on the annual election of their mayor, which took place on the 29th. September, a messenger who waited outside the Tholsel until the oath was administered, was dispatched, in official robes and mounted on a white horse, to inform the authorities in Dublin of the fact, to the intent that they might proceed with the appointment of their chief magistrate, which took place accordingly on the following day".[27]*

In summary, we can see that as soon as the Normans set foot in Ireland they made their presence felt in the Louth/Meath area. Within a mere 25 years of their landing Drogheda had not only been founded, but had been granted a charter from the king. It developed with surprising rapidity and was ranked as an important city – on a par with the four royal cities of Dublin, Waterford, Limerick and Cork.[28] Each of these other cities had a head-start of several hundred years, having been founded by the Vikings. Drogheda occupies first position among the towns founded by the Normans.

This happy state of affairs continued for perhaps four centuries. These were the glory days of Drogheda – days when the town occupied a place of great influence in state affairs, commercial activities and international trading.

Chapter Seven

The Reformation

King Henry VIII's break with Rome was an opportunity which presented him with a two-fold benefit: it not only opened the way for him to re-marry, but it also enabled him fill his treasury with the wealth which the churches and monasteries had accumulated, including their extensive tracts of lands. This was for him a bonanza of unprecedented proportions. Until that time the English crown's position in Ireland was that of a 'lordship', but Henry VIII assumed the title of 'King of Ireland'. Then came the imposition of his newly adopted religion upon the people. An Act of Parliament passed in Dublin in 1536 (the Act of Supremacy) proclaimed that King Henry was **'the only** supreme head on earth of the whole church of Ireland'. Implementing this earth-shattering policy was effected with ease – he simply carved up the territories he had confiscated among his cronies as bribes for their support.

This new legislation was to have devastating and long-term results, causing untold hardship and dissension, dictating the history of Ireland right into modern times. All existing religious establishments were dissolved with a stroke of the pen. The mute evidence of this is still a familiar sight today in the monastic remains that lie strewn throughout the land; examples within Drogheda itself are the ruins of the Old Abbey, the Carmelite Abbey in Mary St. and the Magdalene Tower; nearby we see monastic ruins at Colpe, Duleek, Mellifont, Monasterboice, Skryne, Slane, Termonfectin and many, many more.

All religious establishments were stripped of their icons and their wealth. Items of value went into the coffers of the Crown; everything else that they could lay hands on was burned, including many greatly revered relics such as the precious Baculus Iesu, believed to be the actual staff carried by Jesus of Nazareth.[1] Such sacrileges must have been felt grievously by a deeply religious people. By 1541 most abbeys within the Pale were gone; those outside the Pale went shortly afterwards.

The Franciscan friary in Drogheda was confiscated in 1539 and that of the Augustinians the following year. Later, in the reign of Queen Elizabeth, Mellifont Abbey with its vast land possessions was confiscated and then granted to Sir Garrett Moore, the ancestor of the Marquis of Drogheda, following which the great forest of oak trees adjoining the monastery was cut down and used in roofing many of Drogheda's houses.[2]

Some red tape was employed in completing these seizures, and there was a purpose behind it. The work was rounded off in a diplomatic, tactful manner that was self-serving, being followed by an invitation for the abbot to hand over the assets voluntarily, a nicety which presupposed acquiescence on the part of the donors and the king's compliance with the law. Thus, he could not be accused of acting illegally since he had merely accepted gifts that were "freely" offered.[3] This smacks of a ploy used in much more recent times by the Mafia when, to enforce an unfavourable deal on a reluctant seller, they would " make him an offer that he couldn't refuse".

On the Outside, Looking In: It was a feature of Norman towns that the native Irish population remained outside the towns' walls. This explains why *Irish*town in the Dublin of today is a city suburb, being far outside the walls of Norman Dublin. Irish Street in nearby Ardee is outside the original walls of Ardee; likewise the Bogside in Londonderry and the Claddagh in Galway. In Galway, a municipal ordinance of 1581 proclaimed: 'Neither O nor Mac shall strut nor swagger through the streets of Galway'.[4] Some of the native Irish in the course of time managed to gain access within the walls of Drogheda; they congregated in a region that became known as '*Irish* Street' as early as 1312 – this is the street we know today as the Green Lanes. The minutes of the Drogheda Corporation still referred to this street as 'Irish Street' as recently as 1792.[5]

A few of the principal street names have changed over the centuries. Shop Street was called Bodestrata from the time it was laid down by the Normans (*circa* 1214), then changed slightly to Bothe (Booth) Street towards the end of that century. Laurence Street, which leads to the eastern gate of the town, was initially called East Street. The name Dyer Street has remained unchanged since 1329 and John Street has carried the same name since 1317.

To suppress social interaction with the native Irish, parliament passed the Statute of Kilkenny (1367). Intermarriage, fosterage and intimate relationships of any kind were regarded as high treason, and infringement was punishable by death. To speak Irish, dress in the Irish fashion, take an Irish name or adopt an Irish custom meant confiscation of home and land plus imprisonment – it was a form of 'ethnic cleansing'. The native Irish living in the enclave at Irish St. (the Green Lanes) were allowed to remain, but they were forbidden to speak their native language, an infringement of which carried a similar punishment. The terms of the Statute were found to be unenforceable, and were ignored by both the Old English and the Irish. The ineffectiveness of this legislation is well described in a popular song that contains the line '… they might as well go chasing after moonbeams …'. It is remarkable that the native tongue was still the *lingua franca* in Drogheda well into the 1800s.

By this time the Hospital of St. Mary de Urso (the site is now occupied by the Garda Barracks, but parts of the foundations are still in evidence) had come under the care of the Crutched Friars and was taken over by the Corporation and used to found an alms-house under the title of the Poor House of Saint John. This charitable institution by the year 1660 also embraced another hospital in Magdalene Street called St. Stephen's. 'However by the eighteenth century the services of this institution were confined to the widows of the freemen of the borough, invariably Protestant, and it was not until later in the century, with the establishment of the Infirmary in Great George's Street that services for the sick poor became generally available in Drogheda. By the late nineteenth century this institution had ninety beds and catered for 4,000 extern patients in a dispensary annex'.[6]

Another such hospital, the Hospital Priory of St. Laurence the Martyr, was located near the Cord Cemetery, and a third one, which was named after St. John the Baptist, was on the Meath side of the town.

When the religious establishments were abolished, it seems that much of the charitable work being performed for the sick and the poor went the same way. The turmoil in succeeding centuries brought social upheavals in its wake, and religious preferment became the norm, so that fate dealt harshly with the indigent who were discriminated against – they could sink or swim, and the precept of Christian charity played no part. The Corporation Minutes reveal a discriminatory screening process for admission to the Hospital of St. John, and it was not until the Poor Law system was established in 1839 that District Workhouses were introduced. County Louth had three; another was located on the old 'Balrothery Straight' south of Balbriggan, until it was demolished in the 1980s.

The Munster Rebellion: The 1500s were a time of great upheavals in Munster. The Fitzgeralds of Munster had been very powerful, and had attained the stature almost of kings. Their domains were measured, not in acres but in square miles, and they held 1,500 of these.[7] But because they overreached their authority, they fell foul of London and they were dispossessed of their property, and their lands were planted by new English settlers. This work was mishandled and there were serious blunders. The many tenants who had been evicted were determined to take revenge on the newcomers. There were reprisals, taking the form of sabotage, cattle rustlings and murders. The Butlers of Ormonde became involved. Kilkenny, their stronghold, was stormed, and this was followed by pillage, destruction, looting, burning and raping. Settlements were torched and the newly settled families slaughtered in skirmishes and ambushes. Anarchy prevailed, and sadly, many innocent non-combatants were caught up in the friction and they too were murdered. Refugees fled to the larger towns of Cork, Waterford and Youghal. 'Their cattle and horses had been slaughtered, their farms had been burned, and those who had escaped massacre had been driven and whipped naked, men and women, through the devastated countryside. Mutual hatred was pervasive'.[8]

The attempts by the government in Dublin to establish peace and to restore the *status quo* were no less brutal; helpless prisoners were butchered, more livestock slaughtered and lands laid waste – all this by government forces. This era was known as the first Munster Plantation.

A few years later the entire scene was repeated, when greater atrocities were perpetrated. The devastation affected most of Munster, and vast areas were depopulated. The entire country was affected and became impoverished, resulting in a complete breakdown in the economic structure of the island.

Holinshead paints a vivid picture of the devastation: 'The land itself which before these wars was populous, well inhabited, and rich in all the good blessings of God – being plenteous of corn, full of cattle, well stored with fish and other good commodities – is now become so barren, both of man and beast that, whoever did travel from the one end of all Munster, would not meet any man, woman or child save in towns or cities; nor yet see any beast but the very wolves, foxes and the other like raving beasts.'[9] The Four Masters reported: "The lowing of a cow or the voice of a ploughman could scarcely be heard from Dunquin in the west of Kerry to Cashel". This deliberate campaign of destruction continued for over twenty years, which reduced the countryside to a desert waste.

Special mention must be made of Lord Mountjoy and Sir George Carew, both of whom carried out endless atrocities wherever they went in subduing the Munster Rebellion. Carew in particular detested the Irish (they had killed his brother) and he gave specific instructions to his soldiers to create famine conditions as they penetrated the countryside. In this regard he succeeded well, causing men, women and children to perish of famine by the thousand. It seems curious that an army should include in its arsenal such items as sickles, scythes and harrows – but these formed an important part of the army's equipment, and they were used to good effect in denuding the land and in turning bountiful countryside into deserts. The result was starvation and death for countless innocent people. Since history is invariably written by the victor, the destiny of the vanquished goes largely unrecorded, and as for the populace at large – those who were simply bystanders – their fate can only be guessed at.

The conditions that prevailed were truly horrifying. The inhabitants of Drogheda had in earlier times been very fortunate by virtue of having the protection of the Pale throughout the interminable hostilities. This did not save them during the Munster Rebellion. The peripheral regions of the Pale had been in great jeopardy during those times and the inhabitants suffered unspeakably from incursions. Most of Meath was burned and depopulated, and as was usual in such circumstances, this was accompanied by rampant plague, an adversary which the stone walls that surrounded Drogheda were not designed to repel. One historian provides us with this description of army abuses within the Pale: -

> *"In time of harvest companies of soldiers were in the habit of going with their wives, children, servants and friends, sometimes to the number of a hundred, to the farmers' houses, eating and drinking and paying for nothing. They robbed and sometimes killed the tenants and husbandmen; and the soldiers' horses were turned out to graze in the meadows and in the ripe corn, ruining all the harvest'.*[10]

Silken Thomas: In the course of the devastation and the effusion of blood, the chief of the Fitzgeralds was captured and imprisoned in London (1534). His son, believing a rumour that he had been killed, started a little rebellion of his own. He was the young and fiery Lord Thomas Fitzgerald, Tenth Earl of Kildare but better known to us as Silken Thomas. (He and his entourage were noted for their fine clothing). Impetuosity caused him to lose his head in more ways than one. He repudiated his allegiance to Henry VIII and proclaimed a Catholic crusade. He was captured and taken to London where he was executed along with his five uncles. This severely crushed the power of that family. Earlier, the Munster Fitzgeralds had boldly flouted the Statutes of Kilkenny when the Earl of Desmond allied his forces with the native Irish. He was accused of high treason at the Dominican Friary of St. Magdalene's in Drogheda and was found guilty and executed. This took place in February 1467 at the north Commons, now known as Hardman's Gardens. His head was sent to Dublin where it was displayed on a spike in Dublin Castle as a lesson to other dissidents.

Drogheda was fortunate to have escaped much the carnage that was taking place in the south because it was not involved in any rebellious activities. Figuratively speaking, it kept its head below the parapet at all times. Being ensconced within the Pale, it continued to prosper while many towns elsewhere in Ireland were being destroyed and the countryside laid waste. The restrictive policy of the English Government, namely to deprive its enemies in Ireland of commerce whenever possible, did not apply to Drogheda. The law forbade any trading in an Irish market or fair or with a person who had an Irish name. English ships attacked trading vessels plying between Spain and other parts of Ireland while the merchants of Drogheda, being of English stock, were reaping the benefits of being loyal to the English Crown.

Drogheda at this time had become an important ecclesiastical centre, and St. Peter's Church at the top of Peter Street was used for several centuries as a Pro-Cathedral for the Armagh Diocese. Because of the unsettled conditions, the Archbishops of Armagh, the Primates of Ireland, resided in Drogheda (with Termonfeckin and Dromiskin as alternative domiciles). Synods of the Diocese were regularly held in St. Peter's up to 1559, and many consecrations of Bishops and ordinations were held there.[11]

ST PETERS CHURCH

The Spanish Armada (1588): Fortune favoured England when King Philip of Spain sent a great armada of 130 ships to invade England. They were troop carriers rather than men-o'-war for the most part, carrying 20,000 soldiers. The galleys were scattered by the English fleet, and then Lady Luck played a crucial part, with fierce gales playing havoc with them. The Gaelic princes were quite ambivalent in their loyalty, as many of them favoured Catholic Spain in her efforts to convert Protestant England back to Catholicism, and thus they gave refuge to some of the unfortunate soldiers when their ships foundered. Drogheda was to play a minor part in subsequent events. One vessel, *La Trinidad Valencera* was shipwrecked on the Antrim coast, breaking its keel on rocks. Most of the 500 soldiers on board reached the shore and about 150 eventually made their way back to Spain, but the rest were taken prisoner. Handling the captives in accordance with England's wishes was entrusted to Dublin and Drogheda. There the rank and file were executed and the officers were incarcerated until ultimately ransomed.

69

An Abduction and an Escape: It was during this difficult climate that two figures on horseback furtively approached the southern outskirts of Drogheda one day in 1592, intent on heading north. They were being sought desperately by Government forces. Being in the heartland of hostile territory, it was vital that the fugitives take the utmost precautions. They had experienced many vicissitudes up to this point from the time of their departure in Wicklow, and had succeeded in crossing the Liffey at an unguarded ford outside Dublin, but all could come to nothing if they were apprehended in Drogheda.

Having pondered the position, and being fearful of Drogheda's political sentiments, caution prompted them to avoid entering the town. Along the banks of the Boyne they encountered a poor fisherman's hut. 'The man was at the moment loading his boat, when the fugitives entreated him to row them across, and promised a recompense, to which proposal he agreed, and received accordingly a liberal reward. The grateful man thereupon re-crossed the river, and brought their horses through the town to where they waited at the landing place'. Soon the fugitives were on their way once more. They next reached Mellifont which was no longer a monastery but was the home of Sir Garrett Moore. He provided them with sustenance and a night's rest before they proceeded on their journey with a fresh pair of horses. They then passed through Dundalk and Armagh unhindered and eventually reached the castle at Ballyshannon, home of the O'Donnell chieftains. There they were rapturously welcomed – Red Hugh O'Donnell was back home at last. The other fugitive was Turlough O'Hagan who was his friend and guide on that hazardous journey.

The narration of this episode in history is worth recounting: England was in constant fear of invasion by Spain, and was aware that Ireland's loyalty was suspect. Ireland's chieftains would give Spain wholehearted support in the event of being invaded and used as a stepping-stone to reach England. To prevent any such eventuality, hostages were demanded by the Government from the Irish chieftains. The O'Donnells declined to comply.

When a ship laden with wines sailed into Lough Swilly in 1587 some chieftains accepted the invitation to come aboard to view the ship and sample the stock. Then the trap was sprung. The ship at once weighed anchor and set out for Dublin with its prize. In that devious way young Red Hugh O'Donnell was kidnapped by Queen Elizabeth's men and taken to Dublin Castle and incarcerated – he was a mere boy in his fifteenth year.

Still imprisoned in Dublin Castle in 1591 – this was four and a half years later – Red Hugh together with Henry and Art O'Neill (sons of Shane O'Neill – they had also been abducted) succeeded in filing through their fetters with a tool that was smuggled in to them. They then lowered themselves by a rope to the ground outside and crept through the Castle's sewers to freedom.

A guide was waiting for them outside, and soon they were on their way south. As they hurried towards the Wicklow Mountains Henry O'Neill became separated in the darkness and was left behind – the inactivity behind bars had left his limbs unfit for the exertion. His brother Art, famished and exhausted, had to be carried part of the way. Their inadequate clothing added to their peril and their shoes were torn to ribbons. Finally they collapsed in the fastness of the Wicklow Mountains, obliging their guide to leave them and hurry away for help.

Next day the two snow-covered forms were found. Art O'Neill was dead, but Red Hugh, his limbs severely frost-bitten, was coaxed back to life; he was unable to walk and had to be carried the rest of the way. He sojourned among the friendly O'Byrnes of Wicklow while he slowly regained his health. When news of the escape reached his father in Donegal, help was at once sent to him. When he had recovered sufficiently he set out to return to his kinsmen in the north, accompanied by the trusty Turlough O'Hagan. The eventful escapade, as related here, ended in success.

It will be noted that Drogheda had been a stumbling block for the fugitives on their route to freedom. There was not a solitary person within the walls of the town that could be relied on for succour, hence the need to circumvent the town on the journey northwards. This was an agonising interruption for the young Red Hugh. He was still in great pain, and could walk only with great difficulty, and he had to be raised onto and off his mount. Indeed, it later became necessary to amputate his toes.

Here we have an example of the heavy-handed way that England so often adopted to win the hearts of the Irish. If the authorities wished to placate the chieftains and gain their allegiance, this was not the way to accomplish it. The O'Donnells had been on the side of the Government for generations, but this act of treachery enraged them. The incident also illustrates the presumed mind-set of the inhabitants of Drogheda – their loyalty lay with the Crown.

It was at this time that the penal code was first formulated. Its objective was not only to enforce a new religion, but also to deny the majority of the Irish people of all wealth and ambition. Depriving the country of industry was deemed the most effective way of keeping them in subjection.

THE ULSTER REBELLION: The stronghold of English influence lay within the Pale, but by the end of the 1500s their hold on the rest of Ireland had become tenuous in the extreme, and the area of the Pale was also diminishing. Outside the Pale, Ireland was firmly in the hands of the Irish under the leadership of that great Gaelic hero Hugh O'Neill. He scored a signal victory over the English forces at the Yellow Ford (1598) and held Ireland, excluding the Pale, in the palm of his hand. England's enemies on the Continent were watching his rampant progress with satisfaction. Spain's King Philip called him 'Prince of Ireland', while the Pope was ready to crown him King of Ireland and had ordered a gold crown for the occasion.[12] Many of the new Munster settlers fled back to England. The cherished dream of 'Ireland for the Irish' was within reach. One final heave and the English were pushed out forever. This would be accomplished, it was hoped, with military help from Spain.

When Spain agreed to send help, the next decision to be made was to select the most suitable point at which the expedition should land. This was the subject of much discussion, and Drogheda was deemed to be the ideal spot. Firstly, its proximity to O'Neill's military strength in the north meant that the two forces could quickly combine, and secondly, it was within striking distance of the government's heart – Dublin. However, the memory of the debacle of the Spanish Armada a short time earlier (1588) emphasised the need for caution, especially when it was learned that prowling English warships were stationed at Dundalk and Carrickfergus. Support from within Drogheda itself was an imponderable. These factors caused a landing at Drogheda to be abandoned.

Drogheda played a part when the eventual landing took place at Kinsale. Several Drogheda vessels helped in transporting the 4,000 Spanish soldiers. The difficulty was that Kinsale was a most inconvenient point of entry from Hugh O'Neill's position whose stronghold was at the other end of the country. The Spanish force was too small to act independently, so O'Neill was obliged to march to its relief. An English army under Lord Deputy Mountjoy intervened by besieging Kinsale (1601).

Treachery played a hand, for Brian Oge MacMahon betrayed O'Neill's strategy to the English. This was crucial, not only to the immediate outcome of the battle, but also to England's tenuous hold on Ireland. It enabled Mountjoy score a decisive victory. O'Neill was routed and the Spaniards were sent packing. The defeat was catastrophic for Irish hopes, and the back of the Irish resurgence was broken at a single stroke.

The epilogue of that story involves Mellifont. Its occupier at this point was Sir Garrett Moore; he played a part in the aftermath of Kinsale by riding to Tulloghoge and inducing Hugh O'Neill to come to Mellifont under a deed of safe conduct. There, on 30th March 1603, like a broken reed, he met Mountjoy to sue for peace and to parley for pardon. He was obliged to beg for mercy on his knees, and was left in that suppliant pose for an hour before Mountjoy would deign to allow him into his presence. The upshot was that his life was spared and all was forgiven, and the agreement, which was reached 'in the presence of a great assembly', was known as 'the Treaty of Mellifont'.

However, had he tarried awhile in Drogheda *en route* to the meeting, he might have picked up a vital piece of information that would have brought about a totally different outcome to the negotiations. The English had craftily withheld from him the profoundly important news that *Queen Elizabeth had just died.*

QUEEN ELIZABETH I (1533-1603) A Pen-picture: We have seen that it was King Henry

VIII who first assumed the title 'King of Ireland". If he expected loyalty and homage from his Irish subjects he had gone the wrong way about it. Indeed, for centuries to come words such as 'Crown', 'Kingdom', 'Royal', etc. rankled with a people who were the victims of oppression from monarchs who were utterly uncaring towards their Irish subjects, and it was only towards the letter end of the 20th Century that these feelings abated.

Neither did Henry's successor Elizabeth I endear herself. She introduced to Ireland a debased currency which was designed to deliberately undermine the economy. In this she was all too successful, for that policy played havoc with trade and impoverished the people, and its effects lasted for a whole generation. It is said that Drogheda's bridge and quays lay idle and ruined. As for her attitude towards the Irish people in general, she treated them with lupine ferocity, her fangs sinking deep into Irish flesh when she imposed the notorious Penal Laws – they lacerated Catholics for the next two hundred years.

This she-wolf was Henry's bastard daughter. Her mother, Anne Boleyn, was his royal mistress. (Henry's legal wife at the time being the unimpeachable Catherine of Aragon). On ascending the throne she quickly proved herself to be a chip off the old block, being coarse in manner and given to 'pungent oaths and ribald jokes'. As an illegitimate daughter, it can be said that she had no claim to the throne, but ruled by usurpation.[13] Her craftiness came to the fore in surrounding herself with astute, level-headed advisers, so that in the course of her reign they were the architects who elevated England to a foremost position in European affairs. Her own reputation was one of parsimony, procrastination and equivocation.

Just as her father was renowned for disposing of several of his unwanted wives by lopping off their heads, she had a like propensity. The appellation often applied to her is 'the Virgin Queen', but the word 'virgin' in this context should not be given its strict dictionary meaning. It was said of her that when she took a fancy to a soldier on parade she was likely to invite him to her boudoir, but when she grew tired of him he was destined to tread the same path as several of her father's wives – to the executioner's block.

Be that as it may, many eligible suitors of royal blood, both English and Continental, tapped furtively on her boudoir door. While they entertained the notion of wearing the English Crown, she set tongues awagging by entertaining them in a more intimate manner, much to the consternation of her advisers. However, this Jezebel had no intention of marrying.

She out-performed her own reputation for heartlessness when she produced the over-worked executioner's block yet again, this time to dispose of her own cousin, Mary Queen of Scots.

Irish Resistance Ends: We can readily appreciate why the English contrived to withhold from Hugh O'Neill the news of the queen's death. Her successor was the Catholic king James I (son of Mary Queen of Scots) who was reputed to favour Ireland. Were O'Neill privy to the news of Her Royal Highness's death, he would no doubt have adopted a stiffer attitude during the negotiations, rallying his forces to continue the fight to expel the foreigners in the knowledge that Ireland had almost fully wrested itself from the grip of England. But it was not to be.

On the 3rd April 1603 Mountjoy ushered O'Neill from Mellifont back through the streets of Drogheda and onwards to Dublin where he was made to repeat to Parliament his plea for pardon, and it was only then that the news of Queen Elizabeth's death was revealed to him. It is on record that he thereupon broke down and cried. Whether this emotional outburst was caused by a genuine sense of grief at the passing of 'Good Queen Bess', or by the manner in which he was duped, it is left to the reader to adjudge.

O'Neill's troubles were not over, for four years later Dublin Castle came into possession of an anonymous letter which purported that he was again involved in subversive activities, this time to seize Dublin Castle and kill the Lord Deputy. O'Neill was on a visit to Slane at the time. An urgent message reached him saying that a ship under the captaincy of John Rath of Drogheda was at anchor in Lough Swilly, waiting to take him away from Ireland. It was time for him to depart.

The curtain comes down on this eventful chapter of Irish history with a tableau of the great Hugh O'Neill and his family, together with the O'Donnell clan and several other chieftains of Gaelic Ulster, slipping quietly away to the Continent (1607), never to return – an event known to history as "The Flight of the Earls".

"Duleek"

From an antique engraving by Laurence Fagan, now in the High Lane Art Gallery

Chapter Eight

The Moore Family – Earls of Drogheda

Who was this family who assumed the name 'Drogheda' in their title? When Henry VIII confiscated all church property, Mellifont was initially leased to a Laurence Townley, and subsequently to Sir Garret Moore who was created Baron Moore of Drogheda in 1616 – his father had come to Ireland as a soldier of fortune. The vast tracts of land included six castles, 500 messuages, 5 mills, 10,000 acres of arable land and 20,000 acres of pastures. This was an enormous estate by any standard, and almost completely surrounded the town of Drogheda. A few years later Moore was created 'Viscount Moore of Drogheda' for services rendered.

So extensive were these lands and properties that they were capable of producing £3,500 *per annum* for the Crown. Putting that figure into perspective, it represented a quarter of the Irish Treasury's total annual income. However, Moore dishonestly had the enormous property valued at so low a figure that it is estimated that it cost his family a rent of one penny per acre – and this remained undetected for over a hundred years. The fraudulent manner in which the family attained such great wealth promoted profligacy which in turn led to dissipation among subsequent generations. This caused financial problems in the long term, but once again scruples were set aside by the use of subterfuge – they craftily overcame the difficulty by putting several of their leases into trusts. This was illegal, but it had the effect of keeping the hands of the grippers off their extensive properties.

The munificence of Henry VIII gave Moore ample reason to name his son Henry, who was created Earl of Drogheda in 1661. The Moore family then dominated the surrounding countryside and its people. Their covetousness was further appeased in 1727 when the fourth earl got his greedy clutches on another great estate, again free of charge – he married into and inherited the great estate at Monasterevin which we know today as Moore Abbey.

In deference to the king who had presented the Moores with so easy a lifestyle, they continued to honour his name, and the next successor was once again christened (yes, you have guessed it!) *Henry*. It is said that 'Names of fools are like their faces – they are always seen in public places'. Apparently, this particular Henry Moore, Earl of Drogheda, set out to prove that point in an emphatic way, for he lent his name (indeed, *each word of his name and title*) to a cluster of streets in yet another area which he owned, this time in the very heart of Dublin, viz. **Henry** St., **Moore** St., **Earl** St., and **Drogheda** St. There was also a short lane known as '**Of** Lane' to complete the series, but that lane no longer exists. (The name 'Drogheda St.' was subsequently changed to Sackville St., and later to O'Connell St.). Two other locations carry the family title, for good measure – Drogheda St. in Monasterevin and the Drogheda Memorial Hospital in the Curragh.

Even though the Moore family acquired these several enormous estates without lifting a finger, they were unable to retain them. The expansive Mellifont estate was sold piecemeal to settle mounting debts, and by the 20th Century they were also losing their grip on Monasterevin. It was leased to none other than the great Irish tenor, John McCormack, and later an order of nuns occupied it. In finally relinquishing Moore Abbey the last residing Moore wrote:

> '*As the Irish political situation has developed, I should have found it positively painful to be obliged to live in Ireland. However shameful the state of English rule for over three centuries, nothing can condone the atrocities committed by the IRA and the Provisionals. ... I have no sense of nostalgia and a great feeling of relief that England was to be my home*'.[1]

A distinct taste of sour grapes can be detected in this comment. The generations of Moores, as colonists, had been sustained in a state of luxury and indolence for four hundred years, lording it over their deprived underlings while enjoying the fruits of usurpation coupled with wholesale trickery. To attempt to equate the confiscations of property, the religious persecutions, the pitch-cap tortures, the famines, the evictions and the general misrule that a nation had to endure throughout the cruel centuries of oppression with the thirty years of turmoil in Northern Ireland that started in the 1960s, is specious and an affront to rational debate.

The wheel of fortune turned a full circle when a religious order again occupied Moore Abbey – except that the nuns did not acquire it by usurpation. Apart from continuing to adhere to the actual name included in the title, the Moore family today has no connection with Drogheda. The present Earl of Drogheda lives in England, and remarked that at leaving Moore Abbey and Ireland he had 'no regrets'. Others may well share the same sentiment.

Today little remains of the splendour created by the Cistercians at Mellifont. When the Moores first took possession they adapted the various monastic buildings to their own secular needs. The cloister was converted into a cobbled court-yard and the octagonal lavabo – described as one of the most delicate medieval buildings in Ireland – may have served as a porch. Among the artefacts purloined from the Cistercians were statues of the Twelve Apostles. Sir Edward Moore 'clothed them in scarlet, clapped muskets on their shoulders, and transforming them into British grenadiers, placed them to do duty in his hall'. As for the splendid Chapel of St. Bernard, we are told:

> *'This beautiful specimen of ancient Irish art was converted by the Moore family into a banqueting room, and having once echoed to the voices of the monks hymning their matins, next resounded with the orgies of Bacchanals, but now only answers to the noise of swine, being when last visited by the writer, occupied as a pigsty!'*

The writer who supplied these details in 1833 was born locally. He added that the exquisitely worked stone entrance to the Chapel was taken away to decorate a private residence, and all trace if it has since been lost. King William camped there on the night before the Battle of the Boyne. Later, the ruined walls were 'divided into two or three little tenements'[2] and a collection of wretched hovels occupied the site during the 1800s[3], a fate that continued into the 20th Century. Today the picturesque ruins present a focal point for tourists who come to admire a superb memorial to Ireland's distinguished past.

The burial plot of the House of Moore is in St. Peter's Church at the top of Peter Street, Drogheda, but no monument exists to commemorate their name. When they vacated the Mellifont area, the Coddingtons acquired some of the lands at Oldbridge on the south bank of the Boyne (now the property of the people of the Republic under the name of the Board of Works), and the Balfours/Townleys acquired the abbey and tracts of land on the north bank of the river where they built Townley Hall (now owned by the School of Philosophy and Economic Science).

Chapter Nine

The Siege of Drogheda (1641-1642)

The half century starting in 1640 found Drogheda at the very centre of three events that caused the utmost anxiety to its inhabitants – the Siege of Drogheda (1641), the Cromwellian Campaign (1649) and the Battle of the Boyne (1690). More importantly, they were fundamental to the subsequent history of Ireland, and the fate of its people was to hinge on the outcome of each one of them. They plunged the entire country into an era of wretchedness from which it has taken two and a half centuries and more to recover. We can trace the chain of events back to the Ulster Plantation when the inhabitants were ousted in favour of newcomers from England and Scotland.

THE ULSTER PLANTATION: The vast tracts of lands owned by the O'Neills and the O'Donnells were left vacant when they set sail, leaving Ireland forever. These lands, together with the great estates of other Ulster chieftains who had sided with them, fell into the lap of the English Government. The funding of the campaign of repression in Ulster had not come directly from Government coffers; the wherewithal was supplied largely by English speculators called 'Adventurers' – in other words this entire project had been a business deal whereby the speculators who financed the war against O'Neill would be repaid with confiscated Irish lands.

Joint stock companies had been formed for this purpose, consisting mainly of shareholders who hailed from London. These speculators also funded the erection of the Derry walls, and thereby hangs the tail by which the prefix 'London' was added to the ancient Gaelic place-name of Derry, giving us 'Londonderry'. Lands to repay the speculators were requisitioned from sitting occupiers simply by dispossessing them. There was no more convenient or effective way of settling arrears of pay than to carve up these lands and apportion them among the army officers. In addition, many corrupt officials, paymasters, contractors and opportunists of one sort or another crawled out of the woodwork for a slice of this rich cake.

In effect, most of Ulster, which had to a large extent escaped foreign domination and had always been the great stronghold of Gaelic Ireland, was now planted with Scottish Presbyterians and English Protestants. It was intended that Irish tenants were to be debarred from the confiscated lands. However, this stipulation was not effective because imported peasants were few, and native labour was employed as a necessity to work the land. This, in simple terms, is the origin of the friction in Northern Ireland today.

The Ulster Rising: The net result was that Catholics were now tenants and workers on the land they had previously owned. Resentment smouldered in the breasts of the dispossessed – they were now the underprivileged. Tension mounted, and inevitably the resentment burst out into open rebellion.

The Rising began on 22nd October 1641, instigated mainly by Rory O'More and Sir Phelim O'Neill, the latter being a kinsman of Hugh O'Neill. Although plans for the Ulster Rising had been carefully laid, they went awry, and the scene became a re-enactment of the nightmare that had occurred earlier in Munster, except that this time the planters were the victims. Old scores had to be settled, and revenge stalked the land.

Many of the new Protestant settlers – men, women and children – were murdered, their property despoiled, their crops laid waste and their cattle slaughtered. Estimates of those killed vary wildly, and were greatly exaggerated in England – they varied from 2,000 to 20,000 and more. Propaganda was fostered, sending waves of horror throughout England. Stories gained credence with repetition: 'cutting off the privy members, ears, fingers and hands, plucking out their eyes, boiling the heads of little children before their mothers' faces, and then ripping up their mothers' bowels, stripping women naked ...' However, Antonia

Fraser, in her detailed biography *'Oliver Cromwell, Our Chief of Men'* states 'It should nevertheless be pointed out for the sake of historical accuracy that there is no actual evidence that this deliberate massacre, as such, ever took place[1]'.

What is certain is that many innocent people were massacred in the Ulster Rebellion. Settlers fled in terror. Drogheda in particular, which remained loyal to England, gave them refuge. Once again the busy, thriving town by the Boyne remained safe from the turmoil and bloodshed of insurrection. Indeed, it was growing fat and prosperous on the discomfiture of others.

THE SIEGE OF DROGHEDA: O'Neill issued a proclamation dated 23rd October 1641 stating that he intended 'no hurt to the King, or hurt of any of his subjects, English or Scottish', but that his only object was the defence of Irish liberty. He scored a series of successes at Charlemont, Newry, Dungannon, Castleblaney and Dundalk. Everything so far was going according to plan. His next target, and a critically important one, was Drogheda. This town was recognised as being the kingpin in the strategy for re-conquest; it was a vital link in the line of communication between Dublin and Ulster; it was also Dublin's northern bulwark – if Drogheda were to fall to the insurgents, then Dublin was there for the taking.

Sir Phelim O'Neill
He laid siege to Drogheda.
This was later to cost him his head.

Time and again throughout Irish history a mole was at hand at a crucial moment to frustrate the aims of the rebellious element. The Ulster Rising was no exception – Parliament was kept informed of the insurgents' intentions.

As a loyal English town, Drogheda remained steadfast to the Crown and accordingly barricaded its gates as O'Neill's approached. With the medieval walls standing in his way, he had no option but to lay siege to the town, and this began on 21st November 1641. His army, although numbering about 20,000 men, was ill-equipped for a siege, being deficient in artillery and the other instruments of war, and the soldiers were without tents to provide shelter during the winter months that lay ahead. His men were quartered at Rathmullen and in the villages of Bettystown, Mornington, Oldbridge, Tullyallen and Ballymakenny. We will see that his 'siege' was little more than a partial blockade.

O'Neill established his headquarters in the Beaulieu home which was the principal seat of the extended Plunkett family. The Plunketts had decided to support the insurgents (or Confederates) during a meeting held at Tullyeskar Hill, and it was agreed that William Plunkett would raise a Louth regiment of which he would be its captain. This commitment was to cost him the loss of Beaulieu.

The town's defence was undertaken by Lord Viscount Moore of Mellifont who had six hundred foot and fifty horse under his command. It had been augmented by a force of one thousand foot and one hundred horse which were hurried down from Dublin. The army was under the command of Sir Henry Tichborne who was then appointed Governor of Drogheda.

Sir Henry Tichborne: The dominant character in the siege, and its undisputed hero as far as the adherents to the Pale were concerned, was 'the great Sir Henry Tichborne'. He was an English officer who had come to Ireland in 1620, and quickly gained recognition as an administrator and a general, and at the age of 60 was in command of the military force that was to confront Phelim O'Neill at Drogheda. County Louth was soon to experience a foretaste of Cromwell's bloodthirsty tactics by the manner in which he (Tichborne) swept through the county when O'Neill finally withdrew. When he broke into Dundalk he had many of the burgesses and freemen hanged. '... the number of slain I looked not after but there was little mercy shown in those times[2]', he later recalled. He was 'so great an enemy of the rebels in Ireland, killing many hundreds at his own hands or standing by to see them executed'. As well as being Governor of Drogheda and Meath, he was appointed Marshal of the army and became a member of parliament.

BEAULIEU HOUSE:
This architectural gem is one of the few local residences
still occupied by the original owners.

He incurred considerable personal outlay during his military encounters, but had difficulty in being recompensed. One of his petitions to the throne stated that: 'some drop of the king's flowing bounty may refresh the withered fortune of your decayed pensioner'. Who could refuse a plea presented so elegantly! He later acquired the headquarters used by Sir Phelim O'Neill during the siege, Beaulieu, and the surrounding lands. The townland of his new abode still bears the family name – 'Beltichborne'. The beautiful mansion that we see today was constructed in 1670 and his successors are still in residence. A distinctive feature, unique for that period, is that its appearance is not encumbered by fortifications of any kind. He died in 1667, and the family vault is in St. Mary's C of I cemetery at the head of Mary St.

Details of The Siege: We are fortunate today in having a blow-for-blow account of the actual siege. It is contained in a lengthy, detailed letter (published by Tichborne in book form) that Tichborne addressed to his wife. He had been instructed, he said, to 'forthwith raise a regiment of One Thousand Soldiers, and march with all Expedition unto Drogheda'.
His First Duty on reaching the town was to strengthen the fortifications for the impending siege.

> *'Having duly attended to the quarters of his soldiers, Sir Henry diligently inspected the fortifications of the town, and directed measures for yet further strengthening of the place, and in particular the mill-mount as the stronghold on the Meath side...'*[3]

Secondly, he assessed the stocks of foodstuffs that the town possessed. He wrote that from an inspection of '... the Provision of Victual and the Grain within the Walls, I easily observed

78

that in a short time we should be distrest for want of Provisions; and perceiving that there was a pretty Quantity of Corn in stack at Greenhills, about half a mile without the East-Gate [Laurence Gate], and that the Rebels were quartered a Mile from it', he created a diversion at another gate, then 'went suddenly forth at the gate that led directly unto the Place; and before I was advanced a little above half way I met an Irish Woman that lived without the Walls, who told me that part of the Irish Army, at least three thousand were marching toward me, a thing I little credited, because I had sent forth Scouts'. He claimed to have killed about 200 in the skirmish that ensued. 'Of our men four only hurt', which leads us to suspect that exaggeration played a big part in the relating of some of the episodes that occurred over the next few months.

Thirdly, it was necessary to obtain intelligence on the strength and deployment of the enemy. His enquiries proved to be more difficult than would appear at first sight, for he soon discovered that many of the people around him were not to be trusted. He said:

> '... these Reports were daily strengthened with false Intelligence by some that were employ'd in the Service, being in Truth no other than Rebels in their Hearts and Affections, as afterwards plainly appeared by their flying from our Party, and siding with the Rebels'.[4]

Some of O'Neill's successes up to this point of the Rising had been accomplished by means of subterfuge, and he tried to apply similar tactics with Tichborne. Twice Tichborne reacted to false intelligence by setting out from the town to attack the enemy. He was sufficiently cautious to take out only a small force, 'but found my self deluded; and to have left the Town with the whole Force *(as I conceive was the Aim of Intelligencers)* had been in a sort to put it into the Rebel Hands ... and discovering themselves and their ill Intentions daily more and more ...'

Dublin then sent down 600 additional men, 'who setting forth ... through some Miscarriage on the Way, though they had reasonable Notice to prevent it, yet were they met with by the Rebels, totally routed, and most of them lost'. This is an allusion to what became known as 'the Battle of Julianstown'.

THE BATTLE OF JULIANSTOWN (1641): An urgent request had been sent to Dublin for further help, an occurrence that brought Julianstown into the picture. The additional contingent of Government troops duly set out from Dublin to the relief of Drogheda. The soldiers were 'raw men, newly taken up, not trained nor exercised' and they displayed a marked lack of enthusiasm for the task. The first day's march took them only as far as Swords. The next day they managed 12 miles and encamped at Balrothery where they mutinied, and it took an inducement of double pay to persuade them to continue their march[5]. As we shall see, they did not have an opportunity to enjoy the fruits of their extra pay.

Word reached Rory O'More that this force was on its way, so he ordered a detachment under Colonel Plunkett to intercept it. (The marchers were warned of this, but they did nothing about it). Plunkett's plan was to set an ambush at Julianstown. His men lay in cover to await events while he sent a cavalry patrol ahead as a decoy towards the approaching relief force. On being sighted, they turned and scampered back according to plan, with the Government cavalry in hot pursuit. This force was allowed to pass the concealed position. As the infantry approached, Plunkett launched his surprise attack. The ambush caught the marching soldiers completely unawares and they were almost completely destroyed. Only about fifty horse and a few infantry survived from the force of six hundred and fifty that had left Dublin. The dead were buried in a communal grave in Julianstown Churchyard, and in later times a collection of bones was found in the course of alterations to the church.

A suitably worded plaque commemorating this victory over Government forces was placed on (the present) bridge wall at Julianstown in 1967. However, it should not be presumed that that particular spot was the point where the ambush occurred. Tradition has it that it took place near Dardistown Castle[6] which is 3km. west of Julianstown village. This seems likely since the main route from Dublin to Drogheda passed Dardistown Castle in that period.

JULIANSTOWN BRIDGE
NEAR THIS SPOT IN NOVEMBER 1641
AN ULSTER FORCE LEAD BY RORY O'MORE AND OTHERS
DEFEATED GOVERNMENT TROOPS
MARCHING TO THE RELIEF OF DROGHEDA
THE VICTORY WAS FOLLOWED
BY THE FORMATION OF THE CATHOLIC CONFEDERATION

THIS STONE WAS PRESENTED BY SIR WILLIAM BUTLIN M.B.E.
AND ERECTED BY
MEATH ARCHAEOLOGICAL AND HISTORICAL SOCIETY 1967.

The interception and defeat of the relieving force was a great boost to the morale of those besieging Drogheda. Booty included arms, ammunition and money intended to bolster the Drogheda garrison. Tichborne admitted that that was a disaster, 'for the whole Pale seeme'd to waver … and declared for them and immediately joined for the Northern Rebels'. This proved to be the sole serious reversal suffered by Tichborne.

Around the same time the castle of Stameen was seized by the rebels, and this resulted in further slaughter; and booty was taken during an attack on the village of Colpe. While drawing sand from a nearby quarry in more recent times a quantity of human bones was unearthed – mixed with them were fragments of buckles and military attire[7]. Meanwhile the siege continued.

Progress of the Siege: O'Neill lacked the means of storming the town, and was obliged to attempting to reduce it by famine. Had he put a stranglehold on the town by means of a permanent encirclement of fully alert soldiers, he would have slowly starved Tichborne into submission. This was Tichborne's fear, for he greatly lacked provisions for his men and fodder for the horses. Many of his men deserted by dropping over the walls at night.

The 7th January saw another foray when the quarters at Rathmullen were attacked and 'an hundred of them at least slain upon the Place, many driven by Heaps into the River and drowned'; more were killed the same day in a follow-up escapade before returning with 'many Muskets and Corslets, a few Cows and some other Plunder'.

Tichborne confines his letter to military exploits, and makes no reference to the rationing of food or to the condition or the welfare of the townspeople. The populace, which numbered about 6,000, were in a state of starvation throughout the period. 'Horse-flesh, dogs and cats were the best food attainable for the men'. It was recorded that the better class people were limited to one meal per day, with the diet of the common soldier being merely herrings and water without bread. The influx of the refugees from Ulster had swelled the population, adding to the difficulties of the defenders. O'Neill had sunk ships at the bar on several occasions to block any attempt at relief by sea, but they were blown out of position by gales. A relief ship then succeeded in getting through with provisions.

Negotiations occurred at one stage, and this resulted in prisoners being exchanged. Another time a Dominican prior, Fr. Darcy was sent as an emissary by O'Neill to parley with Tichborne in an endeavour to effect a surrender, but it came to nothing.

In the case of the more renowned Siege of Derry that was to take place 47 years later, the people were likewise reduced to eating candles, dogs and rats. The siege of Drogheda continued for a lengthy 105 days – exactly the same duration as the more famous Derry siege.

Cannon fire caused several breaches to be made in the walls, but the town continued to hold out. February was a month of great activity, repelling attacks, and making forays to capture foodstuffs, etc. On 7th February Tichborne made a sally 'and recovered a little Forage and Provision to refresh us a few Days[8]', inferring that existing stocks were exhausted. He

A LETTER

OF

Sir *Henry Tichborne*

TO HIS

LADY,

OF THE

Siege of *Tredagh*;

AND

Other Paſſages of the WARS of *Ireland*, where he Commanded.

DUBLIN:

Printed by and for AARON RHAMES, and are to be ſold by the Bookſellers, MDCCXXIV.

This was undoubtedly a violent era, and the ire of the dispossessed was unbounded.
*These depictions of the cruelties perpetrated by Catholics during the Ulster Rebellion may or
may not be factual. Either way, they served admirably as propaganda in the book published by
Tichborne. Such rumours inflamed English feelings and set Cromwell
on the path we know so well.*

From that time onwards Tichborne met with little or no resistance – the opposition seems to have melted away. He sallied southwards where he encountered a battalion and 'caused a Party of Horse to meet them at the Bridge of 'Gillianstown' [i.e. Julianstown – here is where he exacted sweet revenge], near the Place where Six Hundred Men, sent at first to assist us, were unhappily defeated; and there in the same Field and about it, Three Hundred and upwards of the Rebels were slain, and Two Colours taken'.[13]

Tichborne mentions townlands such as Colpe, Inch (Laytown), 'Stamine', and Platten south of the Boyne, then 'Tullahallen', 'Bewly', Carstown etc. on the north side where he snuffed out small pockets of opposition. 'I burnt some villages, took a large Prey in Cattle and Sheep, to the great Satisfaction of the Soldiers, who now fed plentifully after their long Penury and Want'.[14] But there is still no mention in his writings as to how the inhabitants of Drogheda fared throughout their long ordeal. One particular prize he mentions is the capture of Art Roe Mac Mahon 'whose head was valued in the Proclamation to be taken or bringer in of him at Four Hundred Pounds'.[15]

Next to suffer were the inhabitants throughout counties Louth and Meath. The soldiers pillaged these areas, and both 'Atherdee' and Dundalk were sacked and plundered, with booty being their main objective. In a complete reversal of the situation of just four months earlier, the people fled as refugees from their homes to the safer neighbouring counties of Cavan and Monaghan. Tichborne wrote 'there was neither Man nor Beast to be found in sixteen Miles between the two Towns of Drogheda and Dundalk, nor on the other side of Dundalk, in the county of Monaghan, nearer that Carick-mac-Cross, a strong Pile Twelve Miles distant'.[16] On a later occasion he states: 'At Kells we took a few Prisoners that were not aware of their Danger, [in other words, he broke his trust and kidnapped them] and among them one Plunket a Popish Arch-Deacon'.[17]

'The History of the Execrable Irish Rebellion': An accounts of the Siege of Drogheda is documented in Borlace's *'The History of the Execrable Irish Rebellion'*, and it tallies, more or less, with Tichbourne's account as given above. It describes Drogheda thus:

> *'Tredath is an ancient City, of great Circuit, the river of Boyne passeth through the midst of the Town; it is encompassed about with an old Stone Wall, without Bulwarks of any kind of Rampiers, or other Fortifications than an ordinary Ditch; it lies about three miles from the Sea, the harbour is but ill yet such as would admit Vessels of good burthen and such as exceed not sixty Tuns may come up to the Bridge in the Town. It is situated in a plain open Countray, plentiful for all manners of Provisions, no Bogs or Marsh-ground near it so as the rebels had all the opportunities and advantages they could desire for making their approaches to the place'.[18]*

Lord Moore of Mellifont had been alerted by his sister of O'Neill's successes in the North, and of his imminent approach to Drogheda, whereupon Moore hurriedly 'repair'd in the middle of the night from Mellifont to Tredath' which he resolved to defend, and he immediately set about making preparations for the siege. There was a great dearth of weaponry, and it was necessary to call into service some old guns that had been 'cast into a Dungeon' as well as 'four [guns] took out of a Merchant Ship for service'.

O'Neill likewise was ill-prepared for a lengthy siege. The account supports this oberservation, stating that there was a 'want of great guns to batter the Walls, skill to undermine them or courage to scale them', so that the only option left to the besiegers was 'to sit still, till Famine within had made them an entrance'.

Several instances are given which clearly indicate that the town's inhabitants in general were hostile to the defenders. 'One [Sir John Netterville] of the two half-Companies in the Town proving afterwards false [and] the citizens themselves (Papists – sic) being no way real [i.e. loyal] … and the Inhabitants being no way assisting'. Time and time again they supplied false information to the commander designed to cause confusion.

When Sir Henry Tichborne arrived with his supporting force he 'was coldly received by the Citizens, not admitted into any Quarters, till himself (after many hours being in the streets) found one'. This experience taught him a lesson, for 'he expelled many of the Papish Inhabitants, which held intelligence with the inhabitants without'.

Relief for the besieged town arrived in the form of several vessels that ran the gauntlet and were able to discharge much needed supplies: this included 'a Pinnacle loaded with Bisket, Powder and Ammunition'. There can be little doubt about the dire circumstances when dogs, cats and horses were gladly eaten.

> *'That whuch discourag'd the soldiers most was the constant duty which they performed in the Night-Watch; the Circuit of the Wall was very large; the Weather (being in the depth of Winter) was very sharp, and the number of the Soldiers (who were to watch) were but small, and thereof very ill-cloth'd so as it came often to their turn than usual, which bred sickness and diseases, and some even fell down and died upon the Walls'.[19]*

Did Sir Phelim O'Neill realise how desperate the circumstances were for the garrison? He had lost a splendid chance. There was now a price of £1,000 on his head[20] and he was eventually captured and executed. The fortunes of the Irish people had hinged on the performance of the Drogheda defenders in the face of the besieging forces. The successful defence saved the day for the Pale, the Government and the King, and O'Neill's failure was eventually to spell the end of the Ulster Rising

THE MEETINGS AT BELLEWSTOWN AND CRUFTY: To the annoyance of the Dublin parliament, the Old English declined to refer to those in arms as either 'rebels' or 'traitors' – they preferred to call them 'discontented gentlemen'. This was a clear indication as to where their sympathies lay. On suspicion of treachery, the government armaments that had been allocated for the defence of Louth were repossessed by Lord Moore, but shortly afterwards his residence at Mellifont was attacked and plundered. Likewise, a detachment went out from Drogheda and repossessed Meath's arsenal which was in the custody of Lord Gormanston. The Old English were in a difficult position – they were unswervingly loyal to the Crown, yet they were being victimised by virtue of being Catholic. Lord Gormanston summed up their position in stating that they were being allowed neither the benefits of education nor employment without forfeiting their souls. The unrest was palpable and was leading them to take action. This could best be accomplished by combining with the forces of the Gaelic Irish. It was arranged that the two sides would meet to discuss the feasibility of a confederation.

The venues for the momentous event that was now to take shape will be familiar to every Droghedean. The meeting took place, not in Drogheda itself, but rather in its immediate neighbourhood, Crufty, located a few kilometres beyond Beamore Cross. This was in December 1641, a brief time after the Battle of Julianstown. Today the exact location is marked with a notice at the roadside.

It involved the principal Old English landholders of counties Louth and Meath, and was spearheaded by Lord Gormanston (Nicholas Preston) who was Governor of County Meath. He called together a preliminary meeting to obtain a consensus of the nobility of the region, namely Lords Fingall, Netterville, Slane, Louth, Trimleston and many other important lords of the Pale. They met on Bellewstown Hill prior to heading down the hill to Crufty where a large gathering had already assembled.

The Gaelic Irish were represented by Rory O'Neill and other chieftains from Ulster, accompanied by a guard of musketeers. Lord Gormanston addressed O'Neill thus: "Why come ye armed to the Pale?" To which O'Neill replied that they had "taken up arms to safeguard freedom and religious liberty of their consciences, the maintenance of loyalty to the king, and making the subjects of this kingdom as free as those of England". This wording smacks of having been stage-managed, but both parties had to act cautiously, and took the precaution of stating their objective from the very outset as being religious liberty coupled with continued loyalty to their king (although there was the hidden agenda of recovering the lands taken from them in the Ulster and Munster Plantations). All concurred, and then both parties 'shook hands together'.[21] This agreement was ratified at a follow-up meeting held at Tara on 7th December. The homes of almost all of the Old English lords named above were situated within a short distance of Drogheda; others who participated were Lord Dunsany, Lord Dillon and Nicholas Darcy at whose home in Plattin another meeting was held. *The upshot was that the Gaelic Irish and the Old English joined forces in an alliance known to history as the Confederation of Kilkenny.* The government side in the conflict preferred to call it 'the Great Popish Rebellion".

Soon the Old English from the other provinces joined. Lord Gormanston assumed overall command. The fact that Sir Phelim O'Neill was not put in charge tells us that the Old English were treating the Confederacy as an uneasy alliance rather than a fully committed union – they maintained a certain mental reservation throughout the Confederation's existence.

THE CONFEDERATION OF KILKENNY (1642-1649): Although the Ulster Rising ended in failure for the Gaelic Irish, they were still intent on ridding Ireland of the English, and were conscious that England's hold on Ireland was very tenuous. The Pale was contracting and its inhabitants felt very insecure. The timing was right to press home their advantage.

Kilkenny lent its name to the Confederation because the Supreme Council normally met in that city. We have seen that townlands in the immediate Drogheda area – Bellewstown, Crufty, Tara, Tullyesker and Plattin – all featured in the Confederation's birth, the inference being that it was these local Old English landholders who, with the Ulster chieftains, initiated the Confederation. However, the town of Drogheda was uncomfortably close to the seat of influence in Dublin for parliament to sit there – Kilkenny was at a safer distance.

The Confederation nonetheless governed two-thirds of the entire country, and held sway for seven years. The remaining Old English landowners of Louth and Meath joined in, and, in particular, Thomas Preston was appointed Colonel of the Confederation's Army of Leinster. He was one of an Old English Catholic family, and his daughter Louise was married to Sir Phelim O'Neill. He later became Viscount Gormanston whose seat was Gormanston Castle, now the Franciscan College and boarding school for boys. The Preston family had been associated with the town of Drogheda from early Norman times. Other leading members were Rory O'More, Owen Roe O'Neill and Sir Phelim O'Neill of Kinard.

Co-incidentally, Sir Phelim O'Neill's son, also called Phelim, was a Franciscan friar and later served as Guardian in Drogheda's friary at the time of the severe religious persecutions of the 1670s. He had been nominated for office by no less a person than Archbishop Oliver Plunkett of Armagh. A subsequent Guardian of the same friary in Drogheda was Fr. Anthony O'Neill, a son of Owen Roe O'Neill,[22] and a grand-nephew of the great Hugh O'Neill of Yellow Ford fame. Thus, the fathers of both of these Guardians were key leaders in the Confederation of Kilkenny.

The Confederates were well placed to converge on the Pale and Dublin in a pincer movement, Sir Phelim O'Neill from the north and the other forces of the Confederation from the west and south, and then to capture the principal members of the Government. In that way the English would be pushed out of Ireland, just as Brian Boru had done to the Vikings six hundred years earlier.

The Battle of Benburb: In 1646 Owen Roe O'Neill, a key leader in the Confederation, inflicted a crushing defeat on the English forces at Benburb, which is located on that same little river – the Callan – that his uncle, the great Hugh O'Neill, had beaten another English army 48 years earlier (at the Yellow Ford). A resurgent Ireland had again sent the new English settlers scuttling behind the Pale, and the net was closing in on its occupants. This victory at Benburb could have been as conclusively favourable for the Confederates as the earlier one at Kinsale was for the English, had Colonel Preston lent a hand in the mopping up operation and in consolidating the victory, but the links in the Confederation were tenuous at best, and there had always been a cold rivalry between Colonel Preston and Owen Roe, and thus a rare opportunity was lost. Disunity!

The entire Pale at this time was still in imminent danger, bearing in mind that the combined encircling forces of Ormonde and Lord Inchiquin were threatening Dublin from another direction. Besides, Dublin's Governor, Colonel Michael Jones, was running short of both ammunition and food. Also, Colonel Preston, who led the Army of Leinster, was poised for attack. And the redoubtable Owen Roe O'Neill was at hand to deliver the *coup de grace*. So near, and yet so far!

Civil War in England: Meantime, a different turning point in history was being enacted across the water which was to have repercussions throughout Ireland, and which Drogheda in particular would have cause to remember. King Charles I was on the English throne. He was a Catholic, but this did not relieve the plight of Irish Catholics. On the contrary, it was divisive in the extreme. He was headstrong and indiscreet, and claimed to rule by Divine Right; he had taken many unpopular decisions against the wishes of Parliament; this was an affront to his subjects, the vast majority of whom had embraced the Protestant faith. The tension reached breaking point, splitting the populace between Royalists and Parliamentarians. The upshot was the English Civil War.

Drogheda found itself in a serious dilemma, and it must have been difficult for the local authorities to try and unify the same perplexing patchwork of factions that Tichborne had earlier encountered. It is equally difficult from today's perspective to assess the divergent moods and loyalties of the citizenry. An anonymous visitor to the town in 1635 observed '… Most of the town's inhabitants are Popishly affected'. Let us briefly review this hotchpotch of political and religious humanity that were thrown into Drogheda's tempestuous cauldron:

- The descendants of the original founders of the town, the Normans (now known as 'the Old English'), had adhered to the Catholic faith, but remained steadfast in their loyalty to whatever king happened to be sitting on the throne, be he Protestant or Catholic.
- Others, who perceived that the wind was now blowing from a different direction, made the tactical change to Protestantism.
- The New English settlers were, almost to the last man, Protestant.
- Most of the native Gaels living within the town were Catholic.
- A section of the native Gaels did change their religion, not excluding some clergy.
- For good measure, the latest newcomers within the town were mostly those refugees who escaped having their throats cut in the Ulster Rebellion and were made up mainly of Scottish Calvinists – zealots who preached fire and brimstone.
- Others among the refugees were marginalised Scottish Presbyterians; although they had recently been dispossessed by the resurgent Irish, they were being persecuted and were downtrodden in much the same way as the Catholics.
- Finally, although Drogheda did not yield to the Confederate forces under O'Neill, there were many Confederate sympathisers among the inhabitants, as Tichborne had discovered.

All told, it was a nice how-do-you-do. But this bewildering complexity of religious and political factions was soon to be compounded by a sequence of events that brought another character onto centre stage – a gentleman by the name of Oliver Cromwell. He had come to prominence in the English Civil War, and he put an end to that troubled episode in the peremptory manner that personified his character. He committed regicide – that is, he severed the king's head from his body. Such was his reputation that any adversary would quail at the mention of his name, and it was a courageous (or foolhardy) force that would stand in his way.

Chapter Ten

Cromwell Comes to Town

The king now sitting on England's throne was Charles I. His policy, both in showing deference to his Catholic subjects (both in England and Ireland) and in levying taxes, did not sit well with Parliament who represented the majority, and they were Protestant. Among those who resented this behaviour was Cromwell, and this brought him into prominence, and inevitably into direct conflict with the king, a situation that escalated into civil war – the Royalists versus the Parliamentarians.

He played a prominent part in the war, and his qualities as a leader in politics and as a skilful general in battle soon became evident. He displayed particular ability with cavalry. The king was defeated in a series of battles, and he was finally brought to trial. Cromwell presented trumped up charges against him, alleging that the king was a "tyrant, traitor, murderer, and a public and implacable enemy of the Commonwealth of England".

The king displayed great dignity throughout the court proceedings, cogently enquiring by what authority he had been brought to trial. In fact Cromwell and his Parliamentarian co-accusers were little more than a self- appointed caucus which was hell bent on ridding itself forever of the king. The verdict was a foregone conclusion, with Cromwell smiling with satisfaction as he signed the king's death warrant.

A few moments after the king submitted his neck to the executioner's block, the executioner, disguising his visage in wig and beard, held up the severed head, and declared "Behold the head of a traitor!" But the king's adherents regarded him not as a traitor, but as a martyr, and their day would come.

Drogheda Takes a Fateful Decision: Drogheda had demonstrated its fealty to the Dublin Parliament and the Crown when Sir Phelim O'Neill was hammering at the town's gates. With his failure to gain entry, the people could breathe easy again. But their respite was short-lived.

The town was to be the centre of a political and military tug-of-war throughout the 1640s and was to remain in the headlines – it started with the Siege of Drogheda. The Governor of Dublin, Colonel Jones, set out to secure Drogheda for the Parliamentarians early in 1649, but the Marquis of Ormonde (who was a Royalist) tells us: 'When I got [to Trim] I understood Jones was gotten before Drogheda; but upon knowledge of my coming he drew back to Dublin'. Lord Inchquin also harried Jones who then consolidated his position while awaiting the arrival of his lord and master, Oliver Cromwell. Ormonde wrote that when Cromwell arrived 'it was resolved to that end held necessary to place in Drogheda a much greater force of men, and an experienced Governor, Sir Arthur Aston was pitched on to command, and above 2000 of our best foot and 250 horse were put in, 55 barrels of powder with victuals for a much longer time than it held out'.[1]

Having withstood O'Neill's Siege, the town was soon faced with another grave decision. It was no longer enough simply to remain loyal to England, where a civil war in full spate. The question now was whether it should support the Royalists or the Parliamentarians – it could not remain on the sideline. Tradition dictated that Drogheda, for better or worse, should take its stand with the Royalists, and this was the course taken. The result was to be writ in blood.

OLIVER CROMWELL (1599-1658) – A Pen-picture: It was a portent of events to come that the house in which Cromwell was born was the site of a confiscated Augustinian monastery; indeed, the very materials used in the construction of his home were taken from the walls of that monastery. This was in the town of Huntingdon, near Cambridge. He was born of lesser gentry stock in the closing years of the reign of Queen Elizabeth I.

There were ten children in the family, three of whom died early. Of the surviving siblings, all were girls apart from Oliver. Being served hand and foot by his sisters and an attentive mother, this upbringing was no doubt a factor in shaping his character into one of dominance and wilfulness. He was used to having his own way. Exceedingly straight-laced and self-righteous in later life, as a boy he was wild, boisterous and obstreperous and was not slow about robbing orchards, breaking down hedges, vandalising dovecotes to pluck and devour all that was within, and generally indulging in horseplay.

His schoolmaster had written a book on the subject of retribution from God, theorising that punishment was to be inflicted on wrong-doers *in this life*, and that God would exact His own punishment in the next. This conviction undoubtedly left a marked impression on him and, allied to his upbringing in a home where he was the only boy, this was to greatly influence the formation of his character subsequently as a Puritan. It also provided him with auto-suggestive justification for the upheavals and the heart-wrenching grief which he inflicted on Ireland and on everything that smacked of Catholicism.

In time he became almost paranoid in regard to the Catholic Church, a trait that was manifest during his expedition to Ireland. When towns surrendered to him under agreement, priests were specifically excluded from the terms[2], and he stabled the horses of his army in the churches as he passed along. He abhorred icons and other church trappings; he closed the ale houses. *He even went to the extent of banning the celebration of Christmas!*

His father had died when he was 18, thus leaving Oliver as the sole male in the household, and shaping his disposition as a leader. However, he attended university in London where one biographer tactfully described his behaviour as being "not altogether free from the wildnesses and follies incident to youthful age". Another writer put it more bluntly: "He became the terror of the local alehouses, whose proprietresses would call out when they saw him approaching: 'Here comes young Cromwell, shut up your doors ... ' [His vices as a buck included dissipation in] drink, women, gambling and personal violence".[3] Like Saint Paul on the road to Damascus, he was later to experience a conversion and he changed his ways – except that Paul stopped persecuting Christians whereas Cromwell entered into this pursuit with single-minded relish.

With the king out of the way, Cromwell was now cock of the walk. He set his sights on Ireland, which, as we have seen, was at this time in full revolt and in imminent danger of being lost as a colony of England. He gave this matter his undivided and thorough Puritan attention, resulting in leaving a trail of blood wherever he went, starting with Drogheda. His stay in Ireland was a mere nine months, but in that short time he had accomplished his objective all too well. He completely snuffed out all Irish resistance, leaving the entire country prostrate. He left the mopping up operation to his son-in-law Ireton and then he returned to England in the certain knowledge that Ireland would not rise again.

As Lord Protector he spent the rest of his life vainly trying to give constitutional permanence to his military régime. His son Richard assumed command as Lord Protector after his death. He was a complete disappointment and was known as 'Tumbledown Dick'. The new political structure was doomed to failure, and it soon fragmented. Within eighteen months it collapsed totally.

The decapitated king's son, then in exile, accepted the invitation to ascend the throne as Charles II. He was also a Catholic, but as it transpired, he made no concessions to the Catholics of Ireland. Indeed, during his reign an Act was passed whereby Protestant clergy were to receive payment by taxing householders in the towns of Ireland, Drogheda being specifically mentioned as one of the towns saddled with this imposition.

It is an irony of fate that the climate of prejudice and hate in which Cromwell so much indulged, and which subsequently led to the execution of another Oliver – Archbishop Oliver Plunkett – should recoil on Cromwell himself. It followed him into his grave. The revulsion of murdering a king lingered in the minds and consciences of the populace, and redress was sought. Within a year of his death his stinking carcass was dug from the earth by an enraged people who dragged it on a hurdle through the streets of London to Tyburn (now Marble Arch, at the entrance to Oxford Street) and there they strung it up on the gibbet for all to revile. Next day the grisly scene was extended in a further irony reminiscent of the death sentence he had contrived for his king. The corpse was taken down and the common hangman hacked the head from its body. The headless corpse was then buried deep under the gallows. And the head itself – warts and all – was implanted on a pole outside Westminster Hall where it was left to moulder away for many more years. *Sic transit gloria mundi.*

THE STORMING OF DROGHEDA: Clearly, Cromwell was nurturing in his heart the stories of atrocities he had heard during the Ulster Rebellion. They were greatly exaggerated rumours, but they gained credence with repetition and they were avidly consumed in particular by the Puritans, who were members of a movement of extreme Protestantism, and their champion was Oliver Cromwell. These stories gave him justification (not that the lack of justification would have deterred him) when his day of retribution came. He despised the Irish and stated that 'I had rather be overrun with a Cavalierish interest than a Scottish interest; I had rather be overrun with a Scottish interest than an Irish interest… all the world knows their barbarism'.[4] He was shortly to prove that he could easily outdo the Irish in barbarism.

Determined to subjugate Royalist Ireland and teach the Irish a lesson that they would never forget, he landed at Ringsend, not far from Dublin, on the 15th August 1649. This was his first and only trip outside England – and he became sea-sick on the way. He was well prepared for the coming campaign, having 35 ships crammed with eight thousand foot and four thousand horse; plus an additional 77 ships bound for the south under his son-in-law Henry Ireton. On arrival, he delivered an oration, which was reported thus:

> *"… As God had brought him thither in safety, so he doubted not, but by his divine providence, to restore them all to their just liberty and property … for carrying on the great work against the barbarous and blood-thirsty Irish, and the rest of their adherents and confederates, for the propagating of the Gospel of Christ, the establishing of truth and peace and restoring that bleeding nation to its former happiness and tranquillity … "*

So, with "the sword in one hand and the Bible in the other", he set out on his mission against the "barbarous and blood-thirsty Irish" (both quotations are his own) to avenge the Protestant massacre of 1641, and to restore tranquillity to that "bleeding nation" – this was his stated objective.

His march from Dublin took him within sight of Gormanston Manor, and legend tells us that he decided to capture it. He enquired of Lady Gormanston as to who owned it, and she said "Lord Gormanston today, tomorrow Lord Cromwell". He was moved by this submissive reply and said "Lord Gormanston today *and* tomorrow". His men encamped there that night, and the following morning he detailed that a tree was to be planted on the lawn for each horse that had grazed there. This was duly done, and the field is still known locally as 'Cromwell's Field'.

He attempted without success to kidnap the infant heir, Jenico, of Lord Gormanston. Had he succeeded, this would have been a strategic coup, but the very attempt to use an innocent child as a pawn in a bloody war gives us an insight into the single-minded and insensitive nature of the man – it besmirches his character even if no other instances were to be quoted. An example of his misplaced sense of justice occurred near Julianstown when he had two of his men put to death in front of his entire army as proof that his justice was impartial – they had stolen a few chickens from an old woman.

His forces then camped at Ballygarth Castle, Julianstown in preparation for the assault – this was on the 1st September 1649. The campsite that they used is still known as 'the Camp Field'. At the same time he captured the principal castles in the area, viz. Athcarne, Dardistown and Bellewstown.

His artillery included two great cannon of eight inches bore and two of seven inches bore – each weighed 5½ tons. Hauling these weighty guns along the rutted Irish roadways was out of the question. He had them shipped to the Boyne estuary from where they were put ashore at Mornington. This was on Monday, the 9th September. They were man-handled over the mud-flats to North Lane, Mornington and hauled along a narrow laneway (now impassable through disuse) that runs parallel to the present Mornington/Drogheda road.[5] Trundling along the road that runs parallel with the Boyne, they reached the outskirts of the town and were hauled up the laneway that ever after would bear the name 'Cromwell's Lane' and placed on a vantage height (Cromwell's Mount) opposite the town's medieval walls and conveniently close to them in preparation for the bombardment.

The defence of the town was entrusted to Sir Arthur Aston, an Englishman who had gained considerable experience in warfare in many parts of the continent including Lithuania, Poland and Turkey. He had lost a leg and had also suffered head injuries in the course of his military career. In England he commanded the dragoons in the battle of Edgehill early in the civil war and was all too familiar with the formidable reputation of Cromwell. He may simply have been instilling confidence in his men when he boasted of its fortifications, saying that 'he who could take Drogheda could take Hell'. His pleas for assistance when Cromwell was nearing the town were not answered, and Owen Roe O'Neill in particular, who could have harried Cromwell, was unable to comply through illness. Indeed, he died on 6th. November of that year.

Cromwell was an astute and well-organised commander, and he did his homework well. He had about five days to spare while waiting for the arrival of the cannon, and he put the time to good use. He reconnoitred the town's defences from every angle. In particular, he spent some time on St. John's Hill (now Highfield) which afforded him a splendid panoramic view of the town. He paid particular attention to its defensive walls, its towers and its gates, probing for the more vulnerable points. Two features in particular struck him. Firstly, the most prominent of these was Millmount – to occupy this lofty position was to dominate the entire town from within the town itself. Secondly, there was but one bridge spanning the river, so *this had to be captured at the same time as Millmount* – otherwise the defenders would retreat across it to the larger section of the town, and a second siege would become inevitable. If he were to achieve this dual objective, he would then have Drogheda by the throat.

His first step was to issue a summons to Aston, demanding him to surrender, adding "If this be refused, you will have no cause to blame me". Like Pontius Pilate, he was attempting to shift the blame away from himself for the perceived massacre that would follow. A bloodless surrender would have well suited Cromwell; long drawn out sieges were notoriously damaging by reducing the strength of besieging armies.

Aston refused to surrender, but was well aware of the consequences of his decision. He had about 2,200 foot soldiers and 320 horse compared with Cromwell's 8,000 foot and 4,000 horse. His supplies of both armaments and foodstuffs were meagre, and there was no hope of having these augmented. Moreover, a blockade was put on the port by Cromwell's fleet – he was leaving nothing to chance.

It will be remembered that during the Siege of Drogheda seven years earlier the loyalties of the inhabitants could not have been more disparate. On this occasion it was marginally worse! – for Aston discovered that he could not trust his own grandmother! She was Lady Wilmot and, instead of doting on her grandson as grandmothers generally do, and applauding his achievements, she opposed him in this time of peril and led a plot to overthrow him. Having to face Cromwell was bad enough, but a confrontation with his grandmother was more than he could take. Bravely, he met this adversity head on, and with a threat to "make gunpowder out of her", he bundled her out of the town. She then stayed with the Moore's of Mellifont until all was over. By that time her grandson was dead.

The Barrage Begins: Cromwell wasted no time. Preparations were begun at once for the concentrated bombardment. Little has changed to the topography since those times; the steep green banks, the deep gorge known as the Dale and the little stream called the Dove (more properly, Dubh, meaning black) running through it are still as they were in 1649. A visit there today will give the reader a clear picture of the confrontation that took place. A storming force with muskets at the ready and laden with personal armour had a difficult task ascending the opposite slope, and was dangerously exposed to withering gunfire from the defenders on the town wall. But once the artillery would have made a breach for the storm troopers to gain entry, Millmount would then be within their grasp, and an armed force in occupation at that point would dominate the entire town. That was the strategy that Cromwell employed.

The cannon guns were aimed across the Dale gorge at a point of that part of the town wall that abutted St. Mary's Church and the adjoining tower. When the bombardment began the church steeple was the first to collapse, then the tower at the corner of the wall crumbled as well as other buildings in the heart of the town. Nightfall brought a lull to proceedings and provided the defenders with the opportunity to further strengthen the defences. We must remember that the walls, then 400 years old, could withstand arrows and hand-held weapons, but not gunpowder and cannon fire. No doubt the soldiers slept little, and the terrified inhabitants not at all.

'NINE ELEVEN' COMES TO DROGHEDA: The constant and concentrated pummelling by the heavy cannon caused an eventual sagging of the walls. They had not been constructed to withstand the abuse to which they were now being subjected. They began to crumble. A breach was eventually made and some Ironsides charged through at Duleek Gate. They killed about 40 defenders before they were thrown back. A second assault was made which was contested with great heroism and much spilling of blood. It, too, failed to make headway and was forced to retreat. The men were despondent at this second reversal, but Cromwell, his leadership qualities showing through, regrouped them and instilled in them a die-hard Puritan spirit, and urged that this was their God-given opportunity to avenge the misdeeds of 1641 by punishing the Catholic infidels within the town. Thus he rallied them for a further onslaught – by now it was mid-afternoon.

They charged once again, and this time, with the Lord Protector himself at their front and fully exposed to every danger, they were more resolute. They reached the breach, and amid the cry of battle, the clash of swords and the discharging of muskets, on this occasion they succeeded in penetrating the gap by sheer force of numbers. They were followed by the cavalry and soon the rest of the army – eight thousand of them – were pouring through. The garrison was soon overwhelmed and it was destined that the day would belong to Cromwell.

Aston and some of his force retreated to Millmount across the roadway from the Carmelite Church where the breach was made. Whatever fortifications stood there we know not, but they were not stout enough to resist the men on the warpath. (The Martello Tower was not constructed until Napoleonic times). It

The Storming of Drogheda
by a contemporary artist

seems that quarter was offered to some defenders and their officers, and they therefore laid down their arms. But Cromwell rushed up and forbade mercy to anyone. Thereupon, everyone was put to the sword, including Sir Arthur Aston himself. It had been falsely rumoured that a collection of gold-pieces was secreted within his wooden leg. Having pulled it off and finding nothing to satisfy their greed, the Ironsides used the leg as a club to beat out his brains.

The description of the slaughter at Millmount is given in Cromwell's own words: -

"Divers of the enemy retreated to the mill mount, a place very strong, and of difficult access, being exceedingly high, having a good graft, and strongly pallisaded. Sir Arthur Aston and divers considerable officers being there, our men getting at them, were ordered by me to put them all to the sword; and indeed being in the heat of action, I forbad them to spare any that were in arms in the town, and I think that night they put to the sword about two thousand men ... I am persuaded that this is a righteous judgment of God upon these barbarous wretches".

Two Cannon Balls fired by Cromwell.
A supply of cannon balls for use in a campaign was too heavy to be carried with the artillery - some weighed 32 lbs. It was usual to cast them on location as required.
These two specimens were fired by Cromwell in storming Drogheda.

In the continuing mayhem the defenders had neglected lifting the drawbridge over the Boyne that linked the two parts of the town. This was a crucial oversight. The storming troops saw their opportunity and quickly seized their goal. Thus the orgy of slaughter was extended to the town's northern and more populous section. The order had been given that all who bore arms were to be slaughtered, but no questions were asked, and civilians were cut down equally with the soldiers.

Many sought refuge in St. Peter's Church at the head of Peter Street in the belief that they would be safe within the sanctity of that building. They were wrong. Colonel Hewson 'caused the seats of the church to be broken up, and made a great pile of them under the steeple; which, firing it, it took the lofts wherein five great bells were hung, and from thence it flamed up to the top, and so at once the men and the bells and roof came down all together, the most hideous site [sic] and terrible cry that ever he was a witness of at once'. Again we will allow Cromwell himself to supply us with a further description of the scene: -

"... I forbid them to spare any that were in arms in the town, and I think that night they put to the sword about two thousand men: divers of the officers and men being fled over the bridge into the other part of the town, where about one hundred of them possessed St. Peter's steeple, some of the west Gate, and others a round tower next to the gate called St. Sunday's, these being summoned to mercy, refused, whereupon I ordered the steeple of St. Peter's to be fired: when one of them was heard to say in the midst of the flames "God damn me! God confound me! I burn! I burn!"

Cromwell seems to have taken a fiendish delight in describing that scene. One individual escaped from the inferno with his life. He had sought refuge in the tall steeple and then taken in desperation a perilous leap to escape the encroaching flames, and on landing on the ground he sustained only a broken leg. This incident was deemed so remarkable that his life was spared 'for the extraordinariness of the thing'.

More gory details were described by Cromwell, and the entire event he attributes to God. He explained that people had:

"set up the Mass in some of the places of the town that had been Monasteries, but afterwards grew so insolent that, the Lord's Day before the storm [viz. the storming of the town] the Protestants were thrust out of the great Church called St. Peter's and they had public Mass there, and in this very place near one thousand of them were put to the sword, flying thither for protection. I believe all of the friars were knocked on the head promiscuously but two ... it is good that God alone have all the glory".

Cromwell also left his mark on the steeple of the old Magdalene monastery, even though it had otherwise withstood the elements remarkably well over the centuries. 'There is, indeed, a breach in the upper part of the east side, and the mullions of one window are removed, but this is supposed to have been effected by Cromwell's cannon to compel the surrender of part of the garrison who had taken refuge in it[6]. The ravages wrought both by Cromwell and by Time were repaired in the 1990s, but, inexplicably, the stonework used was sandstone, not the limestone that the Dominican monks had used when originally constructing the monastery.

Today's generation will recognise the date attaching to the following morning – it has an ominous ring about it – it was the Eleventh of September, or 'Nine Eleven', to use American parlance. This was the date in 2001 that rocked the Western World to its foundations, when the Twin Towers in New York crumbled into dust, bringing violent death to many innocent inhabitants. Curiously, apart from the common date, both events involved towers; in both cases many unfortunates flung themselves from aloft in desperate efforts to escape the inferno, and an unspecified number of innocent people were liquidated; both events left an indelible mark on history.

The exact numbers that were killed in both of these catastrophes will never be known. Those that perished in the Twin Towers is officially given as 2,749, although it is difficult to accept that that figure is accurate, given that an indeterminate number of bodies had been totally incinerated and were simply reduced to dust. Cromwell puts the Drogheda figure at two thousand, Dr. Bates at four thousand and the official verdict is nearly three thousand – a figure not dissimilar to that at the Twin Towers.

The Mayoralty House of the day had stood in Laurence St., next to Keyser's Lane (known today as the High Lane). Regrettably, this was destroyed along with all the official Corporation records relating to Drogheda's past history. (Other official documents were later used as fuel by yeomen in 1798).

The Ironsides were now masters of the town; their blood was up and they showed no mercy; they set about slaying all before them, and their commander declined to stay their hands. Cromwell continues: -

"The next day the other towers were summoned, in one of which was about six or seven score; but they refused to yield themselves, and we knowing that hunger would compel, set only a good guard to secure them from running away, until their stomachs would come down. From

one of the said towers, notwithstanding their condition, they killed and wounded some of our men. When they submitted themselves, their officers were knocked on the head, and every tenth man of the soldiers killed and the rest shipped to the Barbadoes."

In his bulletin dated 27th September 1649 he included a list of the main officers killed, and ominously ends with *'... and many inhabitants.'* An eyewitness account describes how a group of ladies was found by the soldiers huddled in the crypt of a church. They promptly received the same fate as all the others, save one. She was 'a handsome virgin, arrayed in costly and gorgeous apparel' and the commanding officer ordered his men to spare her life. But while he was interrogating her, another soldier ran her through from behind.

Another incident occurred that day when Colonel Boyle (from the defeated army) was dining with Lord and Lady Moore. (Officers often knew their fellows in opposing armies and were on personal friendly terms; they showed courtesy and chivalry towards one another). An Ironside soldier marched over to him to say he must leave the table and go outside. Lady Moore asked him why he was leaving the company so hurriedly. He replied: "Madam, to die". Those were his last words.

The carnage continued with Puritan diligence for five days. It is ironic that Cromwell ended the lives of many fellow Protestants at this time, so thorough was his work. In particular, many who met horrible death in St. Peter's C. of I. Church would have been adherents to that religion. We must remember, too, that the population had been swelled when many Protestants had arrived as refugees during the Ulster Rebellion eight years earlier, when the dispossessed Catholics had risen up against them. Cromwell, in his enthusiasm for butchery, was killing some of the very people whom he had set out to avenge – there is little time for niceties in the heartless prosecution of wars. His pathological detestation of friars and priests meant that none of them was spared – they were treated as if they were combatants.

Contemporary accounts of the slaughter still exist. A chaplain who accompanied the Cromwellian army as a correspondent wrote on 15th September 'Tredagh is taken. Three thousand, five hundred and fifty-two enemy and sixty-four English killed. None spared'.[7] Another contemporary was the Marquis of Ormonde whose army was pitted against the Parliamentarians. He wrote:

'... but much greater was the cruelty exercised by Cromwell's own command, against the desire even of his common soldiers, upon all he found alive in Drogheda, when after two repulses he had gained by assaulting a large breach'. And again, 'This cruelty [at Rathmines] was not to be exampled but in Cromwell, who had at the taking of Drogheda exceeded himself, much more than any thing I ever heard of, in breach of faith and other inhumanity...'. And again, 'The cruelty exercised there for five days after the town was taken, would make as many several pictures of inhumanity, as are to be found in the book of Martyrs, or in the relation of Amboyna....of those that were killed, the better half were butchered an hour after quarter given them, and some after they were brought within the walls of the town'.[8]

We have instanced above Cromwell's exactitude for discipline in the ranks when soldiers purloined a few hens for their supper. Whether this policy towards property was applied to Drogheda, having defied his call to surrender, we are not told. Looting may well have occurred during his men's days of rampaging, but undoubtedly pillaging and confiscations were, by and large, the order of the day. Both the Royalists and the Church would have accumulated wealth and property – this was fair game for the soldiers. Cromwell's bulletin to the Speaker of Parliament immediately after the storming states that *"the war is likely to pay for itself"* – a pregnant statement.

From the historian's point of view, the destruction of the town's past records was an unmitigated tragedy. With the burning of the Mayoralty House (later the site of the Franciscan Church in Laurence St., now the High Lane Art Gallery) everything kept there that related to council meetings and other events since the days of Hugh de Lacy went up in flames. The earliest surviving records of the General Assembly which are held today in the Corporation archives are dated subsequent to April 1649. However, Úna O'Tierney, in her thesis 'Fair Street and Drogheda – the Eighteenth Century Town, the Street and its Houses' surmises in reference to the Minute Book:

> 'It is apparent that the writing [of the April Meeting] is so similar to the next recorded meeting, that of September Meeting of 1649, that both of these meetings were written by the same hand. It is possible that the earlier meeting was edited and/or that meetings were not recorded or else records had been removed. The September Meeting would have taken place after Cromwell had departed from the town. It is remarkable that in the minutes of the General Assembly meetings of the Corporation immediately after this event there is no mention of the loss of life and property, these may have been edited out later. The only reference to the event is in connection with the 1655 records of Corporation leases and the fraternity charters held by the Corporation, which were lost in the "Storm of Drogheda". General Assembly 12th. April 1665'.

The dreadful tidings of the massacre at Drogheda quickly spread throughout the land, striking terror into every Irish and Royalist heart. The neighbouring towns of Dundalk, Carlingford, Newry and Trim speedily opened their gates and thus avoided the slaughter of their citizens. Towns that did not readily submit, such as Wexford, paid in blood for their courage. Terrified, one after another the towns fell to the feared Ironsides. In that facile way the submission of the entire island was gained.

In the earlier battles of the English Civil War there was nothing to compare with the bloodbath that Cromwell wreaked in Ireland, especially in Drogheda and Wexford. In his written report to Parliament (quoted above in part) Cromwell took pains to excuse the massacre by saying that it was done 'in the heat of action' and concluded by convincing himself that the atrocity had the full approval of the Almighty! It can be said that 'He doth protest too much, methinks'. R.F. Foster skilfully sums up Cromwell's performance:

> *"The tone was set by his massacre of the civilian population at Drogheda ... Like the later horror at Wexford, it is one of the few massacres in Irish history fully attested to on both sides; even Edmond Ludlow [a contemporary Parliamentary army commander] described the 'extraordinary severity' that was employed. Cromwell himself affected to see no need for excusing or palliating the action of his troops, but his account betrays an uncharacteristically uneasy tone. As with later wartime outrages, the argument was proffered that such tactics saved lives in the long run by acting as a scare tactic; but this, too, has the tone of an ex post facto rationalisation".*[9]

A row of neat redbrick cottages was built in 1891 under the aegis of the Cairnes Trust Fund on Cromwell's Mount at the site of the gun emplacements. In the course of digging the foundations for these homes a collection of human skeletons was found, and in some cases lead bullets and military buttons lay intermingled with the bones. Evidently these were the remains of soldiers who had perished during the assault on the town.

Chapter Eleven

The After-effects of Cromwell

Cromwell's visit has reverberated through the long, troubled corridors of Irish history, reshaping the country's destiny right into modern times. It started with the Cromwellian Plantation, an event that ensured that there would be no repetition of the settlers becoming 'more Irish than the Irish themselves'. Many of the existing landed classes were unseated and replaced with a new breed, causing resentment, which has abated only in recent times. No longer was England's hold on Ireland restricted to the Pale. Cromwell achieved in a matter of nine months what the Normans had failed to accomplish in almost five centuries – the conquest and submission of the whole island. This was now completed, and in a most thorough fashion. The dispossessed were given the heartless option of "to Hell or Connaught". Of all the unpleasant personages to occupy the pages of Irish history, none is more reviled than Oliver Cromwell.

The last outpost in Ireland to surrender was Inishboffin, off the western seaboard, where the French commanding officers simply surrendered their post without firing a shot. We can appreciate the chagrin expressed by one defender who regarded these supine leaders as traitors, describing them in vitriolic terms thus: *"those bloudie tigers and human bloud-sucker whaspes"!*

The overall mayhem resulting from the campaign and the mopping up operations that followed was devastating. It had an immediate and profound effect on the demographic profile of the island, reducing the population from an estimated 1,200,000 to 850,000 in the short fifteen years between 1640 and 1655.[1]

How many of the soldiers who had been present at the defence of Drogheda were actual natives of the town we do not know, but Drogheda was one of the 15 precincts named in connection with the Act of Transportation. We are told by Cromwell himself that those who escaped death "were shipped to the Barbadoes" and other parts of the West Indies. Between men, women and children, these numbered about 100,000. He devised another scheme of shipping a thousand Irish boys and girls to work in the sugar plantations of Jamaica; this scheme he delegated to his son, but it was not pursued. Those who surrendered in subsequent Irish engagements, numbering some 13,000, were allowed by agreement to leave Ireland and join a continental power friendly to England. Drogheda was one of the ports designated for embarkation. It must not be presumed that those who sailed the ocean blue to Barbados spent their time sunning themselves on the silvery shores of that holiday island. They were indentured or bonded to overlords, and their status was akin to slavery; they toiled under a cruel sun clearing virgin scrubland and working in the sugar plantations of several of the islands that constitute the West Indies. One of these islands, Montserrat, is sometimes referred to as "the Emerald Isle" by virtue of the high percentage of its inhabitants with Irish blood. The indentured men freely interbred with African slaves who had also been introduced to the island, and their progeny today work together in harmony.

The entire country was excoriated by the Cromwellian campaign. Disease and famine swept through the land in its wake, leaving perhaps 20% of the population dead[2]. Such was the devastation that much of the countryside became wild and desolate, and wolves roamed freely 'which of late years had much increased in many parts of this nation' and bounties were offered for their destruction. Taking the exodus of the defeated soldiers into account, the total population of Ireland had been reduced to a figure that was not much greater than half a million souls.[3] Drogheda's population was reduced to about 5,000. Livestock numbers were so reduced that it became necessary to issue a prohibition order preventing the export of cattle so that a restocking of the land could occur, and thus allowing a gradual recovery in the economy.

The Adventurers and the Cromwellian Plantation: The financing of Cromwell's campaign had been arranged in a method similar to that used in the earlier conquest of Ulster – it was a speculative arrangement hammered out with London capitalists, although great difficulty was experienced in procuring investors. The project was looked upon as a business venture or 'adventure', and in consequence those who contributed funds were called 'Adventurers'. In effect they were akin to shareholders, and the money they advanced was secured on the Irish land that was to be sequestered. It was likewise envisaged that the army officers and the common soldiers (of whom there were 35,000) would receive estates or parcels of land in lieu of cash, and this certainly acted as a spur to their performance when in the field of battle.

Cromwell as Governor of Ireland
A contemporary woodcut

The actual work of allocating the Settlement took ten years. The records are deficient regarding the precise parcelling of lands, except to reveal 'that Ireland was monumentally transformed between 1653 and 1660'. A total of 11,000,000 out of a possible 20,000,000 English acres were confiscated.[4] Ten counties were targeted, Antrim, Armagh and Down in Ulster and seven counties between the Boyne and the Barrow, representing the cream of the fertile land.

Many of the soldiers who were allotted holdings had no desire to remain in Ireland, and sold out to wheeler-dealers with greedy paws, so that some of the new settlers/adventurers emerged with thousands of acres – the average new holding was 700 acres.

The English Parliament made sure that enough land was confiscated to meet its obligation. 'By the order of 2 July 1653 all Catholics, regardless of their guilt or innocence under the Act of Settlement, were subject to transplantation to Connaught, and 44,210 names were recorded in certificates of transportation by 1 May 1654'.[5] The existing occupiers were accordingly bundled off to the territory west of the Shannon. This region included County Clare, and thus the total area was encompassed by the broad sweep of the River Shannon on one side and the wild Atlantic on the other. It was perceived as a ring-fence – a Pale of sorts – behind which the 'mere Irish' were to be contained.

> *"Here will be met representatives of the old aristocracy and the minor gentry, lords and ladies of the Pale and elsewhere, knights and baronets, esquires and gentlemen, widowed ladies, grandmothers, orphans and their guardians, aldermen and burgesses of Galway, Limerick and Drogheda, merchants and those of lesser estates suggested in their acreages – all on the way out".[6]*

In that way many landholders from the Drogheda/Meath area were uprooted from their homesteads and estates, and were left to scrape out a living among the inferior lands in Connaught. Thus was created a massive social upheaval. The exodus from east to west had the effect not only of impoverishing the transplanted peoples, but also of eroding the Irish language and old Irish customs, replacing them with the English language and alien ways.

We know that many of the Old English Catholic landholders, whose roots had been implanted for generations in Irish soil, had valuable contacts in government circles and were otherwise familiar with officials in high places in Dublin. A study that focused on County Meath clearly demonstrates this pattern[7]. These managed to hold on to their lands by sending a Memorial to the Lord Deputy, reminding him of 'their services during the rebellion of 1641, and praying to be restored to their former Estates, freedoms and immunities therein and they prayed to be relieved from the oath of supremacy and the direction of receiving the sacraments'. The Lord Deputy acceded to their plea. The Earl of Drogheda made it his business to curry favour with the Drogheda Corporation, for in 1665 its members expressed thanks to 'the Right honourable Henrey Earle of Drogheda for presenting a large Silver Boule' to them.

Others, finding themselves in the dilemma of not knowing which horse to back during the campaign, escaped confiscation by having placed an each way bet on the outcome, whereby some family members supported one side, and some the other side. Heads they win, tails they win! And some are still in possession of their estates today!

Most farm labourers were also left undisturbed, not for humanitarian reasons, but because sufficient replacement peasants from England could not be found – after all, someone had to remain to milk the cows and till the soil. The system could not function without them.

If we seek first hand accounts by the townspeople of the actual siege, the slaughter and the aftermath, we will not find them in the Corporation's Minute Book. As stated above, the first meeting of the Drogheda Corporation following Cromwell's storming of the town was held three weeks later (5th October 1649) and it consisted of men who were determined to suppress any notion of further revolt. Catholics were marginalised in infinite ways, but primarily by being disqualified from voting, and this policy was pursued with exactitude. They were excluded from all public life and positions in administration and commerce; this effectively excluded them from having a say in the future running of their town.

Who were these newcomers to the bountiful plains of Louth and Royal Meath? Whether they were English blue-blooded aristocrats or mere beggars on horseback it is not for us to judge from such a time-distance. Either way, these were the people who now dominated the country and who influenced the subsequent course of events at every level, and their position was consolidated 41 years later when King William of Orange arrived. These newcomers came to be known as 'the Ascendancy'. They were the people on whom the welfare of the population was to depend for the next two and a half centuries.

A proposal was adopted in 1656 stating that 'no Papist should be admitted free [i.e. granted the privilege of a freeman and thus entitled to vote] to this Corporation', thus making the town a ghetto to its native inhabitants. One year later a resolution was passed that 'all Protestants who had faithfully adhered to the interests of the Commonwealth ... should be continued in their ancient freedoms'[8]; The Irish House of Lords thanked his Majesty for his prudent care in securing cities and corporate towns in the hands of Protestants.

MILLMOUNT:

Few Irish towns have a skyline as distinctive as that of Drogheda, with its early Christian monastery towers, its medieval and its more recent church spires and industrial chimney stacks reaching towards the sky – they form an  impressive skyline. The most distinctive of these structures is Millmount; its profile surpasses all else. It featured prominently during Cromwell's visit to the town, and is mentioned several more times throughout this book, including the disturbances created during the Civil War.

There are several theories as to how, why and when Millmount was built. Its origins are obscure and are lost in the mists of the remote past. One theory suggests that it is the burial mound of Milisius who died in 1029 BC. How does one verify that!

Did our distant forebears create the steep grassy mound by hauling up loads of earth in wicker baskets on their backs? We don't know the answer, but that is one school of thought. A more likely explanation is that a prominent misshapen mound had always been there – left by Mother Nature – and that its profile was purposefully altered, then topped by the symmetrical cone-shaped pile we see today. Was it the funeral mound of Queen Scotia? ... or of Amergin the Elder who was killed at the battle of Meath? In his work "Treasures of the Boyne Valley" Peter Harbison proffers the tantalising suggestion that it 'could well be another passage grave *a la* Newgrange ... or could have been a Norman motte set up by Hugh de Lacy when granted the Lordship of Meath in 1172 – or both'.[9] The theories abound.

Whatever its origin, its strategic importance is self evident since it offers a commanding view to every point of the compass, especially eastwards to follow the course of the River Boyne on its approach to the sea. Consider the alarm of observers in an earlier millennium as they spied the dreaded sails of the Viking longboats bearing down on the locality for an orgy of rape and plunder. This brings us to another theory – tradition has it that it was built as a fort for Thurgesius the Dane who occupied the region about 830 AD. It was still a Danish stronghold in 910 AD. Be that as it may, the Danes did not remain long enough to establish a permanent settlement or to leave behind any trace of their occupation, unlike other towns along the east coast such as Wexford, Waterford and Dublin. Curiously, no artefacts of Viking origin have ever come to light in the Drogheda area.

No sooner had the Danes departed than another set of invaders arrived – the Anglo-Normans, and it was they who selected this location by the Boyne – it had been nothing more than a green field site – in which to found a town. To consolidate their control over the native Irish, they adopted the policy wherever they went of building mottes and castles as they extended their range across the land. Drogheda was no exception. D'Alton tells us:

> On this principle, immediately after the invasion, two castles were erected here, the Castle of Drogheda, properly so styled, and the Castle of Blackagh or Ulnagh, as it is otherwise called in some ancient documents, both situated at the Meath side of the Boyne. It may be reasonably presumed that these were erected by Hugh de Lacy, the first Palatine of Meath, and who, by such erection of castles along the marches, best secured the settlement of English rule within the district called the Pale............. In Newcomen's map the castle of Drogheda is distinctly marked as near the bridge, at the south side of the town, and it appears to have been the fortress designed in the corporate seal; not a trace, however, even of the foundations of this, or of the castle of Blackagh now remains to suggest their precise site; and during the lapse of centuries nothing worthy of historical notice is recorded in connection of either.[10]

We tend to regard the round stone structure (the Martello Tower – the actual 'Cup and Saucer') that crowns the conical green mound as "Millmount". More properly, Millmount is the steep hill leading up to it from the Boyne. The Martello Tower is a relatively recent addition – it was erected just two hundred years ago (1808) in anticipation of an invasion by Napoleon, but the name "Millmount" was applied centuries before the Martello Tower was built. The very name Millmount implies that a windmill once stood there. Such an elevated position was certainly ideal to capture every breath of wind from whatever direction it blew, fulfilling its purpose of keeping the breadbaskets of the town's inhabitants well supplied.

Its strategic importance was recognised in 1641. Referring to the Siege of Drogheda when the Confederate forces had encircled the town, D'Alton states:

> "Having duly attended to the quarters of his soldiers, Sir Henry [Tichbourne – he was Governor of Drogheda at the time of the siege] diligently inspected the fortifications of the town, and directed measures for yet further strengthening of the place, and in particular the mill-mount as the stronghold on the Meath side........."[11]

The fortifications were sufficiently strengthened to withstand the attentions of Sir Phelim O'Neill's army, for after a lengthy 105 days – the same duration, by coincidence, as the famous Siege of Derry half a century later. The Siege of Drogheda was lifted, mainly because the besieging force lacked proper artillery and storming equipment. This was to the great relief of the inhabitants – they had been reduced to conditions of absolute starvation. Had Drogheda fallen to the Confederate forces, then Dublin itself would have been in imminent danger, with the consequence of the English being ousted from Ireland forever.

Eight years later (1649) another opportunity arose when the town gates were defiantly closed to Cromwell and his Roundheads. We have seen how Cromwell concentrated his bombardment on the area around Duleek Gate until the walls began to crumble. It was around the area of Duleek Gate/Millmount that he finally succeeded in making a breach, allowing his soldiers to pour in. Governor Aston and many of the defenders had retreated to Millmount and met their end at this point.

Thomas Wright had an eye for historic buildings and has given us a wealth of information, supported by sketches which he published in the mid-1700s under the title *'Louthiana'*. A second collection of his works were never published, and to this day it lies dormant in the vaults of the British Library. The subject is well worthy of pursuit as evidenced by the accompanying sketch taken from a drawing which he had prepared of Millmount. The text states:

> *'In Draugheda on the south side of the Boyne and in county Meath, near the Barracks, there is a large Danish Rath. [Until the early 1900s the many raths throughout Ireland were thought to have been of Danish origin]. It is 100 feet in height sloap away from the ditch which has been large and deep, at present encumbered with gardens, etc. that 'tis not to be measured, it is twenty seven paces broad on the top, and has the ruins of a round tower on it, there is within 15 feet of the trench five small bastions built of stone, at equal distance from each other. On the side of the Rath, the acute angle of each bastion being without forms an area within which might contain a dozen men at arms, but the parapet is only breast high with spike holes in the sides'.*

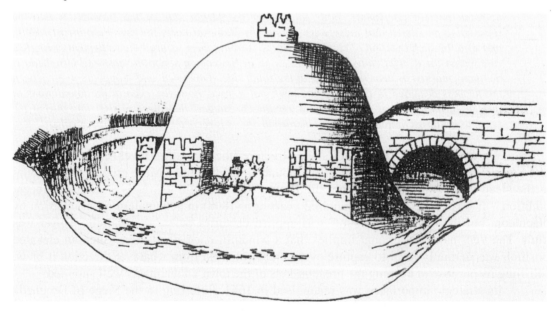

Sketch of Millmount in the mid 1700s
It was surmounted by the remains of a windmill,
and depicted some intriguing military emplacements.

This intriguing snippet gives us a new insight into the fortifications at Millmount. The overall structure is captioned *'Castlemount'*, and the 'small bastions built of stone' tell us that it was more elaborate than has been assumed. They were no doubt in place at the time of Cromwell's onslaught, and were probably built during the reign of Elizabeth I. No trace of them remains today, but no doubt some remnants still lie beneath the grassy mound. The dilapidated windmill which surmounted the pile is mistakenly described as 'the ruins of a round tower'.

What If ?: It is hardly an exaggeration to claim that Millmount has played a pivotal part in the destiny, not only of Ireland, but also of England. When Cromwell, with the backing of Parliament, set out to reconquer Ireland in 1649, his very first objective was Drogheda which was a bone of contention between the Royalist and the Parliamentary/Cromwellian forces. Its possession was regarded by both sides as being strategically important, being the conduit between Dublin and the North.

Everything hinged on Cromwell's performance at that crucial moment in time, with the Pale hanging on by its fingernails. Had he failed to capture Drogheda, or had he been killed in the attempt, the history of these islands would have taken a totally different course. Having risked himself at the head of the storming force he was in an extremely vulnerable position, and a well directed shot or a stray bullet could have brought him down – this would have turned history on its head. Ireland would have escaped the Cromwellian Plantation and the upheavals that ensued. The forces of the Confederation of Kilkenny would have been in complete control.

Half a century later, when King William arrived on the scene to confront King James at the Boyne, we could conclude with a little conjecture that the Confederation forces would have joined James at the Boyne, and their combined strength would have reversed the outcome of that fateful battle; and King William would have high-tailed it back to Holland and be lost to history. These altered circumstances would have put a completely different account on subsequent history. With no imported Ascendancy to cause the cruel era known as the Penal Days, the later imposition of the Act of Union (1800) would not have occurred. Ulster, being the stronghold of the O'Neills and the O'Donnells, would today be the staunchest province in a united, harmonious island. The country would not have been torn apart by religious prejudices and the Ulster of today would not have been beset by turmoil.

As for English history, Buckingham Palace today would be the residence of the Catholic Stuarts, but who knows what difficulties they would have engendered! Fate had taken a hand when Cromwell stormed Millmount and slew Governor Aston and his co-defenders, and, thus, the path of history took the route we know so well.

Millmount's Garrison: It is recorded that a garrison of eighteen men was stationed in Drogheda in 1659.[12] In a military listing of fortifications which were built or repaired in 1664, Millmount is described as a *"citadel"* – this implies that the structure was a very formidable one. In 1702 it was handed over to the Crown for the purpose of constructing a permanent military barracks there. It was known as Richmond Fort and is still in place today. It forms three sides of a rectangle and thus encompasses a parade ground.

There was seething discontent among the underprivileged throughout the late 1700s. Ireland was on the verge of revolt as the century approached its end, and it culminated in the 1798 Rising. The government prepared for this in 1793 by calling for the formation of militia regiments, and it was in that year that the Drogheda Militia came into being, its headquarters being at Millmount.

The barracks had accommodation for little more than 100 men, and a property in West Street was acquired where the remainder of the battalion were billeted. There were shortcomings at Millmount for training men; the parade ground fronting the structure was inadequate for drilling, conducting parades and other martial activities. Also, the approach road, Barrack Lane, was exceedingly steep.

The Martello Tower: When the all-conquering Napoleon Bonaparte was marching across Europe in the early 1800s, England was deeply apprehensive of being invaded. To counter that possibility, a series of Martello Towers were built at likely entry points, including a string of them along the east and south coast of Ireland. Drogheda was allocated a tower, even though it is five miles inland, and the obvious site on which to place it was Millmount, next to the barracks. It was built in 1808, and was equipped with two 9-lbs. cannon on moveable platforms. Any invader sailing up the Boyne was sure of a hot reception from this vantage point. Garrisons continued to occupy Millmount in the decades that followed. In times of prolonged peace the British Army was reduced in size, and this resulted in the barracks being unoccupied periodically, apart from a small caretaking staff and an acting barrack sergeant. A detachment of the Royal Irish Rifles (which had incorporated the Drogheda Militia) was quartered there for a short time in 1881. During the Great War regiments from Britain alternated with Irish regiments as occupants.

The Union Jack at Millmount was finally replaced by the Tricolour when the Provisional Government assumed control in 1922. Sadly, this was followed by the bitterness of the Civil War, and an anti-Treaty force occupied the barracks. When a Government cannon was trained on the building a temporary truce was arranged which enabled the occupants get away. The 'Cup and Saucer', as Millmount tower is affectionately called by locals, and which had withstood the elements so well, was soon reduced to ruins in the bombardment that followed, and it remained in that state for the remainder of the century.

In 1950 a large cross with four transepts was erected on the tower to commemorate the Holy Year. At night it was illuminated and was very conspicuous, even from ships at sea. This enhancement was so approved by all that it was left in place for about four years.

To mark the Eight Hundredth Anniversary (1194/1994) of Drogheda's foundation an attractive postage stamp was issued by An Post acknowledging the town's medieval origin; it features a windmill atop the green mound of Millmount, which is probably an accurate depiction.

Today the barracks continues to be used for peaceful purposes, namely as a restaurant, a museum and a craft workshop, while the Governor's residence is now the headquarters of the Old Drogheda Society. The townspeople may at times be guilty of taking Millmount's presence for granted, but to visitors it is a source of admiration and wonderment. The skyline of the town, with its chimney stacks, its church spires, and of course the Boyne Viaduct, is distinctive by any standard, presenting Drogheda with a most unique profile. But Millmount is its most dominant feature and its crowning glory.

*   *   *   *   *

DAY-TO-DAY ROUTINE IN THE 1600s: A visitor to Drogheda in 1635, Sir John Brereton, wrote 'It is the largest and best-built town I have seen in Ireland, with house neat and well built, and shops well finished'. No doubt he was moving in upper class circles, and was being shepherded away for the squalor that also existed. The Corporation discussed such mundane matters as complaints being made regarding the filth in the streets. They criticised the townspeople for 'the permitting of Hoggs to go up and down the streets' and for 'neglecting to cleane their doores and carry away their dunge'. Those who failed to comply with this order once a week would be fined 6d. (€0.030)[13]

Five years later the problem of dirty streets had not improved, and it was noted that the people 'doe permitt several nusances of Dunge to lye at their Doores, which by ill smells may cause diseases'. We smile smugly today at their conclusion that diseases were caused by '*ill smells*' alone, not by germs! Even during the Great Famine smells were thought to have been the culprit for the rampant cholera and thyphoid that stalked the streets of Drogheda. A further drive towards cleanliness was put into effect whereby the areas around their cabin doors were to be cleaned twice each week 'to witt, every Munday and ffriday and carry the Durte away forthwith"[14] It strikes one that this was a futile ordinance; the people had not been motivated into a sense of hygiene and civic pride once a week by the threat of a fine, so they were less likely to comply *twice* a week, especially as the fine for non-compliance remained at 6d.. The people may well have decided to wait for the Dunge and the Durte to move away from the Doores of its own volition! Even 200 years later Drogheda had the unenviable name of being one of the dirtiest towns in Ireland. We find that in 1700 the Corporation arranged 'that Hugh Tygh be admitted as scavenger during the Corporation's pleasure, and that he be paid a halfe penny out of every house or tenement per weeke throughout the whole Towne for carrying away the Dirt of the Streets'.[15] No doubt the inhabitants kicked up a hullabaloo at this imposition – just as they did when a charge was introduced 300 years later!

We are given a clue in the Minute Book as to the origin of the street name we know as 'Stockwell Street'. There was at this time an actual well in Stockwell Street which was used for watering livestock, and in 1683 the Corporation ordered that: 'the Well in Stockwell Lane be shut up and paved over and that the same be noe more open'.[16]

The members of the Corporation evidently were proud of their town. In 1666 they decreed that the 'Sword Bearer and Mace Bearer sallary be augmented to £10 a peece yearly ... and provide themselves with comly gownes'. Likewise, they ordered that no dwelling be constructed 'within the Town's walls unless it be with slate'[17] This was a commendable directive, since thatched roofs were notoriously fire-prone, and perhaps the city fathers were prescient – the year in question was 1666 – in which the Great Fire of London occurred.

THE PENAL LAWS: Although expelled from their monasteries and deprived of their possessions, the friars did not abandon their flock. They went underground, moving from one place of refuge to another. Some survived by concealing their identity. It is recorded that in Waterford some priests adopted the roles of gardeners and coal porters. Loyal friends who succoured them were at risk of losing not only their property but also their very lives.

Since the expulsion of the monks from Mellifont and the other abbeys throughout Ireland during the Reformation, some embers of the Cistercian flame continued to flicker in Holycross Abbey, Co. Tipperary, and from there they managed to recreate a presence in Drogheda. We find a group of them residing in community there in 1623. Their revival was shortlived, for two of them when discovered were taken prisoner, brought to Newry, stripped naked and hanged from the beams of a wooden bridge.[18] (The ruined abbey at Holycross was restored in the 1970s and presently serves as a parish church). In 1648 Fr. Gormley OFM from the Franciscan community in Drogheda was arrested while preaching near Navan, taken back to Drogheda and hanged.[19]

Religious practice was not forbidden, but the restrictions were such that it was expected that in the course of time the Catholic Church in Ireland would disappear. So discriminatory were the laws of the land that, for tactical reasons, a sizeable number of property holders converted to Protestantism – these were 'conversions of convenience'. Those that remained steadfast to the traditional religion were subjected to restrictions that were designed to deprive them of normal civil rights. They were debarred from all government posts, from joining the army and from practising as lawyers. Priests were hunted, forcing them to celebrate Mass in improvised chapels and on mass rocks in open fields. The screw was to be tightened further in the decades following the Battle of the Boyne. The Oath of Supremacy was reinforced, excluding Catholics from their own Irish Parliament – this applied also to representation at local government level, so that no Catholic was eligible to represent the people of Drogheda in the Corporation Assembly of their home town. (Further examples of penal restrictions are given below).

These iniquitous laws were applied sporadically; and at some periods the authorities seemed to turn a blind eye on the activities of the clergy. At times religious observance was treated with a velvet glove, and at other times with an iron fist. Indeed, it is known that on occasions Protestants took great risk in helping Catholics to evade the full force of the law. The religious orders still held out in Drogheda, but they kept a very low profile.

An extremely virulent outbreak of persecution occurred in 1673 whereby decrees were issued banishing all bishops and religious from Ireland. A £50 reward was offered to bounty hunters who exposed a bishop. An edict was issued: "All papists are to be turned out of the cities, and for priests, friars and nuns, £20 will be given for intelligence of them, and whoever doth harbour them is to forfeit life and estate".[20]

The Popish Plot: A wave of hysteria swept through England in the late 1670s. It stemmed from the discovery of the infamous Gunpowder Plot early in the century. This induced a wave of paranoia, and the flames were now being fanned by a rumour, completely unfounded, that was initiated by one Titus Oates, a defrocked Anglican priest and perjurer. He alleged that the Roman Catholics of England were conspiring to kill the king and massacre the Protestants. He was eventually discredited and duly punished, but not before many innocent people were condemned to death. It was in that climate that Primate Oliver Plunkett was witch-hunted and brought to trial. The personage of King William of Orange later entered this little vignette when, true to form, he demonstrated his appreciation of the machinations that were taking place by arranging that a pension be paid to him – that is, to Titus Oates, not Oliver Plunkett!

A measure of the pervading prejudice can be gauged from entries in the Minute Book of the Drogheda Corporation during that era. Following a discussion of the Assembly in 1656 it was ordered: "that only freemen of this Corporation bee and is hereby from henceforth allowed to grayse two calves upon the Comons belonging to the same ... *and it was ordered by the general assembly that none but the English Protestant shall have libertie of the Comons as aforesaid".*[21] Townspeople, by time-honoured custom, previously had a right to graze livestock in commonages outside the town. However, the wording in the Minute Book quoted here in italics was crossed out in pen in 1672, and in the margin a postscript was appended, which read: *"This pt. struck through with ye pen was done in open assembly July 26th. 1672".*

Another set of orders aimed at the deprivation of Catholics was passed by the Corporation in 1656.[22]

> (a) *"Ordered that noe papist is or for the future shall be made free of any fraternities within this Corporation nor have any such as a freeman at their Halls at Generall days of meetinge, and that noe freeman take a papist apprentice upon paine of being disfranchized".* [Tradesmens' Guilds were known as 'Fraternities']
> (b) *"to shutte up the shoppes and debarr the trade by retayle"* of every person not a freeman.
> (c) *"every papist now resident"* to be likewise disenfranchised".[23]

These three Orders inscribed in the Minute Book are likewise given here in italics to indicate that four years later they were revoked.[24]

OLIVER PLUNKETT (1629-1681) – A Pen-picture:

He was born at Loughcrew Castle, Oldcastle, Co. Meath in 1629 of Old English descent, and having studied for the priesthood in Rome was ordained in 1654. He remained in Rome as professor of Theology, and returned to Ireland in 1670 when appointed Archbishop of Armagh. It is clear that he held Drogheda in high regard, and his letter dated 26th. September 1671 states

"In the most wealthy and most noble city of my diocese and of the whole province, there are three chapels, very beautiful and ornamented; the first belongs to the Capucins, the second to the reformed Franciscans, the third to the Jesuits. There is also one belonging to the Augustinians but it is rather poor. The city to which I allude is called Drogheda, a five hour distance from Dublin; it is, next to Dublin, the best city in Ireland."

Dr. Plunkett's fortitude is evident from his activities within the Pale during these times of persecution. Catholic schools were few in Ireland, and there were none in the Armagh diocese. He set about establishing one in Drogheda. It had about 160 pupils and, surprisingly, 40 Protestants attended it. This indicates that at times the State showed some tolerance towards the Catholic religion and also that local Protestants exercised a benign attitude towards Catholics and were prepared to have their children educated by them.

But soon a severe bout of persecution returned, and after three years the school was closed and levelled to the ground. Dr. Plunkett was then forced to go into hiding. He reported to Rome that '[I] shall retire to a hut in some wood or mountain in my diocese with some candles and books ... until the storm passes". He underwent considerable privation, sometimes being given refuge in sympathetic homes, where the owners were risking their own lives if he were discovered. In one of his letters he states that often did he and his companion run risk of death from fatigue and want of the necessary means of subsistence. "The hut in which they had taken refuge was made of straw. When they lay down to rest they could see the stars through the openings in the roof through which the rain penetrated, and each successive shower 'refreshed them'. A little oaten bread was their only support".[25]

Despite the witch-hunt, he nonetheless persisted in his labours and he was able to report that "during the past four years I confirmed forty-eight thousand six hundred and fifty-five." He also crusaded untiringly against the plague of alcohol abuse.

Capture and Trial: Prophetically, he said that "I am morally certain that I shall be taken, so many are in search of me; yet in spite of danger I will remain with my flock, nor will I abandon them until they drag me to the ship". He was eventually captured in a house in the Naul and taken to Dublin Castle where he was kept in solitary confinement. An escaped convict from Dundalk Jail and others of similar ilk came forward to swear against him, adding perjury to their other crimes. His initial trial was held in Dundalk, but some of the shady characters who were to have sworn falsehoods against him failed to turn up for the hearing.

He was then taken to London where he was incarcerated *incommunicado* for six months. The allegations against him were in line with the rumours concocted by Titus Oates, including " ... that he would raise 60,000 men in Ireland for the Pope's service, to settle Popery there, and to subvert the Government".

Moving the trial from Dundalk to London was a severe setback to him. because in Dundalk he would have been able to expose the characters of the deceitful State witnesses, a few of whom were priests that he had defrocked for perversion, and thus were hostile towards him. In London he was without his files, and was therefore obliged to requisition them from Ireland. Likewise he sent for his supportive witnesses, crucial to his defence, but he was denied the time to have them sent over, and the trial took place without them.

In the climate that pervaded the English Courts it is not surprising that all the refutations of Archbishop Plunkett were futile, and the foreman of the jury announced a verdict of 'Guilty', to which he graciously replied *"Deo Gratias"*. It was the Earl of Essex, the former Irish Viceroy, who initially had Plunkett arrested. A feeling of guilt now assailed him, for he approached the king to intercede, and assured him of the condemned man's innocence. King Charles was afraid to reverse the verdict but was nonetheless disturbed by what he was being told. His response was akin to that of Pontius Pilate in a similar circumstance. He said: "Why did you not attest this at the trial. It would have done him some good then. I dare not pardon anyone. His blood be upon your head, not mine".[26]

Sentence was pronounced, and he died a martyr's death, being hanged, drawn and quartered on 11th July 1681. He was beatified in 1920 and canonised in 1975. Saint Peter's R.C. Church in West Street, Drogheda, which contains the relic of his severed head, is also the Saint Oliver Plunkett Memorial Church.

Chapter Twelve

The Battle of the Boyne

Spare a thought for the poor little rich girl named Mary Stuart. On the face of it, life should have been a bed of roses for her because her father was a king, and so was her own husband. But this very fact caused her some very uncomfortable moments because one of these kings took the throne of England from the other and it was destined that they should dispute the issue in deadly combat a few miles outside Drogheda. Her loyalties lay with her husband, King William III, in opposition to her father James Stuart, the deposed King of England. Indeed, her sister Anne also turned her back on him. When she, too, changed allegiance, King James exclaimed "God help me, for my own children have forsaken me".

The relationship between these two monarchs was further entwined through King James's sister being the mother of William. Thus, James at the Boyne was confronting both his daughter Mary and his nephew William. However they were alienated by the curse of the religious divide. Curiously, although James was born a Protestant, he and his wife converted to Catholicism. William, on the other hand, was a staunch Calvinist.

In Holland, William had earned the appreciation of many through confronting King Louis in his rapacious plans of dominating Europe. The Edict of Nantes, which had given protection to the Protestants of Catholic France, was revoked by King Louis (against the advice of the Pope), and the Protestants were again subjected to persecution. Most European states feared the aggressive Louis and opposed him in his imperialist ambitions. They formed an alliance against him, and their cause was helped when William sat on the English throne. Pope Innocent XI likewise had reason to fear him, and consequently supported King William.

When King Charles II died his brother, the Duke of York, ascended the English throne as James II. While Charles had kept a fairly low profile in religious affairs, James was intent on dismantling all that Henry VIII had done to the Church in the past, and he began by appointing Catholics to senior positions right, left and centre. One of these was Richard Talbot, Earl of Tyrconnell who energetically strove to include Catholics in the Assembly of Drogheda. On 5th November 1687 King James gave Drogheda a new Charter whereby it became a borough and a distinct, stand-alone county; also, the existing panel that formed the Corporation was ousted and supplanted by a new panel of faces and they had a different mindset. This is evident from their gesture when King James was being crowned; the event was observed in Drogheda in splendid fashion:

> '... there shall be a hogshead of wine bought at ye charge of ye Corporation and hung up neere the Tholsell doore, to be drank on that occasion, and that there be a barrell of beere, with tobacco, and pipes, given to every foote company to drinke ye Kings Health ...'.

We may be sure that a section of the town's inhabitants did not enthuse about this celebration, and declined to join in the jollifications. However, they derived consolation from the fact that both James's daughter Mary and her husband William were Protestants, and they were next in line for the throne.

The Kernel of the Conflict: Alarm spread throughout England when King James presented the nation with a son and heir. The majority of people in England, especially among the ruling class, were deeply concerned at the prospect of a perpetuation of a Catholic dynasty. It was an age that was sensitive to any rumours that might have religious connotations. (There existed an undercurrent of paranoia. The Great Fire of London (1666) was attributed to Catholics, and we have mentioned the general reaction that surrounded the Popish Plot). The people readily embraced the rumour being put about that the newly born infant was not in reality his own child, but some creature that had been smuggled into the royal bedchamber in a warming pan! The people of England thus felt cheated at the prospect of the person they considered to be the rightful heir, Mary, being eclipsed, and the matter culminated in Mary and William being invited to take the throne, the upshot being that James was deposed. He fled to France where the powerful and bigoted Catholic King Louis XIV gave him refuge. His reign had lasted only three years. This upheaval, which occurred in 1688, is known to history as 'the Glorious Revolution'.

THE PROTAGONISTS

It was a case of a father opposing his daughter and his nephew over the English crown.

The outcome for Ireland was centuries of strife.

William III

James II

William and Mary had thus come to the throne, not by succession, but by special Act of Parliament. The legitimate successor was King James' son, named James Francis Edward, but to debar his succession as a Catholic, a parliamentary Act of Settlement was passed, restricting succession to a Protestant line.

It was at first envisaged that Mary should become Queen of England in her own right, but William made it clear that he had no wish to play second fiddle to her, and so it was decided to make them joint monarchs. The usurpation and the prospect of a father confronting both his nephew and his daughter in battle must certainly have affected all three psychologically. James wistfully wrote to his daughter saying that she was

> 'a good wife and ought to be so, yet for the same reason I must believe you will still be as good a daughter to a father that has always loved you so tenderly'. Being sensitive to the bonds that link father with daughter, he also said that she must be 'very uneasy all this time, for the concern you must have for a husband and a father. You shall find me kind to you, if you desire it'.[1]

William wasn't sitting on the throne comfortably, since James was making preparations to regain it. He addressed both Houses of Parliament with this rationalisation:

> "It is a very sensible affliction to me, to see my good people burthened with taxes; but since the speedy recovery of Ireland is, in my opinion, the only means to ease them, and to preserve the peace and honour of the nation, I am resolved to go thither in person.[2]

He decided 'to go thither in person' and thus Ireland was to become a pawn in the political chess game being played by Louis XIV, so that Drogheda and the River Boyne were on one momentous occasion to become the focal point of all Europe. This is the background to the battle that was to take place at Drogheda. It was a European battle – the only one ever to be fought on Irish soil. Its consequences for the Irish peasantry were an irrelevance to the

107

heads of the European states; to them the defeat of 'our natural enemy', the menacing Louis XIV, was all that mattered.

The Dutchman who was now sitting on the English throne was the stumbling block to King Louis's ambitions. If only he could replace him with James, England would then be his ally instead of his foe. So in order to topple William he applied the strategy of using England's back door – Ireland. He equipped James with 7,000 troops and arms and sent him to Ireland. This was to divert William's attention from Europe and to force him instead to go to Ireland to protect his crown.

James, the first English monarch to set foot in Ireland for three centuries, was rapturously received. He was greeted by a pageant on entering Dublin.

> *'Forty young and beautiful maidens, selected from the different convents in Dublin, clad in white silk, and bearing baskets filled with flowers in their hands, joined the procession and walked immediately before His Majesty, strewed the contents of their baskets in his path the rest of the way to the castle ... the people rent the air with shouts of 'God save the King! Long live the King!'*

The local landed gentry who rallied to his cause with regiments of Foot included Lords Bellew, Louth, Slane, Dillon and Gormanston. Siding with King William were the Earls of Drogheda and Meath. To help James in his finances the Drogheda Corporation disposed of the family silver including the town's silver mace. Many such treasures were melted down and used as coinage to finance his army, and recruits flocked from town and field to join his ranks. As a Catholic he was the one man who could heal the people's festering wounds. Here, in particular, was the Irish Parliament's opportunity to rid itself of the burdensome Poyning's Law so that 'the Irish Parliament will be made independent of England'. Accordingly, its members drew up a Bill suitable to this end, but James declined to give it his assent – he did not want his royal prerogative to be restricted in any way when he retrieved his crown.

This was not to be Ireland's only disappointment with the king on whom they were pinning their hopes. Other setbacks were to follow, and it soon became evident that James was using Ireland merely as a stepping-stone to regain his throne. The plight of the dispossessed Irish, both as to the recovery of their confiscated lands and the practice of their religion, was of little consequence either to James or Louis.

William's army landed in Ulster, intent on confronting the Jacobites. (The Latin name for James is Jacobus, and thus 'Jacobite' was the term applied to those who supported King James and the ensuing Stuart cause). A major battle was brewing, but James's venture northwards to challenge William was very tentative since Ulster contained too many recent planters and adherents to Protestantism for him to make a total commitment in that area. He retreated southwards and hesitantly placed his army at Dundalk, he then back-pedalled to Ardee, and finally retreated to Drogheda where he took a stand.

Once again Drogheda was recognised as the bastion that was protecting Ireland's capital city. Indeed, his advisers wanted him to retreat further. Writing afterwards in his *Memoirs* (in the third person) he explained "The reason that induced the King to risk such an action with such unequal numbers was his feeling that otherwise he should be obliged to abandon Dublin and all Munster without striking a stroke and to retire behind the River Shannon in Connaught, a province of least fertile in grain of all Ireland and in which, as he had no magazine, he could not subsist long."

In order to take up its position on the south bank of the river at Oldbridge, the Jacobite army had marched in two columns, one through Drogheda and the other by fording the river at Oldbridge. A regiment and other reinforcements numbering 1,300 men had been left within Drogheda under the command of Lord Iveagh to protect the town's bridge. The next bridge along the river – that at Slane – was torn down to impede the Williamites.

We are given a clue as to where King James stayed on the night prior to the battle. On his journey from Duleek to Drogheda in 1860, the writer Thackeray stated '... you pass by a house where James II is said to have slept the night before the Battle of the Boyne (he took care to sleep far enough off the night after!), and also an old red brick hall, standing at the end of an old choce or terrace avenue that runs for about a mile down to the house and finished at a moat towards the road[3]. The Williamite headquarters were at Mellifont, the king himself using a caravan specially designed by Sir Christopher Wren.

King James reasoned that, if he won the impending battle, then Drogheda, Dublin and the rest of Ireland was securely his, and therefore there was no point in causing the destruction of Drogheda at this stage. He therefore positioned his troops outside the town. The populace were undoubtedly greatly dismayed at the influx of strange soldiers and the feverish activity that occurred during the build-up of the military forces in and around the town. A section of the inhabitants would have been overwhelmed with foreboding at the sight of their streets being thronged with soldiers whose allegiance was to a Catholic king, and at the prospect of what might follow.

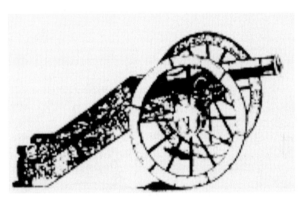

On a point of fact, it would be quite in order for us to substitute the name 'Drogheda' for 'the Boyne' when the Battle of that name is being discussed, and it should be noted that the victorious King William was congratulated by Lord Carmarthen on his victory at **'*Drogheda*'**. Curiously, the site chosen for the battle is the same site of the original Droichead Átha or *Vetera Pons,* viz. Oldbridge which we have encountered in an earlier chapter.

The pastoral, peaceful scene was soon to be shattered by the sound and fury of marching men and belching cannon and of the agonising screams of dying soldiers that followed the brief visit of the two armies – 60,000 soldiers in all. This was far and away the greatest collection of soldiery ever assembled in Ireland, either before or after. They descended like locusts on the area, and no doubt considerable pillaging took place, picking it clean of anything that was edible, The people of Drogheda had been in a state of apprehension throughout the ordeal – they remembered only too well the nightmare of Cromwell's performance just 41 years earlier.

Injury to King William: The two armies were ready for the engagement on the 30th June which was a Monday, but William was a superstitious person and delayed action for 24 hours since he considered it unlucky to fight on a Monday. This could not have helped the nerves of either army; even on the following day action did not commence until 10.15 a.m. The date on which the battle took place was Tuesday the 1st. July 1690 according to the calendar of that time. (The subsequent correction of the calendar, by adding eleven days, revised the date to the 12th. July being the date on which the Orange Order and many others annually commemorate the victory at the Boyne).

Some cannon fire of a sporadic nature did occur on the 30th. June, in which the Jacobite guns killed two horses and a soldier. The enemy field guns responded, which obliged the Jacobites to remove their ammunition to a safer place.

This desultory discharging of guns could easily have taken history along a very different course. While reconnoitring the battlefield, William had cheekily ventured within range of the enemy, and in a bout of sporadic shooting he received a musket shot in the shoulder. The shot had glanced off a bank before striking him and tearing his jacket, so the injury was not severe and he made little of it; his personal surgeon applied a plaster to the wound. 'It is well it came no nearer', he said – a remark that was surely the understatement of the era. He then returned to his headquarters at Mellifont, which was the residence of the Moores. James's headquarters were at a graveyard near the village of Donore.

The Battle Begins: 'A joyful day. Excessive hot. About 6 this morning ye King got on horseback and gave the necessary orders', according to Colonel Thomas Bellingham whose home at Gernonstown (the name was later changed to Castlebellingham) was torched by Irish soldiers. William planned that a detachment of 10,000 men would march several miles westwards in a flanking movement to a point opposite Rossnaree where the river was fordable. The morning of the battle dawned with a thick mist and this greatly aided that plan. Only 750 Jacobites were present to oppose the force. They were soon across, and then set off to attack the enemy's left flank. James made the fatal mistake of assuming that this was the main thrust of the attacking army, and hurriedly sent a major part of his force to combat it, depleting the main body of his men. This meant that when the main Williamite crossing did occur at Oldbridge, the Jacobite forces were depleted, being outnumbered by three to one.

King William's cannon playing on the Jacobite forces
from an engraving by Theodor Maas

The bulk of the Williamite army was positioned opposite the hamlet of Oldbridge, of which nothing remains today. They had been secreted in an ideal location – a defile with a canopy of trees which gave excellent cover, and known today as King William's Glen. Equally important, it was right beside the river, enabling the soldiers to appear as if from nowhere when the critical moment arrived. The river is tidal at this point and at 10.15 a.m. the water was at its lowest ebb, and amid the battle cry of the men, the roll of the drums, the smoke of muskets and the roar of cannon some divisions began to cross the river. The soldiers were then at their most vulnerable, the river's depth at this point being up to a man's chest. Wading in compact serried ranks caused the flowing water to rise higher, and it must be remembered that the average height of a man in those times was merely five feet three inches. They would have entered the water shoulder to shoulder, a row at a time, in order to reduce the damming effect on the flow of the current.

Up to their chests in water and holding their muskets over their heads, they had difficulty in holding their balance and keeping their powder dry. But with covering musket fire from their colleagues on the bank, they succeeded in reaching the opposite bank and they soon established a bridgehead. Others were obliged to swim across. The line was extended as additional forces made the crossing.

Early in the engagement James ordered the withdrawal of his artillery, an act which caused puzzlement, if not consternation, among his French officers; they queried the order, since cannon would have been at its most effective at that stage. The result was that the Jacobite artillery hardly featured in the defence of the Boyne. It points to a fatal lack of commitment on the part of James.

King William Makes the Crossing: By noon King William himself ventured to cross. This was at a point on today's Ramparts we still call 'Pass' or 'Pass-if-you-Can'. He got into difficulties when his mount became stuck in deep mud on approaching the opposite bank – this brought on an attack of asthma, an affliction to which he was prone. An Enniskillen man, seeing his dilemma, rushed to his aid and carried him to safety.

Just for a moment let us stop the movie-camera at this particular time-frame of the historical documentary because a little retrospection is called for. *This was one of the most defining moments in Irish history – and English and European history too – and was to have seismic consequences for Ireland.* Placing his two feet on *terra firma* on the south bank signalled the ebbing of Jacobite resistance and the immanence of King William's victory. It also fixed the destiny of England's Crown unequivocally. More than that, it ended all future disputations as to who should wear it – all subsequent coronations were peaceful affairs with never a hint of controversy, and to this day every Catholic is debarred by law from wearing it. The occasion also affirmed Protestantism throughout England. For the majority of Ireland's population the consequences were catastrophic; it heralded the age of the Penal Days, of the Ascendancy, of landlordism, of a people's marginalisation based on religion, of failed insurrections, of transportations in irons to Van Diemen's Land, of floggings and pitch-cap tortures, of mass emigration, of evictions, of the tithe war, of the land war, and of much, much more. It left a permanent imprint on the map of Ireland which exists today in the form of a divided citizenry demarked by an artificial partition

Williamite regiments continued to swarm across the Boyne. One observer reported "The Jacobite resistance was strong, the fighting was so hot that many old soldiers said they never saw brisker work[4]". Charge after charge of the Jacobite cavalry was made to stem the advancing waves of soldiers, and Patrick Sarsfield featured in these. The Rev. George Walker, the defender of Derry, was killed at this point. King William dismissed the incident by saying that Walker, as a designate bishop, was a fool for having involved himself in the battle. A man who escaped with his life and whose name is today carried by a Dublin hospital was Sir Patrick Dunn – he was physician to the English army in Ireland.

Schomberg's Death: In one of the encounters the Captain-General of the Williamite army, the old Duke of Schomberg, received a series of wounds amid scenes of great confusion. A Williamite soldier, for example, had levelled his gun at no less a person than the king himself, and realised his mistake just in time. 'What! Are you angry with your friends!' – the king is reported to have coolly said. The historian Samuel Lewis describes that, in the course of a melee in rallying the Huguenots, Schomberg was taken prisoner. Then, while surrounded by guards, the French Protestants fired into the

midst of the group, accidentally killing the Duke. The grand old man – he was 75 years of age (some say he was over 80) and a veteran of many battles – died on the spot. (There are other versions as to how he died). His remains now lie in St. Patrick's Cathedral in Dublin. Dean Swift was greatly disappointed that Mr. Millmay (Lord Fitzwalter) ignored his suggestion to erect a worthy memorial, and caustically wrote:

> '... let Sir Conyers D'Arcy know how ill I take his neglect in this matter, although to do him justice he averred that Millmay was so avaricious a wretch that he would let his own father be buried without a coffin to save money'.

The spot where the Duke fell is marked by a small, simple memorial stone, showing merely the date 1690. It is in a field where once the village of Oldbridge stood, close to the latticed Bridge that today spans the Boyne leading from King William's Glen, and a few dozen paces inside a field gate to the south of the present roadway. Today nothing remains of the village – it is part of an open green field, but the site is marked by the work of archaeologists who have revealed the outline of several of the former homes. The overall site has been made a focal point by the OPW and is the subject of some interesting development plans.

Fighting continued to be fierce, with the entire action occupying more than a mile of the river's length. Eventually the Jacobites were forced to give way to an army that was superior in professionalism, resolve and leadership, as well as in numbers. They retreated towards the high ground at Donore. The village at that time was adjacent to the old churchyard. At the River Nanny there was extensive bogland, and this hindered the enemy from getting to grips with the scattering Jacobites who realised that the day was lost. Many were able to escape by crossing the Magdalene Bridge over the river. If the retreating soldiers had time to read the writing etched on the stonework that is still to be seen today on the bridge wall, they might have found time to offer a prayer of deliverance, however hurried, for the couple who built it. The plaque reads: -

"This bridge with the cause[way] – [the causeway across the bogland leading to the bridge] were repaired and builded by William Bath of Athcarne Justice and Janet Dowdall his wife in the year of Our Lord 1587 who soules God take to His mercie. Amen."

Great confusion accompanied the retreat, leading to pandemonium in places. Lieutenant John Stephens became embroiled in a scene while his battalion was marching away:

> '... The [cavalry] came on so unexpected and with such speed, some firing their pistols, that we had no time to receive or shun them, but all supposing them to be the enemy (as indeed they were no better to us) took to their heels, no officer being able to stop the men even after they were broke, and the horse past, though at the same time no enemy were near us, or them that fled in such haste to our destruction ... What few I could see I called to, no commands being of force, begging them to stand together and repair to their colours, the danger being in

DROGHEDA'S SWORD AND MACE
King William III presented them to Drogheda
following his victory at the Boyne
Courtesy of the Old Drogheda Society
and Drogheda Borough Council

TWO ACCURATE TIMEPIECES

The Chamber in the Newgrange Tumulus (left) has captured the dawn rays of the sun at the Winter Solstice for 5,000 years. That of Dowth has been doing likewise at sunset for a longer period. Although its passageway is considerably shorter than that of Newgrange, the rays remain longer in the Chamber. (See Chapter One).

Dowth photo is by courtesy of Anne-Marie Moroney; Newgrqange is by courtesy of Dept. of Environment, Heritage and Local Govt.

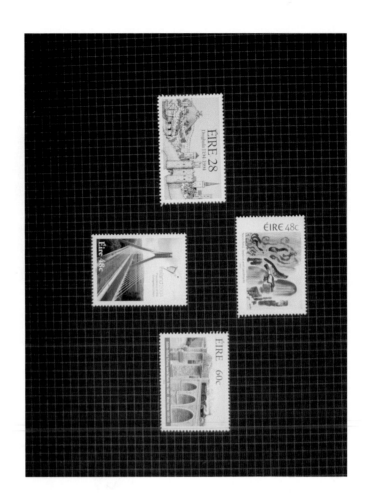

POSTAGE STAMPS

*Drogheda is well represented on
Ireland's stamps*

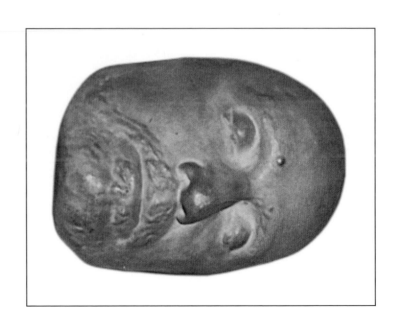

DEATH MASK OF OLIVER CROMWELL

Courtesy Tom Reilly/Jimmy Weldon

These Cannon Balls Pounded the Walls of Drogheda in 1649.

The fragmented ball (left) lodged in the wall at the point where Cromwell gained entry. Covered by ivy, it remained undiscovered for over 300 years.

From a private collection

The Battle of The Boyne

The scene as depicted is reasonably accurate

TWO CHARTERS PRESENTED TO DROGHEDA

King James II charter (below) was of little moment, since he reigned for only three years before being deposed. The charter of King William III, which he presented to Drogheda following the Battle of the Boyne in 1690, had a profound influence on subsequent events throughout Ireland, giving rise to the dominant Ascendancy class.

Photos of Charters by Jimmy Weldon
Ccourtesy of Drogheda Borough Council

THE SITE OF THE BATTLE OF THE BOYNE:

THE M4 BRIDGE NOW DOMINATES THE SCENE

The western end of the Ramparts is below the new housing estate. It was at that point (next to the small island) subsequently called 'Pass' or 'Pass If You Can', that King William III made the river crossing, a prelude to his victory.

THE BULL RING

No motor cars to cause congestion in the early 1800's;

vessels were berthed up to the bridge.

From a private collection

dispersing; but all in vain, some throwing away their arms, others even their coats and shoes to run the lighter ... all scattered like sheep before the wolf'.

By about 5.00 pm. the irresolute King James, seeing the writing on the wall, turned tail and headed for Dublin, which he reached at 9 pm. There he was met by Lady Tyrconnell. Tradition tells us that his initial greeting contained an innuendo that was pregnant with bitterness: "Your countrymen, madam, can run well". Her riposte was equally barbed: "Not so well as Your Majesty, for I see you have won the race". This may well be an apocryphal tale, but it certainly fitted the occasion. Next morning he was racing again – heading south to Duncannon, Co. Wexford from where he took a ship via Kinsale to France. Thus ended another episode where Irish hopes were raised, only to be cruelly dashed, plunging the people into greater despondency.

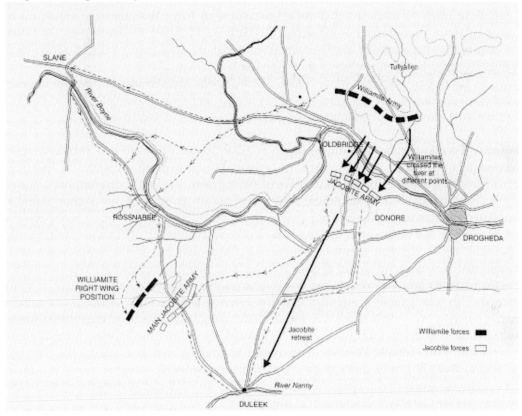

PLAN OF THE BATTLEFIELD
*When King William sent a diversionary force to cross the river at Slane/Rossnaree,
King James sent a substantial portion of his army there in response.
This was a fatal error, for it weakened his resistance when William made
his main thrust at Oldbridge.*

The two opposing forces were indeed unequal in strength. James had 25,000 troops to William's 35,000, and James had much less artillery. Many of his soldiers had no uniforms and some of his Irish troops were barefooted and in rags, were untrained and ill equipped, having to rely on farm implements and wooden sticks with sharpened points to combat the enemy. Whatever uniform or apparel they wore, all displayed a white feather or a piece of white linen as a distinguishing mark; the corresponding Williamite colour was green. The sides were also unequal in leadership, William proving to be the more astute general. As to the number of casualties, accounts vary, but they were surprisingly light, bearing in mind the numbers involved in the conflict. One source stated that there were 'not above 1,600' killed between both armies, the Jacobites suffering the greater losses. The thoughts and prayers of all Europe were focused on Drogheda and the Boyne while waiting for news of the battle's outcome. Defeat for William III would have meant that King Louis of France was free to continue his aggression and his imperialism. For the native Irish and the Old English it would have meant recovery of confiscated lands and an end to religious persecution.

The first people to know the result were, of course, the inhabitants of Drogheda. Now they could breathe freely again – and no doubt the news warmed the hearts of many, for the fortunes of the landed gentry throughout Ireland hinged on the outcome. In Dublin the relief shown by the inhabitants was palpable, and as the early sections of the victorious army trickled into the city they were greeted with cheering and unrestrained jubilation, with dragoons being pulled from their mounts to be hugged and kissed.

The dismay of the dispossessed and of Catholics generally can be imagined, but their fate was of little import to King Louis of France. For him the defeat was a serious setback to his grandiose plans of dominating Europe because, with King William now secure on his throne, England was confirmed as his nemesis. The rest of Europe was overjoyed; *Te Deums* were sung in the churches, and the Pope breathed a sigh of relief, and no doubt got down on his knees for some heartfelt prayers of thanksgiving.

As for Queen Mary aka Mary Stuart, she no doubt had mixed feelings. But although her father could henceforth say goodbye to his crown, her own crown and that of husband Billy were now fixed securely on their royal heads.

Surrender Terms: On the day following the battle a detachment rode into Drogheda under the command of Brigadier Le Melloniere – it consisted of 1,000 horse supported by foot and 8 pieces of artillery – and demanded surrender of the garrison. At first it refused, but a second demand was accompanied by the threat that, if force were to be used, no quarter would be given. The commanding officer, Lord Iveagh, was prevailed upon by the townspeople to avoid bloodshed and destruction, having had first-hand experience of the two earlier sieges during the 1640s. He sent a messenger asking for terms, but if the reply were to be unconditional surrender, he would defend Drogheda to 'the last extremity'. The response to this was that if the garrison were to lay down its arms and march out without delay, it would be spared. This was agreed to, and thus both the garrison and the town of Drogheda came to no harm, much to everyone's relief. The victors had been deadly serious in their threat, having mounted cannon in several positions around the outskirts of the town, poised for a sustained bombardment. Lord Iveagh, however, had used a bargaining tool in effecting the surrender terms that enabled him walk away so freely. It was recorded with a degree of chagrin by the victors: "Tho this barbarity in tying the Protestants back to back and placing them where they expected our Guns to play, ought not to be forgot'.[5]

William was remiss in failing to surround the Jacobite forces. This had been a distinct possibility – but he had 'scotched the snake, not killed it'. They were able to escape intact, and the surprisingly few who were killed is evidence of this. The surrender terms were, in fact, quite generous, with the officers being allowed to retain their swords, and the surrender papers were formally signed by both parties two days later. This speedy agreement allowed William to head for Dublin, which was now securely his, and he was able to enter the city without fear of an attack from his rear.

Drogheda was forthwith garrisoned by a Williamite regiment. According to a historian of the time the officers "took great care to preserve the town from the violence of the soldiers". This policy was implemented in the light of the earlier horrors inflicted at the hands of English forces under Cromwell, and the generous treatment was also to be interpreted as a demonstration to all that the new régime would be a benign one.

The scene where the battle took place has on occasions yielded up a few mementos including musket and cannon balls. In 1929 a dagger was found in a ditch near Duleek. It was described as 'a stiletto with a silver haft, inlaid with ivory. The carved iron blade, though rusted and somewhat jagged is quite sound, and is firmly attached to the haft. The weapon is about seven inches long and of very delicate design. The place where it was found is in the direct line of King James the Second's retreat from the battle of the Boyne, the townland being named Kingsgate in memory King James' entry on his way to Dublin".[6]

* ** A NEW CONTEMPORARY ACCOUNT OF THE BATTLE ***

The known eye-witness accounts of the Battle of the Boyne have been studied by strategists and pored over by historians for centuries. It is therefore of the greatest interest that a hitherto undiscovered source has come to light in recent times. It is in the form of a letter by Sir Henry Hobart (c.1658-98); it provides a new insight into the battle and corroborates the accounts from the earlier sources.

It is of particular interest because the narrator was not only present, but was by the side of King William himself during some crucial moments, and he set down his experiences a mere two days following the event. We already knew that James's army, in retreating from Dundalk towards the Boyne, passed through Ardee; It is now revealed in Hobart's letter that "the Enemy had Pillaged and abandoned [the town]; there his Majesty received intelligence that King James and his Army were certainly Encamped on the other side of the Boyne near Drakeda". [A contemporary who wrote about the Williamite era in Ireland was Roger Morrice, and he also accumulated a collection of letters and reports on that era. They included 'a remarkable and hitherto entirely unknown letter from Sir Henry Hobart (c.1658-98) dated 3 July 1690 concerning the Battle of the Boyne[7]].

He also recounts the reconnoitring by some horsemen of both armies along the banks of the river on the day prior to the great engagement, and of their conversing across the waters to each other. Some casual firing took place, as we know, on that day while Hobart and King William were viewing the terrain. In the course of events they stopped

> "to eate a piece of bread, and drinke, I had two field Pieces fired at me, one of the Bullets fell near me, these were the first Shott, and the King was pleased laughing to tell me I now was Cannon-fire. About one [o'clock] the King dyned upon the side of a hill, where comeing from dinner we could easily observe the Enemy planting two or three great Guns upon us, and though I tooke the liberty to show the King the Gunns and pressed him to shelter himselfe, his great courage would not give him leave to go a jot faster. I had scarce spoke when not from above 250 yards distance they fired in upon us and one of the Bullets Grazed upon the Kings shoulder, tore his Coate and shirt, and made his skinn all black".[8]

Hobart at that moment was in the presence of the King, and saw the wound inflicted on the shoulder, which he says was slight, and he credited God for having taken the 'particular care to preserve him [the King] for the good of Mankind and the support of our Religion, never was there so miraculous an escape and never was there so much a Consternation as amongst us. I was just by him and I saw the hurt. He only stopped a little but never changed countenance, or mended pace'. In 'a narrow lane' [King William's Glen?] the wound was dressed with a handkerchief 'the cannon fireing furiously upon us all the while'.

It therefore seems that this episode was something more than the fortuitous incident that history has hitherto told us, for the 'Prince of Hermanstade had his horse killed at the same, and my cosen Latten the Skirte of his Wastcoat torne'. Indeed, word circulated around the Jacobite camp that King William had been killed. Another point worth noting is that Sir Henry Hobart was riding a white horse at the time, a fact that may have initiated the still current myth that King William's horse was white. In fact, he was mounted on a dark horse.

Hobart explained that he had no particular duty to perform in the battle, so that he 'was at every place and saw the whole fight and were I capable could give as good account as any one'. On the morning of the battle he could see the enemy's tents being dismantled, and as a detachment of the Williamites headed towards Slane, he watched the bulk of the other army heading in the same direction and

> 'our great Gunns Playing all the while upon their March. We could see the Bullets some times clear whole Ranks ... About twelve [o'clock] his Majesty commanded Duke Schomberg with two Battalions of his Dutch foot Guards to wade over at a Foord, there was a village just on the other side of the Boyne ... [They accomplished this manoeuvre] with unspeakable resolution for all their continuall fireing, and some drove off the Enemy out of the Village, and then charged a Battalion of King James's Guard which they Routed. But then came a

Squadron of the Enemies Horse, and we having no Horse to shelter our foot, they gave a little way on one Side, and then Duke Schomberg Fell'.

A short time later most of the Horse and Foot (including the king) were across, forcing the Jacobites to retreat. "We pursued them to the top of a hill where there was a small village [Donore]; there their Dragoons made a vigerous stand". In the confusion the Danish Horse were subjected to friendly fire from the Enniskillen Horse -'they fell foule by mistake of one another'. It must be remembered that the various nationalities that made up the army were wearing a variety of different uniforms, and some confusion was inevitable. At this juncture the king, at the head of the Enniskillens, had a narrow escape, and so intense was the action that they were forced to retreat, or 'to speake plain English, fled'. With Horse support they rallied

'and the enemy made no more resistance only retiring. ... We pursued them till darke night. There is Ten Pieces of Cannon taken, a great deale of rich Baggage, Ledd horses [i.e. pack horses], above 4000 Armes, several Waggons of Powder and Amunition, few Prisoners for our soldiers gave no Quarter. ... I scarce see what I write having not slept these 48 hours above 2 Nor eate but a crust of bread, but thank God I am well else, and came off unhurt. I had a Pass of a Pike or a Halbert in the Village, but it did not pierce my Buff Coate, and my horse fell upon me but only a little hurt my Ribbs. The King is very well, and shewes as much Mercy and moderation as he did Courage'.

A description is also given by another source of the probes made to ascertain the point of the river where a crossing would be feasible. The king enquired as to the actual depth, and five youths entered the water. One was killed, but at least two made it to the other side, one being 'a blackhaired youth' who was able to report that

'the River was fordable, whereupon divers rode over (I thinke some of his Army had gone over at other places before) and he himselfe rode over in safety. The next day his Majesty enquired for that black haired youth, and told him, I both observed what notice you tooke of my words yesterday, and of the Adventure [risk] you made etc. Come to me tomorrow at 9 o'clock etc. The black haired youth did then come to him and his Majesty gave him an hundred Guinneas, and a Commission to be a Captain etc. It's very likely there was some Reward given to others'.[9]

Non-paying Guests: Although the din of battle had died away, the people of Drogheda were not yet finished with military matters, for they were left with several regiments who were ensconced in the town and who had to be hosted as a garrison. In all probability these were foreign soldiers, and their success in battle would have rendered them quite extravagant in their demands.

The locals were soon to learn that victory came at a price, for eighteen months later the soldiers were still being quartered in their midst, and some of the inhabitants avoided the obligation of accommodating them by simply vacating the town. This matter came up for discussion at Corporation meetings on several occasions: '... people doe at present leave their dwellings to avoid quartering of soldiers' and it was agreed that their names would be recorded with a view to denying them 'certain town benefits and freedoms.[10]

The burden of quartering the soldiers remained, and it was later agreed to prepare a petition setting forth the unhappy condition of the inhabitants. ' ... six hundred pounds is due to them for the subsistence of the several Regiments that have from time to time been quartered in this Towne, since the surrender thereof in their Majesties hands ... [and compensation must soon be made] to preserve ye inhabitants from ruine'.[11]

The Orange Connection: The historic city of Avignon in the south of France had been the home of nine Popes during the 14th Century, and their spectacular Gothic palace (the world's largest, and now a UNESCO world heritage site) situated on a massive and prominent outcrop of rock, still dominates the landscape. The sunny slopes of this region of the Rhone Valley produce a delectable wine. Thirty kilometres upriver is a smaller city that, in the heady days of Imperial Rome, was an important post along the Via Agrippa; it contains some magnificent

Roman ruins including an amphitheatre where concerts and plays are still staged today. The Romans called the town Arousio, but that name was later changed to '**Orange**'. Although King William's family seat was in the Netherlands, a connection through marriage was made with this little independent principality of Orange – hence the title 'Prince of Orange'. The mighty King Louis snaffled it for France in 1660, a move which did not endear him to the minor Prince of Orange.

In that circuitous way the outcome at the Boyne has influenced the colours chosen for the national flag of the Republic of Ireland, Green for Ireland (Republic of), White as the symbol of peace and reconciliation, and Orange representing the Protestant connection.

(One wonders whether the Popes, when they resided so close to Orange, had in their autocratic way trodden on the toes of the resident nobility, or committed some other ancient wrong in the course of their stay at Avignon – it would further explain King William's animosity towards Catholics. It is also amusing to speculate whether the much lauded wine of the region ever crossed that king's lips, carrying, as it does, the unacceptably popish title *Chateauneuf du Pape!* – the New Palace of the Popes!)

The New York Connection: James disappointed his followers at every turn; he had the opportunity of redressing Poyning's Law but he refused the request. He was inept as a commander, he made crucial errors of judgement at the Boyne, he blamed 'the cowardly Irish' for his defeat, and then made a speedy and permanent exit to France, leaving his supporters to sink further into the bloody morass that he had created. No wonder his name was held in odium throughout Ireland, earning him the derisive nickname – *Seamus an Chaca* – James the Shit.

We have seen that Drogheda's storied past has been commemorated in the names of several of its streets. We hasten to clarify one particular point – James Street was so named to honour James the Apostle, not King James! All that the latter left behind were bitter memories and shattered hopes.

Curiously, in the United States of America King James is commemorated in 'the Big Apple', the circumstances being that during the reign of his brother (King Charles II) the English were making inroads into the New World, and in 1664 they had seized the settlement called New Amsterdam on Manhattan Island from the industrious Dutch colony who had founded it. They renamed the burgeoning town for the king's brother James who was at that time the **Duke of YORK**, thus giving us '**NEW YORK**'.

The Aftermath of the Boyne: The Boyne was not the last episode in the Jacobite campaign, but it was the one that mattered most. Other battles including Athlone and Aughrim followed, but the struggle had become hopeless. The final stand was taken at Limerick, where negotiations took place with the besieging army. A draft treaty was drawn up and signed – the infamous Treaty of Limerick. The terms were reasonable, allowing the French soldiers to set sail for France and the Irish participants to return to their homes or to join a continental army. It was also agreed that only some supporters of the Jacobite cause would have their lands confiscated.

Most importantly, religious discrimination would cease. This was the clause that the Irish Catholics welcomed most of all. The Treaty augured well for the populace at large. With the hatchet being buried, the several religious factions on the island would henceforth co-exist in communal harmony. Equality and true Christian charity would prevail ... or would it?

(NOTE: The focal point of the battlefield was acquired by the State in 1999 from the various landholders in occupation, with the intention of developing the site as a major historical attraction, and to promote mutual understanding between the differect traditions. This work is being carried out by the Office of Public Works in consultation with the Grand Orange Lodge and other bodies interested in the project for which a sum of €15,000,000 has been earmarked. A highly informative staff is at hand on Sundays throughout the summer months giving on-site information concerning the main participants in the Battle, the course of events during the actual engagement, the type of gunnery used, etc. A visit to this site is highly recommended).

Chapter Thirteen

Drogheda's Fifty Tempestuous Years

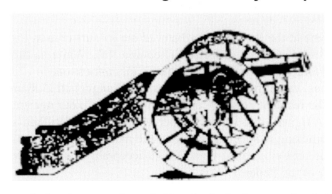

It is curious to reflect on the many historical events of profound importance to Ireland's subsequent destiny that occurred in Drogheda during the half century from 1641 to 1690. No other Irish town experienced so many convulsions in so short a period – the outcome of each of them had deeply-felt and indelible repercussions on Ireland as a whole. A person born in Drogheda in the year (say) 1630 would have encountered a unique series of occurrences, all of them traumatic or life- threatening, in the course of his life-span. Let us retrace his footsteps: -

• When the town was being bombarded by Sir Phelim O'Neill in 1641 the lad was 11 years old. Being under siege, the blockade prevented food from entering the town so that the citizens suffered great privation.

• Apprehension increased further at the news that a Government force was marching to the town's relief. This force was intercepted and annihilated by Rory OMore at Julianstown, and thus the confrontation was averted. The siege continued, subjecting the populace to starvation for four long months.

• When the siege was lifted, a bewildering series of events was soon in train, with Drogheda being caught in the cross-fire of opposing factions. The town was the bone of contention between the armies of the Parliament and the Confederation of Kilkenny. The lad was greatly confused but was too young to appreciate the subtleties of how Drogheda became embroiled in an English Civil War in which Ireland had been an innocent bystander. First the Parliamentary forces arrived (under Colonel Jones), but that was an ineffective posture, and the army retired back to Dublin.

• Hot on its heels came another army – this time a Confederate one. These comings and goings were taking place in a tug-of-war to secure the town for one side or the other, all in the knowledge that Drogheda occupied a pivotal position in the political drama that was being enacted.

• The uncertainty was ended in a most peremptory manner – Oliver Cromwell had arrived. The lad was just 19 years old when cannon were pounding the town's defences. This time the walls came tumbling down; he was fortunate to have escaped with his life in the massacre that followed, but the scenes of bloodshed would haunt him for the rest of his life. Following that, there were heart-rending scenes as many long established estates were confiscated in the Cromwellian Plantation resulting in the families being bundled off to Connaught.

• The years of his mid-life were marked by many upheavals, accompanied by a virulent strain of religious persecution which included the capture and martyrdom of Archbishop Oliver Plunkett. By this time the Droghedean was a man of 51 years.

• More was to come. At the age of 60 he witnessed feverish activity in the town, with soldiers in a variety of foreign uniforms scurrying hither and thither. He again heard the unmistakable reports of gunfire, this time from two opposing sets of artillery; they were facing each other across the River Boyne a few miles upstream from the town. The year was 1690 and the guns were those of King William and King James. The outcome of that encounter elated some, alarmed others.

• On the day following the decisive battle, more soldiers entered the town. This time they were from the victorious Williamite army. A respite came when the garrison that had been detailed to defend the town surrendered peacefully. During the remainder of his life he witnessed a repeat of the distress of long established landholders who had supported the Jacobite cause being dispossessed to make way for a new set of planters.

Drogheda a Cockpit: Ireland's long-term future hinged on the outcome of each of the three momentous events in which Drogheda was the cockpit, when a shift in the balance of power would have sent the course of Ireland's history along a totally different pathway. There were variant sets of circumstances and objectives on all three occasions, with different armies in contention each time. Firstly, the Siege of Drogheda was in the nature of an Irish civil war in which the Confederate forces faced the forces of the Pale. Secondly, Cromwell's arrival was a sequel to the English Civil War; the political scene had changed, and Drogheda was to pay a high price for its loyalty to royalty. Finally, Drogheda was caught in the middle when two English kings were disputing the English Crown at the Boyne. Cannon were spitting fire on all three occasions which occurred within the short space of 49 years. How did the conglomeration of mixed loyalties and religions react to the results? Some people were deeply apprehensive, and not without reason; others were ecstatic. Fate was very unkind to those unfortunates who were native Irish (and for the most part Catholic). *They were the losers on all three occasions.*

*   *   *

Old Minute Book of the Drogheda Corporation

Drogheda itself escaped further turmoil, but the imprint still exists in the form of place names. The site chosen by Cromwell where he mounted his artillery when bombarding the town's defences is still known as **Cromwell's Mount**; and the laneway through which he hauled his guns to that point still bears his name – **Cromwell's Lane.** The martyrdom of Oliver Plunkett is commemorated in the splendid **Memorial Church** in West Street, and his name is perpetuated in **Mount Saint Oliver**. Following the Battle of the Boyne the exultant Mayor and the Assembly changed the name Wynhalier Lane to **William Street** in honour of that king's triumph, and the 'King' in **King Street** was also to honour him. The roadway leading from the Obelisk Bridge towards Tullyallen – a deep, wooded gorge where the Williamites were encamped on the night before the battle, and where the canopy of trees afforded excellent cover – is still known as **King William's Glen**. The western end of the Ramparts we know as 'Pass', or '**Pass-If-You-Can**' – this was the point where King William passed across the Boyne, signalling closure to King James' attempt to reclaim his crown.

*   *   *

The Repercussions: Taking one thing with another, there can be few events that have influenced the course of Ireland's history as profoundly as the momentous occurrences that took place at Drogheda during the mid and late 1600s, especially the Battle of the Boyne. Some of its after-effects are still starkly evident today. A conspicuous consequence is the Border that separates Northern Ireland from the Republic of Ireland. The echoes of the cannon-fire that sounded on the 1st July 1690 have died away, but the beat of Lambeg drums, and the tramp, tramp of marching feet are repeated in celebratory ritual parades that are often contentious, perpetuating an environment that is at best cool, often tense, and at times riven by violence. Today's supporters of the Orange Order regard 'the marching season' as a joyous and innocent celebration of a signal victory which liberated the people from the influence of Rome. To the other side it is a continuing act of triumphalism and an insensitive reminder of wrongs that have been perpetrated on a deprived people that continued for two hundred years.

*   *   *   *

The sectarianism still endures to this day. The factious strife that took place in Northern Ireland during the latter decades of the 1900s claimed twice as many lives as were killed in the actual Battle of the Boyne.

PART 3

THE 1700s

THE TURNING OF THE THUMB-SCREW

At no period were the common people more subjugated than during the period we are about to discuss – the 1700s – when the welfare of the majority was totally eclipsed by the indulgence of the dominant minority. King William's victory was to have profound consequences, shaping the future history, not only of Ireland, but of the whole of Britain, and in addition it curtailed France's dominance in Europe. It secured a Protestant monarch on the throne of England for evermore, as well as entrenching Protestantism throughout Britain. At home the new regime turned its back on social equality and religious tolerance. Instead, the majority became victims of a policy that was utterly divisive. It created circumstances for Irish Catholics that were infinitely worse than any pessimist could have foreseen – they were shorn of civil liberty and remained so until Daniel O'Connell appeared on the scene 130 years later. In the meantime they were inflicted with a series of penal laws that were designed to restrict them in every facet of their lives, and this kept them in a state of deprivation and permanent subjection.

Commercially, Drogheda fared better than most other towns. It experienced a period of unprecedented stability – a prerequisite to industrial growth, and this stimulated a variety of industries (notably linen) which provided a livelihood to the working classes.

What about the privileged few who dominated the scene and who dictated the conditions which the majority had to endure? What are we to make of them? Napoleon said that it is the historian's role to present the facts, and for the reader or student to interpret them, and this directive we should bear in mind in piecing together the major events that occurred in Drogheda during the 1700s – and then extended for a further 120 years during the operation of the Act of Union (1800). However, so unpardonable were some of the measures taken by the Drogheda Corporation on behalf of the dominant few that, in acquainting ourselves of them, it is not always easy to suppress a sense of moral righteousness, and to cry 'Shame!' when natural justice is so blatantly denied to the common people. If personal sentiments seem to have surfaced on occasions in these pages, the reader should point a finger, not at this author, but at the naked, irrefutable facts of history.

Chapter Fourteen

Life Under the Penal Code

AFTER-EFFECTS OF THE BOYNE AND LIMERICK: Radical changes took place overnight in the make-up of Drogheda Corporation. Firstly, the sitting members were given short shrift. On 12th July 1690 King William appointed William Elwood as Mayor; other appointees bore names such as Moore and Tichburne, family names that we have already encountered in these pages, and whose families were to dominate in political and civic matters for the next 150 years along with other names such as Ball, Balfour, Chesshire, Fairtlough, Forbes, Hardman, Leyland, Sandiford, Singleton, Smith, and van Homrigh. These families were now the principal property holders, the merchant princes and the civic representatives both at local and national level for a further century and a half.

The Drogheda Corporation was pleased to accept from the victorious King William a new Mace, a Ceremonial Sword and a new Charter. (The old mace had been melted down for use as coinage to fund King James' battles).

The Protestants were at once restored to 'the rights and privileges' which they had previously legislated for themselves, and the gulf between the peoples of the religious divide widened markedly. Visitors to Ireland subsequently wrote about the appalling poverty resulting from social inequalities that contrasted the peasantry from the landed gentry. The verdict at the Boyne had hammered into place the last nail in the coffin of a possible Irish resurgence. Gone were the leaders of the past like the great Fitzgeralds in Leinster and Munster, and the powerful Ulster chiefs, the O'Neills and the O'Donnells. The cream of the military families, like Patrick Sarsfield, as well as the rank and file, had joined continental armies. Henceforth the native Irish population countrywide was leaderless and helpless and were to become marginalised as never before. What happened to the Treaty of Limerick, one is prompted to ask.

Reneging on the Treaty of Limerick: It was one thing to allow reasonable terms to the defeated army and to guarantee religious liberty, as provided in the Treaty of Limerick (1691), but honouring it was an entirely different matter. The Treaty brought no relief to the native Irish because Parliament reneged on its terms. When it was being ratified, several crucial clauses contained in the draft document were unilaterally struck out – this was done over the head of King William who was more graciously disposed towards the Irish. Contrary to what had been agreed, estates totalling about 1,500,000 acres were confiscated. General Ginkel was created Earl of Athlone and was given 26,000 Irish acres and William Bentink got 136,000 Irish acres. King William granted a vast mount of sequestered land to his mistress Elizabeth Villiers. Parliament was regularly in conflict with the king and later revoked many such grants, selling the land and applying the proceeds to meet the arrears of pay of officers and other miscellaneous outlay incurred in the Williamite War. Little thought was given to the dispossessed owners of the land.

Not only had the victors reneged on the terms of the Treaty, but fresh penal laws were soon enacted and enforced with impunity, further subjugating the Catholics. They were denied everyday civic rights including education, entry to the professions and trades, holding or owning property, taking apprentices or being apprenticed, carrying arms, etc.

The Minutes of the regular Assembly Meetings of the Drogheda Corporation – which form a primary source of information in this book – reveal an inordinate and continuous preoccupation among the governing classes with securing and consolidating their dominant position. This policy was a necessity to ensure their survival as the tiny but dominant segment in the hostile environment that they themselves had created. The basic tenets of Christian ethics were either abandoned or applied arbitrarily. We are presented with the contradiction that the ruling elite were simultaneously applying both piety and pitiless indifference at their own convenience. St. John's Home, for example, was a place of refuge operated by the Corporation for the exclusive use of Indigent Protestants – all others could sink or swim. Many sank.

The workings of the Corporation enforce us to use the terms 'Protestantism' and 'Catholicism' repeatedly throughout this book, but it is deemed more accurate to substitute terms such as 'the ruling class', majority/minority; upper/lower classes; landlord/tenant; gentry/peasantry; etc. when the two sections of the social and political divide are being discussed. The irony is that if the Corporation had adopted a more circumspect and benign approach in running the affairs of the town, this would have been to the certain benefit of both sides. (Conspicuously, most of the national leaders in subsequent upheavals and in the constant fights for justice and independence, starting with the 1798 Rising and continuing right through to the formation of the Irish Free State in 1922 were of Protestant stock).

The Antithesis of Christianity: The 1700s brought economic growth and prosperity sufficient to place the town's populace on a comfortable footing; it enabled the Corporation to construct ambitious and costly municipal buildings (such as the Tholsel) which still proudly stand today. While one section of society thrived, the other struggled for survival. Indeed, both the 1700s and the 1800s would bring hardship for the masses such as, even now, is disturbing and painful to contemplate.

The social attitude of the governing class towards the deprived and poverty-stricken majority throughout those two centuries reveals their hypocrisy and calls into question their professed *bona fides* as Christians. They seemed less concerned with sanctity and genuine religious zeal than with paying homage to the false god Mammon and in the acquisition of riches purloined after their victory at the Boyne. They were mostly of English origin, and the religious motif, as such, played no part. Religion was nonetheless used as a façade or distinctive badge to enable a coterie of conquerors with grasping hands to filch material wealth from a vanquished people, and to secure a place of easy living for themselves and their progeny – they were adamant about retaining this advantageous position in perpetuity – all at the expense of the dispossessed. It is of interest to note that, prior to the 1600s, only 2% of the populace were English/Protestant but shortly after the Battle of the Boyne the figure had soared to 27%.[1] The inherent traits of Anglo-Saxon dominance, cupidity and self-interest asserted themselves, to the exclusion of humanitarianism, religious pieties and basic Christian ethics.

No better example of the callous disregard for the plight of others exists than during times of distress. The country was beset by recurrent famines in the 1700s and 1800s which brought starvation and death to many. Famines have been a regular feature in Ireland's past, causing mass mortality, as in 1739/41 which claimed as many as 400,000 lives; others occurred in 1816, 1822 and 1831. (The Great Famine of 1845/50 was not an isolated catastrophe – its distinction lies mainly in its duration and overall intensity). Drogheda, more than most other towns, was plagued by teeming, poverty-stricken hordes who lived on the fringe of destitution, but only once in the course of 200 years was their plight recorded in the Minutes of the governing Assembly. It voted a sum of £300 to ease

'the distress of the poor who cannot exist without immediate relief ... nothing but absolute necessity and the saving of lives of numbers of the inhabitants shall induce the Assembly' to dispense these alms'.

Why dispense such munificence on this occasion when there was no famine in the locality? Was the Assembly losing the run of itself? 'Though this be madness, yet there was method in it'. We must take particular cognisance of the fact that this uncharacteristic gesture occurred in the year 1800. The significance in the timing of the 'madness' was that it coincided with an act of crass infamy – the people were in the process of being hoodwinked into accepting the notorious Act of Union. Thus, this once-off donation to the poor was less an act of apparent Christian charity than an appeasement, a sop to allay their discontent and to repress impending violence. *Habeas corpus* had been suspended at the time and there was pressing need to forestall rioting.

Another case in point was when so many of the town's freemen side-stepped their responsibility in quartering soldiers after the Battle of the Boyne – many of them simply vacated the town – they took a sabbatical – to avoid their duty. This again illustrates that self-interest predominated over communal duty.

Again, there is the truly scandalous instance of commandeering the Commons outside the town. This was a facility used by common custom for grazing livestock, especially as a 'parking lot' for horses that had hauled produce into the town. Now it was fenced in, and the income derived from lettings was put to use in funding accommodation for the dependents of deceased Corporation members *'and for no other purpose'* (See below). The aggrieved public had no redress, nor had they the opportunity to voice their grievances in the columns of the local press.

Throughout the years of the Great Famine, when there was unlimited scope to highlight distress and to rally support for the starving people, the *Drogheda Conservative Journal* remained silent for the most part, or what was even worse, took a reactionary stance, ridiculing O'Connell for drawing attention to the people's plight.

DISCRIMINATION INTENSIFIES: It transpired that those who had supported the vanquished king had their lands confiscated, leaving the native Irish/Catholic population with a mere one-seventh of Irish land. King William's victory copper-fastened and perpetuated the gulf that separated the dominant sect from the underprivileged, exacerbating the hardship of the majority (80% of the people were Catholic at the time) and gradually reducing many of them to extremes of destitution.

Henceforth the civic affairs of Drogheda were administered by a corporation that was the exclusive domain of Protestantism, notwithstanding the preponderance of Catholics within the town. The Charter granted by William and Mary in 1698 was interpreted as giving the new régime exclusive *carte blanche* to use its authority to legally 'appropriate' land and property by requisitioning or petitioning for leases, and it confirmed the pre-existing 'privileges and properties, and granted anew the power of dividing themselves into guilds of trades, etc. and the exemption from toll, etc.'[2] In that way, coupled with many other commercial advantages, the dominant section of the community in the Drogheda area were sheltered by legislation as landlords, merchants, traders and artisans, while depriving their servile underlings of virtually all civic rights. This artificially created gulf remained for the next two hundred years and beyond, enabling the dominant few to amass sizeable fortunes for themselves.

A perusal of the Minute Book of the regular Assembly Meetings indicates a diligence that was focused on maintaining this dominant position. The two subjects most frequently appearing on the agenda were the granting of leases and the electing of Freemen. Hardly a meeting took place without a new name, or perhaps a brace of names, being admitted to the Borough as *FREEMEN,* and this privilege was normally passed on 'by birth' to the following generation. Only the Assembly members could confer that right, and only Freemen had a vote at election time. It was the Assembly's policy to ensure that their control would be absolute and would continue indefinitely, applying the precept that the most effective way to retain power is to exercise power. Their position was invulnerable.

The pervading mindset of retaining mastery is seen in the preferences bestowed to their co-religionists in the matter of charitable bequests. The Corporation in 1699 made an order concerning a commonage on the south side of Drogheda:

> *'... Knowne by the name of the Cowleyes [these were a commons] that are eaten up and made use of for the most parte by strangers, and Idle Bad people that come and sitt downe upon or neere the said lands, and is only an encouragement for Theives and ill People to come and harboure about the Towne ... to sett out [i.e. to let] the said lands to the Highest Bidder ... and the rent to be wholy sett apart and applied for the releife of poor, decayed Members of the Corporation, their Widdows and Orphans and such other objects of charity as shall from time to time be allowed ... [and to be applied to] no other persons use or purpose whatsoever ... so we do hereby leave it as a charge upon our successors and posterity ... and they will avoide the just displeasure of Almighty God [by complying with this order]'.[3]*

In other words, the commons on the outskirts of Drogheda was now being confiscated by the Corporation 'for the releife of poor, decayed <u>Members of the Corporation</u> ... [and for] <u>no other persons use or purpose whatsoever</u> ...', thereby excluding Catholics. [The location of the 'Cowleys' or commons may have been the green fields outside the walls north of the Green Lanes and Scarlet Street, now occupied by the housing estates of Bothar Brugha, Hardmans Gardens, etc. The name Hardman recurs repeatedly in the Corporation records, and three generations of Hardmans were mayors of the town. Another commons existed on the south side.] The ruling junta was adamant that this arrangement was to continue for all time to come; and for any successor to neglect this stipulation would entail bringing down on him the wrath of God. The wording was later deemed to be insufficiently specific and was open to varied interpretations – it did not mention any specific religion, and was therefore in need of refinement so as to make the intentions of the Assembly absolutely clear. So twelve years later they honed the wording by stating that no donation arising from the Cowleys rents would be granted 'without a certificate from the minister [to the effect that] the petitioner has received the Sacrament three time a year at Least'. This left no doubt that Catholics were excluded from benefiting from the trust.

They were still not fully satisfied with the wording used and they deemed it necessary to spell out their intentions with even greater clarity. To put the matter beyond all possible dispute, their intention was further endorsed seven years later when the Corporation ordered that the document '... be engrost in Parchment ... as a lasting Memorial of the true intent and meaning of this Corporation in setting the said Lands. And the said Lands be sett only to Protestant freemen of this Towne ... [and the income applied] to decayed ffreemen, their widdows and orphans'.[4]

Drogheda Soldiers with 'the Wild Geese': The unbidden visits of both Cromwell and King William resulted in an estimated 34,000 Irish soldiers, including leaders such as Patrick Sarsfield and an unquantified number of Drogheda men, leaving their native shores and entering continental armies. Under the banner of the Irish Brigade they covered themselves in glory in many military engagements. Scattered across the battlefields of Europe over the next 150 years an estimated **two million** Irish soldiers lay dead, having fought in the armies of one side or another of the major European powers. They fought with a special vigour when facing English uniforms.

Droghedamen at Fontenoy: Foremost among these battles was Fontenoy (1745), in present day Belgium, where the Irish Brigade played a crucial part in defeating the English forces. Later in the same year they set about attaining their ultimate objective, namely the defeat of England on English soil. The Jacobite Rebellion, which was still ongoing but was confined largely to Scotland and the north of England at this stage, presented that opportunity.

The invasion fleet that set out from France for Scotland contained a number of soldiers who hailed originally from counties Louth and Meath. But because of the naval blockade only one ship got through to Scotland. The list of the soldiers who were taken prisoner in the captured vessels included the names of two Drogheda men. They were James Norris (29) of whom his English captors said that he "behaved decently", and Edmond Finegan (25). The latter had gone to France with his uncle initially on a business venture and was described by his captors as "a genteel, well behaved lad".

Another Irish regiment that featured at Fontenoy had local connections. This was the Fitzjames Cavalry Regiment. Initially it had been in the proprietorship of Comte de Nugent from Dardistown Castle on the slopes of Bellewstown Hill. He transferred it to Comte de Fitzjames in 1733. It included 27 Meathmen and 8 Louthmen, three of whom were from Drogheda. They were Patrice Shorington (28), Christophe Colwell (27) and Barthelemy McNemy (39) who had a "ruddy, handsome face". This regiment sustained heavy casualties at Fontenoy, and most of those who survived were annihilated fighting for Bonnie Prince Charlie in the Stuart cause in Scotland.

Those soldiers of fortune who had escaped death in France's many battles were not left destitute to wander penniless around Europe. The magnificent hospital *Hotel Royal des Invalides* was set up by Louis XIV in Paris to care for the soldiers who had been maimed in his battles. About 2,000 Irishmen were admitted to Invalides between 1690 and 1769, and that number included 95 'broken soldiers' from the Drogheda area. Did they write home – indeed, were they *able* to write? Did their loved ones back home know where they were? They were, for the most part, illiterate; they lived in turbulent times, and many of those who set sail for far foreign fields were never heard of again. (The case of a specific Drogheda family will be related in a later chapter).

Warfare and its Effects: After the Williamite battles the country was denuded of people. As was inevitable in warfare, plague followed in its wake, and great numbers suffered from sheer hunger; many joined continental armies, or otherwise emigrated. Vast numbers of cattle and sheep had been wilfully destroyed. Resulting from this, cattle that in earlier times was exported to the Continent and America, had to be imported in 1692. Corn was unprocurable. The countryside was desolate, running wild. Tillage was rendered impossible by the fact that a great many horses had been commandeered by the armies, and crops were left to rot in the ground in consequence. The peasants' abodes, where the soldiers had lodged, were bare of food.

> *"After the Boyne and Limerick the greater part of King James's army went to France; the number of emigrants on this occasion amounted to 14,000; and this was but the beginning of a continuous stream of Catholic refugees who poured to the Continent for many years. In 1692 we read that great numbers of Catholics were still emigrating, and in 1694 the stream was still flowing. An attempt was made to renew the Cromwellian system of selling the Irish as slaves, and shipping them to the colonies, and numbers of Irish boys and girls were transported in this way. ... Between 1691 and 1745 no less that 450,000 Irishmen had died in the service of France alone. ... The lot of the Catholics who went abroad, however, was much less terrible than that of those who remained at home, as the period was now beginning when the Catholic population of Ireland was to be ground down and degraded by the infamous system of penal laws, which have done more than anything else to injure the industrial character of the Irish people, and therefore the industrial wealth of Ireland. This orgy of religious intolerance was not only odious in itself, but was doubly odious inasmuch as it was an express breach of the Treaty of Limerick".*[5]

This is but one example of the aftermath of warfare in Ireland, and battles were endlessly fought before the coming of the Normans as well as after it. It can be seen that, tragically, non-participants usually suffered as much privation as the combatants. In prehistoric times the Celtic tribes were constantly at war with one another; in the Christian era the monks were not as sanctimonious and peace-loving as one would expect – they often paid unwelcome visits to neighbouring monasteries, spilling blood in the process. As for the Vikings, Irish chieftains often added fuel to the fire by joining them in their pillaging escapades in order to benefit from the spoils of war.

The Ulster Rebellion and the Cromwellian Campaign saw a repeat of the carnage, reducing the overall population by almost one-third. People were killed simply because they were Catholics; people were killed simply because they were Protestants. Drogheda escaped most, but not all, of this blood-letting. Its luck had held out pretty well until the Cromwellian campaign.

THE PENAL LAWS: Drogheda did not convert *en masse* to Protestantism following the Reformation. The native Irish had infiltrated into the town over the centuries, and despite the upheavals of 1649 and 1690, the Catholic population gradually swelled until it constituted a majority of the town's inhabitants. By 1732 over three-quarters were Catholic. (The first official census to provide statistics on the religious profile was in 1861 – it showed Drogheda's population to be 90.5% Catholic.)[6]

We can perhaps appreciate that the penal laws in Elizabethan times were enacted out of fear of an Irish resurgence, since the old Gaelic chieftains had asserted themselves and were coming close to ousting the forces of the Pale. But when they fled into exile after Kinsale, and the other military leaders joined continental armies, the common people were soft targets. The motivation for the severe laws being introduced was based, not on any fear of reprisals that might arise from a prostrate, conquered people, but on a determination to perpetuate the dominance of the ruling classes. They were being applied more rigorously and systematically than before, and they remained in force for more than a further century. The new laws were instigated, not alone by England, but by the Irish Ascendancy operating from Dublin Castle. A succession of these penal enactments was introduced over a period of time. A brief summary is given: -

- The Oath of Abjuration compelled every Member of Parliament, civil servant, bishop, lawyer and doctor to renounce the Catholic faith. This effectively excluded all Catholic representation in parliament, and all Catholics from key posts.
- No Catholic could teach, either in a school or in a private house; a child could not be sent abroad for education. This meant illiteracy for all Catholics, and deprivation of education. The penalty for non-compliance was forfeiture of all goods.
- Catholics could not accept a legacy. Thus, property could not be passed on to Catholics.
- All Catholics were to hand up their arms; in searching for arms Catholic homes could be broken into at any time. No maker of arms could employ a Catholic apprentice.
- No Catholic could own a horse (which was the equivalent of a car in the times under review) of £5 value or greater. Any Protestant could acquire a horse from a Catholic by tendering £5.
- All priests had to be registered, and provide security for good behaviour. All bishops, and members of religious orders were forced to quit the kingdom, and for any who returned the punishment was death.
- For a priest who turned Protestant: a pension of £30 was offered as an inducement.
- No Catholic chapel could have a steeple or a bell.
- For priests landing into Ireland: imprisonment followed by transportation. To return carried the death penalty.
- No intermarriage with Protestants. A Protestant who married a Catholic lost all his privileges and was treated like a Catholic.

The Irish House of Commons deemed the existing restrictions to be inadequate and in 1704 further repressive measures were advocated, resulting in additional legislation being passed, the main examples being: -

- If the eldest son turned Protestant, he became owner of his father's land to the exclusion of all the other siblings.
- A person who was not a Protestant since fourteen years of age was prohibited from being a solicitor.
- No Catholic could purchase land or take a lease longer than 31 years. If land came by descent to a Catholic, or was given to him, or was left to him by will, he could not accept it.
- No person could vote in an election or could hold any civil or military office without taking the Oaths of Allegiance and Abjuration. (This effectively debarred all Catholics).
- Rewards were offered for the discovery of Catholic bishops, Jesuits, unregistered priests or schoolmasters – the amount of such rewards to be levied on the Catholics.

The military was to play a vital role both in implementing and enforcing these draconian measures and in using its muscle to give protection to the dominant elite – hence the need for a garrison at Millmount. Those who were being suppressed were powerless to take counter measures, and the Corporation voted in 1719 that 'no powder, ball or flint should be sold to any Papist'. The statesman/philosopher Edmund Burke, himself a Protestant, described these laws as 'a machine as well fitted for the oppression, impoverishment and degradation of a people, and the debasement in them of human nature itself, as ever proceeded from the perverted ingenuity of man'.

Depriving the people of education anticipated the code that was later employed to deny literacy to the Negro slaves working in the cotton plantations of the Southern States of America; there is an instance where a Negro child was punished for innocently playing with a set of A-B-C toy blocks that had been given him by a slave owner's child – it was envisaged that this could have introduced him to literacy. A most effective way of keeping a people in subservience was to also keep them in ignorance. In a similar way the Drogheda Assembly was vigilant in denying civic rights to Catholics; they conducted a trawl of their records dealing with corporation leases so as '... to enquire into the state and circumstances of all lands and houses belonging to the Corporation that are now in the possession of Papists or other persons not legally entitled thereto'.

LAURENCE'S GATE

A Policy of Apartheid: These penal restrictions related primarily to education and the holding of property. The laws relating to *employment* perhaps had the most insidious and long-term consequences of all because they ensured permanence to the two-tier system. This policy of segregation based on religion was being applied several hundred years before the term 'apartheid' came into vogue, as applied for a time in the Republic of South Africa. All recognised trades were closed to Catholics by virtue of being debarred from trade guilds or 'Fraternities', as they were called. To become an apprentice or a member of a Fraternity, e.g. of the Shoemakers' Guild or those of the Butchers, Bakers, Glovers, etc. it was obligatory to take the Oath of Allegiance – this policy precluded Catholics from following a fruitful vocation. A system called 'quarterage' admitted them as associate members, but they were ineligible to vote at guild elections or to attain office. It now appears that the rights and privileges claimed by the guilds were contrary to the law.[7] Overall, Catholics were denied career opportunities and the prospect of a livelihood except by the most servile task-work Depriving a people of a proper or realistic means of living was effectively denying them the very *raison d'être* of their existence. Kept in subjection, their position was not dissimilar to that of the caste system that operated in India – they became the hewers of wood and the drawers of water, and these were the types of demeaning occupations that were passed from father to son. Thus, they were shorn of all elemental self-esteem and human dignity.

The absence of any tradition of skills in the workplace was, despite the gradual decline in the power of Fraternities, to become tragically evident during the mass exodus that accompanied the Great Famine. Creative, skilful fingers, manual dexterity and craftsmanship are always at a premium in an expanding community such as the budding cities of the New World, but the hordes of Irish paupers who crossed the Atlantic had no contribution to make, and were thus rejected on arrival with the abominable out-of-hand refusal: 'No Irish Need Apply'.

Being denied the opportunity of apprenticeship to trades, etc. the sole option for many who were unable to scramble on board an emigrant ship was to join the Crown's armed forces. The result was that almost half the British Army consisted of Irish Catholics in Napoleonic times and after. Even with that, the Penal Laws ensured that there would be no prospect of promotion for them – they were debarred from the officer ranks. They were little more than the cannon-fodder used in England's battles and colonial conquests.

A One-way Street to Wealth: The imprint of discriminatory legislation introduced after the Battle of the Boyne was indelible, and its after-effects were still evident even into modern times. The distinguishing factor existed in the form *wealth* among the privileged class, and was sustained by the 'rights and privileges' which they had accorded to themselves and to which they constantly made reference during the Assembly meetings of the Drogheda Corporation. In addition, rank injustice in commercial practices took place in the form of the discriminatory impositions of taxes, etc. – these stifled enterprise among Catholics and effectively precluded them from becoming merchants and engaging in trades.

Some contrasting traits of the Anglo-Saxon/Protestant minority *vis-à-vis* those of the Celtic race exacerbated this imbalance. The admirable characteristic known as 'the Protestant work ethic' paved the way in maintaining their position at the top of the pile in later times – in America today it goes under the acronym WASP (for White, Anglo-Saxon Protestant), and denotes an abstemious, well-heeled, reliable, industrious person. The perceived notion of the native Irish was that they were indolent. Also, improvidence and intemperance are more prominent characteristics in the Celtic profile.

Redressing the imbalance of wealth distribution was a slow process – it persisted well into the 20th Century. Despite the overwhelming preponderance of Catholics in Drogheda – the ratio was 93:7 or perhaps greater at the time of Independence in 1922 – there still remained a pronounced imbalance in the distribution of wealth. Many of the major retail outlets at that time, such as drapers, hardware merchants, builders' providers, etc. as well as members of the professions and executives in industry were Protestant, and as prominent businessmen they occupied the town's prominent residences.

Drogheda, with its wide diversity of industries, was the envy of most other Irish towns. It boasted of about a dozen important industries ranging from textile mills to flour mills to breweries and chemical works, etc. These enterprises provided the bulk of the town's workforce with employment, so that the town's welfare hinged on their performance. They thrived – but every one of them was in the proprietorship of the small Protestant community at the time of Independence in 1922. It was a universal perception that Protestants occupied privileged positions and enjoyed comfortable living standards. These circumstances can be traced back to the discriminatory legislation that followed the Williamite victories at the Boyne and Limerick.

The trend towards a more level distribution of wealth was influenced during the 1930s when the Free State encouraged the establishment of new home-based industries producing footwear, textiles, cement, edible oils, etc. These were limited liability companies and they gave the small shareholder the opportunity to participate in the town's commercial progress. They also provided the man-in-the-street with an *entrée* to positions above the factory floor. It can thus be seen that the *economic* effects of the penal code introduced after the Battle of the Boyne were gradually being eroded in the newly formed Free State – the process had taken upwards of two centuries. The *political* effects of the Battle were more entrenched than ever.

The Fatcats and The Underdogs: Tolls required to be paid on all goods entering or exiting the town, whether by land or sea, but freemen were privileged by being exempted. Likewise, only freemen had the privilege of voting in elections. The records tell us that it came to the attention of the Drogheda Assembly that John Jones, a stone cutter, was married to a Popish wife. 'It was ordered that unless he satisfied the next General Assembly that within a year and a day from the marriage she conformed to the Protestant religion, he would be deprived of his freedom'. Catholics still remained the underdogs entering the 1800s, and the Act of Union exacerbated this situation. The collapse of the linen industry caused havoc, and it was followed by the Great Famine so that there was virtually no economic growth to correct the imbalance of wealth during the ghastly 1800s. Sadly, instances of discrimination at the workplace still occurred well into the twentieth century, and this was most pronounced in institutions such as banks.

The Corporation pursued with singular diligence the policy of allowing only Protestants to become freemen, and was determined to root out freemen who were suspected of being adherents to the Catholic religion:

> 'Upon the petition of John Knight of Drogheda, mason, and Patrick Roal of the same, two free members of the Corporation, setting forth that upon the last election of Members to serve in Parliament of this town, they were not permitted to give their votes, it having been alleged that they were seen at the Popish chapel and that they to remove all objections of that sort, have gone through the several requisites that the Law requires to confirm them established Protestants and praying to be readmitted free members of the Corporation ... they are hereby readmitted free members without paying any fine'.[8]

This John Knight was not yet off the hook because the authorities were still suspicious of his popish connections. His case was again put under the microscope. His Petition has survived, and well illustrates the depth of feelings[9]

The Corporation members were reassured by being informed that 'he hath lately performed the several qualifications required by law to confirm him as an established Protestant...' He was accordingly reinstated as a glover and a freeman of Drogheda. Presbyterians were similarly discriminated against. An exodus resulted, and many

Presbyterians emigrated to the New World as the "Scots-Irish". Ireland's loss was America's gain; they were people of strong character and strict moral code and they were later to prove their worth in forming the back-bone of the emerging United States of America – a dozen of the early Presidents carried their blood. As for the defeated Jacobite soldiers, they found ready employment in the ranks of continental armies, notably those of France and Spain, and they are known to history as "the Wild Geese".

Catholics could not become Members of the Irish Parliament. Later they were debarred from voting in both parliamentary and municipal elections. Indeed, complaints were made that the restrictions being applied to Catholics were not sufficiently stringent and it was pointed out that loopholes had to be closed, so that in 1719 and 1723 further Bills were drafted by the Irish Parliament and sent to London for ratification. Here Poyning's Law, the thorn in the side of the Irish Parliament for so long, came to the rescue, for London refused to endorse the Bills.

THE END OF DROGHEDA'S PROMINENCE: Until the Battle of the Boyne, Drogheda had always occupied a pre-eminent position, both political and commercial, in the affairs of the country. As a measure of its importance, King Henry VI had excluded it from the territory allotted to de Lacy, but instead he retained it for himself. It was deemed suitable as a university city; and it had a licence to mint the coins of the realm. During the Elizabethan wars, the wars of the Confederation, the Cromwellian and the Williamite campaigns the occupation of Drogheda was always regarded as a key possession in any major military campaign. It had influenced the destiny of the entire island not only by reason of its location on the corridor between Dublin and Ulster, but also because it was an important trading centre in its own right and was arguably the busiest port in Ireland. In the centuries ahead the town would feature irregularly in the affairs of the island. Politically, it faded into an era of anonymity, a fate that applied equally to the other towns of Ireland – Dublin excepted. Gone were the prestigious days when Drogheda received kings and hosted parliaments.

Impact of the Penal Code on Land and Property Ownership: The newly appointed members of Drogheda Corporation wasted no time in divesting Catholics of their property. They were at a loss to know the proper legal process to adopt in the matter of leases, and therefore sought enlightenment from their colleagues in Dublin. Only a month after taking office they 'Ordered that there be a letter written to the Recorder to desire his advice, … and to enquire what course ye city of Dublin takes in theirs, that this Corporation may take like'. In 1702 they voted that any leases of corporate property held by Papists should not be renewed.

The landed class represented a miniscule 0.2% of the population, and together with the other adherents to Protestantism they accounted for 20% of Ireland's population, but they were in possession of the lion's share of the land. Prior to 1641 an estimated 59% of the arable land was owned by Catholics nationwide; following the Cromwellian Plantation this was reduced to 22%, and the further carving up after the Boyne and Limerick left a mere 14% in their hands.[10] By 1778 it was a tiny 5%.[11] County Louth had 65% of land confiscated, and in the case of Meath it was 76%. Dublin Castle issued exhortations to the ruling class that the Penal Laws be strictly enforced. They pursued that policy by force of arms and by drafting further oppressive legislation.

Restrictions on Industry: Today's schoolbooks give primary students merely *an outline* of Irish history – they relate the major occurrences, those which were turning points and which set the nation's course in new directions. But there are many underlying events in history, which, although not initially explosive, were injurious through being insidious, and greatly influenced the day-to-day lives of the common people and were the cause of untold distress. They all touched Drogheda directly or indirectly. Let us examine a few of them.

We have seen that in the reign of Queen Elizabeth I a debased currency was foisted onto Ireland expressly to disrupt the economy. This was easily accomplished and it caused havoc to trade and commerce. In later times other ploys were used with effects that were even more devastating. An embargo was applied to all Irish exports to the colonies. Also, to protect English farmers, Irish cattle were debarred from the English market. The effect on the national economy can be imagined. The Cattle Acts together with the Navigation Act almost destroyed the Irish cattle and shipping trades, pursuits in which Drogheda merchants had been heavily engaged.

The Cattle Acts turned out to be a blessing in disguise, because the country switched over to sheep rearing, and pursued this alternative in an intensive way. Suffice it to say, wool and woollen goods became Ireland's major industry, outselling the English product in the open market, and the industry thrived. Alas, this situation would not be allowed to continue. The English merchants cast a covetous eye on the Irish industry and petitioned the king, urging him to suppress it. He responded positively, imposing an export duty on all Irish woollen products.

In consequence of this the entire woollen industry in Ireland was destroyed, and it soon made the population destitute. To make matters worse, the English Parliament prohibited Ireland from exporting wool and woollen goods *to anywhere in the world* except to a few English ports such as Liverpool. In order to keep an eye on activities to ensure that the duties were being properly levied, exports could only be made through a few selected ports, notably Drogheda and Dublin. This wool restriction was the most disastrous of all the trade barriers ever to be inflicted on the Irish economy. It well satisfied the English merchants and it ruined the Irish wool trade, dragging 40,000 Protestants – apart altogether from the masses of Catholic peasantry – into poverty, and forcing 20,000 Puritans to emigrate across the Atlantic to the New England states to escape the burden.

The restriction in the wool trade continued for almost a century and it never recovered its former prosperity. Wool that sold for only 5 pence a lb. when shipped to England, would have fetched 2 shillings and 6 pence in France – six times the price.

It is surely an adjunct to the law of supply and demand that where there are prohibitive tariffs, there will be found smugglers. Trade with France flourished simply by evading the tariff, and the authorities were unable to stop it. Happily, since Drogheda had been favoured as one of the designated wool exporting ports, it found a way of subverting the obstruction. Undoubtedly, when vessels set out for Liverpool, unfavourable winds blew some of them off course and took them (surprise! surprise!) to French ports. The returning ships were laden with contraband brandy, wines and silks. The traffic was accomplished surreptitiously, and all classes joined in this racket, rich and poor, squires, clergy, peasants, Protestants and Catholics alike, and this enterprise continued for a century. Today, locals in remote coastal areas can point out coves and smugglers' caves which were used to receive this illicit traffic, and tracks across mountainsides still exist, some still known as 'brandy paths', along which the contraband goods were taken for distribution.

The loss of the wool industry is best summed up in George O'Brien's *'The Economic History of Ireland in the Seventeenth and Eighteenth Century'*: ' ... the suppression of the Irish woollen manufacture was the most important landmark in the whole economic history of Ireland ... and was the most fruitful source of the dreadful distress that characterised the eighteenth century'.

Not satisfied with snuffing out the woollen industry, the parliament interfered with almost every other branch of Irish trade and industry – beer, malt, hats, cotton, silk, iron, ironware – all suffered from imposed embargoes. Since Drogheda always occupied a primary position as a seaport and trading centre, the effect on its merchants and ship-owners was severe. Evidently, there existed a two-fold policy in England, namely to protect English manufacturers and, secondly, to keep Ireland in a permanent state of debasement.

Chapter Fifteen

Life in Drogheda in the 1700s

Drogheda was still a walled town until the near the end of the 1700s, and the town gates were still being locked at night. A tax was collected at each gate on goods entering or leaving the town. Not surprisingly, this was often circumvented by smuggling goods over the walls at night. The Collector of Customs wrote to the Commissioner of Customs in Dublin on 25th April 1780, pointing out that the battle against smugglers was being lost:

> 'There have been more goods smuggled into this town within these few nights than has ever been remembered in so short a time; nor can our utmost vigilance prevent it, circumstanced as we are; for those villains are so connected in this town that should the officers attempt to watch within the walls they are immediately discovered by some of the many spies...'[1]

For the most part, poverty was never far from the doors of the under-privileged; their fare was poor, their clothes were ragged and only the more fortunate ones were shod. The authorities should not have been surprised that smuggling was taking place on a grand scale, and that taxation in all its   forms was being resisted, given the living conditions and the fact that the privileged few were absolved from paying taxes. Obtaining revenue from the movement of goods was becoming a futile exercise, and towards the end of the century some parts of the town walls were being openly pulled down to make way for other developments. The population was probably in the region of 14,000, making it the sixth largest town in Ireland.

The Streets and Lanes: The main streets were paved with cobbles, and the secondary streets and lanes were dusty when dry and muddy when wet; poultry and other livestock mixed casually with the inhabitants, and dung littered the streets. This was a constant source of annoyance, and the city fathers were urged to take action in the matter. A byelaw was drafted, printed and published pursuant to a resolution of the Assembly as follows:

> "Whereas many dangers and inconveniences may and do arise as well as to the inhabitants as to strangers passing through the town by suffering swine of all kinds to go at large through the streets and lanes and other passages within the said town [of Drogheda] and suburbs thereof.

> "In order therefore to put a stop to so dangerous and offensive a practice, for the time to come it is order'd by the Mayor, Sheriffs, Burgesses and Commons of the County of the Town of Drogheda at their general Assembly held this day that from and after the 20th. day of October instant all persons to whom any swine of what kind soever do or shall belong, shall keep it confined ... and if thereafter any be found so at large, the owner shall forfeit for that end the Hog, Pig, or Sow so found the sum of 1/- which, if not paid within the space of 24 hours, shall be levied by distress and sale of said swine ... and half of said penalty to go to the Informer and the other half to the Poor of the Town; and it is further enacted that copies of this Byelaw be posted up at the Tholsel Gates and other public places of this Town, and that it otherwise be proclaimed by the Bellover [Town Crier] through the streets in the most public manner that it may be known to all persons and that none hereafter plead ignorance.

> Dated this 10th. October 1760   Signed by Order

> Edward Meade, Town Clerk

Undoubtedly, little or no attention was paid to this public notice. Cattle and sheep as well as pigs wandered at will in most Irish towns – and in none more so than Drogheda since it was an important market town. On fair days the scene was often chaotic, and the herds of livestock were a continuing nuisance to passing traffic. 'Consideration being had of the very great inconvenience to the public by the throng of cattle and carriages at the West Gate of the Town on market and fair days by which people are stopt and obstructed from coming and going out of the same to their great danger, delay and detriment, [arrangements were made to] construct a public gate thru the Town Wall to the Turnpike Road leading to Dunleer ... and to pull down so much of said Wall as will be necessary, and of the building of a proper Gate for the same' .

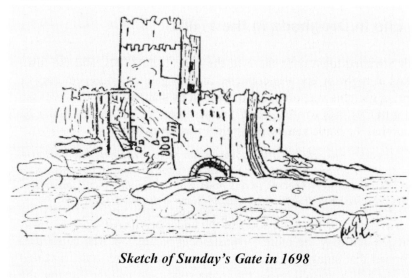

Sketch of Sunday's Gate in 1698

It was not unusual for livestock to be treated with great cruelty. To supply meat for a meal it was known for slices of flesh to be cut from living cattle. There was little variety in the matter of food for the table. Vegetables such as carrots, turnips and cabbage had been introduced in the previous century and were still something of a novelty to the poor.

Forests were relentlessly being cut down for fuel. Bull-baiting had been banned at this stage, but other forms of amusement still involved cruelty:

> *"Owing to the humane exercise of the Rev. Mr. McCann, P.P of this town, that savage custom of throwing at cocks on Shrove Tuesday is nearly abolished. Mr. McCann had been particularly active, and in some degree successful in suppressing licentiousness and dissipation in the lower order of the people'.[2]*

There were apparently several routes leading to Dundalk, for the Corporation issued an order 'for the repairing of the road from Drogheda to Dundalk between Mr. Nicholson's Cottage and Listoke' (which is on the *Ballymakenny Road)*, and to cover the cost of this work they set aside the princely sum of £5 (€6.35).

Unskilled Workers: 'Blind alley' jobs had always been a pitfall for many an impoverished family. Even several centuries later, the 1950s, the child of poor parents would gladly forsake school to take up a job in a mill or as a messenger boy. Many shopkeepers, especially grocers, butchers and fish mongers, would employ these early school-leavers, equipping them with a custom-made bicycle complete with a large frame on front of the handlebars to accommodate a basket in which deliveries were made to private homes. The lure of 7/6 a week (€0.48), however meagre it was, was irresistible to many, because it helped to put food on the table of impoverished homes even in the 1940s and 1950s; but there was seldom the prospect of advancement for uneducated youths holding such jobs, and as they grew older they lacked the skills to perform more meaningful tasks, and thus they were stuck fast in the poverty trap. As grown men they undertook the responsibilities of marriage on such pitiful wages, and the spiral of poverty continued ever downwards. A veteran who was a schoolboy of the 1920s recalled: -

> *"The rest of us were envious when word went round the class that one lad had left school – he had got a job. A few weeks later I was down the town and I saw him at work. He was in a butcher's shop and he had a fly-swat in his hand. His job was to keep the flies off the meat".[3]*

The Corporation in the 1700s set out to regulate the earnings of these messenger boys. We hasten to explain that this step was taken, not to ensure a minimum wage, but rather to avoid disputations among the lowly-paid waifs.

'... It appears necessary that the several carriers of Meat and Fish from the Market to the dwelling houses of the inhabitants should be badged; and that no person be suffered to apply for hire herein without having a badge affixed to the outside of his or her coat, ... that the Mayor do furnish Badges for that purpose to such person as he shall find properly recommended for the Badge Boys and Girls, and that any Badge Boy or Girl not having a clean and sufficient Basket for carrying Meat and Fish be fined six pence ... and on refusal or neglect of paying such Fine, to be deprived of their Badge and struck off the list'.

This regulation applied also to coal porters. It was another blind alley occupation, yet to earn a few coppers men swarmed in that direction like flies towards a rotting corpse. It was found necessary to issue an official scale of charges, based on distance, and starting with ½d. (€0.0026) for deliveries to streets in central Drogheda, and progressing by units of a farthing (¼d. or €0.0013) for deliveries further from the town centre. It is pathetic to observe so many people orientating towards unskilled, labouring jobs; a demand for artisans such as carpenters, tailors, etc. existed, but it was necessary to become a member of a 'Fraternity' or 'guild' and this entailed taking the Oath of Allegiance. Thus the occupations open to Catholics were of the most menial kind, e.g. common labourers, cattle drovers, domestic servants, etc. In 1819 the Assembly pronounced that 'the number of coal porters [in Drogheda] is more than sufficient, and no new ones will be required *until the number has fallen below **180'***. Numerous as this figure is, and lowly as the men were paid, it still leaves unanswered the question of how they eked out a living during the summer months.

CIVIC INFRASTRUCTURE: Apparently, complaints were made about the inadequacy of Drogheda's public lighting, and the existing arrangements were deemed to be unsatisfactory. The Assembly discussed the matter, stating that 'the annual Expense of 60 guineas [€80.00] for Oyle, Lamps and other Material for enlightening the streets and lanes of this Town in Winter and that the same has been, through mismanagement and carelessness, very badly done'. They therefore resolved that a half guinea [€0.69] was to be allowed for supplying the oil and other material. The members of the Assembly must have concluded that an increase in his remuneration might induce the lamplighter to provide a better performance, and so it was agreed to raise his pay to 65 guineas [€86.70] for the half year from Michaelmas to the 25th. of March, his duties to include lighting each of the 86 lamps and 44 globes in the town, and extinguishing them again each morning. Presumably, the lamplighter was to provide his own ladder; the work was not without its hazards, with the poor fellow being obliged to climb up the ladder and down again no fewer than 260 times each day, hail, rain or snow.

We know that Peter Street had been named Pillory Street in earlier times; a pillory was in place there for punishing wrong-doers – it was directly opposite the Magistrate's Court at the Tholsel. We don't know the date or the circumstances as to when it was last put to use, but we find a reference to it among the Minutes of the Corporation in 1767 when they queried

'... a charge of £3.2.11 for Boards got from Mr. John Hathorne to make a Pillory when Thomas McArdle was pillored lately, but cannot get any account of what became of them since, and think the Bridewell-Keeper should have the care of them, that the Corporation should not be put to such expense on every occasion of this kind'.

Workers unions or 'combinations', as they were then called, were illegal, and the *Drogheda Journal* of 1795 published a warning to that effect, stating that they were 'destructive to the prosperity of the manufacture and the true interest of the Kingdom, and they have desired their inspectors to prosecute every person who shall offend therein'. The matter of a fair wage did not arise. The punishment meted out to persons found guilty, as directed in an Act of King George III, was 'imprisonment six months and thrice whipped'. Meetings nonetheless took place surreptitiously, and a man who allowed his house to be used as a meeting place for combination journeymen was punished at the pillory in 1787:

> *'We are informed that a man who on Saturday last was pilloried at the Tholsel for keeping a house of meeting for combinating journeymen, behaved in a most rude and indecent manner to one of our most worthy High Sheriffs who attended on the occasion to see the sentence of the law being executed upon him and was with difficulty restrained from assault on the Magistrate'.*[4]

The following eye-witness description of everyday life, although written in 1690, would still have applied throughout most of the 1700s, since there was no major occurrence in the interim to uplift the social conditions of the underlings:

> *' ... They all smoke, women as well as men, and a pipe, an inch long, serves the family for several years, and though never so black or fowl, is never suffered to be burnt. Seven or eight will gather to the smoking of a pipe, and each taking two or three whiffs gives it to his neighbour, commonly holding his mouth full of smoke until the pipe comes about to him again. They are also much given to the taking of snuff. Very little clothes serves them, and as for shoes and stockings much less. They wear brogues being quite plain without so much as one lift of a heel, and are all sowed with thongs, and the leather not curried, so that in wearing it grows hard as a board, and therefore many always keep them wet, but the wiser that can afford it grease them often and that makes them supple. In the better sort of cabins there is commonly one flock bed, seldom more, feathers being too costly; this serves the man and his wife, the rest all lie on straw, some with one sheet and blanket, others only their clothes and blanket to cover them. The cabins seldom have any floor but the earth, or rarely so much as a loft, some have windows, others none. They say that it is of late years that chimneys are used, yet the house is never free from smoke. That they have no locks to the door is not because there are not thieves but because there is nothing to steal. Poverty with neatness seems somewhat the more tolerable, but here nastiness is in perfection, if perfection can be a vice, and the great cause of it, laziness, is the most predominant. It is a great happiness that the country produces no venomous creature, but it were much happier in my opinion did it produce no vermin ... A little hut or cabin to live in is all that the poverty of this sort hope or have ambition for. Their dwellings or cabins – an English cow-house hath more architecture by far. The Lord Mayor's dog kennel is a palace compared to them; the walls are made of mere mud mixed with a little wet straw...'.*[5]

Tramps and vagrants were a perennial nuisance in the town, and no doubt the streets, the shops and the numerous market places provided them with the opportunity to practice their skills of relieving unsuspecting victims of their valuables. Laws had been passed making it an offence to beg, but notwithstanding that, the town was constantly plagued with vagabonds wandering about the streets and lanes. For some it was a way of life to tramp from town to town, sleeping in hay barns and generally living on their wits. In 1767 Drogheda Corporation had in its employment two men, known as 'Bangbeggars', whose duty it was to keep these unwanted specimens of flotsam on the move, although it seems they were not performing their duty with the diligence that was expected of them:

> *' ... and we are of the opinion that the two persons employed by the Corporation for keeping the town clear of strange beggars and the streets free of the same and including other business for which they are paid £15.12.0 yearly, (viz. €19.80 which works out at €0.19 per week each) and*
>
> *so far from doing their duty and the other works they are directed to do, that they encourage and licence foreign beggars to set down here, to the loss of the real poor of the town and a burden to the inhabitants, and with great submission we hope they may be discharged by the order of this Assembly, and that Mr. Mayor may provide proper persons in their places".*[6]

Tories and Bandits: It must be remembered that many such unfortunates had been thrown out of their homes and farms at the time of the Plantations, and they simply had nowhere to go and were left to endlessly tramp the roads. One school of thought suggests that the itinerants of today may have originated in that way. Other dispossessed people simply took to the hills; they engaged in a type of guerrilla warfare with the planters and were called raparees or *tóraidhe* (tory = bandit), the latter word today having political connotations. Many of these unfortunates had their origins in the Cromwellian Plantation, having been dispossessed, following which they retreated to the hills, and later they were supporters of King James II. The term 'tory' was used derisively and was in time applied to Jacobite supporters, and later still to the Conservative, or *Tory* Party in Britain.

IMPROVED ECONOMIC AND SOCIAL CONDITIONS: The latter half of the 1700s saw a gradual relaxation of the Penal Laws, and places of Catholic worship began to be tolerated, but they were obliged through legislation to keep a low profile, being sited invariably in unpretentious, inconspicuous locations and back streets, being called 'chapels' rather than 'churches'. These chapels were prohibited by law from having a steeple or a bell. The word 'chapel' has been retained in usage into modern times from the penal days, and has always been used to denote any Catholic church building, irrespective of its size, and to distinguish it from its Protestant equivalent which was invariably called a 'church'. This relic in word usage continued in Drogheda right into the mid-Twentieth Century when the word 'church' gradually replaced 'chapel' for major places of worship, irrespective of the denomination, and the latter word regained its dictionary meaning, viz. a subordinate church building.

The improving prosperity of the town during the latter half of the century was reflected in the financial circumstances of the Corporation, the Mayor in 1768 having arranged to provide Watch Coats for two of the Sergeants at Mace, 'who are frequently ordered to sit up at night in the Tholsel'. In 1785 the Assembly decided to provide the Mayor with proper Mayoral chains of office, and a link was to be added each year as necessary. His regalia in earlier times included a sword – this permission was granted by a statute of Edward IV – a distinction which brought him into line with the Mayor of London. The Sheriff also had a chain of office, but this office was subsequently merged with that of Mayor. The Mayor was granted an allowance of £150 in addition to 'the profits from the town cranes'. It was agreed that he should not be required to host more than 'five entertainments' annually to the members of the corporation. He was granted a further increase in 1790, and the five entertainments were to be given on prescribed dates or otherwise 'the remainder of the allowance to be withheld and applied as the corporation saw fit'. Such outgoings on unessential items indicate that the town's economy had greatly improved and had entered an era of prosperity.

(By 1891 the mayoral allowance had been increased to £250, and in 1964 to £500; in 1970 it was £1,000. In 2005 his stipend stood at €16,690).

THE MILITARY: It was inevitable that those who were being denied a share in the increased prosperity would be resentful. This in turn generated sparks of violence and would one day explode into open rebellion. To combat such an eventuality, barracks were set up throughout the country – 150 in all. Towns vied with one another to have a garrison stationed in their area in the knowledge that its presence would provide a fillip to the local economy. A spin-off for army personnel was an improvement in the otherwise dull social life, the officers courting the daughters of the local gentry. The rank and file found entertainment among the lower classes 'although in some places it was felt they had worsened social and economic tensions by fathering bastards, or abandoning wives and children when they were posted away from Ireland'.

Drogheda was an obvious candidate for a barracks. Millmount was handed over to the Crown for this purpose, and arrangements were made for the installation of a garrison. The provision merchants and other suppliers of the town welcomed this move because it helped to fill their coffers. (The added cash flow in Sligo, smaller than Drogheda, was to the tune of £7,000 p.a. – a considerable sum at that time). The Ascendancy welcomed it to a greater degree because it gave them a sense of security. The shadow of Millmount and the military presence would henceforth dominate Drogheda and influence the lives of its people for many generations. Today it is Drogheda's most distinguishing feature, and it houses various facets that are of great interest to the dilettante, but in former times it was for the man in the street the stern symbol of repression.

Indeed, the military played an important part in the lives of the townspeople in a variety of ways throughout the centuries. Not only was Drogheda a garrison town, it also supplied the ranks of the British Army with generations of soldiers for service throughout the Empire. We will follow the history of the local regiment – that one which bore the name 'Drogheda' (and later 'Louth') in its title, and the following pages will portray its performance at home and abroad, and will also give an account of the overall military presence in Drogheda.

The normal policy of the Government in military matters was that Irishmen should not serve within Ireland, and thus it was mainly British soldiers who occupied Millmount Barracks. This was often the cause of misunderstandings and friction when, for example, the locals showed reluctance to join in celebrating the birthdays of Hanoverian kings, as were the first four Georges. Others grumbled at having to pay for an army of occupation whose function it was to keep them in debased circumstances. Whenever a British regiment could not be found for service in Drogheda, it was replaced by an Irish regiment but, as we shall see, they too were no angels and were well capable of raising dust.

Needless to say, it was not from a sense of loyalty to the Crown that these men shouldered a gun and marched away to help England establish her Empire. On the contrary, most of those who enlisted were driven by dire, naked, economic necessity. The prospect for most of them of ever rising above subsistence level at home was remote. In the late 1700s, for example, almost 60% of the population of Ireland existed on £5 (€6.35) *per annum* or less. They lived from hand to mouth, and the attraction of enlistment was that they were assured of an army ration. It was meagre, but it was regular.

The Maiden Tower and the Lady's Finger
from an old etching.

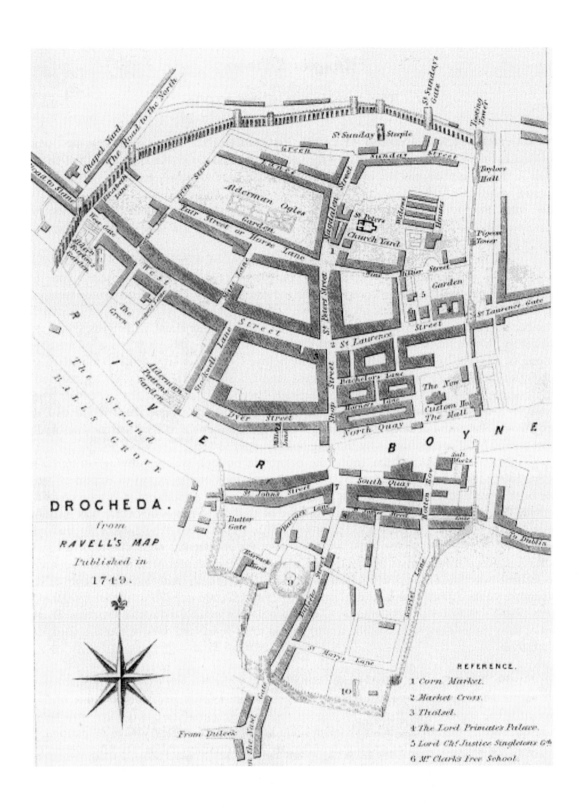

Ravell's Map of Drogheda:
*Notice that Bolton St. has been misnamed 'Irish St.' Irish St. is now called
the Green Lanes. Alderman Ogle's garden encompasses a very substantial
and valuable area – he was a member of the Assembly for many years.*

Chapter Sixteen

The Economy in the 1700s

INFRASTRUCTURE, INDUSTRY AND PROSPERITY: The 1700s saw no major political upheavals until the very end of the century. The Battle of the Boyne had put an end to all further resistance, and the exhausted country had time to slowly recover. This created a vacuum, a lull in which the two main elements of society learned to adapt to their respective new roles that followed the plantations, those of masters and those of servants; the dispossessed knuckled down to menial tasks such as working the land while the overlords enjoyed the fruits thereof.

An English writer divided the social hierarchy of England into four categories, namely: (1) gentlemen, (2) citizens or burgesses, (3) minor freeholders and (4) artificers/labourers. This was in contrast to Ireland where (1) the landed gentry ruled supreme, followed by (2) artisans who had taken the Oath of Allegiance. As we have seen, to become a member of a guild or fraternity of artisans such as bakers, shoemakers, carpenters, etc. it was obligatory to take this oath – it precluded Catholics from rising above the rank of unskilled labourers. (3) The manual labourers and unemployed – they were securely rooted at the bottom of the pile and were by far the biggest segment. (4) An underclass of vagrants and a shiftless mass of paupers was the inevitable result. There was a scramble for any casual work, however demeaning, that was likely to earn a small coin. We have seen above that the Drogheda Corporation deemed it necessary to regulate the number of coal porters – surely the most menial of all occupations – by limiting their number to 180.

Towards the end of the 1600s the economic outlook was improving owing to an easing in the restrictive impositions on trading. Restrictions on the export to Britain of cattle had been lifted to the benefit of Meath farmers, and the rising population in Britain created a demand for most agricultural produce. From the beginning of the 1700s there was no more laying waste of crops and livestock. Exports to English ports were extending, the main items being wool, linen, yarn, wheat, oats, rye and cattle; the continental ports that received these exports included Rotterdam, Cadiz and the Canaries. As the century progressed the economy in Ireland was steadily growing healthier. Both agricultural and industrial output had expanded. Grain exports had increased nationally from £72,000 in 1778 to almost £300,000 in 1798. Slane's flour mill, completed in 1776 was Ireland's largest industrial structure. By the end of the century Drogheda was the fourth largest town in Ireland, behind Dublin, Cork and Waterford.

In 1731 the Dublin Society, later known as the Royal Dublin Society (RDS), was established. (Its initial headquarters were at Leinster House, and in 1924 it became the home of Dáil Éireann). The society was formed 'for the advancement of agriculture and other branches of industry, and for the advancement of science and art'. The landed gentry were its patrons. At that time Ireland was still floundering in antiquated agricultural methods. Farming techniques throughout Europe had greatly improved over the centuries, but Ireland had lagged behind. The result was that yields from corn compared badly with those on mainland Europe, and selective breeding of livestock was not being applied. Cattle weighed 4 to 8 cwt. (200 kg. to 400 kg.) compared with 10 to 15 cwt. (500 kg. to 760 kg.) on the Continent.[7] The proximity of the Louth/Meath landowners to the new source of knowledge that emanated from the RDS created the necessary zest among them, and returns from farmland began to improve.

Flax in particular proved to be a worthy breadwinner and continued to be the main source of Drogheda's rising prosperity. On the River Nanny alone, 17 mills (some producing flour, the rest processing flax) were constructed between Duleek and Laytown. By the end of the century Drogheda had made the linen industry a speciality. In 1795 the Linen Board distributed 37,135 spinning wheels to cottiers in Co. Louth[8]. The evidence still stood in the form of the tall chimney stacks that punctured the town's skyline – they remained in place until the 1950s – as relics of a former chapter in the town's industrial economy. In 1720 Irish exports of linen were 2,000,000 yards and by 1790 the figure had rocketed to 37,000,000 yards, accounting for over 50% of all exports. The farming community benefited from growing the flax while the cottage industries were busy spinning and weaving. The treasurer of the merchants and dealers in the Linen Hall was Jonas Scholes – the lane between Narrow West St. and Fair St. still bears his name.

The Bridge: The municipal buildings in the town were in a poor state entering into the 1700s, and early into the century (1715) the Corporation was faced with the challenging prospect of replacing the only bridge – it was a wooden structure and had fallen into a state of disrepair. The pedestals on which it rested were of stone, but the spans were of timber, and these had greatly deteriorated, and it was agreed that the new bridge would be of stone throughout. It is not certain whether the new bridge was erected in the same precise location as that which then existed. Lack of Corporation funds was a prime consideration in tackling this costly project, and it was the subject of debate by the Assembly for the next seven years.

Another consideration was the inconvenience to traffic during the construction work, especially as there was no other bridge spanning the river before reaching Slane. The city fathers were well aware that the town's shop-keepers and the farming community – like their successors today – would be up in arms if the work were to impinge with their day-to-day business. They therefore:

> 'ordered that the Persons that are appointed to treate about building a stone Bridge take care to keep ye present Bridge up, and that it be speedily repaired, if it wants any, and to be done at the Corporation charge[9]'.

This matter was finally resolved with the construction, as a temporary measure, of 'a Float in the convenientest part of the River for the passage of all Travellers through the Town' and thus the populace were able to continue their daily routine without being seriously discommoded. Work on the project finally commenced in September 1720, and the Corporation was satisfied that

> 'the best men they can work with ... to build a stone Bridge over the River Boyne within the Town, and County, and to that end and others, have been engaged ... The building will put the Corporation to a very great expence, which the Corporation will not be able to bear, and defray, without the very greatest frugality and best management of their revenues... '

The municipal purse-strings had to be tightly guarded; this entailed a retrenchment of all other civic expenditure, and it was agreed to pay 'no money to any person on any account whatsoever' other than in the direst circumstances. A grant was applied for, and to help finance this costly project a toll was imposed on all horses, cattle, cows and carriages using the bridge.

The contractor was Stephen Price, but a difficulty arose when he was due to be paid a moiety of £504.6.8, 'all of which the Corporation hath not at present in cash' to discharge the debt. One of the town's wealthiest men, Alderman Edward Singleton came to the rescue by arranging to advance the money himself, and the Corporation later recompensed him.

The following year they sat down again to 'consider ways and means to raise the sum of £1,000 towards the finishing of the Bridge'. They were obliged to cut back on the overall contract price (which was in the region of £3,000) by omitting some of the elaboration that had formed part of the original plans, and it was agreed 'to build the Battlements of the said Bridge without any niches'. The cut stones came from Ringall's Quarry (location unidentified), but a difficulty was encountered when 'Martha Chesshire, setting forth that she is of great loss by suffering the Corporation to dig stones for the Bridge out of Ringall's Quarry'. A payment of £7 as compensation seems to have kept her happy.

A Christian church had in earlier times occupied the site (presently occupied by Wogan's) at the northwest corner of the bridge. This church had been in a neglected state since the Reformation, and it was deemed to interfere with the construction of the new bridge. 'The East Gable End of St. Saviour's Church is in a ruinous condition and in great danger of falling to the great danger of the neighbours thereunto adjoining. It is therefore ordered that Mr. Mayor employ workmen to pull down as much of the said Gable end as shall be thought convenient'.

The bridge – it was comprised of three arches – finally became a reality in 1722. It is unclear when the name 'St. Mary's Bridge' was first applied to it. It served Drogheda for the next 150 years, straddling the river to provide the crucial linkage between the two sections of the town, and also forming part of the vital conduit that connects Dublin with Ulster. It was replaced in 1868 by another stone bridge that remained in place until 1976.

Where now are the fine, hand-dressed stones that had been wrested from the quarry, meticulously chiselled into the desired shape and then hauled into place to form the 1868 bridge? When London Bridge was being replaced, the old stonework was carefully marked and numbered piece by piece, and then transported across the Atlantic where it was reconstructed in, above all places, the Arizona Desert. Does it serve any purpose there? Yes. It is a focal point, an object of admiration and it has been preserved for posterity's edification. By contrast, a local businessman who values Drogheda's past, attempted to rescue the stonework when the old 1868 bridge was being replaced, but had his request turned down by the authorities, only to find that it was dumped in the slob-lands along the Boyne estuary. (A few inscribed stones have been rescued).

The Jail: At this period the facilities for locking up wrong-doers were inadequate, and notwithstanding the shortage of money at the time, the Corporation was forced to 'consider of a convenient place for a Gaole for criminalls'. A plan was put before them on 29th March 1739 and the site chosen was in James St. where St. Mary's Church now stands. Pity its inmates – its cells were underground and it was badly run. Moneys were raised for this and other such projects by leasing Corporation properties. That jail served until 1818 when portion of a field at Scarlet St. was acquired from Miss Barlow and a new jail was built. Apparently, there was another lock-up which was still in use as late as 1814, for the Mayor made a direction 'to improve the place of confinement for people taken up at Night commonly called the Black Hole'[10].

The new jail came in for severe criticism and, like its predecessor, it was badly run, with insufficient bedding and its inmates often left naked. Inadequate as the food ration was, it was marginally better than in the Workhouse during the Great Famine, and famished people often committed petty crimes deliberately to be given a jail sentence. The building was subsequently used as a bus depot and garage for the GNR and then CIE; currently it is a hardware store. Today, Drogheda has no jail, from which it should not be inferred that all its inhabitants are law-abiding.

Debtors who were unable to settle their accounts were treated very harshly. Thomas Wright, who travelled throughout County Louth in 1748 making sketches of ancient buildings, encountered such a case at Ardee Castle/Jail: 'Here we found a poor old grey headed Man, imprisoned for a debt of six English shillings [€0.38], whom we released... There are many such objects of Charity to be found in the Irish Prisons which would require but a small sum of Money to set them at Liberty'.[11]

The Mayoralty House: With the criminals thus taken care of, the Assembly then focused its attention on a new Mayoralty House. 'The Plan of the Offices and the remainder of the works necessary to complete the Mayoralty House being layd before the Assembly, the same are approved of, and it is order'd that the building thereof be proceeded upon immediately'. This was in 1757. The lease for the site was signed on 8th April 1765 and the building was completed in 1768. When the work was nearing completion, a committee was formed 'to employ proper workmen and cause the Mayoralty House of this Corporation to be fitted up with a fit and proper and decent manner for the reception of the Chief Magistrate and this

Corporation at their quarterly entertainments and for other purposes of the Corporation'. The property was to have the additional function of 'a Court House for Assembly Sessions'. These considerations are compelling evidence of the town's improving prosperity.

Over the many decades that followed, the Mayoralty House has been used as a reception hall to entertain important dignities, for formal dances and balls, a commercial club, a reading room, and a venue for trade exhibitions, etc. During World War II it was used as a barracks by the Irish Army, with a sentry on duty day and night. The building at that time was surrounded by a wall of sandbags, about 2m. in height. Today it is a retail shop for musical instruments, records, etc. At the time of writing the building is due to revert to the Borough Council.

The Mall:
- *Facing the camera is the Mayoralty House, now a retail shop.*
- *At right-angles is the Custom House; it was destroyed in a fire during the 1950s, and the site is now occupied by the Labour Exchange.*
- *Adjoining it was the Masonic Hall, assembly point of the Masonic Lodge, and now demolished.*
- *The splendid building on the right was the home of the Hardman family, three generations of whom were Mayors of Drogheda. Subsequently it was the Provincial Bank, and is now a retail shop.*
- *The Whitworth Monument was sponsored by the people of Drogheda to commemorate a most generous benefactor.*
- *Notice the gas standard lamp in the middle of the square.*

The Custom House: It was built on the Mall at the junction with Mayoralty St. c.1754. Following a fire in the 1950s which gutted the building, it stood derelict for some years. Instead of retaining the façade, it was demolished, the wreckers displaying a Philistine disregard for its fine cut stonework. The Labour Exchange now occupies the site.

THOLSEL

The Tholsel: Discussions on replacing the Tholsel began in 1757. 'The [existing] Tholsel being at present in a very ruinous state' in 1763, the Corporation gave instructions that it be pulled down and a new one erected in its place. In 1758 the Assembly directed 'the auditors and viewers to inspect into the building of the New Tholsel now carrying on by Mr. Darley, and that they take care the same be properly and well executed. And they or any other Gentlemen of the Corporation are requested to report to Mr. Mayor and the Assembly anything that they shall find improper or wrong".

It is evident that the Assembly members were a responsible grouping, for they left nothing to chance, and the result of their supervisory role is still in evidence today in a building that has stood the test of time at Drogheda's main intersection. The contractor George Darley had been given an initial deposit and this was followed by a subsequent instalment of £350. Not having further funds to pay the contractor, the Corporation entered into a bond by way of debentures with one of the wealthy Assembly members (Mr. Chesshire) for £400 'at £5 *per cent per annum*' and a further advance of £350 being made under a similar arrangement with Mr. Barlow in 1767.

In October 1770 Mr. Darley was paid the final payment of £305.8.4½ 'being the balance due for the extraordinary work done by him at the Tholsel'. One final piece of work required to be done: 'it was ordered that Mr. Mayor and Sheriffs be and they are hereby authorised and required to bespeak a new clock on the Steeple of the Tholsel of the Corporation'.[12]

The building remained the seat of municipal administration for 120 years until a Courthouse was built in Fair Street in 1890. The Corporation consequently leased the proud Tholsel into private hands at £100 p.a., a move that raised quite a hullabaloo (as we shall see) among concerned townspeople.

The Church: St. Peter's Church of Ireland building stands on a site which has been a centre of worship since the founding of the town itself – or perhaps earlier. The site was given by Hugh de Lacy before 1186 to the Augustinian canons of Llanthony. Even before that, there may have been an earlier Christian church there, since traces of old tiles found in the churchyard are similar to those found at Mellifont. Some of Drogheda's most influential Ascendancy families, whose names recur in these pages, lie buried here, notably the Moores, Singletons, Balls, Leighs and Ogles.

On 27th January 1548 the church tower, which was described in the church register as 'the highest in the world', was blown down in a storm. The replacement was of wood and it is within this wooden steeple that some citizens of Drogheda sought refuge in vain before it was torched on Cromwell's order in 1649.[13] Cromwell did not demolish the steeple completely, for the Assembly reported eleven years later that 'one part of St. Peter's steeple is in a tottering and falling condition which, if not speedily looked after, may fall and thereby destroy and kill many of the inhabitants' and that it should be pulled down.

A hundred years later (1753) a new church was built, designed by Hugh Darley. The Corporation ' ... Order'd that the Treasurer be and is hereby Impowered to pay the further sum of Two Hundred Pounds Sterling towards finishing the Steeple of Saint Peter's Church and clearing the churchyard, and that he be allowed the same on passing his accounts'.

A new organ had been requisitioned from London, but before it reached the safety of the Boyne, disaster struck. Instructions were given by the Corporation to ' ... pay for the salvage, freight, package, repairing and putting up the Organ lately purchased by the Gentn.of this Corporation for Saint Peter's Church which cost £300 in London, the ship whereby part of the said Organ was being wrecked at Skerries in the late storm, and same to be allowed in his accounts'.

Twenty-five years later there was another storm – this time a financial one – about 'a Ring of Bells' for the church. These had been purchased from John Rudhall of Gloucester to whom £300 had been remitted in 1793, and a sum of £100 was still outstanding in 1796. The Corporation settled the matter by agreeing to remit this outstanding balance 'together with £17.19.3 interest and costs'.

St. Mary's C of I was built at the top of Mary St. in 1807 at the site of the old church demolished in Cromwell's bombardment. It was deconsecrated at the end of the 1900s. This was also the site of a 13th Century Carmelite priory. A portion of the original town wall still exists at this point.

The Cornmarket: In 1785 all seaports were required by Act of Parliament to establish 'sufficient place for holding the market of corn therein'. The Corporation complied in 1796 by erecting a single storey building in neo-classic style in Fair St. to the design of Francis Johnson. The Courthouse was built in 1888/90, having moved from the Tholsel; the cornmarket building was converted into Corporation offices.

Shipping: Dublin port was notoriously unsafe during this era. The Liffey mouth was undeveloped, being still very wide and shallow – the estuary stretched southwards as far as today's Merrion Square. It consisted of a maze of narrow, muddy channels, and navigators found them very hazardous. Vessels for Dublin preferred to dock at Dalkey or Howth, but this entailed the expense of carting the cargoes into the city. A better alternative was Drogheda, which benefited at Dublin's expense. Forty vessels belonged to Drogheda merchants, making the port a hive of activity; they were trading with ports as far distant as the Black Sea, the Baltic, Nova Scotia and the West Indies as well as to Britain.

Non-native seamen were induced to enrol in the local guild, provided, of course, they took the Oath of Allegiance. The sailing ships were berthed on both sides of the river, and extended up to the bridge at Shop St. The cargoes of coal were shovelled into sacks by the stevedores and then carried on the backs of dockers to the coal yards on the North Quay and the South Quay – this provided back-breaking employment for the labouring classes. Maize was similarly unloaded at the mills on Merchant's Quay. Grain became a major export, especially to feed the British Army during the constant wars on the Continent.

A minor English fishing village and port was coming into prominence at this time and was beginning to outstrip Chester, especially with shipping from Drogheda and other east coast ports. It would later emerge to become one of the greatest ports in the world – Liverpool. Six Drogheda merchants were shareholders in Liverpool's fleet towards the end of the 1700s.

Imports on the Boyne included such luxury items as tea and sugar, but the most important traffic by far was in coal. Drogheda merchants then transported it by the new Boyne Navigation Canal for distribution in Navan and throughout Co. Meath

Streets and Toll Roads: The infrastructure of the town continued to develop in line with its economic growth. A visitor in 1752 described Drogheda as 'a well built town, active in trade, the Boyne bringing ships to it. It was a market day, and I found the quantity of corn, etc. and the number of people assembled very great; few country markets in England were more thronged'.

The opportunity was availed of to widen Irish Street in 1796 by utilising a plot of ground 'on the west side of Magdalene Street and north of Irish Street; this enabled the street to be widened by 50 feet. (The name '*Irish* St.' is a reminder that Drogheda had been established as a Norman or English town).

West of the Hay Market was a green bank sloping down to the river-shore from the rear of the shops in West Street's south side. Until this time it comprised the private gardens belonging to the shopkeepers, but were now acquired by the Corporation for the purpose of constructing 'a new quay at the foot of Stockwell Lane where the stalls of the meat market are' to the junction with Linenhall Street (now Dominic Street). The unimaginative name given to this new quay was 'New Quay', but the signal victory at Waterloo later prompted the change to 'Wellington Quay'.

Sunday's Gate
It was still extant, as were the walls , until the late 1700s.

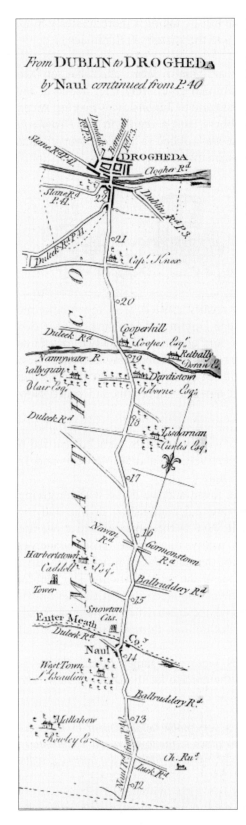

From DUBLIN to DROGHEDA
by Naul *continued from P. 40*

Taylor and Skinner Map
*of the Dublin/Drogheda road via the
Naul. Roads generally passed close
to the residences of
the landed gentry.*

Roads leading from Drogheda to outlying districts were little more than natural tracks with stones scattered over the surface. The regulation whereby locals were obliged to upkeep the surface through a 'six day labour' system was well nigh unworkable. Arterial roadways, if they could be called that, were of a meandering nature, and tended to be aligned so as to pass the doors of the 'big houses'. The surfaces were rutted and muddy in winter, and dusty in summer.

A Jacobite officer making his way from Dublin to take part in the Battle of the Boyne described conditions: '... the road excessive dusty, to that degree that we were also stifled and blinded, and so covered with dust that we scarce knew ourselves'. The weather was very hot, and he looked forward *en route* to slaking his thirst with Lord Gormanston. A disappointment awaited him there, for he described his experience: it was 'at best only a tolerable village. ... Here we made a halt for about 2 hours, but found no refreshment [at Lord Gormanston's], but what we brought with us, unless the coole air and grass. ... All the country between this citie and Dublin is very pleasant, and a good soile, having great store of corn some good pasture, the road in summer is very good, but in winter extreme deep unless helped by an old broken causeway full of holes'.[14]

His route to Drogheda would have taken him via Swords, Ballough, Balrothery, the Hill of Clonard and Gormanston. Here we should note that Balbriggan formed no part of the itinerary – it traversed instead through Man-o'-War which is 3 miles inland from Balbriggan. That was the route adapted in 1732 to form the Dublin/Drogheda/Dunleer toll-road or turnpike. Balbriggan at that time was an insignificant seaside fishing village and was considered unworthy of being incorporated into the toll scheme. With the establishing of its textile industry in 1780, the town soon grew in importance, and the toll-road was realigned 40 years later to pass through it.

The toll-road was constructed in compliance with an Act of Parliament, and it ran from Dublin via Man-o'-War to Drogheda, and then onwards to Dunleer. The extension to Dunleer was probably appended by virtue of the influence of the Foster family who lived at Dunleer – we shall hear more about that family anon. The stagecoach ran from Dublin on Tuesdays, Thursdays and Saturdays from the 'York Minster' in Capel Street, using 'a good set of horses' and stopping for sustenance and a fresh team of horses at the Man-o'-War hostelry. This was a very famous hostelry and was used by such personages at Wolfe Tone who had legal business to attend to in Drogheda. However, it was located on a height, and

147

the road's alignment was later changed to circumvent the hill by taking a more westerly loop. The by-pass inevitably brought an end to business there, and the hostelry fell into decay.

Toll Gates were placed at Santry, Lissenhall and at Man-o'-War, and also on the Drogheda/Dunleer sector at Killineer and Dunleer. Additional gates were later added at the southern approach to Drogheda (probably as Colpe Cross) and at Julianstown, making seven toll gates in all. They were sometimes targeted by robbers, and a report in the *Drogheda News-Letter* tells us that the Julianstown Turnpike House was robbed in 1801 by four villains who attacked the keeper and his wife and then made off with everything of worth.

There was a scale of toll charges, the highest rate being for coaches drawn by six horses – these attracted a charge of 2s.8½d. These original charges were later increased, creating a tendency to circumvent the tolls by taking an alternative route, just like they do today. Nothing changes!

There were two alternative routes used by Dublin/Drogheda traffic, one via Ashbourne and the other via the Naul. An atmosphere of commercial rivalry existed, with the Ashbourne route being misrepresented as being only 22 miles between Dublin and Drogheda. These two roads converged outside the town wall at Duleek Street, and entrance to the town may have been through Barrack Lane, a hazardous undertaking for all horse-drawn traffic. The difficulty was partially alleviated by the corkscrew alignment of that roadway as it passes the steep incline of Millmount. (Today's Mary St. was laid down in the 1840s and called New St.)

Bianconi, 'the man who put Ireland on wheels' did not operate a service to Drogheda, but a Dublin/Drogheda service was operated by other private individuals. Coaches carried 6 passengers inside and 6 more outside, the fare being respectively 7/6 and 5/- (48 cents and 32 cents). The service ran several times per week and took 3 hours.

We encounter no difficulty today in entering the town, and we do so without giving the matter a second thought. We must thank both the internal combustion engine and the labours of our forefathers for having made this possible. But in the times of which we are speaking, the mid 1700s, approaching the town was always an ordeal. From whatever direction one arrived, it was rendered difficult by virtue of the steep valley in which the town nestles, the approaches on the south side of the river being the more difficult. The Dublin Road did not exist. Curry's Hill and Pitcher Hill were much too steep to admit horse-drawn traffic. There was little choice; it seems that one entered the town from the Marsh Road, Barrack Lane or the more westerly Donore Road and Rathmullen through Butter Gate and John's Gate respectively.

The toll-road entered the town through James Gate and James Street. There is mention of 'a very noble improvement' (without stating the precise location) to a road in *'the traveller's guide through Ireland'* (published in 1794): -

> *'Entering Drogheda from the south side, there is a very noble improvement in the road carrying on and nearly finished; the steep bank going down to the town, which was formerly very dangerous and difficult, has been cut away in the highest point and the hollow ground filled up with it'.*[15]

The natural lie of the land presents a very steep bank running parallel with and south of the river, and extending all the way from the present Railway Station towards St. Mary's Bridge. (Indeed, it continues the full length of the Ramparts and beyond – a feature presented to us by the Ice Age, when the land was capped by a covering of ice 100 metres deep).

The route from Cromwell's Lane (and the existing entry to the railway station) to the town's entrance at James's Gate was 'very dangerous and difficult' for vehicular traffic by virtue of the south/north gradient of the terrain. It is reasonable to assume that the 'very noble improvement' was at this point, and entailed levelling the slope, giving a generous width to the thoroughfare and depositing the spoil in the direction of the Marsh Road. A steep embankment was thereby created, and this was kept in place by a buttressed wall rising from the Marsh Road. Hence today we have two parallel roadways running side by side, the Marsh Road and the Dublin Road, but one substantially higher than the other, and separated by the retaining wall.

The names of the trustees of the Turnpike Road reveal to us that almost all of its members were drawn from the landed class, many of whose names feature in these pages; they include: Aston, Bellew, Bellingham, Coddington, Fortesque, Montgomery, Ogle, Pepper and Somerville. The turnpike project had always been inadequately funded, and traffic was able to avoid paying a toll by using one of the alternative routes to Dublin. But what spelled *'finis'* for it was the advent of the railway; and in 1855, when the Boyne Viaduct was completed, the trust was wound up.

We still have a green, grassy slope today between the bus depot and the Bridge of Peace. Let us hope that it is too steep a site to attract the attention of developers for housing etc., and that the surrounding tree-scape will be allowed to remain as a refreshing bank of virgin greenery in the very heart of the town. A similar prospect existed on the Dublin Road until the late 1800s when part of the slope was removed to make way for the beige-bricked Convent of Mercy and the adjoining national school.

St. Johns Gate Drogheda

Likewise, in James St. it was necessary in preparing the site for St. Mary's RC Church to excavate the steep bank and remove considerable quantities of earth. This proved to be a difficult task by virtue of the bank being very steep and the soil being almost rock hard. A section of the face unexpectedly collapsed during the preparatory work, killing a workman. An inspection of the bank immediately to the rear of the church reveals that the natural ground level at that point is more or less in line with *the roof* of the church – this emphasises the steepness of the gradient. A convenient site was found nearby for the excavated spoil – it was deposited a few hundred metres eastwards to infill part of the Dale. Incidentally, on the opposite side of the Boyne an inspection of the rear of St. Peter's RC Church reveals a similar perpendicular bank, and this serves as another reminder of the valley in which the town was built.

Francis Johnson: The eminent architect (1760–1839) was born in Armagh and resided in county Louth. His creations include the GPO in O'Connell St., Dublin and (the now demolished) Nelson's Pillar. He left his mark on the Drogheda area, having designed Townley Hall, and Rokeby Hall in the 1790s, the latter being for Archbishop Robinson of Armagh – that residence cost a very respectable £30,000. Within the town itself his works include the former Siena Convent at the Cord Road and the current Borough Council offices in Fair St. The latter building was designed as the town's Corn Exchange, and the distinctive weathervane still proclaims that fact.

THE LINEN INDUSTRY: The suppression of the woollen industry, as we have seen, had a devastating effect on the Irish economy, and the effects were still being felt generations later. As a sop, Ireland was encouraged to produce linen, an industry in which England showed little interest, so this pursuit would cause no resultant harm to English merchants. Initially, weaving was a cottage industry, beginning long before the 1700s, with the weavers using hand looms within their own little homes. Drogheda was quick off the mark, and the town

149

soon worked its way to the forefront of the industry, providing a livelihood to almost 2,000 Drogheda workers.

GREEN HILLS MILL

WEST GATE FLAX MILL

These large linen mills provided employment to almost 2,000 workers when Drogheda was at the forefront of the Linen Industry.

Today they have been adapted to other purposes. The Marsh Mill (right) was subsequently used to produce edible oils and was demolished in 2006 to accommodate an extention of the Scotch Hall project.

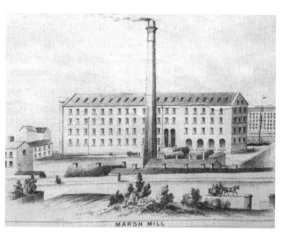

MARSH MILL

In that era of mass deprivation, occasioned by severe unemployment, the need to create an outlet for the labouring class cannot be over-emphasised. If 'King Cotton' dominated the economy in the southern states of America, then 'Lord Linen' was master in the humble homes of Drogheda. The flax was grown in farms as far away as Cavan, Monaghan and Armagh, and supplies of yarn were brought in from Navan, Longford, Roscommon and Belfast, as well as from England and Scotland. Thus, the benefits of this thriving industry extended to many distant communities, and was not confined to those directly engaged in factory work, but farmers, carriers and hand-loom weavers also benefited. Drogheda was thriving on flax and linen. By 1783 there were 7 manufacturers of bleached linen, one-third of the product being exported. Exports went to England, Hamburg and other parts of mainland Europe and the United States.

The marketplace for linen had outgrown its initial accommodation in Laurence Street by 1732 when the Corporation agreed that 'the chiefe dealers in the linnen manufacturing in the Town, for to remove the Linnen Cloath Market from Saint Lawrence St., where it is now kept, to some convenient place in West Street'. The volume of goods changing hands continued to expand, requiring a new, custom-built Linen Hall. It was constructed in 1774 in an area known as 'the Green', where it stood for 200 years. It is now the site of the Abbey car park.

By 1830 mechanical innovations and steam power had arrived on the scene. This encouraged the wealthy merchants and employers to extend their investments into more ambitious projects, namely the construction of large factories, and this changed the skyline of the town. Mammoth buildings rose up, dwarfing the humble cottages that fringed them, and tall chimneystacks pierced the sky. The Drogheda Flax Spinning Mill in Trinity St. employed up to 500 workers; further west along the same road Mell Flax Spinning Mill employed 180, and the Greenhills Cotton Mill employed about 180. South of the river 400 people worked in St. Mary's Flax Mill on the Marsh Road. Sadly, extraneous factors were later to appear, ruining the industry for Drogheda. The chimneystacks have since been pulled down, but the massive five-storey buildings still exist, even though they now serve totally different functions.

The Linen Board, which was instituted in 1711, had the function of promoting flax growing and linen manufacturing. It consisted of 72 members – 18 from each province, and most of them were leading landowners It provided aid in the form of subsidised flax seed for the farmers and spinning wheels for the spinners, and it also undertook the task of conducting inspections and enforcing strict quality standards. The industry was concentrated in Ulster and north Leinster, with Drogheda emerging as one of the main centres. Knowledge of flax growing, and of efficient techniques in spinning and weaving was disseminated by the Board. The linen trade thus influenced the lives of both the farming community and the town dwellers, and it offered better prospects and constant work where fitful employment, blind alley jobs and idleness had been the norm. All sectors of society benefited in consequence – land owners, small farmers, peasants, carriers, spinners, weavers, bleachers, traders and the community at large.

Chapter Seventeen

The Impending Storm

SECRET SOCIETIES: The potato, introduced by Sir Walter Raleigh to his Munster estates in the late 1500s, had by the 1700s become the people's staple diet – it was both bountiful and nutritious. The result was a population explosion, with the overall figure of 2½ million in 1767 rocketing to 4 million in 1781 and to 5 million by the end of the century. The result was a scramble for land, with the landlord sitting pretty at the top of the pile, and this inevitably sparked off agrarian violence. The rancour that ensued spawned a miscellany of secret societies throughout Ireland.

Most towns were adjoined by a 'commons', which from earliest times belonged to the common people and were used for grazing purposes and particularly for horses that had hauled cartloads of farm produce from outlying areas to the market, but now the landlords fenced them in for themselves. Not surprisingly, this was the cause of bitterness, and at night the fences were levelled by secret societies such as the Levellers and the Whiteboys. In 1762 a large force was sent against the latter under the Marquis of Drogheda. He was ruthless in this pursuit; he accused a parish priest of supporting their cause and had him hanged, adding to the peasants' anger. Agrarian unrest continued to escalate and in the Louth/Monaghan area it took on a sectarian mode. In County Louth and east Ulster those that were most active were the Defenders (Catholic) and the Peep o'Day Boys (Protestant, from which body the Orange Order was later to emerge). Atrocities were committed by both sides, and in one skirmish in Armagh the better armed Peep o' Day Boys killed 48 Defenders.

Uneasiness was growing within the ruling class in Drogheda, and on several occasions the Assembly voted sums to be given to the Volunteer Association for the purchase of gunpowder. On another occasion it ordered that 'the sum of £12.5.6 be expended ... for transmitting to Dublin and transporting from thence to America three convicts'. No doubt these men were subversives.

The following extract from a letter dated the 1st July 1788 sent to John Forbes, Member of Parliament for Drogheda, tells us that the Defenders were very active in the Drogheda area, and that the authorities were greatly concerned:

> ' ... You must know that the spirit of that party which are called the Defenders has made its appearance in this town and neighbourhood, so much so, as to create a very general alarm. This day week at a Pattern at Morningtown (sic) a party of upwards of a hundred who had been sworn passed over to Queensberry [Queensboro'] in boats and paraded there for a considerable time, and every night since, parties have been parading and swearing each other in the neighbourhood of this town. And they would certainly have assembled in great numbers at Oldbridge this day, and probably some mischief have been the consequence, but for the timely check given to it by the Speaker, who attacked a number of these insurgents near Ardee on Friday last with two Troops of Horse. A number were cut and wounded desperately, and about twenty taken prisoners – seven only remain in Dundalk gaol – and others were discharged on giving bail.

> 'It appears to me that almost every Roman Catholic in this town of any respectability are happy at this defeat, and the Titular Bishop and some of his clergy here have preached strongly against these riotous meetings – and in consequence have received severe threatenings from those disposed to riot. ... There was no Pattern at Oldbridge this morning, but they expect one this evening. If anything of Riot appears, the Speaker will visit them with his Troops – and the Troops in garrison here will be kept in readiness. I hope these Patterns will be suppressed by an act of Parliament ...

> '(Postscript) The Troops in garrison and the Speaker's Troop met at Oldbridge at half past five or six o'clock in the Louth Side – and the Troops crossed the river [Boyne], cut up the tents, charged the mob and totally dispersed them, without any offence on either side'.

The Volunteer Association: The rebellious undercurrent was ever present, with the underdogs seething with discontent. Notwithstanding their easy lifestyle, the Ascendancy were conscious of the prevailing unrest that surrounded them. The 1715 Militia Act had been passed in anticipation of violence. The county of Louth mustered one regiment of dragoons and a company of foot, and Drogheda as a separate governing unit had supplied two companies and one troop. Apart from dealing with internal unrest, the function of the militia was also to combat any foreign invasion – this real threat from Spain and latterly from France was constant.

The Drogheda Volunteer Association was formed in 1777 under the Militia Act, and Hugh Montgomery Lyons was appointed its lieutenant colonel; it consisted of merchants, landowners and the like. All were Protestants – Catholics, it will be remembered, were prohibited by law from bearing arms. At the same time the Act also made provision for Catholics and all others who refused the Oath of Abjuration to be *taxed double* for the upkeep of the militia, and it also legislated that their horses could be seized by a sheriff in an emergency and then sold to a Protestant militiaman for £5, whatever its value; concealment of a horse or arms incurred a £10 fine. To rub salt in, an extension of the Act forced Catholics to provide refreshments for the militia while they were engaged in training exercises.

At this period of Irish history many aspects of the Penal Laws were still in force; Catholics were still barred from joining the regular army. Enlistment would have served as an avenue of escape from the pervading poverty and hopelessness that was overwhelming the masses. The following notice left no doubt in the mind of anyone who contemplated enlisting:

> *"Any man ... where having produced a genuine Certificate of their being Protestants, and born of Protestant parents, signed by the Minister or Curate of the Parish, or a Justice of the Peace for the County from when they come, they will be immediately entertained and receive Subsistence etc. ... N.B. No man will be enlisted who does not produce a Certificate as above upon his offering to enlist'.[1]*

A Thawing of Attitudes: The thumbscrew on Catholics was slowly easing through the later decades of the 1700s, and in 1771 they were permitted to take on long lease 50 acres of bog for reclamation, provided it should not be nearer than a mile to any town or city. Further ameliorating legislation followed in 1778, 1782, 1792, culminating in the Catholic Relief Act (1793) whereby Catholics were finally granted the franchise. By virtue of these concessions Catholic merchants began to appear on the scene and were becoming successful as traders and shopkeepers and otherwise taking part in the commercial activities of Drogheda. In Dublin about one third of the wholesale merchants were now Catholic; they were also beginning to acquire farmland, and soon one-fifth of farmland was back in Catholic hands.

A cordial relationship grew up in Drogheda between the religious classes – at least among the merchants and the middle class. Some Catholics had risen to prominent positions as property holders and successful businessmen. The Collins family, for example, established a hardware business in Shop Street in 1775 that continued for over two hundred years. The Bird family conducted business in both West Street and Shop Street, and owned other property in Bachelor's Lane, North Quay and the Mall, as well as other premises in Dorset Street and Merchant's Quay in Dublin. The easing of restrictions on Catholics was noticeable, and markedly so when some selected Catholic citizens were surreptitiously admitted into the Volunteers, even though this was officially illegal. Drogheda was the first town in Ireland where a recorded instance of this break-through became apparent:

> *'Saturday last, [circa 1780] being the anniversary of the ever-memorable battle of the Boyne (the conqueror of which gave liberty both civil and religious to the protestants of this once mighty empire) was observed by the Volunteer corps of Duleek. Headed by Thomas Trotter, Esq., the Skreen Grenadiers and the Independents of this town assembled on the Mall and marched together to St. Peter's Church where a sermon was preached by the Rev. Joseph Fairtlough upon the occasion. From there they paraded on the Mall, and then marched to the Tholsel, with colours flying, the fife drums playing the agreeable tune of "King William over*

the Water" ... What gave general satisfaction was that the gentlemen Roman Catholics in the Drogheda Association wore the favour of the day in their hats. The horrid distinction that subsisted between protestants and catholics from which thousands have fell a sacrifice to bigotry in principles of religion is now strongly cemented in the general good'.[2]

This gives us a glimpse of the mindset of the town's inhabitants. The merchants included some 'gentlemen Roman Catholics', to quote the actual phrase used; they marched to St. Peter's C. of I. Church to hear a sermon delivered by the Rev. Mr. Fairtlough. They were throwing their weight behind the ruling class and were beginning to form part of a homogenous fraternity. The parade in question consisting of the combined Duleek/Skryne/Drogheda units held at the Mall indicates the close links that existed in the general area of Drogheda and County Meath, so here at last was a thawing of attitudes, a welcome embrace between the two religious factions – a reconciliation of hearts. But it was short-lived. The overall obduracy towards any form of latitude being granted towards Catholics soon manifested itself and a subsequent meeting called by the High Sheriff at Trim echoed the entrenched hostile mood. That meeting registered a protest at Catholics being permitted to carry arms while engaging in drilling exercises, and resolved:

'That it is improper for any protestant corps of Volunteer association of the county of Meath, to attend at any review of said county, or carry arms with those of the papish persuasion, at any such review, until such times as the laws are altered'.

A review of troops took place on Bellewstown Hill on the 9th. July 1781 under the command of Napper Tandy, whose home was on the actual Hill. The parade was a formidable show of strength, and indicated that the Ascendancy were in a state of readiness to suppress any rebellious action. There were 3,000 troops on parade, consisting of cavalry, infantry and artillery. The officers were the *creme de la creme* of the local gentry, and included Thomas Trotter (Duleek House), Graves Chaney (Plattin Hall), Lieut. Col. Hugh Montgomery Lyons and John Montgomery (Beaulieu House).

Even though Tandy was at the head of this force, he had at the same time been making strenuous efforts to eliminate corrupt practices at government level, and was endeavouring to reform parliament, but all his efforts were in vain. His activities should have provided a clue to those powerful landlords now under his command that he was sympathetic towards the United Irishmen. He would one day risk his life in gaining French help in the Rising of 1798, having set sail on board a French ship laden with armaments to liberate Ireland.

The same year the Drogheda Corporation ordered that 'the sum of twenty pounds be paid by the Treasurer of the Corporation to Col. Lyons to buy gunpowder for the use of the corps of the town, and that the same be allowed in the Treasurer's account'.

A riot occurred in Drogheda in 1780 resulting in the army firing on the crowd, leaving five of the townspeople lying dead at the Tholsel. Whatever the precise cause of the disturbance, it is an example, not only of the pervading unrest, but also of the heavy-handedness with which demonstrations were put down. No questions were asked. A further disturbance occurred in 1782 that prompted Dublin Castle to write to John Forbes, the MP for Drogheda: 'We have just received information of a very unpleasant riot at Drogheda last night and this morning. The Lord Lieutenant thinks you might be of great service by going down and endeavouring to appease them. A party of Dragoons is gone down ...'.

A few years later (1793) an advertisement was published in *The Drogheda Journal* offering rewards to persons supplying information on the Defenders – they were very active in the Down/Monaghan/Louth area. The following news item appeared in June of that year which tells of a local incident. Needless to say, that paper was supported by the landed class and used every opportunity to condemn the actions of subversives:

"Some infamous miscreants, yet unknown, set fire to a new house at Newgrange, County Meath, the property of Mr. Robert Berrill (commonly called the Knight of the Boyne) which

*was totally consumed. Mr. Berrill is in the 96th year of his age and has always supported an
irreproachable character.*[3]

It is evident from the many unpleasant incidents regularly occurring that the people
were not going to be appeased by the appearance of the mild-mannered John Forbes. What
they wanted was equality, starting with Catholic Emancipation, but King George III had no
intention of granting it. In such circumstances the alternatives facing the people were either to
yield to the rule of an iron fist or to engage in open insurrection. As it transpired, they were to
experience both.

The Lavabo at Mellifont

Chapter Eighteen

Drogheda in the Era of John Foster

Until the late 1700s the commerce of the town was in the hands of about half a dozen Protestant merchant princes, notably Edward Hardman and Henry Singleton, and the reader will recognise these two surnames in place-names in present day Drogheda – 'Hardmans Gardens' and 'Singleton Cottages'. Hardman was a general merchant and wine importer. By the granting of a number of alleviating measures, culminating in the Catholic Relief Act (1793), restrictions on the civic rights of the Catholic population were being gradually removed, and Catholic shopkeepers were extending their presence in the main streets. This created the phenomenon of a number of Catholics becoming prominent *property holders* in the town. This was an expressive break-through because the possession of property conferred voting rights.

One particular man was conspicuous throughout this era; he wielded a naked sword which he exercised very effectively on anyone who would deign to oppose him or stand in his way. He was John Foster and he was the champion of the Ascendancy, and they held him in the highest regard. His tenure in the world of politics, both local and national, spanned a lengthy sixty years, and crossed into the 1800s. For several decades both before and after the Act of Union he dominated the Irish political scene. When elevated to the position of Speaker of the Irish House of Commons he then reigned supreme.

He lived in Collon, and this prompted him to dabble in the politics of nearby Drogheda.

What focused his attention on Drogheda was that the town was an independent Borough – separate from County Louth – and the cherry on the cake was that it had been allotted, not one, but two parliamentary seats. He was already a sitting Member of Parliament for County Louth where he held the electorate in the palm of his hand, and he had the confidence and the experience to manipulate the politics of Drogheda with the single-minded objective of preserving the Protestant Ascendancy. To that end he was successful – that is, until 1826 when the voters of the Wee County finally 'kicked the traces' of landlord dominance and set the headlines for the other constituencies of Ireland to follow, thereby shaping the mould for a more just administration and a more contented people.

In discussing the main events that were taking place in that era, we must remind ourselves of the voting rights of the people. Nowadays people going to the polls at election time may take for granted their suffrage rights. In truth, these rights were hard won. The franchise was denied to Catholics until 1793. Even then, a man (and never a woman) had to be registered as a 'freeman' in a Corporate Borough such as Drogheda. This conferred on him the right to vote, but the shenanigans that the Drogheda Corporation employed in scrutinising each applicant ensured that Catholics were excluded. They knew that the most effective way of retaining the *status quo* was in exercising power, and they did so with a rod of iron. With power came wealth. The contrivances and manipulations which they devised became more barefaced in the early 1800s when the Catholic voters began to assert themselves.

For county boroughs (such as County Louth) another obstacle stood in the way of a just society – entitlement to vote applied only to 'forty shilling freeholders'. But these tenants were strictly under the thumb of the landlords who instructed them as to which candidate to vote for. The tenants always complied, as otherwise they were liable to find themselves with their families on the side of the road. All the candidates going forward for election, of course, were Protestants because a Catholic could not sit in Parliament.

Was this state of affairs to continue *ad infinitum*? The Ascendancy had managed to survive the shift in power that occurred in other lands occasioned by the American War of Independence and the French Revolution. In Ireland nothing had changed. Even Thomas Paine's *'Rights of Man'* (1791) had failed to dislodge them. His withering commentary on England's political system he described as 'ridiculous and insolent', pouring contempt on the hereditary powers of monarchs and the aristocracy – he called this 'the vanity and presumption of governing beyond the grave', where the rights of the *living* often counted for nothing, but the wealth of the few was given full protection.[1] It was patently unjust, and someone was needed with the charisma and leadership to make changes and to carry aloft the banner of Catholic Emancipation.

The terms 'freeman' and 'freeholder' are sometimes the cause of confusion to a reader, especially since both terms involve voting rights. A **freeman** was a citizen of a town who was given the franchise by its Borough Council and was permitted to practice his trade and was privileged with several other rights. A **freeholder,** on the other hand, was person who owned land. After 1793 those tenants who held a lease for life or who owned land worth forty shillings (£2 or €2.54) yearly were enfranchised. The numbers of such tenancies rapidly increased after 1793, since landlords sought to increase the electorate on their estates, thereby giving them greater electoral muscle. When voting, the tenants unquestioningly followed the instructions of their landlord. A third similar term is **'freedom'**, as in 'the Freedom of Drogheda'. This is an honour bestowed by the Corporation on an individual (often of great renown) who had performed some beneficial works or noteworthy deeds, such as Henry Grattan, Charles Stewart Parnell, Mother Mary Martin and Kenneth Whitaker, all of whom were conferred with the Freedom of Drogheda.

Prior to the Catholic Relief Act (1793), the Protestant businessmen of the town enjoyed an unfair advantage over their Catholic equivalents in matters of trade and commerce. Apart altogether from the right to vote, discrimination played a vital part in commercial matters. Freemen of Drogheda were exempt from paying tolls, and without exception these freemen were Protestants. Despite the new Act, which was egalitarian in its objective, the members of the Corporation conspired among themselves to continue denying voting rights to whomsoever they considered to be undesirable.

As a self-appointed committee in an exclusive 'club' the members of the Corporation (the 'Assembly') were able to huggermugger transactions among themselves in conclave. This brings into question the probity of their actions, as in the case of corporation property that was sometimes leased out among their members at suspiciously favourable terms such as peppercorn rents or annual rentals of one shilling. Likewise, they engaged in corrupt practices such as which we nowadays call 'jobs for the boys'. Where several candidates (of their own religious persuasion) vied for a particular office, the matter was often resolved by the questionable arrangement of the successful person handing over a stated part of his salary to the unsuccessful one – they divided the spoils.

Abuses and corruption were commonplace, and these wrongs were not restricted to Drogheda. Other administrative centres employed practices that were equally corrupt. An editorial in the *Waterford Chronicle* condemned

> *'every corporation in this country as a charnel house of civil corruption ... a complete nuisance to the community, and an introductory reservoir for the unprincipled abettors of public plunder, and unblushing spoliation' and later it made reference to the 'many crying abuses existing in this body', totally disregarding public opinion.*[2]

This criticism may seem very harsh, but it was well earned, and the abuses continued without interruption. It can be seen that the Assembly held unrestricted control in the running of the Borough of Drogheda, and there was nobody capable of challenging their decisions or of exposing their self-seeking machinations. No redress was forthcoming from the local press – the local newspaper at that time was the *Drogheda Conservative Journal,* and it unquestioningly supported the ruling class. Only the ruling class supported the newspaper with advertisements, only they could read and only they could afford the costly sum of 5d. per copy – this represented about half a day's wages to the labouring class, almost all of whom were illiterate .

The preponderance of Catholics to Protestants in Drogheda was in the ratio of about eight or nine to one, and

> *'the corporation's main preoccupation seems to have been to increase the Protestant freemen as a counterpoise to the Catholic freeholders. By about 1796, it appears that nearly every resident Protestant was a freeman, and that there were many non-resident Protestant freemen besides'.[3]*

With more and more Catholics of the town joining the merchant class and acquiring capital, they became increasingly vociferous, but the corporation still refused to budge. It was they who held the reins of power, and they were determined not to let go.

This whole matter came to a head when a test case was put forward in the person of Sir Edward Bellew of Barmeath Castle, Grangebellew. That family belonged to 'the landed gentry', and they were one of the few who adhered to the Catholic religion. Sir Edward was selected for admission as a freeman because he was a figure of unquestionable character and of moderate political views. True to form, his application was refused. The Catholics of Drogheda then presented a petition to Parliament at this flagrant denial of common justice, and it was supported by no less a person than Lord John Russell who was an advocate of Catholic Emancipation and who later became Prime Minister.

JOHN FOSTER (1740-1828) A Pen-picture:

John *WHO?* ... who does he play for? The name John Foster is rarely mentioned today, but in his time he was a man of very great influence, a colossus striding across the centre stage in Irish political affairs for over 60 years. He lived in Collon. His antecedents were not members of the Aristocracy, having come to Ireland and settling in Dunleer as 'mowers of hay'. In later times they acquired considerable lands from the Earls of Drogheda, the Moore family.

The Moores, as we have seen above, had been given the vast lands of the Cistercians of Mellifont – about 50,000 acres – at the time of the Reformation, but accumulating debts had forced them to sell, first an estate worth £5,000 *per annum* at Ardee, and by the early 1700s the head of the Moore family, Lord Drogheda, had to sell the last portion to clear his debts. This land, amounting to about 6,500 acres, was at Collon and Grangegeeth, and it was the family of the Fosters who bought it. Were they over-extending their financial capabilities in purchasing so much land? John Foster then spent a truly enormous £50,000 in improving the estate. He was either ill-advised or over-

The Right Honourable
JOHN FOSTER,
(Speaker of the House of Commons)
Dedicated to the Glorious 111. Irish Commoners who on the 26th of Jan.y 1799 saved the Legislative Independence of their COUNTRY.

ambitious to have committed so much capital in that way, for in later times he was constantly haunted by mounting debts.

At least the family did not fall into the trap of building an ostentatious mansion. The building which stands today in the main street of Collon was erected in the early 1740s by John Foster's father and is, by the standards of the times, quite modest and unpretentious. No bacchanalian parties or balls were held there – even the occasional visitor had to share a bedroom with a member of the family. This reflects the Foster penchant for pragmatism. Although John Foster rose to great heights in the world of politics, he always adopted the role of an ordinary country squire rather than that of an aristocrat. When attending the Dublin Parliament he lived in a property in Molesworth St., now Buswell's Hotel.

His father had been the Member of Parliament for the Borough of Dunleer. He had gone to great lengths in draining his extensive lands and in rendering them more productive. John Foster, who was educated at the Drogheda Grammar School, had an early introduction to politics, for he succeeded to his father's seat in 1761 when he was merely 21, and he later became an MP for Louth. However, he was a man of great administrative ability and was held in the highest esteem, both at local level and in the Houses of Commons – at Westminster as well as Dublin.

Not only was he an adroit politician, he was also an expert in socio/economic affairs. He was partly responsible for founding both the Botanic Gardens and the Bank of Ireland. The short *cul de sac* next to the existing headquarters of the latter institution was named Foster Place in his honour. He climbed to the highest political offices in the land; in 1784/85 he was Chancellor of the Exchequer and finally he became Speaker of the House in 1785, which was the most prestigious office in the land after that of Lord Lieutenant, and he retained that position until 1800 when the Irish Parliament ceased to exist.

He had the good sense to oppose the concept of union with England, and fought against the Act of Union legislation with the utmost intensity. The Act was rail-roaded through parliament, as we shall see, by employing the most despicable underhand methods, and he was not slow to voice criticism, saying that it was *'carried by the most improper means'*. When he pointed an accusing finger at one of the lords who had succumbed to bribery, he was threatened with legal action, but he maintained his stance and the named lord finally backed down. His attitude had earned him considerable respect and he gained many friends who likewise foresaw the demise of the Irish Parliament as a disaster for Ireland.

By all accounts he was an affable person and in the main was popular with his colleagues. "He bought his meat from my grandfather who was a butcher in Collon, and he would leave it hanging until the maggots fell off it. On one occasion he put his eye on a horse owned by my grandfather. They fell out over the high price of £40, but a short time later my grandfather got his asking price of £40 at the Drogheda fair. The Speaker refused to believe this until he saw the horse coming down the main street and the new owner confirmed the price he paid".[4]

By encouraging his tenants and by good example in farm husbandry the area under his sway became much more fruitful, and he turned the poverty-stricken village of Collon into a thriving community. A visitor in 1776 described Collon as a 'sheet of corn'. He diverted the River Mattock's waters to create a millstream which powered several mills for an industrial estate in which linen and a bleaching green played an important role. In addition, the Collon area had at one time 600 cotton looms and a stocking factory. His family devoted an expansive area to a nursery for propagating trees – the name is perpetuated in 'The Nurseries' located on the Drogheda side of Collon.

But he applied even greater energy towards sustaining the Anglo-Irish Ascendancy class. Any proposal that might impinge on their dominance he vigorously opposed; any move towards admitting Catholics to sharing in political power was anathema to him. To him, Catholics were underdogs, and anyone, even a Protestant who tried to advance their cause, he termed 'a radical' – but by the same token he himself could accurately be described as being a dyed-in-the-wool reactionary. He therefore was only a late and reluctant supporter of the Constitution of 1782 (Grattan's Parliament), and he was ever an effective spokesman against the Catholic Relief Act of 1793, and to the very end of his long life he opposed with every fibre of his being the call for Catholic Emancipation. He died in the year prior to Emancipation, but by then he was resigned as to its inevitability.

He was instrumental in formulating the infamous Corn Act (1784) – indeed, it is usually referred to as 'the Foster Corn Law'. It was designed to subsidise grain exports and to protect landowners from competition from imported grain. One wonders if this shrewd manipulator had a hidden agenda in shepherding the legislation through Parliament. Was the vast acreage of wheat which he himself grew an influencing factor? The price of home grown wheat (and in consequence the loaf of bread) was thereby kept at an artificially high level, exacerbating the lot of the hungry masses for whom bread had become a luxury that was beyond their financial reach. He seemed to have been unmindful of their plight, but was acutely aware of the fact that they had no voting rights at election time, whereas the legislation which he promulgated would have pleased his fellow landlords who kept him in office – 'You scratch my back and I'll scratch yours'.

Evidence of the regard in which he was held by those who mattered is his appointment to Chancellorship of the Irish Exchequer under the newly formed United Parliament in Westminster. Further, in 1821 he was honoured with the title 'Father of the House of Commons' and was later elevated to the peerage as Lord Oriel. He remained active in politics until he was 81, dying in 1828 at the ripe old age of eighty-eight.

Speaker Foster's Home in Collon
Although large, it was not pretentious or in the style of many of the great houses of the other landed gentry. It is located in Drogheda St., next to Collon's main intersection.

Looking back, we can see that Speaker Foster had a rather flawed make-up, despite his elevated status. He pursued a blinkered policy in promoting the Ascendancy cause to the exclusion of others – he was dismissive of the potential Catholic input, overlooking the fact that human endeavour – from whatever direction it may come– is the prime factor in the creation of wealth. Also, the Corn Law lined the well-filled pockets of the landed class, but left the loaf of bread outside the financial range of the peasants, rendering them more fully dependent on their potato drills – with catastrophic results when the blight of the Great Famine descended on the land.

In the running of his estate, his expenditure on draining his many thousands of acres and in making them more fertile was not reflected in the returns therefrom. The many lucrative official posts which he held, including that of Chancellorship of the Exchequer in the Irish Parliament and later Chancellorship of the Irish Exchequer in Westminster when the Irish Parliament was abolished, ought to have left him financially comfortable. The Speakership alone came with a salary of £4,000 p.a. plus fees (which in themselves were very substantial), yet he seemed unable to contain his own debts. So strapped was he for hard cash that he was obliged to take out mortgages and second mortgages on his properties. Social justice, religious freedom and political equality were foreign to his nature, and he failed to see the inevitability of what lay ahead.

The Volunteers were an amateur military force, almost exclusively Protestant, but many among them had a sense of fair play and wished to relieve their Catholic fellow countrymen of the injustices to which they were being subjected. They held a conference in Dungannon in 1782 and passed a series of resolutions that aimed at redressing the existing injustices, revealing a high degree of tolerance and generosity that was out of keeping with the age. The main ones are: -

- That the king, lords and commons of Ireland have alone the right to legislate for the country:
- That Poyning's Law is unconstitutional and a grievance and should be revoked:
- That the ports of Ireland should be open to all nations not at war with the king:

- That as men and Irishmen, as Christians and as Protestants, we rejoice in the relaxation of the penal laws against our Roman Catholic fellow subjects.

Grattan's Parliament: These hitherto undreamt-of resolutions were consummated shortly afterwards. Poyning's Law which, as mentioned above, had been enacted in a parliament held in Drogheda away back in 1494, was now consigned to the dustbin. Ireland at last was given its own parliament – popularly called 'Grattan's Parliament'.

This momentous achievement was largely the work of a Protestant Dublin barrister, Henry Grattan, who spent the rest of his life pressing for Catholic Emancipation. Grattan was an impressive orator and, for that age, a very tolerant and enlightened leader. Instead of using sledgehammer coercion against Catholics, he advocated *an enquiry into the __causes__ of discontent, to be followed by their removal* – he called this "the engine of redress". Even today, world leaders in their pursuit of universal peace and justice would benefit by applying a diplomatic stratagem of this nature when negotiating with an aggrieved adversary.

Corruption in high places is not a recent phenomenon. The Irish Parliament constituted in 1782 was as unrepresentative and rotten a type of parliament as could be imagined and John Foster presided over it as Speaker. In Dublin's House of Commons (it was housed in the building in College Green now occupied by the Bank of Ireland – it is the oldest parliament building in the world) there were 300 members, but only 72 were returned by the people – the rest gained entry through shenanigans of the most blatant nature – and none of them represented the people at large. One particular lord commanded all of 16 seats, and he sold them at election time to the highest bidder; other noble lords likewise held braces of seats; 116 seats were the property of 25 individuals. Some boroughs were purely fictional, while others consisted of perhaps a dozen puppets who voted as directed by the manipulators. Only Protestants had a vote, and only Protestants could sit in parliament. Moreover, strictures on its operation were applied from London. In other words, the new Irish parliament was a sham. At least it was better than no parliament, and infinitely better than being operated by remote control from London where the majority of the Members knew next to nothing about Irish affairs and cared less.

Such as it was, it was destined to be the last Irish elected assembly to represent the entire island. It plotted and developed the progress of Irish commerce, creating a network of roads and, of course, the Boyne Canal. Fairs, markets and banking were developed, including the establishment of Drogheda's Linen Hall. All in all, the country had blossomed into full flower during its operation, and the influence of Speaker Foster's guiding hand was in evidence.

The Influence of America and France: In 1783 America threw off the yoke of colonialism and achieved independence from England. This chunk of real estate was England's sole loss – and a mighty one at that! – until the formation of the Irish Free State in 1922. Gaining American independence was an event that was to have profound repercussions for Ireland and the Irish people more than anyone could have realised at the time – it was to become the escape route and the haven from hereditary injustices for the masses of Irish migrants and the salvation of a nation kept in continual servitude.

For the next hundred years England was extending her imperialism throughout the globe until she dominated one-fifth of the world's land mass. Canada, Australasia, half of the continent of Africa and the jewel in England's crown, India – these and many more possessions became part of the British Empire. They provided endless opportunities for shipping magnates, governors, army officers, civil servants, traders and carpetbaggers of every description to make fortunes for themselves through exploitation, and filling the coffers of England with the spoils of her colonies. But that window of opportunity was closed to a people who were being denied basic civic rights and who were being treated in their native land as second-class citizens – they themselves were labouring under the yoke of colonialism. There was to be no outlet throughout the British Empire for 'Paddy', except as a menial worker, a private in the British army or the butt of music hall jokes. In particular, the magazine *Punch* unceasingly derided him, and portrayed him as a sub-human.

America, by contrast, was the land of opportunity, and America had an abundance of both land and opportunity. Its vastness is brought home to us by the fact that the distance occupied by its great land mass from coast to coast is much greater than the distance from Ireland to its eastern seaboard. Erected in 1886, what first met the gaze of the millions of European emigrants arriving at New York Harbour was the colossal Statue of Liberty bearing aloft the torch of Freedom and proclaiming its heart-warming, reassuring message in a sonnet, the last stanza of which reads:

**GIVE ME YOUR TIRED, YOUR POOR,
YOUR HUDDLED MASSES YEARNING
TO BREATHE FREE.
THE WRETCHED REFUSE OF YOUR TEEMING SHORE,
SEND THESE, THE HOMELESS, TEMPEST-TOSSED TO ME
I LIFT MY LAMP BESIDE THE GOLDEN DOOR.**

No race of people answered that description of wretchedness more than the Irish, and no people responded so eagerly to the gilt-edged invitation: '*Send these, the homeless, tempest-tossed to me*'. The entrance through this 'Golden Door' was to become their escape route from the effects of the Act of Union and their deliverance from the horrors of the Great Famine. Franklin D. Roosevelt in a later time put the American ideal another way: '*... Freedom of speech and religion ... freedom from want and fear*'. These Four Freedoms were unknown to most Irishmen. It is estimated that in the immediate wake of the Great Famine a million Irish people stepped onto America's shore, and today one American in six carries Irish blood. Their endeavours in a just society have earned them both physical comfort and human dignity. It also brought them the opportunity to attain the very Highest Office of the land.

The American War of Independence set in train the French Revolution a few years later (1789) – a major milestone in the socio-economic history of the world. It put an abrupt and bloody end to the system whereby the French Aristocracy and the Church enjoyed all the privileges and luxuries that life could bestow, while the peasants lived in a world of continual want, toiling in the fields and performing the menial and domestic chores. The ideal of the Revolution, 'Liberty, Equality, Fraternity', was the catalyst that turned the existing system on its head. No longer would a penny restrict the God-given rights of a ha'penny. Personal achievement became the reward of every man's effort – henceforth a man could enjoy the fruits of his own labour. It was a spur to the native Irish whose living conditions were not dissimilar to those in France. The unrest created by the Revolution was becoming a matter of deep concern among the British authorities; would Ireland follow suit? These were changing times indeed.

Up to this time the concept of *Nationhood* was absent from the Irish psyche. Prior to the arrival of the Normans those that peopled the land consisted of numerous family septs and minor kingships, all independent of one another. There was never a sense of national identity. The Normans introduced a kingship; this meant little to the native people because the king resided in England, and he was a foreigner. After Henry VIII the people strove for religious freedom rather than national sovereignty. The pipe-dream of nationhood and of national independence began to surface following the success of the American War of Independence and the French Revolution. If others could break free from the bondage of overlords and serfdom, why not the Irish. The seeds of national republicanism were now sown.

The Protestant Ascendancy: The year 1790 marked the Centenary of the Battle of the Boyne, and the Drogheda Corporation did not let the occasion pass without a celebration. It allocated out of public funds a sum "not exceeding £150 to defray the expenses in commemorating the 1st of July 1690 Centenary of the victory by King William'. The occasion included an address delivered by the Reverend Jaime Albey who was awarded the Freedom of the Corporation at its next sitting 'as a mark of approbation of his excellent Sermon preached in Saint Peter's Church on the 1st of July 1790 upon the Celebration of the Victory at the Boyne on the first day of July 1690. Mr. Mayor will be pleased to publish his sermon preached on the above occasion'[5]. Two years later the Drogheda Assembly exhorted its members 'to preserve those laws ... by which the Protestant ascendancy [had been established] and oppose any attempt to alter ... or destroy that repose and tranquillity under which we have so long lived and prospered'.

Here was a naked admission that the "Protestant ascendancy", to use their own phrase, were king of the castle and that they were determined to maintain that privileged situation that they were enjoying. The term 'Protestant Ascendancy' was just coming into vogue at that time. 'The phrase had first been used in 1787 and only in a non-contentious manner. By 1792 ... it had become a rallying cry for the Protestant interest in Ireland and for its right to be the dominant force in the running of the country. From this middle-class origin the term would become identified with the owners of landed estates ... "'.[6]

The Loyal Drogheda Cavalry and the Loyal Drogheda Infantry were embodied for the purpose of maintaining dominance and quelling any attempt at insurrection. Several of the inhabitants also formed themselves into a corps of Volunteers. The Corporation granted 30 guineas 'to provide bed and bedding for the accommodation of two Troops of His Majesty's Dragoons, now quartered on the inhabitants of the town'.

Even though the franchise and other concessions had now been granted by way of appeasement (in the aftermath of the American War of Independence), the matter of equality had still a long way to go, and the Catholic population were still being seriously disadvantaged. Being given the right to vote was one thing, but 36 more years were to elapse before a Catholic could sit in Parliament, and so the struggle dragged on.

Feelings among the masses were coming to the boil. We will see that Louth's role in the Rising of '98 was a non-event, a complete failure. Nonetheless, men of the Wee County played their part in the years leading up to it, and paid for it in 'torchlight executions, floggings and transportation'. The secret organisation known as the Defenders was growing bolder and stronger, and was active throughout County Louth, including Drogheda. A complaint was made to the Earl of Charlemont that "when a thousand men well armed are ordered to disperse by reading the Riot Act they will retire and assemble in other places, to the number of five or six thousand to the terror and confusion of the whole country. Yesterday there were thousands of popish party assembling from Drogheda, Jonesboro and many other places to join those already in this county and by what I can find their whole intent is not to leave a Protestant alive".

The Drogheda Corporation was single-minded in its efforts to defeat the impending violence, and passed a resolution: 'Resolved that His Majesty to preserve inviolate, and to maintain unencumbered the Protestant assembly in this Kingdom ... we are determined to support it from violation, and firmly to resist every attempt to overturn it ...'.

No one was more determined than Speaker Foster in that regard. Any hint of resistance he treated with brutal repression, and he was the nemesis of the Defenders. He arrived at Tallanstown with two troops of Horse when a patron was taking place there. He presumed that they were Defenders, and having read the Riot Act three times, he asked no questions but fired into the defenceless crowd, and the Horse charged with their swords unsheathed. The scene closed with six killed and ten taken prisoner. Napper Tandy criticised Foster for this unprovoked attack and distributed leaflets criticising him. "... are the Catholics attacked in Louth? Yes. By whom? ... by the Speaker! And for assembling at patrons as has been the custom from time immemorial. The army is brought in on the poor people..."

Theobald Wolfe Tone came to Drogheda to try and restore calm. His diary makes many references to the escapades of the Defenders of the area in their quest for firearms. The entry for Saint Stephen's Day 1792 refers to:

> " ... repeated burglaries, breaking into houses and plundering them for fire-arms – twice robbing the mail, robbing some of the 17th. Dragoons of their fire-locks on the high road – by frequent threatening letters and by nightly meetings of large meetings of men in arms, particularly at Tullyesker, Termonfeckin, Port and Clogher ... Crossroads at Grangebellew: It was late in the evening and very dark. Upwards of 1,500 men armed with guns, pitchforks and other implements were looking for guns and awaiting orders to march on Foster's home in Collon ... "

Again, the entry in his diary for New Year's Day 1793 reads:

> "On Saturday they attacked and killed the guard on the Drogheda mail coach at Castlebellingham.

> "Defenders have held nightly meetings at which they have been teaching themselves the use of arms and forming plans for disarming the Protestants. They have broken into nearly forty Protestant houses within a fortnight and wherever they have been unsuccessful they have carried off whatever they can find. Twice they have attacked the Primate's house at Rokeby Hall, where they expanded their ammunition, firing in at the doors and windows but were repulsed. At Mr. Alexander McClintocks their assault was also repelled after the fire of 30 rounds".[7]

Entries for other dates early in the new year (1793) refer laconically to:

- 26th January: "26 Defenders killed near Kells ..."
- 5th February: "13 Defenders killed near Kells. In Drogheda on Friday night nine of the Defenders were taken in arms and put in prison ..."
- 16th February: "Seven insurgents killed and many wounded [at Ardee] ..."
- 23rd February: "£100 for any information about the disturbances in Louth ..."
- 6th March: "On Wednesday Peter McBride convicted of taking arms at Lord Clermonts House. The trial not over till 7.00 p.m. McBride executed at nine. ...
- George McDaniel for administering Defenders oath: transportation for life.
- Twenty-one tried for giving unlawful oaths: 7 years transportation ..."

... and so on. The diary contains many such instances dealing with conspiracies and turbulences that occurred in Drogheda and in adjacent townlands. It makes it abundantly clear that there was no shortage of men in the Drogheda area who were ready to risk their lives to overturn the dominant régime. Outrages were commonplace and, for the most part, the perpetrators were being described as coming 'from the lower order'. The Revd. Lambert in 1797 wrote:

> "The principles of the United Irishmen have advanced to such a stage in Drogheda, that the peasantry who go there on market day are obliged to leave early in the evening to escape abuse and injury, if they refuse an oath, that at every gate an emissary waits to administer".[8]

A Court Case: The emerging wealthy middle class among Catholics in Drogheda did not remain on the sideline; some were involved in the Defenders notwithstanding the fact that others of them paraded with the Volunteers. Prominent among them were the Bird, Hamill and Delahoyde families who had become successful in business and owned substantial properties. These three businessmen were brought to trial at Drogheda in April 1794 and indicted of:

'being wicked, seditious, and evil-minded persons, and of wicked and turbulent dispositions, and contriving, designing and intending unlawfully, unjustly, maliciously, turbulently and seditiously the peace of the said lord the king and the common tranquillity of this his realm of Ireland to disquiet, molest and disturb and as in as far as them lay, to stir up, cause, and incite and procure sedition, insurrection and rebellion within this realm and to bring the government of our said lord the king within this realm into manifest danger ... with force of arms their aforesaid wicked, seditious and malignant purposes and designs to fulfil and effect, did there and then together with divers other wicked, seditious and ill-minded persons to the jurors of our lord the king at present unknown, meet, assemble, agree, conspire, confederate and treat of and about the accomplishing and effecting of their aforesaid malignant and seditious purposes and designs ... '.

This was a verbose, roundabout way, using legal terminology, of saying that these men were being accused of subversive offences that carried the death penalty. Mr. Bird had been aroused from his bed at midnight and taken to Newgate prison in Dublin. There he was deprived of pen and ink to communicate. The person behind these arrests was John Foster.

The counsel for the defence was John Philpot Curran, a Protestant barrister who had established the name of championing the downtrodden. The case attracted widespread interest. The first witness for the prosecution was Thomas Murphy who stepped into the witness box dressed in respectable attire. Curran asked him where he got the coat, and Murphy replied that he bought it. Curran skilfully exposed him as a most disreputable person – he had been in jail several times, once for robbing a priest aged 90 years of money in the Naul, and a further imputation about stealing a pig.

John Philpot Curran
He defended many dissidents in court.

Curran then produced a defence witness, a tailor, who said he had been asked to fit out Murphy for the clothes; he did this by having to go to the jail where Murphy was incarcerated at the time, in order to take his measurements. It was also established that the money which purchased the clothes did not come from Murphy. Both Murphy and the other witness, Bernard Grimes, were led into making many entangling and contradictory statements. The jury, having retired for a few minutes, returned with a verdict of 'Not Guilty'. The defendants, including several others who were implicated in the case, were promptly acquitted, and the two prosecution witnesses were then detained to face indictments for perjury.

It was Speaker Foster who had tried to ruin Bird, Hamill and Delahoyde, and it was Speaker Foster who procured the prosecution witnesses, and it was Speaker Foster who paid for the clothes – he arranged this, not from any sense of benignity, but in order to give the witnesses an appearance of respectability while in the witness box. A measure of his ruthless character is the fact that he later pursued Grimes for having exposed his deviousness, and he eventually got revenge by silencing him on the gallows. He was also the scourge of the Defenders, and would stop at nothing to suppress them, so that they were an ineffective force locally when the day dawned for action.

The outcome of the many instances of unrest in Drogheda and County Louth at this period is summarised by Fergus O'Dowd, TD and former Mayor of Drogheda:

"[These local events] had a profound effect on Wolfe Tone and on revolutionary opinion in Ireland. He had attended the Drogheda trials. He now knew for certain that Protestant ascendancy would never concede one inch of ground to moderate Catholic opinion. Rebellion and revolution would now become the order of the day. His son, Matthew Tone, wrote 'I know that in the year 1794 and 1795 and particularly at the Drogheda Assizes ... on the occasion of the trial of Bird and Hamill where Philpot Curran and Tone were employed as Council he (Curran) opened his mind to my father and that on the main point – the necessity of breaking the connection with England – they agreed'"

It was revealed in the course of the Bird/Hamill/Delahoye case that the Defenders (many of whom were also United Irishmen) had procured a shipment of arms from France, that this had been taken ashore at Annagassan and then distributed among its members. It is clear that the Drogheda/Louth area was rife with unrest, and that there was no shortage of men throughout the area who were toiling to bring matters to a head. Their endeavours to undermine the authorities through force is evident. However, the United Irishmen were later forced to go underground (as were the Defenders), and thus there are no official records of membership. Names subsequently revealed were extracted through torture.

THE DROGHEDA MILITIA AND THE LOUTH MILITIA: Because of the general unrest throughout the land, the existing Crown forces required to be augmented and thus in 1793 each county set about organising its own militia battalion. These were men drawn from the commonality with, of course, a member of the landed gentry at the head of each. County Louth provided two battalions – the Louth Militia and the Drogheda Militia. It was soon found that the financial burden was too onerous for the people of Drogheda to maintain, and thus the Drogheda Militia was united with the Louth Militia six years later. This enabled the Louth Militia's status as a battalion to be raised to that of a regiment. Its name was officially changed several times in the course of its chequered history; in 1854 it became the 108th (Louth Rifles) Regiment of Militia, and in 1881 it formed part of the Royal Irish Rifles. It was finally dissolved, without any shedding of tears, as we shall see, in 1908.

Records are sparse regarding the regalia worn by the Drogheda Militia. The distinctive facings (i.e. the coloured pieces of cloth superimposed on the sleeves and collar of a uniform) were green. We know this from a notice published in 1796 concerning a Drogheda man, one James Cavanagh, who was being sought for desertion and who was last seen wearing his regimentals faced with green.

Later, the ornamentation on the pouch belt was a metal Maltese Cross, above the upper transept of which was a crown; in the centre of the cross was superimposed a disk bearing the words 'County Louth Rifles' encircling a Maid of Erin harp.

It is necessary here, for the sake of clarity, to distinguish between the Yeomanry, the Volunteers and the Militia:

The Yeomanry consisted of *the landed gentry*; it was a part-time citizens' army formed in 1796 at the behest of the government because of the mounting unrest at home and the threat of an invasion by Napoleon. It functioned as a quasi police force, operating mostly in the area local to its members, and it was envisaged that it would assume the role of a garrison in the event of the regular army having to combat a French invasion. With a few exceptions it was a Protestant force and received pay, arms and uniforms from the government; it trained twice a week. Both cavalry and infantry units existed, and at its peak the membership came to a very formidable 85,000. In Ulster it was closely associated with, and integrated with the Orange Order.

We will touch on the inhuman, unlicensed methods used by its members in quelling the peasants' unrest in 1798. The memories of their atrocities remained even after they were disbanded in 1834, only to be mirrored in a later era with the arrival of the infamous Black and Tans.

The Volunteers: During the American War of Independence the Volunteers came into being, and their numbers reached a maximum of 80,000 nationwide. They were an amateur force, and locally based. They were independent of government support and supplied their own equipment. Their initial function was to supplement the police in their duties, but they became a pressure group and were instrumental in the establishing of Grattan's Parliament. Grattan himself was a member. They held moderate political views and exercised an egalitarian policy, especially in the matter of alleviating the lot of their Catholic brethren. They were later suppressed along with the United Irishmen.

The Militia had existed in one form or another from the 1600s, and at first they were exclusively a Protestant force. The body raised in 1793 was different in as much as *it consisted of Catholics, but only as privates,* and they overwhelmed its ranks. They were officered exclusively by Protestants. Full-time service was required and they were invariably stationed outside their local area. Recruitment provided an opportunity for members of 'the lower classes' to engage in employment of sorts. In 1798 they numbered 30,000.

Their loyalty was always suspect, and not without reason. The Defenders/United Irishmen infiltrated their ranks, and in one particular case in Monaghan, for example, four privates were executed in front of their comrades for having taken the oath of the United Irishmen. The Drogheda Assembly did not hold the Militia in high regard, for in 1793 it resolved that 'the appointment of a Chaplain to the body was unnecessary, and that the said office be discontinued from the day the Militia of Drogheda returned to the county'.

In 1816 (immediately after Waterloo, with Napoleon out of the way) they were disbanded, and the release of so many men into the ranks of the unemployed exacerbated the existing plight of the people. The linen industry in Drogheda at that time was collapsing and the town was experiencing unmitigated suffering. At the commencement of the Crimean War in 1854 they were re-established.

An Unwelcome Regiment: In 1796 Drogheda found itself under the "protection" (this word must be given its widest and most generous interpretation here) of the Donegal Militia. That regiment created quite a stir in the town. So unruly were they that a Committee of the townspeople was formed to call upon the Lord Lieutenant and Governor of Ireland to have it removed. The Committee affirmed:

> *"that the peace and good order of the town of Drogheda is and for a considerable time past has been materially interrupted and disturbed by the riotous and disorderly conduct of the private men of the Donnegal (sic) Regiment of the Militia now stationed in this town. That a numerous meeting of the inhabitants of said Town was held at the request of several respectable individuals to the Mayor to call them together, for the purpose of adopting such measures as might appear expedient for restoring and preserving the peace of the Town. Soldiers [were] forcing the country people to give their provisions without any fixed price ... and to take such price as they are pleased to give ... and they have been heard to declare vengeance against the persons and houses of those whom they conceive to have been most instrumental in the measures adopted for procuring their removal".*[9]

Has Anybody Here Seen Kelly?: The locals had good reason to fear these guardians of the peace. An advertisement appeared in the Drogheda Journal which read: **"DESERTED:** By escaping through the Necessary [i.e. the lavatory?] of the guardhouse, Drogheda on Sunday night 6th inst. **Patrick Kelly** of the Donegal Regiment, charged with having committed Murder. Whoever will apprehend him and lodge him in any of His Majesty's Jails in this Kingdom within 6 months of the date hereof shall receive 60 gns. Reward ". A notice in the paper the following week causes one to smile: a property holder was seeking the whereabouts of a certain **Patrick Kelly** (undoubtedly the same tough customer) who had absconded with some of his property together with the price of several sheep. It was suspected that he might have a mind to distance himself from his pursuers by the broad expanse of the Atlantic – as well he might!

Another member of the Donegal Militia, John Daly, in the same year was facing the local Magistrate for "grossly assaulting and abusing" a Mr. Reid. He was found guilty and imprisoned for six months and ordered to keep the peace for seven years. Such incidents were regular occurrences in the town. And these were some of the men who were let loose to quell the insurgents in 1798. At the height of the Insurrection the Donegal Militia was stationed in New Ross, a town where the slaughter was greatest.

Murder in Barrack Lane: A year later Drogheda had the doubtful pleasure of hosting the Armagh Militia. Their reputation for rowdyism differed little from that of the regiment they were relieving. Allegiance to their King meant little to the boys from the County Armagh. However, on one occasion a soldier did express sentiments of loyalty, and he paid for this indiscretion with his life. This caused the Loyal Drogheda Yeoman Cavalry, when on parade in the town, to pass unanimously this resolution:

> *"That we hold in the utmost abhorrence the barbarous and inhuman Murder committed on the person of William James, a private of the Armagh Militia in Barrack Lane on Tuesday night last. We offer a reward of 50 gns. for such further discoveries as may forward the ends of Public Justice by bringing perpetrates of the above inhuman Murder to condign punishment ... We have strong reason to believe that the unfortunate man met his fate for having used Expressions of Loyalty and Attachment to his Sovereign".[10]*

Let us ponder briefly on this resolution because it reveals something of the divergent dispositions of the people of Drogheda at that time. One section deems that someone who voices his loyalty to the king should suffer death. But the members of the Loyal Drogheda Yeoman Cavalry who passed this resolution are the landlords and the property holders – the Ascendancy. They are outraged at the 'inhuman Murder' of a Militiaman because he had "used Expressions of Loyalty and Attachment to his Sovereign'. They specify this as being the cause of their indignation and anger. They offer a reward of 50 guineas (a considerable sum to a poverty stricken people) to lay hands on the perpetrator. But not a mention of a penny to support the widow/mother/dependants of the murdered man – not even a word of condolence. So much for the social conscience of the Ascendancy!

It is clear from the above incident that loyalties within the town are starkly divided. Much of the popular sentiment lies, not with their King, but with their Country – Cáitleen Ní Houlahán. Although Drogheda's plans for the Rebellion (it followed two years later) was to go awry and fail abjectly, many people were not prepared to countenance any posture that ran contrary to their own. It must be remembered that the vast majority (80% to 90%) of the town's population by this time was made up of Catholics. For his indiscretion this soldier was made to forfeit his life. It is reminiscent of a scene from the film *'Captain Boycott'* when the body of an unpopular Bailiff was being fished from a bog-hole. The Constable growled at the onlooking mob in stern disapproval and remarked: "That'll settle nothing". To which one of them retorted: "It'll settle the Bailiff!"

A Mr. Butler from Ardbraccan was duly 'settled' in expeditious Defender fashion in 1792, a deed that incurred the wrath of the Assembly, for they offered a reward of £100 for the apprehension of the assassin. A further award of 50 gns. was offered for the conviction of the culprit who set fire to Mr. H. Nicholson's stables and hay.

We will see that although many priests at parish level were fully in sympathy with the sufferings of their parishioners and actively supported them in their efforts to overcome their misery, the official policy of the Catholic Church was to abide by the law of the land; they condemned violence, whatever the justification. Subversives were denied absolution in Confession and were liable to excommunication. The Drogheda Assembly was particularly pleased with the efforts of the Rev. Dr. Francis Moylan, Roman Catholic Bishop of Cork whom they rewarded with the Freedom of the Corporation in 1797 " ... as a mark of our esteem for his pious exertions and excellent exhortations to the Roman Catholic inhabitants of his diocese, for promoting peace and goodwill at the moment of threatened invasion".[11]

The Dual Threat: Apart from internal unrest, the threat of invasion was ever present, because Napoleon was on the march, and his heart was set on invading England. It was deemed necessary to be on the alert at all times. Accordingly, an advertisement was placed in the

Drogheda Journal under the heading "**INVASION**: PREPARATION FOR RESISTING THE EXPECTED INVASION"[12] listing a set of emergency instructions to the military which included the following:

1. All unnecessary baggage must be removed.
2. No more than 5 wagons and 3 carts to each regiment.
3. Officers' personal baggage to be contained in a small portmanteau.
4. One tent will accommodate 16 men.
5. During a march every officer will remain with his division and never quit it on any account.

Army barracks, some large and some small, were sprinkled throughout Ireland, predominantly in the coastal towns. Many of them were insignificant and were of a temporary nature. Cities such as Dublin and Cork contained very large contingents, including cavalry. Drogheda's garrison at this time consisted of 12 officers and 386 privates, the headquarters of which were at Millmount. No cavalry was assigned there. However, the barracks could accommodate only 116 men and five officers so that a house in West Street was acquired to provide lodgings for the remainder. Drilling and parading was a problem, the square at the barracks being too small, and the steep hill adjoining the square was not conducive to marching. This resulted in the headquarters being moved at a later date to Dundalk. During times of prolonged peace Millmount was unoccupied, apart from a skeletal caretaking staff. From time to time other regiments were stationed at Millmount while the Louth Militia saw service in various parts of the United Kingdom, e.g. Kinsale, Enniscorthy, Taghmon, Curragh, Yarmouth, as well as to distant regions of the far flung Empire, e.g. India, Malta, Canada.

R.C. CHAPEL

St. Peter's Chapel: *the precursor of the existing RC Church in West St. Note the absence of a steeple and bell tower; they were prohibited by law during the Penal Days.*

Chapter Nineteen

The Eye of the Storm – the 1798 Rebellion

The Ascendancy had difficulty in containing the majority of the populace within the straight-jacket of restricted economic, political and religious freedom that was being imposed on them. A reaction was inevitable. By the late 1700s the disaffection was coming to the boil and the rumblings were palpable. Nearly every blacksmith in rural Ireland was a member of the United Irishmen, and with hammers clanging and sparks flying they were busy at their anvils fashioning ingots of red-hot iron into pikes. Trees were openly being cut down to provide shafts for them. The stockpiles of pikes and other armaments were being secreted underground. The homes of the gentry were everywhere being brazenly raided for firearms, and arsenals in many a local parish were being stockpiled, awaiting the day of retribution.

So boldly were these raids for arms taking place that the government was being severely criticised at the state of near anarchy that existed. Steps had to be taken to counteract the anticipated violence. The Assembly in Drogheda made preparations for what might occur, and it voted in 1779 that one hundred firelocks with accoutrements be provided by the Corporation for the Protestant inhabitants, if such firearms could not otherwise be obtained from the government *gratis*.

THE UNITED IRISHMEN: The Society of the United Irishmen originated in Belfast, and its founder members were erudite Protestants and Presbyterians. Its aim was to rid the country of religious injustice, and with it the rule of the dominant 'antiquated and corrupt Ascendancy'. One of its members, William Drennan, coined the eponym 'the Emerald Isle'. The government saw fit to ban it, so, not surprisingly, it went underground as a secret society. Its central directory was then based in Dublin and its leader was Lord Edward Fitzgerald (32), whose family home is now the seat of Dáil Éireann. He was a romantic, and, imbued with the spirit of republicanism, he renounced his title. Branches of the organisation had been established throughout Ireland, and every precaution was taken to maintain secrecy – its members were bound by an oath of silence. This was a prerequisite for the planned Rising, and the date set for it to begin was eventually fixed for the 23rd. of May 1798.

The legal affairs of the United Irishmen was handled by Leonard McNally, a Dublin lawyer, who of course knew all the key leaders, and was privy to every detail of the plans, being entrusted with their innermost secrets. He lived and died in their friendship and gratitude, but he was a mole, and he kept Dublin Castle informed of each and every happening. It was not until many years later, when his heir applied for a continuation of the annual £300 secret service stipend he had been receiving, that McNally's treachery was discovered. The movement was riddled with informers, despite the precautions taken. This information had enabled the army to swoop down at the appropriate moment and arrest almost the entire panel of leaders, and they were promptly hanged. Lord Edward Fitzgerald evaded the dragnet and went into hiding with a price of £1,000 on his head. Once again, a Judas was at hand to betray him to the government and claim the pieces of silver. In the struggle that took place while being arrested he was shot, and shortly afterwards he died of his wounds. The death of this aristocrat was deeply felt by both sides of the sectarian divide.

Being in possession of all the crucial information, His Majesty's forces set about disarming 'the domestic enemy' ahead of any major upheaval. A dragnet was put into operation to recover the arms that were secreted everywhere. Platoons scoured the countryside in a ruthless and unrestrained fashion, employing whatever drastic measures suited them. They availed of 'free quarters', that is, they were let loose to live in the homes of the people while carrying out their searches, and this was the cause of much friction. They plundered as they went.

General Sir John Moore marched five companies of Light Infantry and a detachment of Dragoons around Cork "to show them that I was serious". His instruction to his men was to: "*Treat the people with as much harshness as possible*, as far as words and manners went, *and to supply themselves with whatever provisions were necessary to enable them live well*". In their rampaging, they showed little distinction between the loyal and the disaffected – for the most part they were downright ruffians who revelled in the pillaging and wrecking. Lord Wycombe referred to "the fat sheep, the good wine, and the greasy pigs that have rewarded the valour of the troops".

At first there was a natural resistance by the populace to handing over weapons, but when torture was applied and thatched roofs set ablaze, the desired results usually followed with alacrity. In that way the insurgency was disarmed, and huge quantities of the pikes that had been painstakingly hammered out on the blacksmiths' anvils, and firearms (taken in raids from the landed gentry) were recovered. The authorities "were pleased that the people were humbled and would be civil".[1]

The Policy of the Catholic Church was to support the government and to oppose any attempt at insurrection. The Archbishop issued a Pastoral to be read from every altar denouncing subversive activities, and the hierarchy constantly preached the message of submission to the law, although this was in conflict with the sentiments of some lesser clergy who were closer to the grass roots and who had first hand experience of the abuses of the Militia and more particularly the Yeomanry.

Fr. Murphy, curate of Boulavogue parish, had refused the Sacraments to those who advocated violence, and he co-operated with thirteen other priests and more than seven thousand parishioners in drawing up a testimonial of loyalty to the Government. They pledged their 'unalterable attachment to his Sacred Majesty George the Third'. Notwithstanding that pledge, his little chapel was burned by the forces of law and order. Subsequent reports of torture and murder by the rampaging yeomanry eventually impelled him to defend his parishioners and to lead them in revolt.

County Kildare was a stronghold of the United Irishmen, and was at the butt end of great brutality from government forces in their quest for arms. The square of Athy was the site where flogging triangles were set up; the suspects were tied to these, and the cat-o'-nine tails was applied most effectively in extracting information on the names of leaders and the whereabouts of arsenals:

> '*In Athy the blacksmiths were now tied to the triangle and, with the full authority of martial law, flogged to exhort confessions. [It was suspected that they might have known where pikes were hidden]. A local man called Thomas Rawson was one of the Athy interrogators. He acted on 'speculation' to make men 'whistle' as he termed it. "He would seat himself," we are told by one of the arrested men, "in a chair in the centre of a ring formed around the triangles, the miserable victims kneeling under the triangle until they would be spotted over with the blood of the others". Two of his victims were father and son. Another received 500 lashes, and was then found to be innocent'.[2]*

With almost all the leaders eliminated, the entire movement was effectively decapitated; and with pikes piled high on wagons and brought to the safety of army barracks, it was well-nigh emasculated. Nonetheless, the Rising went ahead, but the arrangements were in disarray: the people were leaderless, without arms, without plans, without discipline. Resistance did not take place nation-wide as had been planned, but was confined to Wexford, Wicklow and Kildare, with lesser episodes in Meath and Carlow. Ulster was a separate issue. Dublin was totally out of the picture, thanks to the informers.

A Hesitant Start: The Rising began in a very hesitant way. Insurgents in small villages on the periphery of Dublin and in County Kildare were first to rally to the cause, and successes were scored notably in Prosperous, Kilcock Dunboyne and in the Quaker village of Ballitore. Wrath frequently gave way to violence, and many atrocities were committed by the undisciplined mobs; Kildare town was set ablaze. The militia and the yeomanry responded in a most malevolent manner, striking terror into the hearts of the peasants, innocent or otherwise, wherever they went. These were the official government forces, but their excesses largely went unchecked – circumstances that were to be repeated in a later age (1920 and 1921) by the Black and Tans.

Innocent inhabitants fled to the hills at their approach, returning only to find their humble cabins smouldering ruins. Jailed prisoners were taken out and murdered in cold blood. To extract confessions they devised a most diabolical form of torture – the 'pitch-cap'. Pitch was applied to a captive's head, and then gunpowder was added. Setting this concoction alight induced many a victim to reveal the names of leaders and the whereabouts of hidden pikes. By such methods was a nation held in subjugation.

At this time the Louth Militia was stationed in County Wicklow, and the Meath Militia was in the Wexford area. One wonders what thoughts ran through the minds of these men on being ordered by their officers to suppress with firearms the endeavours of their fellow countrymen. Doubts were expressed in government circles from time to time (fully justified) concerning the allegiance of many militiamen; they had enlisted ostensibly to defend the King's realm but, privately, their sympathies in many instances lay elsewhere. The United Irishmen had been infiltrating their ranks, and many of the militia throughout Ireland had changed their allegiance. Crucially, those stationed in Wicklow were ready to 'turn coat', i.e. literally to turn their tunics inside out, and join the other side the moment the call was made.

Drogheda took no direct part in the Rising, and it would be unrealistic to have expected any major struggle to have taken place there. It is unlikely that the directory of the United Irishmen in Dublin placed much reliance on support from that quarter. To start with, the underlying cause of the unrest was the *agrarian* factor, but Drogheda, which had a population of 20,000 at the time,[3] was an industrial town, dependent largely on the linen industry, not on agriculture. An eruption of violence would have brought no benefit, but was certain to jeopardise their source of income.

Secondly, the dominant presence of Speaker Foster was felt everywhere. The headquarters of the Louth Militia was at Collon, and he was its commander. The parish (by an Act of Parliament) was responsible for its upkeep, and the money was raised annually by a levy on all the inhabitants. As we have seen, he terrorised the countryside, employing measures of exceptional severity. He successfully drew the teeth and claws from the Defenders in south Louth, rendering them quite ineffective. The name 'Foster' was always associated with the harsh treatment which that family meted out to their tenants in later times, causing great hardship through peremptory evictions during and after the Great Famine.

Thirdly, Drogheda was always heavily influenced by all that took place in the capital city, whether socially, commercially or politically – it was a mere four hours carriage ride away. In a matter of hours the local garrison could be supplemented by armed assistance from Dublin. The traditions of the old Pale were still imbued in the psyche of many of its inhabitants; the loyalists still living in the town ruled with an iron fist.

It is futile for us today to trot out the old *tu quoque* argument, but at the same time it is tempting to enquire what were other counties doing during this valiant attempt at gaining freedom. What effort was the county of Waterford, which is next door to gallant Wexford, making throughout the upheavals; and what about all the other populous towns and cities such as Cork, Tralee, Limerick, Galway, Dundalk and the towns of the midlands. For one thing, they were remote from the centre of power in Dublin. This meant that they were less influenced by Dublin Castle and so were less likely to receive a swift retaliatory response from that quarter, and they did not have that ogre, Foster, to contend with. They were nonetheless very subdued throughout the Rising. As for Connaught, the French had been told that 20,000 men were ready to join their ranks as soon as they landed. But no, the French contingent that arrived at Killala Bay was given a wide berth for the most part, and many a fellow who did join their ranks promptly sold the smart uniform he was given, spent the proceeds on drink, and then queued up for another new uniform. For some shiftless people this was bonanza time.

It is of interest to turn the spotlight on some names in the list of senior government officials and other administrators in Dublin Castle who held centre stage during the drama that was being enacted in those troubled times. These are some of the principal *dramatis personae*:

NAME	TITLE
Beresford, John	Chief Commissioner of Revenue
Camden, John	Viceroy (1793-98)
Carlisle, Frederick	Viceroy (1780-82)
Charlemont	First Earl of Charlemont
Fitzgibbon, John	Lord **Clare**
Fitzwilliam, William	Viceroy (1794-95)
Foster, John	Speaker of Irish Parliament
Gardiner, Luke	Viscount **Mountjoy**
George III	King of England, Scotland and Ireland
Ormonde	First Marquis of Ormonde
Westmoreland	Viceroy (1790-95)
Wycombe, John	Marquis of **Lansdowne**

Many of the main characters are still being commemorated today in the street names of central Dublin, and the reader may well recognise a number of them in the foregoing list. It speaks well for the tolerance (or is it indifference?) shown by today's generation towards the memories of the men in question. For the most part, they were the power behind the institutionalised repression, and they were utterly merciless, despotic tyrants; their only thoughts were to the advancement of their own welfare; they were intolerant of the aspirations of a deprived and hapless people; they were assiduous in meting out to the masses the particular brand of 'justice' that they themselves had fabricated in a parliament which they themselves controlled, and were adamant in denying religious freedom to those who adhered to a religion other than their own. Dominant as they were, they were shortly to engage in the process of securing permanently their own privileged positions by frogmarching the entire Irish people into union with England.

On the other hand, a few characters who held high office – their names are not commemorated on any street signs – were conspicuous in their endeavours to dispense justice in a humane and even-handed way, notably: Sir Ralph Abercromby (he was forced to resign), and Charles Cornwallis (Viceroy 1798-1801) who continually pressed for Emancipation but was hounded at every step until he finally conceded defeat to the radicals. One of their ilk, the freelance Lord Roden from north County Louth, brought as trophies the bodies of mangled Croppies to the Dublin Castle yard. He wrote: "I should look upon [a new] Rising as a fortunate event, as by that means we should have an opportunity of annihilating one or two million of inhabitants who are a disgrace to humanity"[4]. His family name is perpetuated in 'Roden Place' in Dundalk

The Boys of Wexford: County Wexford had always steered clear of aggression and, like Drogheda, seemed to have had but little contact with the directory of the United Irishmen in Dublin. They were unprepared for what was about to happen but reacted in a spontaneous way to the barbarities being inflicted by the militia on the peaceful community. In great fear, they were also responding to the false rumours that were in circulation that the Orangemen were planning a pogrom of the entire Catholic population. The United Irishmen was a non-sectarian organisation and its goal was to secure freedom and religious tolerance for all, but in Wexford the movement soon degenerated into a religious uprising.

Ignorance and fear set in motion a series of events that

culminated in death and destruction of unprecedented proportions. The insurgents rampaged through Wexford town, and the garrison was isolated. Sent to their relief was the Meath Militia (a force of about 70 men) who pushed along the road via Taghmon; they had with them some lethal howitzers that were capable of wreaking havoc. As they approached the town of Wexford they enquired from time to time as to the presence of the enemy, and the locals assured them that the coast was clear. But it wasn't. They walked straight into an ambush, and when the slaughter was over there was not one of the Meath Militia left to tell the tale.

The insurgents were on the crest of a wave, and triumph followed triumph, while the government forces were at sixes and sevens. Everything that happened was more or less spontaneous, but there were no set plans in place, and no ultimate goal – events occurred on an *ad hoc* basis, and the early victories were not properly followed up; the successes were often marred by unruly mobs committing grievous atrocities. Liquor stores were especially targeted and the resulting scenes can be visualised. In one incident, over a hundred Protestants were herded into a barn that was then set ablaze, incinerating everyone inside.

Louth's Non-Event: The efforts of South Louth, though well intentioned, were pathetic in the extreme. Describing the episode in outline today – after the passing of more than two centuries – does not diminish the discomfiture at recounting the scene that took place. It was nothing short of a fiasco. The man who untiringly recruited forces far and wide was Dan Kelly from Ardee. He had tramped the roads of Ireland at great risk to his personal safety as an agent in organising support for the forthcoming upheaval. The insurgency force of Louth was entrusted to Michael Boylan, aged 24 years. He was the son of a prosperous Catholic farmer at Blakestown, Ardee and his homestead was selected as the assembly point for the freedom fighters of the county, and it was planned that under his leadership they would march to Tara to join up with the Meathmen for the commencement of action.

We cannot from this time-distance estimate the strength of the gathered contingent on the night in question, but it may have been in the region of 1,500 men, (other sources put it as high as 4,000) all of them ardent in their resolve, and ready to shed their blood in the cause of freedom. As organiser, Dan Kelly now had the men assembled at the appointed time and place, and then proceeded down the road to report to Boylan that all was ready for him to assume command and to march his men to the rendezvous at Tara.

Kelly was greeted by Boylan with the news, spoken through a bedroom window, that his mother disapproved of his involvement in the affair. His courage had deserted him and he would not go. History fails to supply us with whatever acrimonious words then passed between the two men, but the conversation ended with an oath that Boylan would hang for this crucial act of cowardice, and that he (Kelly) would ensure that this would come to pass. So, leaderless, and without striking a single blow, the assembled men with their pikes at the ready had no option but to return to their homes. Thus ended South Louth's participation in the Rising of '98.

True to his word, Kelly exacted vengeance on the cowardly Boylan, and he invoked the law of the land to accomplish this end. Before the magistrates in Drogheda he swore that Boylan was a rebel. His evidence in court was accepted and the accused was found guilty and sentenced to death. He hoped for a reprieve through his acquaintance with Speaker Foster who was his landlord. Foster, who was a man who carried supreme influence, was not the kind of person to show mercy to a papist, least of all to a rebel papist. So on the 22nd June 1798 – just four weeks after his dereliction from duty in Ardee – the law had taken its full course and the body of Michael Boylan was swinging from the gibbet opposite the Tholsel in Drogheda. The corpse was then taken down and buried in the yard of Drogheda Jail in James Street (sited where St. Mary's RC Church stands today).

This was not quite the end of the story. The Governor's nights became greatly disturbed by a ghostly voice crying "Bring Boylan home". This perturbation of nature continued for a week until the Governor, terror stricken and demented, ordered the exhumation of the body. Boylan's relations then took possession of it and re-interred it in the family grave at Kildemock, Ardee where it now lies in peace. The inscription on the tombstone relates none of these events apart from a few sparse words: "Underneath lie interred the mortal remains of Michael Boylan, who departed this life 22nd June 1798, aged 26 years".

John Kells Ingram's poem about the 1798 Rising *'The Memory of the Dead'*, which has been set to rousing martial music, begins with two rhetorical questions: *"Who fears to speak of 'Ninety-eight? Who blushes at the name?"* Boylan's early demise spared him a great many ignominious blushes.

THE BATTLE OF TARA: Meath responded valiantly to the call to arms. On Wednesday the 23rd May – the day designated to commence action – the Meathmen scored a success when they intercepted a military supply train and captured a consignment of much-needed weaponry and ammunition. Two days later a contingent of Kildaremen joined the 4,000 Meathmen at the appointed assembly place – the historic Hill of Tara which in an earlier, halcyon era was the seat of the High Kings of Ireland.

They waited in vain for the Louthmen. Demoralised by their non-appearance and inadequately armed, they faced Captain Blanche and his Scottish Fencibles who arrived at the scene with a howitzer; they were also supported by the local Yeomanry. The latter were under the command of Lord Fingal who was a member of the same family as Saint Oliver Plunkett, but he had little truck with the peasantry and was greatly disliked. Another leader was Captain John Preston of Gormanston. The predecessors of both commanders had been prominent in the Confederation of Kilkenny. Although Catholic, they formed part of the Ascendancy and their loyalty rested with the government.

The insurgents were unfamiliar in the use of the captured guns, so they induced some Highlanders whom they had captured to enlighten them on their operation. They were without military training or any sense of regimentation, and their 'officers' lacked the crucial quality of authority that comes only with years of experience. Alcohol, as on so many other occasions, sadly enters the story, for a number of men intercepted a dray containing whiskey, the outcome of which impinged on the effectiveness of the insurgents. 'In a short time the boys began to carry away the whiskey in cans, pitchers, noggins, and all manners of vessels'.

On reflection, the rallying point of the Hill of Tara was ill-chosen. Its location as a site of former historical significance had no relevance when confronting a conventional armed force – the glories of the past offer no protection against grapeshot or howitzers. What was the first step for the assembled men to take – to march on Dublin? or Navan or perhaps Drogheda? What then? Who was issuing the orders? To whom were they answerable? What was the final objective? They were ill-provisioned for any sustained action. High ground provides a great advantage to a disciplined army in possession of cannon, but not to an untrained rabble armed for the most part merely with pikes and pitch-forks. The assembled men were totally exposed, apart from the walls of a church ruin, and presented an easy target to the Crown forces. On the other hand, flat land – of which Meath has its full share, with its maze of ditches and hedges – would have provided cover and endless opportunities in the use of guerrilla tactics, a circumstance with which a trained army would have had difficulty in coping.

Aware of these shortcomings, it would have been Captain Blanche's strategy to avoid early contact with the insurgents, and instead to keep them idle throughout the long, hot day; they lacked provisions and, more particularly, water. (The year 1798 was the hottest summer in a hundred years). Some of them had assembled three days earlier. They had been expecting some cannon, but it failed to turn up. Despite his fewer numbers – he was outnumbered by about ten to one – Blanche knew where his strength lay – his men were professional, seasoned soldiers; they were well drilled and well armed, and obedient to a central command. He was like a cat watching a nest of mice, and he bided his time, deliberately delaying action until the evening time.

He then opened with a salvo from his 6-pounder that played havoc on the massed ranks of the insurgents, but nonetheless the resistance was brave and obstinate in the face of the sustained fire. The position became critical for the Crown forces when they began to run short of ammunition; they had no option but to make one last desperate charge. The issue was very much in doubt especially when the cavalry charge from the right flank failed to materialise, (this was later the subject of a court martial), but in the face of the onslaught the Meathmen, who were without cover and were under fire for hours, dispersed in disarray, leaving the green Hill of Tara to soak up the red blood of 350 freedom fighters. The Crown forces easily won the day, having lost only 13 men.

A battle of the Tara type does not have a hero, but in fact it did have *a heroine*. Her name was Molly Weston, and she had reported at Tara with her four brothers; they hailed from north County Dublin. As the United Irishmen fled the field, she rallied the men who were stationed at the church. They put up a stout resistance, followed by a quick sally to try and capture the howitzer that was the cause of such devastation. In this brave feat they almost reached their objective, but were exposed to withering fire. History does not record the fate of this brave woman, but no doubt she fell with her four brothers and the other hundreds.

The yeomanry pursued the insurgents as they dispersed, and tradition tells us that some of them burst into a cottage in Summerhill, not far from Tara, and discovered a baby secreted in a churn. "The Captain stuck his bayonet into the child and then passed it along on the other bayonets, and shortly after they found a girl (probably the child's mother) hiding in the field. She was also killed and was later buried at Bective Abbey in an unmarked grave."[5]

The yeomanry attached to the castles at Dardistown, Ballygarth and Gormanston were returning from Tara on the evening of 26th May when they were set upon by local rebels at Tir-Ri, Stamullen. Once again superior arms and better training won the day, and a number of the rebels were killed[6]. For generations afterwards Louthmen had to endure the bitter invective and insults when confronted by those from their neighbouring county.

Paud O'Donoghue: An individual who scored a personal victory over the military was Paud

*Paud O'Donohoe Memorial
at Curraha*

O'Donoghue from Curraha. He was a well known hurler and was popular through- out the area. As a blacksmith he used his skills in fashioning pikes for the planned Rising. However, his forge was raided by a posse of yeomanry and he was caught red-handed. The captain, with sword drawn, ordered him to kneel, but Paud refused, saying that he would kneel only before God. This defiant pose so impressed the captain that he decided to allow him a little extra time in this world by asking him to shoe his mount. Paud complied, and when the opportunity came, he downed the captain with his hammer, mounted the horse and quickly disappeared. An impressive statue in bronze has been erected to his memory in Curraha.[7]

Undoubtedly, many local patriots who had assembled at Blakestown, Ardee, made their way independently to Tara, but certainly there were no local confrontations such as occurred at Wexford or Antrim, and so Drogheda can claim no glory. We know that the beleaguered government forces in Wexford and Wicklow were constantly appealing to Dublin for assistance – they were facing numbers that at one time swelled to nineteen thousand, and there was only a handful of men in the garrisons of the several local towns to face them.

Camden, the Viceroy, was an ineffective and hesitant administrator, and unfit for office – he hardly knew what action to take throughout the crisis, and the help which he did send to the Wexford area was both tardy and meagre. (Twice he offered his resignation, and he was finally relieved of office). Some of the military officers were equally incompetent. The insurgents were unable to take advantage of these weaknesses because their entire movement lacked the strategy that arises from thoughtful leadership – they were totally unprepared for what was taking place.

Although south Leinster had become the vortex of the violence, the Protestant population around Drogheda were nonetheless in a constant state of panic. The Corporation resolved to collect subscriptions 'for putting this town in a proper state of defence ... at this critical Junction'. The Fermanagh Militia, which had been stationed in the town and had provided it with a sense of security, was deployed elsewhere and this was the cause of great apprehension. In this state of alarm the Assembly appealed to Dublin Castle for additional forces, complaining : -

- that since the departure of the Fermanagh Militia this town has been left with only two Companies of the Carlow Militia which, with one Company of Yeomen Infantry containing 100 men and a troop of Cavalry containing 52 men and a detachment of a neighbouring Troop of 30, form its only defence;
- that in peaceable times the town was seldom left with less than four companies of Regulars;
- that ... few men could be brought to resist the Rebels should they make an attack;
- that the inhabitants of this town and suburbs, amounting to about 30,000 many of whom are notoriously disaffected, [are immediately in need of] 500 Regulars at least, and **two pieces of cannon**'.

This plea was made on the 11th June 1798, just a few weeks subsequent to the Tara affair. We can read several messages into it. Firstly, the danger of a local uprising had not passed, and the powder keg of insurrection could explode once more, especially as many of the Drogheda inhabitants were 'notoriously disaffected'. At this time several United Irishmen were apprehended and hanged at the Tholsel. (A plaque was prepared in 1998 with a view to placing it at the site but permission for its erection was declined). Secondly, the minority who held the reins of power did not hesitate to employ **cannon guns** on defenceless citizens in order to retain that power, should the occasion arise.

We are given here an inkling of the town's population. There are no official figures in this era – the first census was not taken until 1821. However, the city fathers provide us with a guestimate of 30,000 inhabitants. This is undoubtedly an exaggeration by reason of the fact that the local authorities were in a state of panic, and they were making a case that the existing garrison was inadequate in relation to the population. The figure quoted would have embraced outlying villages and the town's suburbs that were veritable rabbit warrens of destitute humanity, consisting of teeming masses of paupers who lived in rows of hovels outside the town walls. The survey of the Rev. A. Lindsay provides us with a figure of 15,225, a figure which probably related to those living within the town walls. A total of 20,000 is taken as a fair estimate.

The battle at New Ross was particularly bloody. The insurgents gained the town in a fiercely disputed contest and then – the same old story – they celebrated their success by looting the wine cellars and wherever else they could find liquor. Once again the Crown forces rallied and, after terrible slaughter, regained the town. The aftermath makes gruesome reading. Having first buried their own dead (ninety-one men), the authorities were then faced with the disposal of the bodies of the insurgents.

> *"The rebel carcasses lay in the streets unburied for three or four days; some perforated over and over with musket balls, or the bayonet; some hacked with swords; some mangled and torn with grapeshot, and worse still with pigs, some of which I have seen eating the brains out of the cloven skulls and gnawing the flesh about the raw wounds".*⁸

Local citizens were engaged to rid the streets of the rotting corpses, which often lay in heaps where action had been bitterest. (The reader will recall that the weather had been exceptionally hot throughout the entire uprising – the stench must have been abominable). A disused gravel pit became a convenient mass grave into which 3,400 bodies were tipped; others were thrown into the River Barrow – sixty-two cart-loads, according to one eye-witness.

These are some of the horrors that Drogheda escaped through non-participation in the Rising. One speculates that the scenes in New Ross may well have been similar to those in Drogheda following Cromwell's massacre. On that occasion there was no one other than the victors to tell the tale, and Drogheda had its own quota of swine to do their handiwork and clean up the mess; the silent Boyne, too, was a convenient vehicle for disposing of unknown numbers of bodies *sans ceremonie*. Tradition tells us that the water remained discoloured with the blood of the slain for some time after that slaughter.

The Rising in Ulster: Northern Presbyterians were suffering discrimination just as were Catholics in the south, and they were at the forefront of the United Irishmen. Prominent among them was a prosperous young man named Henry Joy McCracken. He was imbued with the spirit of liberty, equality and fraternity, and under his level-headed leadership County Antrim rose, and was soon followed by Down. As in Kildare and Wexford, there were some early successes, and the rabble was largely held in check by its leaders, with fewer cases of outrages being committed. But eventually government forces gained control and the insurgents were suppressed; this was followed by cruel retribution.

Fearful of laying down their arms and having to submit to English justice, a large contingent of Wexfordmen headed northwards to join the men from Kildare; but on arrival they were greeted with silence – the memories of the public whippings were too vivid – the freedom fighters of Kildare had had enough. Undaunted, the Wexfordmen marched into Meath, but the story there was the same. They then crossed the Boyne near Clonard and continued marching to rally the Louthmen to the standard – here was their opportunity to redeem their earlier dereliction. The stout-hearted men from Wexford by this time were tired, hungry, bedraggled and dispirited. But no one answered the call – not even a housewife to give them food or shelter or to tend the wounded.

They overnighted near Slane and soon after dawn they continued northwards. They were pursued from one place to the next by the cavalry of Major-General Wemys whose forces were stationed in Drogheda, and Brigadier General Meyrick from Navan. Rebels who lagged behind were cut down, and the main group was overtaken between Ardee and the Boyne. At that point about 1,500 of them formed a line, charged the pursuing cavalry and succeeded in forcing them back, but by then they were truly a spent force.

They escaped into the adjoining bog where they were relatively secure from pursuit[9]. Dejected, they then turned back to face the retributive justice that awaited them[10].

Weymes was the Commanding Officer of the Drogheda garrison and 'the Mayor offered him on behalf of the Corporation their concerns [i.e. property which they owned] called 'the old chapel' outside West Gate for the accommodation of the soldiers'.

Gradually the Crown forces secured the upper hand in both south Leinster and Ulster. The ragged, unruly mobs had no chance of long-term success when facing the ranks of trained soldiers well supplied with ammunition and cannon, and operating to a set design. One by one the rebel towns and villages were regained, and the ensuing punishment was both savage and unrestrained.

Enniscorthy, Wexford, New Ross, Vinegar Hill, ... these are place names that still evoke emotion in the breasts of all who cherish liberty. Vengeance was sweet for the yeomanry. A football match ending with a score-line of 65 – 1 would certainly be regarded as a 'no contest', but that was the final score of Catholic chapels and Protestant churches (in that order) that had been set ablaze. While on the subject of football, tradition tells us that when some of the rebel leaders were captured and killed, the yeomanry played football with their heads.

No doubt many other incidents occurred in the Louth/Meath area, and those who were suspected of involvement paid the full price, but the events remain unrecorded. A story is handed down that two men from Lisdornan, near Julianstown, were arrested for being United

Irishmen. Their hands were tied behind their backs, and then they were tied to horses and made to walk or stumble all the way to Trim where they were tried and then hanged.

A current resident of Lisdornan, Jackie Tallan, states that his ancestors operated a business as nailers and rope makers in Chancery Street (behind the Four Courts) in Dublin during the1600s and 1700s, and were involved in making pikes for the Croppies[11]. At Ballyboghil graveyard a shallow grave was unearthed in more recent times that contained several skeletons with pikes lying beside them – this tells its own unwritten story.

Overall, armaments surrendered or captured included 70,630 pikes, pikes that had been forged in labours of hope and expectation on countless anvils throughout the Irish countryside. Where were those sinewy blacksmiths now, and where were the pikemen who left their loved ones and set out with their lofty ideals of liberty? It is estimated that the Rising claimed about 25,000 lives, 2,000 of whom were loyalists[12]. As for the numbers of demolished mud-walled cabins, grieving widows, fatherless children, and the unspeakable sufferings of the tortured Croppies, history remains silent, but Dublin Castle was well pleased with the final outcome. (Many of the participants in the French Revolution had cropped hair, a vogue adapted by their Irish counterparts – hence the name 'Croppy').

The dawn of freedom had risen just three months earlier in a blaze of triumphs, but now the sun had set on a scene of desolation. The coming night would be long and dark – very.

A hundred years later a committee was elected in Drogheda to mark the centenary of the Rising, and its members attended various commemorative functions throughout the country, but no major event seems to have taken place within the town itself to mark the occasion, apart from a special Mass that was celebrated in St. Mary's church in James Street. At Tara a large crowd assembled, including 500 who travelled by train, with an equal number arriving by road from Drogheda.

The passing of a hundred years had thankfully erased the bitter memory of the debacle in South Louth. For the bi-centenary in 1998 the Old Drogheda Society produced a publication entitled 'Drogheda and 1798'; it deals with various events that occurred during those troubled times culminating in the Rising.

What would have been the outcome of the Rising had South Louth kept its appointment to join the others at the Hill of Tara, or had Drogheda risen in revolt? The Tara engagement was one of the initial events, and success would have made a world of difference. The combined forces of Meath and South Louth might well have tipped the balance in favour of the insurgents in their confrontation with the military, giving them victory, and as word of the good news spread, the resolve of the nation would have been galvanised.

On paper, the total headcount of the United Irishmen in Meath was 10,100 men, and it was reported to be a better disciplined force than most others; it was well organised, having worthy officers at its head, and it had captured valuable supplies of arms and ammunition. Had a serious uprising occurred in Drogheda, the town would have become a vital link, a hyphen joining North with South. The government's attention would have been diverted from both Wexford and the North, thus dissipating its military strength and preventing it from giving adequate support to either North or South. Dublin would have been obliged to maintain a formidable defensive garrison on full alert to keep a constant eye over its shoulder by virtue of Drogheda's proximity.

Thus, Drogheda occupied a strategic position and could have played a pivotal part in events. The non-appearance of the South Louth force at Tara no doubt had a demoralising effect on the gathering, and was a near mortal blow to the overall tactics of the entire movement, because subsequent events would hinge on an initial victory at Tara . In summary: –

- its failure to show up contributed to the defeat at the Battle of Tara;
- this, in turn, removed any threat to Dublin from the direction of Meath and Louth;
- a vacuum was created between the insurgents of the North and the South, keeping them separate;
- the government's hard-pressed forces were thereby released for deployment elsewhere;

179

- news of a victory at Tara would have precipitated immediate wide-scale action and, in particular, the North would have risen *simultaneously* with the south instead of a critical two weeks later;
- it meant that the road to the north was kept open for government forces from Dublin to crush Ulster in piecemeal fashion

JAMES NAPPER TANDY (1740-1803) – a Pen-Picture: A local man who was closely

involved in the Rising had the quaint name of James Napper Tandy. He was a founder member of the United Irishmen in Belfast in 1791. His family were brewers in Drogheda (the brewery which was later known as Cairnes Brewery, Marsh Road). As a Protestant, he was eligible to engage in the administrative affairs of the town; he played a prominent part in this as well as plying his trade as a wool merchant, operating in Dublin and Drogheda. The Assembly voted him a Freeman of Drogheda in 1789. Another member of the family, George Tandy, owned property in the town, and his brother, Burton Tandy, was a member of the Assembly. However, his activities as a United Irishman later brought him into conflict with the authorities. So much so that the Drogheda Assembly resolved on the 9th October 1798 that he

" ... be disenfranchised for being notoriously disaffected, and disloyal, to the King and Constitution, and an outlaw, and for lately having appeared on the coast of this Kingdom in a hostile manner with a body of French troops sent to invade this country".

This disloyalty to king and country must certainly have been an embarrassment to the Tandy family, who were staunchly loyal, and particularly his brother Burton who was elected Mayor of Drogheda in 1800.

> *I met with Napper Tandy and he took me by the hand.*
> *Saying 'How is poor old Ireland? And how does she stand?'*
> *She's the most distressful country that ever yet was seen,*
> *For they're hangin' men and women for the wearin' of the green.*

There is a wealth of both pathos and sardonic humour in the song '*The Wearing of the Green*', but the appreciation is lost on anyone not familiar with the background to the Rising of 1798. The lines tell of a nation yearning for freedom and of the struggle to attain it. The character who enquires about the condition of Ireland is Napper Tandy, an Irish exile, and he is evidently in love with his native land and is concerned about its welfare. However, he is 'on the run' for that very crime – the crime of loving his homeland coupled with the love of liberty – liberty for all. He is a fugitive on the Continent and is being sought by the authorities in Dublin. The reply he receives affords him no comfort: "She is the most distressful country that ever yet was seen". Back home, the laws are so draconian that the government is hanging, not only men, but women also, for one particular crime.

Then comes the line which pokes fun at those in power; yet it is pregnant with satire and derision, making a laughing stock of the law-makers: "Shamrock is forbid by law to grow on Irish ground". Written in jest, the line was not too far off the mark. But the government saw no humour in it. When the song was included in a musical play it was banned throughout the British dominions.

Theobald Wolfe Tone was a regular visitor to Drogheda. He was a barrister on the Leinster Circuit Court and successfully helped in the acquittal, as we have seen, of three Drogheda Catholic merchants who were charged with sedition. Both he and James Napper

Tandy went to France to secure military aid for the Rising. Help was given, but the English blockade made it very difficult for enemy ships sailing the high seas. Instead of operating in concert with the Irish forces, the French help arrived piecemeal and was too late.

Tandy's ship, the *Anacreon*, was one of the fastest ships of its day, and was able to outstrip the pursuit; it was laden with much-needed guns, ball-cartridges and barrels of gunpowder. Also included were bundles of leaflets for distribution; they were designed to rally the Irish people, telling them that French help had landed; " ... James Napper Tandy is at their head. He has sworn to lead them on to victory, or die ... " . General Humbert and his French contingent had scored a spectacular success when the English army simply turned and fled at the very sight of the opposition. It was an event known to history as 'the Races of Castlebar'. (These fleeing soldiers were, for the most part, Irish Militia, and the Louth Militia may well have been among them. The lack of commitment is very evident – they realised that they were combating a cause that they ought to be supporting).

There was no co-ordination with the French help that Tandy had taken ashore in Donegal. The timing was wrong – by that time the uprising in Wexford and elsewhere had petered out. Help had arrived too late.

There is one aspect of Tandy on which all sources agree – his appearance. By all accounts he was strikingly ugly, with a misshapen, bulbous nose – a proboscis which occupied most of his face, as depicted by the several sketches that have come down to us. Indeed, this feature was unkindly referred to on the floor of the House of Commons in Dublin on one occasion, and Tandy handled the incident indiscreetly. Instead of letting the matter pass, he demanded an explanation. Heated exchanges ensued, the upshot of which was that poor ol' Tandy was apprehended and committed to Newgate prison. Parliament, however, was prorogued on the same day, and thus Tandy was spared the indignity of being put behind bars.[13]

The graveyard in Saint Mary's C. of I. Church in Julianstown contains the tomb of the Tandy family. Part of the inscription reads "Here lies Mrs. Ann Tandy: Died 23 December 1820 aged 83: Widow of James Napper Tandy, Irish Patriot and General French Army ...". Tandy himself died in Bordeaux, and it is uncertain where his body lies – a local legend says it was taken back from France in secrecy and buried in Castlebellingham; others say it still lies in France.

The Tandy family lived at Lisdornan House, which takes its name from the townland on which it was situated on Bellewstown Hill's eastern slope – the slope facing the sea. The long, unerringly straight road leading to it from the top of the hill is known locally to this day as 'the Avenue', but this is the only clue to tell us that in days of yore it was the avenue leading down to a tall mansion that once stood at its terminus. No trace of the house now remains – cattle graze unheedingly on the site where it once stood – but a local veteran remembers it well:

"Nobody lived in it in my day, but they say that the Tandy family lived there. I remember when it was standing – there were two basements, one underneath the other – I was down in them. You could see the house from miles away; it was very high – four storeys – and you could see far out to sea from it".

As a boy in the 1930s he had crept up the unsteady staircase of the derelict mansion in search of adventure. His curiosity was rewarded in the form of some unusual objects which he found secreted behind a beam in the decaying roof structure:

"The ceilings were gone, but the staircase was there. I got flares above in it. They were complete; there was a switch and all in them. They were colour coded – orange and green and red. I remember bringing them home and my father, he was going to cut the head off me for going next or near the place. [The building was in a very dangerous condition and was later pulled down] They were up in the top of the building sitting in the walls".[14]

Wolfe Tone
He was a frequent visitor to Drogheda

Here was a tangible link with the Rising. The long sought help from France had been engineered by Napper Tandy as well as by Wolfe Tone, the latter having succeeded in speaking in person to the great Napoleon. (The two United Irishmen were rivals, and worked independently – yet another example of disagreement among Irish patriots!). The location of Lisdornan House, in an elevated position facing the sea and within sight of it, was ideal for making contact with vessels sailing up the coast. It is likely that this was the purpose of the colour flares that lay hidden during all those years after 1798, until discovered by the inquisitive little boy. Alas, these mementoes, which would have been worthy of display in the National Museum, were considered worthless, if not dangerous, and were at once discarded and are now lost to posterity. (In the lean years of the1930s when the flares were found, the people's minds were on more immediate matters).

ECONOMIC RECOVERY: The town had recovered well from the several battles fought during the 1600s, and had taken advantage of the peace that prevailed throughout the 1700s. Especially in the second half of that century there was an expanding market for both foodstuffs and manufactured goods, and Drogheda was more fortunate than most other towns at this period. Corn production and a gradual increase in prices meant that the tillage farmers of Louth were being adequately recompensed, and exports increased tenfold in the last two decades of the century; at the same time the cattle farmers of Meath benefited from a suspension of the Cattle Acts.

Britain was becoming the principal recipient of Irish agricultural produce. Between 1720 and 1800 total exports to Britain increased from 44.4% to 85.4%. Drogheda was prospering as an important market town, and it was a vibrant entrepot centre – this kept the merchants and the ship owners happy. The linen industry was expanding by leaps and bounds – exports of linen goods more than trebled during the century, with Drogheda in particular playing a significant part; and gainful employment kept the populace out of mischief.

A relaxation in the Penal Laws had allowed Catholics acquire property, and this rising number were now engaging to a greater degree in the commercial life of the town. We have seen above that they were being accepted into the Volunteers and were engaging in drilling manoeuvres on the Mall, shoulder to shoulder with their Protestant colleagues. The local newspaper described them as 'gentlemen Roman Catholics', and as such, they were acquiring some of the benefits that hitherto had been denied them.

This resulted in a class division among the Catholic fraternity, the affluent members being as apprehensive of a social upheaval as were their Ascendancy counterparts. However, this made the crafty John Foster grin from ear to ear, the scenario being attributed to his wiles. It is suspected that, far from setting out to patronise any Papist, he had the ulterior motive of driving a wedge between the rising phalanx of local affluent Catholics and the restless proletariat.

'Eager to detach propertied Catholics from radicalism, and prepared as a realist to go a long way to attain that end, he had secured several officerships for Catholics in the Louth militia'.[15]

It seems that religious differences were not the contentious issue locally that they were in other districts, at least among the property holders. Resentment rarely came to the surface and did not escalate into open conflict. In that way Drogheda escaped most of the turmoil and the blood letting that was experienced in other areas during 1798.

As to the Catholic clergy, those who were closer to the common people, namely the curates and parish priests, were all too familiar with the grievances of the peasants and they sympathised with them, but the official line of the Catholic Church did not alter, namely that the faithful were not to engage in violence, but to submit to those in power. This official Catholic Church policy of acquiescence is evaluated with the government-sponsored establishment of St. Patrick's College in Maynooth (1795). Clearly, donating a seminary was out of character with the governing body, but it had an ulterior purpose, being mindful of the upheavals a few years earlier in France when an overworked guillotine cut short the career of many an aristocrat – including those of the king and queen. Students for the Catholic priesthood had been educated in France up to that time, whereas by studying in Ireland their thoughts would be deflected from the influence of revolutionary notions that stemmed from the new, utterly new, France where the ruling class ruled no longer.

An Expanding Population: The improvement of the living conditions of the people was reflected in a demographic way. In mid-century the island's population was about 2½ millions, and by the end of the century it had doubled (nationwide), and within another 40 years, on the eve of the Famine, it had risen to a massive 8½ millions. This was nothing short of a population explosion, the prime reason being that the potato had become the staple of the people. It was nutritious, easily grown, and a small plot would feed an entire family for a year. There are no official statistics of Drogheda's population in that era, but no less a person than Saint Oliver Plunkett tells us that in 1671 the town's population was about 6,000. By 1800 it had more than trebled, reaching 20,000 approximately. We will see that economic condition in Drogheda caused a downturn in the population long before the Great Famine. (See **Population Graph** in Chapter Twentytwo).

Chapter Twenty

A Proposal of 'Marriage'

All of the King's Irish subjects were expected to show unquestioned loyalty to their monarch King George III, but the 1798 Rising revealed the undercurrent of discontent that existed throughout Ireland, and it sent alarm bells ringing throughout the corridors of power. It revealed the continuing threat of mob violence and the need for the ruling minority class to strengthen its link with England. This could best be accomplished by stripping Ireland of all legislative powers and by ruling the country from Westminster. Almost a century earlier Scotland had been led by the nose into union with England, and the attempt was made to take away her national identity by banning such insignia as the wearing of tartan. A similar plan was now proposed for Ireland. If it were to be implemented it would mean that the prime objective of the Rising, which was to 'break the connection with England', would ironically have the exact opposite result to what it had intended.

The ideal solution, concluded some of the Ascendancy class, but certainly not all of them, was to bind the two sets of people into one united kingdom and one big, happy family where all would be equal – Louth and Meath and Cork would be on a par with Lancashire and Devon and Cornwall, with perhaps some provision for later adjustments, and this concept would be effected through the Act of Union (1800). An elaborate web was spun to entrap a naive Ireland. The Lord Lieutenant, Lord Rutland, stated in 1784 that anyone who suggested union should be tarred and feathered[1]. No one was tarred and feathered in accomplishing this end, but the inducement of bribes on a grand scale, as we shall see, succeeded in changing the minds of many of the Ascendancy.

The fruits of the budding Industrial Revolution and the benefits of the expanding British Empire would accrue to all members of an extended kingdom, incorporating those citizens who lived in the annexed island – at least that was the Utopian scenario perceived by some and promulgated by others. This was the rose garden into which Cáitlín Ní Houlihán, like an unwilling bride, was being enticed to enter. This radical concept was spearheaded by the influential John FitzGibbon. Manipulator supreme, he was elevated to Earl of Clare, but was also known as 'Black Jack'. The proposal of Union with England was a very contentious one and was seen by a large section, including many prescient members of the Ascendancy, as being detrimental to their personal interests; it was also detrimental to those who had no say in the matter – the vast majority of the population – because they had no vote. It engendered heated controversy.

Its most vehement critic was Speaker Foster, aided by the MP for Drogheda, Henry Ball. A very forthright prime minister, Gladstone, said 80 years later that it was 'a paper Union obtained by force and fraud, and never sanctioned or accepted by the Irish nation'; he also opined that, if the agreement were to have been referred to a court of law, it 'must at once have been cancelled as a contract hopelessly tainted with fraud and corruption'.

The Petition Sent by Drogheda: The Drogheda Assembly made its views known, and sent a renowned Petition, not to the Parliament in Dublin, but direct to the King, on the 16th April 1800. (A Petition, or plea, was the regular vehicle used in seeking redress from officialdom). Foster, of course, was not a member of the Drogheda Corporation, but we can nonetheless visualise him riding into Drogheda from Collon and standing at the shoulder of the scribe who penned the Petition, where he was able to bring his experience and clarity of mind to good account and assert Drogheda's standpoint most trenchantly – Drogheda was showing leadership and was effectively expressing the view of the entire country. The document was brief and to the point. It was a masterpiece of rational argument. Indeed, the document was to resurface several times in the course of the next century in the pursuit of Ireland's unending quest for freedom. There was not a superfluous word in the Petition, and each of the points made had the directness of a Parthian arrow:

'Under the Constitution of 1782 [Grattan's Parliament], the kingdom has advanced in prosperity with a rapidity unexampled in the history of nations; and to state to your Majesty, that it is with the most heartfelt concern, your petitioners have seen the measure of an incorporate Legislative Union which was rejected in our last session of Parliament ... fraught with inevitable ruin to the Trade and Manufactures of Ireland by depriving them of the protection of a superintending resident Parliament and placing them at the discretion of a foreign parliament where their true interests have never been and probably never can be understood and where in any question of competition that may arise between the two countries their interests will sink under the weight of superior numbers. ... [We deplore] the useless privilege of sending one member to a distant and external Parliament ... [and] your petitioners have observed with grief the flagrant and unconstitutional means to which your Majesty's ministers have resorted to procure a majority in Parliament in support of this union ...'.[2]

Loyal subjects and compliant yes-men as all the Drogheda Assembly members were, their Petition to the King left no doubt as to their opposition to the proposed Union. They stated their case cogently and succinctly, putting the finger precisely on the most controversial point, namely that it would place Irish affairs ' *... at the discretion of a foreign parliament where their true interests have never been and probably never can be understood ... '*.

Furthermore, Drogheda (as a separate county, distinct from County Louth) had previously sent two members to the Dublin Parliament, but under the new arrangement the town's representation would be reduced to 'the useless privilege of sending one member to a distant and external Parliament', and the total representation from Ireland would 'sink under the weight of superior numbers' of English MPs who were ignorant of conditions in Ireland. The Petition also pointed out that the king was being misled with 'gross misrepresentation' through being informed that the Irish people looked upon the project with favour, when in fact it was a 'ruinous and fatal measure', and most people vigorously opposed it.

Lest the king be in any further doubt on the matter, the Assembly also drew his attention to the *'flagrant and unconstitutional means'* that were being used to secure the goal of Union. That in itself should have made the king sit up and take notice. But it was ineffectual.

All other protests were likewise in vain. King George III was dubbed by many as "the Mad King". (He suffered from a malady – *porphyria* – that triggered bouts of insanity, and he died a raving lunatic). Through his ill-advised policy of taxation without representation in government he had lost the American Colonies, but he was determined not to lose Ireland.

Even the weighty influence of Speaker Foster failed on this occasion. Suffice it to say that through bribery and chicanery of the most brazen kind, including the dispensing of peerages, pensions and wads of hard cash slipped under the table, the Irish Parliament was induced to betray the public interest, and to vote itself out of existence. To add insult to injury, these substantial back-handers were saddled on the Irish people, the amounts involved being lumbered onto the National Debt.

Speaking at the John Boyle O'Reilly Summer School in 2001, (the year of the bi-centenary of the Act of Union), Professor Thomas Bartlett, UCD, outlined the dishonesty that took place in rail-roading the Act through parliament:

> *"Bribery was rife, and brown envelopes containing over £30,000 was handed out to woo influential people to the pro-Union side. Although suspected throughout the 19th and 20th Centuries, the hand-outs were confirmed just three years ago when the diaries of a minor clerk who worked in Dublin Castle were discovered in London.*

> *"In this area [viz. Drogheda/County Meath] both Lord Gormanston and Lord Fingal had their titles confirmed in return for their support for the Act of Union. ... The Union was sold to various groups under different guises, with support coming from Archbishop Troy of Dublin, as well as the Catholic hierarchy and from staunch anti-Catholic agitator John FitzGibbon."*

The imposing Ballsgrove Gate that stands close to the south side of the Bridge of Peace today is testament to the ceaseless endeavours of Edward Ball (MP for Drogheda) throughout the controversy. It was erected in 1801 by the people of Drogheda in recognition of the valiant rear-guard action he fought as an anti-Union leader.

It is noteworthy that the Orange Order also opposed the Act of Union. On the other hand, the bishops of Ireland supported it when the carrot of Catholic Emancipation was dangled before them. Emancipation would follow as a matter of course, according to the men who were doing the wooing. But they were speaking with forked tongues.

From the first day of January 1801 the unmitigated evil of the Act of Union became operative, and the affairs of the Irish people were henceforth administered through the Imperial Parliament in Westminster. However, in Westminster the efforts of Edward Ball and the other Irish MPs were snuffed out by the superior numbers of English MPs and were incapable of obtaining any redress for Ireland's ills. Moreover, the will of the vast majority of the Irish people had no representation whatever because Catholics were debarred from sitting in it. It was therefore devoid of all moral validity.

*   *   *   *

The marriage of Cáitlín Ní Houlihán to John Bull was a loveless one. It could be better described as a kidnap, and the bride had been beguiled by promises broken ere they were written, Repeated acts of rape were to follow. There was never any prospect of happiness from a union so ill-contrived, and what followed was a long, dark age of unquenched suffering. The century that followed soon saw the collapse of Drogheda's mainstay, the linen industry – then came the Great Famine, followed by the Land War and its heart-rending scenes of evictions. The inevitable outcome of the marriage was divorce. Even then, the release from bondage was secured only after decades of legalised coercion and acts of violence culminating in the infamous barbarity perpetrated by the Black and Tans. The liberation, when it finally came, was marked by a total lack of grace and clemency, and was the cause of permanent disfigurement.

186

PART 4

'THE UNITED KINGDOM
OF GREAT BRITAIN AND IRELAND'

The Act of Union (1800) spliced Ireland irretrievably to England, over the heads of the people. It soon became evident that this was a union of two countries, but not of hearts. Henceforth, administration and debates on Ireland and on all Irish domestic matters took place in Westminster.

The Industrial Revolution was getting under way at this time, and the British Empire was in the process of encompassing the globe, giving rise to the proud boast that it was an empire 'on which the sun never set'. The produce of the dominions and crown colonies were filling the coffers in the home country with untold wealth. On the principle that all boats rise with the rising tide, this ought to have raised Ireland's economic well-being along with the rising tide of England's economic progress. Alas! Ireland had no boat.

Instead of participating in the increasing wealth of the United Kingdom, Ireland was engulfed by superior industrial forces, and Drogheda's industries submerged when, in particular, the linen industry collapsed. This brought endless misery to its citizens. That collapse was followed by the Great Famine, and then came the evictions and the Land War, making the Nineteenth Century the most harrowing in the country's history.

The lone Drogheda MP, Hardman, no longer went to Dublin to attend Parliament, but was obliged to sail to Liverpool and then take a coach to London. His was a voice crying in the wilderness. The Irish representatives numbered 100 out of a total Parliamentary membership of 660, and thus they were overwhelmed by the preponderance of English members, none of whom had the slightest interest in Irish affairs. As for the House of Lords, its members showed a marked antipathy towards Ireland and its people.

Drogheda had entered the 1800s well endowed with a diversity of industries, but the plentiful times soon turned to an age of pitiful poverty, making the Act of Union one long indictment of British misrule. Conditions would soon grow steadily worse as the Act's predictable consequences began to take effect. Ireland's Dark Ages were about to begin.

Henceforth England dominated every aspect of life in Ireland, and her growing industrial might incxorably suffocated home industries. The textiles for sale in West St. came from Manchester or Leeds, the hardware from Sheffield or Birmingham, the footwear from Northampton, the coal from Newcastle, and the office managers from Bristol or perhaps Shrewsbury or London. Every tool, every artefact, every piece of wearing apparel was stamped 'Made in England'.

Cattle, sheep and pigs converged on the Drogheda railway station from fairs throughout the midlands and the west; and they were then herded down the North Quay to be shipped 'on the hoof' to Birkenhead/Liverpool. Dependence on England was becoming total and was being ingrained in the minds of the populace.

In their search for work and to escape grinding poverty, destitute men scraped together the five shillings one-way fare and walked up the gangway of the *'Irishman'* or the *'Colleen Bawn'* that plied on a daily schedule between Drogheda and Liverpool, then to face a life of labour and loneliness, their only solace being alcohol.

These circumstances were to continue for the following 120 years and beyond.

Chapter Twentyone

An Unhappy Union

THE ECONOMY AND THE PEOPLE'S WELFARE: From the first day of the New Year in the New Century 1801 Ireland became part of a seamless United Kingdom. This change in status was at first barely noticeable in Drogheda. Speaker Foster, disappointed that his resistance to the Union proved unsuccessful, represented County Louth at Westminster. He had already spent 40 years in active politics in Ireland, and another twenty years lay before him, working tirelessly in the London Parliament – he was eighty when he eventually retired to his home at Collon. His vast experience stood to him, and his colleagues recognised his outstanding ability by honouring him with the Speakership of the House of Commons in Westminster. In addition he held several other important offices. At home he continued to influence the politics of the County Borough of Drogheda.

Apart from the Rising which came at the very end of the century, the 1700s had been a time of political quietude at home, creating an atmosphere of stability, a circumstance that was conducive to economic growth, and this trend accelerated as the century advanced. Poyning's Law, which had reduced Ireland's parliament to the role of a mere puppet, had been set aside in 1782. The new legislative independence allowed Ireland more latitude to plan its own destiny, and was guided under the able captaincy of Henry Grattan. It meant that, after a period of three hundred years, Irishmen in Ireland were empowered to pass laws (albeit still under scrutiny from London) for the betterment of the Irish people. These circumstances now ended.

Drogheda's population in 1796 was about 15,000[1] or perhaps more, and it ranked at about fifth in size among the towns of Ireland.

A Buoyant Economy: For some decades leading up to the Act of Union, and for a decade or so after it, Drogheda was on the crest of a wave, experiencing a period of unprecedented prosperity, and fuelled by a diversity of industries. There had been a sustained growth in farm output over the previous decades, and surplus produce was shipped abroad, especially to England where there existed a ready market at steady prices among its growing population. In addition, farmers throughout the countryside were harvesting the flax for the mills, and the housewives in their little cottages were busily engaged at their looms. The mills produced mainly coarse linen, calico and stockings. Everything points to the town being heavily engaged in producing fabrics.

The local ruling class were in a confident mood. The upheavals in the recent Rising were barely felt in the vicinity of Drogheda, and there had been no destruction of property. Trade and industry were progressing hand in hand with agricultural buoyancy. The Napoleonic Wars (1796-1815) were in full swing, creating further demands for horses and foodstuffs to sustain the British army and navy.

The Boyne Canal provided a new and cost effective form of transportation, accommodating barges of up to 50 tons burthen; it linked the town with Navan, and this facilitated trade with the heartland of County Meath and extended Drogheda's catchment area as a market town. Work on the canal's construction had begun in 1759, and with 20 locks throughout its course it was more or less completed in 1792. (The usage of the canal fell short of expectation, and the arrival of the railway service rendered it virtually redundant; but it continued in use until the 1920s). Bulky cargoes, particularly of coal, could henceforth be transported cheaply from the ships that constantly berthed at Drogheda's quays to inland towns; flax and other farm produce entered the town from the broad hinterland of Meath and Louth, with some of these products in their finished form being destined for shipment to England and further afield.

The town was heavily industrialised, and the linen industry in particular was thriving. Great factories, of a size hitherto unknown, were constructed, giving employment to almost

2,000 workers directly. The main proprietors of the mills were John and George Gradwell, Ennis, Richardson & Co., R. Gray & Co., and on the south side of the river was Chadwick & Gradwell's mill. The pay was poor and the hours were long, but the wages were welcome and the work was constant.

BALLSGROVE GATE

The people of Drogheda presented the Entrance Gate to Edward Ball MP as a mark of their appreciation for his valiant but failed efforts in opposing the Act of Union. In the middle ground is the Dominican Church, and to the left is the Linen Hall. Note that the People's Park did not exist and that the river shore extended to the roadway at the entrance to the Ballsgrove Estate.

It is a curious fact that the town may have given its name to a type of cloth. The word 'drugget' is said to have derived from the name 'Drogheda', according to Brewer's Dictionary of Irish Phrase and Fable. It is defined in the Oxford Dictionary as 'a coarse woven fabric used as a floor or table covering', but others say that the word may instead have a French origin. The town also gave rise to a phrase used to describe a workman who has run short of some necessary material: 'Idle for the want of weft, like the Drogheda weavers'.

Many Irish towns operated a distillery, Drogheda's being Preston's. In addition there were three large breweries, the greatest being Cairnes Brewery which exported its celebrated beer to England as well as to the East Indies and West Indies – these industries entailed the use of several malting stores which still stand today, although now used for other purposes.

There were 7 corn mills, 6 salt works, 1 rope-walk and 4 soaperies which included the production of candles. There were 8 tanneries, and Samuel Lewis reported in 1837 that 'tanning leather was formerly very extensive and is still considerable'. Other industries included footwear making, tobacco (of which there were twelve manufacturers) and flour and corn mills. The great flour mill of Smith and Smythe (later known as McCann and Hills and currently adapted for apartments and miscellaneous purposes) on Merchants' Quay cost an enormous £20,000 to build.

The main imports were coal, timber, slates, iron, bark, herrings and rock salt, and luxury items included tea, sugar, tobacco and wine. The principal exports were grain, flour, oatmeal, peas, livestock, butter and, not surprisingly, linen. Shipping was very brisk, entailing the service of 53 pilots as well as a steam tug, and 40 vessels were registered in Drogheda. A major undertaking was the deepening of the river bed by four feet to accommodate vessels with a deeper draught. They plied with ports as far distant as Nova Scotia, New Brunswick and Canada. It can be seen that the town could well be described as a boom town.

Wealth and Poverty: Even in describing it as a boom town, we must not presume that the entire population was living in comfort. Emphatically, they were not. Why, then, should some people be experiencing want, given that the local economy was being fuelled by gainful employment, with the yields from tillage improving, with livestock exports being very healthy and with a thriving linen industry? Here we have an anomaly. The increased prosperity was not being equitably distributed. Handsome profits were being made, but they were being short-circuited straight into the pockets of those who were already rich. The labouring classes were being exploited, and were being denied a fair share of the economic cake.

The discrimination and penal restrictions that were in operation after the Battle of the Boyne had put the Ascendancy firmly in control, and administration was conducted through an unchallenged Corporation. Drogheda's destiny was in their hands, but they eschewed all obligation towards the masses, precluding them from participation in the wealth that was being created.

Furthermore, the unprecedented growth in the population nationwide, which was occurring mainly among the labouring and cottier classes, was creating an ever-increasing demand for land, thereby pushing up rents. The landlords were growing fatter as the rents came rolling in, and the peasants were becoming inexorably poorer. Living conditions throughout Ireland, even before the Great Famine, were deplorable. In 1841 40% of Irish families lived in the most primitive, single-roomed, mud-walled cabins with roofs that were comprised of mere sods of grass laid on wooden boughs and covered with a straw thatch. Most of these hovels had neither a window nor a chimney. Water had to be drawn from wells, and sanitation was of the most primitive kind.

Such living conditions attracted diseases. It was no surprise that a cholera epidemic visited Drogheda in 1832, and in May of that year there were 37 deaths from the 73 reported cases. By the time the outbreak had passes there had been 1213 cases, of which 419 had died, most of them among the poorer classes.

Agriculture was the mainstay of the people, and with living standards ever declining, the potato had become the staple diet. As the population of the island continued to increase, the farmland of rural Ireland was being divided and then sub-divided to accommodate the extended families, until some farms were no bigger than five acres, and often less.

There were regional variations in this trend, with Connaught, (where the land was poorest), having the highest density of pocket farms.

> *'Go to Mayo. You will encounter thousands of men literally nearly dead of hunger. The marquis of Sligo has, in the same province, 70 thousand acres of land, the revenue of which he consumes in England. And should not the law enforce this man to give some of his surplus? Why are so many people dying of hunger in Mayo? Because the landlords find it in their interest to increase their grasslands, and if they can make a little more money, they laugh at us besides. ... It is the interest of the landlords of Ireland to render the people as wretched as possible, for the more the cultivator is threatened by starvation, the readier he will be to submit to every condition they wish to impose on him'.*[2]

This and other observations of a similar vein were recorded by a French traveller to Ireland in 1835. Louth and Meath fared better than most counties. Among the towns, Drogheda was exceptional, as we have noted, in having a wide diversity of manufacturing industries. Drogheda was seen as a magnet of opportunity for the many peasants and broken farmers seeking to improve their lot. It does not follow that, in escaping the rapacious clutches of landlordism, they were free from exploitation. Disillusion attended those unfortunate migrants who were attracted towards the town. It was a fatal attraction – like moths to the flame of a candle.

Those who converged on Drogheda were mainly uneducated and unskilled peasants, and they contributed nothing to the town's economy – they were simply parasitic, an added burden on society. This had the effect of dragging the existing standard of living down towards the level of the migrants. Animosities arose through competition for work, and wages spiralled ever downwards. The suburbs consisted of legions of paupers living in makeshift hovels in absolute squalor. Friedrich Engels, who visited Ireland, wrote '... the poorer districts of Dublin are among the most hideous and repulsive to be seen in the world'. If anything, Drogheda was worse, revealing more starkly 'the unacceptable face of capitalism'.

We are told that a feature of most Irish towns was the number of vagrants who wandered about the streets. Tourists and visitors, when alighting from their carriages, were immediately surrounded by swarms of beggars with outstretched hands, reminiscent of scenes that still obtain today in parts of India. Drogheda, no doubt, had more than its share of these unfortunates.

The nub of the difficulty was the potato. Its twofold advantage – prolificacy and nutrition – meant that a small patch of earth would feed a family for a year. In consequence, Ireland's population had increased by leaps and bounds, but a twofold misfortune was to follow. The second of these was the Great Famine, which we will discuss below, and the first was to deposit a glut of unskilled hands on the labour market. Thus, the merchant princes were in a position to pay minimal wages (especially in the textile trade) to their workers. (Is it any wonder that this scenario led Engels and Marx down the road of Communism!)

The Distribution of Wealth: The workforce was living closer and closer to subsistence level. Living from hand to mouth, chronic poverty ensured that they would never be in the position to accumulate the funds necessary to improve their lot, to acquire better working equipment or to adapt to changing circumstances. As for the capitalists, why should they risk their money on expensive machinery when there was an endless supply of cheap labour – cheap *replaceable* labour at hand? The answer came when the Ulster segment of the industry grasped the nettle of adaptation and made the move into the budding industrial age, leaving Drogheda to flounder in methods that had become hopelessly obsolete.

It must be said that the unequal distribution of wealth was not peculiar to Drogheda and Ireland. The anomaly of opulence existing side by side with poverty was also prevalent throughout Britain where nine-tenths of the country's wealth was in the hands of one-tenth of the people. By today's standards this is an unacceptable situation, and is redressed mainly through taxation and other forms of governmental intervention, but in the 1800s it was regarded as the norm. The concept of a 'social conscience' had not yet entered the minds of those in power.

The government did not deem it its duty to intrude into socio-economic affairs – no regulation, however humanitarian its purpose might be, was allowed to interfere with the precepts of raw, elemental economics. The doctrine of *laissez faire* was sacrosanct, and freedom in conducting business was to remain inviolate. If the weaker elements of society were to be trampled underfoot in the pursuit of wealth, then so be it.

There were a few notable exceptions to this climate of indifference to social needs, but these stood out like beacons and they bypassed Ireland. Robert Owen, for example, created a model community around his mill in New Lanark, where improved working conditions, better housing and schools for the workers' children were introduced as a matter of policy, but in industrial Drogheda the general scene was one of deprivation through exploitation. Despite the enormous quantities of finished linen passing through the Linen Hall in Drogheda, many people were living at subsistence level.

The 'Workshop of the World': The trend in Britain, as in all Western Europe, was for industries to be established close to the sources of raw materials, and with the Industrial Revolution now under way, coal and iron were the crucial components. In the 'black country' in the heart of England industrial towns had sprung up overnight. This scenario was matched by an efficient infrastructure, including the great Manchester Ship Canal which enabled the bales of cotton to sail from the Mississippi straight to Liverpool and then onward to the factory doors in Manchester, Bolton, Burnley and the many other such hives of industry. The upstart princes of enterprise were quick to harness steam technology, and the steam-driven machinery did the rest. A network of canals was soon to be followed by a railway network that was speedy and reliable – these were the arteries and sinews that provided the lifeblood for the burgeoning towns of industrial England.

On the other hand, the Irish economy, already deprived by legislation in so many ways, was at a despairingly competitive disadvantage. Mother Nature had dealt the Emerald Isle a weak hand in the matter of mineral resources, and in consequence she drifted further and further behind England in industrial growth. To try and overcome this handicap, it was necessary to ship coal into Drogheda for the factories, but this added to the cost of production and to the sale price. Where did this leave the cottage industries? They went into free fall.

Britain was well on the way to becoming the world's dominant industrial power through the sheer inventiveness of its entrepreneurs allied to the generous endowment of natural resources, especially coal and iron. Add to this the raw materials that arrived at English ports from her overseas possessions and we are not surprised to find her establishing a position at the very forefront of world trade. Also, she had the prerequisite of accumulated capital that enabled her to adapt to the new industrial age, and to take full advantage of the latest inventions and new techniques. The steam-powered machinery in Manchester was able to turn out mass-produced textiles at prices that poor Drogheda could never hope to match. As one observer put it, Cinderella sat at home in rags while the Ugly Sister, dressed in her finery, was revelling at the Ball.

While Drogheda's schooners lay berthed awaiting fair winds for a voyage, the new packet-steamers from Liverpool and Bristol were able to discharge their cargoes of finished goods on the quays in double-quick time, and the traditional Irish market outlets were being invaded with standardised, flawless, factory-made goods. By contrast, the equivalent Drogheda products were inferior in quality, were often faulty and were more expensive. Drogheda was fighting a losing battle, and it didn't help when the materials being put up for sale in the Linen Hall were found to be degraded with admixtures of cotton. The linen industry was notoriously corrupt, and warnings placed by means of advertisements in the *Drogheda Conservative* by the Linen Board failed to stop the practice.

The linen industry began to collapse early into the new century, and then accelerated. While still grappling with that problem, the potato failed; these joint catastrophes had a drastic and long-term effect on Drogheda's population. All in all, the 1800s would emerge as being the most pitiful in any period of Drogheda's history. An escape outlet for many men was to follow the tradition of joining the army. We will discuss both of these factors in turn.

ENGINEERING AND SHIPBUILDING: One bright spot in providing much needed employment was Drogheda's new ship-building industry. The first vessel to be launched was in 1838, and the occasion was the cause of much excitement. A vast throng had gathered at the North Strand to witness the actual launching which took place on the opposite bank of the river. Other steamers on the river served as additional vantage points for spectators. The most distinguished of these was Daniel O'Connell. He addressed the guests, stating that Mr. Henry Smith, the proprietor of the shipyard, 'had his heart in the right place, and if every capitalist and gentleman acted his part for the good of the country as Mr. Smith had done, we would not now be called 'Poor Ireland', but would be the envied portion of the British dominions'. The ship, which registered 230 tons, was named the *'Lady Maria Somerville'* (Sir William Somerville MP represented Drogheda at Westminster) and was built throughout of Irish oak. It was announced that plans for five further ships were on the books, envisaging employment for 500 shipwrights. In St. James Dock Yard a fine ship was specially built and designed to trade between Dublin and Australia.

Drogheda had been associated with shipbuilding from earliest times. We have seen that as early as 1222 King John commanded that a Galley be built in Drogheda. In 1409 'it was ordered that a ship of war should be built in this town to defend the coast from the invasion of the Scottish enemy'. A miscalculation occurred during the construction of a vessel in a more recent age which resulted in it being of lesser dimensions than had been intended. The shipowners evidently had a sense of humour, for they named it *'The Mouse'*.

In 1826 the Drogheda Steampacket Company was formed, and for many decades its 5 steamers plied from Drogheda to Liverpool and Glasgow, carrying both freight and passengers. The company boasted of several 'firsts': first to have steam steering mechanism; first to use electric light; first to use compound engines; and first to provide berths for third class passengers. Sailing ships continued to operate, and were still seen on the Boyne up to the mid 1940s, the last one being the *Mary B. Mitchell* which regularly berthed at the cement factory on the Boyne Road.

Another important industry was Thomas Grendon's Foundry and Engineering Works. Henry St. George Smith also had an interest in this enterprise. It was established in 1835 at the South Quay. According to the Irish Times in 1921 'In 1845 when the first locomotive was built by Messrs Grendon and Company, and up to 1885, the Drogheda Foundry was one of the most famed of its kind in the Three Kingdoms, employing between 600 and 700 workers, turning out ships, locomotives, weighing machines and all classes of ironworks'. It produced lighthouse equipment and buoys, also railway engines for use on the Irish railway network, and in 1885 an engine was shipped to Liverpool for onward transportation to Brazil. An iron bridge was sent to Malta, and we still see local examples of the firm's workmanship in the Obelisk Bridge and Dominic's Bridge. Further local evidence of the foundry's products is drainage gratings in Fair Street and in other parts of the town. In 1863 it launched the last of three steamers built for the Grand Canal Company in Dublin. This vessel was fitted with high-pressure steam engines, driving screw propellers. Nine such vessels were launched in a twelve-month period, and the company had orders for two further iron vessels of 800 tons as well as several other valuable contracts.

Undoubtedly, this facility had also been used for repairing ships. It is interesting to note that the lane (now demolished to make way for the slip road from the Marsh Road to St. Mary's Bridge) which led from James St. to the shipyard and graving dock was called Graves Lane. Some sources say that a Mr. Graves lived there; but graving is a nautical term which describes the cleaning of a ship's hull and the application to it of a coating of pitch. A veteran (born 1913) recalled another graving dock: 'I remember the slip at Ship St. being used. It had a graving dock for repairing barges, and they were used for hauling flour up the canal to Spicer's bakery in Navan'[3].

Competition from abroad forced the eventual closure of the foundry, but it opened again in 1914 as the Drogheda Ironworks, employing about 70 men. A wide variety of goods were produced including ranges, manhole covers and garden seats. It finally closed in 1970.

The Decline Continues: Unable to adapt to the changing circumstances, the one-time flourishing linen trade, which meant so much to the people of Drogheda, went into decline about 1820, and the spinners and weavers found themselves in straitened circumstances. Great naval battles of earlier decades, such as the Nile (1798) and Trafalgar (1805), had played havoc with the sails of both merchantmen and the great men-o'-war, occasions that kept the linen trade busy. With Napoleon out of the way this outlet diminished greatly. By the mid 1820s the industry was on its knees, and the spinning wheels had virtually come to a halt, plunging the workers into direful hardship.

A news item in the *Drogheda Journal* in 1813 records a submission to the Government that underlines the sufferings being endured by the people under misgovernment from Westminster: –

> *"We the Roman Catholic people of Ireland again approach the Legislature with a statement of the grievances under which we labour, and of which we most respectfully, but at the same time most firmly, solicit the effectual redress. Our wrongs are notorious and numerous. Ages of persecution on the one hand, and of patience on the other sufficiently attest to our sufferings and our submission..."*

This was a *cri de coeur*, and it was presented with measured, dignified restraint. As with so many other petitions, it went unheeded. The position of the cottage industries had become pathetic and, with no means of support, the former spinners and weavers were on the brink of starvation. The Mendicity Asylum in William St. was unable to cope with the mounting destitution. 'The crowds of half famished objects which present themselves at every turn indicate the most unparalleled distress, and great as have been the subscriptions, yet they fall very short in affording anything like general relief. ... The Drogheda Journal of 13th September 1826 warned that deaths for the last fortnight have been numerous beyond any period in our recollection, and all ranks are affected with this distressing malady'.[4]

By 1830 the industry had collapsed completely, reducing the hordes of workers to extremes in poverty. This created an exodus, with many weavers emigrating to seek employment in Rouen in France, to Manchester, Wigan and Barnsley in England and to America.

Drogheda weavers in 1840 were earning 4/- (€0.25) per week,[5] and it was their little potato plots outside the town that kept them alive. Appeals were again made to the government to revitalise the industry, stating that 'Ireland has claims undoubtedly strong upon the Parliament of the United Kingdom for every aid and encouragement necessary to the maintenance and support of the linen manufacture, at least to the extent of the annual parliamentary grant', and for the repeal of laws that were injurious to the industry. Parliament turned a deaf ear on these pleas, and eventually the Linen Board became redundant and was wound down and dissolved.

Prior to the industrial era, the people had little means of support other than being self-employed such as in the cottage industries. Many others looked to the 'big houses' which were virtually the only other source of employment, and where small 'armies' worked in the vast farmlands, the walled kitchen gardens, the livery stables and in the kitchens, working as farmhands, gardeners, gamekeepers, foresters, coachmen, grooms, cooks, butlers, nurses, nannies, etc. However, many of these occupations were taken up by Scottish Presbyterians, German Lutherans or the like. 'The custom of employing foreign domestics was normal in Irish country houses where it was felt that the native Irish did not have the skills required to carry out such work'.[6]

Chapter Twentytwo

Social Conditions in Drogheda in the Early 1800s

Before we view the political scene in Drogheda and County Louth following the Act of Union it is fitting that we should turn our attention to the living conditions of the people. Throughout the 1700s the various processes involved in linen production gave rise, as we have seen, to considerable employment, and this state of affairs continued into the new century. Times were quite good for those in employment during the first handful of years after 1800, thanks to Drogheda being at the very forefront of the linen industry. The small tenant farmer was growing the flax in his little patch, and the town thrived on the scutching, spinning, weaving and bleaching, the several processes which the flax underwent, giving added value to the basic product at each stage of manufacture. The spinning wheels in the cottages were whirring merrily, giving employment to the female population.

Street lighting, which hitherto had been provided by oil lamps, was being replaced gradually by gas from 1819. Private homes were given the opportunity of changing to gas, but acceptors were required to provide security to cover any damage to footpaths occasioned by the laying of the pipes. The enterprise remained in private hands until 1898 when it was taken over by the Drogheda Corporation for £22,250 under a special act of parliament called the Drogheda Corporation Gas Act.

The Linen Hall (now demolished – it was sited at the car park that fronts the Abbey Cinemas) was constructed in 1774 to cater for the demands of the industry. This market place operated under the direction of the Linen Board; it presented a busy scene where the manufactured linen changed hands. The whole neighbourhood of Drogheda and Counties Louth and Meath were involved, and it vied with the eastern counties of Ulster as to the volumes produced. Buyers included representatives from abroad, and shipments of finished goods continued to be exported to America as well as to England and Continental Europe.

The merchant princes were enjoying comfortable circumstances at this time, but it is evident that the town's industries were unable to absorb the total workforce and to sustain everyone with the basic necessities of life. It is inevitable that in times of distress there is a migration of destitute people from rural areas to centres of population in their search for sustenance, and this is an explanation for the hordes of poverty-stricken people who were converging on Drogheda from before the Act of Union.

Undoubtedly, the Assembly members were proud of their tradition and their town. In 1820 they resolved that the Members of the Corporation must wear 'gowns according to rank, Aldermen to wear scarlet cloth, Sheriffs and peers black cloth and common couch Lutherine or proper black stuff'. Meticulous in matters of trivia, it is apparent that they were a grossly uncaring collection of men when it came to addressing the welfare of the people at large, many of whom were living in penury and wearing tattered rags. The elite members of society had created a two tier structure and were cocooned within their own comfortable sphere without applying any deference towards their less fortunate brethren. The religious divide ensured that there would be no integration with them either commercially, or socially; inter-marriage was out of the question.

In perusing the Corporation's Minute Book covering past centuries one is struck by the constant attention given to the admission of freemen to the Borough (by conferring voting rights on these newcomers they were entrenching their dominant position), while the welfare of the townspeople at large and the provision of work for them never featured on the agenda.

Legislation throughout the penal times specifically precluded Catholics from entering trades and professions, and this denial of career opportunities was punctiliously pursued, as repeatedly recorded in the minute book of the Drogheda Corporation. All sense of social responsibility was conspicuously absent, resulting in the economic misery that abounded. The Assembly ruled by exclusion, not inclusion, and it was not intended that Catholics should participate in conducting the affairs of the town or in sharing in the prosperity being created.

They failed to realise that a society's most valuable resource is its own citizens. This was a fatal oversight. By neglecting to utilise this potential asset for the universal benefit they were inadvertently impairing their own welfare, and in time this would bring about their downfall.

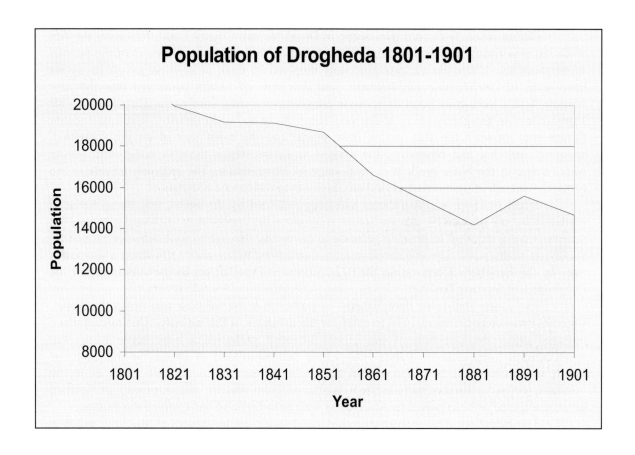

POPULATION GRAPH

*While Ireland, as a whole, experienced a continued growth in population until the reversal caused by the Great Famine, Drogheda had a different experience – **the decline began at the very outset of the 1800s, and that trend continued almost to the end of the century**. This was a clear indication of the adverse conditions that prevailed at local level.*

A primary law of economics is that 'money begets money', and the corollary is that a penniless people kept in idleness and repression can contribute nothing towards a healthy economy. Lacking any purchasing power, they become an incubus to society. The evidence of Drogheda's overall potential for growth and prosperity existed in the form of the diversity of industries that blossomed into full flower in the latter part of the 1700s, especially during the era of Grattan's Parliament. However, the structure of the town's economy was built on too narrow a capital base – this was the exclusive preserve of the privileged few, and designedly so. The dog-in-the-manger policy was restraining the economy, forcing it to operate in a strait-jacket. In the course of time the ruling elite would be overwhelmed by their deliberate partisanship and abuse of power, and this, ironically, would eventually bring about their own demise. This scenario is well described in Goldsmith's pithy couplet:

"Ill fares the land, to hastening ills a prey,
Where wealth accumulates and men decay".

196

A glance at the statistics on Drogheda's population throughout the1800s provides us with no better example of the inherent flaw in the policy being pursued. Myriads of small, insignificant English towns such as Blackburn, Bolton, Bradford, etc. began to develop and flourish, benefiting from the burgeoning Industrial Revolution, and they experienced unprecedented growth, exploding into large, thriving cities. By contrast, Drogheda had entered the economic doldrums early in the 1800s; economic conditions were stagnant and were to grow appreciably worse as the century progressed. The population spiralled downwards, a contraction that continued for a hundred years. By the century's end Drogheda had lost about 8,000 of its inhabitants.

Conditions must have been indeed serious when the plight of the poor came up for discussion during a Corporation meeting in the year 1800. The Minutes tell us that it was " ... agreed in consideration of the extreme distress of the poor, who cannot possibly exist without immediate relief, the sum of £300 [be expended to alleviate their suffering]". This was as close as they ever came towards addressing social reform. The provision of some relief was welcome, but it is disappointing to observe that so much poverty existed at a time when Drogheda was still enjoying favourable economic conditions. The circumstances of the poor were to deteriorate greatly as the new century advanced.

The decline in linen exports was due to competition from Britain as well as to the growth of the cotton industry. The policy of *laissez faire* ordained that protective tariffs be removed, and thus the handlooms in the little whitewashed cottages fell prey to the industrial superiority across the water. Lack of capital meant that the little cottier, however industrious he might be, was at a hopeless disadvantage and was unable to compete with the innovations that accompanied the budding Industrial Revolution, with its scutch mills for dressing flax, its multiplicity of looms in huge factories, its division of labour, and the other advances in technology and steam-powered machinery.

Chapter Twentythree

Speaker Foster's Role in Drogheda's Affairs

John Foster had been MP for Dunleer which was a minuscule pocket borough, the electorate

John Foster
He was a man of great ability and influence,
being Speaker in the Irish Parliament, and
later in Westminster.

consisting of a mere handful of cronies – they were his friends and relations. That constituency disappeared under the Act of Union. For this inconvenience Foster was given the enormous sum of £7,500 as compensation plus an additional £5,000 for loss of the Speakership, kick-backs which softened his cough appreciably. He then represented Co. Louth in parliament. It was inevitable that a man of such energy and talent would involve himself in the politics of the Borough of Drogheda. After all, his Collon residence was a mere seven miles away, and his family held property in the town. He was familiar with many of its inhabitants through having been educated in the Grammar School in Laurence Street.

From the easy times in the Dunleer constituency he quickly adapted to the cut and thrust of politics in Drogheda where there were sharp-minded businessmen and crafty wheeler-dealers. He soon learned that they were open to bribery, and that every political vote had a price tag attached to it. A complication was the question of Catholic Emancipation. In Dunleer this had not mattered, but in the Drogheda borough, where

the Catholic population had climbed to 80% or 90% of the total, it was a burning issue and had to be handled with delicacy, if not duplicity. The challenge was to walk the tightrope of domination over the heads of the underprivileged and discontented masses.

He used his influence in securing government grants for local projects to such an extent as to cause Henry Grattan to demur publicly. State benefits were directed towards improvements to Drogheda's busy seaport, Port Oriel at Clogherhead and other fishing harbours on the Louth coastline as well as in constructing the Boyne Canal. The villagers in Collon had piped water, thanks to his efforts. Such achievements earned him the accolade 'Prince of Improvers'. His prominence in national affairs stood him well, and the Borough of Drogheda recognised his endeavours by awarding him the Freedom of Drogheda in a gold box as early as 1786.

In his home village of Collon he established a factory, a bleach-green and a spinning works. The village and the surrounding countryside grew appreciably in prosperity. When disputes arose, Foster was invariably called upon to settle them. More importantly, his membership of the Linen Board was crucial to the 1,900 Drogheda workers whose livelihood centred on linen production. These factors contributed to his political success in the town.

An example of his interference in Drogheda's internal politics occurred in the Irish parliamentary by-election of 1796. He supported his friend of long standing, Edward Hardman who was the wealthiest merchant in the town, and whose grandfather and father as well as himself had been elected Mayors over the years. Opposing him was John Ball, of Ball's Grove who practised as a barrister in Dublin. Against the odds, Ball won. In the general election held the following year Hardman contrived to be elected, but was immediately unseated when a petition of 'bribery and undue influence' was proved against him, an incident which saw Speaker Foster in a bad light.

The Act of Union had an immediate and direct effect on Drogheda by reducing the Town Borough from two seats to a single-seat constituency. Hardman took the seat, again with the connivance of Foster. A few years later (1807) Foster succeeded in having his son Thomas elected; he was a colonel in the Drogheda Militia (later known as the Louth Militia), and had previously assumed the seat that his father had vacated in Dunleer. His father's muscle at national level and in championing the anti-Union lobby eased the way for him.

There was a regular pattern of intrigue, in-fighting and bribery in the Drogheda constituency, in contrast to cosy Dunleer. While he was engaged in electioneering, he made a point of suppressing his anti-Catholic leanings, and he studiously avoided the slogan 'no popery'. Seats always cost money in bribery pay-outs and in putting on a show of grandeur. His success cost him a very respectable £2,441 in hard cash in buying votes, in distributing largesse and in ostentatiously scattering £12 in coins to the rabble.

As time went on, the accumulating debts began to catch up on the Fosters, and the Speaker's son Thomas, who lacked the political acumen of his father, did not contest the next election. Those Catholics who had the franchise were always glad of an electoral contest – it gave them the option of voting for anyone opposing a Foster. The Ogle family, whose home was in Fair St. opposite the entry to Duke St. became prominent Drogheda representatives for many years thereafter. A trend had developed of playing the Catholic card, and this ploy brought success to the Ogles. Lord Henry Moore, who was a son of the Marquess of Drogheda, threw his hat into the ring at election time but was persuaded to withdraw, as his presence would have split the Protestant vote; anyway, the family of Lord Drogheda by this time were not domiciled locally and were unfamiliar with local affairs.

Another factor in Thomas Foster's decision to stand down after 1812 was the gradual growth in the number of the Catholic electorate in their capacity as freeholders. Families such as the Birds, Collins's and the Brodigans who, under a relaxation in the discriminatory laws, had set up businesses during the last quarter of the 1700s and as property holders and freeholders they were becoming a power in the land. The demographic profile was changing, and to be successful, a candidate in future had to woo the Catholic vote, a gesture that went against the grain of a bigoted Foster. Furthermore, elections involved buying votes and this meant reaching deep into their depleted pockets – they were unable to manipulate the Drogheda voters in the same way as they could with County Louth. Thus, they finally found it necessary to bow out completely from the Drogheda political scene.

'It is easy to trace the varying ratio of freeholder to freeman votes because of the number of contests in the period; and it may be assumed that all the freeholders were Catholic and all the freemen were Protestant'.[1] This observation is a damning indictment on the ruling elite, for it indicates that, while Catholics, as freeholders, were growing numerous through acquiring property and becoming successful businessmen, the freemen were being slipped in through the side door which was left open for them by the Assembly members. It highlights the bias in the legislation and the corrupt tactics being used by the ruling class.

A CORRUPT REGIME: A source of constant resentment was that the Drogheda Corporation was unrepresentative of the townspeople proper. Its members consisted of 24 aldermen, 14 elected representatives of guilds, 2 sheriffs and several others. The 24 aldermen held office for life, and they collectively occupied the seat of power. They were as immovable as the Rock of Gibraltar. When it came to the annual election of the two sheriffs, the nominees of the aldermen invariably succeeded by virtue of their 24 votes outweighing the 14 votes of the elected representatives. In the matter of the admission of freemen they screened every application being submitted for acceptance. In that way they ensured that all successful applicants were of their own religious persuasion and of their own political leanings. In addition, the Assembly was accountable to no one.

Even when the Irish Court of King's Bench attempted to curtail their discriminatory selection procedures, this cabal of graft and bigotry was able to negate the Court's ruling by changing its own admission terms. They simply shifted the goalposts! This was accomplished by applying the expedient of admitting additional freemen who were non-residents, and also by obliging all Protestant traders in the town to register as freemen without incurring any cost. It was an oligarchy that could not be influenced or manipulated except by its own members and they endlessly abused their privileged position to maintain the *status quo*. 'Absolute power corrupts absolutely'.

They never relented. In 1832 they passed a resolution that 'a sum not exceeding £250 be granted by this body for the purpose of assisting the Freemen in ascertaining their Rights'.[2] It can clearly be seen that the Assembly was corrupt and would resort to any underhand measure to retain its vice-like grip, especially when the Catholic assertiveness was beginning to manifest itself. At this time the Protestant bloc represented a mere 8% of Drogheda's population. The legislation already in place was perversely discriminatory, so further restrictions would hardly be deemed necessary. Nonetheless, to stem the tide of the rising numbers of Catholic voters, they passed a resolution in 1820 'that no person shall be admitted to this Corporation unless holding a high official situation, distinguished military character or a Man of Rank and Consequence'.[3] Since Catholics were deprived by both legislation and local manipulation from holding office in these categories, the entry door to the Assembly was effectively being locked, barred and bolted to them.

The existing Assembly members, and they alone, would judge which applicants would conform to the criteria that they themselves had laid down. Notwithstanding their dominance, they redoubled their efforts yet again to enlist freemen of their own persuasion. In March 1820 alone they swore in as many as 215 new freemen. The sole function of these newcomers was to drop out of the sky at election time, vote and then disappear. In relation to the total electorate, this increase would have made a significant difference. In 1830, for example, the total electorate numbered only 1,130. The imbalance is highlighted by the fact that the Protestant population in 1831 numbered 1,437 out of a total headcount of 17,365.[4]

County Boroughs: County administrative bodies (such as County Louth) were distinct from town boroughs, but were no less corrupt. Once again, they were non-elective bodies, their members being (indirectly) political appointees. They were 'notoriously careless in making presentments [for the performance of public works], the works were often indifferently carried out, and [the members] frequently manipulated the system to their own advantage'. Both the town boroughs and the county administrative bodies suffered from a lack of funds to carry out public works such as road and bridge construction. For some civic projects the actual members often made loans at stated rates of interest to ennable contractors be paid for work being undertaken. (We have seen that Assembly members Chesshire and Barlow made loans to the Corporation so that the construction of the Tholsel could be completed).

Apart from the local authorities being constantly out of funds, they were plagued by a high degree of incompetence and abuse. A Government Commission looked into the workings of these administrative bodies and concluded with the damning indictment that they were 'in many cases of no service to the community; in others injurious; in all, insufficient and inadequate...' The system was finally changed, as we shall see, through an act of parliament when Drogheda's Assembly members, along with those of nine other boroughs including Dublin and Belfast, were replaced in favour of an elective town council.

Just as was happening in the Drogheda borough, the balance of power in the County Louth constituency was being slowly tipped away from the landowners by the growing number of 'Forty-Shilling Freeholders'. This was an alarming trend for those currently in power, and they deemed it essential to redress it

REVOLT OF THE LOUTH FREEHOLDERS: Although County Louth had a vast preponderance of Catholics in its population, Speaker Foster hand-picked Protestant tenants for his own estate whenever possible, and he procured them through advertisements, although he denied showing preference. However, the irrefutable fact remains that Collon, most of which he owned, was the most Protestant parish in County Louth. He had also shipped in from abroad a small colony of foreign Protestant weavers, and erected a prayer house in

Collon for their use. When his house was burgled, he hounded his tenants in his efforts to lay hands on the culprit, and he then pressurised the parish priest to have him excommunicated.

The threat of eviction constantly hung over any tenant who was in arrears of rent or who did not toe the line in regard to voting. Intimidation was a regular occurrence; in this regard Foster was served by his own system of espionage. He denied the accusation of 'endeavouring to raise a Protestant Militia in his county, and to keep alive the suspicions and animosity of the Louth gentlemen against the Catholics ... '. He also employed the Louth Militia 'to gratify a wicked and destructive policy', and mention has been made in an earlier chapter of the unbridled tactics he employed in dispersing gatherings of dissident peasants, and in mercilessly quelling anything that smacked of sedition, charging them on horseback and wielding a naked sword indiscriminately upon them. Indeed, the Louth Militia came to be known as 'the Speaker's Bloodhounds'.

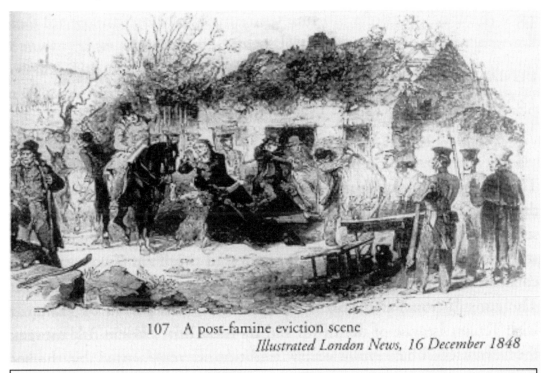

107 A post-famine eviction scene
Illustrated London News, 16 December 1848

The meagre pieces of furniture are thrown outside while men on the roof tear down the thatch while the tenant pleads wit the Landlord.

Whatever their religion, 'Forty Shilling Freeholders' everywhere invariably voted as directed by their landlords – they knew which side their bread was buttered on, and they complied through an instinctive loyalty (or perhaps through a primeval fear) to their landlords' wishes. Here we must not presume that the voting procedure, like today, was by secret ballot. Balloting was a public affair, each voter declaring aloud his preference as he cast his vote. Let it be said that some of these landlords were benign gentlemen and treated their tenants with compassion and humanity. However, in an election held in Waterford in 1826 the tenants bucked the trend of loyalty and voted against the wishes of their landlord. This was a profound break with tradition, but did it signal a new trend? Or was it simply a flash in the pan?

The answer came a few months later when Louth went to the polls in a by-election. A printed circular had been distributed among the freeholders of County Louth, calling on them to unite in putting an end to the 'present unnatural state of the representation of this great (and should be independent) county. [Voters are urged to nominate] one or two liberal candidates who will pledge themselves to support civil and religious liberty in parliament'. This call could not be described as inflammatory; it was a legitimate rallying cry to be heeded by anyone who desired a change. The invincible John Foster was being challenged on his home ground.

The leadership that was expected from the principal Catholic families, notably the Bellews of Barmeath, was not forthcoming. Even Blaney Balfour of Townley Hall, who by this time had shown sympathy towards the Emancipation movement, was not to be seen. Who would oppose the well-oiled electoral machine of John Foster? The opposition, if it could be called that, had no experience in electioneering, no money and, worst of all, no candidate. The call for an Emancipation candidate had not been answered with less than two weeks to polling day which was 21st. June 1826.

An elderly Ardee man with a small estate and who had never aspired to represent the people in parliament was persuaded at the last minute to stand; his name was Alexander Dawson. This meant that now there were three contestants for the two seats, Dawson, and the two anti-Emancipationists Speaker Foster and his cousin Fortescue.

Almost every parish in County Louth rallied to the cause of Dawson, and they raised a substantial £2,174 to cover the electioneering expenses. The local clergy lent their aid from the pulpit. Daniel O'Connell's side-kick Richard Sheil arrived; he stirred up feelings after Mass in Dundalk with "... I tell you that your landlords have no more right to ask you to vote against your religion and your conscience than they have to ask you for the virginity of your children..." (This was an allusion to earlier times when landlords assumed the right, called *droit du seigneur*, of sexual intercourse with a vassal's bride on her wedding night). Engulfed by the upsurge in support for Dawson and by the overall euphoria 'to separate the tenantries from their landlords', the Bellews belatedly decided to swim with the tide and gave their support to Dawson. Balfour, on the other hand, not wishing to stand on the sideline, instructed his tenants to vote for Foster and his running mate Fortescue, the latter being a lightweight and a mere puppet of Foster.

In normal circumstances Speaker Foster would have arranged for the freeholders in his estates to wrap up the whole issue by casting their votes for both himself and Fortescue, but this time he was inconvenienced by the presence of Dawson. He realised that demanding both votes would be pressing the loyalty of the electorate too hard.

An amount of 'jockeying' did take place, with some of the electorate in the anti-Emancipation camp casting a vote for only one candidate and 'sinking' their second vote, a ploy which the inexperienced Dawsonites could also have used. Alternatively, they could simply have given their second vote to the weakling Fortescue in order to edge out the rabidly anti-Emancipationist Foster, but it did not occur to them – they were novices at the game and were somewhat in disarray, the electorate not being versed in the intrigues of politics. This rendered the outcome obscure up to the very last moment; the results were eagerly awaited. *Sensationally, Dawson headed the poll.*

The results of the election were:

Dawson:	**862**
Foster:	**552**
Fortescue:	**547**

With all his know-how in politics, his contacts at every level, raising his hat to some, passing bribes to others and intimidating his tenants, Foster was unable to stop Dawson. Foster himself came within a hair's breadth of losing his own seat – a switch of merely three votes from Foster to Fortescue would have pushed Foster out in the cold.

Balfour's assistance was ineffectual because his tenants had revolted and voted for Dawson. The result was a crushing rebuff to Foster, and he set about taking revenge on his recalcitrant tenantry, 'although it seems that the most extreme of these reprisals was never actually carried into effect'. He reacted to the whole episode in bad grace, drawing up water-tight affidavits for his freeholders to prevent them from ever again reneging on him; he prosecuted others, and considered questioning Dawson's victory by quibbling over minor technicalities. (Note the small number of votes cast; the total electorate was in the region of

3,500, a figure that underlines its exclusivity – most citizens simply had no vote; by comparison, the total electorate today in Louth is in the region of 90,000).

His Collon tenants erected a triumphal arch emblazoned with the words 'Glory, Collon tenantry, in your fidelity to your landlord'. But was this done with tongue in cheek? Was it an expression of jubilation at the electoral victory of their landlord? It reads rather like an exercise in self-adulation – the tenants were praising themselves for having voted for their own landlord! He had just scraped home.

The significant and crucial matter was that the Wee County by legitimate means had broken the bonds of serfdom, and set the pattern for the rest of Ireland to imitate. The genie was out of the bottle, and its master was no longer in control. The immediate upshot was that Counties Monaghan and Westmeath followed suit in by-elections held a short time afterwards. The floodgates were now open.

Dawson acquitted himself well as an MP. After his death a meeting was called in Dundalk with a view to erecting a statue to his honour. Nothing came of it because the timing was wrong – it was 1846 and Ireland was in the throes of the Great Famine. A branch of his family has lent its name to Dawson St. in Dublin.

John Leslie Foster, nephew of Speaker Foster, took over the family leadership when the latter retired, and he was MP for Louth until 1830. He was greatly concerned at the new course that political events were taking. No doubt with the connivance of the elderly Speaker, he conferred with Robert Peel, who was Home Secretary at the time and who later became Prime Minister. A remedy was sought to quell the rising tide, and he pointed out that otherwise the Emancipationists would take both seats in Louth at the next election. The suggested remedy was to raise the bar, that is, to increase the freehold franchise from forty shillings to £20 – a tenfold increase. Following much discussion, a figure of £10 was finally approved. This move substantially reduced the number of Catholic voters in subsequent elections, but notwithstanding these desperate tactics the scales were being nudged in favour of the Emancipationists.

The Fosters were being hamstrung by their financial problems and thus they found it increasingly difficult to sustain their role of spearheading the Ascendancy dominance. Indeed, in later times they committed an unforgivable act of dishonesty. Speaker Foster had refused, quite correctly, to hand over the Mace of the Irish Parliament when the Act of Union became operative. He maintained that it was given to him by the Irish Parliament *for safe keeping, and he would return it* when Ireland again had its own parliament. The establishment of a separate Irish parliament finally occurred, as we know, in 1922 (though not in circumstances that Foster would have approved!). But by then the Fosters were not in possession of the priceless Mace. They had sold it. (The Bank of Ireland later bought it at a public auction, and it is today on display at their headquarters in College Green).

They had acquired very little additional estate in latter years, and the more recent set of landlords in Louth and Meath had names like O'Callaghan and Fitzgerald, men who had acquired land and were setting up freeholders on their estates who favoured Catholic Emancipation. In consequence, around 1820 the Louth electorate shot up spectacularly from 850 to 2,830, and the Fosters were not in a position to counteract the trend by greasing the palms of voters. In the past they had always gained their successes the easy way – between 1768 and 1826 their seat was uncontested and thus they had walked into parliament without incurring any outlay. Those easy days were now gone.

Many of their colleagues, such as the Fortesques who lived nearby, and the Earls of Clanbrassil and Roden who ruled the roost in Dundalk and the north Louth region were also in financial straits, with the bogeyman of bankruptcy waiting in the wings. Their antecedents, for the most part, had acquired their expansive estates either as conquerors or as planters, which meant that the income enjoyed by the subsequent generations had fallen effortlessly into their laps, and this provided them with an easy lifestyle. Some became debauched and profligate spendthrifts – easy come, easy go. Now the dismantling of the barriers that had precluded Catholics from participating in the running of their country was beginning to take effect, and the tenantry were making their presence felt. Times, they were a-changing.

CATHOLIC EMANCIPATION: Following the earth-shattering result in the Louth by-election, the electoral successes in Monaghan and Westmeath came as no great surprise. What was now needed was someone with leadership qualities who would bind the common people in a common cause, someone around whom they would rally and press home their success. All the essential qualities were present in the Kerryman Daniel O'Connell. He had been educated in France and then became a barrister. He had boundless energy, and the underprivileged peasantry responded *en masse* to his powers of oratory.

Daniel O'Connell

When another by-election was held in 1828, this time in County Clare, O'Connell himself stood as a candidate. It was necessary to organise the Forty Shilling Freeholders into a well-drilled unit intent on attaining a fixed objective. This was duly accomplished, mainly by exhortations from the pulpits and by self-imposed absence from drink for three full days, 'a phenomenon which left the eyes of commentators wide with amazement'. O'Connell won in a canter.

The threat to those in the citadel of power was evident. They set about shoring up their electoral base of freemen. They had already scraped the bottom of the barrel at local level for the enlistment of suitable freemen. Now they appointed a committee of its members to devise whatever further means would enable them cling to power, and on 30th January 1829 they passed the following resolution:

> "Resolved
> "That we feel it our duty in order to prevent
> "the increase of Popery in this Country, and to check the dange-
> "rous consequences to our religion and Liberties should the
> "proposed infringement on our Constitution succeed to recom-
> "mend to the General Assembly the necessity of admitting the
> "following persons to the Freedom of this Corporation agree-
> "to the order of Assembly.
> "(Signed)   "J.B. Fairtlough"
> "J. Anderson
> "Obadiah Wisdom
> "Francis W. Leland
> "Thomas North"

'RESOLVED That we feel it our duty in order to prevent the increase of Popery in this Country and to check the dangerous consequences to our religion and Liberties, should the proposed infringements on our Constitution [viz. the granting of Catholic Emancipation] succeed, to recommend to the General Assembly the necessity of admitting the following persons to the Freedom of this Corporation...". [5] *[followed by five signatures]*

There followed a list of 67 names with addresses in Dublin and in such other unlikely places as Ardee and Ballybay, there being none of the desired voters in Drogheda; it included such staunch, died-in-the-wool names as John Claudius Beresford and John Bull. These were absentee freemen, and their sole function in Drogheda was to vote and then depart. We have seen that, so small was the electoral base, the admission of these 67 new names would have been a critical factor at election time.

Realising that the move towards Emancipation was well nigh unstoppable, the Corporation was still determined to grimly hang on as long as possible, by fair means or foul. King George IV (of whom we shall reveal more anon) was their hero because he had always declined giving royal approval to an Emancipation Bill, but the difficulty was that by now he had become an imbecile through a life of debauchery, and there was no point in approaching him. (He died the following year). So in desperation they resolved in January 1829 'that a Petition be forwarded to both Houses of Parliament against any further concession to the Roman Catholic Body', the motion being carried by 31 beans for the motion, with 5 against. The Petition was carefully drafted and then brought over to the House of Commons by the local MP George Ogle Moore, and the Earl of Enniskillen was entrusted to present it to the Upper House. The document itself is lengthy, and the first page, which is reproduced on the following page, indicated its overall tenor.

Slane Castle

"To the Right Honourable and Honourable
'the Lords Spiritual and Temporal in Parlia-
'ment assembled.
"The Humble Petition of the Mayor Sheriffs Bur_
'gesses and Common Council of the Corporation
'of the County of the Town of Drogheda
'Sheweth,
'That your Petitioners are deeply sensible of the many
'and invaluable Benefits which have been conferred on these
'Realms by the Settlement of the Constitution at the Glorious
'Revolution of 1688, when the ascendancy of Protestantism
'was fully established in every Branch of Legislative and Ex-
'ecutive Authority, and when in pursuance of that Principle,
'the House of Stewart was expelled, and the House of Bruns-
'wick placed on the British Throne.
'That your Petitioners fully convinced that such
'Benefits have flowed from a strict adherence to the Principles
'so established cannot view, without the most serious alarm,
'the prospect of any further extension of political power to
'His Majesty's Roman Catholic Subjects, nor can they conceive
'that persons professing that religion can now be admitted to
'a share in the Legislature of the Empire without violating
'thereby the Principle by which the Houses of Sardinia and of
'France are at this moment excluded from inheriting the
'Throne of it.
'That Petitioners most earnestly beg to call the
'attention of this Honourable House to the existence of a Body styling
'itself the 'Roman Catholic Association' assuming to itself all
'the functions of a Parliament and professing to be the represen-
'tatives of the people of Ireland; levying money from his majes-
'ty's Subjects for purposes unknown to the Constitution, issuing
'its mandates, and sending out its emissaries through all parts
'of the Kingdom, with a view to excite disunion and distrust.

*The first page of a Petition presented by Drogheda Corporation to Parliament
against the granting of Emancipation to Catholics.*

THE TITHES WAR: A perennial cause of friction was the imposition of tithes, which were a church tax on agricultural produce for the support of Church of Ireland clergy. The levy was one-tenth of produce and was payable by all denominations. Resentment was felt especially by Catholics and Dissenters who found it unacceptable that they should be forced to support a religion of which they were not members and whose doctrines differed from their own. The tax brought them no benefit of any kind; indeed, to the majority the levy was an imposition designed to support that very symbol of despotism that was directed towards their repression. They saw it as a patent injustice.

Tithe collectors were known as Procters, and opposition to their demands had resulted in centuries of passive resistance, constant conflict, agrarian disorder, and the spilling of blood. To worsen this scenario, grassland farmers were exempt from paying tithes, and thus the burden fell heaviest on those who were providing employment, the tillage farmers, and also the Catholics with their potato plots.

Melees were commonplace, constantly involving police, sheriffs, proctors, peasants and the military whenever property was seized for the non-payment of tithes. The duty of having to distrain goods on peasants who were living in penury was distasteful work for police and soldiers. Resistance strengthened following Emancipation, and the situation came to a head when an unpopular Protestant curate demanded tithes from a parish priest in Graiguenamanagh, seizing his cattle for non-payment. The locals became involved and the agitation spread throughout Ireland – the government soon had a Tithes War on its hands. Eventually, the Tithe Rentcharge (Ireland) Act 1836 relieved the difficulty by converting the tithe into a rent chargeable on the landlord. This gave him justification for increasing his rents – he simply passed the buck.

Desirable as the granting of Emancipation had been for the masses, it had some unfortunate and long-term consequences. It widened the chasm between the adherents to the two main religions, accelerating the polarisation of the nation along sectarian lines, a pernicious result that is still virulent in a section of the island.

The Protestant Contribution to Nationalism: Notwithstanding the bigotry and oppressiveness in the laws of the land, some of the conspicuous leaders in the liberation of Ireland have been Protestants. Leafing through these pages we find that Henry Grattan – champion of the independent Irish Parliament – devoted his life to redressing Catholic injustices. *Others of them were instrumental in creating **a national consciousness**, an essential requirement if the goal of self government was ever to be achieved.* This had been lacking prior to 1798. Almost all of the main players in the 1798 Rising, including Lord Edward FitzGerald, Napper Tandy, Wolfe Tone and Henry Joy McCracken were Protestants. It was they who created the first stirrings of Republicanism in Ireland. Likewise were the leaders in subsequent agitation and risings: Robert Emmet in 1803, William Smith O'Brien in the 1848 Rising, Isaac Butt in the Home Rule League, Charles Stewart Parnell in the Land War and Arthur Griffith in the War of Independence, the last named being also the founder of Sinn Féin. These men, and many such others worked tirelessly in their quest to attain justice for all; some risked confiscation of their estates, some were thrown into prison, while others gave their very lives in that cause.

In later times other Protestants spearheaded the Celtic revival movement, and others again were conspicuous contributors in the realms of art and literature, with names such as Beckett, Goldsmith, O'Casey, Shaw, Sheridan, Swift, Synge, Wilde, Yeats, etc., whose works grace the libraries of the world. They have given us such fictional and memorable characters as the Village Blacksmith, Fluther Good, Eliza Doolittle, Mrs. Malaprop, Gulliver, the aristocratic Lady Windermere, while audiences are spellbound in their seats while waiting for Godot.

The first and fourth persons to occupy Árus an Úactarán were respectively Dr. Douglas Hyde and Erskine Childers, Protestants who 'have done the State some service' in the role of President of Ireland.

THE MUNICIPAL CORPORATIONS REFORM ACT (1840): The ruling junta in Drogheda throughout past centuries elected mayors who bore quaint, strange-sounding names such as de Rock, de Bath, Faunt, Snackberd, Wywall, Jebb, Foxtheth, Stubber, Sankitt, Ogle, Shegog, Keapock, van Bobbett, van Homrigh, Chamney, Knaggs.

The legislation which excluded Catholics from Parliament and also from borough membership had been in operation since 1641. Emancipation meant that Catholics could now sit in Parliament, *but at local level control still remained in the hands of the same few*, and they would not budge an inch; it was they alone who selected the MP. They would never countenance a Carty, O'Brien or Murphy wearing the mayoral chains. The Assembly still constituted an *impasse* that frustrated the operation of Emancipation. Nothing had really changed in Drogheda.

Abuse by the dominant aristocracy was quite common in Europe, but the situation in Ireland was unique in as much as a small minority was dominating a very large majority, and this had continued for centuries. An enquiry into the conduct of municipal corporations was instituted by the government in the 1830s; it exposed the rampant sleaziness and corruption that existed. Steps were taken to restrict their powers, and this resulted in 58 of the 68 corporations and boroughs being abolished.

The remaining 10 corporations, which included Drogheda, were to be replaced by governing bodies elected by a municipal franchise, and the instrument drafted to effect this change was the Municipal Corporations Reform Bill. The day was nigh when the hitherto invulnerable Drogheda Assembly members would be obliged at last to share power with colleagues of a different religious persuasion.

They saw the impending legislation as tearing down the final barricade that protected them in the comfortable world in which their bread was being earned by the sweat of the brow of others, and they were greatly alarmed when the Bill was passed by the House of Commons. The final barrier in their self-serving structure of total dominance was crumbling, and their backs were to the wall. What were they to do? In defiance of the inevitable, they made one final, frenetic bid to hang on to power. They drafted yet another Petition and sent it to their staunch allies, the House of Lords.

The Cord Road
Note the open sewer, with several planks thrown across.

TO THE RIGHT HONORABLE THE LORDS SPIRITUAL AND TEMPORAL OF

THE UNITED KINGDOM OF GREAT BRITAIN AND IRELAND
IN PARLIAMENT ASSEMBLED

The Petition of the Mayor, Sheriffs, Burgesses and Commons of the Town and County of the Town of Drogheda

Humbly Sheweth,

That Petitioners view with undiminished apprehension and alarm the renewed introduction to your Lordships' House of the Bill, which has passed the House of Commons, for the professed purpose of Reforming the Municipal Corporations of Ireland, and which, as Petitioners humbly submit, is not a Bill for their reform, as at present constituted, but for the total annihilation, so far as Petitioners are concerned, of their Corporate rights, privileges, immunities and vested interests in property and otherwise, and for the transferring of the same, without just cause to others, in violation, as Petitioners respectfully submit, of the trusts and purposes for which they were originally granted.

That the cause assigned for the intended change of the Municipal Institutions, is the substance of a report made by the Commissioners of Corporate Inquiry, in which conclusions are drawn, and charges, in general terms, made, which are not only unwarranted, as Petitioners submit by the evidence taken, but in many instances, in direct contradiction to it, and against which report, Petitioners respectfully, yet earnestly, repeat their protest, as being the result of a prejudicial and illiberal view of the case, as far as respects your Petitioners.

That as regards the exclusion of Roman Catholics from the Corporations of Ireland, now made one of the pretexts for the introduction of said Bill, Petitioners beg to remind your Honourable House that such exclusion was in strict accordance with the purpose and design of their original establishment, – the object of which was to encourage the Protestant Religion in Ireland, and to assist in maintaining the connection with Great Britain. That although such exclusion has been made the cause of complaint against them (but which, since the Legislature thought fit to sanction their admission, has not been universal in this Corporation, and doubtless would have been much less so but for the decided hostility uniformly evinced by them for all Protestant establishments); yet there is little doubt if the Bill, now before your Honourable House, shall become the law, that the exclusion of Protestants will be equally, if not more rigidly acted on by the successors of Petitioners and that the future Corporations will consist wholly of Roman Catholics.

That should your Lordships enter upon consideration of the measure, and introduce such alterations and amendments as may serve to ensure the Protestant trusts and purposes which it was the object and intention of the original framers of Corporations to perpetuate, and also endeavour to continue and preserve British connection. Your Petitioners respectfully hope and trust you will be graciously pleased to make such enactments as will clearly and indisputably ascertain and declare the rights, privileges and interests of Petitioners and their successors to the charitable trusts, political franchises and vested estates in the Corporate property to which they are entitled by immemorial usage and Bye Laws, as Petitioners are fully and conscientiously convinced from experience, of the facility with which enactments and even securities for their observance are defeated and perverted, unless expressly defined, that through a political hostility and jealousy every means which ingenuity can devise will be used to harass Petitioners and impede the acquisition of their rights and which will be the more necessary to be guarded against when those privileges, franchises, and vested rights are to be sought for and required from the adverse body; and who instead of assisting to carry out the just intentions of the Legislature for the Petitioners and their successors, would more prolong, obstruct and frustrate them.

Relying, therefore, as Petitioners do with perfect confidence on the justice of your Lordships, they trust that if it shall appear expedient to pass the Bill, your Lordships will introduce such restrictions and provisions as may effectually secure to your Petitioners all the rights, privileges and immunities to which they are at present entitled. And petitioners will pray.

In testimony whereof we have caused to be hereunto affixed our common Seal at Drogheda.

This   day of   in the year of Our Lord 1840
Certified by
Town Clerk   SEAL

The Petition:[6] The Petition itself lacked the clarity and incisiveness that John Foster would have contributed, but he was now dead. Instead, the document reads as if it were drafted by a committee, with everyone having an input. Its main point was based on the questionable argument of vague probabilities rather than on irrefutable facts, namely that the petitioners were apprehensive of what they *might* experience under Catholic administration. They expressed alarm at the prospect of 'the total annihilation ... of their Corporate rights, privileges, immunities and vested interest in property and otherwise'. They were aggrieved that these 'rights' etc., would no longer be theirs in perpetuity. They challenged the conclusion of the Commission that had been set up to investigate the blatant irregularities that existed, stating that it was 'unwarranted' and was 'the result of a prejudicial and illiberal view of the case. ... The exclusion of Roman Catholics from the Corporations of Ireland ... was in strict accordance with the purpose and design of their [viz. the Protestant] original establishment – the object of which was to encourage the Protestant Religion in Ireland ...'. The penultimate paragraph is particularly weak, being tantamount to an admission that the Bill in any event was destined to succeed. In summary, it was a whinging tale of woe, begging the House of Lords to indulge them by retaining *ad infinitum* their ill-gotten privileges which they had purloined in consequence of the Battle of the Boyne.

This time the pleadings to their cronies in the House of Lords fell on deaf ears. The Bill was finally passed, thus ending at last the era of non-accountability by the Ascendancy.

The First of November 1842 was a red letter day in Drogheda's history. This was the day on which the law of the land gave effect to the operation of the Municipal Corporations Reform Act (1840). (Co-incidentally, it was also the very same date which in 1412 the two separate municipalities were united into one single town by Fr. Bennett, as described in an earlier chapter). A Catholic could now represent the people by serving on the Corporation, by becoming Mayor of Drogheda, or even representing the people of Drogheda in Parliament. The election of the first Catholic Mayor of Drogheda's reformed corporation was a momentous occasion and was greeted with great jubilation by the populace. The event was reported in the Drogheda Argus:

> 'The Tholsel [which was the venue for Corporation meetings at that time, and where the Mayoral election took place] and the different streets in its vicinity, were crowded almost to suffocation by persons anxious to witness the novel event ... The ceremony [of placing the chain of office on the new Mayor, Thomas Carty] was the signal for one universal shout of acclamation, such as was never before heard in Drogheda ... The shout was renewed again and again, re-echoed by the thousands who thronged the avenues leading to the Tholsel...'.[7]

On the occasion of the first freely elected Mayor of Drogheda for 200 years the Drogheda MP, Sir William Somerville, spoke in glowing terms of the attributes of the new Mayor. He said the mayor was elected by the free suffrage of the people, and he acknowledged that 'there is no mark of inferiority fixed upon [any particular religion] by the law – they are eligible for every office'.

Root and Branch Reform: A breath of fresh air wafted through the chamber of the Tholsel when Mayor Carty assumed the Chairmanship of the Reformed Assembly. An official notice convening the first meeting, dated 1st June 1844 and bearing the signature of the Mayor, had been affixed to the front door of the Tholsel, and this formality was adhered to for future meetings, inferring that all discussions would be above board and open to public scrutiny.

The first matter tackled was the deplorable condition of the town's 'streets and footways'. Although the main streets were in a reasonable state, 'the suburbs were in a most neglected and filth condition', manure heaps outside many doors being s feature. A Paving and Cleaning subcommittee was appointed to ensure that all the lanes and byways were properly cleaned, and for many years thereafter that submitted a progress report to the Assembly.

The town sweepers were called in to a meeting and they revealed that their wages varied between 2s/3d. and 2s/7d. (0.14 and 0.17 Euro) per week. An abuse immediately came to light – they were being cheated by their overseer. He never paid them more than one shilling in cash, and they were obliged to accept the balance in the form of bread for which they were being charged 2½d. for a 2d. loaf; they were also obliged to accept tea, sugar and butter as part payment; this practice, known as 'trucking', is illegal. Moreover, but they were never given the full weight. Under interrogation the overseer 'admitted that every word was true.'[8] Other flagrant injustices of the past came to light, and were immediately reversed.

Reading between the lines, we can now clearly see why the previous junta had fought so strenuously to cling to power – it had been nothing short of a fellowship motivated to promote a series of nefarious practices to further their own interests. Now their shady world of corruption was exposed. The newly constituted Assembly set about undoing them:

- Tolls and Customs were abolished. (We have seen that Freemen were exempt from paying these taxes).
- A Firefighting Service was inaugurated. In tackling any threat from fires in the town, 12 coal porters were to be drilled. In the event of a fire they were to receive 'not in any case exceeding 2s.6d'.
- Arrangements was made to take out insurance policies on the Municipal properties (the Tholsel, Mayoralty House, etc.) Also, necessary repairs were carried out. They agreed '…to take such steps as are deemed necessary and advisable in impeaching the Deed of Rent Charge which had been sealed and executed by the Late Corporation to the Trustees of the Protestant Orphanage Society and which was granted in opposition to the opinion of the Recorder'.
- The Proctors of the Poor of St. John, George William Evans and Graves Ackland, were dismissed, and replaced by Messrs. Drew and Kelly.
- They considered 'the best and most effectual mode of obtaining possession of lands known as 'the Aldermens Acres' or 'the Cowleys'. These lands, in a time honoured way, had belonged to the people as a commons, but had been purloined after the Battle of the Boyne for the exclusive and perpetual benefit of the Protestant community.
- They set out to curtail financial allowances that had 'been applied or attempted to be applied solely to the personal aggrandisement of a few individuals without even the pretext of public service to sanction such a disposition of the public Funds, thus that which was originally bestowed and intended for the benefit of the community at large was unjustly converted into a source of private emoluments'.[9]

The bluntness of the wording used in several of these minutes is indicative of the feelings felt by the new Assembly members at the baseness of the misdeeds of the previous members. Also, elementary community matters such as a fire-fighting service and insurance of municipal property had been shamefully neglected.

Some of the official Corporation posts were undoubtedly sinecures, appointments that carried salaries but with few if any duties attached. Henceforth these people had to earn their salaries. Their duties were now spelled out in great detail, notably those of the Town Clerk, Treasurer, Sword Bearer, Mace Bearer, Sergeant at Mace, Chief Constable, Clock Keeper, House Keeper, Keeper of the Mayoralty House, Caretaker of the Corn Market, Public Crier (or 'Bellover'), Inspector of the Fish Market and Inspector of Paving. The duties of the Curfew Toller were 'to toll the curfew bell at 6 o'clock each morning and evening for the regulation of the Trades people and also in cases of houses taking fire'. A curious office was that of the 'Halbertman and Bangbeggar' (a halbert is a type of pike). Thankfully, his services are no longer required nowadays – his duties, which may have called his halbert into play, were to 'preserve order and prevent beggars and to remove swine from the streets'. One wonders if the swine were 'banged' as vigorously as the beggars!

A HARDENING OF ATTITUDES Within a few years the political sentiments of the Reformed Corporation became more evident. They voted on 3rd April 1843 to send a Petition to the Houses of Parliament decrying the Act of Union, deploring its effect on Ireland and making a case for its repeal. The arguments which had been set out in the famous Petition of 1800 (see Chapter Twenty) were repeated, but this time they added some remarks which were even closer to the bone, stating quite bluntly that 'the Union was carried by the **grossest Corruption and Bribery** [emphasised in the records as shown here] added to force, fraud and terror...' They added further examples of how approval for the Act was contrived, stating that the Irish people had never assented to it, that Martial Law was proclaimed and enforced during the time that the Union was carried, that the Habeas Corpus Act was suspended, that people were not allowed to assemble but were 'dispersed at the point of a Bayonet' and that in effect it had 'annihilated Irish manufactures'.[10]

The ardour of the Reformed Corporation is very evident from this Petition and it reflected their frustration. It clearly spelled out the trickery that had been applied in having the Act of Union passed. However, it was short on diplomacy. Whatever chance of success it would have had if pitched in an obsequious, boot-licking manner, its tone ensured dismissal in Westminster. Acceding to the Petitioners wishes would have been tantamount to admission of the skulduggery that the Government had used. Needless to say, their answer was NO.

Attitudes were hardening, and at the Assembly meeting in November 1844 it was agreed that no person would be proposed as Mayor who did not espouse the Repeal Movement, and further, that he would propose 'a Repeal Toast at all public Dinners'.[11]

Daniel O'Connell was in jail at this time for his efforts in seeking Repeal so they wrote him a letter of condolence. When he was set free they congratulated him on his ' release from his illegal and unmerited imprisonment'.[12]

Several further Petitions were sent to parliament pleading for repeal of the Act of Union, but by this time the Corporation were drinking from a poisoned chalice. Potato blight had made its appearance and the Great Famine was in full spate. They were virtually powerless in helping the unfortunate sufferers, mainly because of the economic conditions in which they found themselves, and there was no money in the kitty. They applied the only means they possessed – sending Petitions. One of these (April 1848) referred to the 'long suffering and much wronged people of Ireland ... the main cause of the misery is that her laws are not made by an Irish Parliament'. This argument was self evident; Ireland was in the grip of the Great Famine at the time, and it exposed the London Parliament's shameful neglect of the Irish people throughout that nightmare. A year later (February 1849) the Corporation repeated its plea to Parliament, stating that the Act of Union was 'calculated to keep alive religious animosity and sectarian hostility which has been the bane of Ireland' – a point well made.[13] London remained intransigent. All these efforts, however ineffectual, give weight to the fact that the true Drogheda spirit ever had been to wrest Ireland from England's grasp.

At local level the Reformed Corporation made some impact. The boot was now on the other foot, and within a decade or so Catholics were dominating the Corporation. In 1856 a slogging match was in progress between the two local newspapers, the right-wing *Conservative* and the partisan *Drogheda Argus*. Week after week the *Conservative* was complaining of the bias being shown in the matter of allocating municipal appointments. Of a dozen or more positions, only one had been assigned to a Protestant. It expostulated that this was unfair. Moreover, it grumbled that at a recent Official Dinner the Mayor had omitted to drink to the health of Her Majesty Queen Victoria. This matter was to remain unresolved.

The Repeal Movement: Daniel O'Connell's next task was the repeal of the Act of Union and to this end Monster Meetings held throughout Ireland were the order of the day. The first was held in Trim. Agitation reached fever pitch and was nationwide, and 1843 was announced as 'Repeal Year'. A total of forty of these mass gatherings took place in various parts of

Ireland, including one in Drogheda which drew an enormous crowd of 60,000. O'Connell also addressed a rally at Bellewstown on 2nd April 1843. He was very familiar with that area, having attended conferences in the home of the Caddell family at Harbertstown House, the Naul. The Caddells were an old Anglo-Norman family who elected not to change religion at the time of the Reformation, and they supported the nationalist cause.

The greatest of all the monster meetings was at the Hill of Tara, the scene of so many historic occasions from earliest times. It is estimated that about 800,000 people attended on the 15th August 1843, with many of the attendees camping overnight. 'They were spectacular participative occasions with O'Connell's speech perhaps the least important element. There were bands, banners and coloured sashes for the different trades and a great procession to meet O'Connell that passed through triumphal arches. Greenery was carried, and loaves of bread raised on poles as a symbol of poverty'.[14]

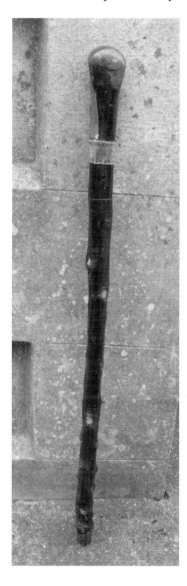

Walking Stick presented to Daniel O'Connell
on the occasion of the Monster Meeting held at Tara.

The local newspaper in that era was *"The Drogheda Conservative Journal"* and was priced at 4½d per copy which was about half a day's wages for a labourer. Since that social class had no disposable income and was almost totally illiterate, the paper was exclusively the mouthpiece of the landed gentry. It detested O'Connell and was virulently opposed to his latest objective. His efforts had already destabilised the Ascendancy to its foundations, and Repeal was seen as an even greater menace to them in their seat of absolute power, and so it knifed him whenever it had the opportunity. He was known to his supporters as 'the Liberator' but *the Drogheda Conservative Journal* called him 'the Agitator' and on occasions 'Old Humbug' and 'Old Bag'; it ridiculed and severely criticised him for collecting a monthly penny for membership to the Catholic Association, a body that bound the populace in a common cause. By 1846 O'Connell was a spent force, dying in the following year, but the paper harassed him with invective to the very end, the issue of 10th January 1846 saying:

> *"It appears that Mr. O'Connell, constituting himself the sole Election of the liberal Constituencies of Ireland, has patronisingly extended to Sir William Somerville [the sitting MP for Drogheda], in the case of a general election, the representation of Drogheda. It is really absurd to hear the Agitator complain of the limitation of the franchise as regards Ireland when he usurps in his own person the disposal of 70 Seats. ... His dupes go through the mummery of appearing at the hustlings to do his bidding just as his shoe-black polish his boots and in as servile a manner too... The whole force of the Repeal interest could not oust [Somerville] from the representation of Drogheda".*

The *Drogheda Conservative Journal* needn't have worried about the Repeal Movement, and those of the opposite camp who expected its early success were to be greatly disappointed. Another event, of cataclysmic proportions, was to intervene. It would focus the people's attention on much more immediate matters – famine.

Chapter Twentyfour

Drogheda in the 1800s – A Pen-picture

We can visualise strolling through Drogheda's main marketplace at Bolton Square during that era: a variety of smells assail the nostrils, smells of fish, of hay, of potatoes caked in mud, of manure – they all mingle into one inglorious stench, and the mud underfoot is carpeted with rotting cabbage leaves, offal, animal manure and other accumulated rubbish. All the sights and smells are compounded on market day in the babble of voices, the cries of vendors, the squawks of cockerels, the quacks of ducks and the squeals of pigs. Women talk, men shout, children laugh, dogs bark. Ragged, barefooted urchins worm their way to the front of a crowd who are watching a tethered bear performing some clumsy tricks. A gaunt beggar extends his cáibeen in the forlorn hope of receiving a copper coin in charity. An old soldier rocks on his crutch as he lurches his weary way to his tumble-down hovel where his cupboard is bare and his fireplace is cold; he lost his leg in Spain during the Peninsular campaign; apart from that distant journey, he has never been but a few miles outside his native town

A gang of scantily clad children play leap-frog outside a row of thatched mud-walled cabins, whose rude floors are of beaten earth, often damp; some of the roofs leak, and the straw thatch is bedecked with dandelions and clods of grasses. These hovels are their homes; they consist of two rooms – the kitchen is also the living room, and at night it doubles as a bedroom for the parents while the siblings sleep in the bedroom; the bed is a bundle of straw heaped on the floor. The bedroom has been the delivery ward of innumerable offspring, some of whom died at birth. Most families consist of ten to fifteen children, or perhaps more. School is not for the underprivileged; anyway most children would be unable to attend school simply because their parents could not clothe them. Furniture is sparse and basic – there is a rickety cupboard, a table, a few chairs and a few wooden boxes that serve both as chairs and receptacles for rags that pass for clothes; a pitcher of drinking water stands in the corner. There are two tiny windows that are shaded by the over-hanging thatch, restricting God's sunlight so that the gloom conceals the cobwebs that bedeck the smutty rafters.

A comment in the *Drogheda Conservative Journal* in 1847 tells us that:

> *'The poor of this large town – with its very extensive and filthy suburbs – (suburbs erected by small Capitalists in order to make money) and many of the houses more fit for pigs – not even pigs – but in dung-holes, than for human habitation'.*

A bundle of twigs lies near the fireplace, and the glowing embers produce an acrid but homely smell. A large black pot is suspended from a bar over the fire; the potatoes in the pot are 'lumpers' – similar to those cultivated throughout the land. This variety of potato has a soft, watery texture and is grown for quantity rather than quality or wholesomeness. Trevelyan said of 'lumpers': 'The potatoes used by the people of Ireland were of the coarsest and most prolific kind, called 'lumpers' or 'horse-potatoes' from their size...' Nonetheless they fill a vacuum in the stomach and are washed down with a mug of buttermilk – this fare is their main meal, day in, day out. Wheaten meal bread is a rare luxury, and the smell of cooked meat is almost unknown.

This family is fortunate – their fireplace has a chimney – many of the other cabins lack chimneys so that the smoke lingers long, leaving a deposit of soot on every surface, including the clothes, faces and lungs of the family, until it billows through the half-door. Water is drawn from the well down the road; the dry lavatory is at the end of the small patch of garden and is emptied occasionally among the potato drills, or onto the footpath. A mongrel raises his leg and marks his customary territorial posts.

The local newspaper of the day singles out Drogheda as being the worst town in Ireland in regard to the water supply and cleanliness, being 'destitute of all sanitary regulations'. Water, it points out, is the mainspring of health and cleanliness, but there is only one pump, which is at the Linen Hall, catering for the town's population. A further clue of living conditions in the town is given in the local paper:

> 'It is disheartening to see children and females waiting for hours at the only pump in our town for a scanty supply of water. ... It would melt the heart of any man but our present Corporation who seem callous to the sufferings of the poor. The filthy state of our streets, lanes and avenues is a reproach to the inhabitants generally. Indeed, it has become a bye-word among travellers, their exclamation being 'Dirty Drogheda, what a filthy town!'.[1]

There are 2 or 3 deplorable tenements in Peter St., and others in Laurence St. and West St. and these are described as 'wretched hothouses of disease'.

It may surprise the reader to learn that there were habitations answering that description in the 'respectable' main streets of the town almost a century later. Some of them were at the top of Peter St. Several veterans recall:

> "There were two tall tenements at the top of Peter Street on the right hand side. I remember one Ascension Thursday about 1938 coming home from ten o'clock Mass and the entire front of the building had collapsed. You could see each of the rooms with the bits of furniture in them. This fellow was still sitting there at the fire – his name was 'Hen Egg' Farrell. The new fire brigade was able to take him down only because it was equipped with an extended ladder".[2]

> "I saw the collapsed tenement in Peter St. with the front gone. One woman was supposed to be half nude, about 2 or 3 storeys up. Pearse Park was being built at the time and the tenants were moved there from Peter St. and Scotch Hall".[3]

Farm animals live in close proximity to the dwellings. Some residents keep a few hens that scratch for scraps as best they can in a nearby dung heap. But 'the treasure of the Irish cottier is his pig. There is scarcely the tenant of any cabin who is not possessed of one hog ... To the sale of this animal they look for the sum from which they are to pay the rent of their cabin and potato garden, and of course he becomes their chief care. During the day he is suffered to range about at large, and return when he is in want of food; his potatoes, and those nearly of as good quality as the family subsist on, are boiled for him, and with as much care as for themselves'.[4]

At night the pig takes its place in the parlour, and is almost one of the family. Sophisticated generations in later and better, much better, times will look askance at this feature of Irish life; but in fact the pig, with a little training, is a spotlessly clean creature, a pet to the whole household, the younger members of which will grieve when the butcher arrives to take the creature away; but needs must, especially when the rent is overdue. People of the poorer and unemployed classes never handle cash – they operate largely in a cashless economy, giving of their labour in lieu of money to settle debts. The pig is their 'piggy-bank'. 'To sell his pig [is] to fall back on the last trench against starvation'.

John's Court, at the junction of John St. and the Donore Road was a warren of the most decadent habitations imaginable, only to become more degraded in the early part of the twentieth century, until they were eventually pulled down by the Corporation. The Sisters of Mercy regularly visited the occupants of these hovels after they had performed their normal duty in the classrooms, bringing sustenance at weekends and doling out a few precious shillings which had been gathered at a church door collection held once a year. They were able to describe conditions first-hand of scenes in the early 1930s:

"The poverty of the inhabitants in John's Court was appalling. They were tiny two-roomed cabins. We visited them on a regular basis. In one of them a mother raised seven boys – aged from one upwards. They ate raw turnips for their dinner, and we helped out by giving her a half crown [€0.16]each week. The husband in another of these had a horse and cart, hoping to earn an occasional few shillings as a carrier. The inner room was so dark that your eyes could barely make out through the dimness the sick wife lying in the bed with a few rags over her. There was no back door and no yard. The horse was in the front room. Sometimes you wouldn't know whether he was talking about the horse or the wife".[5]

The Pay Packet: The wages earned by a rural labourer in the first half of the nineteenth century varied from about sixpence to a shilling (€0.03 to €0.06) per day. The discrepancy in these two sums is caused by the fact that the former figure relates to the number of days actually worked – there were valley periods when farm hands were laid off. Financial records for the 1850s of one particular 'big house' in the Drogheda area show that a regular worker was paid six shillings per week (i.e. €0.06 per day), but this payment was not a constant one – on occasions it was five or four shillings, and leads us to the conclusion that nothing was paid on wet days or when other factors such as sickness prevented work being done.

Sunday was the day of rest, but it could be argued that, since wages were paid on a daily basis, the 'day of rest' and church holidays were taken at the worker's own expense. As for annual holidays, there was no provision for these – a man worked through each of the 52 weeks without a respite. Women earned about half of the sums paid to men. Daniel O'Connell stated in 1825 that in the poorer and more remote counties the average rate was not more than sixpence per day, and that some were prepared to work for tuppence (one cent) rather than be unemployed.

The Devon Commission (1843) reported that for counties Louth and Meath the average daily agricultural wage was ten pence in summer and eight pence in winter (€0.05 and €0.04 respectively). In such circumstances it was impossible to break out of the poverty trap, and for the common man there was no discretionary income. In that period the price of the local weekly newspaper (the *Drogheda Journal)* was five pence, and from this we conclude that, so niggardly were peasants being paid, it entailed the labour of not less than half a day to earn the price of a newspaper. This in itself should not be regarded as a deprivation because almost every member of this stratum of society was illiterate.

Spalpeens – The Wandering Workers: Many a poor soul survived by tramping the roads in search of work, spade on his shoulders, especially in springtime and harvest time. Some migrated seasonally to England for work. These were known as *'spalpeens'*, and the many hookers plying between Drogheda and such ports as Liverpool were availed of for this purpose. The prospective employee walked from his home in Cavan, Westmeath or wherever else in the heartland of Ireland, paid the passage of five shillings (€0.32) to Liverpool and then walked the roads of rural England in search of employment. His neighbours helped to raise the necessary passage money, otherwise where was the money to come from? A man from Mayo explained: "I sold my pig myself to enable me to go. I thought little of my pig when I had the good English wages before me".

The *spalpeens* arriving in England were resented by the English labour force because they tended to depress the level of wages and increase unemployment. To make matters worse, hordes of vagrants traipsed around the English countryside and towns, and this trend escalated greatly during the 1820s and 1830s. Their destination was not restricted to Liverpool or Glasgow, but the South of England was also inundated with these wandering souls. Select committees were set up to tackle the question of removing these Irish paupers who had become an intolerable burden on English parishes. Then further committees and sub-committees were formed and they talked about it and talked about it and then made reports, but nothing constructive was ever done, and the reports were invariably shelved.

> *"During the first half of the nineteenth century the condition of the Irish peasantry was miserable in the extreme. ... The houses in which the cottiers dwelt were the merest hovels, unfit for swine to inhabit. They were constructed for the most part of mud, and were sunk in the ground so that the walls of the upper part could be constructed from the mud excavated to make room for the lower part. In the not uncommon case where these hovels were constructed by the farmers, the cottiers were forced to pay a most exorbitant rent for their use, often amounting to fifty per cent annually of the capital expended on them, this rent being generally paid in labour taken at the lowest rate, and exacted at the most inconvenient or pressing time of the year, when a poor labourer could obtain employment elsewhere at a higher rate of wages. The clothes of the peasants were of the rudest and roughest description; neither men nor women in general wore shoes or stockings".*[6]

Meantime, the crisis at home increased, and the people became more impoverished as the island's population approached 8,500,000. Finally it was agreed to extend the Poor Law (which was in operation in England) to Ireland. This step was prompted, not so much to alleviate the lot of the Irish at home, but to act "as a sovereign remedy for the evils with which England is menaced by the migratory tribes of pauper Irish". In that way a Bill was eventually passed in the House of Commons in 1838 which established the workhouses in Ireland. So primitive were these institutions that they were regarded by the populace not so much as places of refuge, but rather as the ultimate in destitution, and those who were compelled to cross their doors would have preferred to enter a jail.

The Drogheda workhouse, within whose stark, stone walls many a cadaverous poor soul was forced to seek refuge, stood cold and forbidding on the Dublin Road for 125 years – the institution was always referred to colloquially as 'the Dublin Road'. It cost £7,1450 to construct, plus £1,440 in fitting it out, and was completed in December 1841. This timing was very fortuitous, for within a few years its capacity was strained to the utmost. During the 1840s its inmates sometimes exceeded 1,000. The complex consisted of six buildings; one of these was a general medical hospital that also admitted children. (It must be remembered that there was no other hospital in Drogheda at the time other than St. John's Hospital, admissions to which were screened by the Assembly in a most discriminatory manner). The other buildings were a county home for men, a separate but similar one for females (including maternity cases), a fever hospital, a chapel and a Board Room for the Board of Guardians who supervised the overall running of the institution. The capacity was 230 persons who were accommodated in wards intended to contain 14 beds each, although the number of inmates swelled to over a thousand during the Famine. Most of the buildings were demolished in 1964. The Sisters of Mercy have always been closely associated with the Drogheda workhouse. One of these nuns, who spent her adult life in religion caring for the inmates during the mid-1900s said:

> "They never caused any trouble. The only fear was that they might cause a fire from smoking a pipe in bed. You could always tell an ex-soldier because his bed and locker were so neat.

> "We always gave tramps a good wash when they arrived. I took this poor old fellow to the washroom, and put his feet in a basin of water. He was very talkative at first. But when I was on my knees working away at his feet I noticed that the talking stopped, so I looked up to see if anything was wrong. The tears were streaming down his face. He just explained that no one had ever washed his feet before, but he mustn't have known the story of Mary Magdalene and Jesus".

In his book *'Drogheda Before the Famine'* Ned McHugh paints this depressing pen-picture of the town:

> "Encircling the town centre on all sides were rows upon rows of dilapidated thatched hovels. It was not possible for a visitor to reach the town centre without passing through some of these suburbs, where poverty and destitution were omnipresent. Open sewers, filthy streets and suburbs, miserable dark cabins constituted this less than wholesome side of Drogheda's split personality. Travellers were appalled by the sights they witnessed in these areas ... rows of the most wretched mud cabins extended at least a mile from the town ... "

So serious had the matter become that a meeting of the more affluent townspeople was called in 1830 to discuss ways and means of alleviating the distress. The notice convening the meeting was published in the Drogheda Journal and was addressed:

"TO THE WEALTHY AND HUMANE INHABITANTS OF DROGHEDA:

At no period within the recollection of the aged were the working classes of Drogheda in so forlorn and destitute a condition as of this moment. The linen manufacturing which employed such a number of the townsmen has unfortunately totally failed. Here and there as you pass the dreary abode of the once cheerful weaver the noise of a solitary shuttle is heard and recalls the gay and jovial rondo which used to fall in just though untutored cadence to the pauses of the loom ... here are to be met groups of families perishing under the severest privations of want ...". [7]

The notice, from which the foregoing extract is quoted, is couched in flowery language, but was sufficiently heart-touching as to elicit a response that appeared in the next edition of the paper. The respondent, who signed himself 'A Friend of the Poor' confessed that he had been unaware of the wretchedness in the town, and admitted that he had thought 'that no such misery existed'. However, he had now taken the trouble to see conditions first hand and then he suggested a remedy: -

> '... A more deteriorating state of society can scarcely be imagined than that where the produce arising from industry is carried to a foreign country to enrich our greatest enemies, and impoverish those who are the legitimate source of all comfort.

> 'Absentee gentlemen should, in times like the present, return some of those funds which are wrung from the labouring poor, to keep them from perishing from cold and hunger. It is to be hoped that the gentlemen possessing properties in this town and vicinity, who live in distant countries, will contribute to the sums now raised among the shop-keeping and industrious for the relief of the indigent. ... [The well-off people should] examine their wardrobes, and send to

the clergy, of every persuasion, whatever articles of clothing could be spared to cover the limbs of shivering humanity'.

The wealthier people seemed to have little or no conception as to how the lower classes existed. In the case quoted above, what motivated the correspondent was a report in the previous week's local paper. 'I went the rounds of the dreary abodes and found the sad reality ...'.

Happily, in this instance the response was positive. A committee of prominent citizens was formed under the chairmanship of Peter Van Homrigh (the sitting MP for Drogheda – his Dutch sounding name indicates that he may have been one of the many who benefited from the Battle of the Boyne), and it was resolved that funds would be raised by a weekly subscription to help the poor, and this would continue 'until the great distress, under which they are at present suffering, shall have abated'.

It is necessary here to point out that this effort to raise funds for the poor occurred in the year1830 – it tells us that the spectre of destitution and hunger had taken up permanent residence in the hovels of Drogheda *a full fifteen years before the Great Famine,* a subject which we will discuss separately.

An advertisement appeared in the *Drogheda Journal* offering a building for letting – it was the Black Mills at Annagassan, located '200 yards from the river'. It tells the tale of further unemployment, for the closure of that factory brought misery to another area of County Louth. George O'Brien, who covers the economic history of Ireland exhaustively in that era, singles out Drogheda for special mention, and describes the plight of the inhabitants in this harrowing description:

> *"In no town had the decay of the [linen] industry produced so much distress as in Drogheda, where the condition of the weavers was shocking. The total number continually or casually employed in 1840 amounted to 1890 workers; wages were very low and supplementary employment almost impossible to obtain. By means of begging and of planting a few potatoes on patches of ground given to them by neighbouring farmers for the sake of the manure, they managed to supply themselves with the lowest species of vegetable food, and provide a place of shelter, if shelter it can be called. ... The cabins that the weavers live and work in are fearful specimens of what habit will enable a human being to endure; I am persuaded that no part of Europe, or I might add of the world, present such a specimen of dwelling for human beings as part of Drogheda".[8]*

What was the Corporation doing about the problem? With the rare exception mentioned earlier in these pages, no reference is made anywhere in the Assembly minutes- spanning several hundred years – to indicate concern for the masses of Drogheda's poor.

THE NIGHT OF THE BIG WIND: When it seemed that the people could take no more punishment, they were dealt another cruel blow, this time by Nature, and uncaring overlords were in no way responsible, indeed, they also suffered. A hurricane swept across Ireland, the likes of which had never been experienced in recorded history. It started on Sunday evening, the 6th. January 1839. The wind began to rise at 5 p.m. and by midnight it was howling with unprecedented force, reaching hurricane force. It wreaked havoc, lifting roofs, knocking chimney stacks, destroying homes, uprooting trees and killing both people and livestock. No county or town escaped the devastation. By morning it had abated, having moved eastwards to England and Wales where it continued on its path of destruction.

Even stone buildings collapsed, and sturdy castles such as Ballygarth at Julianstown and Gormanston Castle were damaged, but it was the humble mud-walled cabins and shacks that suffered most, with their thatched roofs being lifted and scattered in every direction. Others caught fire from upturned tilly lamps and candles. Giant trees were flattened like hay before a scythe. In Gormanston demesne 'all the Elms, the pride of the place, perhaps some of the finest in the country, are laid prostrate. ... The Gormaston of 1839 is certainly not the same as the Gormanston of 1838'.[9]

The following morning Drogheda presented a scene of complete devastation. Debris was strewn everywhere. Fallen chimney stacks, gable ends, slates and thatch blocked the roadways. Houses in Laurence St., West St., and William St. were damaged. Of some 90 dwellings in the Windmill Road, 32 had their roofs stripped off and scattered far and wide. Mell Flax Mill, Greenhills Cotton Factory and other industrial premises suffered. On the Mall, the roofs of the Mayoralty House and those of the several millers McCann, Smith and Smythe were also extensively damaged. The subsequent demand for thatchers and slaters enabled them demand ten shillings a day for their services. Public thoroughfares were rendered impassable by fallen trees.

The mansions of the landed gentry outside the town, notably Balls Grove, Oldbridge and Beaulieu did not escape, and many hundreds of the great trees in their adjoining woodlands were flattened. A description was given in a letter written the next day about two other estates: 'The Marquis Conyngham's demesne has suffered much, but Beau Parc, the once charming demesne of Mr. Lambert, has fared still worse. ... The grove of trees at the back of the garden that formed so great a feature has vanished. The buildings have been but little damaged, though some of them are so surrounded by fallen timber that they cannot be approached except by creeping under trees. The character of the place is wholly changed: and that which on Sunday night vied in beauty with any place in the united empire, is now completely shorn of its splendour'.

Curiously, in the Drogheda area there were neither lives lost not serious personal injuries sustained in the course of that night of terror.

An Uneven Playing Pitch: The laws concerning the Irish nation, now being passed in the Union Parliament, were based on the false premise that conditions in Ireland were identical with those in England, and therefore the two islands should be treated alike. This was the nub of the evils that were plaguing Ireland. Ireland, as we have seen in an earlier chapter, had been systematically stripped of her staple industries, and with the linen industry now a thing of the past, she had become an agricultural country pure and simple. Most manufactured articles were imported from England, but since the people were relying heavily on the potato as their diet, there was virtually no cash crop (flax in the north-eastern counties excepted) with which to pay for the other necessities of life.

On the other hand, Britain had entered the age of industrialisation and was becoming 'the workshop of the world'.

At home, prices for farm produce had remained buoyant as long as Wellington and Napoleon were locking horns, but agricultural prices plunged in the aftermath of Waterloo. Dauntlessly, Henry Grattan continued to fight Ireland's cause in Westminster. When the Corn Bill was introduced in 1815 (its aim was to restrict imports of wheat to the benefit of the farming community and to the certain detriment of the poor by increasing the price of bread) he argued that England had an obligation to buy Irish corn, pointing out that Ireland's entire manufacturing industries had already been extinguished by wilful legislation, and it would be grievous to compound the injury.

The doctrine of *laissez faire* was fundamentally flawed in its application to Ireland, in as much as it presupposed that the competing elements inherent in healthy trade and commerce were operating on 'a level playing pitch'. The legislators seemed blind to the fact that England was already vastly more wealthy than Ireland, a circumstance that was exacerbated by maladministration from London of Irish affairs.

In addition, many of the landed gentry had moved to England after 1800; this diverted the flow of their income away from Ireland where it had arisen, and instead it was enriching England. About one-third of Irish landlords had left the running of their estates and the collecting of rents to agents, while they resided in England. These absentee landlords had little knowledge of the state of affairs in Ireland, nor had they empathy with their tenants. They were drones who were contributing nothing to the common purse while being sustained abroad in an extravagant lifestyle.

Union with England meant a universal application of legislation and a sharing in the common wealth, or at least that is what it should have meant. But there was a serious downside to this arrangement in the matter of financial obligations. The protracted European wars with Napoleon were exhausting the common purse. (It was at that time that Prime Minister William Pitt first introduced Income Tax 'as a temporary measure'). As the 1800s advanced, so did the boundaries of the British Empire. South Africa, Sudan, Zululand, India, Hong Kong, Singapore and a host of outposts known as Crown Colonies were purloined from the natives and were now added to the list that had begun 6½ centuries earlier with Ireland.

Apart altogether from military and naval personnel and their armaments, armies of civil servants and administrators had to be maintained in all these destinations, and the Irish Exchequer had to foot the bill for a proportion of this. It would have been pertinent to ask what Ireland received in return.

Ironically, less than two decades before Waterloo, Ireland was seeking (and receiving) help from France in her struggle for independence, and now in a complete turnabout Ireland was contributing to a war to defeat France, and swelling the ranks of Wellington's army to boot. Funding the various wars of Great Britain was something that Ireland could ill afford – it was a serious drain on the Irish economy, and it diverted much needed capital from investment at home.

Highway Robbers: In their struggle for survival, some men yielded to the temptation of operating outside the law, by stealing, poaching or robbing. In November 1847 Mr. and Mrs. Greene were returning home to Mornington when 'two armed ruffians presented pistols at them and demanded their money. They searched both of their victims and carried away Mrs. Greene's pocket containing about fourteen shillings, and then allowed them to proceed'. Later that night they stopped another vehicle; in the scuffle that followed pistols were discharged, but the intended victims 'drove off as fast as they could'. The view was expressed that 13 constables was an insufficient force for the town.

Captain Morgan was returning to his home in Baltray when he was held up by two renegades. They relieved him of 17s. 6d. which was all he carried in cash, and his watch. But when he said that he could identify them in a court of law, they returned the loot and fled. Carriages were frequently waylaid by highwaymen who forced passengers to hand over their valuables. One of Ireland's most notorious highwaymen was Collier the Robber (1780-1849). Michael Collier was born in Lisdornan, Bellewstown, and his main sphere of operation was Louth/Meath/Cavan/North Dublin. He led a colourful career, living at times in Drogheda, Trim, Australia, Africa and the United States. He had a reputation for 'robbing from the rich to give to the poor' through relieving wealthy persons of their gold watches, etc. The long arm of the law put him behind bars on occasions and this brought his expertise as an escape artiste into play. His brother Richard was transported for life to Australia in March 1834 for robbing Patrick Downey, a farmer, outside Drogheda. Michael's career came to an end in 1849 when he was struck down with cholera; he lies in an unmarked grave in the Cord Cemetery.

One of the local landed gentry had first-hand experience of a robbery. He was H.B. Coddington Esq. who was High Sheriff of Meath and lived in the stately mansion at Oldbridge. He was accosted "by two highway robbers who were armed with pistols, on his return from Church to his residence at Oldbridge, near this town. Two persons of notorious character named John McParland and Laurence Dignam who were fully identified by Mr. Coddington and forthwith committed to Trim to abide their trial for the offence. Both of these ruffians confessed to their guilt." Their characters having been tarred in advance by the press in that manner, the outcome of their trial was a foregone conclusion.

The former Coddington estate adjoins the river Boyne at the site of the historic battle, and it included fishing rights. Even in more recent times the proprietors were plagued by latter day 'ruffians' who constantly poached salmon on that fruitful stretch of the river. They sometimes took offence when apprehended, and the proprietor deemed it necessary to explain that his forefathers had not, in fact, taken the land from the natives by force, but had actually purchased it. The validity of this argument was countered with the rejoinder, which contained a grain or two of logic, that a person cannot acquire a better title to property than the seller, and thus the purchaser was the receiver of stolen property – it had been sequestered from the

Cistercians! Today the estate is back in the hands of the people under the custody of the OPW who plan to develop it as a tourist attraction.

Joining the Army and Navy: Men who would otherwise have been chronically unemployed found a place of refuge in the British army or navy, but these outlets were about to be shut to them. An interlude of peace followed the turmoil of the Napoleonic Wars, and this meant that the need for a large standing army diminished. Accordingly, the entire British army was scaled down in 1816 and this included the Louth Militia. The military authorities in future could afford to be selective as to who should be retained. "No man under five feet five inches or five feet six inches should be retained, as a better size is abundant" – according to a recruitment notice in the Drogheda Journal.

They may not have realised it, but the undersized men who were rejected were the luckier ones. Two unfortunates, "James Martin and Michael Tracy, serving in the 44th. Regiment in Cawnpore [India] received *six hundred lashes each* on 14th May for attempting to maim themselves in order to be discharged". Soldiers occasionally died from such excessive punishment.

It is difficult for us to adjudge from today's standpoint whether life was harsher inside the army or outside it. Conditions must have been intolerable for soldiers to have deliberately injured themselves in their efforts to obtain a discharge. It is known that a few went to the extreme of blinding themselves to this end, and we will discuss below the general conditions of barrack life. At best, the army provided an outlet for men who had no other prospects of earning a wage. When the army was scaled down it resulted in added distress in many homes, leaving families penniless.

In 1835 a barracks was in use in Fair Street, opposite the entry to Duke Street – in later times this building served as a convent. It had been rented in 1796 for use as a military hospital accommodating twenty patients, and it also served as an infantry barracks. D'Alton states that 'the parade ground is large, but the house small'. At that period Bolton Square was completely open and devoid of buildings, occupying the entire area between Bolton Street and Fair Street. The square was admirably suited for many outdoor uses, being very spacious, and was deemed to be one of the finest town squares in Ireland. Thus there was ample latitude for military exercising, drilling, etc. It was also used by the populace as a market place.

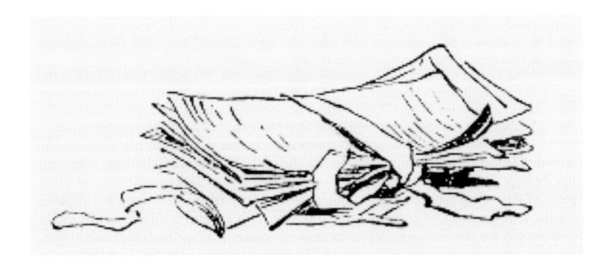

Chapter Twentyfive

A Royal Visitor

The sufferings of the people of Drogheda leading up to, during and after the Great Famine make harrowing reading, and we will encounter that subject in some later pages of this book. But at this point let us partake of a little diversion that will provide a welcome relief and some amusement at the expense of royalty. Nor will this interlude be out of place, because the royalty in question was a king to whom the people of Drogheda paid homage – well, at least some of them did. He was the Hanoverian King George IV who carried the impressive title of King 'of Great Britain and Ireland and of Dependencies Overseas'.

In the course of Drogheda's history, royalty has visited the town on a number of occasions. Let us enumerate them. Not long after the town's foundation, King Henry II arrived to inspect his new domain. His son John came in August 1210. Then in 1394 King Richard II stayed with both the Franciscans, close to the present Mall, and the Dominicans in St. Magdalene's at Sunday's Gate. Although Oliver Cromwell paid Drogheda a visit, we cannot include him because he had turned down the offer of a kingship. In the fateful year of 1690 two kings arrived in the town within a few days of each other – they had come to settle a dispute as to who should wear England's crown, James II arrived just a few days before the battle and a few days later came William III, who must have been in a jubilant mood, because he is said to have written on a drumhead at Kilcullen the promise of a new Charter, which was fulfilled in1697 when he also presented Drogheda with a new Sword and Mace as well as the Charter.

In more recent times (June 1961) Drogheda was pleased to welcome Prince Rainier of Monaco and his beautiful wife, Princess Grace. Pope John Paul II arrived by helicopter on a memorable sunny day, the 29th September 1979 bringing a message of love and peace. Northern Ireland at that time was suffering from a lengthy period of turbulence, punctuated by bombs, bullets and bloodletting. In his address to the crowd estimated at 300,000 that had assembled on the slope of Killineer, a few miles outside the town, he made a plea that was delivered with great fervour: "On my knees I beg you to turn away from violence ... ".

When another king visited Ireland, there must have been great excitement in Drogheda, because several venues along the picturesque valley of the Boyne were included in his itinerary, and it was hoped that perhaps the town would also be honoured with his presence. No doubt the streets were given an exceptionally good scouring, the poultry and pigs shoo-shooed away out of sight, and the main buildings festooned with flowers, flags and bunting to honour the presence of His Royal Highness. How pleasing it was that within a mere *three weeks* of his Coronation in Westminster Abbey on 21st July 1821 the king should deign to visit Ireland and, in particular, the Boyne Valley area.

The king in question was none other than George IV. No sooner had he donned the crown of England than he expressed the wish to visit Ireland, a gesture that must have seemed very flattering to its inhabitants. A vast crowd of sightseers numbering 20,000 converged at Dunleary's shoreline to bestow a timely *Céad Míle Fáilte* on the day of his expected arrival.

Wherever he made a public appearance in the course of his visit, it was recorded in meticulous fashion by a dutiful Boswell-like follower who later published his jottings. Dubliners cheered as he was escorted down Sackville Street and other parts of the capital city. But the highlight of his entire Irish trip was a visit to Slane Castle. It is generally believed that the roadway from Finglas to Slane was specially constructed for the occasion, so as to ease his passage along the otherwise rutted, circuitous route to the gates of the castle. His itinerary in the area also included a visit to Annesbrook, Duleek, where a ballroom was specially added to the mansion for the added pleasure of the royal visitor.

KING GEORGE IV (1762-1830) – A Pen-picture:

*George the Third
Ought never to have occurred.
One can only wonder
At so grotesque a blunder.*

*George the Fourth
Lacked any worth.
When from earth he at last descended
God be praised, the Georges ended!*

> **King George IV** *in caricature.*
> *He was highly unpopular*
> *throughout his kingdom.*

This doggerel reveals the average Englishman's disrespect for the Hanoverian Georges. The first of these Georges was an unknown quantity to the English people – and for that matter, to the Irish people. He was grabbed in haste as one out of 57 contestants for the English throne simply and solely to bypass the hereditary heir James Stewart – son of King James II, – the selfsame person who, as an infant, was alleged to have been slipped into the labour bedchamber in a warming-pan, and despite his tender age, was therefore the prime cause of the Battle of the Boyne. But because he was a papist he was passed over to wear the Crown of England – just about anyone else would fit the bill.

George I came from Germany, and the aristocracy who greeted him as he stepped on English soil were faced with an insignificant, middle-aged man with bulging eyes. He was accompanied by 'a flight of hungry Hanoverians, like so many famished vultures [who] fell with keen eyes and bended talons on the fruitful soil of England'. His rude retinue were unable to resist the finery that they saw around them and outdid the Huns and the Vikings of old as they plundered. The next George to wear the Crown of England yelled 'Dat is one big lie' in broken English when informed of his father's death, but the news was perfectly true. He had a vile temper, and was known to have kicked his wig around the palace when in a rage, especially when he was suffering from piles.

This background as to how the Hanoverian Georges reached the throne is given here because all four of them ruled over Ireland as of right. The average Irish citizen had little cause to respect them – George III was the monarch who could not find it in his heart to grant Catholic Emancipation to his Irish subjects. The Ascendancy, however, never ceased to grovel before them.

The son of George III was of the same mind in regard to his Irish subjects when he became king as George IV. Apart from that, there was no similarity between these two monarchs. Be assured of that. In truth, they bore a mutual detestation towards each other. The father was a diligent, self-righteous man who promoted and practiced good, clean living. The son and heir to the throne was the exact opposite – he was a bounder, morally reprehensible, licentious and dissolute. Among other notable events in his life, he had contrived to secretly and illegally marry a glamorous widow, Maria Fitzherbert. That was bad enough but, horror of horrors, she was, of all things, a Papist! This was the cause of endless embarrassment and complications both inside and outside Parliament. In particular, it did not go down well with his straight-laced Daddy.

We are told that George III went insane during his reign. His delusions were such as to enable him to see his beloved Germany with the aid of a telescope. If he expected filial support or sympathy at this sad turn of events he was in for a disappointment: "Damn him! He is as mad as Bedlam!" his son said of his affliction. Nonetheless, the prospect of taking control of State affairs appealed greatly to him, and he set off for Windsor Castle in the expectation of becoming Regent. He would make a superb ruler, thought he. And what a splendid abode from where to rule his great Empire – Buckingham Palace. And surely he would be provided with resources galore to enable him continue his profligate and hedonistic lifestyle.

But the very idea of his son ruling 'Great Britain, Ireland and the Dependencies beyond the Seas' was enough to bring a timely return of sanity to the father. He recovered sufficiently to physically beat hell out of his dissolute offspring who whereupon set off to pursue his life of debauchery.

His intimates called him 'Prinney', and at the risk of being accused of familiarity towards his royal personage – as commoners like ourselves should never do – we will refer to him in like manner. 'Prinney' then returned to his wildly extravagant ways, where his massive corpulence continued to expand apace with his ever accumulating debts. Gambling was another of his many weaknesses; he had racehorses, but such were his shenanigans that the authorities saw fit to warn him off the course at Newmarket. This vice caused his bank overdraft to grow alarmingly. His debts reached proportions that were absolutely staggering –

about €75,000,000 in today's money – a matter that he treated with total indifference. He also indulged his passion in a variety of middle-aged mistresses, not all of whom were widows like Mrs. Fitzherbert.

Insanity later returned to King George III, and this time for keeps, poor fellow. By 1810 his mind had totally collapsed. Blind and deaf, and suffering from dementia and abdominal pains, he still retained a tenacity in clinging to life, and this kept 'Prinney' from planking his outsize bottom on the throne for another ten years, the king still lingering on in a vegetative state. All told, he would have made it into the Guinness Book of Records through reigning longer than any other king in English history, but 'Prinney' did not consider this a praise-worthy achievement at all, at all. Indeed, had he been allowed near his father's bedside, he would assuredly have abbreviated his longevity with a generous dose of arsenic.

Cartoonists had unlimited scope in lampooning 'Prinny'. This sketch depicts him wallowing in alcohol, with a chamber pot on his head as a crown.

Anyway, to make a long story short, in the year of Our Lord 1820 the Crown of England finally passed into the fat, clammy hands of this dissolute and self-indulgent sloth. The Drogheda Assembly came to the fore with a long palaver offering some consoling words on his father's death, plus a pledge of continued loyalty expressed in the most unctuous terms:

"Most Gracious Sovereign,

We, Your Majesty's most dutiful subjects, humbly entreat your permission to beg before Your Majesty the expression of our unfeigned Condolence on the lamented death of Your august Parent and late venerable and well beloved Monarch. ...
"Divine Providence has called Your Majesty to the Throne of your Forefathers. Permit us, Royal Sire, to offer our most cordial congratulations on the Event. We have experienced the Wisdom and Vigour of Your Majesty's Councils. Under your Auspices a War unexampled in duration and content has been brought to a glorious termination by a Series of the most splendid Victories in the annals of any country.

"We beg Your Majesty to accept the declaration of our unshaken loyalty, our inviolable attachment to your Sacred Person and our steadfast support of Your Majesty's government ...".[1]

... and so on and so forth et cetera, et cetera – it was as grovelling an example of bootlicking obsequiousness as one would encounter in a lifetime. All this, it must be remembered, was done of behalf of the people of Drogheda.

Prinney was then prevailed upon to enter into a legal marriage, just to keep the records straight, and the unfortunate victim was Princess Caroline of Brunswick. He spent the wedding night getting blind drunk, and thereafter he cruelly ignored her. (She, too, was not averse to indulging in sexual entanglements on the side). Their one night's encounter was sufficient to   produce an offspring, a daughter called Princess Charlotte, and the unfortunate girl was destined to be treated with equal indifference by her father throughout her short life.

His coronation in Westminster Abbey was costly beyond words, a most elaborate affair that beggared all description. The occasion called for decorum and dignity, qualities that were not forthcoming from the new king. He acted in an unseemly manner throughout the coronation ceremony, as journalised by a friend of the Duke of Wellington: 'The king behaved very indecently; he was continually nodding and winking at Lady Conyngham and sighing and making eyes at her. ... Any body who could have seen his disgusting figure ... would have been quite sick'.[2]

The people of Ireland, the reader is again reminded, were the subjects, loyal or otherwise, of this newly-crowned buffoon, and the members of the Drogheda Assembly, most devoted as they were, did their utmost in paying him homage on the occasion of his Coronation. They passed a resolution ordering:

"that the sum of £50 sterling be laid out in fire works to be burned on the 19th inst. to commemorate the King's Coronation, and that the public offices of the Corporation be illuminated on that night".[3]

However, the occasion of his Coronation was more noteworthy for the absence of one particular guest, namely his wife and Queen, Princess Caroline. On her arrival to take her rightful place at the ceremony, the great door of Westminster Abbey was slammed shut in her face by burly guards. 'When she got to the door, and made an attempt to enter, she was actually thrust back by the hands of a common prize-fighter'.[4] Within three weeks of this rebuff the poor jilted woman was dead.

The Duke of Wellington said "By God! You never saw such a figure in your life". The Duke was ashamed to walk beside him, and as Prime Minister, he had the misfortune to serve under the scoundrel when he ascended the throne as King George IV. He said of him that he was "the damn'est millstones about the neck of any government that can be imagined[5]" and that he suffered from 'the effects of strong Liquors taken too frequently and in too large quantities. He drinks spirits morning, noon, & night', and he summed up his general conduct with the remark: 'He is selfish' – a gross understatement if ever there was one. He could have added that he also indulged in laudanum (a form of opium) 'in immoderate quantities'. Another close associate, Charles Greville, who was a politician and a diarist, gives us a succinct description: 'A more contemptible, cowardly, selfish, unfeeling dog does not exist than this king...'

It is fortunate that these comments did not come to the king's attention. The illustrious writer Leigh Hunt indiscreetly put his views in writing: "This Adonis in loveliness was a corpulent man of fifty". Innocuous enough, you might think, and close to the mark, but since it appeared in print in *The Examiner* in 1812 it earned its author two years in jail.

He had at one time tried to divorce Princess Caroline, but Parliament and the public would have none of it. He was stuck with her, and she with him – at least in theory. His friends were few both in Parliament and outside it, which is not surprising, because he constantly quarrelled with everyone around him, even with his troupe of middle-aged female companions. Devoted friends were dropped at the snap of his pudgy fingers.

So unpopular had he become that he had completely forfeited the respect of his English subjects, and his carriage was often pelted with stones as he passed through the streets of London. Afraid of being attacked and apprehensive of being laughed at by virtue of his inflated, degenerate body, he avoided being seen in public altogether in his later years and he became a recluse. He was in the habit of ringing the bell in the middle of the night simply to ask the time – even though he had a clock right at his bedside. The excesses of his lifestyle inevitably caught up with him, and he developed gout, venereal disease and a host of other complaints; as well, he became partially blind. Mercifully, in 1830 he obliged mankind by snuffing it. But before he died he had deluded himself into thinking that he had ridden winners at Goodwood and also that he had distinguished himself by commanding a division in the Battle of Waterloo. All in all, his subjects were overjoyed to be rid of him.

Royalty Comes to Slane: This is the gent who was hosted in Ireland. He could hardly wait to get to the Boyne Valley after his Coronation. A detailed itinerary was planned, but things did not work out as envisaged. To start with, a great disappointment awaited the crowd which, as we have seen, had flocked to Dunleary to welcome him – the expected vessel failed to arrive! Unfavourable winds had blown it back to the Welsh coast – a sublime instance of pathetic fallacy. This turned out to be a fortuitous occurrence for Prinney, because he was then given the sad (or glad!) tidings that his estranged queen was dead. "Is she, by God!" was his reaction when given the news. This occasion, no doubt, caused him great jubilation, and the protracted sea voyage now presented him with ample opportunity to celebrate his release from the bonds of matrimony (not that the same bonds were an impediment to his licentious conduct).

We can visualise his state of inebriation in setting out for Ireland the second time, and the commendable Captain Skinner took it upon himself to exercise a degree of discretion. The spectacle of the besotted human cargo staggering down a gang-plank in sight of 20,000 onlookers at Dunleary had to be avoided at all cost. Suffice it to say that, to obviate grave embarrassment in official circles, the resourceful captain changed tack and headed instead for the insignificant harbour at Howth with his very intoxicated charge.

While the patient throngs were waiting dutifully at Dunleary pier, a bemused handful of fishermen at the little fishing village of Howth witnessed the stotious personage lurching onto the pier with all the finesse of a deranged hippopotamus. One member of the entourage remembered the occasion more vividly by being relieved of 'a watch valued sixty guineas by the light fingered gentry'.[6] The king was speedily whisked away from Howth, but not before one of the horses – and horses are noted for their sensitivity – expressed its resentment by bolting, and was subdued only with difficulty. The spot where Prinney first planted his unsteady feet on the pier's granite flag was later indented with an imprint by a local stonemason, and this can still be seen today near the end of the west pier. The date was the 12th August 1821.

Blind drunk as he was on arrival, at least he must be given credit for being the only English king ever to have set foot in Ireland without having either a sword or a gun in his hand.

He performed several State functions in Dublin through a haze of alcohol over the next week or so, including an appearance in College Green and Sackville Street where he wallowed in the adulation of the rabble which had come to have a good look at him. Presenting his royal personage to the people of Ireland was not his objective, however. His thoughts instead were focused on the Boyne Valley. It would be wrong to suppose that it was the natural beauty of the river Boyne and its environs that drew him to the area. Nothing could be further from the truth. He was coming to receive the favours of his current love, the Marchioness of Conyngham who lived in Slane Castle. (By this time he had dumped Mrs. Fitzherbert and a litany of others).

The King Arrives at Slane Castle: Off he romped on Friday the 24th August in the direction of Slane Castle, changing to fresh horses at Ashbourne. For the record, and contrary to a widely held fallacy, the route that he traversed had been laid during a scheme of road development carried out about fifty years earlier, and thus we can breathe a sigh of relief that its characteristically straight alignment cannot be attributed to any sense of devotion towards the royal scoundrel but to a standard in road construction that had been ordained in the previous generation. His train of attendants had difficulty in keeping up with the eager monarch as he bowled past Kilmoon Cross. The hills around Slane village blazed with a string of bonfires as an obsequious manifestation of the peasants' loyalty (or was it curiosity?) towards the royal guest.

He had a predilection for damsels who were fair, fat and forty. His hostess at Slane fitted that criterion, apart from the qualification of age. The Marchioness was a fat, fifty-one-year-old grandmother. The king himself was no chicken at this stage – he was all of fifty-eight years old, but that did not inhibit him from demonstrating a degree of immature passion towards his plump paramour. That took place during a crowded reception at Slane Castle. The Duke of Wellington relayed to a friend the following love scene that Prinney performed in the presence of the local gentry: -

> *'The King [said] ... that he had never known what it was to be in love before, that he was himself quite surprised at the degree to which he was in love, that he did nothing from morning till night but think what he could do to please Ly C [Lady Conyngham] to make her happy, that he wd do anything upon earth for her for that he owed his life to her, that he shd certainly have died in his illness if it had not been for her, & that she was an angel sent from Heaven for him. He cried, Lady C cried, & Madame de Lieven [who was a witness to the spectacle that was taking place] said that, being nervous & easily agitated, she had cried also; & all this passed in a crowded drawing room. One never did hear such folly!! from a man, too, of 58!!'*[7]

Now that we have eaves-dropped on the king in one of his amorous moods, let us take a surreptitious peep at one of his love-letters to the same Lady Conyngham: 'Our Hearts ... do, I think, understand one another, & beat so completely in unison ... you are one of the brightest Ornaments, and to Me, one of the most indispensable ingredients, if everyone is to be happy...' The king was 63 at that time, and his weight was all of 17 stones and 8 pounds.

Another female who was a victim of his amorous emotions described her experience of being in his obese clutches:

> *'[He] threw himself on his knees, and clasping me round, kiss'd my neck before I was aware of what he was doing ... I should make my own terms!! I should be his sole confidant, sole adviser – private or public – I should guide his politicks ... I must have laughed out at the comicality ... and then that immense, grotesque figure flouncing about half on the couch, half on the ground'.*

The entry of the king under her battlements presented Lady Conyngham with the splendid opportunity of inducing him, omnipotent as he was and head over heels in love, to relieve the burden of the Irish people by granting Catholic Emancipation. This particular subject was a running sore with one Prime Minister after another, causing one of them to resign because of the king's continued intransigence. All it needed was a nod from him. There were many opportune moments for her to pop that question while he was purring and whispering sweet nothings in her ear. She was very adept at engineering high positions for her friends and relations, including her cuckolded husband and her son Lord Francis Conyngham.

A little feminine guile accompanied by some gentle persuasion and the whole vexed question of Emancipation would have been a *fait accompli*.

The King and Lady Conyngham, both of whom were endowed
with outsize posteriors, romp around the garden.

The opportunity went a-begging, however. She was evidently as self-centred as her lover-boy, and was pleased to accept all the jewellery that he showered on her, and her interests extended no further than that. Wellington reported that 'whenever the King spoke to her about Politicks she told him that she did not understand the subject'.[8] A close associate, Princess Lieven, summed her up admirably with this feline assessment: 'Not an idea in her head; not a word to say for herself; nothing but a hand to accept pearls and diamonds with, and an enormous balcony to wear them on'.

What a pity she did not beguile her victim towards alleviating the suffering Irish populace. This was a brief moment in Irish history when their grievances could have been redressed at a stroke of the pen. It would have put sleepy Slane on the map. Other geographical locations have lent their names to legislative milestones, for example the Treaty of Rome and the Statutes of Kilkenny. The title 'the Slane Protocol' sounds grandly important – it would have elevated Slane to a position of everlasting prominence by attaching its name to an Act that ended the deprivations being endured by Catholics throughout the kingdom. But it was not to be. The fact remains that politics and Emancipation were outside the sphere of this self-indulgent pair's interests – mundane matters such as these were never to interfere with their passionate pursuits. The visit to Slane was simply for the gratification of base desires, and nothing more.

As for the sober Duke of Wellington, a few well-balanced words from him would have provided added weight – after all, the king was a guest in the Duke's very own County Meath, and the same Duke, the victor of Waterloo, was of such political stature as to be later appointed Prime Minister of Great Britain and Ireland. Although conscious of the injustices

230

being perpetrated on his fellow Irishmen, he always regarded Emancipation as a hot potato; indeed, he opposed the concession at every turn.

Lady C's penchant for acquisitiveness was most evident by making it her business to loiter around Windsor Castle when Prinney was gasping his last. Here she gave a display of opportunism at its best. 'Before leaving his death-bed Lady Conyngham purloined as much booty as possible, and her subsequent hurried journey from Windsor to Ireland, in a coach laden with baggage full of her paramour's costly presents and other extravagant items of a provenance at best dubious, was a gift to the satirists'.

By way of diversion from their romps under the blankets in Slane Castle, the lovey-dovey couple took a trip a few miles down the road to the Obelisk, the scene of the great military victory of 1690, the issue of which cleared the way of securing the German Georges on England's throne. This was on Saturday the 25th August 1821, and it was as near as the king got to Drogheda where, no doubt, the Mayor and his cohorts were standing to attention, dressed in their Sunday best, in anticipation of his arrival. They were in for a disappointment. Instead he went across the road to Townley Hall where Blaney Balfour received him and where, we are told, he 'partook of a sumptuous collation'.

The King at Duleek: Next port of call was Annesbrook, Duleek. This was the stately abode of Henry Smith, the gentleman who had strained his financial resources to the uttermost to build a ballroom so that His Majesty could disport himself. (Indeed, Smith later became a bankrupt!). Prinney was renowned for being grossly inconsiderate, and he had an in-built propensity for disappointing the many guests who continually went to great pains to please him. At the drop of a hat he was liable to change course, leaving would-be hosts open-mouthed and frustrated. The itinerary planned for him in Dublin, for example, had included a visit to the RDS, bastion of the Ascendancy; they knew of his gluttonous appetite and had prepared their own version of 'a sumptuous collation' for him. And why shouldn't they – after all, it was he who was protecting them in their privileged position as lords and masters. No doubt the principal hosts had their speeches well polished for the occasion. He simply failed to turn up, disappointing the cream of society which had made such elaborate preparations – it had taken all of forty tents to lay out the dishes for the banquet. The tables, laden as they were with expensive wines and foodstuffs, were left on their hands.

The day set aside for the visit to Annesbrook, Duleek dawned bright and sunny, prompting the royal guest to elect to have his next 'sumptuous collation' *al fresco* – out on the lawn under nature's blue dome. Suffering from a bowel infection, Prinney had occasion to enter the house to use the privy. This was as near as he got to the ballroom – he never saw it.

Had Prinney entered the town of Drogheda, how would he have reacted to the scenes of destitution? When his niece, as Queen Victoria, was passing through English towns on the recently constructed railway system, the blinds of her carriage were pulled down so that she would be spared the sight of the abject squalor that existed around her. Drogheda's Mayor and the other fawning dignitaries would have been determined to usher King George in like manner. It is improbable that he would have been moved at seeing the plight of his Drogheda subjects, where living conditions were even worse than in England.

The Drogheda Assembly did not let the occasion pass without having an input, nonetheless. This took the form of a donation of £100 sent to a Dublin bank for his use. Such a sum would have gone some way towards alleviating the distress of Drogheda's poor, but to the visiting king it mere 'pocket money', a drop in the ocean, a peanut to an overweight elephant. The inmates of Drogheda Jail were in an expectant mood, having had reason to be jubilant a few weeks earlier. We are told that the Assembly had made a disbursement of '£1.13.9 [€2.14] provisions for prisoners confined in the gaol at Drogheda on the day of His Majesty's Coronation'[9]. This time they were left languishing in their cells with not as much as a stale crust to mark the occasion.

He cancelled his planned trip to the races at the Curragh on Wednesday the 29th. August because the weather was not to his liking, but the Clerk of the Weather held back the excessive downpour that had been set aside for Prinney, for when he arrived at the racecourse two days later we are told that: 'The rain poured down in torrents'.

A vast congregation converged on Dunleary to bid *Slán Abhaile* to him on his departure on the 3rd September 1821. Jarveys had a field day. Their normal fare for carrying passengers to Dunleary from the small village of Ballsbridge that lay outside Dublin was sixpence, but on this occasion, those who were able to hail a jarvey were parting with 10/- and £1 – up to forty times the normal rate – to see him off. The port at that time was much less significant than it is at present, and the great piers that we see today were not completed for another thirty years, so the congestion at the departure point was severe. The crowd was so unruly that four of the *hoi polloi* toppled into the harbour, one having to cling to the rudder of the departing vessel to avoid drowning.

Thankfully, Drogheda escaped the mayhem that was experienced at Dunleary. Had the august Prinney entered Drogheda, perhaps he would have renamed the town 'Kingstown' in his memory. Perish the thought! However, the fawning Drogheda Assembly of 1821 have saddled later generations with the names George's Street and George's Square. As for Dunleary, he inflicted the doubtful honour of a name change there, and accordingly, that port was thereafter known as Kingstown – that is, until 1922 when the old Irish name was restored, and variously spelled Dún Laoghaire or Dunlaoire.

Did the Lady from Slane make a last-minute plea on behalf of the suffering Irish people? Robert Huish, the king's contemporary and biographer, answers this question for us: '[He was] kept in a whirl of pleasure and dissipation, and left the Irish coast as ignorant of the internal discord and misery of the country, as when he landed on it'.[10]

232

Chapter Twentysix

Education

Books published during the 1700s generally had a religious or scientific subject-matter – novels and penny dreadfuls were not in vogue. Drogheda had several circulating libraries, and in 1802 a bookseller in West St. advertised 'books lent to read at 6½d per week'. Literacy was confined almost exclusively to the upper classes and the landed gentry, and it was only they  who could afford the price of a newspaper, but an emerging Catholic middle class began to appear towards the end of the 1700s. Booksellers, of which there were several in Drogheda, were also newspaper proprietors. The first local newspaper appeared about 1760; it was *The Drogheda Newsletter*, and it was followed in 1774 by *The Drogheda Journal or Louth and Meath Advertiser.*

We get an inkling of the official religious policy in Louth and Meath during the Penal Days from an official Order which stated that 'severall Popish schoolemasters doe reside in severall parts of the Counties of Meath and Louth, and teach the Irish youth, training them in Supersticion, Idolatry and the evill Customs of this Nacion' … and they should be suppressed and 'that further Order may be given for their due punishment as shall be thought fitt'.

Notwithstanding official opposition, the Popish schoolmasters remained active. Foremost among these was Oliver Plunkett, who wrote of the Jesuits: 'They cause more annoyance to our opponents because they are at Drogheda, only four hours journey from Dublin, where no Catholic school is allowed … And indeed many Protestant boys come to them, belonging to the principal families, who afterwards assist us in defending them…'. The school had about 180 boys, mostly 'of the Catholic knights and gentry'.

Following the easing of restrictions on Catholicism, brought about by the Catholic Relief Act (1782), the schools often contained pupils of mixed religions. Protestants occasionally funded them. At Mornington one Protestant and seven Catholic children were taught by Elizabeth Brabazon, a member of the landed gentry, in a little school which she funded from her own purse. The Brabazon residence is now the Ozanam Home.

It goes without saying that a significant cause of the continuing inertia and destitution among the masses was the lack of proper education. Ignorance prevented them from improving their living condition, and kept them in a state of unending intellectual darkness. Government endowments for education were granted from 1733, and institutions such as the Erasmus Smith Foundation made a presence from the late1700s. But since they were regarded as having a proselytising role, they were not supported by Catholics. Barns and out-houses often afforded accommodation to Catholic school children, and in fine weather classes were held in the open – these became known as 'hedge-schools'. A State-controlled, centralised system of elementary education was established in 1812, but once again early suspicions of covert proselytising agendas gave way to outright accusations, and these were later proved to be well founded.[1]

In 1831 the National Board of Education was established whose function it was to administer a centralised system of undenominational elementary education. Illiteracy stood at an appalling 72% in 1841, and slowly the position began to improve. By 1855 one-third of the juvenile population was receiving an education[2]. As the century advanced the literacy rate became quite comparable with that of most other European countries, thanks mainly to the arrival of religious orders of teaching sisters and brothers. In addition to the three Rs, the curriculum usually included a familiarisation of the English language – a crucial acquisition, especially for the many who lacked manual accomplishments, and for the huddled masses who were making their way in the emigrant ships in search of a better life.

AG LABHAIRT GAEILGE I nDROICHEAD ÁTHA: The gradual erosion throughout the island of the Irish language in favour of English was only to be expected. By the mid 1800s only 23.3% of the entire population could speak Irish, and a preponderance of these lived west of the Shannon, more especially in isolated pockets. Through commercial and social intercourse it had largely disappeared throughout Leinster and most of Ulster and Munster.

What is surprising is the fact that the Louth/Meath region was an exception to this trend, notwithstanding the influence of nearby Dublin. The Cooley Peninsula was a pocket where Irish survived as the vernacular into the twentieth century. Owing to its proximity to Dublin, one would expect English to have been the *lingua franca* in Drogheda, but it is equally surprising to discover otherwise. (It is possible that many of the Gaelic speakers were migrants). A German visitor named Johann Kohl who travelled extensively throughout Ireland in 1844 had this to say about Drogheda:

> *"Drogheda is a very Irish town – the last genuine Irish one the traveller meets on this coast as he travels northward. Nay, Drogheda is perhaps more Irish than many a town in the south or west of the island. The population is almost entirely Roman Catholic, but few Protestants are to be found there. The suburbs of Drogheda are genuinely Irish, miserable, filthy, falling cabins, and many persons are likewise to be found in the neighbourhood who understand and speak the old Irish language and say they cannot speak English with comfort or fluency. Nay, according to what I was told by the inhabitants, I must believe that the Irish language is far more general in and around Drogheda than at any other point on the eastern coast of Ireland".*

The Drogheda Grammar School: Erasmus Smith was a London Alderman who was given title to large tracts of Irish lands under the Cromwellian plantations. He created charitable trusts in 1657 which were directed towards education 'in the kingdom of Ireland'. The first appointment of a master was to the Grammar School at Drogheda. The Governors recorded: 'And as for Drogheah wee have purchased … two very convenient houses whereon is roome enough for master and usher and schollers that are boarders, a good garden and large unwalled yard for ye boyes to play in …' Erasmus Smith's sons visited the town in 1709 and were 'presented with the ffreedome of this Corporation'. About 1770 the pupils gave proof that boys will be boys – and sometimes to an excessive degree: 'the boys took possession of the school and house, and held it for some days; they had baskets hung out of the windows, into which the trades-people put provisions for their sustenance'.[3]

The critics of today who oftentimes castigate the Christian Brothers for their use of the cane should take cognisance of the performance of the headmaster of the Grammar School in the period 1859/63:

> *'He flogged knowledge into his pupils, and enforced discipline with a cane … His temper was ungovernable and once aroused he lost all self-control … [On one occasion when the pupils remonstrated with an unpopular German teacher he went berserk] … Without a moment's delay he rushed to his study, seized a bundle of canes, ordered all the school to assemble in the Prep. Hall and thrashed everyone soundly, breaking in the process a dozen canes'.*

The liberal use of the cane did the boys no long term harm, for the school was proud to have launched an array of church dignitaries, including bishops, as well as most of the local landlords including the Coddingtons, Filgates and Balfours, and such luminaries as Henry Flood, Henry Grattan and Speaker Foster. A pupil who attended school by travelling along the Boyne by boat was Arthur Wellesley, but it has not been established whether the school in question was the Drogheda Grammar School. His most noteworthy achievement was the defeat of Napoleon, and he affirmed that 'the battle of was won on the playing fields of Eton', but perhaps the 'good garden and large unwalled yard for ye boyes to play in' far away in Laurence St. Drogheda also made a contribution to that signal victory!

The school was in dire financial straits in 1956, and was rescued by being adopted by the Religious Society of Friends. Subsequently the numbers of students exceeded one hundred and a Regency building on the Mornington Road, Eden View, was acquired with the aid of a Government grant. Today it educates about 220 boys and girls, some of whom arrive from Germany, Japan and Russia; pupils of all religious persuasions are welcome.

The Convent of Siena: The foundress was Catherine Plunkett, a grandniece of the martyred Oliver Plunkett, and in 1722 she established a convent in a mud cabin on the south side of Drogheda, near Ship St.. The community conducted a school for poor girls – it may have been the only Catholic girls' school in Ireland at the time. When a three-storey house in Dyer St. became available a few years later they moved to it. The penal laws were still in force and it was necessary for them to maintain a very low profile. They dressed as lay women during the day, and only at night, when the doors were locked, did they change into their religious habits. They were presented with a rare saint's relic – the severed head of Oliver Plunkett, but such were the circumstances of the times that they found it necessary to keep it secreted in the base of a grandfather clock. Had the authorities known that the premises was a convent, they would have torn it down and scattered the nuns. The nuns described the building as a 'boarding house', a title that sufficed to explain the presence of the several occupants. When an official called to probe their activities and to enquire if any of them were nuns, Mother Plunkett's reply was a classic example of Delphic ambiguity: 'My companions are as much nuns as I am'.[4] The enquirer went off probably scratching his head in puzzlement.

The renowned architect Francis Johnson designed their next building which was at the Cord Road. They first occupied it in 1796 and continued their role in educating girls, which then housed boarders. Their pupils included Mrs. Sadler who wrote 'The Old House by the Boyne', Nano Reid, RHA and this author's mother. They became a completely enclosed, contemplative order in 1930 and their educative work ended; henceforth their only contact with the outside world was through a grille. A veteran recalled: 'I used to do plumbing work for them. Two nuns would walk in front of me down the corridor and they ringing a bell to indicate that there was a male in the house'[5]. In 1994 the convent was gutted by fire and they moved to a custom-built property at the Twenties.

The Presentation Sisters: The school was opened on the 7th June 1813 in the basement of No. 12 Fair Street. Its purpose was 'the uplifting and education of the poorest and most neglected girls in the town'. The first items of furniture, a table and some chairs, were supplied by a kind Protestant lady, as the building was otherwise completely bare. The nuns – there were only two of them – were poor, and often hungry. 'On one occasion they were on the point of selling some lead from the roof to a plumber in order to buy food, when an unknown man handed in an envelope containing a £1 note'.[6]

Many of the pupils were also partly fed and clothed as well as being taught sewing, cooking, etc. With the passage of time more and more children flocked to the school and the community was able to acquire adjacent property to accommodate the classes. In 1923 a substantial house at Greenhills (Smith's) was purchased, and to relieve further overcrowding a new school was built on the Ballymakenny Road. Today only 9 nuns remain, and most of them qualify for the Old Age Pension.

The Sisters of Mercy: Fr. Mathews, a member of the Mounthanover family, was instrumental in arranging for four nuns from their convent at Tullamore to establish a new one in Drogheda. They set off by canal barge to Dublin and from there by train to Drogheda. This was on 8th. November 1854 following which they set up home at No. 2 Dublin Road until a more suitable home was available. Their first postulant arrived two months later – she was Aloysius Healy from a well known family of chemists in West St.

They took possession of their new home in 1879, and a 'bazaar largely helped to defray the cost of its erection … [and much of] the rest was supplied by the community and their relatives…'.[7] An expanding population saw a Boys' National Primary School being constructed in 1953 – it was designed to accommodate 500 pupils, and a Girls' Primary

School followed some years later. In 1992 a lay principal was appointed, and the lay staff increased as the numbers of nuns diminished. A secondary school to accommodate 500 girls was constructed to cater for the requirements of the new housing estates in the parish.

Education formed only part of the work undertaken by the nuns. The present age of affluence tends to obscure the former age of deprivation and that, since their arrival in Drogheda, the nuns were also deeply engaged in works of mercy, in alleviating the lot of those who were destitute – and Drogheda had more than its share of these. When their daily work in the classrooms ended they made visitations to the sick and the poor. Some spent their lives in the nearby Workhouse, dedicated to catering for the needs of society's rejects and life's failures. They continued this work for over a hundred years until the workhouse eventually closed. They earned money by making jam with the fruits from their garden, and used the proceeds to replace the crude tin plates and chipped enamel mugs that the Workhouse inmates had been using since famine times. One elderly nun told this author that shortly after entering the Order her brother came to visit her (in the mid 1930s). He was so appalled at the grim, primitive conditions of the Workhouse and the dismal circumstances under which she was working that he went back and informed their father. "He came over [from the Navan area] to take me away, but I wouldn't go. I loved it."

The school curriculum did not include preparing girls for their role as housewives, so the nuns taught them the domestic essentials, such as cooking and sewing after normal classroom hours.

With dwindling vocations many of the cells in the Convent were unoccupied, and the building was put up for sale in 1993 and the remaining six sisters took possession of their new Bungalow Convent located in the garden at the rear of the convent.

The Daughters of Charity: Previously known as the Sisters of Charity, they are a French order, and they first arrived in Ireland in 1855 – just one year after the Sisters of Mercy. They selected Drogheda as their first home in Ireland, and undoubtedly the pressing needs of the town's poverty-stricken multitudes were an influencing factor, so that 'the street was their cloister' as they attended to the wants of the poor and the infirm. Their first home was Harpur House in William Street. Financial help came from an unlikely source, akin to an impecunious Peter receiving alms from an impoverished Paul – a Franciscan priest, Fr. Dardis, had received a legacy which he passed on to them.

They operated an industrial school for boys as well as an orphanage catering for an average of about 150 children. 'On a Sunday morning after Mass (in the 1930s) you'd see the young boys going down the Green for a walk, about 50 of them in a crocodile line, and usually holding hands. A nun in her blue flowing garb and white butterfly bonnet would shepherd them, and they were always spick and span in their short pants and grey pullovers'.

The very distinctive bonnets worn by the nuns, called 'coronets', were of stiff, starched, white linen, which earned them the nick-name 'Butterfly Nuns'. This head-gear was modified after Vatican II.

The Christian Brothers: They arrived in Drogheda in 1857 and took charge of a school that had been established in 1787 at West Gate under the auspices of the Patrician Monks. A stone slab on the wall states:

> **"This institution was founded through the benevolent exertions of the Rev. Matthew White, Curate of St. Peter's Parish, under the patronage of the most reverend Richard O'Reilly Roman Catholic Archbishop of Armagh in the year 1787, and a lease of this ground at a nominal rent has been liberally granted by the Corporation of Drogheda. The charitable inhabitants thereof caused this school to be erected A.D. 1802".**

Initially it catered for 120 boys, and by 1840 the pupils, including infants, numbered 340. The ever increasing numbers prompted a new school to be built, this was in 1859 at Sunday's Gate. A second storey was later added and in 1936 a separate primary school was built, adjacent to the existing one. The school at West Gate closed in the 1950s and became the Star and Crescent Club; the older one at Sunday's Gate was relocated to Newfoundwell in the mid 1990s, and meanwhile another secondary school was built on Beamore Road catering for the needs of families living on 'the Far Side'.

The foundation stone for the monastery house, which was constructed of limestone and Belfast brick, was laid in 1869. It is sited in Palace St., next to the schools; it provided for 17 apartments. Public subscriptions were raised to defray the cost, one of the contributors being Benjamin Whitworth, whose name as a generous benefactor to the town will constantly recur in these pages. With ever dwindling vocations this building was sold and converted into a hotel in 2005.

Other schools included the Blue School, St. Peter's Male and Female School, established in 1723, and several private schools and academies such as the English Mercantile and Mathematical School, O'Reilly's Academy in Fair St. and Miss Tighe's school in Duke St.

A dearth of religious vocations has brought closure to some of the religious orders in Drogheda. The Franciscans, the Irish Christian Brothers and the Medical Missionaries of Mary saw but a year or two of the new millennium before closing their doors forever, and the members of those communities that remain are fewer in number and older in age. The benefits which these religious orders have bestowed so selflessly on successive generations throughout the many dark decades of the past can never be properly evaluated or fully appreciated and acknowledged. Suffice it to say that the groundwork they instilled in their pupils has removed the stigma that accompanied Irish immigrants in earlier generations; those who seek employment in foreign lands today do so by choice, not necessity, and are competing on equal terms with all others. Their professional expertise is much sought after, and this is due in no small measure to the commitment and selfless dedication of their teachers, both lay and religious.

Teaching a classroom of pupils, whether bright or dull or simply unruly, is never less than a formidable challenge. The roll-book in this author's CBS classroom in 1941 contained all of 72 names, and there were instances where numbers well exceeded 100. Controlling classes of that magnitude entailed the use of *an bata,* and such usage has occasionally been the cause of criticism. Unquestionably, undue corporal punishment is to be deplored, but it is unfair and irrational to judge the circumstances of the past by the standards of today when resources are more plentiful and classes are considerably smaller.

The generation of accomplished, well-instructed students that entered the twenty-first century would be remiss if it lost contact with the fullness of Ireland's past, particularly that era of repression when generations depended on the 'hedge school' for enlightenment. It should be ever mindful of the selfless efforts that were taken in establishing in the Irish people a rightful sense of self-esteem and self-assurance that comes only with a sound education.

Chapter Twentyseven

The Great Famine

The famine of 1845/47 was not a unique, isolated occurrence – there had been frequent famines during the 1700s and early 1800s. The famine of 1817/19, for example, claimed 60,000 lives. Nor were they confined to Ireland – Belgium and other countries had experienced famines during that era. Severe frosts, excessive rain, droughts, as well as blights, had been the cause of great hardship and deaths in the past.

The dreadful news of potato blight that descended on the Drogheda area was first reported in the issue of the Drogheda Argus on 20th September 1845. The agricultural correspondent wrote: –

'... I regret that my observations and enquiries on the subject establish the appaling fact that [the potato crop] has suffered to an alarming extent. ...

'It was asserted that drilled potatoes were safe and that the rot was confined to ridges. I was making the observation last Tuesday to a gentleman who has a large farm in my neighbourhood, but he shook his head significantly and observed '... I have 14 acres of as fine looking drills as were in the country a few weeks ago; in one night they were all blasted and I am sorry to inform you they are nearly all rotten...'

Warnings about the undue dependence on the potato crop by a people who were already living at subsistence level went unheeded, and the authorities were totally unprepared for the great catastrophe when it struck. There were several aspects which distinguished the visitation of blight in 1845 from its predecessors, namely its duration and its unprecedented magnitude. It was the greatest peacetime calamity to visit Europe since the Black Death 500 years earlier. The situation was exacerbated by the victims being notoriously disadvantaged

through being shorn of the wherewithal to combat it, and being at the mercy of a failed, uncaring and corrupt régime.

The official in charge of famine relief was Sir Charles Trevelyan, and a more insensitive, unsympathetic official could not have been selected. He was utterly unbending, and adhered rigidly to a policy of minimal state support and maximum self-reliance. He said: "Ireland must be left to the operation of natural causes", and again "The great evil with which we have to contend is not the physical evil of the famine, but the moral evil of the selfish, perverse and turbulent character of the people".[1] Conducting affairs from his remote mahogany desk in London, he declared: 'It is my opinion that too much has been done for the people'.

He endeavoured to justify his stance by reporting: 'There were separate committees which raised and sent over [from England] large sums of money. There were ladies' associations without end to collect small weekly subscriptions and make up clothes to send to Ireland'. He rationalised this heartless *laissez faire* policy that he pursued so exactingly by arguing that government intervention would have been counter productive in the long term – all this while people were dying by the thousand.

There can be no doubt but that many charitable organisations in Ireland, Britain and elsewhere sprang into action in relieving the people's distress. Foremost among these was the Society of Friends (or 'Quakers') who initiated a subscription list and sent a deputation to Ireland to set up soup kitchens. Since the governmental response was too tardy, the speedy action of the Quakers during the earlier months of the famine saved untold suffering. The value of their relief amounted almost to £200,000, and sums were distributed among the 32 counties in accordance with the extent of the distress in each. County Cork received £35,000, Skibbereen being absolutely decimated. Meath got the smallest amount, indicating that the suffering there was much less acute than in other counties.[2]

At local level a meeting was arranged in the Tholsel where it was agreed to raise funds by calling on the generosity of the more affluent townspeople. The poor could also be employed 'for work of such utility as are absolutely necessary and which should be executed at public cost, [e.g.] repairs at Ulster Lane, Patrick St., the Rope Walk, the road leading to the Strand and several others'. Accordingly, it was decided to prepare a schedule of landlords and to name 'those who contribute and those who neglect this duty [and have it] laid before his Excellency the Lord Lieutenant'.

This request for alms met with a most satisfying response, as reported in the Drogheda Conservative Journal on 25th March 1846: –

> "We seldom witness a more gratifying scene than was presented at the Tholsel on Monday last when the clergy, gentry, merchants and others met. ... It was very pleasing to behold the Protestant Vicar with the Roman Catholic Primate, the Presbyterian and Wesleyan ministers and men of all shades of political feeling joining cordially..." Donations were freely handed in, and were acknowledged in the columns of the press.

The blight worstened and the potato harvest of 1846 brought the prospect of a second year of famine to the people. To make matters worse, the crop planted was smaller because in desperation many were forced into consuming the seed potatoes intended for planting, so that the conditions of the poor had greatly deteriorated. Another public meeting was called in December of that year which, as reported in the *Drogheda Conservative*, demonstrates the workings of an impersonal bureaucracy:

> "Pursuant to a respectably signed requisition addressed to the Mayor, his worship convened a meeting in the Tholsel on Tuesday last [8th December] for the purpose of devising the best mode of allaying the great distress under which the poor are suffering at present.... Nothing further was transacted than the appointment of a committee from the general Relief Committee to draw up resolutions, etc. and an adjournment took place to Thursday at one o'clock ...
> "On Thursday the adjourned meeting took place, when the court-house was crowded in every part, a large number of the labouring class having attended, for whose benefit the meeting was called ...
> "The Rev. Dr. Crolly said 'A committee was appointed to make arrangements to provide employment for the destitute poor until the public works presented for at the sessions can be commenced. The committee met from time to time in order to make the arrangements as perfect as possible and in such manner as to allow as many as possible to take part in the good work to be performed. I must say that, after eleven years experience on this subject, I always see that the laborious part of the public duty is left to be performed by the active and zealous few, while the absenters are generally those who complain of the manner in which the business is done (hear, hear). The gentlemen who acted on the committee during the past season had a great deal to do in making their arrangements; they had to wait on the Lord Lieutenant; and on the Relief Commissioners; they had to wait on the Harbour Commissioners; and to have applications made to the Board of Works; they had to wait on the Railway Companies. The Board of Works did nothing for them. The Railway Companies did not see their way very clearly. ... The poor must be employed and fed – they cannot wait for the Board of Works or any other Board (hear, hear)".

The Rev. Mr. Wynne, Vicar of St. Peters, supported the previous speaker and said the poor people of this town deserve the highest credit for the great patience and good order exhibited by them throughout.[3]

The parish priest in Stamullen was treasurer of the local relief fund, and several times he was obliged to denounce the gentry for failing to make donations – they often treated the collectors with contempt. Likewise, the Drogheda Conservative Journal in an editorial dated 29th January 1848 castigated the wealthy section of the community who were found wanting in the matter of Christian charity:

> '... as we view the hordes of destitute poor – famished men and children, and even the weaker sex, in piteous accents crave a morsel of bread at the doors of the wealthy who rudely repulse them as an inferior class of beings, and direct them to the workhouse in a stern tone of voice, as a remedy for all their evils – we cannot avoid exclaiming with indignation: unfortunate country, after centuries of misrule, has the climax of thy misery arrived at last? ...

A more pleasing report emanated from Collon. "We rejoice to learn that the benevolent Lord Massereene has contributed liberally" in relieving the destitution. "Soup kitchens by the ladies of Collon should cause the ladies of this town [Drogheda] to blush for their negligence[4]," an observation that tells us that the upper class was leaving the throngs of destitute citizens of the town to their own devices.

A widely circulated rumour was prevalent that Queen Victoria's personal donation was £5 when contributions were being sough. Other sources say she donated £2,000. Parnell, who showed scant affection towards the royal family, stated in a letter to the press about the contribution made by the 'Famine Queen' as she was called on occasions: '...the Queen gave nothing to relieve the Famine in 1847 ... [but I might add] with perfect accuracy that not only did she give nothing, but that she actually intercepted £6,000 of the donation which the Sultan of Turkey desired to contribute to the Famine Fund.[5] The government expenditure on maintaining garrisons of 50,000 soldiers could have been better deployed in feeding the poor. On the other hand, some sympathetic landlords spent their fortunes in providing relief, bringing them to the brink of insolvency in their efforts to keep their tenants alive.

At this day's market there was not a dozen of Eggs offered for sale, an occurrence which we never before remember to have taken place. Our Potatoe market, which in former years were filled with that article is now deserted, and turned into a depot for stone breaking.

This report epitomises the conditions endured by the people throughout the famine years. It appeared in the local newspaper in the week prior to Christmas 1846.

FAMINE? – WHAT FAMINE? Ironically, there was no lack of food in the country at the time – there were fields of golden corn and endless pastures on which beefy cattle grazed – but the people lacked the means of purchasing food. Since Ireland had been shorn of its industries throughout earlier generations, it would be proper to say that there was a famine, not of foodstuffs, but of capital and the opportunities that capital creates, rather than the absence of food.

The dictionary defines the word 'famine' as 'a severe shortage of food' and it has often been pointed out that the Great Famine would more accurately be described as 'the

Great Hunger' because food *shortage* was not the issue. In the five year period 1821/25 the average annual exports of live cattle were 46,714; ten years later the figure was 98,150, and in the period 1846/48 when the famine was at its height the cruel irony is that it had risen to 190,828 head of cattle.

This anomaly is borne out by the wagons laden with produce that made their way through the country lanes converging on Drogheda port, all bound for export. The compelling evidence appeared in the weekly reports of cattle fairs and corn markets that were held in Drogheda, as published in the *Drogheda Conservative Journal* throughout that era. They tell the tale in a matter-of-fact way: the newspaper quoted statistics on the week by week activities at the port. For example, the issue of the 17th November 1848 contained this snippet:

"EXPORTS: The '*Irishman*' for Liverpool: 231 cows, 551 sheep, 7 horses, 9 boxes eggs, 11 do. Butter…".[6]

Scarcity of food was not the issue, there being no general food shortage. Simply put, the people were harnessed to a political economy *which left them too poor to buy the fruits of their own labour*. In one particular week 2,670 cattle and 2,342 pigs left Drogheda port for Liverpool, and this was a regular occurrence. The local paper routinely reported the prices and the quantities on offer at the Drogheda market. A random extract taken during 'Black Forty-seven' states in casual, every-day language: "There was a large supply of grain at the market today …" and the report enumerated that 140 cows, 270 sheep, 340 pigs and quantities of wheat and barley arrived at the docks for shipment, just as it had been doing for centuries past. Thus the vessels sailing down the Boyne were laden with foodstuffs, and as one ship departed, another arrived – the service ran on five days each week: Mondays, Tuesdays, Wednesdays, Fridays and Saturdays. The Irony of the super-abundance of foodstuffs existing side by side with a starving populace is well illustrated in the reports reproduced here from the *Drogheda Conservative Journal* dated the 14th November 1846.

The newspaper cutting shown hereunder is taken from the *Drogheda Conservative Journal* issue dated 14th November 1846. By coincidence, the weekly report of the Guardians of the Poorhouse was positioned immediately below the weekly report headed 'EXPORTS' which listed the week's shipping movements out of the Boyne. One report is in stark contrast to the other. This anomaly well illustrates the cornucopia that existed cheek by jowl with starvation. A total of **13 cargoes** left for Liverpool, Barmouth and Ayr during the week, laden with a combined total of 1,914 cattle, 1987 sheep and 2,759 pigs, plus some horses, eggs and large quantities of flour, oatmeal, wheat, peas, etc., and such exports of foodstuffs were quite routine. At the same time the Guardians of the Workhouse were grappling with the ravenous needs of the inmates, and were also faced with the bank's rejection of an application for a loan.

EXPORTS.

(Week ending 14th November, 1846.)

Faugh-a-Ballagh for Liverpool—9 boxes eggs, 198 cows, 696 pigs.

Irishman for Liverpool—170 cows, 80 sheep, 470 pigs, horses.

Fair Trader for Liverpool—100 cwt oatmeal, Morton; 9 casks ale, Cairnes, 618 cows, 60 sheep, 240 pigs, 2 horses.

Grana Uile for Liverpool—142 cows, 370 pigs, 3 horses.

Rodolph for Liverpool—250 cwt oatmeal, H. Crolly.

Anne and Catherine for Barmouth—200 cwt flour, 160 cwt oatmeal, 30 quarters wheat, 10 do peas, Smith and Smyth.

Faugh-a-Ballagh for Liverpool—186 cows, 200 sheep, 76 pigs, 9 horses.

Brian Boiroimhe for Liverpool—120 cwt oatmeal, Chadwick, 17 boxes eggs, 145 cows, 318 sheep, 217 pigs.

Sisters for Ayr—800 cwt oatmeal, J. and R. Morton.

Irishman for Liverpool—9 boxes eggs, 117 cows, 271 sheep, 230 pigs, 2 horses

Brian Boiroimhe for Liverpool—120 cows, 200 sheep, 10 pigs, 8 horses.

Fair Trader for Liverpool—80 cows, 120 sheep, 80 pigs.

Grana Uile for Liverpool—140 cows, 700 sheep.

DROGHEDA POOR LAW UNION—Thursday.
Weekly Meeting.

The following guardians attended at the Board-room—
Francis Donagh, Esq., Chairman.
Thomas Brodigan, Nicholas Markey, H B Coddington, P Matthews, Esq.

The minutes of last meeting were read and affirmed.

Master's Report—Admitted during the week 47; remaining from last week 339; discharged 9; died 1; born 0; remaining 376. Expenses for the week £36 15s 11¼d average 1s 10¾.

Doctor's Report.—In hospital during the week 48—discharged 8; died 1; remaining 39; in lunatic ward 17; vaccinated 0. In temporary fever hospital 12; discharged 1; died 0; remaining 11.

The Chairman stated that he and Mr Brodigan waited on the Manager of the Branch Bank of Ireland in this town to ascertain the likelihood of obtaining a loan of £2,000 upon the terms contemplated by the board at the last meeting, for defraying the expense of the fever hospital erection, &c. It appears that the Manager is not at liberty to make the advance in the manner which the board desires.

The Chairman suggested an application to the Consolidated Fund Loan Commissions.

Mr Coddington thought the Consolidated Fund Commissioners would make no further advances of money for Irish Poor Law purposes, as the instalments of the last advance of Workhouses in Ireland are not been paid.

43 poor were admitted.
The Board adjourned.

DROGHEDA POOR LAW UNION –
Thursday
Weekly Meeting.

The following guardians attended at the Board-room:

Francis Donagh, Esq., Chairman
Thomas Brodigan, Nicholas Markey, H.B. Coddington, P. Matthews, Esq.

The minutes of last meeting were read, and affirmed.

Master's Report – Admitted during the week 47; remaining from last week 339; discharged 9; died 1; born 0; remaining 376; expenses for the week £36 15s 11¼d; average 1s 10¾.

Doctor's Report – in hospital during the week 48; discharged 8; died 1; remaining 39; in lunatic ward 17; vaccinated 0; in temporary fever hospital 12; discharged 1; died 0; remaining 11.

The Chairman stated that he and Mr. Brodigan waited on the Manager of the Branch Bank of Ireland in this town to ascertain the likelihood of obtaining a loan of £2,000 upon the terms contemplated by the board at the last meeting for defraying the expenses of the fever hospital erection, &c. It appears that the Manager is not at liberty to make the advance in the manner which the board desires.

The Chairman suggested an application to the Consolidated Fund Loan Commissions.

Mr. Coddington thought the Consolidated Fund Commissioners would make no further advances of money for Irish Poor Law purposes, as the instalments for the last advance by them for the erection of Workhouses in Ireland have not been paid.

43 poor were admitted.
The Board adjourned.

An excess of printer's ink used in the original printing has rendered the Workhouse Report difficult to read, and it is reproduced here for the reader's benefit.

The same weekly paper also regularly quoted, again by way of routine notices, a list of the 'Duties on Foreign Grain' for wheat and other cereals being imported from America. These duties were imposed by virtue of Foster's Corn Laws, their purpose being to protect land-owners from outside competition, but they had a direct effect of the cost of flour, and they put the loaf of bread further out of reach of the penniless people. At this time (1847) Morton's Mill on the Mall (the ground floor is presently a restaurant and other sections serve as apartments) was constructed, to join Smith and Smythe's other flour mill down the quay; their output was stacked in the holds of waiting paddle steamers and shipped to England.

It is surprising how restrained the people remained, and reports of food riots were relatively few in the area despite the appalling circumstances that surrounded them. However, it was reported in 1846 that the unemployed of the town had collected in parties of 50 (these meetings were evidently prearranged) and called on influential businessmen of the town, demanding food and work. They made the point that, after paying rent, they had merely 3s. 6d. (22 cents) remaining per week to buy food for their families. No intimidation was otherwise involved, and promises were made to the suppliants, the nature of which was not specified. In January 1847 four people were taken to court for raiding a bread van. One of them, a woman, was given a fortnight in jail. The barrister seems to have had a humane streak in him, for 'he ordered straight away that the bread be given to them'.[7] Subsequently, nightly meetings were held in Duleek Gate, and a bread van was later intercepted on the Ballymakenny Road. Thereafter a police escort accompanied the van.

A year later a complaint was reported in the *Drogheda Conservative Journal (12/2/1848)* that 'during the past week parties of able bodied labourers have stopped the bakers' carriers and robbed them of bread. ... Policemen have now to escort the bread carts through the town and suburbs'.

Fever: As was to be expected, the emaciated people were easy prey to disease, and epidemics of typhoid and cholera followed in the footsteps of the blighted potato crops. It became necessary to open a separate fever hospital as a temporary expedient. This was located on the Marsh Road. It was reported on 16th. October 1847 that 'Disease is on the increase, with 170 patients in the Marsh Fever Hospital and there is no more room for applicants'. A week later a report stated that 'a quarter of the weavers of the town have fallen victim to the disease'. The Grim Reaper was plying a wide swathe in securing his deathly harvest. The Board of Guardians was concerned at the numbers being housed in the fever hospital, and advocated that they should 'make searching enquiry to ensure strict economy' because the cost of maintaining inmates was 50% higher (viz. about €0.04 per day) than in the workhouse.

EMIGRATION: this was not a phenomenon that originated in the Famine; we have seen that in earlier times such as the Comwellian campaign, people were forced to seek a better living outside Ireland. Periodic famines in the early 1800s accentuated this trend. In 1835 the fare from Drogheda to Quebec was £2. The organisers of a state-aided scheme from Munster to Canada had an unenviable task when 50,000 applied for the 1,500 places on offer[8]. The sea crossing regularly took forty or perhaps sixty days in adverse weather conditions so that rations, including water, had to be severely curtailed. Cholera and typhus accompanied them on the voyage, and the term 'coffin ships' was well earned. It was commonplace for perhaps 20, 40 or 60 deaths to occur on board, and the numbers who had their journey shortened in that way will never be known. Bodies were wrapped in sail

TO SAIL FROM THIS PORT
On the 13th April
FOR ST. JOHN'S N·B·
With Passengers
THE FINE NEW COPPER-FASTENED BARQUE
WARRIOR
SIX HUNDRED TONS BURTHEN.
JAMES TIERNAN
COMMANDER.

THE above Splendid Vessel present a most favourable opportunity for persons desirous to emigrate to the flourishing Provinces of New Brunswick, Upper or Lower Canada, or to the United States, as St. John's is convenient to either. Persons desirous to go by this Vessel should make as early an application as possible, as the owner intend to limit the number of Passengers, so as to afford every accommodation in his power—and Captain Tiernan's civility and attention to his Passengers is so well established need no comment.
For Freight or Passage apply to the Captain on Board or at Mr Hoylan's Office, North Quay.
Drogheda, 8th March, 1846

canvas coated in tar; a heavy weight was attached and the remains were then consigned, feet first, to the deep. When in sight of land the passengers found the aroma of the pine forests a welcome change from the claustrophobic, fetid stench that surrounded them in the overcrowded holds of the ships. Their journey was not yet over. The relief of stepping ashore was delayed because a quarantine period of 15 days still had to be endured while the ships lay at anchor off Grosse Ile – this was Canada's version of Ellis Island in New York harbour – on the St. Laurence River.

> *'Before the emigrant has been a week at sea he is an altered man. How can it be otherwise? Hundreds of poor people, men, women and children of all ages, ... huddled together without light, without air, wallowing in filth and breathing a fetid atmosphere, sick in body, dispirited in heart, the fevered patients lying between the sound, in sleeping places so narrow as almost to deny them the power of indulging, by a change of position, the natural restlessness of the disease; by their agonised ravings disturbing those around. ...'.[9]*

The Voyage of the 'Ajax': [This was not an isolated event, but is a fair representation of the experiences encountered by the million emigrants who crossed the Atlantic during the era of the Great Famine]. A contingent of 110 emigrants from County Meath on 30th May 1847 set sail in a vessel called the *Ajax*. The captain, a severe man, was accompanied by his wife who was the very essence of kindness. The sole cabin passenger kept a diary which today provides us with a window into the experiences suffered by emigrants. He remarked that 'the passengers were dressed in their best clothes and presented a better appearance than I expected … they were divided into two parties, those who spoke Irish and those who did not'. Within a week several went down with illness and 'the Mistress was occupied all day attending the numerous calls upon her. She already regretted having come on the voyage, but her kind heart did not allow her to consult her ease'. Great alarm was caused when a blaze commenced in the fore part of the brig and was eventually doused with water. Owing to the slow progress of the ship food rations and drinking water had to be curtailed. Later, a sample can of drinking water was shown to the captain: 'it was quite foul, muddy and bitter from having been in a wine cask … some of the casks were beyond remedy, and the contents, when pumped out, resembled nauseous ditch water'. A week later the diarist recorded more passengers having fallen ill, enough to 'terrify one having the charge of so many human beings, likely to fall prey to the unchecked progress of the dreadful disease'. Others complained to the captain of 'starvation and want of water for their sick wives and children' and they threatened to break into the provision store; they were subdued only when he fired a blunderbuss over their heads. Meanwhile the contagion spread, even among the crew.

> *'It was awful how sudden some were stricken. A little child, playing with his companions, suddenly fell down and for some time was sunk in a deadly torpor, from which, when he awoke, he commenced to scream violently and wreak in convulsive agony. A poor woman who was warming a drink at the fire for her husband also dropped down quite senseless and was borne to her berth. ... It made my heart bleed to listen to the calls of 'Water, for God's sake, water'.*

The sick list continued to grow longer as the *Ajax* yawed with its empty sails flapping in mid-Atlantic. Four week out the figure for those down with fever was 30, soon it was 37, and by July 6 almost half the passengers were sick. Corpses were often slid silently over the side unceremoniously and without last rites to avoid undue distress on board. When all the spare canvas had been used up, corpses were wrapped in meal sacks.

The normal time taken for an Atlantic crossing was about 3½ weeks but these emigrants from Meath had to endure all of 57 days before the *Ajax* finally dropped anchor on the St. Laurence with its depleted cargo of humanity. One individual, whose morose demeanour was in keeping with his pock-marked face and having but one eye, carried his child in a silent, surly manner and went below decks. A sailor explained to the diarist that the man had just retuned from having watched the soil being placed over the body of his wife. He snatched up two shovels and lay them in the form of a cross atop the little mound of fresh earth and then uttered: 'By that cross, Mary, I swear to revenge your death. As soon as I earn my passage home I will go back and shoot the man that murdered you – and that is the landlord'. A passage to Canada was the expedience used by the Meath landowner – and by many other landowners throughout Ireland – to rid broad, fertile estates of unwanted tenants.

'By the end of May forty ships lay at anchor [off Grosse Ile awaiting medical inspection or undergoing quarantine, some from continental Europe], stretching a mile down river, and there would have been two more but they were lost at sea'[10].

On finally stepping ashore, most emigrants were penniless and lacked the wherewithal to move away from the port of arrival. There was absolutely no 'disposable income' among the peasants and weavers who were earning 4/- [€0.25] a week in Drogheda. They were shunned wherever they went, having brought contagion and death to many thousand residents of Ottawa, Montreal and Quebec.

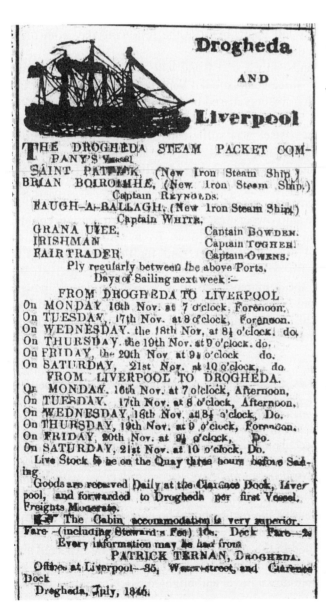

The Drogheda Steampacket Company operated 'a splendid fleet of first class ships', the 'Faugh-a-Ballagh', 'Grána Ueile', 'Fair Trader' and 'Irishman'. They plied between Drogheda and Liverpool – one sailing each day, and as one vessel left another arrived. Passengers could escape the misery at home by tendering the one-way deck fare of 3/- which exposed the unfortunates to the vagaries of the weather, dressed as they were in the most flimsy, threadbare attire; the more affluent passengers paid 10/- which gave them the luxury of a berth.

Paradoxically, these were the same vessels that were laden to the gunwales carrying away the cargoes of livestock and other foodstuffs produced throughout the plentiful plains of Louth and Meath.

The throngs taking the boat to Liverpool were so great that the Drogheda Steampacket Company saw fit to increase the deck passenger fare to 5/-. This tended to put a check on the number of immigrants, and at the same time it increased the profits of the shipping company. One report states that 'During the past week the influx of Irish passengers [nationwide] to the port of Liverpool was:

Monday	1,035
Tuesday	677
Wednesday	825
Thursday	1,105
Friday	1,010
Saturday	667
Sunday	2,445
TOTAL:	7,764

A family from Ballina, County Mayo joined the throngs setting out for England in search of better times, and they reached Drogheda intending to catch the boat on Thursday 18th February 1847. However, their plans fell apart, because the following day both of the children died and the parents ended up in the workhouse.[11]

Those who were able to lay hands on £3 or £4 and who wished to put a greater distance between destitution at home and some semblance of hope in another land could take the barque 'Jane Dixon' of 600 tons, which was advertised in the Drogheda newspaper as 'To sail from this Port [Drogheda] for New York' – the date of sailing was not specified, and presumably it weighed anchor when the vessel was sufficiently packed with its cargo of emaciated humanity – it was not uncommon for vessels to lay at anchor for a month, and meantime the intending passengers' savings were being dissipated on lodgings and sustenance.

For the most part, the vessels had taken cargoes of timber from the New World, the journey taking about three weeks. But the ship owners learned that the return journey could be made very lucrative by packing the holds with human cargoes. Even with a fair wind, the westward journey usually took about 4 or 5 days longer, and for the vast majority the 'farewell' was forever.

Not having the price to board the emigrant ship to America, hordes of poverty stricken souls continued to invade England. What faced them when they got there? Under the heading "Irish Paupers in London", the Drogheda Conservative Journal dated the 9th December 1848 answers this question for us:

"The inflow of beggars into London is, as appears by the following police report, calling for very stringent measures to prevent it. Much better for Paddy to speculate on turning 'an honest penny' into 2/6 [€0.16] at home than run the risk of a flogging or six months imprisonment as an incorrigible vagabond. At the Guildhall there was no less than 49 charges yesterday for begging in the streets ... Out of the whole batch only two were discharged as they were going to Wales. The rest were sentenced to terms of imprisonment varying from 7 to 14 days. Two had just arrived in London. ... Steps are now being taken to punish them as rogues and vagabonds when they can either be whipped or sent for trial to the sessions where they will get six months".

It seems strange indeed that citizens of the realm should be punished with a whipping simply because they were hungry. A disappointment was in store for poor 'Paddy', as the wandering Irishmen were collectively called in the above pronouncement, if he expected alms or even sympathy on arrival in London. Six months in jail or a whipping is what awaited him having tramped all the way from his tumble-down hovel and blighted patch of potato stalks to another part of the same United Kingdom which he was inveigled into joining 45 years earlier.

Press Coverage: Daniel O'Connell, although nearing the end of his days, criticised the authorities for their abject efforts in handling the crisis, pointing out that the nation's population was being eroded by both death and emigration. *The Drogheda Conservative Journal*, staunch supporter of the ruling class as always, saw fit to contradict O'Connell:

> "... *the alleged diminution in the numerical amount of our population, imputing it, as a matter of course, to British misrule. On what data he found the rather statistical assertion we cannot clearly understand, nor does he himself satisfactorily explain*".[12]

This was quite an extraordinary standpoint to take in the light of the prevailing emergency, and indicates a marked degree of irresponsibility by the local newspaper. Clearly, it was spokesman for the upper classes, and the attitude taken underlines the disregard being shown for the destitute people during the crisis. The famine was then in its second year, and the country lay prostrate. The phrase 'a diminution in the numerical amount of our population' – a classic among euphemisms – is used to describe the tragedy of countless deaths by starvation. Worse, the phrase is preceded by the cautionary word 'alleged', suggesting that the circumstances as described by O'Connell were open to question and were perhaps spurious. The jaundiced eye of the correspondent failed to observe the damage being wrought by the Act of Union and by general British misrule. The 'rather statistical assertion' of the decline in the population was all too clear from the throngs making their way to the workhouse and the unending strings of uncoffined bodies being carried to Bully's Acre at the top of the Poorhouse Lane.

The local press during these harrowing times is singularly lacking in accounts of the distress being suffered by the poor, although any journalist would have had unending scope to highlight these circumstances. However, the above rebuttal of O'Connell's criticism is an indication of the piteous scenes that were left unreported. By adopting that attitude, he was discouraging the moneyed class from making charitable donations; he may well have been influenced by *The Times* of London. Neither support nor sympathy might be expected from that source, which unceasingly made use of the harshest, most brutal and insensitive wording in pouring scorn on the Irish people in their plight. The Irish people were

> 'men of idle hands ... who hug their indolent misery as a treasure ... they have tasted of public money, and they find it pleasanter to live on alms than on labour. The alternative raises no feeling of shame or self abasement ... [but has the effect of] corrupting them with a fatal lethargy, and debasing them with a fatuous dependence". And again, "Kind Heaven has blessed [Englishmen] with a nobler fate and more auspicious laws: they can, therefore, afford to look with contemptuous pity on the Celtic cottier suckled with poverty which he is too callous to feel, or too supine to mend'.[13]

The true causes of Ireland's affliction failed to penetrate the cast-iron heart of *The Times*, but by 1860 the reality began to dawn on that newspaper. At last it realised the injustices that had been committed, and presciently set down in writing the consequences of misgoverning a race of people for generation after generation:

> "We must gird our loins to encounter the Nemesis of seven centuries' misgovernment. To the end of time a hundred million, spread over the largest habitable area of the world and, confronting us everywhere by sea and land, will remember that their forefathers paid tithe to the Protestant clergy, rent to absentee landlords, and a forced obedience to the laws which these had made".[14]

This observation by *The Times*, belated as it was, spelled out clearly the main wrongs that were being committed against an entire nation, and provided abundant justification for those who harboured rancour against the perpetrators. Even today it may cause dissident men of Irish blood – who are often more impassioned abroad than at home – to grin a sardonic grin, and to provide paramilitaries with the motivation to commit acts of violence. (Witness the activities of the Northern Ireland Aid Committee – NORAID). The Irish Diaspora has not yet quite reached *The Time's* forecast of a hundred millions, but it passed the very formidable figure of 70,000,000 globally by the year 2000. The affluent and tranquil living conditions which, thankfully, came with the new Millennium have helped to dispel notions of reprisal, and betoken the dual hope that latter day patriots will overlook the past and that England wont.

Some landlords were wholly sympathetic to the plight of their tenants and funded those who wished to seek a new life by emigrating. One of these was Vere Foster from Ardee whose kindly treatment of tenants stands out in stark contrast to his kinsman Speaker Foster. The local paper stated that he arranged for '46 girls and 2 lads' to go to Canada, 'with preference being given to those in large families. Mr. Foster will despatch another party of young women in the course of the next month'. Boatloads of young men and women, numbering 25,000, were able to escape the poverty trap in that manner through the munificence of this benevolent landlord. He travelled with them, enduring their privations of many Atlantic crossings, to ensure that they were properly treated in transit and on arrival. So generous was he that he completely exhausted his estate and ended his days in virtual poverty.

Those who were forced to emigrate, either to America or Britain, were shunned on arrival. Employers, when advertising for workers, and landladies offering lodgings often appended the damning sentence 'No Irish Need Apply'. (Indeed, that abominable sentence was still being used as recently as the 1950s). So commonplace had this become that the notice was often abbreviated to its initials 'N.I.N.A.'. Illiteracy and the lack of manual skills were serious drawbacks. Many found back-breaking labouring work in the construction of railways and canals – dug by hand for the most part – that brought them to regions as far apart as Lake Erie, San Francisco and New Orleans.

The author found evidence of such work in a remote part of Mexico. The rail journey to Mexico's Pacific Coast encounters a most formidable obstacle, the Sierra Madre Mountains – it is a continuation of the Rockies. It takes several days while the train labours arduously, climbing endlessly upwards on a winding, tortuous track, clinging to precipitous cliffs that look down on awesome chasms. High in the remoteness of these wild mountains and far from civilisation is a tribe of Indians called the Tarahumaras. They remain uncontaminated by the influences of the white man, and to this day they mostly live in caves. It is therefore surprising to find them playing the violin. They were taught it by the Irish navvies who went there to construct the railway.

A Cashless Society: In comparative terms the general Louth/Meath area together with east Ulster fared better than most other regions during the Famine. Since flax was the predominant crop in northern areas, the reward for labour was *cash*, not a potato plot that was subject to infection. The effects of the potato blight were felt at their severest in Connaught and west Munster. Most of the peasants of these regions operated on a cashless basis; it was usual for them to settle accounts for rents, provisions, etc. by performing labouring tasks for their landlords and creditors.

Thus, when the potato crops turned putrid in the fields they had neither food on the table nor the wherewithal to acquire it. As Isaac Butt put it: 'They lived upon the produce of their potato garden and had been customers of no shops'. In the Louth/Meath area that practice was less common and thereby these counties escaped the full brunt of the hardship. The statistics which show the estimated average annual rate of excess mortality in the years 1846-51 indicates that Louth/Meath fared much better than most counties. Louth is positioned near the bottom of the table with 8.2 per thousand and Meath with 15.8. But it is hardly necessary to stress that we are speaking only in relative terms. The western seaboard fared worst, with an excess mortality rate of 58.4 being sustained by Mayo.[15]

Public Works were devised by the government to enable people earn a wage that would put a little money in their purses. In Drogheda the Mayor ordained the continuance of employment 'of the poor at stone-breaking until some other work is provided'. This is seen as a pathetic gesture at providing a remedy. Schemes that were devised were accompanied by many restrictions; landlords were prohibited from benefiting from the laying of new roads near their estates, and in consequence some roads led aimlessly into bogs.

Furthermore, abuses were widespread. These projects were later abandoned, but not before an improvement was made to the Termonfeckin/Drogheda road. It had previously meandered southwards from Beltichburne in the general direction of Newtown, taking a circuitous route (now closed off and totally overgrown) that led via Greenhills to the Boyne Road. Thanks to a local relief scheme and the toil of a team of gaunt, skeletal beings, the alignment of this road today leads straight from Termonfeckin to Newfoundwell, and is more in keeping with today's speeding traffic than with the donkeys and carts that meandered along the rutted roadway in the eighteen-forties.

The Drogheda Harbour Commissioners discussed the possibility of advancing a loan of £500 free of interest for 6 months, but there is no further record of its implementation. At Plattin Hall work was provided by the felling of trees on the estate.

The local newspaper, so supportive of the ruling class in earlier times, at last gave voice to the silent masses of human misery, and castigated both the Drogheda Corporation and the Imperial Parliament for their inadequate handling of the crisis. In a hard-hitting report it implied that there was no margin whatever to cover what is today called 'discretionary expenditure', even for essentials such as clothing, medicines, caring for the aged, etc.: –

'... Let us take a case in point, a labourer earns 6 shillings [38 cents] per week – he has a family of five to support out of this, and we speak of a town like Drogheda. His expenditure may be reckoned as follows:

	s.	d.
Rent per week	0	9
Fuel	1	0
1 stone oatmeal	2	2
1 stone cooking meal	1	7
Milk etc.	0	6
	6	0

'Thus the whole of his miserable pittance is spent on procuring a scanty supply of food – as for potatoes, they are out of his reach. ... Agents who collect the rents of 70 cabins weekly, that in almost every instance the inmates are destitute of bedsteads, blankets, sheets and coverlids, that they have seen several grown girls who toil from early dawn to eight in the evening in the factories, lying on straw with no other covering over them, save the clothes they wore during the day'.[16]

At local government level there was never adequate cash in the kitty to arrange sufficient public works to provide employment for the famished hordes. A further difficulty was the government's reluctance to infringe on the sacrosanct domain of the private sector – the central government was obliged to be cautious at all times in that regard. Notwithstanding this, occasional intrusions were deemed to be acceptable, such as in the improvement of the civic infrastructure, e.g. roads, bridges and harbours – this stimulated some degree of economic activity.

Formed at this time was the Board of Works; it rendered relief by spearheading some public enterprises through grants and loans. One of its officers reported that he had 'poor, wretched, half-clad wretches howling at the door for food'. The returns from the fishing industry at this period had been in decline for years, brought about by a dearth of capital investment. The government allotted £750 for the development of Clogherhead pier, and its harvest of fish meant salvation for some of the famished masses. Putting a herring on an empty plate gladdened many a dejected poor soul.

Soup Kitchens: The gratuitous distribution of food replaced the schemes of public works as a means of alleviating the distress, and it was found that this form of relief gave less scope for abuse. Through the Soup Kitchen Act committees were appointed to administer the work. The headquarters of the Relief Commissioners was in Dublin, and they requested the Drogheda Relief Committee, who operated from the Tholsel, to indicate how the scheme was administered locally. Their report, dated 12th March 1847, described that this was done by means of ration coupons. These were issued on parchment …

'in preference to paper or card, as the tickets remain in the possession of the poor person and get rumpled and soiled in their keeping, circumstances which would be destructive to paper or card. They were issued to last six months. The committee man ... makes a puncture with a large awl on the date [12th March on the sample furnished]. This prevents the return of the ticket for the day, whilst the ticket still remains good.

'To avoid the danger of dysentery, white bread is generally used, and for the same reason beef is preferred to pork. ... The mixture of Indian meal with the rice gives satisfaction. No soup is allowed to remain over, lest the vegetables might ferment and occasion disease. The soup is nutritive and conducive to health. The poor look better since we commenced distribution, now about eight weeks. I am of opinion that if arrangements could be made to sell soup at cost price to persons in employment on railways, public or private works, it would improve their capability of working as they have not the utensils nor the knowledge necessary to prepare wholesome and nutritive food economically; coal, besides, is dear and they have no other fuel. There are three or four factories, for instance, in which large numbers of females and children are employed. Their wages are small and by the loss of potatoes they can barely find themselves sufficient food. If a boiler was opened near each factory, these persons could be better fed, and as cheaply as now, by getting bread and soup at cost price ...'

> **Pat Rogers, the holder of the above Soup Ticket lived in Morgan's Lane, now called Francis St.**

However, in regard to the Soup Kitchen Scheme, the sting was in the tail: the outlay in acquiring foodstuffs was defrayed by drawing on the *local* rates, and wherever these funds were insufficient, it was supplemented by loans, and these loans were to be repaid by increasing subsequent rates of the *local* property holders, causing the local economy to implode. The burden thus fell partly on the landlords, a circumstance that in time led to the collapse of many estates.

In Drogheda a house at the west end of Fair Street was used as a 'Soup House'. This house was subsequently the home of Peter McCann, building contractor who, on first occupying it, found that there was already someone in residence – *a ghost!* The hauntings ended when a Mass was celebrated in it.[17]

The Workhouse: To enter the workhouse was the ultimate in hopelessness and degradation. Even then, heartless bureaucracy stood in the way of those seeking refuge there. The infamous Gregory Clause precluded those with more than a quarter acre from obtaining 'outdoor relief' without surrendering 'all rights to any land over and above … one quarter of a statute acre.' Thus, a broken farmer had to sell all his land, for which there was no demand, or die of starvation. In consequence, he could never hope to re-establish himself and become self-sufficient. This 'quarter acre clause' also overlooked the plight of the owner's dependents, for his wife and children were deemed to be ineligible for relief unless the holding was surrendered. The homes that were abandoned in favour of the workhouse were in many cases never seen again, for the landlords seized the opportunity to level them. A report on the village of Duleek made to the Board of Guardians in 1849 stated that:

> '*Most of these persons present the most pitiable appearance, half-clothed, with scarcely any food, and yet hardly any one could be induced to enter the workhouse*'.

The policy, known as 'clearances' was to make way for grassland farming, because cattle and sheep-rearing had become more profitable when Foster's Corn Law was abolished, and thereafter the need for farm labour greatly diminished. In the year 1850 alone, an estimated 104,000 families nationwide were turned out on the roadside. Leaving their homes, miserable as they were, in favour of the workhouse acted as a forbidding deterrent to many. The case of one poor woman who opted to starve rather than enter was discussed by the Drogheda Board of Guardians:

Advocate:	If the family left the house it would be thrown down by the landlord.
Response:	Not if she left it in [the Board's] charge.
Advocate:	The landlord would then serve notice on the Board [to have it demolished].
Response:	Their powers *are most unconstitutional!*

The fate of evicted families 'was terrible in the extreme. Great numbers flocked to the country towns, on the outskirts of which they congregated in the most miserable cabins imaginable; others migrated to Dublin [and no doubt to Drogheda] in the fruitless search for employment'.

The Board of Guardians was comprised of the landed gentry, including such persons as Mr. Coddington of Oldbridge, Mr. Balfour of Townley Hall and Mr. Preston of Gormanston. Weekly meetings were held in the boardroom to supervise the efficient running of the Drogheda Workhouse, and to receive the Master's Report which included details of expenditure. As the effects of the potato blight began to bite deeper in 'Black Forty-seven' the challenge of accommodating the growing numbers seeking admission became extreme. The workhouse facilities had been constructed to accommodate a maximum of 800 inmates, but it could clearly be seen that the existing facilities were becoming inadequate, and the numbers later exceeded a thousand, resulting in suppliants being turned away. With accommodation bursting at the seams, a resolution was passed at their meeting on 11th February 1847 to instruct:

'their architect to give a plan and estimate for erecting temporary floors on brackets in the upper dormitories and to increase ventilation in the same to effect greater accommodation which is now found necessary'.[18]

A contractor was engaged to construct the 'sleeping galleries' at a cost of £38. The following week the Board was informed that three attacks had been made on the bread store, and the entrance door had been broken. The meal store also needed to be secured more firmly.

The dormitories at this stage were being described in the workhouse's Minute Book as 'sleeping galleries'. Readers who have seen pictures of the Nazi concentration camps of World War II will have some idea of the skeletal figures who were crowded like sardines into these spaces. In the matter of overcrowding, a Board member asked if any distinction was made between adults and children. The answer, as reported in the local newspaper was: 'No. A child consumed more air than a grown person (laughter)'.

The members of the Board lived in a different world from the unfortunates whose welfare was in their hands. When one guardian drew the meeting's attention to a particular man who was dying of neglect, Mr. Balfour washed his hands of the matter by saying that it was 'a matter for the Relieving Officer'. He was then given the reply that "the clergy, both Catholic and Protestant, were more cognisant of the distress of the poor than any Relieving Officer. ... If [the destitute people] came to the workhouse they were informed that there was no room for them – were they to die of starvation?" The case was then dropped without a decision being taken.

Taken as a sample, the weekly Report on the 6th February 1848 reads:

Persons in house (previous)	928
Admissions during the week	34
	962
Died during the week	9
Discharged	47
	56
Inmates Remaining	906

The Report further stated that the Expenditure for the week was £89.9.5 and that the cost of keeping and feeding each pauper worked out at 1s. 3¼d. per week, which is approximately one cent per day in Euro currency.

No doubt the Guardians were relieved, judging by the above statistics, that they had 22 fewer inmates on their hands at the end of the week; 'only' nine had died during the week and they saw fit to usher out onto the streets of Drogheda a further 47 inmates, and their subsequent fate is unknown to us. A few weeks later the figure being housed had risen again.

In Christmas week 1848 the case of a family was discussed by the Board because 'the husband crossed the wall and fled from the [work-]house. The Guardian was of the opinion that the walls should be elevated so as to render the escape of paupers impossible'.[19] This implies that the inmates were compulsorily confined, as in a jail.

A woman was accused by the Drogheda Board of abandoning her young family. But when they were brought before her, she denied they were hers, and she surreptitiously signalled to the eldest one not to identify her as their mother.

The officer in charge of Termonfeckin requested £1 (€1.27), but was told that supporting information was required. He said it was 'to pay for coffins and to purchase bread'.

Unscrupulous traders, intent on feathering their nests, sometimes added to the sufferings of the recipients, and in this regard Drogheda was not without its 'gombeen-men'. They even stooped to short-changing the helpless inmates. The Chairman of the Drogheda Poor Law Union called the attention of the Board to the quality of the bread being supplied by the Contractor which in his opinion 'was of a very inferior description'. Samples placed before the Board were pronounced to be 'decidedly sour'. The supplier, a Mr. Whearty, was then called in to the meeting, following which he 'promised to be more careful in future'. The milk supplier also fell in for criticism, and the Board remarked that: "It is very hard to make him send in good milk".

Regarding the price of flour, the local newspaper queried why flour was 7 pence per stone cheaper in Birmingham. However, it commented that "A new era has commenced here – a liberal feeling has sprung up in favour of the destitute. It is a strange anomaly that while Smith and Smythe [millers at the Mall, later acquired by McCann and Hill] are buying wheat at 42 shillings a barrel, the same quantity of wheatmeal may be had at their stores at 40 shillings.[20]

Meanwhile, the Ascendancy's pursuit of pleasure continued. A schedule of fixtures for the Louth Hounds, the Meath Hounds, the Trim Hounds and the Ward Stag Hounds appeared in the paper under the heading 'Hunting Appointments' and the dates of local race meetings at Bellewstown and at 'Bettystown Strand' were also given.

The Rates-in-Aid Act (1849): In fairness to Trevelyan, he was a most diligent worker, and the gaslight in his office was regularly seen burning after midnight. But he stuck incorrigibly to his principle of minimal interference with the laws of elemental economics. He devised a solution in 1849 called 'Rate-in-Aid' whereby those regions that had become bankrupt and unable to fund the workhouses would be assisted by the better off regions. Great! Here was the one great benefit of having joined the United Kingdom. Although help was not forthcoming from the Exchequer, help was nonetheless at hand. The counties such as Lancashire and Devon and Cornwall would come to the aid of Louth and Meath and Cork, etc. – they were all members of the one big happy family brought together under the Act of Union. Those who thought that this would happen were left gaping, because they soon learned that their expectations were ill-founded. No assistance was forthcoming from that source. Ireland was cut adrift and left to fend for herself in isolation. Isaac Butt presented the situation with devastating logic:

> *'Ireland has been deprived, by the Union with England, of all separate power of action ... She cannot ... draw upon her own resources, or pledge her own credit, for objects of national importance. Irish men were told that, in consenting to a Union which would make them partners with a great and opulent nation like England, they would have all the advantages that might be expected to be realised. How are these pledges to be fulfilled if the partnership is to be one of loss, and never of profit to us? If, bearing our share of all Imperial burdens – when calamity falls upon us we are to be told that we are then to recover our separate existence as a nation, just so far as to disentitle us to the state assistance which any portion of a nation, visited by such a calamity, had the right to expect from the governing power? If Cornwall had been visited with the scenes that have desolated Cork, would similar arguments have been used? Would men have stood up and denied that Cornwall was entitled to have the whole country share in the extraordinary loss?'[21]*

The End in Sight: The thoughts of the nation were constantly focused on the weather and the harvest prospects. Each week the newspapers gave reports of conditions in various parts of the country. Would there be yet another visitation of potato blight? The local paper made a valiant effort of instil a glimmer of hope into a prostrate people in 1848 when it wrote 'The crops present in every direction a most cheerful appearance ... indicating that Providence will bless our land with a plentiful harvest'. By the end of 1848 the numbers in 'the Dublin Road', as the Drogheda workhouse was familiarly called, had fallen to 496 and in the week ended 4th November 'only' three deaths occurred. By 1849 the worst was over.

In the five years from 1845 to 1850 about 1.1 million people nationwide died from hunger and the diseases that attended it which included typhus, diarrhoea, dysentery, cholera, etc. And to escape the horror an additional million emigrated. The luckier ones were able to buy a passage to New York or Boston, but the one-way fare of £3 might as well have been a barrier of £3 million to the majority, because they were penniless.

By the mid 1850s the average number of workhouse inmates was about 450. The weekly statistics occasionally disclose that a birth had taken place in the workhouse. One wonders at the prospects of success in life for an infant born under such circumstances.

The Great Famine has cast a long shadow. So indelible on the minds of the people were its horrors that the psychological scars have impacted on subsequent generations and the collective trauma has been passed on by word of mouth. During a school history lesson in 1941 the author recalls being told of the sufferings endured by the people. The lay teacher described how wretches were regularly found dead with green stains on their mouths from resorting to eating grass and the tops of nettles through sheer desperation, and that the leaves of the hawthorn bush were still known in some parts of the country as 'bread and cheese' from being consumed as a food. The teacher, in emphasising that the famine was a more recent occurrence (in relative terms) than people seemed to realise, looked earnestly at the pupils seated before him and said "Your own grandmothers were probably alive at the time of the famine". The point was well made.

"My grandfather lived through the Famine", said former Mayor of Drogheda, Patrick Buckley who hailed from Dromcollogher. "He worked for a penny a day and he was 101 when he died. There were 8 boys and one girl in the family – he was the youngest. There was a row of houses just where we lived at home, maybe a hundred or more houses, and only about a couple still lived there after the Famine – the rest either died or emigrated".

Thankfully, these harrowing stories seem incongruous amid the opulence enjoyed by the generation that crossed into the third Millennium, and a passing reference in the school history book is deemed adequate today. It is not the intention in this work to dwell further on the sufferings that the nation endured – many works on the subject are available. Suffice it to say that the population of the island was 8,175,121 according to the 1841 census. It is generally taken to have reached its peak at 8,500,000 on the eve of the Great Famine, making it the most densely populated country in Europe at that time. It fell to 6,552,385 by the 1851 census – a drop of about two million, caused by a combination of starvation, disease and emigration.

The seepage through emigration continued for over another hundred years. That, in itself, is another human tragedy. The Irish Diaspora has reached every continent. Of every one hundred people claiming Irish ancestry today, only seven live in Ireland. This infers that 70,000,000 people throughout the world carry Irish blood.

The flames of nationalist sentiments that manifested themselves in the Rising of 1798 were now well and truly extinguished, and the ill-timed Rising of 1848 was a pathetic failure, thanks in part to the efforts of the Catholic clergy – an uprising might have jeopardised governmental support for Maynooth College.

Mary Robinson, President of Ireland (1990/1997) put it this way:

"History is not about power and triumphs nearly so often as it about suffering and vulnerability. The Famine was a central part of our past, a motif of powerlessness that runs through our national consciousness. It is also a human drama upon which we, as Irish people, place an enormous value and by which we have been radically instructed".

Aftermath of the Famine: Drogheda had great difficulty in shaking off the effects of the famine. Even ten years after it had ended mass unemployment still persisted and many were still in a state of chronic destitution. So pressing were the conditions that in 1857 a committee under the chairmanship of the Mayor was formed with the aim of redressing the plight of the poor, the numbers of destitute having grown alarmingly. The meeting was attended by the local clergy of all denominations and by businessmen of the town. Funds were raised to supply coal to the needy. In 1861 the situation had worsened. The *Drogheda Argus*, ever critical of Whitehall's administration, was outspoken:

'When distress prevailed in 1857 we suggested to apply the labour test to the poor, with a view to effecting local improvements [e.g. repairing roadways, harbours, etc.] and keeping the people employed so that they might be imbued with the idea that they were not the recipients of mere 'charity'. Otherwise this would create a habit of idleness most injurious in its consequences. This kept the able-bodied employed while at the same time the thoroughfares leading to the town were improved; the cess-pools which fronted the cabins of many of the poor all around were filled up and thus was a sanitary improvement effected which was to the benefit of the population at large. The epidemic diseases which lately have visited Drogheda with unfortunately most disastrous results were owing in their origins to the prevalence of stagnant pools in front of the cabins of the poor and they – out of mercy to the miserable creatures themselves – should be filled up without delay ... The cabin holders should be made to understand that the prevalence of such nuisances before their houses is as dangerous to their health as to the community at large, and that their physical condition can only be improved by cleanliness ... There are a great many females who are in a wretched state and are incapable of manual labour.

'The poor law system in Ireland during periods of distress acts injuriously instead of beneficially. When the head of a family falls in want of employment and becomes destitute, if he apply to the poorhouse for outdoor relief, he will not receive it. He must either break up his house and imprison himself in the poorhouse or starve.

'Such is one of the evils of English legislation. Were the Parliament in Dublin, such an obnoxious state of things would not exist'.[22]

This exposé from the *Drogheda Argus* pointed an accusing finger at where the blame lay, but the authorities were unmoved. It demonstrated how insensitive the poor law was in its operation – it broke up homes and families, and it deprived farmers of their farms and of their livelihood forever – for them there was no going back. Most of the menfolk were unskilled labourers – and gainful employment was scarce in a land where the economy was dormant and capital investment almost non-existent.

We are here presented with a glaring example of the syndrome that resulted from the constant outflow of cash to Britain which is where the absentee landlords abided. Much of the wealth that was generated at home went straight into the pockets of the Ascendancy, and a large proportion of these (about one-third) had departed like rats from a sinking ship following the Act of Union. Living conditions in England were congenial, and the rents continued to be extracted from tenants. By depriving Ireland of capital investment in the land where it was sourced, it was impossible to kick-start the economy. This continuous haemorrhage of wealth meant that the country was languishing in a permanent state of monetary anaemia, and thus the prospect of the workhouse or the emigrant ship was ever present for the masses. The result was economic misery, unrelieved suffering, destitution and pestilence. The pernicious effects of the Act of Union were now fully in evidence. The hopelessness of the situation was compounded by the fact that Ireland was cut adrift economy-wise, and the people had to fend for themselves, despite the Act of Union which should have rallied common support from the Motherland. On the contrary, each townland of Ireland was ring-fenced and was obliged to support its inhabitants from its own internal resources. To put the case another way, the people were expected to extricate themselves from the quagmire by pulling on their own boot-laces. (Thankfully, the outstanding famine debts were later remitted when a more humane prime minister, William Gladstone, arrived on the scene).

Unwittingly, the conditions wrought by the Famine also contained the seeds of self-destruction for the Ascendancy, for in time the 'big houses' were engulfed by the same tragedy, eventually sucking them into the same quagmire of impoverishment as the tenants they distained. In the long term it was instrumental in the eventual collapse of landlordism in Ireland.

Chapter Twentyeight

The Dublin/Drogheda Railway

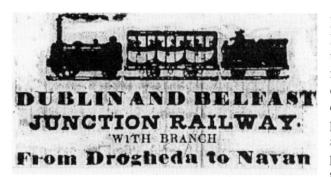

During the 1840s the Dublin/Drogheda railway link was under construction, followed by the mammoth engineering project of erecting the Boyne Viaduct. When discussing the costs of the project the promoters considered a quotation of £80,000 too high, and they resolved to pursue other quotations. When the structure was finally in place, it constituted a vital artery with both Dublin and Belfast, not to mention the bonus of the branch lines which brought the farm produce of north Leinster within easy reach of Drogheda. As an engineering project, it created enormous excitement and was regarded at the time as 'the eighth wonder of the world'.

Controversy had raged during the 1830s as to the route that the line should take. Some favoured an inland line via Ashbourne which was 4 miles shorter than the coastal route, but that would entail a branch line from Duleek to Drogheda. At one stage it had been envisaged that the Dublin terminus would be sited opposite the GPO in Sackville St., and the Drogheda station in the very town centre at Pitcher Hill.

Areas that had hitherto been remote from Drogheda, such as Cavan, Monaghan and Westmeath became part of a single market economy, and the produce from these regions could henceforth be transported swiftly and economically both for sale in the local Drogheda market and for shipment from the port to England and the Continent. Hotels such as the White Horse, the Imperial, the Central and the Railway catered for the needs of visitors and commercial travellers. The arrival of the railway system was thus a valuable fillip to the town's economy, without which the pervading depression would have been felt more severely, and it enabled the town respond more rapidly when conditions improved.

The construction work of the railway and the bridge itself were a powerful boost to the local economy, and there were many ready hands to engage in this work which ranged from quarrying, to haulage of the material, to stone-cutting and masonry, to steeple-jack work. Much of the dressing of the stone was performed in the yard at the foot of the (new) Cord Steps, and the entire project was indeed a boon to local homesteads through the employment that it created. The bridge, which was completed in 1855, was proclaimed as a marvel in engineering. The celebrated engineer who designed it, Sir John McNeill, spoke highly of the workforce:

> "An Irishman is the most active fellow possible if remunerated for his work; there is no idleness among them if they can turn their work to a fair remuneration ... No man will do more, or undergo more hardship for the sake of his children, than an Irishman".[1]

The first railway trip took place on 25th March 1844. *En route* to the starting point in Dublin for the inaugural trip from Dublin to Drogheda, the train stopped at Pilltown Bridge to pick up Thomas Brodigan and some friends. Brodigan, who lived in Pilltown House, would be called in today's parlance a 'VIP'. He was a prime mover and a substantial shareholder in the railway project, and was called 'the Father of the Railway'. He was presented with the Freedom of the Corporation in a gold box in recognition of his efforts.

The Boyne Viaduct under Construction
A veritable forest of wooden poles was used as scaffolding.

A clash of personalities evidently occurred among the people in power, for within a few years Bettystown Station was pulled down 'in order to gratify a private pique against an individual'.

The appointments and furnishings in the carriages were of the most luxurious kind. 'On every side beautiful mirrors are set at the particular angle of inclination, which permits the dandy or dandizette to have the gratification of ascertaining that no one of their points, from the ambrosial curl to the shoestring, has been discomposed', according to the local newspaper.

Needless to say, this description of opulent travel referred to the first class carriages. Travel for third class passengers was anything but comfortable. They had to stand in trucks that were open to the elements, while Puffing Billy smothered them in smoke and smuts.

The passengers on the inaugural journey included most of the moneyed landowners of the surrounding countryside, including Major Peppard (Ballygarth Castle), Colonel Coddington (Oldbridge Estate), George Hamilton (MP for Antrim), Thomas Grendon (Proprietor, Drogheda Ironworks), John D'Alton (author of *History of Drogheda*) as well as Thomas Brodigan (Pilltown) and two of Daniel O'Connell's sons. The train was cheered by sight-seers at the various bridges as it puff-puffed its way towards Drogheda. It pulled into the station one hour and 18 minutes after leaving Dublin. What a vast improvement on the horse and carriage!

Flags and bunting floated in the breeze, shouts from 10,000 throats rent the air and 'three pieces of cannon roared out their vociferous welcome' and the joy bells rang their merry peals. The Temperance Band vied with that of the 34th. Regiment in a musical duel. There were then 'mountains of confectionery and the produce of a vintage of fine old Sherry', not to mention a cask of Cairnes best Drogheda ale. Thus was launched the age of the steam engine in Drogheda.

Chapter Twentynine

The Military Presence at Home and Abroad

The option of joining the armed forces was a godsend to the hordes of idle men who were so crucially lacking in marketable skills. Many Drogheda men campaigned under the Duke of Wellington. Under his skilful generalship they took part in many successful battles in the course of the Peninsular War. The finale was the crowning victory at Waterloo in 1815. During the Napoleonic wars as many as 200,000 Irishmen, or one-sixth of the Irish adult male population saw service in the British Army or Royal Navy. As many as 16,515 served as Jack Tars in Admiral Nelson's fleet, and 63 Irishmen served on his flagship '*Victory*' at Trafalgar[1] when he hoisted his famous but questionable signal prior to the start of that battle: '*England* expects every man to do his duty'. As part of the recently formed United Kingdom, the renowned Admiral was surely remiss in omitting Ireland's name from the signal, although the mention would have made it unduly ponderous. Or perhaps it was a Freudian slip on Nelson's part, being conscious of the unprincipled manner in which Ireland was duped into joining said United Kingdom? The fact remains that service in the armed forces constituted a vital safety valve for the surplus male population.

Drogheda's Part in Napoleon's Downfall! It is of interest to speculate on the part played by Drogheda and Louth/Meath in the defeat of Napoleon Bonaparte. Apart altogether from the harassment and defeats inflicted by the British Army on the French forces during the Peninsular War, the *coup de grace* was delivered at Waterloo by Wellington who hailed from Trim (and was schooled in Drogheda). Also, it was the victories scored at the crucial naval battles at the Nile and at Trafalgar, in which so many anonymous Irishmen, some of whom undoubtedly were from Drogheda or Baltray or Clogherhead, took part, that effectively destroyed Napoleon's navy and put paid to his plans of invading England.

Napoleon
All his brilliant victories were cancelled out by Wellington at Waterloo.

Much of the linen produced in Drogheda was of the coarse variety for use as sail canvas, which was taken up by English buyers at the Linen Hall and destined for use in the Royal Navy. By the same token, the rigging in those men-o'-war may well have originated in the cabins of the Rope Walk – ropes on naval vessels required to be replaced regularly, (say) every three years. Incidentally, when Wellington signalled his ranks to make the crucial push against the faltering French fusiliers at Waterloo, the unbelievable happened. Napoleon's invincible Imperial Guard were forced to turn tail and run. At that moment, when Wellington had raised himself on his stirrups and waved his plumed hat signlling the advance, he was mounted on his favourite mount '*Copenhagen*', an Irish-bred charger which may well have caught his eye at the great Drogheda Horse Fair held annually on 12th May. Wellington said "There may have been many faster horses, no doubt many handsomer, but for bottom and endurance I never saw his fellow'.[2] Napoleon's mount was another Irish-bred horse.

There was a preponderance of Irishmen in the British Army in terms of their proportion of the population of the British Isles. *It is an astonishing fact that 42 per cent of the British Army consisted of Irishmen* in 1830,[3] and thus it can be said with a modicum of truth that Irishmen played a significant part, not only in ridding Europe of Napoleon, but also in extending the tentacles of British Empire. Apart from a presence in the armed forces, many of the landed gentry joined the civil service and were given senior administrative appointments overseas. The brother of the Duke of Wellington, Richard Wellesley, was Governor-General of India, and many others of the Ascendancy class served abroad in senior positions; a member of the Gormanston family was Governor of Tasmania during the 1880s.

The problem in Drogheda had always been that the principal industry, textiles which involved looms and spinning wheels, provided work for females, leaving the men in idleness, and their main outlet was the British Army. We can conclude from this that Droghedamen were over-represented in the army. They soldiered in India, South Africa, Canada and in many other parts of the burgeoning Empire. Others served in the Royal Navy.

Not all Droghedamen fought exclusively for the British Crown. The founder of the Equadorian navy was Thomas Charles Wright, a member of a very old Drogheda family. When he heard of Equador's struggle to rid itself of Spain's dominance he offered his services and was

Wellington and (inset) *'Copenhagen'*
Both Wellington and Napoleon were seated on Irish-bred mounts
during the Battle of Waterloo

instrumental in achieving important maritime successes throughout South America. His brother Richard took part in the naval battle of Lake Maracaibo in 1823, which was a turning-point on Columbia's anti-colonial war.

To govern a truculent nation being held down under duress, a strong military presence, supported by coercive legislation, was essential. Even when England was grappling with Napoleon, there were as many as 30,000 regular troops scattered throughout Ireland for the purpose of quelling unrest, and just prior to Emancipation the figure topped 35,000, inclusive of police, militia and coast-guards.

The Crimean War: The outbreak of the Crimean War in 1853 brought relief to the unemployed, and the local Regiment was reconstituted. The Drogheda Argus reported in May 1855: 'The Louth Rifles were inspected in the large market square in Fair Street'. Britain was seeking men to help defend the Turks from the expansionist aims of Russia. The supply of apparel and equipment for the new Drogheda recruits was inadequate in many ways; but let it be said that there was a like deficiency in the ardour of the men. They were badly clothed and some of them tore what clothing they had to escape being drilled. At first no uniforms were ready for them and the apparel that was eventually provided could hardly be described as uniforms, being of forty shades of green, and the suitability of their garments to combat the severity of a Russian winter seems to have been completely overlooked.

Whatever enthusiasm they had possessed when they signed on speedily ebbed away when they received the dismal tidings that their full kit – whatever motley shades they might be – had to be purchased by the recruits themselves in hard cash. Scope for disputes or for negotiating extended credit terms was obviated by having the cost docked from their pay. The regiment lacked such basics as a bugle, but one recruit fortuitously possessed *bagpipes*, and it was to the mournful wail of that instrument that they awoke at morn. This situation was later resolved by a pensioner 'who fortunately had a bugle of his own'.

Fights and brawls were commonplace among the recruits, many of whom came from neighbouring counties, and the local Drogheda people did not take kindly to them. At least one recruit did not reach the front at all. The records tell us that, being imprisoned in West Street barracks for some unspecified misdemeanour, he attacked the sentry and was bayoneted to death. From time to time several others were dismissed for misconduct. Another was tried and reduced in rank for making away with the sergeants' mess money.

Thus the rag-tag recruits set off to tackle the Russian Bear. The sufferings which they underwent in that campaign were unspeakably severe. The officers were grossly inept – as exemplified in the debacle known to history as 'the Charge of the Light Brigade' – and this exacerbated their unhappy lot. It is acknowledged that for every soldier who died from enemy action, three unfortunates perished as a result of the incompetence of the officers. Many who escaped enemy action fell victim to frostbite, cholera and other epidemics which were rampant. Nor was there any respite for those who were hospitalised. The conditions in the wards were dreadfully primitive, and unhygienic in the extreme. The untiring efforts of Florence Nightingale helped greatly to expose these shortcomings. One participant wrote home:

> ' ... *The few horses that are left are scarcely able to carry their hides, and the poor men, from the cold and the hardship they are going through, are scarcely able to walk. The roads are knee deep in mud and to see the poor men and horses dragging and pulling along the road it would strike pity into any person's heart. There is a good deal of the men dying...*'.[4]

From peering through this little window of script we get a glimpse of the hardship which the soldiers endured. Why did they enlist in their droves if such experiences lay before them? We must realise that at this time Ireland was still reeling from the effects of the Great Famine, and no doubt many a destitute young fellow preferred the rigours of army life to the bleakness of the workhouse.

In the Crimean War 'forty per cent were Irish [including] a considerable Irish presence in the cavalry'.[5] A large proportion of the 11th Hussars and 17th Lancers of the Light Brigade who made that fateful charge into "the Valley of Death" were from Ireland.

One senior officer was a native of Duleek – he was Lieutenant-Colonel Richard D. Kelly of the 34th Regiment. (He ended up in a Russian POW camp). Incidentally, the bugle that sounded the charge on that fateful day is inscribed with the name of the maker 'J. McNeill, 148 Capel Street, Dublin', a firm that was established in 1834 and still trades today at the same address.

The Charge of the Light Brigade: Those soldiers who survived the vicissitudes of warfare returned only to find that circumstances at home had not improved. They were left to their own devices which meant, for the most part, a return to a desolate life of penury.

One such 'soldier of fortune' was hauled before the Mayor of Drogheda's Court in 1891 for being drunk and disorderly. He had acquired a wooden leg in the course of his nineteen army years. He was Jeremiah O'Sullivan who had served in both India and the

Crimea. When asked by the court how he earned a living, he replied: "By limping along from town to town, singing my songs as I move along. I served Her Majesty for 19 years, and I am one of the men that fought in the Balaclava Charge of the Light Brigade". This light-hearted troubadour and veteran of many a far distant battle was shown no sympathy; he was given a month in jail, and this, no doubt, was an experience with which he was already all too familiar.

In the graveyard of Saint Peter's C. of I. church in Drogheda there lies a tombstone near the left hand side of the church with the following inscription:

"Sacred to the memory of John Duggan who died in Drogheda 22ⁿᵈ March 1881 aged 67 years, late private 17ᵗʰ. Lancers and Sexton of St. Peters Church. He fought in the battles of the Alma, Inkerman, Sebastopol and Balaklava."

Another Drogheda participant in the Balaclava Charge was the 'blue-eyed, brown-haired' Robert Moneypenny (19). He was awarded the Distinguished Conduct Medal for 'praiseworthy and gallant service throughout the campaign'. He was admitted to the Royal Hospital in Kilmainham in the autumn of his life and died there in his 80ᵗʰ year.

A local veteran of the Great War, Harry Banks, who was known to this author, stated that he regularly spent the customary sentence of 'seven days' behind bars for being drunk and disorderly. However, being well known to the jailer, he was quietly allowed to walk the streets by day under a gentleman's agreement that he would report back to his cell at nightfall. This enabled the jailer to keep the records accurate.

About the mid 1850s a set of five Drogheda brothers enlisted. They lived in Bryanstown Lane (the entrance is opposite Glanbia at the Black Bull) where there were two small thatched cottages. One of these contained a family of twelve, consisting of the two parents, seven boys and three girls.

> *"They were unemployed. A recruiting officer came around looking for recruits and five of them joined up – they got a shilling [when signing on]. The youngest of them was only 15; you had to be 16 to join the army, but he gave the wrong age. They done their military training in Dundalk, and they set off marching [for embarkation to some part of the far flung Empire, possibly Mesopotamia, now Iraq] on a Friday with their regiment for Kingstown [Dún Laoghaire]. On their way through Drogheda their mother met them on the Dublin Road at the Black Bull and gave each of them a pillowcase with some thick marching socks and a brown cake. They were never seen after. They were my grandfather's brothers".⁶(DF)*

Such incidents provide us with a valuable insight into living conditions at that period in Drogheda. The remark included in the above narration about the five brothers that *"They were never seen after"* was stated in a casual manner. It is nonetheless pregnant with pathos. It was given to the author in a matter-of-fact manner by a grandnephew of the five young brothers who enlisted, but undoubtedly it was representative of countless similar instances in homes throughout Ireland. It implicitly tells us of the unrequited foreboding and the untold grief in many an Irish mother's heart.

Once a month the *Drogheda Argus* included in its columns a lengthy list headed *"Stations of the British Army"*. It contained specifics as to the location of about 150 regiments throughout that vast Empire on which the sun never set, located in barracks varying from Mallow to Aldershot, and from the Curragh to the Cape of Good Hope. Readers today might register puzzlement at seeing such seemingly irrelevant and meaningless listings being published in the local newspaper on a regular monthly basis, but it must be remembered that at that time many Drogheda men served in one regiment or another scattered throughout the globe, and through this medium parents were able to track the whereabouts of a son – or several sons – who had joined up.

The King's Shilling: With whatever country Britain was at war, and in whatever decade, there were always Irishmen available to 'take the King's shilling'. In 1870, for example, no fewer than 47,131 Irishmen were wearing British Army uniforms[7]. By comparison, the Irish Army today is a force of about 11,000. That trend continued up to (and after) the Great War. An elderly resident of Francis Street, formerly known as Morgan's Lane, recalled the circumstances in the 1930s:

> *"This street was full of them [ex-soldiers]. Next door was Peter Moore's father — he was a sergeant in the First World War. [Peter Moore was a member of Drogheda Corporation and wore the Mayoral chains on eight occasions]. Then there was the Fallons, Joe, Jemmy, Tommy and Frank. Joe and Jemmy was in the Connaught Rangers in India. That was the regiment that mutinied when they heard that the 1916 men were executed. All of the Rangers were going to be shot, but in the end they only shot one of them — Daly from Waterford; the rest were pardoned. There was a lot of soldiers in this street, but I can't remember their names — I was young. Those that were not in the Army were in the Navy. Then they got pensions, but a lot sold their pensions back to the government, and then they were finished — they spent it on drink'.[8]*

> *"There was one ex-soldier where I lived in Dooley Gate, and we used to shout after him 'Kiss the Queen' — that was his nickname. Then we'd run for it'.[9]*

The Louth Militia returned from the Crimean War in 1860. Following the din of battle and the hardship they endured, one would have expected these heroes to immediately head for home to be reunited with their loved ones and to relish a degree of peace and tranquillity. However, on being discharged at Dundalk, pandemonium broke out:

> *'... Many of them indulged to such a degree in intoxicating drink that they kept the town in a state of uproar. The Market Square was the scene of much tumult, two or three of the intoxicated men having commenced to drag each other about. One of them who was in a state of uproarious drunkenness, fell several times and cut his face, and a comrade who was nearly as helpless, having endeavoured to take care of him — the drunk leading the drunk — got his clothes covered with blood'.[10]*

The Irish Papal Troops (1860-1870): For over a thousand years a large chunk of central Italy was under the jurisdiction of the Pope. But in the mid 1800s there was a move to unify the fragmented country, which meant that the Papal States were in jeopardy. The Pope sought help, both financial and military, to repel the impending invasion. Over 1,000 Irishmen answered the call, a significant number coming from County Louth, including the commander of the force; he was an officer in the Louth Militia, Major Myles O'Reilly. Departures from Ireland began in May 1860 and each volunteer was handed £3-15-0 (€4.00) travelling expenses; no uniforms or kits were given. The British Government disapproved of these enlistments and issued a *'Proclamation against Enlisting in Foreign Armies'*, and in June a ship about to set sail from Drogheda was boarded and the names of 50 volunteers from Drogheda plus 30 from Dundalk were taken.

On reaching Italy each man was given three days pay and a uniform. The pay rapidly disappeared when they were introduced to the local *vino*. Then the uniform was promptly sold to locals to enable them indulge more freely in further sampling of the same. The arrangements were chaotic from start to finish, language being a major cause of confusion. This was followed by bickering with other nationalities, complaints about the unfamiliarity of the Italian food, inadequate washing and toilet facilities, damp straw bedding, etc.

On marches they soon learned to live off the land, a practice that proved to be highly unpopular with the local farmers whose sheep began to disappear from the fields. Villagers barricaded their homes at their approach, and shopkeepers put up their shutters. Major O'Reilly endeavoured to establish some semblance of order, weeding out the main troublemakers and sending them home, and others he put behind bars — not public house bars, but the other type — the ones made of iron.

In the several skirmishes with the enemy the Brigade suffered about seventy casualties, but most were taken prisoner. The final outcome was inevitable, and in six months it was all over. The men were now stranded and they lacked the fare to return home. When they turned to the Papacy they were told that its coffers were empty. Eventually, through subscriptions being raised back home, they finally reached Ireland again, and on arrival each was given a hero's welcome. Sixty were back in Drogheda by November. One of these who had resigned as a constable in the RIC was found a job as Officer of the Night Watch by the Corporation.

The *Drogheda Argus* in 1861 reported on the funeral of a former member of the Irish Brigade: 'Patrick Mullen at Mell (near the town) had shown fearless courage, and acted heroically at Spoleta. [Elaboration on the precise nature of the 'fearless courage' and heroism was not supplied – the reporter was undoubtedly indulging in a journalistic flight of fancy, but at least it fitted the occasion and read well in the obituary, and no cad was going to contradict it]. Fellow soldiers Matthew McKenna and John Connolly were the chief mourners. A great multitude marched after the hearse the entire road to Monasterboice, four Irish miles from Drogheda, and only separated [Here the suspicion of further journalistic licence asserts itself] after the last sod of green Irish earth was slowly and mournfully placed on the grave'.

Disquiet in Italy flared up again in 1870, but this time there was much less enthusiasm in Ireland about taking up arms and coming to the Pope's rescue. On this occasion the force was known as the Papal Zouaves. Resistance in Italy to the invading forces was half-hearted at best, and in a short time the Pope raised the white flag of surrender. Thus Italy became one united nation from the Alps to Sicily. It is presumed that the Irish contingent found its way home without undue difficulty. One of these men, who later lived at Oldbridge, was a familiar character in Drogheda and was known only by his nickname – 'the Pope' Heeney.

The American Civil War (1861-1865): The civil war in America is regarded as the first "modern" war, when rifle fire proved its worth and performed its function with deadly efficiency. To replace the multitudes who fell in battle, Federal agents from the U.S.A. came to Ireland seeking recruits. Canvassing had to be undertaken surreptitiously since this was a breach of Britain's neutrality whose leanings, in any event, were towards the Southern (Confederate) side. (It was not any moral righteousness that prompted this bias, but rather the impact of the Union's blockade which prevented the cotton-laden ships of the Confederates from reaching Liverpool and the mills in Manchester).

The inducement of a small cash advance and having their passage paid were compelling factors for many an Irish lad. They were so destitute, said an agent, 'that the temptation of a little ready money ... would lead them to go anywhere'. The resulting exodus brought almost 150,000 to the Union ranks, many joining the famous Fighting 69th and a further 40,000 joined the Confederate Army.

'Colonel' Leonard: Some of them cherished the dream of returning to Ireland when the war ended, to gain freedom for their native land. One of these was Patrick Leonard from Tullyallen who had risen to the rank of Lt.-Colonel in the Union Army. He was a deeply committed Fenian and a close personal friend of John O'Mahony, founder of the Fenian Brotherhood. On his return home when the war ended he became involved in the Fenian Rising, and was an instigator in Drogheda's aborted rising at the Potato Market and was soon arrested at his mother's house at Begrath, following which he was imprisoned at Ardee goal. He died at his sister's house in Drogheda aged 52, an occasion that was honoured by a great assemblage, and several bands accompanied his remains to his final resting place at Monknewtown graveyard. On the anniversary of his death in 1877 fifteen bands and a crowd estimated at 10,000 marched from Drogheda to his graveside in homage to his memory. The Colonel Leonard Fife and Drum Band (now known as the Drogheda Brass Band) was named in his honour.

With the ending of the American Civil War many men remained in the U.S. Cavalry and were engaged in patrolling the frontier areas for the settlers who were setting up homesteads during the inexorable push westwards. The way of life for both the settlers and the soldiers in those remote parts was much harsher than that depicted in some John Wayne westerns – we are told that living conditions for the soldiers were only one step above those of the Negro slaves toiling in the cotton fields. And many of them came straight from the emigrant ships that left Queenstown, Galway, Drogheda and Liverpool.

They sometimes found themselves in frontier posts and remote forts (now restored and preserved as historical sites) of the wastelands and semi-deserts of Texas and Arizona. Adjoining the forts are silent and lonely graveyards that cause the visitor to muse at the many familiar names inscribed on the headstones, names such as Maguire, Kelly and Daly. Did they accidentally fall from a horse or did they succumb to an Apache arrow? The inscriptions do not tell us.

Polarisation of the Classes: What was the attraction for so many Irish men to join the army? The living conditions of the populace and the absence of any uplifting prospects were the underlying factors for the vast majority. The 1798 Rising was immediately followed by the Act of Union, the effects of which have been outlined above. The century that followed was the most distressing one in Irish history, marked with recurring epidemics, famines, social unrest, evictions and agitation for land reform. Evictions were not confined to the depressed areas on the western seaboard – Louth/Meath also experienced these distressing scenes.

The motivating factor for the Ascendancy class in answering the call to arms in times of war was the preservation of the *status quo*. This was a self-serving motive. It stemmed from an instinctive response to protect their stately mansions and vast tracts of lands from the deprived masses. The castles and great houses that still stand today on the fertile lands of Louth and Meath supplied in their time colonels and other high-ranking officers to the British Army. These were the men on horseback. It was an age of clearly defined 'haves' and 'have-nots' in Ireland.

What prompted the ordinary foot soldier to join up is delicately explained by Brian Griffin in *The Irish Sword*: " ... There is less evidence of Irishmen in the non-officer ranks enlisting from a desire to witness bloodshed first hand, or from a misguided sense of glory of war. Many who enlisted in the militia or army did so from mainly economic motives and not from any overwhelming desire to serve Queen Victoria or to fight Russians".

In other words they enlisted under the duress of want, to escape the grinding poverty that engulfed them in their home environment. This point is expressed with a tinge of bitterness by a contemporary observer: 'Starvation is a good recruiting sergeant, and many poor fellows enlist to escape from the hunger to which misgovernment consigns them in their own fertile land'.

Living Conditions in the Army: The catchment area for recruitment to the Louth Militia was not restricted to Drogheda or to County Louth; about half the members came from adjoining counties. The total strength of the regiment varied as circumstances demanded but averaged 600 men. When a contingent of fresh recruits entrained at Drogheda Station for Dundalk, the moms and sweethearts were present to see them off. Amid cheers and tears the band of the Regiment struck up *'The Girl I Left Behind Me'*. The press reporter was pleased to note that 'The soldiers looked well and not one had to be left behind for drunkenness'.

These recruits were not paragons of perfection. Newrymen in particular made themselves conspicuous for all the wrong reasons. It was reported that they "did not at all look like the class of men who would make soldiers", having reported for annual drill being clearly 'under the affluence of ilcohol'. They were lustily singing "*God Save Ireland*", a sentiment that was distinctly at variance with the disposition of the Queen whose empire they had pledged to protect. One of the Newrymen, when ejected from a pub, thereupon challenged all and sundry to a bout of fisticuffs, 'at the same time proclaiming that he was a *'Newry mon'* – which was quite unnecessary as his accent and behaviour were sufficient evidence of the locality he hailed from'.

Their loyalty was further suspect when they shouted *"To hell with Bloody Balfour"*. (Arthur James Balfour was the English statesman who was Chief Secretary for Ireland and who vigorously opposed Home Rule. This earned him in Ireland the sobriquet "Bloody".)

These were the "have-nots" and they were for the most part, but not exclusively 'from the lowest, most despised levels of society'. Although they won many a battle for Wellington, he referred to them as 'The scum of the earth – the mere scum of the earth'. If their reason in joining was to escape the deprivation and hopelessness of their home environment, then a disappointment awaited them:

> 'Many had joined out of desperation, to escape poverty, criminal charges, unwanted marriages or debt. The ranks included tramps, adventurers, outcasts, and idealists. The British Army of the 1840s was ... a symbol of tyranny known for its almost unmitigated misery as to the life it offered a ranker. Crowded barracks, bad food, sickness, poor pay and abuse all greeted a new recruit ... Soldiers slept sometimes four to a bed – less room than prison provided. Clothes were seldom washed, and urine tubs doubled as wash-basins in the morning. Sickness was rampant. The same room was used for eating, sleeping and lounging, and bachelors lived in a common room with the married men and their wives and children. There was no privacy and little decency'.[11]

We get a glimpse of living conditions in Drogheda from a report in the *Drogheda Argus* in 1861 concerning goods stolen from Millmount Barracks. A certain Patrick Sullivan was hauled before the magistrate because he did not give the Constable a satisfactory account of a blanket in his possession. He was accused of having 'knowingly in his possession a blanket belonging to the ordnance department of the Queen's stores'. The case had been adjourned because the witnesses for the defence did not turn up. At the adjourned sitting they were still absent – the accused explained to the Court that he thought that the prosecution would arrange such matters. The Court chided him for expecting this to be done for him "... while you are sitting on your bottom". His wife took the witness stand:

> *Wife: I went for water to the barracks. I was in the habit of going for water every morning, but the pump was locked. A man there asked me if I wanted to buy a blanket.*
> *Court: Did you know him?*
> *Wife: I would if I seen him. He wanted a shilling (€0.06) for it. All I had was eleven pence so I brought them over and gave them to him. I thought there was no hurt or harm about it, and I thought the man had the power to sell it.*
> *Court: The worst of it is that your husband is responsible for your actions. It is a very serious thing to purchase anything belonging to Her Majesty.*
> *Wife: I thought there was no harm in it. If I were to die and never see the Almighty at the Day of Judgement I declare I did not know the harm of buying it. I even washed the blanket and put it out drying for three days.*
> *The Court enquired as to the value of the blanket, and the Constable stated that 'it appeared not to be worth a shilling'. He added that Mr. Sullivan was known to be an honest man.*
> *Capt. Gardiner (prosecuting, for the Army): It could be bought in a pawnbroker's auction for a shilling.*

These were magnanimous statements by the prosecution, and it is clear that they were sympathetic towards the poor woman. The mayor imposed a fine of one penny plus three shillings being three times the price of the blanket plus three shillings and sixpence court expenses. He cautioned the guilty party: "Be more circumspect in future and do not buy military blankets". Patrick Sullivan thanked the Mayor and promised to pay the fine at the end of a fortnight.

Boredom prevailed. This was relieved by such fatigues as picking stones from the parade ground. The wage of the private soldier was 1s/1d. (€0.07) per day in 1864 – the same emolument as he would have been paid 64 years earlier, or at the time of Waterloo. It is no surprise that dissatisfaction permeated the ranks, and that loyalty to the Crown at that army level was conspicuous by its absence.

An occasional injection of cash into their pockets was certain to dispel, however temporarily, the pervading despondency. This had the desired effect, but it produced unwanted (but predictable) consequences. The serving men were entitled to a periodic bounty, and this was doled out to them quarterly. The amount in question was 5s/5d (€0.35), and how this was spent can easily be guessed at. Largesse of such magnitude in their possession had the tendency of making them rather incautious. A ready outlet was at hand. It enabled them to escape the drudgery of barrack routine in a brief but glorious bender. The revelry continued until the pockets were again empty. When the dust settled and the scene returned to normal, then the recriminations began. It is on record that the bacchanals that ensued led to many a court martial. This in turn caused further difficulties, for the barrack cells were unable to cope with the influx. The guilty parties were obliged to wait their turn for the inevitable confinement in the stockade, and this pause gave them time to reflect and to cool their heels and their heads.

Social Life Among The Officers: For the officers, conditions were much different. The appointment of officers was governed by the Militia Act 1793. Everything hinged on the *wealth or income* of the applicant – the bigger the estate, the higher the rank in the army, and this criterion remained in force until 1869. Those with the largest estates received a colonelcy, followed by lieutenant colonel, then major, captain, etc.

News items of a military nature in the *Drogheda Argus* illustrate the gulf that existed between the "haves" and the "have-nots" in the army. One short paragraph in 1875, for example, stated that the Louth Rifles "arrived to complete their training and take over the Millmount barracks after being vacated by the 75th Regiment. In physique and military bearing the men present a marked improvement on former years...".[12] This is in stark contrast to the lengthy report of a social occasion in the following week's paper (14th August 1875) which is headed "LOUTH RIFLES BALL". It reports:

> *"This fashionable event came off in the Whitworth Hall last night with complete success. The invitations, which included the elite of the locality were responded to by a large and brilliant company. All the arrangements were admirable. The decorations, under the directions of Mr. Bellingham and Mr. Jameson, displayed much taste. Some large mirrors, interspersed among the floral devices that were placed along the walls, multiplied the effect when the company assembled. Mr. Liddell's band was in attendance. As heretofore, the newsroom was converted into a supper-room. The company assembled at about eleven o'clock and did not separate until an advanced hour of the morning. The list of invitations included: ... "*

A lengthy list of the revellers follows, commencing with the Colonel of the Regiment, then a glittering array of named Lords, Ladies, a Marquis, a Duchess, several Viscounts and their ladies, Captains, Majors, Knights, the Attorney General, the Mayor of Drogheda, and many others representing the *crème de la crème* of society of counties Louth, Meath and Dublin.. It is interesting to note that the ball commenced at the late hour of 11 p.m. and the revellers "did not separate until an advanced hour of the morning" – probably about 4 a.m. or 5 a.m. which was the norm in that era. Combing through that long list of distinguished revellers today, it would be difficult to identify even one family name that is extant.

Here we may reflect on the grandiloquent spectacle of the carriages and coaches trotting up Laurence Street to the Whitworth Hall, the officers in their colourful dress attire festooned with medals and decorations, the coachmen quickly alighting to hold the horses' heads, the footmen in their livery scurrying to open the carriage doors, and bowing as the ladies step down in their long, flowing dresses and being escorted up the steps of the Whitworth Hall to commence the night of revelry. Meanwhile, a collection of ragged, barefooted urchins gaze in silent awe.

Friedrich Engels, who had visited Ireland, had the measure of them and was not taken in by such shows of opulence and pomposity. He took a more circumspect view of such scenes, and his shrewd observations were set down in a letter sent to Karl Marx:

> *'These fellows are droll enough to make your sides burst with laughing. Of mixed blood, mostly tall, strong, handsome chaps, they all wear enormous moustaches under colossal Roman noses, give themselves the false military air of retired colonels, travel round the country after all sorts of pleasures, and if one makes an enquiry, they haven't a penny, are laden with debts, and live in dread of the encumbered estates court'.* [13]

One wonders what military skills and battle-craft these gentlemen possessed, bearing in mind that the lives of the rank and file rested in their hands when they were deploying a regiment in the field of battle. They were the occupants of 'the big houses' and the vast estates, and the pursuit of pleasure was their wont. During the Crimean War, for example, Field Marshall Raglan, who infamously gave the order to charge the Russian cannons, had his private yacht conveniently tethered where he could sleep in safety. Day to day fatigues in the dreary barracks were not for them. They avoided the banality of the officers' mess by engaging in pursuits such as hunting, cricket and other sports, and nights were often spent in revelry. Many managed to secure week-end leave. Others who came to dislike the routine of army life simply resigned.

The aristocracy and landed gentry in the Louth/Meath area almost without exception held military titles e.g. **Colonel** Coddington and **Major** Coddington (Oldbridge), **Major** Law (Rossnaree), **Major** Lambert (Beauparc), **Lieutenant-Colonel** Pepper (Ballygarth Castle), **Captain** Osborne (Dardistown Castle), **Colonel** Cairnes (Stameen) to mention but a few. Their names were very familiar to every Droghedean, but by WW II most of these families had succumbed to external pressures, mostly of a monetary nature. An exception is Montgomerys of Beaulieu whose family produced daughters but no sons covering many generations and they still occupy the family residence. Earlier generations held military posts, and an illustrious military relation of theirs visited Drogheda after World War II – he was Field Marshal Bernard Montgomery (of El Alamein fame).

The army posts they held were handed down from one generation to another. Factors such as crippling death duties have resulted in many of these families being forced to sell out, and most of the 'big houses' had changed hands by the end of the twentieth century. Their proud homes are now in the possession of individuals whose sympathies do not necessarily orientate towards the British Crown.

THE ZULU WAR (1879) & THE BOER WARS: Few wars attract more discredit to Great Britain than the Boer Wars (1880-1881 and 1899/1902) in the matter of their execution – and even more so in regard to the moral justification for initiating hostilities. First came Zululand. It was expedient for Britain to acquire the traditional land of the Zulus, so Britain took it – just like that! Fearless as the Zulu warriors were, their spears were no match for the rifle fire and Maxim machine guns of the white man in the red tunic, and as they charged in waves towards the barricades they were mown down mercilessly. The resistance shown by the Boers in the struggles that were to follow shortly afterwards was much more obstinate – the Boers were using guns, not spears.

The Louth Militia (which by now had formed part of the Royal Irish Rifles) had not long returned home from service in India (1899) when they were recalled to don once more their tunics and depart for southern Africa to tackle the Boers. The Boer settlers, who originated in Holland and Germany, had set sail for southern Africa to start a new life by ploughing new furrows in a strange land. They were industrious, God-fearing, hard-working sons-of-the-soil. Having set up their homesteads, they succeeded in turning the virgin lands of the Orange Free State and the Transvaal into productive farmland.

But the discovery, first of diamonds and then of gold, caused an influx of newcomers from England. British imperialism speedily asserted itself. The farmers did not yield without a heroic fight. Their sharpshooters skilfully picked off the Redcoats, and humiliated Britain in

267

many battles and skirmishes. But their lands were laid waste and their homesteads systematically torched. A new concept in warfare was created in handling the womenfolk and children while the men were absent – they were herded into compounds that provided the dictionary with a new term 'concentration camps', confinements which were lacking in water, sanitation and medicines. This caused 26,000 innocent inmates to die of starvation and disease. The native blacks over whose lands the fighting took place fared worse. Those who were not assigned to slave labour were herded into other 'concentration camps' – 30,000 people in all – and their fate can only be guessed at. The final outcome was that the Boers were overwhelmed by vastly superior numbers. It was thus that a massive chunk of a continent, known as South Africa, became part of the British Empire.

It was ordained that the Louth Militia/Royal Irish Rifles should engage the Boers in combat. (For the record, other Irishmen sympathised with the Boers and fought on their side). The usual influx of new recruits had signed up, but they seemed greatly confused as to what was motivating them. As in earlier wars, poverty in their home environment was the motivating factor. The prospects of obtaining employment at home or of improving their life style were non-existent. Further, they were sadly lacking in manual skills, and it is pathetic to observe how many of the Drogheda men who enlisted were without trades or accomplishments of any kind. The occupation of 85% of the rank and file is given as "labourer". Most were illiterate.

The imminent departure of the Louth Militia in late 1899, as described in the *Dundalk Democrat*, is surely the ultimate in farce. Many relatives and friends had gathered at the Dundalk Barracks to see them off, and the occasion was marked by both the recruits and their friends imbibing excessively in alcoholic refreshments. The *Democrat* revelled in describing the scene of the departing warriors, stating that they

> 'were unable to support the weight of their accoutrements without the aid of the arms of their friends ... Cheers for Kruger and the Boers were called for and loudly responded to. A more ludicrous sight than that of a mixed crowd of Royal Irish Rifles [incorporating the Louth Militia] and civilians cheering themselves hoarse for the doughty enemies of England could not be imagined'.

It need hardly be explained that the *Dundalk Democrat* had strong Nationalist sympathies! General Kruger, the subject of the exultations, was President of the Transvaal and a bitter enemy of England. Departing regiments in other parts of Ireland expressed their sentiments in like fashion. In that era, Irish children at play were apt to honour their leaders by nicknaming them "Kruger" – he was the 'goodie' in the school playground and in every schoolboy escapade. One colourful and nationally known character from Dingle was "Kruger" Kavanagh. Another was "Kruger" Sheridan, a beloved lay teacher in the Christian Brothers School, Drogheda, who taught a generation of boys up to the 1950s. Such men carried their nicknames throughout their lives. (The name was invariably mispronounced 'Kru**dj**er').

The regiment was stationed at Sheffield for training, the intention being to ship it to South Africa while, inexplicably, an *English* regiment was being posted to *Ireland*. Deep concern was expressed at home at these raw, inexperienced Irish recruits being sent to the front. The *Dundalk Democrat* again dipped its pen in vitriol, and stirred up dissension:

> "Louthmen to the front! Louth Rifles to face the Boer sharpshooters. Had anyone suggested it a month ago, we would have been laughed at. But it is a fact. We cannot wish these Militia reserves better fortune than to be speedily taken prisoners ..."

New recruits were enrolled to replace those who sailed away, and these were also drilled in Sheffield. Then the entire battalion was asked, as a unit, if they would volunteer for South Africa. (It must be remembered that militiamen were not regular soldiers, and service abroad was not compulsory; they had the discretionary right to refuse foreign service). What happened next caused great confusion. It seems that the men were asked if the would volunteer to oppose the Boers, and while some agreed to go, others did not, but to put it delicately, the unit may have been "volunteered". The *Dundalk Democrat* went into overdrive:

> ' ... it is nothing short of wilful murder to send men like the Louth Militia, unfamiliar with the use of arms ... to fight against the deadly shots and practised warriors like the Boers. What chance have these poor fellows – raw lads, many of them, scarcely out of their teens, unused to hardship such as soldiers in the field have to endure – in a struggle that has already proved too much for the cream of the British army, men trained in England's little wars, hardened in campaigning, and expert in the use of rifle and bayonet? If these lads be sent to the front, they are sent to the certainty of death, wounds or a Boer prison ... And these are the sons of poor people in Dundalk and Drogheda and other parts of Louth; in many cases the breadwinners and sole dependence of aged parents ... Are they to be sent out to be shot like dogs, to die without the spiritual aid of a Catholic priest – victims of a cause that, almost to a man, they know to be bad and unjust, and which, for all this humbug of "volunteering" we pledge our conviction that nine tenths of the battalion do not and cannot sympathise with'.

Here was criticism of a most trenchant nature. The *Democrat* thus left no doubt in the readers' minds as to where it stood on the issue! It wrung the very last drop of emotion and pathos from the event. The arguments as set out were irrefutable, and were uncomfortably close to the truth. Serious repercussions were to follow.

Questions were raised in the House of Commons as to the manner in which the men were consulted. And why, asked one Nationalist MP, had Irish Militia regiments been removed *from* Ireland while British Militia regiments had been brought *into* Ireland to serve in their place. A good question.

The newspapers of Britain took up the case, some supporting and others deprecating the issue. The article in the *Democrat* reach the men and it freely circulated around the Sheffield barracks. The Louth Militia were again paraded, and the question of volunteering was again put to them. In the normal course of events it is the assenting persons – those who are agreeing to volunteer – who are asked to step forward. But not this time. Inexplicably and confusingly, it was those who were *not* prepared to go to South Africa that were to take one step forward. Clearly, the authorities were indulging in moral blackmail – they had hoped to expose and shame anyone contemplating a refusal to volunteer. It misfired. One hundred and seventy six men left their line and stepped forward.

This was startling. It was almost mutinous. It caused dissension and consternation in the barracks (a section of the militia was from Belfast and County Down, and their reluctance to volunteer for service abroad was perhaps less marked), some denying that they had sympathy with the Boers, others claiming they had wives and children to support back home; others again denied being influenced by the reports in the *Democrat*, others arguing that they had been misled by their officers.

His Eminence Cardinal Logue entered the fray on behalf of one reservist who was illiterate and who "never was asked and never consented to volunteer for foreign service", but was nonetheless ordered to report for embarkation to South Africa along with several others who had been equally hoodwinked.

Some English newspapers covered the 'mutiny' in their columns. One of them deplored the fact that " ... Sheffield [was] the place to bear the shame of the first exhibition of disloyalty to the Queen in the present crisis in national affairs ... ". Another paper mooted that the *Democrat* was guilty of a felony by encouraging traitorous and mutinous acts. It was sedition, they said!

Never missing an opportunity to tweak the Lion's tail, the *Dundalk Democrat* stirred up more trouble by reporting that the Louth Militia in Sheffield were " ... hooted by loyal English mobs, composed of men who take very good care to keep their own skins safe and whole, while driving unfortunate Irish militia men to fight their battles and sustain their precious Empire". The same paper reported on a bizarre occurrence in Scotland. When a thousand Highlanders on parade were asked to volunteer, not one answered the call. Using the pragmatic logic of the Scots, they had said they would go to South Africa if they were given a share in the gold mines out there, but otherwise they were not prepared to risk their lives for a shilling a day. Who could argue with that!

The order for the Louth Militia to embark was eventually cancelled, and thus the controversy petered out. For the record, 175 men did answer the call and went out to South Africa to fight the Boers.

A scrutiny of the statistics covering the first year of combat presents a puzzling picture, and for this little exercise we will combine the Royal Irish Fusiliers with the Royal Irish Rifles by virtue of the fact that the statistics are similar to each other, but conspicuously different from those of the other regiments, e.g. the Royal Dublin Fusiliers and the doughty Royal Enniskilling Fusiliers.

In the case of the two last named regiments, the ratio of those reported as 'Missing or Prisoners' to 'Killed or Died of Wounds' was approximately **125 : 100** – in other words, slightly more soldiers were taken prisoners than died in battle, whereas in the case of the Royal Irish Fusiliers/Rifles the figures were *ten times greater*, viz. **1,120 : 100**. These figures indicate that the Royal Irish Rifles/Fusiliers were amazingly adept at dodging enemy bullets, and in addition they had the remarkable propensity of falling unscathed into enemy hands!

A member of the Royal Irish Fusiliers who had been taken prisoner wrote home:

" ... *We were all then taken prisoners ... While we were in the laagers we were treated extremely well and they [the Boers] gave us food and tobacco. All you read about the Boers in England is absolutely untrue. They are most kind to the wounded and prisoners, looking after them, and anything they have got they will give you if you ask them, even if they deprive themselves...".[14]*

Stories of that nature gaining currency in the ranks – where hunger, thirst and privation prevailed in the raw, hostile environment – were certain to influence others in being counted among the "Missing or Prisoners", more particularly if they were deficient in the fortitude and the enthusiasm necessary to extend the territory of the British Empire.

A period of tranquillity followed the Boer Wars, and this was to spell 'the end' for the Louth Militia. A certain amount of rationalisation took place within the army, some battalions being amalgamated. One of those destined to disappear was the Louth Militia. Existing members were assigned to the Royal Irish Rifles – this took place in 1908. A rare souvenir of the South African campaign is held locally. It is a scarlet tunic in the proud possession of the Quinn family, whose grand-uncle served in the Boer War. [JQ]

The *Dundalk Democrat*, looking back on the past exploits of the Louth Militia, and being mindful of their role in 'the Races of Castlebar' in 1798, switched into a nostalgic mood. It recalled:

' ... *The Louth Militia and part of the Kilkenny regiment [when facing the invading French forces at Castlebar] threw down the English colours and went over in a body to the French and in an hour were completely equipped as French soldiers. Poor fellows, they paid the penalty for their rashness, for in a field at Ballinamuck, ten days later, Cornwallis hanged 90 of them...'*

The general reaction to the demise of the Louth Militia is best summed up in the concluding words of the book *The Louth Rifles*:

'*Alone among the militia battalions of the Royal Irish Rifles, the Louth Militia was disbanded in 1908. A curious factor relating to their disbandment is the lack of debate or controversy. No voices were raised in protest. The Louth Militia passed unlamented by Unionist and Nationalist alike into history and was quickly and quietly forgotten'.*

To that conclusion we feel tempted to add a not very pious *'Amen'.*

Chapter Thirty

The Fenian Brotherhood and The Rising

There was another reason why men joined up – some had an ulterior motive, a hidden agenda. Smouldering resentment served well in breeding discontent and revolt. These feelings crystallised in the Fenian Brotherhood. It was founded in the United States and soon reached Ireland. The Drogheda branch was inaugurated in 1862 in the back yard of Keapock's Hotel (now the Westcourt) by Thomas Clarke Luby.

Its members looked upon the British Army as a fruitful source of trained recruits for their own ranks. By 1860 thirty-one per cent of the rank and file of that army were Irishmen. Even regiments with non-Irish names such as the Prince of Wales Own and the Gordon Highlanders contained a sizeable proportion of Irishmen.

One local youth became a trooper in the Tenth Hussars. His name was John Boyle O'Reilly. The ulterior motive for this young man in enlisting was to surreptitiously gain recruits, not for the regiment in which he was serving, but for an objective that was much nearer and dearer to his heart. "By his personal magnetism, as much as by the force of his eloquence, he turned many a stout fellow from allegiance to the Queen, to the more dangerous path of devotion to country". [1]

> *'There were good men as well as good soldiers, thousands of them, in the rank and file. It was always the good men and good soldiers among the Irishmen who were most easily converted to the doctrines of Fenianism. This is one of the commonest fruits of misgovernment'.*

A nonagenarian explained to this author why his mother, on the morning of her wedding, was not 'given away' by her father:

> *"My grandfather, Samuel Clifford, was over the Fenians and was jailed for a short period. When he heard his daughter, my mother, was marrying an Englishman, he put her out of the house and she had to get married out of digs"* [2]

The author's own great-grandfather Hugh Greene was an active member of the Fenian Brotherhood. He 'was the Head Centre for the Fenian movement in Meath and took part in the battle of Tallagh in the ill-fated rising [CG]'[3]. He also had close ties with members of the Franciscan community in the High Lane Church at Laurence Street, and it is an intriguing possibility that he was in some way connected with the cache of old firearms that was discovered there in the 1980s; they had been secreted under the roof of that church and had lain undisturbed there since Fenian times. Coincidentally or otherwise, he had donated a pair of statues to the church – two large winged angels, each bearing aloft a lighted orb; they were placed on pedestals one on each side of the main altar (and were still in place when the church finally closed its doors on being deconsecrated in the year 2001). Was this a *quid pro quo?* In Hughes's *"The History of Drogheda up to Date"* there is a reference to the liaison between the Fenians and a Brother Furlong who secreted arms "under the high altar in the Franciscan Church[4]".

JOHN BOYLE O'REILLY (1844-1890) – A PEN-PICTURE: In 1865 the strength of the British army in Ireland was 26,000 regular troops, 60% of whom were Irish. John Boyle O'Reilly was one of these. His aim in enlisting was to penetrate the army for the recruitment of men for the Fenian Brotherhood – an 'army within an army'. He pursued this objective with a rare passion, and within four months he had gained 80 new members into that oath-bound society.

He was born on 28th June 1844 in Dowth, a stone's-throw from the prehistoric tumulus at the Bend of the Boyne, and nine km. from Drogheda. He became a printer's apprentice in the *'Drogheda Argus'* at the age of eleven. The day was long, and he worked from 6 a.m. to 8 p.m. for 2/6 (€0.16) per week with the prospect of an annual increase of 6d. (3 cents) per week. He completed his apprenticeship in Preston, Lancashire where he lived with an aunt. While there he also learned shorthand and journalism, accomplishments that were to be of benefit to him in later life. On returning to Ireland he enlisted as a trooper in the Tenth Hussars, which put him in daily touch with prospective 'recruits' for the Fenians.

The British Government was acutely aware of the disaffection in the ranks. They had spies and informers everywhere, and these men did their work well. O'Reilly's activities were exposed; he was found guilty of treason and sentenced to death. This was subsequently commuted to twenty years penal servitude, and at the age of 23 he was transported in chains to Western Australia, never to see his parents or the banks of the Boyne again.

On the long, tedious voyage to Australia he whiled away the time for those on board by producing a remarkable periodical called *'The Wild Goose'* in association with some of the other 280 convicts, 62 of whom were fellow Fenians.

By a curious twist of fate, the fabric in the garb that he and his fellow convicts wore was woven by the mill girls in Drogheda, Ireland.

Fremantle, in Western Australia was considered to be escape proof, and prison conditions in the jail were diabolically cruel. O'Reilly, as Convict Number 9843, later described the cells as being 'dreary, seven feel long by four feet wide, and a little over seven feet high. They were oppressively warm in summer, and dismally cold in winter[5]. By comparison, they were one-third smaller in capacity than the notorious cells in Alcatraz, which measured 5' x 9' x 7'. Only those who have spent time within a cell of those dimensions know the restrictions they impose on the human mind as well as on the body. The tiny window admitted light, but it was positioned too high to provide a view of the world outside. The bed was a hammock slung between two hooks, and cell space was so confined that it was necessary for the captive to detach it by day if the seven feet of the cell's length were to be used to allow the endless pacing up and down in such a restricted area.

He was punished with loss of privilege for six months for a minor infringement. His warder at one stage showed him a letter that was address to him. The cover bore the portentous black border of a mortuary notice, and the warder then threw it in a drawer. It was not until the six months had expired that O'Reilly learned of his mother's death.

Drawn by W.Greenlees   DROGHEDA from the Dublin Road   October 20 1838

TWO PANORAMIC VIEWS OF DROGHEDA
Drawn by a travelling artist in 1838

From a private collection

OIL PAINTING OF THE OBELISK BY JOHN CASSIDY

Cassidy was born in Slane and spent much of his successful career in Manchester where he was given many painting commissions.

From a private collection

SALMON FISHING ON THE BOYNE C.1940
An oil painting by Nano Reid 1901-1981
From a private collection

**GEORGE IV DEPARTING FROM DUNLEARY,
FOLLOWING HIS VISIT TO SLANE (1829)**

The cartoonist had a distorted concept both of Dunlaoghaire and of the Irish people.

From a private collection

Lady Conyngham Returns to Slane Castle Laden with Booty.

(See Chapter 25)

THE NORTH QUAY IN THE 1800S

Idle men sit on the Quay wall

MAGDALENE STREET IN FORMER TIMES

Portion of the Town Wall in evident

From a private collection

The Earl of Drogheda (c. 1880)

*Chapter Eight gives an account of how the Moore family assumed
the name of Drogheda in their title.*

From a private collection.

A spirited young man like O'Reilly was determined not to remain confined in the hell-hole of Fremantle Jail. The epic story of his escape in a whaler called the *'Gazelle'* that took him to America, of his editorial work with the prestigious *'Boston Pilot'* newspaper which he subsequently owned, make absorbing reading. In particular, the escape in the *'Catalpa'* which he later engineered for six Fenians from Fremantle Jail from under the noses of their watchful British jailers is worthy of a separate volume.

He had an untimely death, with one of the pall-bearers at his funeral being the great Fenian leader O'Donovan Rossa, and it is reputed that the cortege was the largest ever seen in America until the death of President John F. Kennedy. This is not surprising, for John Boyle O'Reilly's name was very widely known. He had the distinction of holding the office of president of the Papyrus Club and the Boston Press Club; he enjoyed a wide reputation, and held many distinctions including a degree of Doctor of Law. He lectured widely, and left behind a legacy of poems and writings that are truly endearing. President Kennedy was familiar with his works, and when he was addressing the joint meeting of the Oireachtas in Leinster House he made the point of quoting a couplet:-

> *"The world is large when its weary leagues two loving hearts divide;*
> *But the world is small when your enemy is loose on the other side".*

The poet Francis Ledwidge was present at the unveiling ceremony of O'Reilly's monument in Dowth graveyard in 1903, and an annual pilgrimage is still unfailingly made there on the anniversary of his birth.

THE FENIAN RISING: The editorial in the local newspaper, the *Conservative,* gives an account of Drogheda's part in the abortive Fenian Rising which was set to commence on Tuesday night 5th. March 1867. It was to have formed part of a general plan whereby a simultaneous uprising would take place throughout the country. It was a pathetic failure, and the effort in Drogheda was as feeble as the episode at Ardee in 1798.

> *'Many peaceful inhabitants were startled on Tuesday last by the rapid stamping of feet in every direction, and their alarm was considerably increased by the sound of firing in the neighbourhood of the Market Square. ... A contemplated attack had been defeated, blood had been shed, and a large number of prisoners captured. The 'outbreak' – if that can be so called, which was so promptly arrested – formed part of the general plan'.*[6]

The 'Catalpa', a converted whaler, successfully snatched six Fenian convicts from captivity in Australia. O'Reilly was closely involved in the plan.

The local garrison had been forewarned, because an anonymous letter marked 'Desperate Rising' had reached them, alerting them of the impending insurrection. They informed the police and the Mayor, and thus all was in readiness at officialdom. When word reached the barracks towards midnight on Shrove Tuesday that men were assembling at the marketplace they marched up Georges St. and captured a few who had been posted there as look-outs, taking them into custody. At Bolton St. they encountered the assembled crowd and fired at them. Some men fell. And there was then an immediate stampede, and 'men tumbled over each other in their effort to get out of the way. ...

The Fenians were completely routed at the first discharge, and their flight was of the most hurried and disorderly description'. (If we are to judge the mood of the townspeople by the accounts of the rout as reported in the local press, there was little sympathy for the subversives).

The crowd was estimated at 800 to 1,000. There were 25 policemen and they took 26 prisoners. 'One poor fellow was so far gone that he had to be carried to the barracks where, on examination, it was found that he had sustained no injury whatever'. The county infirmary turned away some wounded men who had sought medical aid the following day.

In the morning the police found the area around Bolton Square strewn with guns, ammunition and weapons of all kinds. Millmount barracks was immediately strengthened with 90 men from the 39th. When the steamer St. Patrick from Liverpool docked, 20 men on board were arrested 'and marched to the Tholsel two by two with an armed constable on each side. They were followed by a large crowd and were loudly cheered while passing along the quays'. A few weapons were found on board. The men were then handcuffed. The newspaper described them as 'an evil looking lot', but nonetheless the women who followed them gave three cheers for the Fenians as they passed through the iron gates of the gaol.

Thus ended Drogheda's effort in the Fenian Rising – elsewhere in Ireland the results were not too dissimilar. It was a dismal failure. The occasion serves well to illustrate the futility of relying on an indisciplined body of men, however ardent they may be, who lack the firm resolve and rigorous military training, and crucially, are without strict leadership.

John Boyle O'Reilly
as a convict

Political Prisoners: In the course of a trip to Australia to retrace the footsteps of John Boyle O'Reilly and the other Fenian prisoners, the author conducted some research on the penal colony records in Hobart, Tasmania and at Fremantle. He was struck by the great number of unfortunates who were transported for very trivial offences, both political and non-political. A perusal of the records for the penal colony of Port Arthur, Tasmania, reveals that the minimum punishment usually handed down by the courts was a term of seven years.

The records show that persons who stole an ass or a cow in Ireland, for example, were sentenced to transportation for life. Pilferers caught stealing trifling items such as a hat or a pair of shoes or a book earned seven years. One pickpocket was given the customary seven years for having stolen a handkerchief – he was a mere youth of sixteen; a culprit from Stamullen was transported who was a boy of 14 years. Another chap – call him a felon or a patriot depending on your political leanings – was convicted and sentenced to transportation *"for being present when treasonable songs were uttered"*.[7] It need hardly be pointed out to the reader that, although as a general rule songs are 'sung', the authorities on this occasion stated that they were *'uttered'*. Also note that the guilty party had not in fact 'uttered' anything, but was merely *present* at the time. The verdict – banishment!

The usual sentence for political prisoners who escaped the death penalty was penal servitude for life. While in prison, the slightest infringement of the rules drew the most severe punishment. A particularly recalcitrant prisoner was the one-eyed Dennis Doherty. He seemed determined to take on the British Empire single-handedly and thereby incurred the wrath of the warders many times. In the course of his incarceration it is estimated that he received close on three thousand lashes of the cat-o'-nine-tails. Oddly, he survived this fiendish treatment and lived to eventually gain his freedom.[8] The regulations clearly designated that the person dispensing such punishment should have unrestricted latitude in wielding his whip. Nothing was to impede its wide arc as it descended on the human flesh. Hence the phrase of having 'room to swing a cat' – it has no connection with our domestic tabby, but to the infernal appliance with nine leather thongs designed by man to inflict pain on man. Victims regularly died from the ordeal.

In all, 38,907 convicts (including political prisoners) were shipped out from Ireland. Most of them, including John Boyle O'Reilly, never saw their loved ones or their native land again. It is pertinent here to enquire whether we fully appreciate that the political independence and economic prosperity enjoyed today by the people of the Republic was bought with the untold sufferings and sacrifices made by earlier generations of freedom fighters.

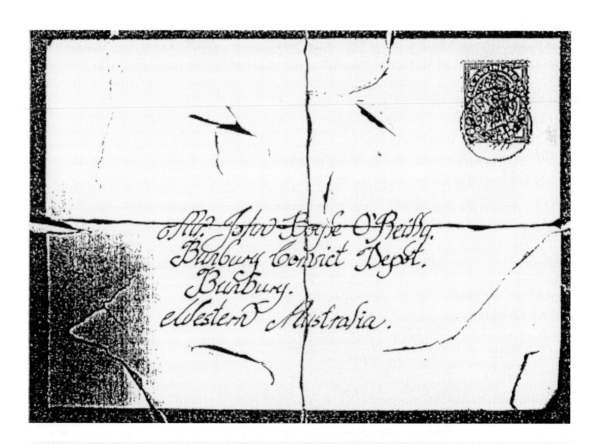

The Envelope containing news of the death of O'Reilly's mother.
It was shown to him, and then withheld for six months.

275

Chapter Thirtyone

The Town's Infrastructure

The good times of the 1700s saw a marked improvement in the matter of Drogheda's municipal buildings. The authorities had the ambition and the wherewithal to tackle the construction of the Boyne Canal, a new Tholsel, the Mayoralty House and the Linen Hall; the town's bridge had also been replaced. The dire conditions that prevailed during the first half of the 1800s prevented any further grandiose projects being contemplated. The latter end of the century saw a gradual improvement in the economy, enabling a series of projects, both civic and private, to be undertaken.

Living Conditions: Before we mention the main civic buildings and better-class homes that were constructed, we must firstly attempt to envisage the conditions under which the commonality existed. This subject, insofar as it dealt with the early part of the 1800s, has already received our attention, and the reader may have presumed that, with the passage of time, a curtain could be drawn across the scenes of squalor and destitution that previously existed, and that the general populace were now living in improved circumstances. Famine conditions had thankfully gone, but apart from that, living conditions were no better; indeed they were horrifying, if the observations of a lecturer, J.B. Gray MP are to be accepted. They were truly appalling, and there is no reason why we should doubt their veracity. They were reported in the columns in the local newspaper of the day, *The Conservative*, in the issue of 11th. November 1860 and are presumed to have been presented in a spirit of candour, and delivered in the hope that a remedy would speedily follow. The account of the address was given under the title *'Important Lecture'* held in Drogheda's Hall of Mechanics Institute. The meeting was chaired by R.B. Daly, founder of the auctioneering firm that still bears his name, and the audience was evidently in concurrence with the tenor of the address, for they constantly broke into applause.

> *'You see in numerous localities the poor crowded in stifling dens wherein the rich would not consent to keep their domestic animals, so used are the inhabitants to pass by an overflowing rank, offensive sewer, so accustomed to send out and beg or borrow a can of water ... The slight remove from a state of barbarism as regards a people at large cannot be better illustrated than in the imperfect arrangement existing for the distribution of water for ventilation and drainage ... A dirty population who cannot remove the impurities from their person and garments will almost always be found depraved and immoral'.*

He singled out the Dale and the Marsh Road as having furnished two-thirds of the victims in the recent outbreaks of cholera that had occurred in Drogheda, and he identified four main causes:

- Overcrowding
- Defective drainage and ventilation
- The use of foul water
- The privation of solar light

Mr. Gray then related the impressions of an American who had recently visited the town:

> *' ... many of the dwellings I saw upon the roadside looked to me like the abodes of extinguished hopes, grovelling, despairing, almost idiotic wretchedness. I did not know there were such sights in the world. I did not know that men and women, upright and made in God's image, could live in sties, like swine, with swine, – sitting, lying down, cooking and eating in such filth as all brute animals.... I scarce saw one hovel, the mud floor of which was not excavated several inches below the ground level without, and as there is no sill or raised*

threshold, there is no bar – I will not say to the water – but to the liquid filth that comes to its lower level within.

'A few miles from Drogheda a woman sitting in a hovel at work with muddy water up to her ankles, and an enormous hog scratching himself against her knee. These disgusting animals were everywhere walking in and out of the hovels at pleasure, and jostling aside the naked children or wallowing in the wash outside or in – [The swine are] the best conditioned and most privileged inmates of every habitation.

'All this, of course, is a matter of choice, and so is the offal-heap situated in almost every instance and nearly before the door and draining its putrid mass into the hollow under the peasants' table.

'As we drove into Drogheda we entered a crowd – it was market day, and the streets were so thronged that you could scarce see the pavement except through the feet of horses, and the public square was a sea of tatters ... the beggary at Drogheda fully came up to the travellers' description. They were of every possible variety ... The sight was awful, old age in shapes as hideous. I should think the most horrible never had conceived. The rain poured down upon their tangled, uncovered heads, seeming with its cleaning torrents of faces so hollow, so degraded in expression and in also clothed in filth and neglect, that they seemed like features of which the very owners had long lost, not only care, but consciousness and remembrance; as if in the horrors of want idiocy, they had anticipated the corrupting apathy of the grave and adorned everything except the hunger which gnawed them into memory of existence'.

Mr. Gray then presented a further illustration of Drogheda, as penned by the English novelist William Makepeace Thackeray (1811-63) who visited the town. His descriptions tally with those already given above:

"... But as the coach arrives near Drogheda and in the boulevards of that town, all resemblance to England is lost. Up hill and down, we pass low rows of filthy cabins in dirty undulations. Parents are at the cabin doors dressing the hair of ragged children; shock-heads of girls peer out from the black circumferences of smoke, and the children inconceivably filthy yell wildly and vociferously as the coach passes by. ...

"The town itself, which I had three-quarters of an hour to ramble through, is smoky, dirty and lively. There was a great bustle in the black Main Street, and several good shops, though some of the houses were in a half state of ruin, and battered shutters closed several of the windows where formerly had been 'emporiums', repositories and other grandly titled abodes of small commerce. Exhortations to 'repeal' were liberally plastered on the blackened walls, proclaiming some past or promised visit of the great agitator. ... The quays were grimy with the discharge of the coal vessels that lay alongside them. ... Numerous factories and chimneys were vomiting clouds of black smoke. ...

"There is a very large and ugly Roman Catholic Church in the town and a smaller one of better construction. It was so crowded however although on a week-day, that we could not pass beyond the chapel yard; there were great crowds of people, some praying, some talking, some buying and selling. There were two or three stalls in the yard such as one sees near continental churches presided over by an old woman with a store of little brass crucifixes, beads The church is large and commodious within and looks as if it were frequented unlike most churches'.

The impressions of Surgeon Wilde, medical doctor, writer, archaeologist and father of the famous playwright, were then quoted. He had been knighted for his work on the decennial censuses of Ireland and was very familiar with the Boyne valley and with Drogheda. Referring to the town's ecclesiastical ruins, he said the Old Abbey

'spans a dirty lane, now principally used as a stable yard. [The Magdalene Steeple] is surrounded by the most miserable of hovels inhabited by the most wretched portion of the population and not only is the adjoining locality a disgrace to the town, but the very site itself stands in need of a Sanitary Commission than any other place we know in the British dominions. As soon as the Corporation of Drogheda cleanse their city we hope to conduct the Boyne tourist round some of its other memorable ruins'.

Mr. Gray concluded by describing the habitations as being 'stifling rooms crowded to excess with human beings' and that houses in the main streets that outwardly appeared to be respectable 'too often conceal deformities worse than hideous, a repulsive background of ghastly squalor and reeking filth'. By comparison, the neighbouring town of Navan had a considerably better drainage system. He castigated both the town's merchants and the Corporation for failing to remedy these appalling conditions. 'Can our merchants look back with any pleasing retrospect on their outlay for the benefit of the town? No! Have [the Corporation] fulfilled the high functions for which they were originally destined? No! They are lamentably deficient.'

The above descriptions of the living conditions in Drogheda during the latter half of the 1800s are startling. In 1863 the local paper refers to 'the filthy lanes which form so large a part of the town'. The Corporation was certainly remiss in failing to install even a rudimentary sewage system and a supply of potable water. The Ascendancy by this time had been ousted, so they cannot be blamed. Nor can we point a finger at the Act of Union for the malodorous dung-hill (invariably pronounced 'dunkill') that sat outside so many doors. As for the seepage of foul, brown gunge that trickled to the lower level within the hovels, surely a few shovels of earth at the threshold would effectively serve as a buffer. It is difficult from today's standpoint to pass final judgment on these matters, but there would appear to exist a marked lack of initiative and self-dependency. God helps those who help themselves.

St. Johns Gate   Drogheda

Sketch 1.:

We are able to glean details of the occupations of the townspeople from the roll book of the Presentation School during the 1860s. The register of pupils additionally states the father's occupation in each case. It lists a handful of bakers, carpenters, shoe-makers and other such tradesmen, but what makes lamentable reading is the inordinate number of fathers who were devoid of all marketable skills. They include coal porters, 'dealers', drovers, a fiddler, a piper, a rag man, hawkers, huxtors, jobbers, labourers (a great preponderance of these), watchmen, as well as washerwomen and widows. From a total of 738 occupations as listed, as many as *461 (62%) were without a recognised trade or regular employment*. What is even more touching are the descriptions 'pedler' and 'pauper' – surely no more poignantly hopeless 'occupations' exist than these. These statistics reinforce the point made in an earlier chapter that depriving the populace of the opportunity to learn trades kept them in permanent poverty, and rendered them unable to make a contribution, however slight, to the advancement of society. Wholesome meals were unknown to them. The nuns were providing a glimmer of hope by placing these children onto the first rung of the ladder that would lead them towards improved living conditions.

The primary duty of the nuns was to teach pupils, but they worked tirelessly to provide some essential sustenance for the children, even though they themselves were often hungry. "We hadn't enough to eat. We lived in poverty, I tell you", said a nun speaking of conditions in the convent 70 years later. As recently as the 1940s many children arrived in school hungry and in their bare feet, and were given bread and hot milk by the nuns to sustain them. One pupil in the early 1940s remarked to the nun that she didn't like weekends because she got nothing to eat until the following Monday when she was back at school.

Earthquakes: Events which certainly cannot be blamed either on the Ascendancy or the Act of Union were acts of God – earthquakes. One occurred in November 1852 which was felt in the town centre, but lasted for merely a few seconds. The following year an earthquake occurred in East Meath and lasted for ten minutes. Of all the days in the year for it to happen it was on Halloween Night, a night when a superstitious populace must have been truly terrified. There are no records of deaths or of damage being done.

A news item in 1877 stated that Typhoid Fever had been rampant in the town for six weeks; also that 'scarlatina, measles and whooping cough are rather prevalent and have been for several weeks past'. Contagious fevers prowled around the streets and lanes of Drogheda, a circumstance that should have surprised no one. What lay at the root of the outbreaks were the open sewers, the polluted drinking water and the pervading filth in the hovels.

A survey on the sanitary state of Duleek in 1849 states that, although some of the homes in Main St. were clean and well ventilated, others were in a filthy state. As for the street itself, 'stagnant water is allowed to remain in some of the channels until it creates the most disagreeable smell. The sewer in the lower part of the street is entirely choked ...'. The condition of the side streets was worse, dung-heaps being a feature in each: 'It is impossible to describe the filth created here by stagnant water and manure heaps up to the very thresholds of the doors, and even the interior of their houses are shocking, either from the negligence or laziness of the inhabitants, they scarcely take the trouble of sweeping their floors'. Of Larrick St. it states that the 25 families were comprised of 176 individuals, and it was there that 'the principal wretchedness of the town is concentrated. Some of the houses have no through air, no ventilation, no light except that admitted by the door; hence the persons living in these huts inhale and exhale mostly the same air. ... The whole street may be said to be one mass of cesspools and dung-heaps which, if allowed to remain until the heat of summer, it will be quite impossible for any person not habituated to such an atmosphere to pass through, from the malaria which must necessarily arise, when the manure is undergoing the process of decomposition. In one house without a door to exclude wind or rain, there are 5 families huddled together'. This description was made in the immediate aftermath of the Great Famine and when evictions were commonplace.

CHURCHES: St. Peter's C. of I. Church: It had been built in 1750, and in 1847 was 'thoroughly renovated with a magnificent steeple and spire. The vane and weathercock have been completely and substantially fitted in a style which reflects credit on the eminent architect'. This work may well have been undertaken as a means of providing employment and of alleviating distress in 'Black Forty-seven'. In addition, a new type of lightening conductor was added which was claimed to be the first of its kind in Ireland.

The grounds surrounding the church contain many graves, including that of the brilliant James Ussher, Bishop of Meath and later Archbishop of Armagh and Primate of All Ireland. It was he who concluded from an excessively detailed study of the Bible that the world was created in 4004 BC and would end on 23rd October 1997. This calculation was a taken as a widely accepted fact at the time but, as we now know, that fateful date came and went without as much as a hiccough.

St. Mary's C. of I. Situated at the top of Mary St., this church in pre-Reformation times this was the site of the Carmelite monastery. The structure we see today was built in 1810 and deconsecrated in 1998.

Methodist Church, Laurence St. was built in 1811 and is now a commercial establishment.

Presbyterian Church, Palace St. was built in 1828 and continues to hold services regularly.

Catholic Churches: The repression of the Catholic religion has already been dealt with. In the year of Catholic Emancipation (1829) the Franciscans built their church (colloquially known as 'the High Lane') in Laurence St. It continued in use until it was deconsecrated in 2001. The Augustinian Church ('the Low Lane') was completed in 1866. The members of that Order were relieved when the priory was completed in 1870, for they had previously rented the property adjoining the top of the High Lane steps and were 'tossed about ... I can scarcely have a moment to myself, as my bed is in the sitting room', diaried the prior. During the following few decades three further churches were built. The Dominican Church opened in 1878 and cost £8,000; the adjoining priory was built on the site previously occupied by an old thatched church. The two parish churches, St. Peter's and St. Mary's, were

279

completed towards the end of the century. Our Lady of Lourdes Church in Hardman's Gardens was completed in 1959, and to cater for the expanding population and the construction of extensive housing programmes on 'the far side' of the town in the Ballsgrove area the Holy Family church was built in 1973.

Bridges: The need was felt for a second bridge within the town. The position chosen was at the Haymarket. An advertisement was consequently inserted in the local paper in 1838 inviting tenders for 'a stone bridge with one arch, across the Boyne, opposite Stockwell Lane'. Nothing further was heard of the project, and people continued to use the ferry service which plied between the Hide Market at the foot of Linenhall St. and Ballsgrove. Eventually, Dominic's Bridge was constructed at this point.

Two other bridges that had fallen into disrepair, namely St. Mary's Bridge and the Obelisk Bridge, were later replaced. The latter bridge was built in 1869 of steel lattice construction and cost £2,540. As far back as 1862 a committee was formed which undertook the formidable task of replacing the existing structure that connects Shop St. with the Bull Ring, and six years later, in May 1868, it was officially opened by the Mayor of Drogheda, Alderman Thomas Greene. The construction work was the cause of difficulties, plunging several unfortunate contractors into bankruptcy, and taking exactly two years to complete.

> *'We really forget how many contractors failed, from one cause or another, in constructing the bridge. The foundation stone was laid on the 16th. May 1866 by the then Mayor Ald. James Matthews J.P. Mounthanover. A large crowd collected to witness the opening of the bridge. The Mayor rose and pronounced the bridge open in the name of God, as Saint Mary's Bridge. A great cheer went from the people following the announcement. Flags were flown from shops in the area. Several barrels of ale were ordered for the populace. At the Imperial Hotel bottles of champagne were cracked by gentlemen of the committee in honour of the event'.*

The Courthouse: Coming towards the end of the 1800s the Tholsel was no longer deemed suitable as the seat of local government. The plans submitted by Francis Johnston for a new building at the corn market in Fair St. were accepted, and the new offices were opened in 1890. The change in location resulted in the Tholsel becoming redundant, and the Corporation took the decision to dispose of it. The prospect of that fine building falling into private hands caused uproar among both the businessmen and workingmen of the town when its sale was proposed. The Mayor called a meeting to obtain a consensus – it was held in the Crown Court of the Tholsel in May 1889. A resolution was read by the spokesman, Rev. Fr. Woods:

> *'That we, the inhabitants of Drogheda, in public meeting assembled do hereby protest against the Tholsel being given away for any purpose other than for municipal and public purposes'.*

He added that the old building had witnessed many stormy scenes in the past, and he spoke of the era prior to the reformed Corporation when the Ascendancy ruled the roost, and when an 'ermine judge' might come and thrust away the Mayor. Others spoke in emotional terms, one saying that it was 'the people's property', another that 'the future of the building lay in the hands of the workingmen of Drogheda for they had a claim upon the Tholsel as they were the support of the town'. Another speaker alluded to a former Mayor (presumably of Ascendancy vintage) who had taken a very unusual course

> *'to preserve it against contact with the lower orders; and how did he manage it? He got it tarred. ... That man has been known ever since as 'Tar the Tholsel'. ... And when this island will be governed by its own Parliament (loud cheers) under the development of Home Rule, this old building in the hands of the Corporation of Drogheda will stand erect, grand and beautiful in its old age; and the Tholsel clock will beam down on manufacturing industries increasing in their town (more cheers)'.*

These eloquent and emotive words were of no avail, for a lease was granted to the Hibernian Bank (now part of the Bank of Ireland group, and the name 'Hibernian Bank' consequently disappeared) at a rent of £70 per annum for 75 years. The duration of 75 years of the lease became very elastic, and the valuable and well beloved property, which still stands 'grand and beautiful', remained in private hands until 2006.

In opposing the resolution it was stated that the building should be disposed of at once and the proceeds 'spent in providing suitable dwellings for some of the poor people of the town who at present are compelled to live in miserable hovels, which are veritable hotbeds of disease. ... At present all the roughs and loafers in the town congregate within its hallowed precincts, and people either passing down Shop Street or across West Street are seriously impeded by those characters'.

In September 2006 the building reverted to the Corporation. 'We haven't really decided what to do with the place just yet', according to the Town Clerk. Occupying such a prime location, it would serve well in providing some civic amenity for the convenience of the townspeople such as a motor taxation office, etc., alternatively as a tourist office, etc.

Creations of P.J. Dodd, Architect: The civil engineer/architect who designed many local buildings during this period was P.J. Dodd. Dublin born, his skills were employed in the county surveyor's office in Dundalk; later he conducted a private practice in Drogheda, residing in the Cord Road. The fruits of his work are still evident in Drogheda and the surrounding district, and include the premises forming the rounded corner on the Bull Ring and also the red-bricked building at the Peter St./Laurence St. corner – it was known for many years afterwards as 'Dodd's Corner'. He also designed many private homes.

Up to that time no. 32 Laurence St. was the site of a desolate tenement. This was pulled down and Dodd designed a new branch for the Belfast Banking Company which opened in 1886. They remained there for about 35 years, but moved away from Drogheda at the formation of the Irish Free State. The bank's crest is still shown on the tympanum.

P.J. Dodd designed a new church at Laytown – it was dedicated in 1876 and replaced a timber structure. The building material was taken to the site by boat at high tide and then hauled up the beach, there being no coastal roadway at the time to provide access to the site; likewise, the worshippers were able to approach the church only via the strand. Dodd then prepared the plans for the new road running parallel with the beach connecting Laytown with Bettystown. Other projects designed by him included the new bridge at the Obelisk, St. Mary's Bridge, maintenance of the Boyne Canal, several schools throughout the general area, the Sisters of Mercy Convent, the boathouse for the Drogheda Rowing Club and several other churches and parochial houses throughout Louth and Meath.

A major project was St. Mary's RC church in James St., construction work for which was begun in 1881; it was completed *circ.*1884 at a cost of about £8,000. Subcontractors were engaged for various sections of the work. The slating contractor was Peter McCann, Fair St. (who was also engaged in the building of the Dominican Church). When it was discovered that one consignment of slates differed in colour to the rest, the difficulty was overcome by laying the slates to form a simple design, as the finished work today shows.[1] The construction, by a different subcontractor, of the church spire was the cause of difficulty, and the faulty workmanship on the spire is still in evidence by viewing it from the vestry area – a slight tilt can be detected.

P.J. Dodd's busy and creative life came to an end in 1892 – he died prematurely aged 47 years, but his legacy of architectural heritage is a matter of which Drogheda and counties Louth and Meath can be justly proud.

Benjamin Whitworth: These and other civic projects undertaken toward the end of the nineteenth century indicate that the town was recovering well from the collapse of the linen industry and the effects Great Famine. The town's workforce was given a welcome boost with the arrival of an industrialist from England. He was Benjamin Whitworth, whose textile factory, Boyne Cotton Mills, provided employment to a workforce of over 800. As a benefactor he presented the people of Drogheda, entirely from his own resources, the Town Hall in Laurence St. Of particular note was the £21,000 that he contributed towards a sorely needed water supply for the town. The reservoir was built at Killineer in 1865.

The following year Whitworth was elected MP for Drogheda. However, the result was declared null and void due to massive intimidation, but his son Thomas was then put forward and was duly elected. An act of Parliament was passed in 1872 called the 'Secret Ballot Act' resulting directly from the Drogheda intimidations.

A grateful public in 1875 funded the erection of a monument opposite the Tholsel in his memory at a cost of £450. It took the form of a fountain surmounted by an ornate spire 13 metres in height and was yet another creation of the architect P.J. Dodd. So many memorials throughout Ireland have a political motif that it was refreshing to seeing one being erected commemorating deeds of philanthropy and kindness. The inscription stated:

'**This fountain was raised by public subscription in recognition of the many valuable services conferred upon the town and the trade of Drogheda by that true philanthropist and generous benefactor Benjamin Whitworth.**

The Home of James Dunne at Belpatrick, Collom
He was evicted by the landlord Captain Singleton c1889.
He died on the side of the road a few days later.

THE LAND WAR: The agitation generated by Daniel O'Connell towards the dream of Repeal of the Union lay face down in the water when the Great Famine had done its work. It took several decades for ardour to resurface, and when it did the list of grievances was lengthened to include Tenants' Rights and the Land Question in addition to Home Rule. Discontent festered among tenant farmers, and their demands were summarised in 'the Three Fs.' – Fair rent, Free sale and Fixity of tenure. Famine reappeared in the late 1870s, and many smallholders were unable to meet the demands of their landlords for rents, so that evictions once again became the order of the day. These heart rending scenes were accomplished simply be posting a notice on the tenants' doors to settle arrears 'otherwise summary steps will be taken to recover same'. Then the Peelers and the army moved in to unroof the cabins and knock the walls. The scenes that followed were distressing beyond words.

'THE BATTERING RAM HAS DONE ITS WORK. 1772. W.L.'

The Battering Ram
It was a very effective instrument at eviction time

Tenants who had no lease – 'tenants at will' – were particularly aggrieved because they were not compensated for improvements made during their occupation. Nor could they expect sympathy, if we are to take cognisance of Lord John Russell, Home Secretary and later Prime Minister. He dismissed the notion of compensation with: 'You might as well propose that a landlord compensate the rabbits for the burrows they have made'.

Evictions occurred mainly in the west, but Louth/Meath did not escape completely. The Fosters of Collon featured in them and the name Freke, who was the resident magistrate on the Foster Estate, notoriously turned families out on the roadside. However, the 12th Viscount Massereene, who succeeded to the Foster Estate in 1905, was blessed with a more benign disposition and reinstated evicted tenants, and also negotiated with others for the transfer of lands previously leased.

Evictions were not the prerogative of Protestant landlords alone. The homesteads around Gormanston were also vulnerable to a landlord's rapacity. The 14th holder of the Gormanston title, who was Governor of Tasmania in the late 1800s, turned several families from their nests, although in general terms the Gormanstons were regarded as considerate landlords.

The scourge of evictions did not cease with the Nineteenth Century – instances occurred during the memories of people who entered the new Millennium. As recently as 1920 a news article under the heading 'The Evicted Flynn Family' reported that: –

> 'A meeting was held in Stamullen on Sunday after Mass to advocate the re-enstatement of the Flynn family in the lands of Cock Hill [Stamullen] on the Gormanston Estate. ... [They] expressed the hope that a friendly settlement would be arrived at between the representatives of an old a respected family of the district and the owners of the Estate...'[2]

It is naive to enquire why so many people of Ireland were imbued with feelings of hostility towards their overlords. The landlords were Irish, too, but the tenants did not see things that way – they regarded them as 'West Britons' – an apt term, and always applied pejoratively.

CHARLES STEWART PARNELL (1846-91) A Pen-picture: Who would challenge the

abuses of the landlords and spearhead the tenants' demands? The leader who appeared on the horizon was Charles Stewart Parnell, a member of the Protestant aristocracy from Co. Wicklow. He seemed an unlikely candidate, but he championed the cause of the undertrodden, focussing on Home Rule and fundamental rights for tenant-farmer. His great-grandfather was Chancellor of the Exchequer in Grattan's Parliament, and evidently the quest for justice was in Charles' blood, because other members of the family had written works dealing with the causes of discontent and the unfair treatment of Irish Catholics under English rule.

He first stood for election in the strictly Conservative stronghold of Co. Dublin, but was defeated. When a vacancy occurred in the more nationalistic constituency of County Meath in 1875 the people rallied behind him and he headed the poll, securing twice as many votes as his nearest rival. He made a telling point in his maiden speech in Westminster: "Why should Ireland be treated as a geographical fragment of England? ... Ireland was not a geographical fragment, but a nation".[3] This underlines his intense desire for justice, and of redressing the anomaly of having Ireland, systematically impoverished through legislation for centuries, welded under the Act of Union to a rapacious England. Meath had opened the door to a man who was to prove himself truly worthy of the fullest support of all who strove for reform.

At Westminster he witnessed for himself Parliament's offhand treatment – so very predictable – of Irish affairs; its members showed a total indifference, if not ignorance, whenever subjects pertaining to Ireland were being debated. By the time parliament dispersed at the 1877 recess, for example, fifteen Irish bills were proposed, but not a single one had been passed into law. Parnell responded to this apathy in a very effective way – he adopted a policy of showing an inordinate interest in English affairs – it was a policy of obstruction, aimed at consuming parliament's time by speaking interminably on matters that were of little or no consequence.

He and his colleagues on occasions kept the House sitting continuously for as long as 45 hours in a process of filibustering on subjects that were irrelevant to Ireland. The English MPs did not take kindly to being deprived of their sleep by the representatives from Ireland, but Parnell let his sentiments be known: "I care nothing for this English parliament, nor for its outcries. I care nothing for its existence, if that existence is to continue a source of tyranny and destruction to my country". He had something akin to Fenian fire in his belly, and he was speaking the mind of the common man back home.

Sadly, the Irish MPs at Westminster held disparate views on how best to achieve legislative independence, and some were constantly at loggerheads with Parnell. Even the other champion of land reform, Michael Davitt, was at odds with him on occasions. Parnell ceased speaking at county meetings in Ireland for two years, but an exception was made in Drogheda in 1884 at which he criticised Davitt's solution which was to nationalise the land, and in addition Parnell poured scorn on the naive suggestion that Ireland should team up with English 'democracy'. 'The poor Irish will have, I fear, to rely upon themselves in the future, as they have had to do up to this moment,'[4] he said. He had had enough of English 'democracy' already.

Laurence Gate

as seen from the Cord Road (1898)

The Home Rule Bills: The late 1880s saw several successive bad harvests, bringing famine to the land once more, and once more tenants were evicted in their thousands. Concessions were eventually wrung from the government under pressure. An air of optimism became apparent when the Parliamentary Party held the balance of power at Westminster.

A few days prior to the introduction of the Home Rule Bill, Waterford Corporation issued to Prime Minister Gladstone a communication which had originated in Drogheda. It was a copy of the celebrated letter which Drogheda Corporation had written to King George III 86 years earlier urging him against passing the proposed Act of Union in 1800 (reproduced in Chapter Twenty). Waterford Corporation had requisitioned a copy of the letter, and it was now countersigned by their council members, because that Petition, so succinct in its argument and so trenchant in its expressiveness, would surely win the day and persuade the legislators to grant Ireland a separate parliament, and to celebrate the Bill's anticipated successful passage through Westminster, a Banquet was held in Waterford prior to the council members travelling to London with their tails wagging in gleeful expectation, but a constipated House of Commons declined to pass it! It was back to square one.

Parnell was one of the initial shareholders of the *Drogheda Independent,* and was offered a directorship but was unable to accept that role owing to his many other commitments. (His shareholding later passed to Kitty O'Shea). However, he was a regular contributor to the columns of the newspaper. An indication of his burning idealism is the fact that he refused to accept from the Corporation the Freedom of Drogheda until he could

The Cook Family

Tenants evicted by the Fosters – Collon 1896

receive it from a Nationalist Mayor. This came to pass in 1884 when Casey Connolly was elected Mayor. The occasion was followed by a banquet in the Mayoralty House when 400 joined in the celebrations. It was not the first time that this honour was bestowed on a Parnell – his ancestor the Rt. Hon. Sir John Parnell, who served in Grattan's Parliament and replaced John Foster as Chancellor of the Exchequer, had been given this honour in 1787.

His popularity rose to new heights following the exposure of the Pigott Forgeries. His letter condoning the assassination of two important politicians in the Phoenix Park was published in *The Times*. The purpose was to discredit Parnell. In the subsequent trial the correspondence was sensationally exposed as being bogus and his signature as a forgery, and the climax of the episode was reached when the perpetrator, who was a Meathman named Pigott, shot himself.

Parnell travelled extensively in America, securing substantial sums to aid evicted farmers and the other causes he espoused. Under his dynamism the cherished dream of Home Rule was still being pursued, and unity of purpose among the Irish members at Westminster would surely win the day. However, constant infighting and dissention bedevilled real progress.

The disarray escalated into open hostility when the Kitty O'Shea affair entered the public domain. Many followers including the Catholic clergy, bishops, archbishops *et al* clamoured to topple him. Support from Drogheda was split; a portion greeting him at the railway station with several bands when he arrived to rally support in 1891.

However, worn out by attending public meetings often in pouring rain, by constant travelling, by a vile press and by endless harassment from fellow Irishmen, his health gave out, and at the early age of 45, in the arms of his beloved bride of five months, there cracked a noble heart.

James Joyce was an ardent admirer of Parnell and perhaps he had this tragic turn of events in mind when he penned the observation, unpalatable as it is, that Ireland 'is an old sow that eats its own farrow'.

THE 'TURN OF THE CENTURY': The curious and rather lyrical term 'the turn of the century' was widely used to indicate the passing from the Nineteenth into the Twentieth Century. The world was in transition from the pedestrian pace of the donkey and cart into that of the automobile and, soon afterwards, to the aeroplane, and who knows what other inventions might follow in the decades ahead.

Let us now visualise the living conditions of the people when Drogheda was at the threshold of the Twentieth Century. The shop assistants – whatever their age – are called 'shop-boys' (in parallel with farm hands on the American prairies who were called 'cowboys'). They are men who had joined the staff as teenagers having left school at 12 or 13 and 'served their time' for perhaps four or five years for a pittance of a wage (perhaps starting at €0.32 per week or less as in the case of John Boyle O'Reilly). They are easily identified by their khaki dustcoats stretching to the knees.

Many shops remain open until 9 pm or 10 pm which makes it a long working day for the 'shop-boy', but at least he has Sunday free; his wage permits no entertainment more extravagant than 'a walk round the Obelisk' on the one day of rest. If he maintains a record of being scrupulously honest and proves himself diligent in every possible way, his loyalty may be rewarded by being retained until old age catches up – most staff cherish this ambition and entertain the hope that, unless they blot their copybook, their own eldest boy may have the good fortune to be selected to join the firm under the same conditions of employment.

A feature of the shops in the principal streets is that they habitually display their wares outside their doors. The first duty of the 'shop-boy' each morning is to place a selection of wares at the entrance; shoes and hob-nailed boots are attached to a pole that leans against the front window; the hardware merchant places a row of galvanised iron buckets, shovels and other farming instruments along the footpath at his frontage; the corn merchant leans an array of sacks of seed-corn against the window; the frontage of the butcher's shop is completely open – no glass window – and the exposed carcasses of mutton and beef are suspended from hooks along the shop front to attract the dust as well as myriads of flies, but the word 'hygiene' is unknown; the kerb opposite the publican's premises is occupied by a row of empty barrels – these are wooden beer barrels that had been shaped by the skilful hands of coopers of which Drogheda has several. (The 'iron lung' is fifty years into the future).

The era of the multiple chain stores is still 80 years away, and the shops in West St. are family businesses, and the families live on the premises – even bank managers reside overhead. An exception is Tylers (footwear merchants) which, along with R.B. Daly (auctioneers), Martin Butterly (coal merchants) and the Drogheda Independent (newspaper publishers), will have the distinction of being that little handful of enterprises that will see out the Twentieth Century that lies ahead.

Most of the side streets of the town feature hucksters' shops. These are private homes of which the front parlours, small as they are, have been converted into shops, and are used to stock groceries and everything else from a needle to a ball of wool. Hucksters are the lifeline of the community because they dispense provisions in minimal quantities, (say) one cigarette or a single egg for the man of the house; a brass weighing scales sits on the counter for doling out tea by the ounce, or a quarter lb. of margarine, etc. Many people live quite literally from hand to mouth because the humble homes of Drogheda lack the wherewithal to purchase items in larger quantities. Records of purchases are entered in little jotters, and accounts are settled on Saturday which is the universal payday. Where there is no wage-earner in a family, survival is a daily challenge.

The town hosts several pawn shops; they provide short-term credit facilities. Granddad's fiddle went there years ago and will never be redeemed; personal items now form part of a weekly routine – suits, overcoats and other personal possessions that had been handed in on Monday are redeemed on Saturday to enable the owners wear them to Mass on Sunday. Monday morning again sees long queues outside the pawn shops when the clothing is being returned as pledges for a half-crown (€0.16) to enable the owner struggle along for another few days. This routine is perpetual. People are not embarrassed to be seen near a pawn shop – this is simply part of the everyday scene, and frequenting a pawn shop is as commonplace for many households as attending Mass on Sunday.

The Whitworth Monument, originally erected at the foot of Peter St., was caringly transported six years ago, stone by stone, to a new site at the Mall where it continues to honour Drogheda's great benefactor. Its dual fountains dispense water to all who need to slake their thirst; horses and cattle are catered for at the trough at the foot of Mary St.

There are several wells and water pumps throughout the town, and drawing water is a daily chore because most homes have no running water. Neither have they flush toilets. The luxury of running water and flush toilets is unknown to most of 'the lower classes'. (A veteran recalled: "We got a flush toilet in 1933 and we thought we were in heaven"). They use a privy, a wooden or corrugated iron shack housing a bucket surmounted by a plank which constitutes the seat – it is located in the back yard (that is, if they have a back yard); the less fortunate homes use a chamber pot which is kept in the bedroom. 'Slopping-out' takes place as conditions dictate, but this chore can be curtailed if bladders are emptied individually in the garden; the solids (called 'night soil' in horticultural circles) are then dumped in the garden, a separate pit being used each time. In the course of time this will be the source of a splendid crop of floury potatoes.

It is a different matter for those who have no back yard or garden – some households simply deposit the contents outside at the kerb, and it will be shovelled by Corporation workmen[5] into an open cart which will then trundle along with its dripping contents to the town dump which is sited where, in the late 'Thirties, a much needed Corporation housing estate called Pearse Park will rise up.[6] The town dump will then be moved to the slob-lands along the Mornington Road.

Apart from those in the main streets, many of the homes of 'the lower classes' (a phrase in general use) are abject, mud-walled cabins and miserable hovels comprising of merely of two rooms, or perhaps just a single room. Even many of the more recently constructed cottages consist of simply two rooms. Furniture is of the most basic kind since there is no 'disposable income' (a phrase not in general use at this time) for spending in that direction; a bed is often a palliasse (this is a mattress filled with straw or chaff) and is spread on the floor. The floor is beaten earth – there is no covering of any kind. Because families are large, sleeping accommodation allows little privacy, the boys being separated from their female siblings by means of a makeshift curtain of sacking suspended across the room, while the parents sleep close to the open fireplace in the kitchen/living room.

Living Conditions: The quality of life for the underprivileged in these conditions is truly pathetic, and life expectancy is short. The island's population as a whole had continued to rise during the first half of the 1800s until it was brought to a sudden halt in the years of the Famine, following which it plunged dramatically. Drogheda was different. The town's population, as we have seen, had peaked at about 20,000 when the Act of Union was passed in 1800, and the decline began straight away – this was largely due to the collapse of the linen industry which brought untold distress. On the eve of the Great Famine it had fallen to about 15,000 and it continued to fall, and now stands at about 12,000 – **a catastrophic fall of almost 40% over the century.**

Serious as the population decline is, the ratio of Roman Catholics to the other Christian religions has actually increased from 90.5% in 1861 to 92.4% in 1891, the inference being that the Protestant section of the population has fallen by 35% in the course of 30 years (albeit from a narrow base).[7]

The terms 'tuberculosis' and 'TB' are not in use, but the disease itself is rampant – it is called 'consumption', and all too often one hears another current phrase 'He/she died of decline'. This killer disease finds easy prey within the dark, damp conditions of Drogheda's many hovels, and it seems to take particular delight in claiming the lives of handsome youths and lassies. It sometimes sweeps away entire families in a matter of a few years. 'I remember a house where three coffins were taken out within a week or so'.[8] To enter the Workhouse is the ultimate in degradation, but TB patients occasionally are obliged to seek refuge there (the district hospital) where 'St. Theresa's Ward' is set aside for victims of consumption, and it is permanently full of patients coughing away their final days. The town's hospital is in the Workhouse, but many invalids are tended in their homes by the local communities of nuns who are dedicated to visiting them when their daily work in the classrooms is finished.

The medical needs of the population are served by just four general practitioners, and they are named in a popular piece of local doggerel:

'I have a pain in me belly, says Doctor Kelly.
Rub it with oil, says Doctor Boyle.
I have a hump like a camel, says Doctor Hamill'.
[The other doctor's name is Parr.]

Most children are provided with footwear in wintertime, but in the summer they attend school barefooted. They all wear happy faces, and boredom is unknown to them because they make their own fun, the girls with hop-scotch on the pavement or skipping with a length of discarded rope, and the boys play marbles and spin tops. "The tops were turned by Mick Noonan of Newfoundwell on a lathe in his home, and we got the steel spikes off Gull Tiernan, a fitter in the Boyne Mills. The spikes came from the nose of discarded wooden shuttles which, after many years of usage the wooden part would be worn out, and the spikes came in handy for tops. The chant was 'Gloss the length of my lace, and tally hokers'. Gloss was the name of the game and the lace or twine was wound around the top which was then flicked away to generate the spin; 'tally hokers' was the punishment inflicted on the loser – his top was split by the winner".[9] The footballs are made from the bladders of cattle (obtained in the abattoirs). "They wouldn't burst when you kicked them because you were in your bare feet". Old bicycle wheels and tyres serve as excellent hoops – they are propelled with a stick. On summer days some boys are off to the countryside adding to their collections of birds' eggs. "I was mitching from school one day in Beaulieu Wood and I saw some fellows eating blackbirds. They'd put them in yellow clay, and when they were baked the clay and the feathers would fall off neatly".[10]

A special treat is to take a trip on the pleasure boat from the tideway at Oldbridge along the Boyne Canal to Navan, passing some spectacular scenery akin to the Canadian Rockies on the way. The return journey is by rail or charabanc, and the fare (inclusive of the initial jarvey trip to Oldbridge) is 4 shillings (€0.25).

The quays on the South side of the Boyne
They contained several important industries, including a brewery and a chemical manure factory, the latter giving employment to 200 workers. There was also a shipyard, the town's gas works and a textile factory nearby. Smoke belching from chimneys seems to have been a status symbol. Retail shopping outlets now occupy most of these quays.

Trade and Commerce: The Boyne Mills and Robert Usher produce textiles which are exported to destinations as far apart as New York and Bombay, which is akin to taking coals to Newcastle. The work provides employment for many hundreds of mill girls. Some are only 12 or 13 years old and ought properly to be attending school. They are called 'part time workers' and the authorities turn a blind eye at them if they attend school in the afternoons; their contribution to the family budget, miniscule though it is, is the salvation for many a household. The other workers face a 12 hour day at the looms, with a short break for breakfast at 8 am and another one at 1 pm.

Cattle, sheep and pigs arrive at the railway station from fairs throughout the Midlands and are herded through James St., over St. Mary's Bridge and down the quays where they are held in stockades until sailing time. The scenes are reminiscent of the Wild West and are enacted several times a week. The livestock is destined for export on the paddle steamers that are berthed at Steampacket Quay. These ships and many sailing boats discharge their cargos of beams of cotton yarn (like giant spools of cotton thread) for delivery to the mills, as well as coal and sundry manufactured goods.

The celebrated Cairnes Ale is known internationally and is shipped across the Atlantic, the mills despatch great bales of *dhooties* which are worn by the coolies of India; also consignments of flour and famous pin-head meal from McCann and Hill and Morton's Mill. Like the females in the textile mills, the men's working day commences at 6 am and continues until 6 pm and they are the envy of all the neighbours because they have a secure job until their retirement at about 72 – or until they drop.

* * * *

A BRAVE NEW WORLD: Drogheda was more fortunate than most other towns at the cross-over into the Twentieth Century. It had escaped much of the agrarian distress associated with the Land War of the previous quarter century, and evictions in the area were much fewer. It enjoyed the reputation of being an industrial town and was the home to a variety of industries, although this did not fully eliminate the endemic problem of unemployment, especially among the male population.

Its status had been enhanced by the construction of some fine municipal buildings as well as private homes for upper class families during the opulent times of the 1700s. The harrowing decades of the 1800s brought stagnation, but the economy began to improve towards the end of that century. This is reflected in the unprecedented attention being given to the housing needs of the labouring classes. The year 1898 alone saw 26 working class houses being constructed in Patrick St., 24 in the Windmill Road and a further dozen in Scarlet St. and Francis St. Rows of cottages had also been built through the munificence of the Cairnes Trust, the architect being P.J. Dodd. The Cairnes Trust was responsible for constructing a total of 54 houses, including those at St. Mark's Terrace, Clinton's Lane and the Green Lanes. These statistics are laughable by today's standards of house construction, but they were an enormous break-through at the time. Fine terraces for the professional class were also being built, such as the red-bricked Albany Terrace in William Street; and tumble-down buildings in West St. and Dyer St. were being replaced with tall, sturdy structures.

The needs of the faithful of the Roman Catholic persuasion were catered for with the construction of St. Peter's and St. Mary's parish churches as well as those of the Augustinian and Dominican orders. All of these superb structures were completed within a time span of only 30 years, the last one being St. Mary's in James St. in 1892. The raising of funds for these costly projects imposed a heavy financial burden on the populace and this in itself is indicative of the town's emergence from the depressed times experienced in the earlier part of the 1800s. At the century's end Drogheda was entering a brave new world.

The captains of trade and industry had recently formed the Drogheda Chamber of Commerce (1894) to direct the town's business affairs, but there was a perennial scarcity of jobs for the male population. Idle men congregated by the dozen at street corners where they stood day after day after day without any prospect of work. Virtually all of them were unskilled. Others, to escape the hopelessness that surrounds them, enlisted in the armed services of Her Majesty Queen Victoria; they embarked for South Africa to fight the Boers, or for some other part of the far flung Empire quelling the restless natives.

There were 'restless natives' at home, too, but they counted for nothing and could safely be ignored. They could be ignored because the 'Uncrowned King of Ireland', Parnell, was dead, and the country was without leadership. Agitation at local level for Home Rule had abated and the people of the area were complacent. After all, Drogheda had ever been a town secure within the Pale and, with the 'Pale mentality' being dominant, the inhabitants seldom showed that spirit of assertiveness for independence associated with the south, and they were imbued not with anything resembling virulent nationalism.

Unfinished Business: Where did all this leave Daniel O'Connell's unfulfilled dream of Repeal? Since the death of Parnell the objective of Home Rule seemed further away than ever owing mainly to an unsympathetic House of Lords and its repeated use of the veto. Furthermore, the town had lapsed into a state of complacency, and was resigned to permanently hosting an army of occupation in its midst, with the Union Jack still fluttering from the flagpole at Millmount.

The vast majority treated this matter with total indifference, although it was an issue that continued to rankle with a few die-hards who still considered Ireland to be, as Parnell had defiantly told the House of Commons, 'a separate Nation'. This handful of idealists perceived that negotiating with Westminster was utterly futile, and their resolute conviction was that only through armed revolt could the stranglehold of the Act of Union be loosened. *Sinn scéal eile.*

PART 5

THE TWENTIETH CENTURY

To ask some of 'the present generation' a few questions about conditions in Drogheda during the first half of the Twentieth Century may cause disappointment – most of them have a dearth of knowledge about that era. The garrison of British soldiers at Millmount, the depredations of the Black and Tans, the Civil War, the lifestyle of the people – most of the younger folk are not conversant about these and other such subjects. We cannot blame them for this because they have grown up, for the most part, in an age of peace and plenty, and topics such as abject poverty, British rule, the Black and Tans and the War of Independence are now beyond the experiences even of their grandfathers.

I must confess that in my own boyhood days I was equally vague about those turbulent times, although my elders had lived through them and had often made reference to them. I had vaguely bracketed the year 1921 with 1922. These years were collectively called '*the Troubles*'. In my own mind they were indistinguishable, but subsequent enlightenment revealed the deep chasm that separated these two periods, as well as the umbilical connection that joined them – the War of Independence and the Civil War. Collectively, they formed a defining moment in the history of our green island; that was a time when the nation was suffering birth pains and when, to quote Yeats's forceful oxymoron, 'a terrible beauty was born'.

The scene in Drogheda in the first score years of the Twentieth Century was one that was influenced – indeed completely overridden – by British occupation. The townspeople did not need to see red letterboxes or to hear '*God Save the King*' being played at the end of a concert to be reminded of that fact. The local newspapers contained scant news of local interest. News items emanated mainly from London, and the people were indoctrinated with newspaper reports on debates taking place in the Imperial Parliament at Westminster and with events that occurred in various corners of the British Empire which at that time was at its zenith.

Most manufactured goods were shipped into Ireland from England because Irish industries were few – breweries and distilleries always being the exception. Clothing and footwear, hardware and kitchen utensils, motor vehicles and farm machinery, these and most other manufactured goods were being imported because for centuries Irish manufacture was unable to compete with the industrial might of England.

A large wall-map in every schoolroom depicted '*The British Isles*'. Another map displayed prominently a world that was dominated by one particular colour – red. The school atlases presented the same message. Great landmasses such as Canada, Australia, India and South Africa were coloured red on the map; so were a myriad of disparate islands such as Jamaica, Trinidad, Ceylon, Cyprus and New Zealand. The significance of the colour was to proclaim that together they formed the British Empire. *One of these islands shown fully in red was IRELAND.*

Why were letterboxes painted *red?* Why were images of *Queen Victoria* and later *King George V* on the postage stamps? Why was there a garrison of soldiers – of *British* soldiers – stationed in Millmount Barracks? Why were emaciated children setting off to school in bare feet and with empty stomachs? Why so much *poverty?* At the conclusion of a concert in the Whitworth Hall why did the audience stand to attention to the strains of the anthem '*God Save the King*'?

The reason is not hard to find. We have now come to an era of Drogheda's development of which 'the present generation' is, at best, indifferent. That era is light years away from the scene today in the bustling town by the Boyne where there is close to full employment, family cars, nightclubs, well-nourished children, as well as supermarkets laden with luxuries that arrive from every corner of the globe.

No excuse will be accepted if to-day's generation fails to record current happenings for the edification of posterity because we have the benefit of such modern appliances as tape recorders, cameras and camcorders to facilitate the work of recording and storing current events. Besides, we live in a more tolerant age and are at liberty to speak our minds without the risk of being clapped in irons – as many were – and being banished to the penal colony at Fremantle or Van Diemen's Land.

Eyewitness accounts are best. With that in mind this author set himself the task of capturing first-hand the impressions and the experiences of some of Drogheda's oldest citizens, and they now provide us with a glimpse of the town as it was in their childhood and youth. Some of the events they have recalled were mundane, everyday experiences, and were not in themselves of sufficient moment to reach the pages of the school history book. Nonetheless, they constitute part of the overall circumstances that depicted the quality of life in the early part of the century that is now behind us. Within their lifespan there occurred the most fundamental changes in the history of Mankind, ranging from the first flight of a heavier-than-air flying machine to walks on the Moon and the marvels emanating from the microchip and the computer.

That period was also the most momentous one in Drogheda's – and Ireland's – history when, like a butterfly emerging from a lengthy metamorphic state, the nation was at last entering into bright sunlight and freedom. Tragically, the sunlight was suffused by the dark thunderstorm of civil war, an event that forms a core part of our history.

'History in the Making': The remaining pages of this book constitute 'history in the making', aimed to record *live,* everyday scenes, scenes that include some momentous episodes that were seminal to the Nation's birth as experienced *by those who witnessed history as it was happening,* and before it faded into the nebulous mist of legend. It is therefore based neither on the discoveries of archaeologists nor on historical records, but on the recollections, experiences and 'verbal snapshots' of our own contemporaries, people who have recounted scenes of life in Drogheda a century ago. These were everyday folk describing both everyday events and some occurrences that were central to the nation's history. This is as near as we can get to *live, contemporary history,* to coin a phrase.

To have been taken on 'a memory tour' by contemporaries who lived in the early decades of the last century is an experience that is akin to peering through a powerful telescope and seeing life on a distant planet. We have since passed into, not only a new century and a new millennium, but also from the era of the pony and trap into that of space travel. These 'memory tours' were conducted by Drogheda veterans who actually saw the British soldiers when they were garrisoned at Millmount, who heard the sound of the bugle every morning and night, who waved good-bye when many young men of twenty marched away to the killing fields of France, and when young ladies knitted socks and prepared bandages to be sent to them in the trenches of the Great War. Such anecdotal tit-bits are not found in hidebound tomes or musty archives, but nonetheless they constitute some of the pieces in the jig-saw which, when positioned into their proper places, form a more complete picture of the town's eventful past, affording us an authentic glimpse of the human, everyday side of life in the Drogheda of yesteryear – the Drogheda that never again will be.

Chapter Thirtytwo

Drogheda in the Early 1900s

THE MILITARY PRESENCE: The bugle call that sounded in Millmount Barracks was a familiar sound in earlier times to the ears of the populace of Drogheda. Even though we have now moved into a new millennium there were still a few survivors who vividly remembered it. The sound of the bugle was part and parcel of everyday life in Drogheda. Its resonant notes were heard morning and night – Reveille, Last Post and Lights Out – and the routine continued until 1922 when the soldiers of the newborn Irish Free State replaced the British forces at Millmount.

In its day the bugle-call resonated over the roof-tops of the town and it re-echoed over the surrounding suburbs – not that the townspeople needed a reminder that a garrison of Crown forces was in occupation. The military parades, the unfamiliar accents, the martial bands, the bugle calls, the army uniforms, the playing of *'God Save the King'*, all these were indications of the military presence and of occupation by a foreign power. They were an everyday experience.

A Drogheda-born veteran who survived into the Twenty-first Century well remembered those early years of the twentieth century; he lived during his childhood days at the Nuns Walk, close to the Cord Cemetery. Nearby was a green patch where he was wont to play with the neighbouring children on summer evenings. When in his nineties he was able to recall:-

> *"You could see across to the Cup and Saucer [Millmount]. At nine o'clock [in the evening] you could see the bugler. He'd come out and he'd parade round and he'd blow the bugle. Then mother would come out. 'Come on, children, it's time to go to bed. There's the Last Post – it's nine o'clock. All hands to bed'. It was getting late and we weren't allowed to play any more. By the time Lights Out was sounded at ten we were all asleep in bed. I don't remember Reveille because at that hour of the morning we'd be still in bed asleep. We were only five or six years old. Reveille was sounded each morning at seven o'clock. It went like this [miming a bugle call]: 'Get out of bed – get out of bed, you lazy boy. Get out of bed'. The bugle call was heard all over the town"* (JQ).

Being a garrison town, the populace were well used to the presence of Crown forces in their midst. Not so familiar were some of the accents of the soldiers who occupied the barracks – they may have been from an English, Scottish or Welsh regiment. Irish regiments, too, were occasionally stationed in Millmount.

> *"Before the 'Munsters' there was the 'Leinsters'. When they were disbanded, one of them remained in the town and married a Drogheda girl. He had been a bugler in the 'Leinsters' and so he became a member of the local Brass and Reed Band. His name was Condron. When the regiment was disbanded he was made a present of the silver cornet, which was a rare gesture in those days. There was a special press in the corner [of the band's premises on Georges Square] and his cornet was put in it, and he kept the key. I was a member of the band at the time – I was only a learner – I played the cornet and the tenor horn. When the 'Leinsters' were disbanded the instruments of the orchestra were auctioned, and I remember our local band bought two drums, and I think one of those drums is still above in the band room – a bass drum"*(JQ).

It is impossible to quantify the impact made on Drogheda by the military presence. Flirtations between the soldiery and the local girls was as inevitable as night follows day. No doubt this sometimes blossomed into marriage, with the soldiers remaining to become part of the local citizenry – some non-Irish surnames in the town today have originated that way – not to mention other entanglements that prompted a hasty departure under a cloud.

"Sometimes they were left in the lurch – the soldiers went away and never came back".[1] Even an occasional Black and Tan in later times remained to become integrated into the local community – not all of them were ruffians.

The economy of the town – especially as it affected the publicans – certainly benefited from the presence of a garrison. At the time of the disbandment of the Louth Rifles in 1908 it was estimated that their presence in Dundalk was worth £5,000 per annum to the shopkeepers, and the loss in circulation of that money was a matter of concern to all. The Chamber of Commerce sent a deputation to the military authorities in an endeavour to extend the regiment's tenure, but this proved fruitless.

The military presence in the early years of the last century was remembered by a Drogheda man who lived to celebrate the new Millennium:

"I remember Millmount when the soldiers were there. When I was about seven years old I used to be sent out with a nurse to go for a walk; she used always bring me home by James Street where the soldiers from Millmount – the Munster Rifles – used to go to ten o'clock Mass [in Saint Mary's Church]. And after Mass they lined up in the street and formed fours, and they had a band and all the girls of the town went with them. The band played for an hour in the square and all the girls waltzed around – hundreds of them. Those that came to Drogheda after the Munsters were not so popular – there was no dancing with them. When the war started [the Great War] the Munsters were sent to France – Mons – and they were practically all wiped out; there is a monument. When the British retreated they stayed back to hold up the Germans – it was at an orchard – and they were all killed"(MC).

"You would hear the bugle, and the flag [the Union Jack] would be flying. Soldiers used to parade to 11.30 Mass, down Mary Street and into James Street. Father Norris used to organise it – he was the Chaplain. One garrison was the Cornwalls (Welsh); there was always trouble with them; they were nasty boys – insulting – especially when they had drink. They were here at the time of the Black and Tans"(DF).

A humorous incident occurred which tells us of the fraternising that invariably took place between the soldiers and the local girls. The Ramparts was a favourite lovers' lane where the couples regularly took a walk, and one rascally Droghedean decided to play a practical joke on them:

"There was a fellow named Mullen; he was an apprentice butcher in Smith's of West Street. He joined the army and became a bugler. One time he had been home on leave. Well, the girls were going up the Ramparts with their soldier friends. Through his connections with the butchers, Mullen went one evening into the slaughter-house yard bringing his bugle with him. And he sounded the Last Post. Well, when the soldiers heard that they all had to scurry back to the barracks" (JQ).

Thus their amorous perambulations came to an untimely end! This little story has a sad ending; the narrator concluded that the poor fellow with all his merriment and pranks later sailed for France, only to be numbered in the carnage of the trenches during the Great War. His grave is somewhere in Belgium.[2] Several soldiers from the garrison died of natural causes during peace times in Drogheda. "I remember a few soldiers' funerals. The band played Saul's Dead March: 'dum, dum, de-dum'; it would take them an age to go up the Poorhouse Lane, and they were buried in Bully's Acre".[3]

Many local soldiers ended up in pitiful circumstances when they were discharged from the army, because there was no gainful employment for them in Drogheda. The author recalls seeing one such character in Camden Street, Dublin during the early 1950s who was a regular busker on the street. Alcoholism was written across his face, but when he put the bugle to his lips the golden notes sounded as if they were played by the Angel Gabriel. Such men were expert buglers, but there were few to appreciate their talent. They formed part of the flotsam that was beached after the Great War. "There was another fella, named C------ who lived at the bottom of Mary Street. He was an official bugler in the army, and was

WEST ST. in the early 1900s

engaged to sound the Last Post. He finished up on the streets of Dublin busking – playing the bugle and trying to earn a living" (JQ).

LIVING CONDITIONS IN THE EARLY 1900s: At the outset of a discussion on living conditions, it must be stated that social benefits were virtually non-existent. A great leap forward was the provision of a pension to the elderly. When the Old Age Pension was introduced in 1908 a weekly sum was 5 shillings (€0.32) was given to persons who had attained the age of 72 years.

Sanitation: Until 1865 Drogheda had no municipal water supply. Women and children queued for hours to draw pails of water from wells and a few inadequate pumps. In 1860 there had been a cry for 'a proper supply of wholesome water', but the Corporation did nothing about it. An editorial in the local newspaper, *the Conservative*, stated:

> *'The dirt and squalor that exists is fearful, and the contagious effluvia proceeding from unsightly hovels that everywhere meets the eye is most disgusting. We can hardly be surprised that when pestilence stalks abroad, death should revel here triumphant in 1832 and 1849. During those direful years the havoc committed by cholera in Drogheda was far greater than in any other town in Ireland. ... So long as utter indifference is manifested in those matters, so long will Drogheda be a disgrace and a byword'.*

The townspeople were greatly indebted to Benjamin Whitworth who stepped forward to provide the solution. Largely from his own personal resources he provided the town with wholesome, running water which was sourced at a new reservoir at Killineer. He also built the Town Hall which he presented to the townspeople. His textile factory at Greenhills provided 800 females with employment for generations, until it finally closed in the 1970s.

The luxury of domestic tap water took many years to reach the small cottages of the town. By about 1930 taps were being provided in the terraces of Magdalene St.; they were not installed in the kitchens, but in the back yards. Prior to that, families were relying on wells and public pumps. As for flush toilets, that era still lay ahead, as these reminiscences demonstrate:

• "*There was a pump across the road [in Magdalene St.], and my brothers would go over with a bucket. If my mother was washing, they would have to go over a few times. The houses had dry toilets in the yard, and the ashes from the fire would also be thrown into them. On Thursday night Dad and my brother would shovel the contents into a container, carry it through the house and dump it at the kerb down the street. This sounds disgusting today, but we knew nothing else. The Corporation men would come the next day with a horse and cart and shovel it on to an open cart*"(BT).

296

•	*"There were no flush toilets in Dooley Gate. We sat on a board with a hole in it and the bucket was underneath. It was in a small shed of corrugated iron in the yard, and my father would dig a hole in the garden and dispose of the contents that way. There was a pump at the end of Priest Lane – that is the only pump I remember, but I'd go to Patrick's Well in the Dale for water – it was ice cold"(PM).*

•	*"Along Trinity St. there were no flush toilets in the houses on the left hand side. Our house, which was opposite McCrumish's pub, had a flight of steps at the back leading down to a little privy that extended over the river and what you did was flushed by the passing tide. It was like that up to 1956 when I left. There was a tap in the kitchen, but no sink. So I broke a hole in the wall to let the water run outside through a pipe, and I got a solicitor's letter complaining that I had damaged the wall. There was a gas mantle over the mantelpiece. The houses in Greenhills were the same – the buckets of sewage would be left in the passageways between the houses for collection by the Corporation"(PB).*

•	*"There was a shed at the bottom of the garden. You left the bucket outside once a week and the Corporation came and collected it. They had specially built carts, banana-shaped and made of wood; no matter which way it wobbled, it wouldn't spill anything"(PF).*

•	*"Francis St. was all dry toilets. I remember the wet toilets going in about 60 years ago [in the late 1930s]. You'd use a bucket and peg the ashes in on top of it, and the Corporation would take it away about once a week"(KF).*

•	*"You emptied your ashes at the side of the street, and they'd come along and shovel it on to a cart. The town dump was where Pearse Park is now. It occupied the area between Crushrod Lane and Hardman's Gardens. When they built the houses in Pearse Park in the mid 'Thirties the dump moved to the sloblands along the Marsh Road where Flogas was later built. They'd occasionally set fire to the refuse; it would burn for days and when the wind was from the east the town would be smothered with the smoke and the smell"(JM).*

•	*"The borough boundary was at the 'Navan Bridge', so we were outside the town limits [at the Black Bull]. The privy was at the far end of the garden; there was a white enamel bucket in it, and every night there'd be a hole made in the garden and the contents would be emptied into it. We kept a bag of lime and we'd scatter it over it. Others would manure the garden with it. We got flush toilets when I was ten [viz. 1933] and we thought we were in heaven"* (CM).

•	*"The Dale contained a small mill called Fagan's Mill and about a dozen cabins of the most pitiable description. They had no back door – just a room and a kitchen in each, and some of them had eight or ten in the family. A public toilet served the twelve or thirteen families. There was a cement floor in it and two holes in the ground with a division between the two compartments (DF)". In reply to a query from the author: "I suppose one compartment was for ladies and the other for gents?", the interviewee replied as follows: "No, you took your choice – or whichever one was empty. There was no seat, just a hole in the floor – you backed in and put your feet in the loops. If you were a bad shot you got it on your heels! The women used to use a bucket and then throw it into the stream [the Dale Brook or Dubh]. Maybe you'd be goin' to Mass, and if they didn't see you comin' – swooosh! – across the footpath, and you'd be trudgin' through it in your good Sunday suit"(DF.)*

•	*"West Street was always very dusty, fierce dusty. The streets would be watered by the Corporation to keep the dust down. There was a big tank of water on a cart pulled by a horse. And a big perforated pipe the full width of the cart and extending round the corners. The urchins of the day would follow these carts in their bare feet enjoying the novelty of water and mud squeezing through their toes. Another cart would follow with four strong spikes, the depths of which could be adjusted – this would scarify and rip up the surface. A steamroller would then arrive and compact the material into the ground. Another task was to collect surplus mud in a cart; it would be taken to Hungry Hall [opposite the present bus depot] and tipped into the quarry"(DM).*

•	*"The Corporation used to keep a heap of stones at the bottom of Mary Street where the cenotaph is now. It was to fill the potholes – they would roll them in with a steamroller – there was no tarmacadam then"(DF).*

• *"The local TD James Murphy continually pressed for the surfacing of West Street with concrete. When this was finally achieved the cynics contended that he had been pressing for this simply because his business premises were in that street – this was in the 1920s"(DM).*

HOUSING: There was but little improvement since the 1800s to accommodate Drogheda's poor, and conditions throughout the rest of Ireland were no different. The employees of Cairnes Brewery, however, were well looked after, with several terraces of sturdy cottages being built in selected area of the town for them. For most others, a two-roomed cabin was the norm, notwithstanding the size of some families.

• *"There were five cottages in our row [a terrace that joined the west side of Magdalene St.] They had just two rooms and no upstairs. Our family consisted of three boys and two girls and Mam and Dad. They slept in one room and we, the children, slept in the other one, with a curtain separating the boys from the girls".*[4]

• *"We lived in a two-roomed cottage; one room and a kitchen, that's all there was in it. It was in Duleek St. – that's a grand name for it – in my day it was 'Dooley Gate', and every Saturday night there would be fights among the men coming out of Samson's pub and the Barber Callans. There were nine of us in all, four boys and three gerrils plus our parents. Father and Mother slept in the kitchen beside the fire. We slept in the other room. A curtain was pulled across the centre, dividing the boys from the gerrils. At the back there was a small garden and a cobble-stone yard. My mother kept pigs in the yard, two bonhams, which she'd buy from a red-faced man from Dunleer."*[5]

• *"The family opposite us kept pigs – they were kept in the yard, not the house. The boys and girls would go round the houses collecting slops. You didn't throw anything out, you put it in the slop bucket and that was all collected for the pigs."*[6]

• *"There was no back entrance, so they used to bring them out through the house to take them away. And the roars of the pigs coming out! You'd think they were murdering them!" (JS)*

• *"A lot of people kept hens, and at dawn every morning you'd hear the cockerel crowing – it was heard all over the town. My mother would save the scraps and potato skins for a neighbour who kept hens. When the bucket was full I would bring it down to them, and they would occasionally give me a boiled sweet – that was my reward. The sweets were kept in a paper bag near the top of the dresser. But their boy, who was my own age (about five or six years) watched me getting my sweet, although he was never given one himself. Sweets were too expensive to be dispensed like that"(TG).*

• *"A man used to go round with a donkey and cart selling sticks. He'd bring the donkey through the house to the back yard where it was stabled. There were dozens of jarveys in the town, and the horses were kept in their back yards. Since most of these homes had no hallway, this meant bringing the horse in and out through the living room each day"(PM).*

• *"Chaff beds were great for sleeping in, chaff beds and pillows – most people had them. My mother would folly the thrashing mills in the autumn to wherever they were operating, and then sell it. The chaff would be changed once a year"(PF).*

• *"We all slept on chaff ticks – three or four of us lying on the one bed"(PF).*

• *"When it was thrashing time people would go along with these huge white bags and fill them with chaff, and that was their new mattress for the year, and they'd burn the old chaff. It was the warmest and most comfortable bed you could lie on"(CM).*

SHOP ST. in the early 1900s

Thomas Sherlock, veterinary surgeon, employed a washerwoman who lived at the top of Mell, and when she became ill, Mrs. Sherlock sent her daughter Georgina to the house with a basket of food and to give a helping hand. This gave her an insight into living conditions among the poor:

"My mother cooked some food and sent me up to tidy the place and to wash the two children and get them ready for bed. I was amazed when I walked into the house – the floor was made of clay [an earthen floor, without floor covering] and every time you swept it, it got dusty again. Just two rooms – no upstairs. They were very, very poor. There was no bed in the bedroom, just a mattress on the floor – a straw mattress – it was known as a palliasse"(GK).

PUBLIC AND DOMESTIC LIGHTING: The Drogheda Gas Works was located on the Marsh Road and it supplied gas to the homes of the town for both cooking and lighting; it also illuminated the public thoroughfares. Prior to that the average Irish family existed in almost total darkness once night fell if they did not possess a paraffin lamp or a candle. Before the era of electricity, the gas equivalent of an electric light bulb was the 'mantle', which was a small, white, dome-shaped mesh about the size of a hen's egg, and very delicate – it was liable to disintegrate at a slight touch The smuts that it emitted eventually left their mark on clothes, curtains and the other articles in the room while the fumes had a long-term effect on eyes and lungs. In terms of brilliance, it compared with about a dozen candles, but it took a hundred candles to equate with the light from an electric bulb. Reading and close eye work was a strain. "We didn't have gas. If we were out of paraffin for the lamp, we'd sit as kids in the dark until my mother would come home with a candle."(SC).

The life of a mantle was quite short and it had to be replaced when the light grew dim. The homes were supplied with gas meters into which a penny was inserted. A diminution in the pressure was indicated by a reduction in the light being emitted, and this entailed an urgent search for another penny. The alternative was to light a candle or else to sit in the dark. The public gaslights were usually suspended from brackets placed at street corners and were not very effective in illuminating the streets, but at least they was better than the light shed by the moon.

"My grandfather was a lamplighter. He came to Drogheda from Julianstown and got a job with the Gas Works as a lamplighter. He had to go round with a taper, a box of matches, a

rag and a ladder. He used to clean the glass with the rag [when smuts collected], light the lamp and then go to the next one. There were four lamplighters in the town He used to do Dooley Gate and all that area. Then someone invented a clock which was fitted to the bottom of the thing, so that at 4 o'clock in the evening [in winter] the gas would come on itself and it would go off in the morning.

" *While he was at it he had a fishing rod with four little bells at the top, and he'd rap up the mill girls – they had to be at work at six. And he'd get a penny a week from the families for rapping them up – it was a lot of money that time! [The exclamation mark is the author's. The weekly payment of a penny per household equates to €0.005, or half of one cent]. Bobby Churchill of Ship Street was the last lamplighter I knew – a little man with a cap"(DF).*

The author recalls another lamplighter; he lived at the Potato Market and he, too, was a little man with a cap, and at dusk he would be seen trundling along the footpaths from lamppost to lamppost carrying his ladder balanced on his shoulder. This public service was supplied by the Corporation and was still in operation in the mid 'thirties. Every day of the week, hail, rain or snow this routine was performed. The routine was repeated each morning, this time to extinguish the flame. A song in later times nostalgically recaptured the scene:

> *He made the night a little brighter wherever he would go,*
> *The old lamplighter of long, long ago.*

It might seem a formidable task, from today's standpoint, to have the entire town of Drogheda covered by only four lamplighters. We must remember, however, that in the early 1900s the town encompassed a much smaller area than now – it has since expanded beyond all recognition with housing estates as well as several industrial estates. North of Sunday's Gate there were, for the most part, green fields (no Hardman's Gardens, no Pearse Park, no Cross Lanes, no Moneymore etc.), and the North Road consisted of a simple row of thatched, white-washed cabins. On 'the Far Side' there were virtually no houses in the direction of Donore Road past Dominic's Bridge or the present bus depot; beyond Duleek Street were wide, open spaces, the domain of cattle and sheep. Housing developments such as Moran's Terrace, Halpin Terrace, Congress Avenue, Ballsgrove, etc. did not begin to appear until twenty/thirty years after Independence (1922).

"THINGS WERE HORRID BAD": The economy of the entire country was at a low ebb throughout the first half of the century; the commercial life was stagnant and could not be stimulated. There was insufficient capital with which to prime the economy into meaningful activity, and there was a lack of confidence among the entrepreneurs. The result was a veritable army of idle men.

The regime that ruled from Westminster is apt to be blamed for many shortcomings within Ireland. What is certain is that over the centuries Irish industries were designedly restricted by legislation so as to favour England at Ireland's expense. The thriving wool industry of the 1600s, for example, had been extinguished to appease jealous English producers – this had a devastating effect on the Irish economy. Other Irish industries were likewise hobbled by the imposition of tariffs. After the Act of Union the thriving linen industry in which Drogheda excelled (it was initially a cottage industry) had been overtaken by virtue of the Industrial Revolution which launched England into a position of absolute dominance, making her "the workshop of the world". This left Ireland out in the cold. and an uncaring Imperial Parliament in London gifted Ireland with a heritage of idleness. This resulted in a populace that lacked any worthwhile tradition in craftsmanship and manual skills.

A precept of economic doctrine is that 'labour follows capital' and in consequence of the demise of the native industries there had ever been a deplorable paucity of any tradition of talented expertise. The Penal Days marginalised the majority of the population, and one of its impositions in particular, as we have seen, was the prerequisite of taking the Oath of Allegiance in becoming an apprentice to a trade. This effectively excluded Catholics from

300

joining a Guild and thus from learning a trade or profession. Even though the relaxation of the penal laws gradually opened the door to opportunities that had previously been denied, the establishment of a tradition in the workplace was a slow process. Even after Independence and the formation of the Irish Free State in 1922 the Great Depression and the Economic War of the 1930s continued to retard the growth in the national economy so that Drogheda, a so-called industrial town, was plagued by unemployment.

Corner Boys were a sad feature of every town in Ireland. They occupied many of Drogheda's street corners – they were a devalued segment of the community, lacking skills of any kind, and the prospect of work for them simply did not exist. Although the term used to describe them was 'corner *boys'*, they were in fact adults of every age, ranging from youths to able-bodied men, to elderly, grey-haired veterans. It would be an injustice to dismiss these people as lay-abouts and idlers. For the most part they were decent, God-fearing citizens.

Idle men used to congregate – each had a favourite street corner in some part of the town – from about mid morning and remained throughout the day until evening time, standing against the wall with their hands in their pockets, standing, standing, standing, their thoughts obscured by the nebulous uncertainties of what the morrow might bring or where their next meal might come from. In the evening they drifted home for a mug of tea and a few cuts of bread. A veteran who was a youth in the 1920s summed up the scene: 'You know, things were poor at that time – there was no money'. (KF) The stubble on their faces failed to camouflage their cadaverous, undernourished features; they wore threadbare jackets and baggy trousers, most often of navy serge. Patchwork on a garb was the norm – this was able to extend the life of clothing; the criterion for all apparel was any material that covered the nakedness of the wearer. All wore headgear, and for the most part this was a cloth cap, but some wore bowler hats, the latter being a relic of an earlier age, and the last of the bowler hats disappeared in the 1940s.

A corner boy's comfort was his pipe, and this he would occasionally light up to dispel temporarily the tedium of the day. A companion implement was a pen-knife with which to pare his precious Mick McQuaid plug tobacco. It was, of course, a clay pipe – priced at tuppence (€0.01) in the shops. It was very fragile, and the shank, or stem, invariably came to grief early in its life, but this was never sufficient reason to cast it aside and purchase a new pipe. Instead, the abridged instrument simply became a 'nose-warmer' and continued to give satisfaction to its owner. A centenarian recalled: " ... There used to be a woman selling vegetables in West St. at the entrance to the Meat Market, sitting there on a stool. I used to be fascinated at that old creature with her clay pipe upside down and she smoking away [c. 1920]" (GK).

A few brought a slice of bread with them, and this obviated the need to return home during the day. Even when the men had gone back to their homes for a mug of tea, the areas that they had vacated were unmistakable because they were well marked with the brown stains of tobacco spits left by the men who chewed tobacco. Spitting was a universal habit, and spittoons in private homes as well as in pubs were a common sight. Every bus displayed a sign to be read by all passenger: it was bilingual after 1922 and read *"Scaoileadh Toirmische – Spitting Prohibited'* – but the notice might as well have been in Greek – nobody took notice.

As a young boy, this author was most familiar with the areas adjacent to the quays and, retracing his steps in the direction of the Viaduct, it is an easy matter to visualise the many favourite corners of sheds along the river where men congregated every day. The Round House (now reconstructed) at the junction of Shop Street and the North Quay was the first corner – up to a dozen men occupied the corner, or on a sunny day they would cross the road and sit on the quay wall. Next was at the Mayoralty House corner at the North Quay/Mayoralty Street junction (now the Sound Shop), and the next corner at the junction of the Mall/Constitution Hill also had its quota.

The sheds and warehouses further down the quay also provided cosy corners where men congregated – they arrived from the homes in Hand Street, Oulster Lane, Thomas Street, and the Cord Road areas. The direction of the wind was an important consideration – they moved from one side of the corner to the other as circumstances dictated. The quay thus provided five or six corners; dozens of other corners of the town were frequented in the same way.

By far the most popular corner in the town was the Tholsel – and the evidence is still there today on the stone walls whose surface in places has been worn to a glassy shine by the untold numbers of idle, hunched backs that leaned against it, year in, year out. The stone ledge which is inset in the building's eastern (Shop St.) wall was never intended as a convenient public seat, but it nonetheless serves as silent testament to a past that is best forgotten. Limestone it may be, but its surface has been worn to the shiny smoothness of polished marble by the threadbare trouser-seats of countless men who were condemned to a featureless future.

The men whiled away their idle hours by watching the hustle and bustle of West Street, and witnessing how the other half lived. Some favoured the red-bricked building that is diagonally opposite the Tholsel 'and when the sun would move, they'd move too – they'd follow the sun'(CM). The civic authorities occasionally gave these men short shrift, and they were sometimes moved away by the officers of the law with the aid of a cane. A member of the Corporation in 1889, in an effort 'to preserve it against contact with the lower order', advocated the application to the Tholsel walls of *a coat of tar*, and he was known thereafter as 'Tar-the-Tholsel'.

One veteran recalled: "I used to go down of a mornin' from Dooley Gate to stand at the Tonesil [i.e. the Tholsel] with a pain in me belly with the hunger. They were horrid times". (JO)

Many were ex-soldiers, men who had seen service in the Boer War or the Great War, or both. Some of these men were conspicuous through having lost a limb. Men with disabilities were generally left to their own devices, although a committee met regularly in the Whitworth Hall to assist impoverished ex-soldiers. " ... This man from Thomas Street – he lost a leg in the First World War and he used to stand at a corner down the quay every single day, and he had two crutches"(DM). "One ex-soldier lived near me. He had gas gangrene in the leg. He just lay there on a litter inside the door and children passing by would come in to see him"(MW). Another had the empty sleeve of his jacket trust into the pocket – he had lost an arm.

One conspicuous character had no legs. He regularly came to Drogheda from the direction of Balbriggan. His mode of conveyance was a home-made, four-wheeled, self-propelled, make-shift hand-cart – a velocipede of sorts. It posed no serious threat to Henry Ford or General Motors. It was a contrivance consisting simply of *a discarded fish box to which was attached a set of four old rusty pram wheels*. Thus, he was positioned close to the ground in the contraption, and he propelled himself along the foot-path with the aid of a wooden peg gripped in each hand. He was given several nicknames: 'Nippy' and 'Jack-in-the-Box'. In a later age he would have been called 'Porgy', since he was a carbon copy of that character in Gershwin's musical 'Porgy and Bess', especially if he were to sing the show-stopper *"I'm on My Way"!* To watch him passing over West St. – more often drunk than sober – was a sight to remember.

A more abject sight than 'Nippy' was the unfortunate Vincie Dunne. He, too, survived the trench warfare, but only just. He was a victim of shell-shock, and every bone and muscle in his body shook violently and incessantly, and he walked only with a slow shuffle. Presumably he was dependent on others to be fed, because his hands and arms likewise had a severe and permanent shake. His tongue protruded from an open mouth from which a stream of saliva endlessly issued, dribbling onto his waistcoat which was permanently wet. He was the epitome of the horrors produced by the Great War. His journey to Heaven must certainly have been a happy release.

'What's on the Menu'? : The fare on the kitchen table in working class homes was both unvaried and sparse. The only point at issue is how far back in time these scenes and these circumstances extended. It was very common to see schoolchildren with boils on their necks and on their bottoms; sties on their eyes were also very common afflictions – undeniable evidence of malnutrition. Conditions in the previous century – apart altogether from the distressful conditions of the Great Famine – were undoubtedly worse. Poor families were able to keep hunger at bay for their off-springs by buying stale bread from bakers:

- *"They would queue up of a Monday morning at Lyons's or Galbraith's [the town's principal bakery shops] and get two shillings worth of stale bread in a big pillow slip, and haul it home on their backs – that done them for the week"(PMy). [The author witnessed this practice still occurring in the 1940s]. "Some bakers would break a loaf in half, and sell it that way."*

- *"Mothers would sprinkle water on the stale loaves – that would prevent them getting too hard"(CM).*

- *"You'd go down to Peter Lyons's or Galbraiths. You went off with your pillow case at half past seven in the morning and there'd be a queue. Maybe you'd get the full of a pillow case for a shilling, and that bread would do the family for the week. You'd make 'bitties' by pouring hot milk over the stale bread – this was a better way for people to live. I didn't know what it cost to buy a loaf [of fresh bread, because it was beyond our financial reach]"(BT).*

- *"I was passing down Laurence Street one Saturday evening in the 1930s, when a servant who was employed in a professional's home called me to the door and, handing me a sixpenny piece (3 cents). She had not permission to go shopping herself. She said: "Go down to O'Hagan's in Shop Street and get me a rabbit". It was Easter Saturday and she was bringing this home as a special treat for the family dinner the next day"(TG).*

- *"At Easter I'd get an egg for breakfast – that's the only time I remember getting an egg"(Anon).*

- *"[Others would get] sixpence worth of stale cuts of meat from the butchers, because in the summer a butcher would want to get shut of it. There was no fridges then. The butchers would stay open until half nine on a Saturday because you wouldn't get paid until a Saturday night. The meat that was left over would be sent down to the Oil Cake [the Irish Oil and Cake Mills on the Marsh Road]; they had a cold storage plant. It was kept there until Monday morning and butchers paid so much a pound for the storage"(PMy).*

- *"We were reared on yellow meal and goats' milk – that was your breakfast(DF) [Indian corn had several local names, e.g. 'yellow meal' and 'Indian buck" This particular family had a regular supply of fresh milk – they kept goats].*

- *"You got stirabout – it wasn't called porridge – and you'd take it with buttermilk. You couldn't afford to buy new milk, but you'd get a big can of buttermilk for tuppence. I can't ever remember having meat, except maybe sausages. Roast beef or that, no, no, no. At Christmas you might get meat. A turkey? ... (laughter) ...You must be joking"(BT). [Note the use of the term 'new milk'. This was the term commonly used to describe fresh milk, as distinct from buttermilk].*

Some Drogheda veterans recalled the bleak times of their schooldays during the earlier part of the century: –

- *"I used to bring my lunch to school. The boys would be looking for a slice of bread off me. 'Hadn't you your own breakfast?' 'No. There is nothing in the house – I had no breakfast'. I don't know how those poor fellows existed at all"(MC).*

- *"I remember a chap from Dunne's Lane [off the North Road]. He was poor, and poverty was written all over him. He was slapped by the teacher for failing to bring a penny 'school money' [for school books]"(DM).*

- *"The poverty was frightening – I'd be a prime example of the poverty [in the 1930s]. I'll give you warts and all – we had nothing. I went to school in my bare feet. I remember my mother sending one of us to a neighbour to know if they could lend us a right boot. You'd be lucky to get a slice of bread for your breakfast. At lunch time [in the Sisters of Charity school] we got lovely white bread and a mug of hot milk. My father was a docker – he herded cattle onto the B.& I. boat which was every Tuesday, so that was the only day of the week he worked. My mother took in people's washing; she sat up with people when they were dying; she laid out corpses; she assisted at childbirths using her own experience – there were ten of us in the family. [In later life] I was told 'Don't pray for her – pray to her'. The mothers of Ireland were great, they carried Ireland on their backs"(Anon).*

- *"You hadn't the money to buy anything [other than essentials]. It was through sellers coming to the door selling bedclothes, a bicycle or things like that. And you'd pay so much a week"(BT).*

- *"The furniture would be taken from your home if you couldn't pay. They were called 'the grippers'. I saw that happening – they were hard times"(CF).*

- *"Jack-the-Jew used to come round selling shoes and things"(SC). [Jack Horowotz operated from a run-down premises in Dyer St. He was one of the very few Jews living in Drogheda]*

- *[Recollections of a nun]: "A young pupil asked me what day of the week it was, and I told her it was Friday. 'O, I hate Friday because tomorrow is Saturday and I have nothing to eat. At school we get breakfast and lunch, but at weekends I get nothing'. They'd be delighted to be back at school on Monday because we gave them bread and milk"(RO).*

- *"They'd be watching my lunch because they knew I wouldn't eat it all. They'd grab it – they were that poor. They'd be in bare feet and [the girls] would have a cotton dress and underneath that they'd have nothing"(MS).*

The Local Huckster Shop was the lifeline of most working class and lower class homes. These were small family-run groceries, using the front room (the 'parlour') of their homes as makeshift shops; and most streets had one. They sold everything from a needle to a ball of wool, but in minimal quantities, because most families lived from hand to mouth, quite literally from meal to meal. Foodstuffs were generally bought 'on tick' because ready cash was never to hand. Settlements were made on a Saturday night when the wages were paid.

- *"We all dealt in them. You went down and got your little bits of tea and sugar, or a quarter pound of butter – no one would buy a pound – they wouldn't have the price of it, and it [a record of the transaction] was kept in a little book"(PMy).*

- *"You couldn't do without the hucksters. They were part and parcel of everyday living. Everyone had a book [a note book which was kept by the huckster]. Whatever you got during the week was put down in it. If you had enough money you paid at the end of the week, but if you hadn't the money you'd pay it off at tuppence or thruppence a week extra – that way you'd gradually get the bill down" (BT).*

- *"If your Dad wanted an egg, you'd go down to the shop and buy just one egg – that was for the man in the house. You'd never buy a half dozen. Or maybe just one rasher. Tea was sold in half ounces, there was no such thing as a packet of tea"(BT).*

- *"I often went in and bought just one cigarette. Shopkeepers would sell a half loaf to those who couldn't afford a complete loaf. You certainly had no need of a trolley like today!"(CF).*

- *"You couldn't buy a big packet of tea or sugar. Tea came loose in a big tea-chest, and for each transaction, say an ounce, they'd weigh it out on a little brass scales on the counter every time. The same with sugar and butter"(BT).*

- *"[My father was a small shopkeeper ...] I can remember women coming in and buying a fish or a couple of eggs. If there was a boat in, this meant that the husband had a job emptying the coal boat – it meant she could afford to buy food. She would pay for it at the end of the week, otherwise she'd have to delay settlement. They depended very much on the goodwill of the shopkeeper – they'd give them credit. The dockers were mostly casually hired. If there was two coal boats in together there would be great jubilation for the second band of dockers – there would be money, shovelling like hell"(MW).*

The huckster shops gradually disappeared (and, with them the 'corner shop' and many of the larger family grocery shops) with the arrival of supermarkets and a more affluent society in the nineteen-sixties. The first supermarket to arrive in Drogheda was Egan's, at No. 115 West St., in the year 1960 – it was a normal-sized shop with a frontage of about 14 ft., with the counter and other such furnishings removed.

Wearing Apparel: The concept of 'designer clothes' is very much a phenomenon that is distinctive of the affluent times that began in Ireland in the late twentieth century. Schoolchildren, for the most part, wore hand-me-downs; bare elbows protruded through sleeves, but modesty dictated that patches were applied to the seats of boys' trousers. No notice was taken of shabby or ragged attire, because that was the norm. Used flour sacks were always put to good use – being white, they served as sheets, and were otherwise fashioned into shirts by nimble-fingered mothers – even though endless scrubbing still left the blue telltale proprietary names and trade-mark that denoted their source.

- *"The best dressed people were the breadmen and the Corporation workers – men like that had constant money, and also the girls who worked in Ushers and the Boyne Mills. You'd leave school as soon as you could get a job, maybe at twelve or so, maybe as a messenger-boy, or out thinning turnips or picking spuds"(DMcE).*

- *"When I was about 9 or 10 I used to mind fowl for a neighbour [outside the town], and put them in at night. At Christmas the woman gave me a 'shop shirt'[i.e. a shirt that was bought in a shop]. Up till then I never wore anything but home-made shirts. My mother would get empty flour sacks from McCann and Hills [millers] and make shirts out of them. They were white, but you couldn't get the blue writing off, so 'Miller's Pride' [the brand name] was always on my back"(JW).*

- *"Kids were better off if their fathers worked on the railway. The men were issued with a fresh corduroy rig-out every year, and a dressmaker would cut up the old one to make up clothes for the kids – so all those kids were dressed the same"(PMcK).*

- *"Women would come down from Dublin on Saturdays selling second-hand clothes in the Market. They would gather people in a circle and auction the clothes. I saw this in 1931"(PF).*

- *[Recollections of a nun who made charity visitations to destitute homes]: "Some women used to go to early Mass especially because it was dark so that others wouldn't see the rags they were wearing. One poor woman we used to visit saw that I was a postulant; she asked me if I intended joining the Order, and if so could she have my clothes when I entered. This was in the early 'thirties. I came from Kerry but I never saw real poverty until I came to Drogheda" (RO).*

- *"One man was voted on to the Corporation; he was elected Mayor and he was going to Dublin [on official business]. He came to my father [a major shopkeeper] for the loan of a suit"(MC).*

- *"The eldest boy got a suit for his First Communion; the rest all wore that suit when their turn came – it didn't matter if it was too big for you"(BT).*

- *"My father's boss, Joe Birthistle, gave my father an old suit. My mother cut it down and cut the legs off. That's what I was confirmed in"(PM).*

- *"One thing I remember about them days, the mothers were great. There were 7 of us and I don't know how she managed. At times my father wouldn't be working, but there was no Children's Allowance then. Padraig Pearse wrote: 'Generations will remember them and call them blessed'(TM)*

- *[Class distinction provided a clear dividing line that separated the more comfortable sector from the lower classes; women in the latter sector invariably wore shawls]. "Going out of doors they'd have a shawl around them, and young children were nursed in the shawl because they were warm and comfortable. My mother wore a shawl; she'd wear it every day"[Anon].*

- *"In the country every woman wore a shawl out of doors. They'd wear a hat only on a Sunday, and it would last years and years"(RO).*

- *"Tinkers still wore shawls for decades after that trend had ended. That way you'd always know a tinker, and invariably there'd be a little infant inside it. They'd be along the footpath and knocking at the doors begging for alms. The infant was a 'prop' for them"(TG).*

Pawn Brokers: Bassett lists six pawn shops in Drogheda in 1886, and by the 1930s there were still four in existence, one each in Peter St., Laurence St., West St. and Shop St. Each one displayed the familiar pawnbroker's sign above the door – three large brass balls; the bracket of Curtis's sign in Peter St. is still in place at the time of writing. The service they offered was crucial to the poorer classes, providing them with a little ready cash to tide them over a few days. All kinds of personal possessions were put in hock as a pledge for a modest short-term loan. A sum of a half crown (viz. 2s./6d. or €0.16) would exchange hands for (say) a suit or a pair of shoes which would be redeemed on the following Saturday which was the universal pay day; this enabled the owner to wear the suit to Mass on Sunday. This was the routine, week in, week out. The transaction usually cost the borrower 2d. or 3d. – this approximates to an annual interest rate of about 500%, a consideration that was never taken into the reckoning, especially when hunger was knocking at the door of a large family.

- *"We used to have to go to the pawn shop of a Monday morning with whatever clothes or shoes that was good, and go back on Friday or Saturday when my mother would get the wages, and take them out again. They'd be back in on Monday. The pawn shops were called 'my uncles'. James Curtis was the one in Peter St., but there were others"(DM).*

- *"You paid tuppence or thruppence as a charge for the deal. If you didn't redeem the item it was sold off in two or three months. The shelves were packed with brown paper parcels tied up with twine containing unclaimed stuff. Courtneys in Laurence St.[at the top of the High Lane Steps]had a side door on the lane for those who were a step above buttermilk"(PF).*

- *"Everyone called them 'My Uncle's'. My mother used to say 'Go down to me Uncle's with this ...'"(PF).*

- *"You couldn't go down to the shops to buy anything [other than essentials] – you hadn't the money. There would be a queue outside the pawn shops on a Monday morning. They'd put the clothes in for the week and they'd get half a crown (€0.16) and that would keep the family for the week. On Saturday morning the queue would be there again taking the clothes back out. The men would have their suits for to go to Mass on Sunday"(BT).*

Clogs: Wooden clogs are not exclusive to Hollanders – they were in common use locally, since the cost of leather boots were beyond the pockets of many families. "I used to wear my father's army boots"(P. Farrell) The observations of several veterans is given: "The kids used to wear clogs – the other kids would call them 'Cloggie'. You'd hear them coming clip-clop, clip-clop. They were made below in Donaghy's boot factory by a carpenter"(DF) "Bare feet was the accepted thing, and summer was always a godsend. You saved your shoes for the winter".(DM) "The school playground in January would be covered in ice. And you'd see the lads in their bare feet hopping from one foot to the other on the cold ice – they couldn't afford to get shoes. I went to school in my bare feet and often grazed my big toe! Kids would stand on the iron grating on the footpath at Sheill's bakery in James St. and the heat coming up from the ovens would warm their feet"(JM).

By the mid 1940s the children of Drogheda were better shod, although bare feet were still a common sight in rural Ireland. "I went to school in Fieldstown [near Ballymakenny]. We'd all be in bare feet as soon as the 'three borrowed days' were over – these were the first three days in April which were supposed to have the same bad weather as March. That is why they were called 'borrowed days"(JW).

"The Evening Herald launched the 'Herald Boot Fund' that was responsible for introducing bare feet to leather shoes for the first time for many a poor child. You'd always know kids who got boots through the Herald Boot Fund because they'd put their bare feet straight into the boots – they didn't have socks"(PMcK).

A former resident of Donacarney recalls attending his local school in the 1920s: "We all went to school in our bare feet. And there were clogs – leather uppers with wooden soles, and big tips around them – you'd hear them coming. You got them in Gustie Murphy's in West Street. I went to Donacarney School – you brought your own sticks for the fire. The four teachers were principal Doherty of the Boyne Road, Kitty Sheehy, Miss McCann and

Mrs. Hughes. There was a dry toilet. And if there was no bread in the house, you might get a penny and buy a round of Lyon's bread with butter from the little huckster's shop beside the school, it was called 'the Doodle Collins "(PMy).

The Scotch Hall in Profile: The Scotch Hall of today is a symbol of the affluent society of which today's generation has the good fortune to be members. The name itself 'Scotch Hall' is derived from the word 'scutch', a term used in the linen industry. Scutching was a process of pounding used in separating the fibres from the wooden part of flax, and the workers were paid a subsistence wage. The stone building stood on the Marsh Road and belongs to a past era. It was later adapted as a tenement and it was an abode of sheer destitution.

> *"The poorest of the poor lived there. They had no running water; they had to bring up a bucket of water from a tap outside. This was in the1930s; before that there was no tap at all. Each family – some of them very large – usually lived in just one room, luckier families had two. They were eaten alive with fleas and creepy-crawlies. To foil them they'd put the legs of the beds into four little tins of paraffin oil, but then they'd crawl across the ceiling and parachute down. What else was one to expect, with the rent being a mere sixpence a week[€0.03]" (DF).*

> *"I was born in Scotch Hall. There were only two rooms, and grandfather slept in one room beside a big open fire – I don't know how the place never went on fire – it was the kitchen as well. My aunt, who was his daughter, lived in a room beside it. The window was only about 12 x 18 inches. She had three kids in that room. She worked in the Boyne Mill; she'd have to be in at six o'clock until six at night.[The building had] one hall and three families living in it, and the back door was never closed. At night the front door would be pushed over – no lock or anything like that. There was no heating, only the open fire [with no electricity], and an oil lamp or a candle for lighting.*

> *"Nothing was thrown out – you et (sic) everything you got your hands on… . [Regarding one particular family]: At school the eldest boy would ask to be let home because they got no breakfast, and the breadman was after coming. There were 7 or 8 in that family and they all went to England except one"[Anon].*

> *"McConnon lived in one part – he was a basket weaver. We used to be looking at him working and the rats coming up through the floor. 'They're all right, they won't touch you'. He lived in one room – worked, et (sic) and slept there as well. No electric ligh - it was lamp light or a candle. Upstairs was Danny Byrne. Another was Monkey Brennan. He was deaf and dumb; he wasn't always like that – he used to box.*

> *"There were no toilets in any of the houses. A bucket would be kept in the bedroom and brought down the next day and dumped in the pit. There were three dry toilets at the back – no locks or anything, and a pit with a wall around it, and we'd dump the bucket into it. This man, Paddy Brodigan, used to come with a horse and cart with packing all around the sides [to prevent the liquid escaping] and he'd empty the pit and away down to the sloblands [further down the Marsh Road] every 3 or 4 weeks.*

> *"There was a tap outside that we used, and it was stuck on a pole in the ground; before that there was a tap at the far side of the arch across the road leading to the Dale – you pushed down a lever and the water came out. You'd keep the water in a dish and when it was dirty you just threw it out the front door into the channel.*

John's Court was located at the end of John Street, opposite the present Bus Depot. It was a cluster of the lowliest mud-walled hovels imaginable, each of them consisting of two small rooms, and the single tiny window admitted a minimal amount of light. Living conditions were appalling. Vagrants used to come into the town seeking odd jobs; they congregated in the vicinity of John's Court and John's Gate:

"They had no business or no work – 'gippos' they were called; they were at the Old Wall in John Street – John's Gate. Some used to sleep there in tents – rows of little canvas crawls. Some of them got little bundles of straw and made little thatched covers. They'd put a few ash plants together and then another one across, and tie them at the top. The police would come along and shift them, set them on fire and everything"(DF).

Another den of destitution was the Dale. Through it flows the stream called the Dale Brook or *Dubh* (= 'Black'. Cromwell referred to it in his report to Parliament as 'the Dove'); it rises at the Black Bull and it enters the Boyne through a culvert opposite Constitution Hill. The following incident was graphically related by a veteran who lived nearby all his life:

"[At night time] you wouldn't see any light [gaslight] until you came to Conway's of the Dale. There was an old fella in the Dale called Jumbo Farrell and he used to let in the travelling people – 'gippos' they called them. There was a small little square window on the front of the cabin. And if the weather was bad the wet would come through the roof; he'd let them in and you'd see eight or ten of them lying on the floor. After that another man and his woman took over – oul' Jumbo Farrell's house they got. She was only a young one, and we used to go down to hear the rows – we used to sit in the Sally Gardens to hear them fightin'. Mickey would come home drunk – she'd have a few on her, too, and she'd go mad. She had a baby and it wasn't more than a week or ten days old, and it was in the shawl. Mickey would come home, but she wouldn't let him in. Anyway, he went off and got a big stone and busted in the door. So she ran out.

"Another night he wouldn't let her in so she asked him to let the child in. "Keep your old bastard" he said. "He's not my bastard, he's yours. If you are not goin' to let me in, here he is for you". With that, she just took the child up, bashed the pane of glass and bashed the child in through the window. Mickey opened the door and she ran – she went like a gazelle. Now, the child must have been lyin' on the floor and Mrs. Keegan ran in; I seen her afterwards with the child in her arms. She [the 'gazelle'] ran down the Height and him afther her. When she come to the top flag [or step] she caught howlt of the lamp-post and she swung round it. He tried to stop, and one leg went each side of the lamp-post. He went out – as dead as a door nail – the back of his head hit the ground. Next thing you see the police comin' and draggin' him away.

"That was about 1917. In 1932 they all moved to Congress Avenue and the houses were flattened. Since then the Corporation built a sort of a garden there, and made a lovely job of it, but it has gone wild again" (DF).

D'Alton makes reference to the Dale in his *History of Drogheda*, a work that was published just before the Famine. The work covers many aspects of the town's past but it bypasses the living conditions of its inhabitants. An exception is a passing reference to the Dale which he describes as 'a picturesque valley ... but is now nearly filled with miserable huts'.[7] We can conclude that there had been little or no improvement during the ensuing eighty years up to the period now described.

Reminiscences of a Nun: A girl who was born in Donegal in 1922 answered the vocational call at the age of 17 and joined a Drogheda convent:

"I left home in 1940 in a taxi – this was my first time in a car – and went to Derry to get the train which brought me to Drogheda. When I started in the school there were 72 youngsters in the class with nothing to eat. They would come in at half past eight and they would get a wee bit of breakfast before starting school. They would be mostly in their bare feet, and perished with the cold.

"There was a wonderful set of helpers in the town who would collect second-hand clothes; they would wash and iron them in 'the work room' of the Convent. On a Saturday the mothers would come in and tell us what their needs were, and we'd put the items [discretely] in a bag to take home. The Boyne Mills would send us bales of cloth so that we could make pinafores for the children. This work was all done by hand in 'the work room'. Then someone presented us with a sewing machine and we learned to use it; this was a great boon because it speeded up the work greatly. Sometimes when a child was given a pinafore she might come in the next

day still in rags. Her sister would have taken it – it was literally a case of 'first up, best dressed'.

"A bread van would arrive every morning with fresh bread straight from the bakery, and a farmer would bring a few gallons of milk. We'd heat the milk and add cocoa, and that is what the children got for their lunch. We [in the religious community] would envy them and sometimes say it would be nice to be one of those poor children coming in. We didn't get this. We lived in poverty, I tell you. Some porridge and a slice of bread for breakfast. My brother came down to visit me and he was shocked to see this skinny person, I had lost so much weight after about six months. We simply hadn't enough to eat. When one nun went to hospital for an operation they were unable to operate on her for seven weeks because she was mere skin and bone. Novices entering the convent brought a lump sum with them which was put in the bank, and the interest it earned was supposed to support them for the rest of their lives.

"We were an enclosed order until the mid 'Forties; after that we were allowed to walk on a Sunday afternoon from Fair St. to our [recently purchased] residence at Greenhills by a designated route. Previously we'd go in a horse and enclosed carriage that was provided by a farmer – it accommodated about seven or eight. On one occasion the horse sat down in the Cord Road and wouldn't budge, and we were stuck there with all the people watching, and we could see them through the curtains. A man then enticed the horse forward by holding out bread in front of him.

"Under the Capitation System the government made payments in relation to the number of pupils, and this money was used to provide heating, etc. We were not allowed to teach, but after the war we qualified by going in twos to Carysfort Training College and were then entitled to draw a salary. We would simply sign the back of the cheque without knowing the amount. We were better off then, and would sometimes get an egg for breakfast. On a church holiday we'd get a slice of cake and two sweets"(RO).

Works of Mercy: We associate the Convent of Mercy with the education of Drogheda's children, but the services rendered by the nuns to the less fortunate members of society extended far beyond that of teaching, and the charitable works which they performed to the underprivileged members of the community has never been fully recognised or acknowledged. The assistance that they administered to the poor was always accomplished without the glare of publicity.

They also operated a laundry to provide work for school leavers, and taught girls other skills such as lace work and hosiery (This operation provided employment for 30 girls, and much of their finished work was taken up by the Army Camp at Gormanston). In keeping with the ideals implicit in the name 'Order of *Mercy*', the nuns were constantly engaged in charitable works. When not teaching in the classrooms, they went out in pairs, usually consisting of a senior nun accompanied by a younger one or a postulant, on visitations to the poor and the infirm, and to give succour in places such as Scotch Hall which is here briefly described by a nun who made regular visits there:

"The stairs were shaky and rickety; the rooms contained but the barest furnishings – just a few chairs, a table and a ragged bed. The poverty was beyond description. On the top floor lived this couple; they had just the one room; the husband was a coal porter at the docks and his face was perpetually black with the coal dust. There was no running water. Whatever little wages he got was spent on drink. We used give the woman a half crown [€0.16] to buy a few morsels of food.

"We were able to dispense small sums of money to the poor through a church collection which was held once a year on the first Sunday in Advent. The families of the members of our own religious community were also very generous. Three girls from one local family entered the order; then their father would call once a month with small bottles of whiskey and tobacco that we would give to the inmates of the Workhouse.

"If pupils got the chance of a factory job working on the looms, they jumped at the opportunity; their age would be about 12 or 13 years. But they would still attend school for part of the day. They were called 'half time workers' and their earnings, such as they were,

were most welcome at home. The School Attendance Officer was Mr. Shanley; he was kind and understanding and he overlooked what was happening. The girls had a jingle:

> *Shanley is an honest man.*
> *He goes to Mass on Sunday*
> *And asks for grace to catch the girls*
> *Who are not at school on Monday" (RO).*

THE HIRING FAIR: A feature of most towns was the assembling of men and women of all ages at appointed places where they offered themselves for hire. "They were treated like cattle". DF The duration of service was usually a single season, and if the hired hand was found to have been satisfactory during his term of hiring, he had the prospect of being re-engaged for a further term. In Drogheda there seems to have been several assigned areas where people seeking employment would gather, Trinity Street and the Tholsel.

- *"The farmer would come along and look at them, look at their hair to see if there was any lice in it, and feel the boy's muscles. They'd go and live, get boarded, get their grub, and the father would get the wages. That was the old fashioned way. The last I seen was at Trinity Street   outside the school [the CBS, now the Star and Crescent premises]. I think they were from Tullyallen – a family of two girls and a boy, and the father standing along with them on the footpath"(DF).*

- *"I used to attend fairs around the country. I remember the ones in Ballybay and Ballyjamesduff – they were held in May. They got about 7/6 [€0.48] a week. Women and all used to be hired. They were usually hired for six months"(TMcC).*

- *"There would be a line of them standing at the corner of West St. and Peter St. stretching over several shop fronts. The farmers would give you a shilling [to seal the engagement] and call for you on the way back" (PM).*

- *"The farmers would come in to hire chaps – about £20 (€25) a year they'd get. They'd be there on a fair day, at the Fair Green, maybe a dozen of them"(DMcE).*

- *"There would be dozens of them there on the Twelfth of May; they got £26 a year"(JW).*

- *"My grandfather, he was a ploughman and he used to hire out to different farmers, one this year and a different one the next year. He was after doing a year with M------- in Clogherhead, and when the year was up he went back to the hiring fair in Drogheda, and he was hired back to the same farmer again. On the second hiring he got a rise.* **And the rise was tay (sic) for his breakfast.** *[Tea was something of a luxury, but whether this was the fair equivalent of a wage increase is a moot point; it is a stark reminder that it was a buyer's market in the times that we are discussing]. A son of his – my uncle – told me this, and I asked what in the name of the Lord was he getting for his breakfast before he got this rise. His breakfast was stirabout and buttermilk, a can of each, and he got it out in the ploughed field. The horses got fed before the ploughman got his. The maid would come up from the house and hold the horse while he got down on his two knees with the two cans and the big spoon and that is how you had your breakfast"(TW).*

- *"I remember the hiring. If a fellow wanted a job around harvest time, he would go down to the Tholsel. This was the only way they had of communicating. [The sophistication of inserting an advertisement in the local paper was out of the question]. He would have a rake with him, and a reaping hook attached to his belt hanging out of him. John Collins [hardware merchant, Shop Street] was a great centre for selling reaping hooks. A farmer would want someone to cut the corn, and he would offer him a job – those were the days before the binders and combines. The hiring was usually for six months, doing general farm work. They called them 'servant boys'. He would go and live with the farmer, and he would live in a bed in the loft or somewhere, maybe over the stable – and the cattle would be a form of central heating"(SK).*

One veteran, when asked to relate his experience of hiring, made his reply in the form of a song:

"Come all ye loyal heroes And listen to my tale
Dont hire with any farmer For you know what your work will be.
He'll rise you bright and early And from the clear daylight of the dawn
And still I'll never be able To plough the rocks of Bawn
... And my shoes they are well worn And my stockings they are thin
And my heart is always trembling I'm afraid they might cave in". (PMy)

A visit to a country homestead was always a novelty to a 'townie', and the author has fond memories of many visits during the 'thirties and 'forties to one such farm located in the Tullyallen area. It was a substantial farm; its total acreage was of little consequence to a schoolboy, but the existence of an orchard was what really mattered to him, and returning home with pockets bulging with apples or with some additions to a collection of birds' eggs (depending on the season) are fond memories that still linger.

The collie helped in bringing in the cows for milking, and it was fascinating to observe that each cow had its own individual stall that it occupied on every occasion. Hygienic operations (such as sponging or washing down the cows' udders) formed no part of the routine; the udders were moistened by dipping a knarred hand into the bucket of milk taken from the previous cow. Both the farmer and Barney – he was 'the servant boy' – undertook the job of milking the cows, a chore that required to be done twice a day, every day, every year without any break for the farm hand. And all was done manually. An oil lamp that swung in the breeze hung from a rafter, and tried rather ineffectively to penetrate the darkness in wintertime.

The Town Walls
A few small sections still remain. This portion is at Laurence Gate.

311

Barney had a room to himself – it was an annexe off the shed where the cart was kept; it had concrete walls and concrete floor – a veritable ice box in winter; the only furniture were the bed and a wooden chair, and the only drapery were the hanging cobwebs. The cattle occupied a separate building, so that Barney was denied the benefit of nature's 'central heating system'. The best that could be said about this abode is that it was dry, a benefit which the rodent population of the countryside fully availed of in winter time, and Barney seemed quite indifferent to their presence. The daily routine of separating the milk and then churning the cream into butter was performed by the farmer's wife in the 'dairy' – a small room off the kitchen. Again, this routine was accomplished by hand, for the magic of Rural Electrification did not arrive in the Irish countryside until the mid 'fifties. There was no tap or running water either in the house, in the milking stable, in the 'dairy' where the milk was separated, or anywhere else on the farm, so that scouring out the churns and the milk buckets was an added burden. Water was a scarce commodity because it had to be drawn bucket by bucket from a well located some distance from the farmstead.

The Brodigans were 'landed gentry' who lived in Pilltown House. The family had been merchant princes as well as holding extensive farmlands. The steward's name was McCormack:

> "About 20 men worked at Pilltown. They were paid much more – about half a sovereign [€0.64 a week] – than the local farmer around, who got 7/6 [€0.48]. My father would pay the men out of his waistcoat pocket on a Saturday night. And the men who came in on a Sunday to milk the cows got an extra shilling [6 cents] – you could do a lot with a shilling then. But my father learned after a while not to pay them until Monday. Otherwise they'd spend it on Saturday night and they wouldn't come in to mild the cows on Sunday"(TMcC).

The Mill Girls: Drogheda was fortunate in being home to a variety of industries. The textile industry in particular gave constant employment to about 1,000 women. (In the earlier part of the 1800s the linen industry provided employment for close on 2,000 females). The factory hooter was a familiar sound, calling the mill girls to their place at the looms each morning. We have seen above that the local lamplighter was able to supplement his income by knocking on the windows of the mill girls each morning. Work started strictly at 6.00 a.m. in the earlier part of the century; to arrive a minute late was to face a shut gate, and then a dejected walk home.

The roadways leading to these factories were thronged every morning with females of all ages in their shawls, converging from every corner of the town to Robert Ushers and to the Boyne Mills at Greenhills. They always walked on the roadway, sometimes singly but mostly about three to six or seven abreast, taking up the full width of the road, and chatting, babbling and laughing among themselves as they stepped smartly along. There was a break for breakfast at 8.15 a.m. when relatives would arrive down at the factory gate with billy-cans and hunks of bread. Other workers ate their breakfast walking to work along the roadway. There was no vehicular traffic to disrupt the waves of workers – apart from an occasional cyclist, and few could afford these. All of the women wore shawls, usually black. 'Coming home after work, the Cord Road would be black with them – about 600 women all in shawls. From about 14 or 15 years of age every working class female donned a shawl, and she would never go out of doors without it; she continued to wear it until the day she died – that was the unwritten code of the times'.

The following conversation took place between the author and an elderly woman who worked at the looms in the Boyne Mills all her working life:

> **Question**: *"What wages did you get".*
> **Answer**: *"I got seven-and-six [seven shillings and six pence = €0.48]"*
> **Question** *"That was that per hour, I suppose?"*
> **Answer** *(which came swiftly and very reassuringly)* *"Oh no, per week – **per week**".*
> **Question**: *"And how much of this would you hand up at home?"*
> **Answer**: *"All of it, of course".*

- *"I remember this woman scurrying along the middle of the road in bockedy shoes in the direction of the Boyne Mills long after the hooter had stopped and everyone else had passed. Like all mill workers, she wore a shawl, and the tears were running down her face as she cried out loud. Even though I was a child of about five I could see that she was distressed, and I felt sorry for her. Why was she late for work, and why was she crying? Perhaps she had been attending to her husband in bed dying, or her sick child – who knows? But there were no hard luck stories accepted at the factory gates – she would certainly be turned back"(TG).*

- *"I worked in the Boyne Mills [starting in 1931]. My two sisters worked there – there was nowhere else until Mell factory started. They saw a notice in the window: 'Apprentice Wanted' and they told my mother. She brought me down and Cowdy [the Managing Director] said 'What reason have you for wanting this job'. I said: 'My two sisters work here'. That was a Monday evening. 'Start in the morning'. I started off at 8 shillings [€0.51]a week and I was there for 45 years, in the 'Making-up' Department. The manager was Ken Whitaker's father. One morning he forgot his glasses and I got the job of going back for them. I was delighted – I spent a couple of hours about it!(TM).*

- *"I left school at fo'teen [in 1927] and worked in Mell factory. I got 6/- [€0.38] a week operating a button-hole machine. I handed up the whole lot and got sixpence [€0.03] back for myself. I'd go to a 'hop' which was fo'pence. You worked from 8.30 am until 6.00 pm with a 15 minutes break for lunch. If you were late, the gate was closed and you had to stay at home until the following morning" (BT).*

- *"My father worked in the dyeing department of the Boyne Mills [at Greenhills]. He started work at six in the morning and finished at six in the evening. He got out at eight for his breakfast, walked home [to Magdalene St.], then back down by half eight. My mother would give me a box with his lunch and a billy-can of tea and we'd meet in Donor's Green, and then he'd smoke his clay pipe. He could neither read nor write. An old woman told me she remembered the day he came to Drogheda with his mother [circa 1890?]. She had a shawl, and he was a little chap in bare feet. I don't know where he came from – he never spoke about it, and he had no relatives" (BT).*

The prospects of advancement for girls from rural areas were minimal – they never had the option, as the menfolk had, of enlisting in the army, and so were pleased to secure employment as domestic servants in the big town of Drogheda where the going rate in the 1940s was 10/- (€0.64) per week with their keep. Twenty years earlier the going rate was 5/- (€0.32) per week with keep. "Brigid was so good that my mother gave her an extra 1s./3d. [€0.08 per week]. But there was murder among her friends for giving a maid so much money"(GK).

LEISURE TIME:

- *"We used to walk to Termonfeckin on a Sunday – the roads were clear then. You wouldn't get to the seaside for a swim because you couldn't afford the fare on the train [to Laytown]. There was no such thing as togs – [girls] just wore a dress or a shift or something"(BT).*

- *"There used to be excursions by boat to Dublin. The boat was down the quay. It would leave at seven, and a crowd would go down to see them off. The band would go with them, and they'd be back about ten at night, half of them drunk"(BT).*

- *"Fr. Lavelle, who ran the Holy Family confraternity, would hire the Mail Boat 'Mellifont' when it would be anchored here at the weekend and it would go to Kingstown [now Dunlaoire] or Warrenpoint. Coming back up the river the band would be playing hymns or saying the Rosary. Others would be drunk"(JM).*

- *"There was no television that time – the only thing the women had was leaning over the half-door with their arms folded, talking away to the neighbours. You'd see them in Magdalene St. and the Windmill Road – they'd be standing there and they talking to one another. There were great neighbours then; they would help out one another(TM)*

313

- *"Some people would take a Round Trip of the Boyne Valley. The boat would be at Greene's where there were steps leading to the river, and go by the canal to Navan, and then take a brake [a four-wheeled horse-drawn vehicle] back to Drogheda. At the same time others would go the reverse way. I don't know the fare – I was young. [The adult fare was four shillings]"(PM).*

- *"They used to play Pitch and Toss. It was at Dolan's Corner [Sunday's Gate], and another school was at Newtown Crossroads on a Sunday. And when the guards would come they'd scatter – it was illegal"(BT).*

- *"In the mills they got one week holiday a year. They'd just go down the town, or maybe go to Laytown for the day". (KF)*

- *"There used to be cockfighting at Ducksy Cummins Lane, off Thomas St., but kids would be chased away – it was illegal"(JMy).*

- *"The biggest job the guards had that time was keeping the kids from playing football on the road, [there being little vehicular traffic to interrupt play]. You'd put two coats down for the goal-posts. Then you'd hear 'Here's the guards!', and we'd all run for it"(TM)*

- *"I lived right beside Magdalene Park. There used to be railings around it and a caretaker would open it at three o'clock and close it at six. You couldn't be rowdy or damage the bushes. The Drogheda Band would be playing on a Sunday [on a bandstand that was provided]"(BT).*

- *"For Bellewstown Races the jarveys used to come down from Dublin to shuttle people from Drogheda to the races, and they'd stable their horses in the Barber Callans [in Dooley Gate]. Coming home, the passengers would be roarin' drunk – five or six of them on the car with the driver. We'd meet them at Dooley Gate and shout 'Grab a ha'penny, sir'. So they'd throw us money and there'd be a mad scramble for the coins"(PM).*

CHRISTMAS: With so many of the populace living from hand to mouth, there was seldom the wherewithal to provide extra fare or family treats at Christmastime. If a family indulged in meat on Christmas Day, belts had to be tightened subsequently to pay for the luxury. Santa's sack was very light, and he failed to come down the chimney for many a child. Some recollections:

- *"The only time we got meat was at Christmas. We'd hang up stockings and you might get a rag doll in it or a pencil"(RO).*

- *"In my young days there were no toys. We'd get an apple – apples were a rarity in our part of the country [County Limerick]; no oranges or anything like that"(PB).*

- *"We'd get an apple or an orange, some ribbons or a slide for your hair; the lads might get a Jew's Harp"(RO).*

- *"You'd get a tin whistle; my brother Seán got a toy drum" (TM)*

- *"I'd get an orange in a stocking; later on it was a cap-gun or a liquorice pipe"(PF).*

- *Another veteran recalling Christmas said: "I can't remember getting any toys"[Anon]*

- *"You'd be lucky if you got a little cap-gun"(PF). [Priced at a penny, a cap gun was about 4 inches in length, made from tin. A small box of 'caps' was purchased separately for a ha'penny. They were made of paper and shaped like confetti, and contained a few grains of sulphur; when struck by the gun's hammer they emitted a sound and a spark similar to that of a Christmas cracker].*

- *"Back at school after the Christmas holidays I asked my desk-mate what Santa had brought him, and I clearly recall his reply: 'I got an orjin [i.e. an orange – the pronunciation of the word he had got from his parents] and a new pair of shoes'. This was about 1933" (TG).*

TUBERCULOSIS – TB: This disease was rampant throughout Ireland, and it sometimes swept away entire families. A programme was broadcast by Radio Eireann every Wednesday during the 1940s and 1950s called 'Hospitals Requests'. It constantly broadcast tunes requested by patients receiving treatment in Peamount Sanatorium, Crooksling Sanatorium, Newcastle Sanatorium and many other such institutions throughout the land.

> *"First of all, if you knew where it was, you were not supposed to go into those houses, or associate with them or anything. I had cousins and I never went into the house; two or three of the girls died of it. I was 10 or 12 at the time and we were told not to go near the house"(PB).*

> *[Recollections of a nun who taught in school]: "As a matter of routine we always washed our hands after school as a precautionary measure, with handling pupils' school books, etc. One of our congregation died of T.B."(RO).*

> *"I remember one tumbledown, thatched house at Sunday's Gate and four boys died in it within six months – they were in their 'teens. Shortly after the last one died the corporation pulled it down. In another case a father was dying upstairs while his little child aged three was dying downstairs – this was in Bredin St. and they were only eight years married"(BT).*

> *"Two of my cousins died of it – one was a lovely looking girl – and their mother also died of it"[Anon].*

> *[Recollections of a nun who regularly made visits to the sick]: "They would have open TB sores on their legs. We used to make bandages and bring them to the patients, and burn the old bandages. There was a special ward in the Workhouse. It was called St. Theresa's and there were six beds in it. There was nothing we could do for them – beautiful girls, aged about 17, dying of TB"(RO).*

> *"My mother died when I was young – she was about 26 when she got it; she died in the Dublin Road ['the Dublin Road' was a colloquial name for the Workhouse, as was 'the Spike'] and the three of us were then reared by several aunts.* **'Consumption'** *they called it, and if you had it at all, you were done. My father was about 40 when he got it. My brother Leo died of it, too – he was in his twenties"(KF).*

How The Other Half Lived: It was not all doom and gloom in Drogheda during the early years of the century. The families must certainly have felt superior to their counterparts in rural areas when flush toilets were installed; they were known as water closets or w.c.'s. But they were *outdoor* flush toilets – no doubt the concept of having them outside the home was ingrained in the people's minds from the earlier era of dry lavatories, the object being to keep them as far as possible from the house for a reason that need not be explained here. They were located at the far end of the back yard or garden. "So if it was raining, you had the simple option of scurrying along the back yard and getting your head wet, or staying put and getting your pants wet!". Night-time was a different matter especially in the depths of winter, and no bedroom was without the essential piece of domestic convenience variously called a commode, a chamber-pot, or 'po' or facetiously as a 'goes-under', although rude ruffians gave a grosser name to it.

The homes in fashionable West Street and Fair Street were no exception. It was the duty of the domestic servant to dispose of the contents each morning. Some decades into the century the shopkeepers began to construct toilets *within* their homes. No more dashing out of doors in the rain and getting wet. Moving the toilet indoors usually entailed breaking down the rear window on the first landing of the stairway and converting it into a doorway and then appending a 'little room' onto the exterior wall of the house. In other words it was stuck onto the back wall.

But the general advancement towards indoor toilets was long and slow, some householders adapting more slowly than others in installing this blissful convenience. The author recalls quite vividly, although it was in the mid 'thirties, being sent one morning by his mother with an errand to a lady in Peter Street. Like all shops at that time, the proprietor and his family lived over the shop. The lady was still in bed, but she had left the chamber-pot on the landing outside the bedroom door, and not having a maid servant, her evident intention was to empty the contents thereof into the outside closet at some more propitious hour of the day. This delay in the performance of a domestic chore was unfortunate for the young messenger because, having climbed the stairs he was out of breath, and his lungs took in a full inhalation of the unpleasant aroma that permeated the stairway. This prompted a hasty exit down the stairs and back onto the street, and never was the fresh air of Peter Street more appreciated.

If the lady in question was more up-to-date in matters of domestic comfort, and if she had pressurised her husband into installing a flush toilet, all she had to do was to contact the shop a few doors down the street. It was the premises of a plumbing contractor. Some decades earlier (perhaps about 1915) this author's mother was an assistant in it – her uncle was the proprietor. The demand for baths and shower units in those bleak days, as can be imagined, did not cause the shop to be constantly thronged with customers, and she was wont to vacate her post at the counter on occasions and while away the time in chin-wags with her pals nearby. This created the opportunity for a practical joker to raise a laugh at her expense. (Here we must remember that livestock passing through the main streets was an everyday occurrence). On one occasion when her uncle returned home he passed through the shop and went out to the yard, but returned a moment later exploding with invectives, and demanding an explanation, for, amid the baths, the lead pipes and sundry plumbing equipment, what immediately met the startled man's gaze was *a cow!*

Baths seldom entailed plumbing; most upper-class people used portable bath-tubs; they were shaped rather like reclining armchairs minus the legs. A convenient place to store them was under the stairs, and they were taken out as circumstances required – which was not often because taking a bath entailed preparing several kettles of hot water, following which came the job of mopping up after the operation.

For families who lacked the luxury of bath-tubs their only douche was if and when they went to the seaside. Shower units belonged to a later age. A well known architect who practised in Drogheda during the mid-twentieth century recalled a bathroom suite being installed in a home in West Street in the early 'forties. It was a sight to behold, he said, and the neighbours flocked along to admire the wonder of it all. As for toilet paper, the older folk of the town must smile a bemused smile when they see the endless stacks of these indispensable items piled up in today's supermarkets; yesterday's newspaper had more uses that one in former times, and we should not forget that the very name 'toilet paper' is of fairly recent origin.

The veterinary surgeon Thomas Sherlock lived on the Mall, and his surgery was in Stockwell Lane. The regular charges for a call out were 5/- and 10/- (€0.32 and €0.64). His contact with animals provided opportunities to acquire several domestic pets that provided great enjoyment for the family. His daughter recalls:

> *"We had a pet donkey at our country house in Termonfeckin, and Georgie [her brother] used to ride it into Drogheda. One day it disappeared, but a man said 'Are you looking for your donkey? You will find him up at the altar in Saint Peter's church'. And right enough, Dad went up to Saint Peter's and there was the donkey, bold as brass, near the altar rails. He was familiar with West Street because he used to go up to Peter Lyons' bakery shop for a bun every morning.*

> *"We got another little donkey: Dad was going out on a case and he saw these gypsies abusing this little thing – it was only a few months old. Dad got out and warned them that he would report them. And on the way back the poor little thing was still tethered to the caravan and running behind it. So Dad got out and after some exchanges bought the donkey for half a crown[€0.16] and brought it home in the back of the car. We were thrilled with this new pet, and every morning we would go out to the stable with two big bottles of milk with two great big teats at the end of them and feed it. He became a great pet and would come walking with us like a dog"(GK).*

Their pet fox had the liberty of running the length of the garden next to a rope that was staked at each end; a secondary rope was attached with a ring to a collar around the fox's neck. Their pet ferret's favourite perch was sitting on the shoulders of anyone who encouraged him, 'but when the ladies were having afternoon tea with Mom it gave her great amusement to whistle up the ferret and then watch all the ladies screaming, holding up their skirts and getting up on the chairs'. But the creature that needed most watching was the pet monkey:

> *"I think he was a marmoset – he was always up to some mischief. He would lie in wait for the boys coming home from school. He would snatch their caps and then throw them away, sometimes into the river. It cost Dad a small fortune replacing them! One day he was missing and was found in Mr. Mitchell's house, and when the maid went in to retrieve him there was the little monkey in the dining room squirting the soda siphon all over the place. And another day he went down to the kitchen where Brigid [a servant] and Paddy [the groom] were having a meal, but they wouldn't give him anything. Well, Paddy was called up to harness the horse for Dad and Brigid was called elsewhere, so they tied him to the mangle. He knew how to get his revenge. He reached over and caught a corner of the tablecloth and, whoops, pulled everything onto the stone floor.*

> *"A friend asked my parents could they borrow the monkey for a while, but we never saw it again. They said it died of sunstroke!"(GK).*

IN PROUD MEMORY OF

Fenian John Boyle O'Reilly

HUMANITARIAN, AUTHOR, POET, LECTURER
BORN IN IRELAND 28th JUNE 1844
DIED U.S.A 10th AUGUST 1890
ABSCONDED FROM A CONVICT ROAD PARTY, COKELUP SWAMP
18th FEBRUARY 1869
AND ESCAPED FROM THIS AREA ON THE WHALING SHIP GAZELLE
3rd MARCH 1869
ALSO DEDICATED TO ALL CONVICTS
WHO BUILT, SWEATED AND TOILED IN THIS DISTRICT

THEN HERE'S TO BRAVE JOHN BOYLE O'REILLY
WHO FIRST BLAZED A TRAIL OWER SEA
BY ESCAPING FROM BUNBURY TO BOSTON
AND VOWING HIS COMERADES TO FREE.
CATALPA BALLAD

ERECTED BY THE SOUTHWEST IRISH CLUB AND LOCAL COMMUNITY
UNVEILED BY AMBASSADOR DESIGNATE TO IRELAND
MR. BRIAN BURKE 11th MARCH 1988

A Droghedaman's memorial in Australia

Chapter Thirtythree

The Great War (1914-1918)

The balance of power in Europe went askew when the Archduke of Austria, Francis Joseph Ferdinand, was assassinated on 28th. June 1914; this quickly led to war. The upshot was that Great Britain, France and other nations (the Allies) declared war on Germany (the Axis) 'for the freedom of small nations'. Here was a golden opportunity for local lads to escape the banality of life in Drogheda. The soldiers who set off in high spirits at the outbreak of the war in 1914 "to free little Belgium" and "to teach the Kaiser a lesson" expected to be back home by Christmas.

Recruitment drives took place to entice young men into the army. "I remember the band parading over West Street with a lot of recruits behind it, and they were in khaki – not the official uniform"(JQ). Enlisting for army service was often alluded to as "taking the King's shilling" – a reference to the fact that each recruit obtained a shilling (about six cents and representing a soldier's wage for one day) when signing on, and this sealed his contract of enlistment. The shilling was soon dissipated, by which time it was too late for the recipient to change his mind on the matter. Others were resentful of Irishmen marching away to fight England's battles, and these feelings surfaced with the rise of Republicanism. A couplet commonly chanted was:

> *"They took the dirty shilling*
> *To do the dirty killing."(DF).*

Harry Fairclough worked in Preston's Distillery from an early age. 'On his 16th birthday the manager called him into the office and said 'Now you must do your duty for the King and join the men who are fighting in France'. He refused, so he was sacked without a reference'.[1] (HFJ).

The band played as the men marched away to the rousing strains of *'It's a Long Way to Tipperary'* and *'Come Back to Erin'*. In all, about 2,500 Louthmen joined up, but tragically, some 800 did not come back to Erin, their final resting place being in France. More and still more men were required to replace the multitudes that fell in the muddy, blood-soaked killing fields of Flanders and France during World War I. For decades afterwards the walls of many tiny Drogheda parlours displayed portraits of fathers or brothers in British army uniforms, photographs taken while the men were home on leave. Of the total number (nationwide) who joined Irish regiments, estimated at 250,000, about 70,000 fell in battle. The Cenotaph at the bottom of Mary Street commemorates those local lads who lie buried somewhere in the killing fields at Ypres or the Somme.

> *"My grandmother had 22 children, 14 boys and 8 girls. My mother was at the tail-end and so she didn't know all their names. Four of the boys joined the Merchant Navy and were lost at sea, and the boy in the army was killed in the battle of the Somme"(PMcK).*

> *"There were recruiting bands marching round the streets, and my father joined up. I didn't see him for 5 years; he was out in Salonika [in Greece]. I remember the night he came home – he woke me up. He was wearing a discharge badge"(JM).[He was also wearing a glass eye and had a damaged arm, having been in the wrong place when a German shell exploded].*

The payments made by the Crown to the wives or widows of the soldiers were their salvation. The army was an outlet and seemed a better alternative to standing at a street corner every day. The majority were complaisant and accepted the conditions in which they found themselves, while others saw too clearly the anomaly of fighting for the freedom of other small nations while their own country was still in bondage. It created rancour in some hearts. Feelings that lay dormant in others came to the fore following the 1916 Rising.

"The Marsh and Sunday's Gate were all pro-British. They were poverty areas, so that the men joined the British Army out of desperation. And a lot of the soldiers' houses were in Barrack Lane, and the soldiers' wives were pro-British. The pension was from 5/- [€0.32] per week upwards, depending on your service and medals.

"Father Norris started a band – Saint Mary's Pipe Band – and they marched out to a feis in Termonfeckin. When they were coming down Barrack Lane all the women were there with stones to throw at the band because they had green, white and yellow ribbons on the bagpipes. They had a rhyme about it:

> *Dirty Biddy Owens*
> *Had an apron full of stones.*
> *She got married to a soldier*
> *And his name was Packey Owens".(DF)*

Such incidents tell us of the factionalism that existed. Whatever sentimental notions of nationalism smouldered in the breasts of some soldiers, they suppressed them, and they derived some satisfaction from the knowledge that a little increment, however meagre, was reaching their homes and families while they were abroad. Loyalties were divided, with the mothers and wives placing more value on pragmatic matters such as the shillings that put a crust of bread on the table rather than on high-minded notions of Home Rule.

Conscription: The British Government found it necessary to take the precautionary step of interning people of German origin; accordingly, several Drogheda citizens were held in detention for the duration of the war. These were the Duffners (jewellers) and Kerns (pork butchers) both of Shop Street, and Weherleys (watchmakers and tobacconists) of Laurence Street. The Kerns had no family, but the Weherleys and Duffners had children. "They [the parents] were interned in case they were spying – it was British law at that time".(PM) In World War II no such circumstance arose because of Taoiseach de Valera's policy of neutrality, but a member of one of these families throughout his life persisted in the belief that the concentration camps of Auschwitz, Buchenwald, Dachau etc. never existed, but were merely figments of British propaganda!

There was much agitation and controversy when it was announced towards the end of the war that conscription was to be introduced in Ireland. John Redmond, the leader of the Nationalist Party, favoured this as a means of attaining Home Rule that would (hopefully) follow when the war ended, and he actively encouraged men to enlist. He said it would be a tragedy 'if young Ireland confined her efforts to remain at home to defend her shores from an unlikely invasion, and shrank from the duty of proving on the field of battle that gallantry and courage which has distinguished our race all through its history.'[2] Such rhetoric was intended to inspire volunteers, but many held opposite views, and did not respond. Redmond was encouraging men to serve, not Ireland but England, and it caused a split in the Nationalist movement. England, some argued, was merely making a *promise* of Home Rule, and a half-baked promise at that, especially since a hint of partition was mooted.

Conscription was a thorny issue. Local agitation culminated in a monster torch-light procession to the Mall. "The biggest procession I remember was for anti-conscription. There was a procession with torch-lights and banners all through the town and down to the Mall [where speeches were made opposing the order]"(MC). So vehement was the resistance to conscription that the proposal was finally dropped. Irishmen were likely to join as volunteers, but not under duress. This was the general consensus, and it underlines the fact that many people regarded Ireland as a separate nation, notwithstanding the Act of Union that bound Ireland to Britain.

"One of my uncles had gone to America to seek his fortune. He returned to Drogheda on several occasions on holidays in the 1950s to see his relations. He sailed only on United States liners, refusing to use a Cunard liner simply because of his abiding hatred of everything British: 'Give my money to an English company – never!' One brother he deliberately neglected to visit – he had never forgiven him for having joined the British Army, and never spoke to him again"(TG).

Not all of the men who enlisted were impoverished or destitute. Some did so from a genuine sense of loyalty to their sovereign, and they were leaving behind a beloved family, a successful business or a career. They were simply answering the call of duty. The head of one Drogheda family was Thomas Sherlock, V.S. His daughter related:

"There was a recruiting campaign – I think it was Kitchener who spearheaded it   – and Georgie [her brother] came home and said he had joined up.   He was only sixteen.   He was tall for his age and he said he was eighteen.   He joined the Royal Irish Rifles and went off to the war.   And Dad [Thomas Sherlock, Veterinary Surgeon] also went. He was a captain in the Royal Army Veterinary Corps and was badly gassed. He was at home recovering when a letter came for my mother informing her that Captain Sherlock was missing and presumed dead; they had found his horse but not the Captain. He used to cry a lot when he came home – it was pathetic to see him.   Georgie was injured, being hit very badly with shrapnel. He died later of his war wounds in a Putney hospital – he was only 24. And I had two brothers in the Royal Navy. Billy was invalided out. He got a bite of something that was in his shoe [a scorpion?] and a doctor was sent home with him."(GK)

"The Smythes at Newtown were good friends of ours – it was a family which consisted of seven sisters. We used to go to them for afternoon tea and they would make bandages and I would knit scarves and socks for the soldiers at the front. Also, we used to collect in the streets for the Red Cross. This was around 1915"(GK).

It was quite a common occurrence for over-enthusiastic or misguided youths who were under age to enlist by overstating their age, as instanced in several of these pages. No questions were asked. When one particular set of human bones was unearthed in Flanders long after the war had ended, the soldier was identified by the number embossed on his leather boots. It revealed that he was a boy from Waterford and was the youngest soldier to die in the Great War – he was two months short of his fourteenth birthday.

Key buildings and vulnerable structures throughout the town were guarded by the British Army during and after the war. Soldiers occupied Millmount while others were billeted in the end building in West Street (opposite Barlow House) and a wall of sand bags to a height of about five feet was put in place around it as a protection. The Boyne Viaduct was also guarded, and soldiers were on permanent sentry duty there:

"We'd see them up on the bridge walking up and down and smoking. They used Winter's field [Maple Drive housing estate now occupies that site] where they had canvas bell tents and where they slept"(DM).

Marching to the Somme
These light-hearted fellows were cut down by machine-gun fire during the disastrous Somme offensive, sometimes at the rate of 20,000 a day.

GORMANSTON AERODROME: When the Wright brothers invented a heavier than air flying machine (1903) it did not take long for the war-mongers to recognise its potential in warfare. The Great War saw planes being used for the first time as a means of killing people and destroying property. The Military Camp at the sleepy little village of Gormanston was chosen as a base for an aerodrome and for use in training pilots who had come from the USA. – America had entered the war in 1917. No doubt the presence of the adjacent railway line figured in its selection, as well as its proximity to Dublin. The construction work for this project provided employment for Drogheda workmen. The three hangers housed nine flights of planes, with over 60 planes in each flight. There was non-stop activity in training the pilots, the work continuing from first light until dusk, and accidents were frequent.[3] The son of one construction worker recalled:

"My father was at the building of Gormanston aerodrome. The job wasn't finished until 1918 when the war was over. They were all plain wooden huts. It was for the training of the American pilots, and some of them were billeted in Millmount. My father brought us up in the train to see an aeroplane on the ground – we had never seen one before.

"They had no batteries for starting the aeroplane. They started them with the propeller – two men rotated the propeller by hand. Now, I didn't see this, but my father told me, one day they were starting a plane and it started too quick and it cut the head off one of the men – it severed the head off completely"(JQ).

To see a plane in the sky was a great novelty – it was little more than a decade since the first flimsy contraption took to the sky at Kitty Hawk, North Carolina. The railway line immediately south of the Drogheda station was a favourite place for young boys to watch the planes making training flights from Gormanston Aerodrome, always hoping for some added excitement:-

"There would be crash landings every day – maybe two or three a day. There was no parachute in those days. We'd lie on the railway looking across. There is a long narrow field above where the sewerage plant is on the Marsh Road, and the planes used to come down there in an emergency. I seen one fellow and a bough of a tree through him – down at Stagreenan – down the Marsh. He landed there and then tried to take off again and flew into the trees at Stagreenan. Your man was hanging out of the trees, he was dead and they were cutting the branch to get him down. The bits of the plane were scattered everywhere"(DF).

Another boy who was an eye-witness to several fatal accidents at Gormanston, was Maurice Collins. He spent his summer holidays in nearby Laytown, and recalled:

"I remember when Gormanston aerodrome was being built. The Americans came over and they were learning to fly. I was stopping in Laytown and we used to go up onto the bridge [the railway bridge that spans the River Nanny]. We'd nearly always see a plane coming down [crashing]- nearly one a day – the poor devils! There was nearly always a mortuary coach on the train with a coffin. It would stop at Gormanston and bring the bodies up to Dublin. They [the trainee pilots] used to come into Drogheda. Their transport would stop at the Tholsel when they were going home, and all the money they had in their pockets they threw out to the crowds. You can imagine the stampede!"(MC).

An incident with a remarkable sequel was experienced by one particular airman. In the course of an aerial exercise involving the use of the machine gun, the trainee accidentally shot off the wooden propeller of his own aircraft. He was forced to ditch in the sea off Gormanston, and a rescue team succeeded in bringing him to safety. ... About 35 years later a stylish American car pulled up for petrol at Holden's garage at the bottom of Mary Street. It was driven by the same pilot who had been rescued from the sea, but he was now retired from the U.S. Air Force. He enquired from Tom Holden the directions to Gormanston – he wanted to visit again the scene of his air force days and his close encounter with death. One word borrowed another, with Tom Holden inviting him to his home close by. There, hanging on a wall, he showed him the broken propeller that slewed from the plane all those years earlier – and carved on it was the pilot's name that he had etched during some idle moments. It had been washed ashore and Tom had found it while strolling on the beach and he took it home as a souvenir. The story ends with Tom setting off in response to an invitation to visit the pilot's home in the U.S.A. (DF).

An official notice dated only nine days before Armistice Day was published by the Royal Air Force in the Drogheda Independent. It warned that members of the public were taking their lives in their hands by venturing near the beach at Ben Head. Under the caption "BOMBING" it read: 'Live bombing will take place on His Majesty's Foreshore between Gormanston Station and Ben Head on or after this date (2/11/1918). All persons trespassing on this foreshore do so at their own risk'. The notices were still appearing in the weekly issues of the Drogheda Independent two months after the war had ended.[4] No one seems to have informed the authorities at the airdrome that hostilities had ceased!

Gormanston Camp continued to be occupied by British forces until it was handed over to the Black and Tans. It was used as a base for most of their transport, and all repair work was performed there during 1920 and 1921. The Camp with its vehicles was taken over by the Irish Free State government in September 1922. But when the soldiers prepared to take away the transport, they found that the Black and Tans had put sand in the petrol tanks and sabotaged the wirings. The vehicles were nonetheless driven away within 24 hours. It remained vacant until World War II when about 2,000 troops were stationed there.

A local pilot in the air corps is worthy of mention. He was Captain Cumiskey, and his initial claim to fame was, when stationed at Baldonnell Airport, he was the first person to greet a lone pilot who had just touched down having completed a solo crossing of the Atlantic. It was a *cause celebre*. The circumstances are that the U.S. Government had prohibited airmen from making solo flights across the Atlantic by virtue of the hazards involved. One airman, named Corrigan, planned a non-stop flight from the East coast of America to California on the West coast – at least that is what he told the authorities. But as his plane, laden with fuel, trundled along the runway and took off, his instruments seem to have gone awry for, instead of flying over the Prairies, the plane headed *eastwards* across the broad expanse of the Atlantic towards the green isle of Erin. He landed at Baldonnell Airport, a feat that attracted much publicity and earned for himself the tag 'Wrong Way Corrigan'. Captain Cumiskey, always ebullient and effervescent, was the perfect character to bid a hearty Irish welcome to the 'disoriented' navigator.

Captain Cumiskey, who was later stationed at Gormanston, was a dare-devil pilot in his own right. "There was Cumiskey. He used to fly down as far as Baltray, then up the river and straight under the Bridge. We used to be thrilled watching him" (JQ). Not surprisingly, regulations in the air corps have since been tightened. His family home was a little further along the coast, in Termonfeckin, where he owned a farm. During World War II when foodstuffs were scarce it was not unusual for him, when on routine exercise, to return to base laden with a basket of fresh eggs and butter for himself and his colleagues. Suffice it to say that one of his fields in Termonfeckin was long and level – a perfect landing strip!

THE VICTORIA CROSS: Great excitement surged through Drogheda in 1915 when one of its sons was awarded the Victoria Cross – a medal on which are inscribed just two simple words – *'FOR VALOUR'*. This inscription is a deliberate understatement, and serves well to illustrate its primacy as a citation – it is in fact Britain's highest military award for gallantry. Today there are only 15 living recipients, and a collector recently paid over €200,000 for a specimen.

Some sources claimed that the policy of awarding military honours, at least in Ireland, was a deliberate attempt to glamorise military life and to gain Irish recruits for an army that was becoming increasingly depleted through the carnage in the trenches. Such comments sound cynical, but they were certainly in circulation. They should not be allowed to detract from the heroic and selfless deeds of truly brave men.

Two local soldiers earned the V.C. One was Drum Major William Kenny from Greenhills; he had joined the Gordon Highlanders. His citation reads as follows:

'William Kenny, No. 6535. Drummer 2nd. Bttn. The Gordon Highlanders – For conspicuous bravery on 23 October 1914 near Ypres in rescuing wounded men on five occasions under very heavy fire, in the most fearless manner, and for twice previously saving machine guns by carrying them out of action.

On numerous occasions Drummer Kenny conveyed urgent messages under very dangerous circumstances over fire-swept ground.'

"I remember Drummer Kenny well. He lived beside me. He was a relation of Con O'Brien [Mayor of Drogheda in 1985/6]. He was always dressed immaculate"(JM).

Drogheda Corporation honoured him with the Freedom of Drogheda. The unique occasion is recalled by Georgina Sherlock:

"I remember Private Kenny, the Victoria Cross man. When he came back to Drogheda – I remember it as if it were yesterday – he was sitting in the back of a motorcar, he and his mother sitting there. I think it was Saint Patrick's Day. The car went over West Street [in a parade of honour]. I met him and asked him for a button off his uniform. He cut one off and gave it to me. I still have it in a box upstairs – it is one of my treasured possessions" (GS). [The souvenir button was graciously donated to the Drogheda Museum in 2006 by the owner's daughter].

Another eyewitness added: "Luke J. Elcock was the Mayor, and he was with them [in the parade]. He had a beard and a tall hat"(DF).

One Drogheda boy had several reasons for remembering that occasion and he, too, acquired possession of a souvenir of sorts! His mother had been a surrogate mother to his four uncles because their own mother had died while they were still young boys and all lived together in the same little home. As in so many Irish dwellings at that time, the future for them seemed bleak and the only course open to them was to join His Majesty's Forces; four of them did so. Two enlisted together in 1893, Kitt in the army and Michael in the navy.

"My father's four brothers joined up – there was no work. Michael was too young for the army – you had to be 16 for the army, but at that time you could join the navy at 14. He was only 13 but he got into the navy by saying he was 14. You joined for 21 years, and their time had been fully served in 1914, but then the war broke out and they stayed on for the duration of the war. The only mother they ever knew was my mother, and they were home on leave together, and they stayed with us. This was the first time they had seen each other for 26 years"(DF).

***Drummer Kenny VC** (right). **The two Fairclough brother** were little more than boys when they joined the armed forces. They were now meeting (on furlough) for the first time in 26 years.*

A reunion of the two brothers after so lengthy a time gap – 26 years – was the cause of great rejoicing – and who would begrudge them a little amount of imbibing! William Kenny, V.C., who was home on leave at the time, joined them in their home for the celebrations, and this, of course, made the occasion even more memorable. "My father [who worked in Cairnes Brewery] got a quarter cask in the brewery. It was sitting in the corner over there [in the kitchen of their home in St. Mary's Cottages at Cromwell's Mount]" (DF). There was music and dancing, and at one stage of the festivities the hero Kenny accidentally stood on the foot of young Dermot Fairclough. (He was the narrator of this anecdote, and lived until 2004 having reached the age of 92 years – he was a child aged six years at the time of the incident). It displaced a bone, causing a sizeable lump on his foot, and the bone never properly set, causing a permanent lump – a souvenir of sorts – and he carried the disfigurement for the remainder of his life.

No such revelry attended the presentation earned by the second local hero – it was awarded posthumously. The soldier who earned it was 2nd. Lieut. James (Jim) Samuel Emerson. He was born in Collon and was the youngest of seven sons. His father was an official in the Labour Exchange in Drogheda and had died of anthrax in the Cottage Hospital. His mother was unable to attend at Buckingham Palace for the Award Ceremony, so, accompanied by his brother Alex, she accepted the medal on his behalf in a ceremony that took place in the Whitworth Hall in 1918, the Mayor making the presentation.

Jim Emerson was educated at Mountjoy School, Dublin, and joined the cadet corps attached to the school. At the outbreak of the Great War he answered the call along with about 500 other past pupils who came forward voluntarily to enlist in His Majesty's Forces. He joined the Royal Irish Rifles and served in France until severely wounded at Hooge. After recovering, he returned to France in 1916 where he transferred to the Royal Enniskillen Fusiliers as 2nd. Lieutenant.

The War Office issued the following citation of his action on the 6th. December 1917:

'For repeated acts of the most conspicuous bravery. He led his company in an attack and cleared 400 yards of trench. Though wounded when the enemy attacked in superior numbers, he sprang out of the trench with 8 men and met the attack in the open, killing many and taking six prisoners. For three hours after this, all the officers having become casualties, he

remained with his company, refusing to go to the dressing station, and repeatedly repelled bombing attacks. Later, when the enemy again attacked in superior numbers, he led his men to repel the attack and was mortally wounded. His heroism, when worn out and exhausted from loss of blood, inspired his men to hold out, though almost surrounded, till reinforcements arrived and dislodged the enemy'.

His C.O. wrote: 'He led his men for 24 hours in the hardest fighting I have ever yet seen, and he was cool, calm and collected the whole time. I cannot say too much for his behaviour'[5]. The regiment's Chaplain supplied an additional detail '... A few hours before he was mortally wounded a German grenade hit him on his steel helmet and exploded, tearing the crown out of the helmet but leaving his head untouched. He was also slightly wounded in the thumb but like the brave man he was, he carried on the fight as if nothing had happened to him ...' It was a sniper's bullet that brought his young life to an end later that day. He was aged 22. The cruel and chaotic fortunes of war have denied him a final identifiable resting place.

2ⁿᵈ Lieut. James Emerson VC
Inset: His brother Alex and mother receiving the medal in a ceremony held in the Whitworth Hall.

His name is inscribed on the cenotaph at Collon Church, and on the War Memorial at Mary Street, Drogheda, as well as at Cambrai in France, close to the scene of his gallantry. "Some of his possessions came home – his watch, his whistle and lanyard, and his ceremonial sword. These are now in the Enniskillen Museum"(PE).

Two of his brothers, Gordon and Egerton, also fought in the Great War. The latter brother, known to his friends as 'Teb', served in the Connaught Rangers. His regiment had just returned home from India at the outbreak of the Great War, and after a week's leave he was sent to France. Within a very short time he was taken prisoner by the Germans and he spent the rest of the war in POW camps. Some of the time was spent at Danzig (now known as Gdansk) where he was given the task of breaking the ice on the river.

"He had two cats which he always carried in his rucksack when he went working, and he shared his meagre rations with them. He named them 'General Haigh and 'General Gordon' after the two English generals. The cats went missing one night, and it transpired that the French prisoners were hungry, took his cats and ate them! He could never countenance a Frenchman after that"(PE).

All those who fought in the Great War are long dead. A ceremony took place for many years afterwards on Armistice Day when people assembled at the Cenotaph (erected at the bottom of Mary St. in 1925) to commemorate the local men who fell in both world wars, but the occasion was later allowed to lapse for 30 years. The republican sections of the community in particular looked askance at such demonstrations (including the wearing of an emblem on Poppy Day), interpreting them as symbols of British imperialism, and on at least one occasion the Cenotaph was defaced by being smeared with an oily substance. It is interesting to note that the cenotaph in Castlebellingham makes clear the motive of those soldiers who gave their lives in the war, the wording being that they 'died for Ireland in the Great European War of 1914 – 1918'. The wording was intended to dispel any doubt as to which country they fought and died for.

In 1999 the commemoration ceremony was revived, and representatives of the Drogheda Borough Council, several church bodies, the Organisation of National Ex-Servicemen, the British Legion and other associations annually attend the ceremony. Wreaths are laid, two minutes silence observed and the Last Post and Reveille sounded. These gestures demonstrate that there has been an erosion of memories of bygone injustices, and a maturing of minds among the populace.

It is regrettable that there are so few records of the experiences of the local soldiers who fought. To the boyhood memories of this author, the town was home to many 'ex-soldiers', or 'ex-servicemen' as they were called, and they freely gave of their experiences of war in the trenches to anyone who would listen, but such tales were only of passing interest to the listeners, and for the most part remain unrecorded.

However, one such incident is recalled by the author: the groundsman in the Drogheda Rowing Club, who was an ex-soldier, was describing his experiences to some club members when this author asked him if he actually killed anyone while in the battlefield. He explained that it was virtually impossible to identify a specific 'hit'; however, he instanced one occasion when, having pulled the short straw amid a group of fellow soldiers, it fell to him to dispose of their company officer! When men were ordered to 'go over the top' i.e. to leave the relative safety of a trench and make an attack across no-mans-land, it was the officer's duty to ensure that no one remained behind, and he had the unenviable task of using his drawn revolver on any laggard. Disposing of the officer in charge gave the foot soldiers a better chance of survival. The judgment on the veracity of this story is left to the reader, but it was certainly not uncommon for officers to be 'killed in action' in that manner, and confusion in the trenches made detection impossible.

A more mundane incident was related to this author by a soldier who saw service both in the Boer War and in the Dardanelles. Referring to the Dardanelles, he spoke, not of the withering enemy machine-gun fire, but about the flies, the millions and millions of flies that plagued the entire battle arena. When partaking of a meal (which consisted of a piece or two of hardtack and jam) he described how the flies arrived in myriads and settled on the jam which in an instant became black with them. Here we must remember that, as the men came ashore from the troop ships, they were mown down in their thousands by Turkish machinegun fire; it was often impossible to recover the bodies and thus they lay unburied under the Mediterranean sun. It need hardly be added that the rotting cadavers became the breeding ground for flies and food for worms.

ARMISTICE DAY: The slaughter in the trenches continued unabated for over four years. The guns finally fell silent on the eleventh hour of the eleventh day of the eleventh month in 1918. The welcome announcement was to have been made in the House of Commons on the afternoon of that day by Prime Minister Lloyd George. But he was furious that the House was empty when he got there. No one seems to have told him that the official hour to mark the Armistice was brought forward to eleven at morning, and the venue for the momentous announcement was changed to Buckingham Palace. (It seems that the timing was changed simply to line up all the 'elevens' of that memorable day). Thus he was denied the kudos that attended the occasion. Drogheda celebrated too:

> *"Anyone who was there that day couldn't but remember it. Up the Boyne came this big thing – a Zeppelin, a barrage balloon – and underneath it was a basket affair as big as a motorcar, and it had windows on it. Underneath was a big long rope with a thing like a pot hanging out of the bottom to balance it like a keel. Music came out of it. We were scared it might hit James Street chapel because we used to hear horrible things about the British, and that they were going to knock down the chapel. We sat there with our mouths open! It followed the course of the river towards Dominic Street. It then turned around towards Millmount, which was packed with troops looking on. It then went on in the direction of Gormanston Airdrome"(DF).*

"A great barrage balloon appeared, and our next door neighbours, a Protestant family, ran inside and took a Union Jack flag out into the garden and began waving it like hell towards the barrage balloon"(DM).

"There was a big flag – a huge big Union Jack – on the North side of Millmount. Someone hoisted a Green-White-and-Yellow Tricolour near the Union Jack. We started shoutin: 'There's a Green-White-and-Yellow flag up in Millmount' and everyone stopped and looked. I thought it might be an Irish officer who did it, and he'd later pay for his trouble!" (DF)

(Note the use of the word 'chapel' for St. Mary's Church; also the third colour of the Irish tricolour being described as 'yellow'. This was quite a common error in those times, and this continued well into the 'Forties. Schoolboys were apt to chant "Green, white and yellow; he's a dirty Irish fellow" – a chant which may well have originated in the northern part on the island).

Any occurrence that smacked of republicanism was quickly quelled. Another incident (which may or may not have occurred at the time of the Armistice) happened when the townspeople "got up one morning and they saw a Tricolour at the top of Laurence Gate. Constable Jackson went up and took it down" (GS).

THE GREAT FLU PANDEMIC: In the course of the four years of the Great War the headcount in the slaughter was 21 million people dead. But the world was given no time to recover from the carnage. Nature was to prove that it could outdo man's efforts with ease for, just as the war was coming to an end, an epidemic of global proportions descended to afflict mankind, and countless people succumbed; 'they died like flies'. Much about the pandemic is poorly understood, especially the rapidity with which it exploded on the world, targeting young adults and those in their prime rather than the elderly. It was known as the Great Spanish Flu although it knew no political boundaries. Since accurate statistics in the third world could not be provided, there are no exact figures of the numbers that it claimed. "It was not less than twenty million and probably more like fifty million. Some estimates have put the global total as high as a hundred million". Drogheda did not escape. A few residents who lived through the pandemic have survived into the twenty-first century, and those who were questioned by the author recalled the outbreak:

- *"My mother was one of the first to get it, but she had a cure. My father used to go out and collect the herbs and wild seeds and make it up. And as soon as she was better the Colonel's wife got it. [Colonel Cairnes was proprietor of Cairnes Brewery where both parents of the narrator worked]. The colonel asked her if she would go and help in his house, [now Boyne Valley Hotel] so we didn't see her for three weeks. The whole lot of them got it, but they survived. People died like flies. They'd wrap them in canvass – they hadn't enough coffins for them" (DF).*

- *"I was only a child at the time, but my godfather, Mr. McIntosh died of it."(MS*

- *"There were lots in school had it. But I was too young to know if anyone died with it. I got it, and my grandmother cured me with whiskey – that's what she gave me! After that I was jumpin' mad in the bed!"(JM).*

- *"A Drogheda family called Goodfellow got it and all of them died except one girl – she later joined a convent."(RO)*

- *"In 1919 I became very ill with the Flu. I overheard the doctor telling my parents that I would not last the night. [In fact, she celebrated her Hundred-and-Second Birthday in 2005!] Some weeks later when I was convalescing Doctor Parr called. I was at the top of the stairs. When he looked up and saw me he said 'Behold the Resurrection!' Others were less fortunate; the two Miss McAuleys died, leaving behind their elderly mother."(GK)*

Chapter Thirtyfour

The Easter Rising (1916)

Subsequent to passing into the 20th Century the Irish people continued to be fully resigned to seeing the Union Jack fluttering on flag-poles, and none more so than Droghedeans. For the most part they accepted unquestioningly whatever laws were being passed in far off London, and they were enveloped in a cocoon of complacency. Such attitudes were prevalent, not only among the fast fading Ascendancy, but also among the commonality of people, and they stood to attention when the anthem *'God Save the King'* was being played. It is hardly an exaggeration to say that many had become 'more English that the English themselves'.

Most middle class people favoured England; shopkeepers and other established businessmen in Drogheda were doing all right, thank you very much, and did not want to upset the apple-cart. Ireland's economy was wholly agriculture-based, and the farming community was grateful to an England that took surplus cattle, sheep and other farm produce off their hands; the country was thus conditioned into being totally dependent on England. As for the soldiers' wives, who else but the British Government was feeding their large families. The upper class was, almost to the last man, fully supportive of England. In other words, the Act of Union (1800), which had spliced Ireland *as a country* to Britain, had now almost fully succeeded in joining its *people* as well. There was agitation for a separate parliament, and apart from that the people were copper-fastened body and soul to the United Kingdom.

A New Home Rule Bill was enacted in 1914 (It followed a curtailment of the powers of veto exercised by the House of Lords). This belated Act pleased nobody because its implementation was suspended with the outbreak of the Great War. Those in the south were frustrated, and the response in Ulster was one of deep apprehension. To repel its pending implementation, a paramilitary organisation was formed in Ulster called the Ulster Volunteer Force (UVF). It was well organised and generously funded, and its determination in resisting Home Rule was such as to include the use of firearms should the occasion arise. To this end it imported an arsenal of 25,000 rifles and 3,000,000 rounds of ammunition from Germany in the spring of 1914. This traffic, of course, was contrary to the law of the land but nonetheless the operation was accomplished quite openly, and the authorities turned a blind eye as the ship discharged its cargo. In addition, the army officers in the Curragh refused to go north to coerce the people into accepting Home Rule – an event known as 'the Curragh Mutiny'.

In the South the people were in fear of the UVF and it was deemed necessary to form a similar body as a counter-measure. However, it was ill-organised and was deplorably lacking in funds. Forty years later (1953) the Mayor of Drogheda responded to an invitation to address the local Rotary Club at one of their weekly luncheons. The mayor in question was Alderman Larry Walsh TD, a man who had risen in the ranks of both local and national politics, and represented County Louth in Dáil Éireann. The subject of his address was 'the Development of the Irish Republic', and nobody was better qualified to speak on that subject. He explained the need that had arisen to form vigilante groups (the Irish Volunteers) in the South. He had been assigned the task of forming the Drogheda branch, but he stated that this was a very great challenge. *'The town never had the force, the leaders or the initiative that was later to be revealed in the South and the Midlands'*, he said. This observation underlines the extent of the pervading apathy within the town. It was supported by the very active Harry Fairclough who said *'There were only about 18 active members of the IRA in Drogheda'*. Those who were suspected of harbouring nationalist sentiments were likely to be shunned by the average citizen, and Republicans were regarded as reprobates,

A small shipment of arms – it consisted of 900 rifles compared with the consignment of 25,000 landed by the UVF at Larne – successfully reached Howth in the *Asgard*, but on this occasion the reaction of the authorities was in stark contrast to that in Ulster. The Irish Volunteers were met by the police and the King's Own Scottish Borders with fixed bayonets (although the arms were spirited away in a few vans). A crowd of men, women and children jeered at the soldiers as they passed along Bachelor's Walk. The soldiers opened fire on them, killing four and leaving 37 wounded.

Meantime, the subversives in Drogheda had secured a cache of arms for themselves, as is implicit in the disappearance of officially held guns. A committee, of which several former mayors were members, used to meet in the then Sheriff's office of the Corporation. Their duties included the arranging of a drilling schedule for volunteers. They had 50 rifles that were secured in locked boxes, bolted to the floor of the meeting room in the Corporation premises, but one Monday night they discovered that the arsenal had mysteriously disappeared. Despite police investigation it was never recovered.

Dissention in The Volunteer Movement: To curry favour with Westminster, John Redmond (the successor to Parnell who was the champion of the Home Rule movement) called for recruitments to step aboard the troopships and assist Britain in winning the war against Germany – this would help in securing Home Rule, he surmised. Others reasoned the matter differently: one of the emotive slogans in circulation at that time was 'Free Little Belgium', a nation that had been invaded by Germany. Not without logic, they perceived the freedom of Ireland as a priority over freeing 'little Belgium'. This rent the Volunteer movement in twain, although there was nothing unusual about such an occurrence in Irish revolutionary movements!

One segment recognised that England's dilemma as Ireland's opportunity to strike for freedom, and they set about making plans. However, a glance at Irish history reveals that hardly a generation passed without a section of the people taking up arms in revolt. All of them were dismal failures if for no reason other than that they were uncoordinated; but in addition their ranks were invariably riddled with spies and informers. None seemed so hopeless or pathetic as the Rising now being planned by the idealists and dreamers of 1916. They fully realised that their chances of success were minimal – a handful of die-hard amateurs were about to tackle the British Empire which at that time was at its zenith.

In Drogheda the pervading apathy was a prime obstacle in rallying support at local level. Out of a population of 12,000 *only 17 men answered the call for recruits.* But for those who responded, the commitment was total, and several of their names feature on these pages. These were men of upright character, and for the most part they were professionals or prominent businessmen of Drogheda. The names are:

Frank Bateson, James St. Newsagent

Dr. W. Bradley, Laurence St. Medical practitioner

William Branigan, Shop Street

Joseph Finnegan, Peter Street

Tom Gavin, Duleek Street

Michael Harkin, North Strand: Journalist

Sean Kiley, Cord Rd.: Teacher

Michael Keenan, Beamore Rd.: Railway clerk

Fintan Lawlor, North Strand

James Monaghan, James Street

Philip Monaghan, Cord Rd.: Science Teacher

William McQuillan, Fair St.: Sack factory owner

Malone Brothers (2), West St.: Butchers

James Murphy, West St.: Draper

James O'Mara, Shop Street

Larry Walsh, Duleek St. Grocer

On Holy Thursday in 1916 Larry Walsh, who was the principal organiser at local level, received orders to have his section of Volunteers mobilised on Easter Sunday morning. The assembly point was at the top of Mell where they were to await further instructions. (These instructions were to proceed to Slane where the Dundalk contingent would meet up with them, and together they would head for Dublin, probably to guard the western approached to the city centre). These Volunteers who had reported for action had everything to lose, including their very lives. The first name on the above list was Frank Bateson. He was a newsagent in James St. and he had good reason to act cautiously, having had some close brushes with the military forces, as had a neighbouring shopkeeper, Mattie Corcoran. It was necessary for them to be constantly on the *qui vive* to avoid capture.

"This lady came down from the station and went into Bateson's shop and she bought some trivial item. When she was leaving, she gave her skirt a tilt, and on the hem of it there was a green ribbon. That was a sign that the soldiers were coming [to capture Bateson and Corcoran]. The shop had a cellar and both of them went down the trap-door, so when the soldiers arrived there was no sign of them. The lady was Maud Gonne"(RO).

Maud Gonne, the daughter of English parents, had initially come into prominence by campaigning against evictions in Donegal and she later became a leading republican activist. She married John McBride who was executed following the 1916 Rising.

However, the entire plans for insurrection received a profound setback on Good Friday when a second boatload of arms sent from Germany in the *Aud* was intercepted by the ever vigilant Royal Navy. To avoid the armaments falling into British hands the captain of the *Aud* scuttled his ship, and all hope of a successful Rising sank with it.

The man who had gone to Germany to arrange the gun-run was Sir Roger Casement. Casement abhorred oppression, was a Dublin Protestant and he earned fame in exposing the abuses of the native people in the Belgian Congo and in the Amazon where grave atrocities against the natives were committed and colonial exploitation went unchecked. His sterling work earned him a knighthood from the British Government. He likewise identified similar oppression in his native land, Ireland, and sought to remedy it. He succeeded in arranging a shipment of German weapons for the republicans and was now returning from Germany in a U-boat. The trip was not without incident, but he eventually reached the Kerry coast. Misfortune attended those who were to have signalled the shipment from the coast, for their car took a wrong turn and plunged from the pier, ending the lives of the occupants. Meantime, Casement emerged from the coning tower of the U-boat and reached Banna Strand soaked to the skin. Disoriented, he called to the nearest farmstead. At this point a nun who came to Drogheda in 1931 as a postulant and remained to teach several generations of schoolgirls links us to a crucial moment in Ireland's past: she tells us that her granduncle, Patsy McKenna, was taking his cattle out to the early morning grass when he met a stranger who enquired as to his location, and McKenna was able to enlighten him. Later in the day the presence of the tall, distinguished stranger alerted the RIC and he was taken into custody. He was soon to learn that the type of work for which he had been decorated was provisional, was subject to selective procedures and did not have universal approval – in particular, it was not to be applied in the case of Ireland. Casement was stripped of his knighthood, found guilty of high treason and was executed.

The Countermanded Order: The last minute loss of the vital shipment of rifles was a disaster which forced Eoin McNeill, president of the Irish Volunteers, to countermand the order for mobilisation. The little band of Drogheda Volunteers, amateurs all, by that time had duly met at the appointed place in Mell on Easter Sunday morning, awaiting their instructions. One of their members was Dr. Willie Bradley of Laurence Street who possessed one of the very few telephones in Drogheda at the time – it was telephone number 78. When his phone rang that morning it was an urgent message informing him that the Rising was being called off. This was profoundly important information and he thereupon mounted his bicycle and peddled up the hill of Mell and relayed the news to the waiting men. They then tried to contact the Dundalk volunteers, but endless confusion ensued.

The order to disband must certainly have been a bitter disappointment to the little group of 17 Volunteers. Later that day when Larry Walsh was on his way home, he recalled that it was with difficulty that he was able to pass the police barracks at West Gate. By that time word of the intended Rising had circulated throughout the town, and the general reaction was one of anger and resentment – most people were enraged with the subversives, and the area around the barracks was thronged with townspeople, all clambering to support the constabulary against any attempt at insurrection.

Notwithstanding McNeill's countermanding order, a small faction of diehards nonetheless resolved to proceed with the Rising a day later. Being without an adequate supply of arms and ammunition, they fully realised that their mission had become suicidal, but this did not deter them. Thus the brave hearts who took up their positions in Dublin to face the might of the British Empire numbered only 1,600 Volunteers in total. It is not known what independent plans were made by the 17 Drogheda Volunteers. Dr. Bradley was seen marching quickly down Shop St. that Easter Monday morning, heading for the railway station. [Dr. TB]. In Dublin he was passing quickly along Clare St. clutching tightly a case. His heart somersaulted when an army officer approached him. It was too late to get rid of the incriminating case – it contained a gun. The officer stopped and spoke to him. Never were street directions given so readily – the officer simply wanted to know the way! [Gerry Bradley]

'Life Springs from Death': The leader of the Rising was Pádraig Pearse, born of an English father and a County Meath mother. He was a visionary, a writer, an educator and a republican; he is noted also for his eulogy at the grave of O'Donovan Rossa. O'Donovan Rossa, a Fenian leader and an implacable enemy of serfdom, was well acquainted with the inside of English jails by virtue of his sentiments on Nationhood. When he died in America in June 1915 his body was taken back to Ireland and an armed escort of Irish Volunteers flanked the hearse on its way for burial in Glasnevin Cemetery. An immense crowd attended, and when the funeral rites were completed Pádraig Pearse stepped forward:

> *"Life springs from death, and from the graves of patriot men and women spring living nations. We stand at Rossa's grave not in sadness but rather in exultation of spirit. ... This is a place of peace sacred to the dead, where men should speak with all charity and with all restraint; but I hold it a Christian thing to hate evil, to hate untruth, to hate oppression, and in hating them, to strive to overthrow them ... [The English] think they have pacified Ireland. They think they have purchased half of us and intimidated the other half. They think they have foreseen everything and provided against everything – but the Fools!, the Fools!, the Fools! – they have left us our Fenian dead, and while Ireland holds these graves, Ireland unfree shall never be at peace".*

These stirring words proved shortly afterwards to be startlingly prophetic in regard to Pearse's own fate, when he and a handful of companions trod the same martyr's path of many earlier Fenians. In that way they became the catalyst, the inspiration, the motivation, and by their martyrdom, the ultimate victors in that struggle for which their predecessors had so vainly fought. They didn't realise it, but the wait of seven-and-a-half centuries which the native Irish people had to endure was about to end.

When the small band of Volunteers occupied Dublin's GPO on Easter Monday 1916 he read the Proclamation of Independence outside the building to some indifferent onlookers, and soon the lethal fireworks began. A Royal Navy gunboat was brought up the Liffey and soon reduced O'Connell Street to rubble. Artillery placed in D'Olier St. caused similar havoc in Eden Quay. By week's end most of those who were inside the inferno that had been the GPO, including Pádraig Pearse, Michael Collins and the injured James Connolly, had retreated to Moore St. The inevitable outcome was that the white flag of surrender was raised.

The Battle of Ashbourne: There had been virtually no action in the provinces – McNeill's last minute order had seen to that. The sole important exception was at Ashbourne where 13 deaths occurred. The Drogheda Independent of 6th May reported:

> *"In the North County Dublin, in Swords, Donabate, Lusk, Rush and Garristown districts, strong and well organised branches of the Sinn Fein Volunteer movement have been in existence and they have been supported as far as Swords in concerned by the Larkinites of whom a branch was formed in that district during the strike operations two years ago.*

> *"When on Easter Monday the 'fiery cross' was sent out in Dublin and the Sinn Fein Volunteers took possession of part of the capital, the first of the revolutionaries to spring to arms were those of the North Dublin contingent".*

Groups of men under the command of Thomas Ashe attacked the barracks at Donabate, Swords and Garristown and seized arms, the occupants having surrendered without a fight. The Kilmoon barracks, having been forewarned, put up a stiff resistance, with showers of bullets being exchanged. The explosion of a massive bomb on front of the barracks induced the occupants to surrender. Ashe marched forward to receive and disarm them, but at that moment reinforcements of some 60 police arrived from Slane and then all hell broke loose. The battle continued for 5 hours, with both sides taking shelter in ditches and behind shrubs, etc. as the bullets continued to fly. One by one the police were silenced. The upshot was that they eventually surrendered, but not before 11 were killed and 15 wounded. The insurgents lost 2, with 6 wounded. They were then devastated to learn of Pearse's surrender. Accordingly, they were rounded up and jailed. Ashe was later to die on hunger strike.

> "[Men were] shot and killed. ... My father [Dr. Byrne, Slane] was the Medical Officer to the Drogheda RIC and he went to Ashbourne House. He was captured by one of the Sinn Féiners and he spent the day in the laurel bushes at King's house – near the road to Curraha. He was eventually released and came home." (TB)

The GPO in Dublin
The scene at the end of Easter Week.

A person who had a different purpose in visiting Dublin on that Easter Monday was Hugh Balfe, Cord Road. He had planned to attend a football match – or so he said – but he witnessed pandemonium, with the city centre being turned into a flaming shambles. His grandson, Ray Dempsey described how he eventually returned to Drogheda: 'It took him three days to get home, at one stage hitching a lift on a farmer's cart. All public transport had come to a halt'.

Both parents of Tom Munster, Cord Road, had republican sympathies. There were seven children in the family, one (Tom) being merely ten months old when his father went missing on Easter Monday. When in his nineties he related:

> 'The neighbours were great at that time – they looked after the children. Another neighbour came to my mother and put me in a shawl and took me away to look after me while my mother went around all the barracks in Dublin looking for my father. He had been taken away to a POW camp in England – I forget the name of the place. He was released after a while and came home' [TM].

And so it came to pass that when the Volunteers submitted to unconditional surrender, Dubliners gave vent to their feelings by hurling abuse at them, and women jeered and spat at them in contempt as they were being marched away to await execution in Kilmainham Jail. Housewives gathered at Christ Church (adjacent to the tenements and Corporation flats, which were the homes of many soldiers) and shouted expletives at the prisoners as they filed by – yet another example of the average person's sentiments. The 'gunmen' were reviled and were looked upon as upsetting the *status quo* of a people who had become inured to the political circumstances that surrounded them.

These contemptuous gestures of resentment and disapproval, however, did not extend to the protection of private property. On the contrary, the opportunity was taken by many of the women to loot the shops of central Dublin that had been damaged – they were picked clean.

One national newspaper described the event as 'An Orgy of Fire and Slaughter' and a headline screamed 'The Darkest Week in the History of Dublin'.[1] Reaction throughout Drogheda was no different to that in Dublin; the *Drogheda Independent* reflected the general view by criticising the volunteers. They were 'a silly crowd of irresponsible fools, the mere dupes and pawns of others'. The paper also quoted the chairman of Trim Urban Council who said the insurgents were: 'ill-advised, uneducated, hot-headed young fellows led by scheming fanatics'. Drogheda Corporation likewise passed a resolution condemning 'the futile and deplorable occurrences in Dublin'. The parish priest in St. Mary's church said 'many people had bade good-bye to reason and allowed themselves to be ruled by feelings of a most exciting and dangerous kind'. Reaction in Dundalk and the rest of Ireland was no less adverse.

The condemnations thus were universal. Referring to the Ashbourne ambush, Navan Urban Council said 'we deplore and depreciate the recent disturbances', and praised the police 'for the heroic discharge of their duties'. The Bishop of Meath joined in the condemnation and visited the wounded policemen who had been taken to the Meath Infirmary in Navan. The local Administrator said 'I believe the annals of the happenings of Easter Week 1916 will form the darkest records of Irish history'.

Here we have a clear insight into the mood of the populace at large. They were supporters of the Crown for the most part, and they opposed whatever few mad-caps sought to overthrow the Act of Union and sever the cast-iron links with the Imperial Parliament in London. In particular, overt hostility towards Sinn Féin emanated from the families of the soldiers who were facing death in the muddy trenches and the pock-marked fields of Passchendaele and the Somme. These republicans were looked upon by the majority as being fifth columnists and trouble-makers. Persons acting suspiciously were apt to be reported to the RIC. Michael Walsh, son of former Mayor Larry Walsh, TD, put it this way:

> *"The people were no great lovers of the republican movement because of the many sons and husbands who were enlisted in the [British] armed services. The men were away fighting in the trenches, and the wives at home – who would otherwise be destitute – were getting government pensions".*

A member of the Corporation later publicly criticised Sinn Féin for making 'personal attacks on fellow Irishmen' and he referred to them as 'arrogant revilers'.[2] In the previous generation, that of the Fenian Brotherhood, it was through an informer that the authorities learned of the undercover activities of John Boyle O'Reilly, earning him the death sentence (later commuted to transportation and penal servitude for life). It was the co-operation of informers some years later that enabled the Black and Tans to single out homes for torching, and men for summary execution.

A Turn-about in The Mood of the People: The history of Ireland was to take an unexpected U-turn when the firing squad in Kilmainham Jail had performed its task. Pearse and the other leaders were now dead. There was a complete *volte-face*. No sooner had the echoes of the rifle-fire died away than the pervading apathy and distain vanished and was replaced by feelings that ranged from sympathy to indignation to seething outrage. Here was a paradox probably unique in history because the ultimate goal of the men who were executed – that long, long sought liberty – was at last assured.

The RIC records show that support in Drogheda for Sinn Féin grew after the Rising, and anger within the town smouldered. In the next general election Sinn Féin scored a land-slide victory over all opposition. A Sinn Féin military parade marched through the streets in July 1917. They carried flags and regalia which still caused offence to the wives of the soldier-husbands who were fighting in France, and they gave vent to their feelings by pelting the marchers with bottles and stones. The RIC intervened to enable the parade to continue. The following night the soldiers' houses were attacked in retaliation, and windows were broken.

The Balfe family, like most others, had been upset at Pearse and his companions 'for destroying most of Dublin'. A year later Dempsey's mother Kathleen became a founder member and secretary of the women's segment of the Irish Volunteer movement, called *Cumann na mBan*. Her brothers became active in the campaign against the Black and Tans. The *Cumann* raised money by organising *céilí* nights and concerts for the purchase of arms; they held a tea party in the Mayoralty Rooms which was attended by Countess Markievicz. Kathleen Dempsey was later awarded the Military Service Medal and a pension of 12/6 [€0.40] per week, and later still she became the first lady member of the Drogheda Corporation.

> *'Irish history has tended to portray Irish revolutionary movements as occurring in cycles which always ended in disaster until the triumph of self-immolation of the 1916 leaders, whose sacrifice and courageous example put new heart in the Irish people, and gave rise to an independence movement from which came liberation and prosperity.'*[3]

There are good reasons to remember the insurrections that occurred in the past – those of 1798, 1803, 1848 and 1867 – but there are better reasons to forget them. 1798 transpired to be little more than a serious but spontaneous peasants' revolt and very localised, and the others were deplorable, pathetic damp squibs. One common denomination among them all was a lack of coordination, and they were predestined to failure by virtue of internal dissention, lack of leadership and by the work of informers. The authorities were able to swoop down each time and capture the leaders, emasculating the entire movement. Even the plans for the Fenian Rising of 1867 were betrayed by an informer, despite all the precautions – this time his name was Nagle – and although the firebrand leader James Stephens went into hiding, another informer was at hand to reveal his whereabouts. As for resolve, or rather the lack of it, no better example exists of the futility of relying on an untrained, indisciplined mob than Drogheda's performance in the Potato Market in 1867. This is not to disparage the men's good intentions, but unless pious ideals are matched by total commitment and firm leadership, the outcome will invariably end in failure.

1916 was different. Even though the all-important armaments were intercepted at sea and the ship scuttled, thereby leaving the insurgents critically short of weapons, the men were not deterred. They knew the inevitability of the outcome, but they did not flinch. These men were intellectuals of strong character and firm resolve, with no riff-raff among them. Well educated, the inner council included a teacher of mathematics, a professor of Irish history, a trade union leader, a shopkeeper, a schoolteacher and a poet. The same applied to the assembled Drogheda men at Mell; a glance at the list of names tells us of their calibre; they were businessmen, professionals, or otherwise men of substance and had everything to lose. For once, the régime that operated from Dublin Castle and London was wholly unprepared for what was about to happen – *there were no informers this time*. This meant that by the time the insurgents were rounded up at the tail-end of Easter Week, they had made their point.

The government could easily have regained the situation, because it had the full support of the people, but their heavy-handed treatment of the men when they surrendered was to turn the people against them. They had learned nothing from having 'left us our Fenian dead'. Pearse was right. This time his disembodied voice could almost be heard repeating his earlier emotional expletive: 'The Fools! The Fools! The Fools!' This time they had 'left us our Republican dead'.

This time the execution of the men – there were fifteen of them including Pearse – was soon to bring about the birth of modern Ireland.

Had I a golden pound to spend,
My love should spend and sew no more.
And I would buy her a little quern,
Easy to turn on the kitchen floor.

And for her windows curtains white,
With birds in flight and flowers in bloom,
To face with pride the road to town,
And mellow down her sunlight room.

Francis Ledgwidge, Slane, is known as the 'Poet of the Blackbird'. He was one of the 70,000 Irishmen who fell in the Great War.

Chapter Thirtyfive

The Black and Tans and the War of Independence

The agitation for Home Rule that marked the later years of the nineteenth century lay dormant for a while, but a mild undercurrent still existed. The pressure later increased until a new Home Rule Bill was prepared in 1914. Self-government at long, long last was at hand! But then the Great War intervened and everything was put on hold. Understandably, this was the cause of further frustration. The people were becoming more and more impatient, and the subversives, known as the Irish Republican Brotherhood were aware that 'England's difficulty was Ireland's opportunity'. They were hungry for guns and were actively raiding police barracks and collecting arms.

The *Drogheda Independent* reported in March 1919:

"a daring raid was made for arms at the Collins town aerodrome, near Santry ... and about 80 service rifles were taken and carried off. ... It was found later that a number of military motorcars in the aerodrome were damaged so as to make them useless for the purpose of pursuit. The news of the raid has created a sensation; this is the biggest raid that has yet taken place in any part of Ireland".[1]

The raid had a touch of professionalism about it. The sentries had been tied and gagged, and the entire event was performed with precision. There were to be many more such raids, in some of which, sadly, constables were often shot and killed.

MONSTER MEETING AT THE MALL: Feelings ran high when Crown forces swooped down and detained several hundred suspects, including some Drogheda men in January 1919, and lodged them without trial in Wakefield Prison and other POW Camps. These arbitrary detentions succeeded only in incensing the people's feelings, especially when representations for the release of the prisoners were continually ignored. In Drogheda, the archdeacon of St. Peters parish, Rt. Rev. Monsignor Segrave, complained that men were being held "in detention without charge or trial against all principles of equity or justice".

A protest meeting was held at the Mall, and was attended by one of the biggest crowds ever assembled in Drogheda, according to the local newspaper report. People flocked to the town from outlying parishes including Tullyallen and Julianstown. The Drogheda Volunteers and Cumman na mBan headed by the Sinn Féin Pipers Band were also present. The number that attended was estimated at 10,000.

The speeches were reported in the *Drogheda Independent*, but it should be noted that the news columns, which bore the heading "Great Drogheda Meeting", also contained the sub-heading in brackets: – *"(As Passed by Censor)"*. Comments of an inflammatory nature were liable to result in confiscation of the printing machinery, as Joe Stanley, printer to the Republican movement and later the proprietor of the re-launched *Drogheda Argus*, found to his cost.[2] Publishers were obliged to be cautious lest they contravene the Defence of the Realm Act 1914.

"Though the Tricolour was very much in evidence, several beautiful banners being carried in the procession through the town, the meeting was by no means confined to Republicans. All sections of the Nationalists joined in the demands which had the support of the entire clergy. Soldier and sailors were present sporting the Sinn Féin colours ... and the meeting concluded with the singing of the Soldier's Song".

Larry Walsh presided and Dr. Willie Bradley delivered a rousing address, calling for "the release from English dungeons of Irishmen and Irishwomen who have been imprisoned by the despotic alien military Government of England in Ireland because they dared declare for Ireland the right that her people should self-determine the sovereignty under which they wished to live".[3]

The agitation paid off and the British Government, realising its mistake, reluctantly bowed to public pressure, because it was announced in the House of Commons two months later that the interned prisoners were to be released. On St. Patrick's Day three of them arrived back in Drogheda. They were F. Thornton, M. Reynolds and P. Monaghan, the last named who shortly afterwards became Mayor. They were met at the railway station by a welcoming party which included the Fife and Drum Band. The occasion presents us with yet another example of Drogheda's split personality in the matter of allegiance towards the Crown. Fr. Norris, who was in charge of the band, confiscated the instruments for having been used to fete republican prisoners. As they marched down the Dublin Road towards St. Mary's Bridge they were pelted with stones by the occupants of Duleek Gate, the Old Hill and Barrack Lane, the last named street being disparagingly called 'Peelers' Paradise' by the republican element. The occupants were mainly the wives of men who were fighting in the trenches in France and were in receipt of army allowances.

The procession proceeded to the Mall and, accompanied by bands and banners, they were addressed by the ever active Larry Walsh and Dr. Bradley. Once again, the occasion was reported in the Drogheda Independent together with the now familiar note that gagged candid comment: *"(As Passed by Press Censor)"*.[4]

ONE NATION – TWO GOVERNMENTS!: Sinn Féin was gaining the full support of the people, and in the general election of November 1918 they swept the deck, winning 73 seats to the Home Rule party's 6 seats. They refused to take their seats in Westminster, but had the mandate to convene 'an Irish parliament for a sovereign independent Irish Republic' – it was set up in the Mansion House, Dublin as Ireland's first Dáil Éireann, and it sat for the first time on 21st January 1919, operating in parallel with Westminster. Some of its members were absent – they were serving time in English jails. It was declared illegal in September, but for nine months there existed the extraordinary situation of two separate administrations in diametric opposition endeavouring to govern Ireland simultaneously. This meant that there were two separate sets of Courts in operation, the Dublin version dispensing justice with the aid of Volunteers who assumed the roles of judges and policemen. Accounts of both courts were reported in the *Drogheda Independent*. The voluntary Sinn Féin courts were called 'Guardians and Councils', and wrongdoers who were brought before them faced 'Courts martial'. Likewise, a separate postal delivery system was inaugurated, with (unofficial) postage stamps specially printed for the purpose.

The 'alternative Government' issued its own postage stamps (although their face values were not shown!).

Week after week the editorials in the local press harped on Prime Minister Lloyd George's handing of the situation. The newspaper was reflecting the changed mood of the man-in-the-street. English newspapers, too, were unceasingly criticising Lloyd George, and their columns were being quoted in the local press with glee.

Local elections were held in January 1920. For the first time, the Proportional Representation system was in operation. It confused only a handful of the Drogheda electorate: 'some voters disenfranchised themselves by giving first preference to three, four, five and six of the candidates...'[5] Interest in the election was exceptionally keen in Drogheda. 'The results of the poll were declared to a crowd waiting outside the Mayoralty House. ... They were loudly cheered. Before dispersing, the people on the Mall brought their vigil to a close with *'The Soldier's Song'*.[6] (The reader hardly need to be reminded that the National Anthem in this period was *'God Save the King'*).

The results shocked the authorities. A Sinn Féin candidate headed the poll in each of the three Drogheda wards, making a clear statement of the people's preference. Ten sitting members of the old Corporation were ousted, and Sinn Féin took a total of twelve seats. The express train of Nationalism was gaining momentum and was now unstoppable.

A state of near anarchy existed. The republican movement was in need of weaponry, and the countryside was being scoured, the homes of the landed gentry being prime targets. Lord Dunsany, he who had encouraged the blossoming Francis Ledwidge in his poetic works, was fined £25 at a British court martial for failing to secure arms and ammunition under proper lock and key.[7]

Lloyd George had the Answer: The Royal Irish Constabulary (RIC) had their hands full and were simply unable to cope. The situation was *de facto* ungovernable. Then Prime Minister David Lloyd George stepped in to provide the solution. He resolved on implementing a scheme that would put an end to the turmoil – it was **an official policy to** *'meet murder with murder* – his own words**. It is worth noting that this was a statement of intent issued by the Prime Minister to commit murder on his very own subjects! It was to be accomplished by reinforcing the RIC with a collection of armed men who were to become notorious, and known as 'the Black and Tans'. They left behind a reputation for drunkenness, looting and murder.

EYE-WITNESS ACCOUNTS OF TANS' LAWLESSNESS: This author has had the good fortune to interview, late in their lives, a number of the townspeople who lived through that era. Their memories of the events were still crystal clear and are recorded in the pages that follow. Many of the incidents described were minor in themselves, but taken in totality, they allow today's observer to form his/her own opinion as to the character of the Black and Tans and the type of government that inflicted them on its own citizens.

Many of these *quasi* policemen were ex-soldiers who, with the war being over, were redundant. Recruiting posters were displayed outside police barracks in London and other large cities offering ten shillings per day with keep and the prospects of promotion to recruits. Since there was no other work for them in the aftermath of the Great War many jumped at the opportunity of a trip to Ireland and of being handed ten shillings a day all found. Ten shillings a day was a handsome wage to idle men – it was ten time what they had been getting as soldiers in the trenches in France, and this tells us that these men were not prompted to enlist from any high-minded motive of loyalty to King and Country. They were neither ordinary policemen nor regular soldiers but were more akin to *mercenaries*. "They were sent over to subdue the Irish, and they did so in the way that soldiers would do – at the end of a bayonet. They caused no end of trouble" (TB).

We are given proof, if proof were needed, that the pronouncements of politicians must sometimes be taken with a pinch of salt, and we turn to Winston Churchill for a classic example of codswallop. He announced that the new recruits being shipped to the North Wall were selected 'on account of their intelligence, their character, and their records in the war'.[8] He must certainly have uttered that statement with tongue in cheek, and it does him no credit. Clearly, Mr. Churchill had not inspected these men and was therefore indulging in a flight of fancy.

> *'Actually they were a terrorist force for implementing a British Cabinet policy and were not responsible to local police control ... There had been a boycott imposed on the police. They were ostracised socially. No one was expected to salute them, serve them drinks or give them food or help them in any way ... Police would order a drink, be refused, draw their revolvers and threaten the shopkeepers, and if he persisted, the RIC and Tans would help themselves, with or without payment'.*[9]

Their official title was 'Temporary Constables'. However, they came to be known universally as the Black and Tans – this was the name of a pack of hounds in the Limerick area and, on arrival there, that was the name these men were given, and it stuck. (They even applied the term themselves).

There were insufficient supplies of the regular dark green uniforms of the RIC to clothe them, so they were given whatever came to hand, and the result was a medley of khaki tunics and green trousers or *vice versa*, black leather belts, green caps or even civilian hats. This served very well to confuse the pubic, and they often wore mufti, which made identification difficult when girls were molested, pubs robbed, men killed in cold blood, and other such outrages were being committed. Some sources suggest that they were purposely being denied official uniforms to avoid having the good name of the RIC and the British Army being sullied.

Whatever experience they had gained of warfare in the trenches was of no use whatever in handling a civilian population. They had no training in the subtlety or sensitivity that was required in communing with the general public, be they co-operative or truculent. They had even less training in combating the guerrilla tactics employed by the IRA. They operated outside the control of the RIC – they were a law onto themselves. These were the men who were now being supplied with weaponry and to be unleashed upon the Irish people.

The strength of the Auxiliary Division of the Royal Irish Constabulary, familiarly called 'Auxies', was planned to number about 8,000 ex-soldiers and officers from the British Army. In fact, its strength never exceeded 1,500 but they made their presence felt wherever they went. They were feared more greatly than the Black and Tans because they were recruited from the officer ranks and so had the capacity to commit outrages in a more thorough and systematic way. As officers they were paid £1 per day – double what the Black and Tans were getting – and they considered themselves superior to the Tans, and insisted in having accommodation separate from them.

Their commanding officer, General Crozier, was a martinet and was accustomed to applying strict discipline within the ranks. He was disturbed at the unruly behaviour which he was now faced with, especially following the sacking of Trim. He dismissed 21 men, and other dismissals followed. This action was overruled by his superiors, and they were reinstated. General Crozier reacted by saying that he 'could not go on leading a drunken and subordinate body of men', and he resigned his post.

> *'The Auxiliaries appeared to be answerable to nobody and had a reasonably free hand. They worked independently of the RIC and the Black and Tans, but on occasions the three branches were involved together, on various types of operations, some of which ended with outrages being committed'.*[10]

THE COUNTER MEASURES: There was no one in authority to challenge their depredations. The RIC had been a well-respected force, but it had now become 'the eyes and ears' of the new arrivals. De Valera announced that 'they are spies in our midst'. Circumstances now put the RIC in a different light since they were being strengthened by the Tans and the Auxiliaries, and they were henceforth looked upon as a hostile force. The IRA targeted the RIC barracks for arms and ammunition, committing atrocities in the process. Having raided barracks, they then set them ablaze and killed members of the RIC in the process, and this became their declared policy.

The local newspaper over the course of the years 1920 and 1921 continually contained reports of the activities of the subversives – variously called activists, Irish Volunteers, republicans, nationalists, Sinn Féiners, and IRA/IRB; the Drogheda area saw its share of their activities. There were constant raids on 'big houses' throughout Louth and Meath by masked men in search of weapons; motor cars were commandeered, RIC barracks and other government premises were set ablaze, Crown forces were ambushed, constables were injured and occasionally killed.

A concerted, nationwide operation took place on the night of the 3/4th

April 1920 which illustrates their cohesive structure. 153 RIC barracks were reduced to burned out shells throughout Ireland in a single night. The following month saw a further 56 barracks being destroyed, including those at Collon and Omeath. Another piece of action could have caused a horrific scene but for the speedy intervention of a local citizen: –

> *"Mr. Smith used to live at Bridge House on the Bettystown Road. One of his sons was J.R. Smith who was a coal merchant on the Quay. The [railway] bridge at Pilltown was blown up by the IRA; the Tans were in Gormanston at the time. The mail train was coming and he asked the IRA 'do you mind if I stop it'. They said they had done their job – 'we were sent to blow up the bridge, so now you can do what you like'. So John Smith ran along the line and stopped the train before it got to the bridge and saved all the lives. The GNR [Great Northern Railway] gave him a gold watch for this act."(TMcC)*

The counties where the IRA were most active were in Munster, but in assigning the newly arrived Tans to posts around the country, Dublin Castle recognised County Louth as one of the hot spots or 'counties proclaimed to be in a state of disturbance and require an additional establishment of police'.[11]

> *"The headquarters were at Gormanston; the Auxiliaries stayed in Smith's lodging house at the end of West Street, opposite the RIC barracks (the barracks at Barlow House was subsequently handed over to the Civic Guards). Sandbags were built 5 or 6 feet high all around it. They hadn't an official uniform. They wore a black cape and extraordinarily wide trousers, so wide as to accommodate a Webley revolver. And they wore leggings, some of which were black and some were tan. Getting up in the morning they might be in a hurry, and they'd put on the wrong leggings, taking the leggings of the fella next to him. That is how they got the name of the Black and Tans. We were only schoolboys, and we were all afraid of them. When we walked along the footpath they'd come along and pass you. They'd say 'Get out of the way, you Irish bastards' (JQ).*

> *"Drogheda was a relatively quiet town during the War of Independence. There was nothing happening there. There were two reasons for that: the Black and Tans were beside us in Gormanston, and the other thing was that Drogheda was a sort of a 'rest home' for fellows who were on the run. There was a place in the Sisters of Charity – did you know Mickey Stubbs? – He was the gardener – well, he kept them. There was always a crowd of IRA men there, and for that reason the IRA did not want to draw attention to themselves, and they never shot anybody, or anything like that"(MC).*

The Sisters of Charity operated an industrial school in Fair Street for young orphan boys. Note that the narrator of the above information made the enquiry: "Did you know Mickey Stubbs?" This was quite an unnecessary question to ask any contemporary Drogheda person, because Mickey Stubbs was well known to almost everyone in the town; he was a very bubbly character and had a greeting for everyone he met. A question mark accompanied his birth: "The nuns got him in a parcel at the door, and no one ever claimed him, so they raised him"(DF).

More than that, on reaching adulthood they retained him as a general *factotum*. In an establishment that contained a coterie of nuns and about 150 orphans, his services were indispensable, and his skills were always in demand, painting gates and railings, mowing lawns, patching roofs, attaching electric plugs, etc. In particular, he taught the orphans several skills – this was an industrial school.

> *"Before they went to bed every night they had to polish their boots and leave them in a row. They had a lovely garden with fruit trees and all that. Mickey Stubbs was an orphan himself, and he was very handy – he used to teach the boys how to mend boots and that"(JQ). [He also held a part-time job as the groundsman in the Drogheda Rowing Club].*

It should not be inferred from the foregoing that the good Sisters of Charity (known today as the Daughters of Charity – both titles well describe the vocation they follow; their lives were spent helping the poor and the downtrodden) – connived with their workman in harbouring felons. Here we must apply to the nuns that virtue which they themselves constantly practiced – *charity*. As law-abiding citizens they would be averse to breaking the law of the land. We must therefore assume that they were unaware that a gang of desperadoes who were 'on the run' had taken up residence in the tool shed at the bottom of their garden.

A problem was that these fugitives had to eat, and the prodigious appetite that Mickey Stubbs had suddenly acquired was no doubt a source of puzzlement – nay, of total bafflement – to the innocent nuns! Mickey was a diminutive fellow, and the Gargantuan appetite that he had lately acquired may well have been the subject of many perplexing whispers in the corridors of the convent. Be that as it may, Mickey's impingement of the law seems to have escaped the attention of both the angelic nuns and, more importantly, the demonic Black and Tans, although the arrangement was otherwise fairly common knowledge in the town.

It is a curious fact that a property of the Sisters of Charity was to feature once again in the activities of the IRA about fifty years later. The nuns made use of the building only during summer vacations, and it was otherwise unoccupied throughout the wintertime. They were alerted to the fact that several men were squatting in their rest home at the seaside in Termonfeckin. They immediately went out to investigate the matter, and to their astonishment found their neat home occupied by a nest of what were purported to be IRA activists – on the run during the bombing campaign in Northern Ireland. These men were duly warned that the gardaí were being informed, following which they hastily departed.

The regular Constabulary in Drogheda soon became disenchanted with the Tans, especially as some of them were billeted in the town. When two were charged with the larceny of bicycles from outside a local pub, District Inspector Egan said in court 'We are anxious to have these fellows properly punished. ... There were a lot of very bad boys among them and we want to weed them out as quickly as we can'.

These guardians of the law set fire to Patrick Street, the principal street in Cork City, and followed that by puncturing the hoses of the firemen who tried to extinguish the flames, leaving the street a smouldering ruin. One of their numbers 'shot an old priest and a young man in Cork, without provocation of any kind, thereby causing yet another scandal and further angry exchanges in the House of Commons. The criminal responsible on this occasion was later tried for murder and found guilty but insane."[12] The Auxiliaries had by this time become so notorious that Sir John Anderson advocated disbanding them.

A delightfully innocent way for a group of young Drogheda lads to spend a Sunday afternoon was to organise a horse and cart and take a jaunt out to Termonfeckin, and then return home by the scenic Boyne route. This is what a group of youngster did one Sunday in 1920. It had a sequel:

> "A lot of fellas were knockin' about Newfoundwell. And there was a fella named Bohill – there are relations still there in the fireplace business – who had a horse and cart, an old box cart. Some of our fellas – about ten or twelve of us – got a loan of the horse and cart one Sunday to go for a drive. So off we went around Termonfeckin, turned up towards Baltray and along by the estuary at Banktown and Queensboro'.

> "We knew the sound of the Crossley tenders so well, and we heard them coming. So we said we better get out of the way. So the fella in charge of the horse whipped him up and off we went. This was at the Coastguards [the Coastguards Station was a row of fine, red-bricked houses torched a year later by the IRA] – it wasn't burned down at the time. And at Beaulieu Bridge the Crossley came round the bend and caught up with us and, I remember it well, the Lewis gun was erected on a tripod. We met at the bridge and the Tans went rat-tat-tat-tat-tat-tat.

> "My brother and myself dived for cover on the river side. Some of the others went for the Beaulieu wood side. The leaves and branches came down on top of us, with the bullets flying. The chap that was in charge of the horse gave him a whip and let him go, and we then crossed over Beaulieu Wood to get back to Newfoundwell. The horse went the whole way home by himself. That was in 1920" (JQ).

The narrator of this story, John Quinn, was ten years old at the time. It is most unlikely that a payment was required for the use of the vehicle, for he and his mates would not have had sixpence between them. Vandalism or violence would not have entered their minds, nor would they have abused the horse; in those times even youngsters knew the basics in handling a horse. There was little to fear on the road in the matter of motorised traffic – there were but a few hundred motor cars in the whole of the Drogheda area, plus a handful of motor cycles; it was an open road, and no danger could befall the little band of playmates.

Consider, then, the sudden alarm and the scattering. They had recognised the sound of the tender in the distance, while it was over on the Termonfectin Road, and they availed of the time span to make haste. But the Tans caught up with them at a most awkward spot. Instead of waiting until the horse and cart had passed the narrow bridge at Beaulieu, the trigger-happy Tans opened up with their machine gun, spraying the overhanging trees with lead. Imagine the effect on the horse. Imagine the effect on the young fellows. Was this the Tans' idea of a prank? It was an act of sheer, irresponsible, gratuitous thuggery.

The following accounts are a series of experiences that illustrate the unruly, lawless behaviour of the Black and Tans in the Drogheda area. They were given to the author by eyewitnesses: -

The Collins family operated a substantial hardware business in Shop Street; it was established in 1775 and continued in the Collins' family for over two hundred years. The proprietor's son, Maurice, was a schoolboy at the time of the War of Independence. He recalled:

- *"I remember the Black and Tans well because my friend at school was Jack Kealy [later to become a solicitor, with a practice in Laurence Street]. His father was Clerk of the Court, and coming home from school we would always call into the Court House and he would give us a message to give in to the West Gate Barracks [Barlow House]. The Tans were in it and they had another barracks in the South Quay."(MC)*

- *"At the Confirmation in Saint Peter's church Cardinal Logue was there – the cardinal with the snuff. We were all there, the boys on one side and the girls on the other. Four Black and Tans walked in the front door. They did not carry rifles, they only had revolvers – they were that size [indicating the length of the revolvers, about 18 inches]. The late Fr. Segrave was in the pulpit. He said "Now children, be very quiet; all will be well". So the four of them walked up the centre aisle, and round to where St. Oliver's head now is. Then they went out."(JQ)*

- *"They had Crossley tenders – they were something like today's pick-up trucks. And one evening we were coming home from school, and this Crossley tender was coming along the Ramparts. They had come in at Pass, and when they came to where Dominic's Park is now, they couldn't go any further because the bollards were there. Where the Park is now – that wasn't always a park – there was about eight foot of water – the tide used to come in there. Across Dominic's Bridge there was a blacksmith's forge – Cooney's. A Tan was sent over to Cooney's to get a sledgehammer to break the bollards. But they couldn't break it, much as they tried. The pathway is so narrow that they had no room to turn. So they had to reverse the whole way back to Pass. And we schoolboys had a good laugh"(JQ).*

- *"Our house was raided on a couple of occasions. My father worked for Pratts Oil Company [now Esso Petroleum]. They were looking for the keys to the petrol store; he wouldn't hand them over and they threatened to shoot him. Their superior then came in and ordered the blackguards out. There were some good Tans"(PM).*

- *"An oil lamp was the only light you had. If my father heard footsteps outside, he'd put the lamp out [to avoid attracting them], and we'd have to keep quiet. They were the scum of England"(BT).*

- *"My father had a narrow escape. He was coming down the Dublin Road with a basket of clothing, but he had a couple of guns at the bottom. He was stopped by a patrol of Tans and some soldiers. Fortunately, one of the soldiers was billeted in our house and he gave him the go-ahead."(PF)*

Two Black and Tans (first and third from left)
with a Dublin Metropolitan Policeman and a regular soldier.

A household that was known to have republican sympathies was Munster's on the Cord Road, in which there lived seven children and the parents. Mr. Munster took part in the 1916 Rising, and spent time in jail; his wife's family were Kellys, Grangebellew, and they, too, were closely involved in subversive activities. 'Her brothers used to be in and out of the house, here on the Cord Road. It was a great 'get-away' place. [When they would hear the Tans coming] they used to get out the back door and down towards the North Strand. There was a steep decline ending with a drop of 14 feet to the ground', recalled Tom Munster when in his nineties, 'and that is how they would elude the Tans'. He remembered a raid on the house while he and his siblings were in bed: 'I remember them raiding the house and tapping the chest-of-drawers and looking for guns'. He further recalled an incident in his childhood:

- *"I used to go down to the granny's place [in Grangebellew] – the Tans used to raid there. I was afraid when I saw them arriving to raid the place, so I ran out to the field and hid in a cock of hay. There was one good Tan – the head man. He said to my aunt 'Bring that young fella in or they'll have a shot at him'. They could see my face through the hay"[13].(TM)*

343

- *"They used to come into our shop [a large hardware premises in Shop St.] and say 'Give us that, there'. They would take anything they wanted, but they would pay for nothing. They would put a revolver on the counter and say "Charge that up to King George". The D.I. [District Inspector in the Royal Irish Constabulary] was Carbury, and my father knew him well. He said "I think I will go down to the Barracks and complain. Carbury said 'I'll tell you, either of two things will happen to you: either you'll be beaten up and thrown out, or you'll be SHOT!'(MC).*

- *"Their tenders were always parked outside Gannons pub at the top of Stockwell Lane, and at Dowd's 'Beehive Bar' in Laurence Street. I remember them sitting there with their dirty, scruffy faces and uniforms. The 'Monk Reilly' – he was a holy person – used to walk up and down outside Gannons, holding up a crucifix and advising them that if conversion was needed, they could make enquiries through him and he would do something about it"(DM).*

- *"They [the Tans] came to Slane one night and set up a machine gun on the wall of our house. The Free State soldiers had just come in and were in the barracks. They aimed the guns at the barracks but I don't think they hit anything, but my parents told me in the morning about what happened during the night."(TB).*

- *"The Tans used to frequent Connolly's public house at the corner of Dyer Street and Shop Street, ... Tommy Morgan was his name – he was in charge of the hide and skins in the abattoir. He was a busybody. But this Tan was in the pub this morning. Morgan put his hand down [into the Tan's wide pocket] and took out the Webley and said 'How do these things work?' There was a bit of a scuffle. Now, I didn't see this – I was only told this – I was only ten. The gun went off and he was shot dead"(JQ).*

- *"I remember another very sad case. Their lorry pulled up at the Hibernian Bank [at the Tholsel, now the Bank of Ireland – it is surmised that the Tans were in John Dowd's pub across the road]. In the back there was a coffin, and there was a lady lying over the coffin with a shawl over her, and she was crying. He was shot down the country and he was being brought back to be buried. I always felt that someone should have given the woman a cup of tea. And underneath the lorry were three or four children and they playing marbles"(MC).*

- *"They drank in John Dowd's pub [54 Laurence St., now Sean Freeman's gents' outfitters] and there would always be one or two of their tenders parked outside. They used to have a hostage with them, and I used to feel sorry for the poor fellow. He would have a handcuff around his ankles and he would be sitting there in the rain on a pouring wet day. He would have no overcoat or anything, sitting there miserable. People would be afraid to talk to him and afraid to bring him out a drink in case the Tans would interfere"(MC).*

The public house in the last mentioned case was 'the Beehive Bar', the proprietor of which was John Dowd – he later served on the Drogheda Corporation and was elected Mayor in 1932/33. A chant at the time went: -

> *"In the year of 'Twenty-one when they need a rich man*
> *Johnny Dowd was a friend of the bold Black and Tan.*
> *He housed them and fed them and gave them all beer,*
> *And now he's a hero and we all cheer".*

Although the Headquarters of the Black and Tans were in Gormanston, they needed additional accommodation with the arrival of reinforcements from England. The people of Drogheda drew their breath in apprehension when it was announced that some were to be stationed within the town itself. So reviled were they by this stage that even the local RIC said they would refuse to co-operate with them.

They were billeted in several premises locally, and they simply commandeered whatever buildings took their fancy. The hostel at the end of West Street (opposite Barlow House) which they occupied has already been mentioned above. Another building occupied by them was the home of the McCann family. Peter McCann was a building contractor whose private home (now vacant) was next to the former Boyne Cinema in Fair Street. The adjoining workshop, sheds and builder's yard occupied the property west of the private house and extended towards Georges Square. Even though the house was commodious, the disruption caused to the household, which consisted of the parents and seven children, can be imagined. The author (whose grandmother was a member of the McCann family) recalls being told of the general mayhem generated by these uninvited cuckoos who were occupying the family nest, and particularly that when they eventually departed, the family had to contend with a *plague of fleas* which the visitors had left behind!

A shop that regularly received the attention of the Tans was O'Donnell's, No. 15 West St., a drapery shop owned and operated by two sisters. In their efforts to promote the native tongue they traded under the Irish version of their family name, so that the wording on the fascia above their shop front read *'Clann Uí Domhnaill'*. This did not meet with the approval of the Black and Tans; they arrived one night and smeared the wording with black paint or tar. In defiance, the two sisters engaged M/s Munster, the sign-writers, to restore the name, only to have it again obliterated by the Tans. This game continued repeatedly. On several occasions the private residence of the two sisters above the shop was raided, and the guardians of the law left their trademark behind in the form of a bullet hole in the ceiling.[14](MMcG)

Throughout this period a curfew was in operation – it had been imposed prior to the arrival of the Black and Tans. This had become necessary since the RIC were manifestly unable to contain the unrest. The populace were required to be indoors by 9 p.m. This indicates the seriousness of the situation and the fact that, not alone Drogheda, but the entire country was simply out of control. "I served Mass in the Franciscans; Devotions used to start at 7.45 p.m. but they had to change the time to half seven [so as to be indoors in compliance with the curfew]."(DF).

A local person, who described the following scene, explained that he was not a member of the IRA, being a mere child during the Black and Tan era (born 1912). His four uncles had joined the British armed forces, as also had his five grand uncles a generation earlier. However, enlistment in His Majesty's Forces was no indication of loyalty to the Crown. On the contrary, his family held deeply rooted republican beliefs; one uncle, for example, had served 26 years in the British Army in India; he was an artillery expert and he trained gunners who put their knowledge to use in the Great War. When home on leave he passed on knowledge to his nephew Harry on aspects of explosives, and supplied him with literature on the subject.

> "Harry joined the IRA, and he used to make bombs in the shed out there [at the end of the garden]; I used to be out there watching him. These crude explosives were used to blow up bridges and military barracks and holes in the road and things like that. The bombs were big cement things about the size of three cement blocks with a hole in the middle of them which was packed with explosives"(DF).

> "A party of 10 or 12 of us would go out on bicycles three nights a week on raids [searching for arms], arriving home at about four or five o'clock in the morning. Then we would report into work as usual, as the military would check your workplace and if you weren't there it would make them suspicious"(HF).

When discharged from the army at the end of WWI, an uncle (Kitt) of the narrator became involved in subversive republican activities that obliged him, in the interest of his continuing welfare, to 'go on the run'. He was being actively sought by the Black and Tans. Terms such as 'the Troubles' and 'on the run' were familiar ones during and after that turbulent era. Many men who were thus involved were known to the authorities and were being urgently sought 'for questioning'. Sadly, when freedom came, some of the same men were once more obliged to go 'on the run' because they actively opposed the newly formed Free State Government. A truncated Ireland was not what they had fought for, and so they continued the struggle.

> "The Tans raided our house one night in 1921. I woke up and this fella was lifting me, and his waxed moustache was that [indicating] length. I was crying and screaming with fright, and I pissed all over him. He lifted up the mattress to see what was under it and then he threw me

back. He didn't know that the goat shed was full of guns — the goats were lying on top of them. – guns, bombs, everything. Harry [his older brother] used to make them"(DF).

The narrator's father worked in Cairnes' Brewery, Marsh Road, throughout his working life, as did the narrator himself on leaving school. In the Black and Tan era he was a mere schoolboy of about 9 years. Despite his tender age, he was able to make a contribution in his own small way towards throwing off the yoke of foreign domination, as this example shows:

> *"I was too young to be in the IRA. But I used to bring lots of messages and packages of cigarettes for Kitt [his uncle] when he was on the run. I'd meet him or leave it in Briody's pub in Peter Street. My mother would put food in a biscuit tin and clothes in another biscuit tin. I would change my name to R----------.*

> *"My father started work every morning in the brewery at six o'clock and he'd bring the two tins with him and give them to the man in the grain pit. They would be put into a sack, and the hot grains poured on top of them. I'd bring it in a hand-truck up the Poorhouse Lane to avoid the sentry at the 'Navan Bridge' – there was a sentry at all the bridges. You could hardly get up the lane it was that mucky. There was a gap in the hedge and I'd whistle. One of the R---------- family would come along and we'd lift the truck into the field and go up to the house. I'd come back by the Bryanstown lane and out onto the Beamore Road and home by Coolagh Street and bring the truck up the Hundred-and-One Steps and then home. They wouldn't stop in the one place every night, but they'd collect the sandwiches in R----------'s house"(DF).*

A local factory that gave much needed employment to the male population was the Drogheda Foundry, located on the South Quay opposite the Custom House (now the Labour Exchange) on the Mall. At 6.00 each morning the darkness of the night would glow with the sparks belching like a volcano from the chimney of the foundry furnace. It played its part in the fight for Irish freedom, although this was done without the knowledge of its staunchly West British proprietor. It was being used as a minor munitions factory.

> *"If the boss knew what was going on, he'd blow a gasket. Barney M---------- from Dooley Gate was a 'moulder' in the foundry. He used to make the moulds for the grenades, and they'd put the plungers in afterwards. We used to keep them in a hole in the ground in the shed [at the end of the garden of their home] under the goats"(DF).*

The armed forces regularly raided premises that smacked of republicanism.

Another such 'munitions factory' for the production of landmines and grenades was Cooney's forge, off Dominic St. (a cinema now occupies the site). The mines were of concrete, measuring about 1m. x ½ m., and the explosive material was known as 'war flour'. Examples are presently in the National Museum. They were assembled by an employee, Harry Fairclough, who was in the local Active Unit of the IRA. He led a platoon to assist in planting the first landmine; the chosen target was the bridge over the little Mattock River at Rossin on the Slane Road. First, he took the precaution of calling on the cottage nearby. The occupant was an elderly man; the hour being some time after midnight, he refused to leave, so he was manhandled out of his house in his night attire. 'The keystone of the bridge flew up in the sky, then down through the roof of the cottage and smashed through the bed that the old man had just been lying in'[15]. Colonel Coddington soon arrived in his automobile to investigate. His car, for which he was handed a receipt, was commandeered and pushed into the gaping hole in the bridge.

Moves were then made to blow up the Boyne Viaduct, but when the plan was put forward for approval it was turned down. Common sense prevailed, it being deemed that the national economy would suffer in consequence.

A Drogheda veteran recalled another incident concerning soldiers who guarded the Viaduct: "I remember some soldiers painted a slogan in big letters on the parapet of the Big Bridge. The officer in charge found that it was done without authority, and after two days it was painted out" DM. He was unable to remember the particular lettering. However, another veteran, who, as a child residing in the Cord Road, had a clear view of the actual incident as it was taking place and was able to complete the story. The soldiers in question were members of the Kings Own Royal Yorkshire Light Infantry. They were given the task of painting the Viaduct with red lead paint. They demonstrated their loyalty to their regiment in a truly unique, if hazardous, manner. Two soldiers held another one upside down by the ankles while he painted the initials of their regiment on the stonework – it read: **'KORYLI'** (JM).

The same young resident of the Cord Road experienced his own share of risks while the soldiers guarded the Bridge. "The republicans would be in the Cord Cemetery firing over our house at the Bridge. We were in 'No-Mans-Land'. We used to sleep on the floor under the window for safety"(JM).

LAWLESS BEHAVIOUR FROM THE LAW ENFORCERS: We are apt to forget that the Black and Tans were sent over to Ireland to maintain law and order – they were an official Government force. Their behaviour and the treatment which they meted out certainly did not endear them to the populace. The acts of lawlessness which they committed were astonishing, almost to the point of disbelief. Whatever they wanted, they took, and in particular they had a limitless capacity for free booze. There was no one in authority to challenge their actions or keep them in check. The employees of the local factories were fair game for the Black and Tans on pay day:

> *"The brewerymen [in Cairnes Brewery] used to be paid on a Thursday night. The Tans would come in from Gormanston and line the men up against the wall and snap the wages off them. My father had his money up his sleeve and said he did not get paid until a Friday. They would do different places at different times. A lorry load would go down to the Boyne Mills – they used to be paid on a Friday"(DF).*

In the current era of tranquillity we find such acts of lawlessness difficult to believe, and they beg the obvious question: "Why didn't the people report them to the police?" The author naively put that precise question to the interviewee. The reply, which exposed a plentiful lack of wit on the part of this author, was delivered in a resounding tone: ***"THEY WERE THE POLICE!"***

Some further examples are given: -

An experience has been handed down to a grandson of 'Big Peter' Mohan who lived at 19 Mount St. Oliver. His work consisted of delivering petrol in a horse and cart. Four Tans arrived one day demanding petrol, but 'Big Peter' had none – the tank on his cart was empty. They didn't believe him, or thought he had a supply elsewhere so the order was given 'Take him out and shoot him'. He was thereupon taken from the house to a field opposite (there being no houses in it at that time). After further interrogation he was released.(PlR)

- *"The Black and Tans were the scum of the British Army. They were always in tenders and they were fully armed. They raided our house [in the Cord Road] one night. They ripped open the mattress with their bayonets, looking for guns or something"(DM).*

- *"They were terrible, they ransacked the place. Bobby [brother of the narrator] was out in Laytown picking fruit for a man, Bucky McKeown who had a big fruit farm near the station. It was lovely going to Bucky McKeowns because we got tea out of jam jars and that was a treat for us. Bobby was coming home from the station with a little bag of fruit for my mother that Bucky had given him. But there was a Tan coming up the Dublin Road and he said "What have you in that bag", and Bobby said he had fruit for his mother. The Tan said "Give it to me and if you don't I will throw you over that wall [and down into the Marsh Road]. With that, a man came running up, and he gave the Black and Tan a clout, and then told Bobby to run 'but don't say where I came from'. It turned out he was an IRA man"[He had seen the incident from his hiding place which was a house across the road]"(GK).*

- *"A vegetable man from the Marsh Road, Matthews was his name, used to go out to the Black and Tans in Gormanston Camp with a supply of vegetables every day. They would unload the produce at the gate because no one was allowed inside for security reasons. This day there were some big cart covers lying on the grass inside the gate. 'Any chance of one of them covers?' The sentry said 'O.K. Take that one.' There were three bodies [of Tans] lying underneath the cover. There had been a shooting match and they had shot one another. They were probably coming back drunk and shot one another"(DF).*

- *"Kirkpatricks had a shop at the bottom of Laurence Street, and at Christmas they'd sell toys. I was looking in the window when a Tan came up. 'What are you getting for Christmas',? he said.. "My Daddy is buying that train for me". So he took me by the hand, brought me in, handed me the train, but he didn't pay for it. I went home and told my father, so the following day he went in and paid for it"(JM).*

- *"I was at the pump at the bottom of Mary St. when I saw them putting a few cans of petrol in a van and then setting it on fire"(PM).*

- *"They raided our house for no particular reason. My father was in bed sick with malaria – he got it while serving in Salonika, in Greece. They just heaved the mattress out of the bed to see if there was anything underneath"(JM).*

- *"I remember Ted Quinn telling me he was going over the Cord Road one night and he heard a girl screaming in Oulster Lane. Ted was over six foot and well built – he worked for the Drogheda Harbour Board. It was a Tan molesting some young one, and he gave the Tan the father and mother of a hiding."* The veracity of this incident was reinforced by John Quinn [son of Ted Quinn] who added some further details: *"There was a row of bushes half way up the lane, and the Tan was in the habit of molesting women. There was a fellow who lived nearby called Dotts Banks, and he said 'Ted, there is a blackguard up the lane and he's annoying all the women'. When my father went up the Tan jumped out on him and there was a scuffle. The culprit got up and ran. My father follied (sic) him as far as the Old Jail – where Eddie's Hardware is now. At that stage the Tan got away, but my father got his cap – I remember it well, I was eleven years old – and he brought it home. "Oh, my God", said my mother. "Burn that cap quick. If the patrol comes, they'll burn the house down"(JQ).*

- *"This young man hit one of them with his cap in West Street and then ran off. He was identified and the Tans were going to his house to arrest him. He and his father went on the run, and when the Tans arrived at the house only the boy's mother and younger brother were there. They were about to take the young boy away when they noticed a picture of Queen Victoria on the wall, and this seemed to have an effect on them, so they changed their minds and left"(MR).*

- *"Three of my uncles were members of an IRA flying column. They were constantly away from home – on the run. Their home was the subject of many raids by the Black and Tans, whose bullets pock-marked the walls of their home on the Cord Rd. They found refuge in the Sisters of Charity, and they often hid there. One brother was eventually caught and imprisoned in Ballykinlar Camp in Co. Down, where his inmates included Sean T. O'Ceallaig who later became President of Ireland"(RD).*

THE SACK OF BALBRIGGAN: An event occurred in the neighbouring town of Balbriggan on Monday night, 20th September 1920 which had momentous repercussions for the entire town and its inhabitants, so much so that it reached the world press.

A row broke out in Mrs. Smyth's pub (now John D's) in the centre of Balbriggan. It was a favourite haunt of the Black and Tans. According to the report in the *Drogheda Independent*, the RIC were sent for, but 'on coming to the scene, and seeing who the visitors were, declined, it is stated, to interfere.' In consequence, the Volunteers were requisitioned 'and in the scrimmage that ensued to clear the pub shots were exchanged and two of the unwelcome visitors were shot, one fatally'. The man who was killed was Peter Burke, head constable of the RIC. Retaliation was swift.

(There had been a few earlier cases of Crown forces being shot and killed in the Balbriggan area).

Straight away a large body of Tans set out from their headquarters down the road in Gormanston, thirsting for revenge. The *Drogheda Independent* reported what ensued; it was 'a hell upon earth. For the sacking of Balbriggan there is no parallel save Cromwell's massacre of Drogheda. ... The men ... proceeded systematically through the streets, firing indiscriminately, breaking windows and burning selected houses'. They commandeered petrol at bayonet point from a garage that was then taken away on a handcart to torch the homes; many pubs were also targeted.

> *'The spacious hosiery factory ... in which some 400 workers had been employed, was a mass of smouldering ruins ... several of the leading business premises were also smouldering ruins, and one street containing some 30 houses, Clonard Street, had been virtually reduced to ashes. People of both sexes and all ages were leaving the town as though it were stricken with plague'.*

At that time the economy of Balbriggan centred around the hosiery and fabric industry, and the town enjoyed a highly prestigious position in the global market; its goods were much sought after, and were exported throughout the world. The quality of the product of the largest factory, Smyth's, was so esteemed that it was appointed as supplier to Her Majesty Queen Victoria, and was the recipient of many international awards. So renowned were the fabrics of Balbriggan that the town's name has the distinction of lending its name to the English language and has a place in the Oxford Dictionary alongside Calicut (which gives us 'calico'), Worstead ('worsted') and Damascus ('damask'). *The Oxford English Dictionary* defines the word 'Balbriggan' as: 'a knitted, unbleached cotton fabric used for underwear, etc.'. The Black and Tans were intent on including this target in their rampaging, but were miraculously prevailed upon to desist only 'by the persuasive efforts of Dr. Fulham, a member of the local RIC force and some other residents of the town'. So terrified were the people that many families spent the rest of the night outside the town huddled in ditches. Next day there was a general exodus by over 800 citizens, with mothers pushing prams and herding children along the roadway; others went by train to Drogheda and Dublin. A terrace in the town was later named Fulham Terrace in honour of the doctor for the heroic role he played during that night of convulsion.

The shooting of Constable Burke was witnessed by several bystanders in the pub, but not surprisingly, they remained tight-lipped thereafter. The Tans wanted blood, so they dragged from their homes two men at random,[16] and it was not until the following morning that the bodies of James Lawless, a barber, and John Gibbons, a young farmer, were found. A witness described the two bodies lying in a shed on old sacks. A bandage tied around Jim Lawless' head was soaked in blood. His left eye was closed and bore all the traces of having been battered in by the butt end of a rifle. All around his neck were bayonet wounds, and his clothes were torn to shreds. His legs also bore the signs of torture; Gibbons' body was similarly mutilated. Neither body had shoes or socks. They had been arbitrarily bayoneted to death without trial. Today a Celtic memorial headstone marks their burial place in Balscaddan Cemetery. (These outrages were soon to be repeated in other towns, including Drogheda).

> 'Their Devil's work completed, the maddened braves who are said to have had their lust for destruction still further whetted by deep potations of looted alcohol from the five public houses they destroyed, retired upon their base, and yet another great British victory in Ireland awaits due record at the hands of the historian.
>
> 'As they drove out of the town in the direction of the aerodrome they cheered loudly and sang 'The Boys of the Bulldog Breed'.[17]

Relief committees were set up in Balbriggan and Drogheda in efforts to accommodate the families whose homes had been torched. A disused flour mill was used as a hostel, and beds were supplied by the Balrothery Workhouse. Donations exceeding £100 were paid into the Drogheda Independent to assist those most in need. A week later the Tans were back in Smyth's pub. They 'drank and made merry' until the small hours, but paid for nothing. A few months later the pub was sold.

The Sack of Balbriggan was an outrage that caused indignation and deep concern not just in Ireland but throughout the civilised world, and it was widely reported throughout Britain and America; it was also raised on the floor of the House of Commons. The prestigious *'The Times'* of London was a constant critic of the Government's policy on Ireland, and delivered several broadsides against the government's inept and cruel handling of the Irish question:

> 'The accounts of arson and destruction must fill English readers with a sense of shame. ... The name of England is being sullied throughout the Empire and throughout the world by this savagery for which the Government can no longer escape, however much they may seek to disclaim responsibility.[18]

Dr. Fulham appeared as a witness at the subsequent Court hearing in Green Street, Dublin, and was asked to give an account of the occurrences on the night in question. While the Tans were burning house after house he cried "Do not harm that house; there are only two girls in it". He saw the whole street practically aflame, and he remonstrated with the Tans.

Recorder:	*What uniform did these men wear?*
Witness:	*The police uniform.*
Recorder:	*Have you any doubt about their being police men?*
Witness:	*Not the slightest. [Witness further described the continued acts of arson].*
Recorder:	*Did you go to bed that night?*
Witness:	*No. No one went to bed that night.*
Recorder:	*You spent most of it in the street, I suppose?*
Witness:	*Well, in my own street.*
Recorder:	*You endeavoured, yourself, in aiding in the putting out of the fires?*
Witness:	*Oh yes, and when they saw us trying to put out the fires they fired at us.*
Recorder:	*The armed forces?*
Witness:	*Yes. I may say that some of them came to my surgery and vowed vengeance. They were going about in gangs.*
Recorder:	*How many of them were engaged in this?*
Witness:	*There would be at least one hundred, or very close to it.*

Another witness described how there was a knock at his door and the keys of his garage were demanded of him at the point of a bayonet. 60 gallons of petrol were taken, and his windows were subsequently smashed.

Recorder: *The work of burning and destruction was effected by means of petrol?*
Witness: *Yes.*
Recorder: *And by whom?*
Witness: *By the forces of the Crown – and no one questions that.*

> *"I was at school in the Loreto Convent. The Tans were terribly drunk. What did they do, only put petrol cans all around the Convent, and the children and nuns in it. These drunken blackguards had it all set up. One of the head lads came along and said 'What are you doing?' They said 'We're burning the factory'. 'That's not a factory, that's a Convent and it's full of children and nuns'. The nuns were in an awful state. That's the God's truth.*

> *"They were terrible. I lived five miles from Balbriggan. The McGowan family had a public house [it was named the Gladstone Inn] and they had to get out on the roof, and go from one roof to another to get away. They had to throw the baby from one to the other, and over a wall onto a spread-sheet. This pub is now the Milestone Inn – right in the middle of the town"(MS.).*

Clonard Street, Balbriggan
The scene following the visit of the Black and Tans.

The factory owners and workers of Drogheda held their breath; were they next to be targeted? They took the precaution of having their fire-fighting equipment at the ready, and the mill girls were worried that they might find themselves out of work and on the bread line like their colleagues in Balbriggan. Subscription lists in Drogheda were opened, and donations arrived from all directions for the relief of families whose homes were gutted.

The Tans let it be known that they would not hesitate to retaliate in their own special fashion if the occasion were to arise. The Mayor of Drogheda at a meeting produced a copy of a poster which had been distributed around the town and pasted on several house doors:[19] The poster read:

DROGHEDA BEWARE!
IF IN THE TOWN OF DROGHEDA OR ITS VICINITY A POLICEMAN IS SHOT,

TAKE NOTICE THAT FOR EACH MEMBER OF THE FORCE SHOT, FIVE OF THE LEADING

SINN FEINERS WILL BE SHOT WITHOUT TRIAL.

IT IS NOT COERCION – IT IS AN EYE FOR AN EYE.

WE ARE NOT DRINK-MADDENED SAVAGES AS WE HAVE BEEN DESCRIBED

IN THE DUBLIN 'RAGS'. WE ARE NOT OUT FOR LOOT.

WE ARE INOFFENSIVE TO WOMEN. WE ARE AS HUMAN AS OTHER CHRISTIANS, BUT WE HAVE RESTRAINED OURSELVES TOO LONG.

ARE WE TO LIE DOWN WHILE OUR COMRADES ARE BEING SHOT IN COLD BLOOD BY THE CORNER BOYS AND RAGAMUFFINS OF IRELAND?

WE SAY 'NEVER', AND ALL THE ENQUIRIES IN THE WORLD WILL NOT STOP OUR DESIRE FOR REVENGE.

STOP THE SHOOTING OF POLICE, OR WE WILL LAY LOW EVERY HOUSE

THAT SMELLS OF SINN FEIN!

REMEMBER BALBRIGGAN!

BY ORDER

THE BLACK AND TANS.

Balbriggan was merely the first of many Irish towns to suffer at the hands of this force which was charged by the Government with maintaining law and order. That same day as these scenes were taking place in Balbriggan a young student in Dublin – he was just a lad of eighteen summers called Kevin Barry – was arrested in Dublin, then tortured before facing the hangman. Within days the towns of Ennistymon, Lahinch and Trim were to suffer the same fate as Balbriggan, and Drogheda had not long to wait before experiencing similar rough justice. At Ennistymon:

> "... they then killed a boy of twelve who was carrying water to help put out a fire that was consuming a neighbour's shop. The Tans and the RIC, warmed by the night's work through fire and drink, made a bag of five houses and the Town Hall before they came to Lahinch. ... Flanagans was the first house to be sprinkled with petrol, and when four houses were on fire the constabulary stopped for another thirst quenching. They gave no notice to the sixth house once they had put Mick Vaughans aflame. Inside was an old woman, a young woman and a young child. The woman had watched the killing squads but they thought that their house was safe. Here was used an incendiary bomb which fired the house at once. Luckily the child was brought down the stairway by her aunt who collapsed on the way down but all got out safely. Even then they were fired on as they came out the front door in their night clothes.

"Susan Flanagan had an invalid sister who was bed-ridden. On her knees she begged the RIC not to burn her house as she would not be able to carry out her sister. "We don't give a damn if you have five invalid sisters; we are going to burn" was the hopeful answer as they spilled petrol on the furniture. She had to go upstairs, drag down her sister and then carry her out on her back as far as the end of the yard, where she left her.

"An east Clare man, Sammon, who had come for a seaside holiday, was killed as he was helping to bring a woman from a burning house. Pat Lahane ... was asleep over a shop when the police put the house on fire and he was burned to death.

"Great numbers of people made for the seashore where they lay on the wet grass or on the damp sand. They lay low until dawn came, for fear they would be seen ... Mothers sheltered their young babies in their arms, but elderly people shivered in the moist sea air, for few had time to clothe themselves properly..."[20]

In the area of the Golden Vale they vandalised many creameries in the knowledge that dairies provided the sole source of income for entire townlands, and destroying them would cause maximum harm to the economy and widespread deprivation to the people. These acts of violence, destruction and cold-blooded murder were committed indiscriminately against a people who were, for the most part, entirely innocent. The scenes were not dissimilar to the crimes committed in WW2 by the Nazis who destroyed whole villages as reprisals against partisan activities.

The home town of former Mayor of Drogheda, Patrick Buckley, was Dromcollogher on the Limerick/Kerry border. This area was a hotbed of IRA activity:

"There would be raids on our house because we had a first cousin involved in the IRA. You had to put a list on the back of the door each night of those who slept in the house. He'd be staying quite often, but we couldn't put his name on the list. They took my father and my uncles away and interrogated them for a whole day.
"One time the Tans dropped leaflets on the town from a plane. It was the first time I saw an aeroplane. I don't know what the message was – I was more interested in the plane – I was only 6 or 7 at the time. They burned down half the street in Charleville and Dromcollogher, and they pulled men out of their homes and shot them." (PB)

There were endless criticisms both in newspaper editorials and in reported speeches by politicians, by churchmen and by other public figures such as Sir Horace Plunkett, of misrule, and the subject was constantly raised in London's Houses of Parliament.

Under the heading *'Ireland's Octopus'* a script read by Prof. Oldham revealed that in the 50 years between 1820 and 1870 £360,000,000 was extracted from Ireland in taxes but only £120,000,000 was spent on Ireland.[21] Thus Ireland was helping to fund the expansion of the British Empire and was being short-changed to the tune of £240m during the most harrowing period of her history, and spanning the Great Famine. This imbalance continued, and Ireland was subsequently being taxed to fund the Great War, a war in which Ireland would certainly have played no part but for the Act of Union.

The discontent was coming to the boil as the tit-for-tat sequences of retaliations continued. Loyalist homes were torched by the IRA, not excluding many stately mansions that also went up in flames. Then the owners of the as yet untouched country seats pleaded with the British Government to desist from such short-sighted activities, pointing out that a castle was an unfair exchange for a pub or a humble cottage.

Ballykinlar Prison Camp: A concentration camp was opened in Ballykinlar, Co. Down where suspects were taken and incarcerated without trial. County Louth was well represented, and one inmate obtained signatures of his colleagues in an autograph book, samples of which are given here:

Several elected Members of the first Dáil were unable to attend sittings, the reason being that they were detained as 'guests of His Majesty'. The signature on the left is that of Seán Mulroy TD. The Prison Camp is depicted on the right.

Captives amused themselves through various sports activities. Here a Louth team played Kerry

The above entries in the Autograph Book are those of two Drogheda men, Thomas Devin and P. McEnaney, the latter revealing his talent at sketching. Many entries were in Irish, indicating an ardent desire to create an Irish Ireland.

Dundalk and Ardee: The Crown forces assigned to north Louth were no different to those elsewhere, and outrages were committed both in Dundalk and Ardee. The two Watters brothers, Patrick and John, were taken from their beds in Dundalk and shot dead. It is thought that these killings were of a random nature in reprisal for the earlier killing of a Tan. Buildings were also burned to the ground.

October 1920 saw a series of events at Ardee: Premises in the town being searched; no weapons were found, so the raiders emerged with quantities of liquor and cigarettes. The following month a Tan was hospitalised having a bullet in his thigh resulting from a fight with one of his mates. A week later two men were taken from their beds sometime after midnight and shot dead. They were Sean O'Carroll and Patrick Tierney who were known republicans. At the military inquiry held later in the day it was announced that the hearing would be held *in camera*. A protest was made by the solicitor representing the next-of-kin to the effect that this was unconstitutional, but the court was nonetheless cleared of the press and all outsiders.

It was subsequently learned that Tierney's father, from whose home the son had been taken, had apprehensively retraced the steps of the military mob in search of his son, and soon came across the bodies of the murdered men. His son had been shot in the head and the brains lay scattered on the ground, his stomach had been ripped open and his limbs were broken.

THE KILLING OF HALPIN AND MORAN:

Thomas Halpin   John Moran
They were taken from their homes at night and shot in cold blood by the Black and Tans.

Ash Wednesday morning, 9th February 1921 was cold and crisp – there had been a hard frost during the night. As a workman named O'Brien was making his way to Drogheda from Mornington at about 7.30 am he was horrified in peering through the darkness to make out two human forms lying at the roadside close the Viaduct. A sprinkling of frost covered their bodies, and the blood that had oozed from wounds had congealed. The RIC were quickly alerted, and in a short time a large congregation of townspeople had gathered at the scene of the tragedy and prayed for the repose of the souls of the deceased persons. They had obviously been murdered.

The pathos was compounded when a middle-aged man arrived, fell on his knees at the corpses and identified one of them as that of his own son, Thomas Halpin (26). The other body was that of John Moran (33), who worked in Drogheda, but was a native of Enniscorthy.

Halpin's young widow, dazed at hearing the news, explained that shortly after midnight a group of men in mufti entered their home in Georges Street and arrested him. He went without the slightest protest, she said, only asking what they wanted with him. The next morning, thinking that he was still in the barracks, she sent down his breakfast, and only then did she learn the dreadful news. A similar story was related by the widow of the other victim whose home was in Magdalene Street.

'Drogheda was plunged into horror and consternation. ... The dread affair is the one topic of conversation in town', according to the local newspaper. Both men had republican sympathies, Halpin being an Alderman and one of the ablest members in Drogheda Corporation. It seems that when being dragged over West Street he clung to the railings of St. Peter's Church in a vain effort to evade his fate, but rifle butts and bayonet slashes did their work well.

The occasion was remembered by several Droghedeans – they were mere boys at the time – but were still able to recall the atrocity when in their nineties. One was the son of a well known hardware merchant whose premises in Shop Street were patronised by one of the victims: -

> *"They took out two fellows and killed them. I remember that clearly. I knew Halpin very well – he had a place in Dyer Street. They were coopers, and he used to be in our shop nearly every day buying nails. He was a good singer and he used to sing patriotic songs at the concerts – that's why he was whipped. The other fellow [Moran] was from County Wexford, and he was on the run – that's why he was in Drogheda" (MC).*

> *"I was serving Mass in James St. the day they were shot. It was Fr. Nulty [unrelated to the parish priest of the same name in St. Mary's Church in the early 2000s] who was to say Mass, but he was so overcome when he heard the news that he was late going out on the altar"(PM).*

> *"There was no such thing as an ambulance that time. The bodies were brought up on the back of a lorry to Millmount. And the strange thing about it is that the person who laid them out was a relation of my own – she was known as a mortician. They were employed by the undertakers, and they laid out people when they died. She was a Quinn – she married a Duff afterwards"(JQ).*

There can be very few who actually witnessed the killings – apart from the perpetrators themselves. Strange to relate, *one local boy did witness it.* He was Jack May, aged eight years at the time. He lived in the family home at Cord Terrace, close to the Viaduct and overlooking the Boyne. In his ninety-third year the event was still vivid in his memory: 'I saw the shooting of Moran and Halpin. I could see from our bedroom window right across to the Marsh Road. I saw the flashes of the guns'(JM).

A military enquiry was arranged for the following day, but an officer announced that it would be held *in camera,* and therefore closed to the press. The remains of Thomas Halpin were taken from Millmount Barracks the following evening to St. Peter's Church, and in the morning the coffin, draped in the Tricolour, was borne by his comrades to the New Cemetery. A massive congregation followed it, and all business in the town was suspended, the shop windows being shuttered (as was customary at the time in deference to all passing funerals) as the cortege passed. A force of military and Auxiliaries surrounded the cemetery, but no confrontation or scenes of violence took place.

The remains of John Moran were conveyed to the Railway Station to be entrained for Enniscorthy, his native town. Two military lorries and three caged-in lorries of Auxiliary Police preceded the cortege. On arrival at the station cordons were drawn across the road and nobody except the deceased's relatives, the coffin bearers and members of the Corporation were allowed through to the platform.

Could Halpin and Moran have evaded being killed? The matter of intelligence had been well sewn up by Michael Collins. He had seen to it that the IRA had infiltrated the RIC; whenever plans were made to raid a home or to conduct a midnight swoop, advance warning was invariably sent to the men being targeted. There were many such warnings, most of which proved to be false alarms. (Two different names were given to the author as being the person who relayed the vital tip-off in the Halpin and Moran murders, but it must be remembered that the narrators were mere boys of eight years or so at the time, and the information they heard was hearsay; otherwise the facts tally): –

> *"The story is that Madden warned them not to be at home that night, but they didn't take the warning. Moran was a Wexford man in digs in Magdalene Street. It was a Wednesday after Shrove Tuesday night. They were brought through the town and the people heard the roaring. And the fellows who were supposed to be minding them were hiding down in the Hibernian vaults [the Tholsel building reverted to the Borough Council in 2006] – this is the story I heard.*

> *"The missions were on, and the frost was that thick on the steps [of St. Peter's Church] that you couldn't stand on them. And it stands out in my memory that there was an eclipse of the*

sun. At school we were detailed to use smoked glass to look at the sun. We were told there was murder down on the Marsh – that was the first we knew about it. Tom Halpin was the salt of the earth – he worked in the Kirkpatrick Sawmills – that was long before Murdocks or Bogues [These latter firms had continued in the sawmills business when Kirkpatricks ceased trading. The buildings, known as the Linen Hall, have since been demolished and the area is now a car park fronting the Abbey Shopping Centre, next to the river. This car park is still referred to as Murdock's car park].

"His father, John Halpin, was a cooper and he had a deformed leg. He later became a councillor because of his son, and was elected to the Council. He used also sharpen butchers' saws.[The narrator was a butcher, and spent his entire working life with Byrne's in West Street]. The other man, John Moran, worked in Cahills the Bookbinders, the building which was later occupied by Bogue's Sawmills"(JQ).

"Jimmy Didman worked in the Munster and Leinster Bank [the premises at 13 West St., now occupied by First Active Building Society] as a janitor – a small, little fellow. He got the warning about a raid and duly passed it to each. He would simply touch them on the arm, and then he could swear on the Bible that he had not told them. In that way he told Halpin who was not long married – after that it was up to you [whether or not to heed the warning]. Moran was away travelling and wouldn't be back until late. So Jimmy wrote a note and then gave it to his landlady which she left on the hall-stand for him. He was only in when they came in after him and got him – he wasn't even undressed. Halpin was only half dressed, because we were looking at the clothes the next day – his dressing gown. Halpin said to the wife: 'Another false alarm – I'll take a chance'. The first house they raided was Jimmy Didman's – he lived at the end of Toberboice Lane [in Upper Mell]. Jimmy heard them coming down the lane and he took to the river and crossed to the Ramparts and then over to Donore" (JQ).

A third man had also been ear-marked for death that night. He was Tommy Grogan who lived in a small cottage on the Marsh Road with his five siblings and their mother – their father had died when the children were very young. The house was opposite the present Memorial, but it has since been demolished. "The two youngest sons, Larry and Tommy, became involved in the IRB/IRA – they did prison and all the rest of it".[22]

It was to that house that Halpin and Moran were taken with the intention of rounding up the third victim, but when the Tans got there with their two captives, the bird had flown. Thus, the Memorial marks the spot where two bodies, rather than three, were found the next morning. Nuala, the daughter of the escapee, described the occasion:

"They wanted my father as well. They marched the two men down the Marsh Road. My father heard the racket and got out the back window and away with him. He was on the opposite side of the road behind some bushes watching the two men being murdered. That affected him badly. ... On another occasion they were out looking for him and he escaped to Ship Street where he got into a boat and escaped"(NE).

This scenario was corroborated by a person whose family had close republican connections:

"One of the first places the Tans always raided was Grogans of the Marsh. It was a labourer's whitewashed cottage opposite where the Monument is now. But that night there was nobody at home. Their normal escape route was up the field [immediately to the rear of the cottage] towards the railway station and into the goods yard, then out the front gate and on to the Dublin Road. They would get refuge in the 'Spike'[a nickname for the workhouse, which was adjacent to the entrance to the station]"(DF).

It seems that Moran was 'on the run' and was being sought by the Crown forces as an activist. It was thought that Halpin was simply an elected Sinn Féin councillor, and was not an Irish Volunteer. This is implicit in the inscription on the Memorial on the Marsh Road; it provided Moran with an army ranking, but not Halpin. It reads: -

'In loving memory of the heroes
Thomas Halpin and Captain Seán Moran
who were murdered by English soldiers
on the 9th. February 1921'.

The Crown forces later tried to confuse matters by hinting that the deaths were the result of an internal feud within the IRA, but this theory is rejected out of hand. Why did they hold the inquest *in camera* if they had nothing to hide? Secondly, the murderers spoke with English accents, and thirdly, they had said to Mrs. Moran that they were taking her husband because he was 'the chap who shot D.I. Wilson [Wilson was a member of the RIC in Gorey, Co. Wexford]'.

Cardinal Logue, Archbishop of Armagh, must have had difficulty in controlling his feelings at seeing his flock being pillaged and murdered. He referred to the raids that were being made under the pretext of searches, and that money, and anything that could be carried, especially booze, was being seized at the point of a revolver. He wrote:

> *'Hitherto it was only robbery in the Drogheda district. Now bloodshed has commenced. ...[Regarding the murder of Moran and Halpin] there is not even the excuse of reprisal for this action. There was no crime in Drogheda and the district, except robbery [which were being committed by the Black and Tans]'.*

The murders of Halpin and Moran caused IRA activities in the Drogheda area to escalate. Until then, that region had been relatively quiet. New recruits now flocked into the ranks of the IRA. The Coastguard Stations at Laytown and Clogherhead went up in flames, trenches were dug across roadways, bridges were blown up, Crossley tenders were ambushed, men wearing Crown uniforms shot.

Funds were being collected in Drogheda and throughout Louth and Meath for the benefit of the 'Munitions Fund'. This arose from the fact that dockers at Liverpool had gone on strike in sympathy with the Irish nation, and refused to handle munitions that were intended for use in Ireland. Parishes everywhere contributed to the support of the families in Liverpool affected by the strike, according to the newspaper report. In stark contrast, two advertisements appeared in the same edition of the paper, the first for the promotion of a 'Subscription Dance' held at the Mayoralty Rooms, and the second being 'an American Tennis Tournament' at Mrs. Coddington's stately mansion at Oldbridge, both events being organised to support a named charity, the nature of which may well be the cause of puzzlement, in not amusement, to the reader – it was '**the Louth Hunt Fowl Fund.**'[23]

Ambivalence: Throughout the pages of Irish history we encounter many instances of double standards in the matter of loyalty among the lower classes, many of whom joined the British Army ostensibly 'to fight for king and country', but when weighed in the balance they were often found wanting. However, the moot matter of justification or otherwise for their ambivalence is not for discussion here. What interests us are the several strata of social classes that were influenced by the conflicting ideals of nationhood and loyalty to the King. The traits of infidelity were not the sole prerogative of the lower classes, as the following incidents indicate: -

The Brodigans of Pilltown were a family long established in the area who held vast tracts of farms including lands at Beauparc, at the Black Bull and 'half of Drogheda'. They were merchant princes, and Colonel Brodigan had a town house on the North Quay, also a house in Dublin and a villa in France; his vessels were regular callers at Drogheda port, and he was instrumental in forming the Dublin and Drogheda Railway Company. His land steward, who came to Pilltown in 1907, was a reliable and steadfast Protestant. One of his duties was to 'go over to Beauparc every Sunday morning in a horse and cart and give instructions to the farm hands what work to do in the coming week'. Brodigan was a Catholic, and his wife was a Protestant. To shuffle this deck of cards more thoroughly, his son was a Catholic and his two daughters were Protestant (Indeed, one of the latter entered a convent of Protestant nuns). Where did the allegiance of this household lie in the event of subversive activities taking place all around them, one might ask. Read on:

"They used to hold parties for the army officers. The Black and Tans used to come with their commanding officer for a party. The Tans used to circle around the house on patrol. My father told me they were going to accidentally shoot a man there. Someone came out of the house onto the garden to spend a penny, and they held back just in time – it was Captain Osborne of Dardistown Castle!"(TMcC).

The officers of the British forces on that occasion were being entertained in the family mansion, but meanwhile, back at the ranch (or rather, at the loyal steward's house on the estate), their nemesis, the IRA, were also being entertained, although not to the same lavish degree, and under a much more discrete profile. The circumstances are described by the steward's son:

"These men [viz. the IRA] used to sleep in our house in the loft. My father used to come up to them in the morning and say 'Well lads, what did you do last night'; this time they had blown up the bridge [the railway bridge mentioned above]. My father gave them the oil store where they used to keep the ammunition and clean the guns. I remember as a lad of about seven or eight they used to go down the lane where the graveyard is now and fire two shots; they would wait for someone at Julianstown to fire two more; then two more would be fired at Colpe. This was to indicate that everything was o.k." (TMcC).

It is uncertain whether the lord of the manor, Colonel Brodigan, was party to this duplicity, but it was common knowledge that one of his forefathers was complicit in the gun-running episode at Annagassan strand during the 1798 Rising .

MICHAEL COLLINS: A well known visitor to Drogheda was Michael Collins, whose nephew later married a member of the McCullough family – they operated a public house in Tullyallen, and subsequently at 37 West Street and who are still in business in garden furnishings at Oldbridge. On one occasion the Black and Tans paid them a visit at Tullyallen and commandeered their motorcar.[24] Michael Collins had further connections with the town; his faithful secretary, Paddy Matthews, lived in Drogheda and later became a reporter with the Drogheda Independent.

Many books have been written about Collins, who was often referred to as 'the Big Fellow'. He was a man who was larger than life, oozing charisma and good looks. He also had more than the normal quota of good luck as a Scarlet Pimpernel, judging by the tales of the narrow escapes that he made when being pursued by the Black and Tans – he was 'Number One' on their hit list. This did not prevent him from cycling about the streets of Dublin quite openly. The police journal *'Hue and Cry'* published photos of him and offered a reward of £10,000 for his head, but warned bounty hunters that he was 'a dangerous man. Care should be taken that he does not fire first.'[25]

He led a charmed life, often boldly operating under the very noses of the 'bloodhounds' who were baying for his blood night and day. (His luck held out throughout the entire War of Independence, but tragically it deserted him in the subsequent Civil War when he was shot by a fellow Irishman – possibly by one of his own men – at Béal na Bláth, in his native County Cork). In Drogheda he had at least one close encounter: –

"Michael Collins was in the White Horse [now the Westcourt Hotel] having a drink, and he was in disguise. Dad [Thomas Sherlock, V.S.] was there, and he was in his uniform, on leave from the army. [Being a veterinary surgeon, he had answered the call of duty and enlisted in the Veterinary Corps of the British Army during the Great War]. But he recognised Michael Collins and said: "I know you. The Black and Tans are outside, and you'll be captured. Stay where you are and don't move until I tell you'. In that way Dad got him safely out of the hotel"(GK).

This tip-off may well have prevented a major shoot-out in Drogheda's main street, and it succeeded in balking the Tans of their greatest prize. This was yet another incident in Collins' charmed life. A year later, when Thomas Sherlock had returned to civic life and to his practice as a vet., his good deed was reciprocated:

"The IRA were very good to Dad; they never bothered him. On one occasion when he was going to a farmer, they advised him not to come out in his khaki trousers, so Dad had them all dyed brown. ... He was going out on a case one night, and two men jumped out from a hedge, and they held up the car. But a voice on the other side said: 'O, that's all right, that's Mr. Sherlock, let him go on'. ... On another occasion he had a Black and Tan sent back to England. Whatever misdemeanour he did, Dad objected to it, and he reported him. He said he'd have them all sent back if he could. Everyone was terrified of them" (GK).

The world press, including that of England, was fully in sympathy with Ireland at this time, and *The Times* of London continued to severely criticise the British Government. The *Drogheda Independent* regularly published quotations from a variety of journals, e.g. the weekly review *'Everyman'* which asked a few rhetorical questions: 'How long are we in this country [Britain] going to tolerate this nightmare of misgovernment over one quarter of the British Isles? How long are the taxpayers to bear the expense of this farcical and ignominious parody of Prussian government? [British] rule in Ireland has made us the laughing stock of civilisation. ... It is impossible for Ireland to be governed by a display of bayonets at every crossroads and by patrolling all her highways and by-ways with armoured cars'.

The week ended the 22nd May 1920 was a particularly busy one for republicans in the Louth/Meath area, for the local paper contained reports on a variety of IRA raids:

- Parsanstown Police Barrack, near Lobinstown, was set on fire on Sunday night and partially burned.

- Mountnugent Barrack and Courthouse: a claim was admitted for damages.

- Gormanston Barrack Burning: 'from details to hand it would appear that this barracks was raided on Saturday night by a large number of armed and masked men who saturated the floor etc. with petrol and paraffin and then set the building on fire'. The damage was not great, so the men returned the following night and made a more thorough job of it.

- Claims were reported in the same issue of the newspaper relating to the destruction of barracks at Ballivor, Killyon, Summerhill, Dunboyne and Ballinabrackey.

- Kells: 'the Income Tax office of Mr. G. Brophy was raided by a party of armed and masked men on Wednesday night. He was compelled to hand over the books and records connected with the collection of taxes and rates and these were burned in a nearby field. Meanwhile, a separate party searched the premises for arms and made off with a shotgun'.

- Oldcastle: on Saturday night the office of Geo. O'Brien, Income Tax Collector was raided by a party of armed and masked men. The records were placed in a sack and taken to the cemetery where a match was applied to them.

These operations – all of them dangerous and involving great risk – were performed by flying columns. An occasion is recalled by a Drogheda woman whose mother related an experience concerning them:

'My parents lived in a rural area near Castlepollard and one night they were wakened by a group of about a dozen men who requested a pot of tea. 'I'd be a long time trying to light up the stove to boil water', said my father, 'but we have any amount of buttermilk'. They sat down and enjoyed their buttermilk. Meantime my mother was at the top of the stairs looking down and listening. She saw all these guns propped up and lying against the wall. Going out, the men thanked my father. Next morning the courthouse in Castlepollard was blown to pieces'.[26]

The likelihood is that the perpetrators of these widespread actions were not men from the local areas, but that they were flying columns based in areas further afield, and far from the scenes of action. What was their mode of transport? It is an unlikelihood that any one of them was the owner of a motorcar. It may or may not be relevant to point out that Larry Walsh, whose line of business was the grocery trade, also operated a car hire business in Drogheda, incongruous at these two enterprises may seem, during those troubled times!

By coincidence, another freedom fighter of the past, Joan of Arc, was canonised in Rome on the Sunday previous to these events, and the Venerable Oliver Plunkett was beatified on the following Sunday. Both of these martyrs had been actively engaged in unshackling the bonds of the oppressed. A gathering of 10,000 of the faithful attended the ceremony in Drogheda to mark Oliver Plunkett's beatification. 'The town was *en fete* and magnificently so. An elaborate decorative scheme was everywhere evident, and neither trouble or expense was spared to ensure that Drogheda was arrayed [in finery]'.

A week later the taxpayers of Drogheda wakened to the glad tidings that the Income Tax office in West Street was raided and the books and records vanished.

This was the period when law and order had almost totally collapsed throughout Ireland. Many RIC members had been shot dead in raids on barracks throughout Louth, Meath and elsewhere. Some individual constables had quit the force, others resigned *en bloc*. Meantime Dáil Éireann was continuing to govern the country with the aid of its Volunteer police force. The local press reported that:

> '... [Last week] Volunteers took over the duties of maintaining order at Bellewstown Races, which duties were relinquished by the R.I.C. Headquarters were established convenient to the course, and Volunteers detailed for the regulating of traffic, preventing disorder, etc. At the conclusion of the first day's racing some cases were dealt with by a court of Volunteer officers. Two women suspected of attempted burglary were cautioned, and a young man, convicted of theft of an overcoat, was fined and bound over, the overcoat being recovered.
>
> 'While the Volunteers were on duty the second day, a large party of military suddenly appeared on the scene, in full war kit. Questioned by the Volunteer commandant, the British officer in charge stated that his orders were to arrest any person wearing an insignia denoting the presence that day of Irish Volunteers. This evidently referred to the armlets worn by the Volunteers, and the Volunteer commandant demanded that he be given an hour to consider the matter, which was acceded to, and at the end of this period he informed the British officer that he would accede to superior forces on the question of armlets, and would cause his men to remove them conditional upon he being allowed to deal with the men direct, and upon their not being interfered with in carrying out police duties. These terms being also agreed to, the armlets were taken off voluntarily and retained. The military party then proceeded to search the Catholic Church close by, nothing being removed.'[27]

It is interesting to note that the Volunteer Courts, sometimes called 'Dáil Éireann Courts' or 'Guardians of Courts', were not conducted in a surreptitious manner. The British Government stood by, knowing that having unilaterally *declared* independence was a much different thing to *getting* independence. The first occasion on which the courts were held in Drogheda was on 11th August 1920, and the venue was the Assembly Room of Drogheda Corporation. Reports of proceedings at Volunteer Courts held at Murray's Cross, Grangebellew and elsewhere appeared regularly in the local press. Not having access to official state penitentiaries such as Kilmainham Jail or Mountjoy Jail to punish convicted wrongdoers, the 'alternate government' was handicapped in the matter of imposing sentences. At the Grangebellew Court a man pleaded guilty to stealing £10. The sentence handed down was that he would be 'paraded after the principal Mass at Dunleer the following Sunday, bearing a printed card stating the nature of his offence'.

One of the Volunteer Justices was Larry Walsh. He later recalled having sentenced two ne'er-do-wells to be expelled to England for their misdeeds. They were thereupon frog-marched to Larne and deposited on a steamer bound for Liverpool. By the time the escorting officer had returned to Drogheda, the culprits were also back!

The policing scenes at Bellewstown Races were repeated a few weeks later at Laytown Races when 'the Forces of Occupation attempted to provoke a breach of the peace in the district', as reported in the local press. A Volunteer policeman on traffic duty at the crossroads near Julianstown was approached by the military. As expected, they demanded that he remove his armlet. He explained to them that he was performing a duty which 'a certain section of the enemy forces in Ireland were supposed to perform and for which they were being paid [but were nowhere to be seen]'. The Colonel stated that he 'did not want to cause any trouble and conveyed the impression that he was not altogether keen on his job'. The Volunteers on duty at the race meeting continued to display their armlets without hindrance.

Christmas 1920 passed rather quietly – at least by the standard of the times. The populace had become inured to events that, in normal circumstances, would have been headline news: -

- At least a dozen houses in the Rathmullen and Tullyallen districts were visited by persons in military-style uniforms (viz. forces of the Crown), sometimes saying they were looking for particular individuals, and invariably making off with property.

- On Christmas Eve some members of Crown forces held up people in Shop Street and searched them.

- A Black and Tan created a scene in the Post Office in West Street. He was not happy with the manner in which he was treated at the counter, especially as he was wearing the King's uniform. 'The warrior lost his temper, produced his revolver, and made an averment that only because the clerk was of the female sex he would make her smell powder. He then proceeded upstairs to the Postmaster's private office where he gave out his views on how a Post Office should be run.[28] He next presented himself in the telephonists' room and brandished his revolver there. He left behind a brace of expletives that were out of keeping with the season of goodwill.

- A public house in the Cord Road was visited by a group of men and goods were taken.

- The Hibernian Bank (at the Tholsel) was mysteriously relieved of a very substantial £3,600 during the night. No locks were broken, and the night watch slept soundly throughout the operation.

- The Christian Brothers' residence at Sunday's Gate was raided by Crown forces and it was subjected to a search. Nothing was taken away.

- On Christmas Eve Ownie and Tommy Kierans (butchers) were on their way home with the day's takings when they were stopped by two men in uniform. A voice said 'Put them up' but they did not comply. Instead they took to their heels, following which a gun was discharged, but they got safely away. Ownie Kierans was a well known businessman and was later elected Mayor of Drogheda.

On a Sunday evening a few weeks later a group of youthful merrymakers were dancing at Beaulieu Bridge to the sweet strains of an accordion and some mouth organs. Several lorry-loads of Crown forces arrived and said 'Hands up!' The women and children were ordered home, and the youths, about 35 in number, 'were rounded up and marched to Millmount barracks where they are still detained'. They were later transferred to Arbour Hill barracks where they were incarcerated for several weeks before being released.

Meath County Council was issued with an Order to make haste in repairing the roads and bridges throughout County Meath that had been sabotaged 'by disaffected persons', as the military described them. The order continued: -

'If further damage to communications is done, or if the present damage to communications is not forthwith repaired, it will be necessary in order to maintain order to restrict movement in the County, and I shall be forced to prohibit the holding of fairs and markets and all meetings.[29]

A list of 11 bridges and roads throughout Meath accompanied the Order, and an immediate response was sought. Blowing up bridges was an effective way of thwarting the Black and Tans. When the IRA had run out of primary targets such as police barracks, they turned to bridges and other lines of communication.

The wholehearted co-operation of the County Council in repairing the roads, etc. did not materialise, so a month later the Black and Tans' threat was put into effect. Every shop in Navan was visited by Crown forces and handbills were distributed which proclaimed the banning of all Fairs, Markets and Meetings in public places in County Meath (Duleek and Oldcastle excepted) as a reprisal for the destruction of roads and bridges. Shopkeepers were ordered to put these notices on public display. The following day the same shops were visited by men with opposite political views and they removed the handbills. They thoughtfully provided receipts for the shopkeepers reading 'Seized by I.R.A.'

Combating the Black and Tans was a deadly serious business, and civilians who were suspected of being informers were ruthlessly 'rubbed out'; it was very distasteful, but deemed necessary. Even Cork, dubbed 'the Rebel County', nonetheless had its share of suspected informers who were known as an 'Anti-Sinn Féin Society'. During a one year period 24 civilians were shot.

Banner headlines in newspapers in those times were unknown. All news items, however sensational, were presented within the confines of single columns in closely-typed, small print, and were given in inside pages – the front and back pages were devoted to advertisements. The columns of newsprint were unrelieved by photographs of any kind – that era also lay ahead. A glance at the news pages of the issues of the *Drogheda Independent* gives a clear indication of the escalating violence throughout the Louth/Meath region during 1921/22. Some of the headings contained in the issue of 20th. May 1921 tell of the turmoil: -

*

GOODS TRAIN HELD UP NEAR KELLS: *Armed men destroyed selected merchandise. A boycott had been put on goods emanating from Belfast because of its policy on Home Rule*

*

STATEMENT OF MR. DE VALERA: *…in which he explained his attitude to Dominion Rule.*

*

BALBRIGGAN COURT: A *Tan was convicted of stealing an overcoat*

*

SHOOTING AFFAIR IN NAVAN: *Man being abducted escaped and was then fired at. Perhaps he was a suspected informer*

*

BICYCLES COMMANDEERED IN DROGHEDA: *Crown forces took bicycles from front of Church and issued receipts for them*

*

QUEENSBORO COASTGUARD STATION: *25 armed men seized and took away telephone equipment at 3.30 a.m. See below*

*

BEAULIEU BRIDGE BLOWN UP: *…and rendered impassable; trees felled across road*

*

DROGHEDA CIVILIANS COMMANDEERED: *…and forced to repair Beaulieu Bridge damaged by subversives*

*

BALBRIGGAN RELIEF COMMITTEE: *A meeting to discuss ways of helping workers left idle following the Tans' destruction of their factory*

*

DROGHEDA HOLD-UP: *Crown forces search dozens of attendees at Fun Fair*

*

DUBLIN CUSTOM HOUSE BURNED DOWN: *Gandon's masterpiece at Butt Bridge torched and all records destroyed*

*

ARMS FIND NEAR NAVAN: *Crown forces found cache in an old tree trunk*

*

REPORTED CAPTURES AT DROGHEDA: *200 rifles, etc. found at Beamore, and 89 in another location*

*

DROGHEDA FATALITY: *Man killed by Tan in Shop Street pub*

*

BALBRIGGAN SHOOTING: *...police sergeant shot dead*
*

COURTMARTIAL ON TWO NAVAN MEN: *They had fired on police*
*

MOTOR CAR RETURNED: *Commandeered car taken by*
Crown forces returned. Cars taken by Tans were common occurrences
*

MAILS SIEZED AT SWORDS: *Postman held up and his mails taken*
*

All the above events occurred within the time-span of a single week in Drogheda and in the general area of Meath and south Louth (excepting Gandon's masterpiece – the conflagration at the Custom House, was, of course, in Dublin). They provide us with some idea of the subversive activities that were relentlessly being carried on throughout the region. Several lesser news items of a violent nature were also reported in the same issue of the paper. It should be noted that throughout this period the 'Crown forces' did not always wear the black-and-tan type clothing. They had raided gents' outfitters premises and taken away lorry-loads of clothing. This enables them wear mufti, a strategy that made identification difficult when outrages were taking place, although an English accent often revealed what the apparel was intended to hide. Public houses were popular targets, providing the culprits with free liquor.

The episode at the Coastguard Station in Queensboro' mentioned above was a prelude to its subsequent destruction. In a co-ordinated effort the stations at Queensboro' and Laytown were destroyed on the same night. The platoon assigned to blow up the Laytown station was led by Harry Fairclough who, in later life, described the occasion. Before demolishing the station, they took the precaution of tying up its occupants and destroying the stock of flares. To their consternation, some flares soon illuminated the sky. One of the occupants had freed himself and used emergency flares to alert the Tans in nearby Gormanston. The ditches from Gormanston to Laytown were raked with machine-gun fire as the Crossley tenders raced through the country roads that night. But the platoon had set off for Drogheda along the railway lines and they were lying on their stomachs on a bridge as the Tans passed underneath. This was a close call, but the men finally reached their homes safely. It was the norm for the Tans to call on the workplaces of suspected activists immediately following an IRA raid, and a vacant workplace indicated to the Tans that a worker had been active the previous night. Fairclough explained that both his workplace and home were raided on many occasions, but he always ensured to report punctually for work on the morning following a raid.

The Coastguards Station at Queensboro' was a substantial red-bricked building; it then lay roofless, derelict and with gaping windows for a quarter of a century until it was taken over and adapting as private homes after World War II.

THE TRUCE: Eventually a Truce was called, and on 11th July 1921 hostilities ceased. How long the war could have continued is difficult to say; Great Britain had unlimited reserves of manpower, but the IRA were probably at the pin of their collar. Drogheda celebrated the occasion of the Truce with the sounding of factory horns. The RIC stowed away their firearms, and the Black and Tans retired to their barracks in Gormanston. The populace breathed a sigh of relief and were pleased that the curfew was lifted. They were once again able to walk the streets of Drogheda without fear of interference or molestation. The guns fell silent at last.

The Prime Minister throughout this period was David Lloyd George, and the concept of subduing Ireland by means of the Black and Tans was his brainchild. He was a conniving, slippery, wily little Welshman. He undeservedly enjoyed a respectable reputation among the Allies through his achievements in the latter part of the Great War, and later in placating the trade unions who were in a belligerent mood.

'... Yet it was all dust and ashes. Each success lowered his reputation instead of adding to it, [and he later became] the most hated and distrusted figure in British politics. This was partly due to his method that in his own words was: 'I was never in favour of costly frontal attacks, either in war or politics, if there was a way round'. ... He did not browbeat his followers. Instead he led them with much blowing of trumpets in one direction until the moment when they discovered that he had brought them to an exactly opposite conclusion ... Ireland was the supreme example. Lloyd George's successful peace was preceded by **THE BLACK AND TANS, ONE OF THE MOST ATROCIOUS EPISODES IN BRITISH HISTORY'.**[30]

David Lloyd George, Prime Minister: *Devious and deceitful, the Drogheda Independent was not taken in by his powers of persuasion - it described him as a 'tricky little playboy' and repeatedly castigated him.*

The foregoing assessment of Lloyd George's character is indeed remarkable. Not only is it nakedly frank, but also we must take particular cognisance of the fact that its author was one of the most eminent authorities on the politics that lay behind modern warfare, a specialist who has written many books on the subject. The emphasis given here in bold italics is this author's, but the actual words, so candidly expressed, are those of the well known author A.J.P. Taylor, who established a reputation as a lecturer and diplomatic historian; he had much to say about the career of devious David Lloyd George, unmasking him and exposing him for what he truly was.

For that matter, Lloyd George's sleight-of-hand performances failed to hoodwink the people of Drogheda; the *Drogheda Independent* continually referred to him in a disparaging way, even before he let loose the Black and Tans on the Irish people, and before he foisted the Truce on Collins, as *"that tricky little playboy"*.[31]

It was within his power to redeem England's wrongs of the past by bowing to the legitimate demands being made during the Truce negotiations in London. But he lacked the necessary grace. Smart as he thought he was, he and his wiles achieved nothing constructive – indeed, they were counter-productive. The strong-arm tactics employed by his heavies, the Black and Tans, had created mayhem, and had the effect of turning the main body of the Irish people against Britain. It is hardly an oversimplification to say that the tragedy of the Civil War which immediately followed the Truce can be laid at his feet, for in foisting his version of a solution on a reluctant Michael Collins, he effectively set one half of Ireland's population against the other half, causing immeasurable anguish and creating the bloodbath in which the infant State was born.

AMBUSH AT THE BLACK BULL: Violence unexpectedly erupted again in Drogheda on 30th April 1922. The incident that occurred next was a portent of things to come, a prelude to what would later develop into the Civil War. The Treaty had been in force for four months at this stage, but a group of dissidents were not happy with its terms. They did not recognise it and they set about continuing the struggle with Britain.

The Black and Tans were lying low in Gormanston Camp. It had become a regular occurrence for one of their members to drive to Drogheda every Sunday to convey a clergyman to the Camp for a religious service. The dissidents knew this routine. There were no Crossley tenders or armed guards involved; it was a simple case of an unarmed driver in a private car entering Drogheda to collect a passenger. An ambush was planned.

A better place could not have been chosen for an ambush than the main Dublin Road at the point where it abuts the Drogheda Railway Station. This was, and still remains, a singularly narrow point of the road. The banks on each side are very steep, and overhead is the railway bridge carrying the line connecting Drogheda with Navan, and known locally as 'the Navan Bridge'. Running parallel with the main road on the north side of the main road is the route leading to the actual station and, on the south side, the feeder laneway (Cromwell's Lane) leading to St. Mary's Villas. Both of these side-roads are fringed with stout stone walls. Men positioned behind them and also overhead on the 'Navan Bridge' are in an elevated and impregnable position, and a quarry passing along that route was a prime target that could be picked off at will in an ambush.

All that was now required was a road-block, and this, too, was at hand. The substantial house immediately to the south of this narrow section of the road stands in its own elevated grounds and is surrounded by a coppice of mature trees known as 'McKinney's Wood'. (Mr. McKinney was the owner of the property – he was proprietor of the Drogheda Chemical Manures, Marsh Road). One of the trees, if toppled onto the road, would effectively stop all traffic.

> *"The IRA had a tree half sawn down when someone squealed on them. The Tans, instead of coming along the Dublin Road, came round by Beymore, and the lads were nearly caught"(DF).*

The plan was swiftly abandoned, but some weeks later they selected another point just half a mile further along the Dublin Road that was almost equally suitable for an ambush – at Stameen, at the entrance to Colonel Cairnes' estate (now the Boyne Valley Hotel). At that time there was a significant rise on the roadway immediately to the north of the entrance to the then private avenue. (The rise in question was eliminated in the 1930s when the level of the roadway was lowered by about two meters, but the evidence of the former rise is still to be seen today, with traces of the old tarmac surface remaining on the eastern bank of the existing road). Moreover, this part of the road incorporates a sharp bend. This meant that an obstruction on the road could not be seen by an approaching vehicle in time to allow evasive action to be taken.

> *"Opposite Stameen [the entrance to Boyne Valley Hotel] there is a small lane, and there were two brothers Coyle – they were farmers. The IRA went up the lane and took down two carts and put them across the road, and then they laid in wait in the wood. When the Tans came they saw the carts when it was too late, and they tried to turn around. The IRA opened up and shot the driver."[The narrator claimed that he knew the three persons involved in the ambush, but he took this secret to the grave](DF).*

In the ensuing gunfire the driver, Constable Bentley (22) was mortally injured, following which the attackers dragged him from the car and then sped away in it. Patrick Reilly lived at that time in close proximity to the scene of the ambush, in a short cul-de-sac that presently abuts the gable end of the Flogas premises:

> *"This particular Tan was to bring a minister for a religious service in Gormanston – I don't think he was armed or anything. The Republicans knew their movements and they stopped him*

there at Stameen and shot him. It was around the front gates of the hotel. There were marks of the bullet holes on the stone wall – I think they are there still. My memory of the shooting is that it was a terrible thing to do [because a truce was in operation].

"However, they used to go in to Crilly's pub [now the Black Bull delicatessen, pub and restaurant] and upend everything, demanding drink and all that. The Tans in Crilly's wouldn't pay for drinks. There were bullet holes in the ceiling in my time where they were firing the bullets up, and you'd be unlucky to be above in the bedroom. They would be falling out among themselves with the drink"(PR).

THE SACK OF DROGHEDA: The Black and Tans were incensed by this murder for which there was no provocation, and they were understandably eager for revenge. Millmount had been taken over by the Republican faction at this stage, and the Tans gave the occupiers timely notice of what was about to happen. "They threw a note over the gate at Millmount to say they would be in Drogheda the following night, and if the perpetrators were not handed over, they would burn the place down" DF.

Needless to say, no response was forthcoming from the Republicans. The history of Ireland was now in the process of taking a most painful twist – those who were in possession of Millmount *were anti-Treaty men.* Up to this point Irishmen were united in fighting a common enemy, but the scenario now evolving was cleaving the nation into two opposing factions, and the powder-keg of civil war was about to explode, with all its nightmarish consequences.

The local anti-Treaty men knew what was in store for the town, and they called on numerous houses, seeking volunteers to resist the expected onslaught from the Black and Tans, but the response was most disheartening for them. Most people were content with the terms of the Treaty, and they had already been through enough turmoil.

"John Tully, Davey McDonnell and Harry Fairclough went round St. Mary's Cottages – Legavoureen Park wasn't built at that time. They then went down the Marsh and over the Black Bull. But they only got two recruits, the two McKeowns of the Black Bull, that's all they got. So the following day they [the Tans] arrived in their tenders and drove over West Street breaking windows. They shot up the town and said they would be back the next day to burn it. Singers, the sewing machine shop at the bottom of Laurence Street was set on fire"(DF).

The Tans were hell bent on seeing Drogheda going up in flames. In the dead of night the armoured cars from Gormanston rolled into Drogheda. Some of the tenders surrounded Millmount to prevent the occupants from taking defensive action in the planned rampage. Others cruised around the town, concentrating on the main streets, spraying the shop walls with machine gun fire and breaking many of the shop windows.

"I remember it was the eve of a church holiday. We were going to Mass the next morning in St. Peter's. All the debris was all around the place. They had driven over West Street in the tenders. They threw a can of petrol through Singer's plate glass window – a two gallon can. On the way back they threw a hand grenade in. And up goes the place. They burned Singers to the ground [Singers Sewing Machine shop was the red-bricked building at the corner of Laurence Street and Peter Street; upstairs in the Central Hotel next door was the administrative offices of Sinn Féin]"(JQ).

The ordinary, law-abiding citizens who had always steered clear of politics and subversive activities were so alarmed at this turn of events that numbers of families fled the town to avoid injury or death. A farmer who lived outside the town said: "I remember the time they sacked Drogheda. The people were terrified. We had some cousins in the town; they left all behind them and came out to us" SK. Another town dweller said: "There was a report that our terrace of houses, 'Sandy Row' [in the Black Bull, opposite Glanbia], was going to be burned down. So we took all we could carry and took them up to Stameen House where we stayed the whole night. But the burning did not take place and we came home the next day"[JM]. Others took to the fields.

After the Tans had retired to their lair in Gormanston, some leaflets were found in the smouldering buildings reading:

'This is a reprisal for the shooting of Constable Bentley. Further cases of murder will be more drastically avenged – Black and Tans.'

The good news was that no lives were lost and no blood was spilt. It was essential to restore calm. To this end the Mell curate, Fr. McCooey (later parish priest of Clogherhead) ventured into the lion's den in Gormanston Camp and pleaded with the Tans, explaining that the people of Drogheda were not responsible for Constable Bentley's death. The Tans seemed to accept this, but they demanded the return of the vehicle that had been abandoned at Millmount and then appropriated by the anti-Treaty men. This was complied with by driving it to Julianstown Cross where it was left for collection, and peace was thereby restored.

The IRA were past masters at using propaganda as a tool in winning public sympathy and support. When a constable was killed in Thurles, for example, the RIC retaliated by breaking windows in the Sinn Féin Hall, and then firing a few volleys down the street; this was the extent of their reprisal, a minor incident in which there were no injuries and the damage was minimal. But the IRA tried to fan the flames of discontent by describing it as 'the Sack of Thurles' in the full knowledge that propaganda is a powerful weapon, and they overlooked the fact that the 'sacking' was sparked off by the IRA themselves. The 'Sack of Drogheda' falls considerably closer to the incident at Thurles than to that at Balbriggan.

The upshot of the two years of turbulence was that a Treaty was brokered in London. The talents of Michael Collins cannot be denied, but haggling with devious politicians was not among them. He was bamboozled by Lloyd George during the negotiations, and the signing of the Treaty was to plunge the country into civil war as well as to lead directly to the tragic death of Collins himself.

The final chapter of British forces being stationed in Drogheda was marked by a Military Ball. Eighty-four year after that event took place Georgina Sherlock was still able to recall the occasion: "Before they left, the officers held a Ball in the Mayoralty Rooms and my parents and I were invited. It went on until 2 o'clock, playing foxtrots, the Gay Gordons and the like. The officers were in red tunic and navy blue trousers" GS. Another youngster saw the rank and file departing by steamer:

> "They were disbanded at Millmount, and they were going home. We were all youngfellas, and we were there to see them going home on the 'Coleen Bawn' or the 'Mellifont'. They were all in Jemmy Kiernan's pub [on Steampacket Quay opposite where the ship was berthed], and they were all drunk, and they had Verey Lights going up like fireworks. That was in 1922"(JQ).

And so ended eight centuries of the occupation of a portion – but not all – of Irish land by a foreign power.

Chapter Thirtysix

A Nation at War with Itself: The Civil War

De Valera rallying support at the Tholsel

Wednesday 15th March 1922 was an auspicious day in Drogheda's history. On that day the RIC Barracks at West Gate and the South Quay were vacated by Crown forces, and the occupants headed for Gormanston Camp for the last time. The local Active Service Unit of the newly formed Irish Free State, under Commandant Thomas Gray marched over West Street to the stirring tempo of the Owen Roe O'Neill Pipers' Band and took possession of West Gate Barracks. A large crown was present for the historic occasion, and they cheered lustily 'showing that they were in sympathy with the fall of Drogheda's Bastille'.

It had been 753 long years since the Normans arrived, and most of the intervening centuries had been marked by unrest, deprivation and bloodletting. At last the Irish people could settle down to enjoy the freedom and tranquillity for which so many patriots of the past had striven. But it was not to be.

When Michael Collins and Arthur Griffith returned from London following the treaty negotiations, de Valera refused to accept the terms. Tragically, Ireland was soon to be rent asunder by civil war. Friends who had fought shoulder to shoulder in a common cause were now mortal enemies. Neither Collins not Griffith would survive to see the end of this new conflict.

Drogheda was to experience its full share of action during the ensuing year. An anti-Treaty force (variously called Irregulars, Rebels, IRA, IRB or Republicans) had taken control of both Millmount Barracks and the Railway Station. These vantage points were then besieged by the Regulars who cut off the water supply, also the gas. One of the Irregular soldier, Liam Leech, was killed by a sniper at this point.

Barricades were set up on all roads leading into the town, and check-points were established; permits were required by any person wishing to enter it. West Gate barracks came under fire from snipers who had scaled the tower in the Old Abbey. Sporadic sniping also occurred throughout the town over a protracted period. Scenes reminiscent of the Black and Tan era were now repeated, with many frightened families fleeing their homes to seek refuge with relations in the countryside.

Since the Free State soldiers (or Regulars) in Drogheda were few in numbers, reinforcements were sent from Mullingar. Several civilians were shot and killed by stray bullets in the course of continued sporadic fighting. "The bullets at Millmount were flying. I was so afraid, I had to hug the wall coming home to the Cord Road because I could hear the rifle-fire coming from the direction of Millmount".[1] The Mayor, Alderman Philip Monaghan, one of those who had been jailed earlier without charge and held in Wakefield Prison, received a bullet wound in the neck and was taken to hospital, but the injury was found to be slight.

"They had an armoured train with steel sheeting. As kids, we used to sing 'The engine and carriage were shaking as the bullets were passing by" (JQ). The train, manned with government forces, crossed the Viaduct to dislodge the men occupying the station. These were worrying times for the townspeople, since those with weapons were not experienced soldiers, and guns were being fired indiscriminately. Many families slept on the floor to avoid being shot from stray bullets entering the windows. Even the nuns in the Mercy Convents were not secure. Bullets came through their windows, leaving tell-tale marks on the walls of their cells and the evidence remained for many years afterwards; they were obliged to lay their mattresses on the floor at night. As an infant in his cradle, a bullet struck the wall over the head of Pete McNally, Dyer Street.

A railway engine (protected by sandbags) with Irregulars ran the gauntlet by darting across the Viaduct, heading north. It was sprayed with machine gun fire which came from the Cord cemetery, but little damage was done. It halted at Cartown Bridge because the Regulars had removed the rails at that point, and the occupants were able to make their escape across fields. Railway tracks at several other points were also removed.

The Regulars reconnoitred the area to consider the best way of dislodging the occupants from Millmount. It was decided to use cannon-fire, and a gun was accordingly brought into Slane on the evening prior to the bombardment. The Irregulars, who numbered 35 men, were in fact trapped, being surrounded by the augmented forces of the Free State Army. With no prospect of relief, death was staring them in the face. The cannon arrived at Slane the previous day and was placed in the barrack yard at Slane overnight in preparation for the assault. The last time that Drogheda had heard cannons being fired in anger was in 1690 when a Dutch king confronted an English king. This time it was Irishmen against Irishmen.

Throughout these few years the subversives had been excommunicated because they had refused to take the oath of allegiance to their king. They could not receive Holy Communion in such circumstances, although the priests of the religious orders such as the Franciscans, Capucins and Dominicans were sympathetic to their cause. The impending cannon-fire was a matter of deep concern to the Parish Priest of St. Mary's church – the church steeple was in close proximity to Millmount and was in a most vulnerable position. He entered Millmount and appealed to the occupants to leave. They refused. Under cover of darkness Fr. Purfield OP attended to their religious needs.

Dr. Byrne and his family occupied the house standing at the south-west corner of Slane's intersection. His son, who followed in his father's footsteps as a medical practitioner recalled the occasion:

> "There might have been one or two of the officers in our house [at the cross-roads in Slane]
> and my father entertained them. They said they were going to blow the IRA out of Millmount,
> and they would be operating at three o'clock the following day. That was giving the show
> away [by allowing the Byrne family watch the excitement]. As a result of that little bit of

information I remember my father, who had a long telescope, brought me up to the Hill of Slane and put the telescope on a wall to view what was happening. You could not see very much except a cloud of smoke now and again. But it blew up the place. One of them was Captain Crean – he became fairly important in the Army"(TB).

The cannon guns were then brought into Drogheda the following morning 4th. July and placed close to Cahill's book-binding works at Dominic Street (now Murdock's car park). This location was close to the target, and offered a clear line of fire. Several further accounts of the shelling were given by nonagenarians who, as boys, witnessed the episode from lofty vantage points within the town. One lived at the Nuns' Walk, and from the adjoining Cord Cemetery he had a panoramic view of the southern slope of the Boyne and of the action that was about to take place at Millmount:

- *"The Irregulars were squatting in Millmount at the time, and they wouldn't leave. The others gave them an ultimatum: 'Be out by Monday morning or we'll blow you out'. It was a Church Holiday – the 29th. of June [the Feast of Saints Peter and Paul – the date quoted is at variance with the other date given for the shelling] and we hadn't to go to school. We were off that day and we were prepared for it. Where we lived – it was very convenient – we could see across from the Cord Cemetery" (JQ).*

- *"There was a puff of smoke before we heard the noise. The story is that the gunners were only looking for the range with the first shot. The shell missed and landed somewhere in County Meath [It came down in Beamore in a field, the property of the McCullen family]. But the second one landed in the ball alley and blew the whole place out of it. And every shell that went in we could see the rubble going up every time, but we couldn't hear the sound [for a few moments], and then we'd hear the sound coming across. The gun was placed where the Abbey car park is now. It was Cahill's the bookbinders [employers of John Moran who was killed by the Black and Tans], later Bogue's sawmills. Before that it was the Linen Hall"(JQ).*

- *"The day of the shelling of Millmount there were about 300 Free State soldiers in the town, and most of them were Drogheda men"(DF).*

- *[The proximity of the homes in Duleek St. to the target placed the occupants in a very vulnerable position]. "The soldiers came and told us we all had to get out. Our family was put in a house in Tullyallen for a night or two. I was eight at the time and I slept in a makeshift bed – it was an upturned tea chest" (PM).*

- *"It started spilling rain, and the people blamed the gunfire"(JM).*

The bombardment continued for six hours, and the Martello Tower, which had withstood the elements for 120 years, was seriously damaged and was to remain in a derelict state for almost 80 years. There were no deaths or injuries, as the occupants had already fled, but they were obliged to leave their firearms behind; they also vacated the railway station the same morning. This enabled the Regulars to occupy these strategic points.

The Irregulars were then 'on the run'. Being without weapons to continue their struggle, they set about scouring the countryside, targeting the 'big houses' where they surmised they might acquire replacement weapons. Twelve of them broke into Smarmore Castle and tied up the occupants. A flying column from Dundalk arrived to relieve them and enable them get some sleep. All their plans went awry when one of the servants of the castle undid his bindings and alerted the authorities. They awoke looking into the muzzles of guns held by Free State soldiers. They were then handcuffed, thrown into lorries and taken to Mountjoy Jail.

"They went to Smarmore Castle at Ardee looking for arms. All these places had rifles and arms for their protection. Harry [brother of the narrator] was captured there. He was taken to Mountjoy Jail and shared a cell with Rory O'Connor and Sean T. O'Kelly [later to become President of Ireland]. Then he was put in a cell with an Ardee man called Melia. At about 4 o'clock in the morning he heard footsteps coming down the long corridor. They stopped near

his door. He jumped out of bed and looked through the slot. Rory O'Connor and his cellmate Sean McBride were marched away. McBride came back. They used to go to Mass every morning at 8 o'clock. The chaplain said 'I have something very sad to tell you this morning. There were four men taken out and shot this morning without trial: Rory O'Connor (Dublin), Liam Mellows (Cork), Dick Barrett (Mayo), and Joe McKelvey (Belfast)'. This haunted Harry all his life"(DF).

Fairclough was caught attempting to escape, and this earned him a spell in solitary confinement. He then went on hunger strike for 26 days. Drogheda Irregulars in Mountjoy at this period were Tom Clarke, George Owens, Larry Grogan, Christy Gerrard, Paddy Stafford and Johnny Stafford. They were aggrieved that, although their Protestant colleagues received visits and gifts of tobacco, etc. from their ministers of religion, no such kindness was shown by Catholic priests. They were not given the Sacraments because when asked if they were prepared to take the Oath of Allegiance to the King they answered 'No'. They were later moved to 'Tin Town' in the Curragh Camp; the last batch to be released included Fairclough in 1924.[2]

The Regulars were now fully in control of Drogheda, and they rounded up about 50 known Irregular activists and sympathisers. Additional arrests were made during the months ahead. However, a feature of arrests and the taking of prisoners was the relative ease with which the captives were able to escape. Shortly before the shelling of Millmount 5 Irregulars had been captured and locked away in West Gate barracks. Within two days they were back with their associates in Millmount. It seems that the soldier guarding them had Republican sympathies, so he proceeded to set them free and then decamped with them, taking 9 rifles with him for good measure.

Other prisoners who were detained in the South Quay barracks also escaped. Gormanston Camp (lying idle since the departure of the British forces) was then used as a prison camp, but when a group of POWs was being taken there from Dublin, 18 of them disappeared before reaching their place of confinement. A problem for some participants was in deciding which side they should support. Some Regulars were also imprisoned because they supplied ammunition to the other side.

Throughout the month of July intermittent firing occurred within the town, but no casualties were reported apart from a few unfortunate citizens who happened to be in the way of stray bullets. The action kept the populace indoors, and business in the town came to a standstill. A dance, at which some Regulars attended, was held in the Mayoralty Rooms. The entertainment was interrupted when bullets were sprayed through a window of the dance hall; but only one minor casualty was reported.

An attack was made on Millmount barracks and on the railway station in October by the Irregulars. Its aim was to sabotage telegraph communications with Dublin and Dundalk. A local nest of Irregulars had been joined by a group of 16 who had entered the town on bicycles. Machine guns and bombs were used in the ensuing encounter. Again, no casualties were reported.

Michael Collins, Commander-in-Chief of the Free State Army, had occasion to visit Drogheda periodically. Some schoolboys, dallying on their way home from school, had a brief experience with him:

"A few of us were coming home from school. There were flags and bunting outside the White Horse Hotel [now Westcourt Hotel, West Street]. And there were soldiers with Sam Brown belts – they were dressed lovely. They were Free State soldiers. And this big man came and said with a real Cork accent: 'Hello boys, were you at school today? Good boys!' And he shook hands with me. I didn't know it at the time, but the next day it was in the papers that Michael Collins had a meeting in the White Horse"(JQ).

The 'Long Fellow'   # The 'Big Fellow'

Sketch by Sean O'Sullivan, RHA
Courtesy Old Drogheda Society

Bust in Bronze: Michael Collins
From a private collecrtion

Both of the leading protagonists in the Civil War had connections with the Drogheda area. Eamonn de Valera (sometimes called 'the Long Fellow') was a constant visitor, especially at election times. He married Miss Sinéad Flanagan who hailed from Hampton St., Balbriggan where her parents were shopkeepers. Michael Collins was also a regular visitor. His nephew followed in his footsteps and joined the Free State Army. When stationed at Gormanston he met and married Miss Bridie McCullough whose family were in the licensed trade at No. 37 West Street.

Collins' visit to the town was reported in the *Drogheda Independent* when he inspected the three local barracks, viz. West Gate, South Quay and Millmount. It stated that 'He made a splendid figure in his brilliant uniform, and was accorded a hearty reception by the townspeople'. Little did anyone anticipate that within a month Collins would be dead and buried. Word of his death stunned the nation. Despite the lack of speedy means of communication, the news of his death travelled fast. A resident of John St. recalled a message being passed by word of mouth to a neighbour: "A terrible thing is after happening. They shot 'the Big Fellow"(CF).

In April 1923 de Valera ordered a cease-fire, bringing an end to that tragic episode in Ireland's history. The War of Independence and the Civil War together claimed about 3,300 men who had died violent deaths, most of them occurring in the latter war. Few details were ever revealed of action by individuals at local level – stories of Irishmen being killed by their former comrades were too tragic to be retold; participants always remained tight-lipped. Many of them were unskilled workers, and being idle, they remained in straitened circumstances long after the troubles had ended. A veteran recalled that the matter was given attention:

> *"What is to be done about the old IRA fellows. So Larry Walsh and five others got together. They collected sixpence a week, and if you got sick you got a few shillings – it didn't matter which side you had been on. The women in Cumman na mBan also got together and they would make a quilt"(DF).*

373

Chapter Thirtyseven

The Years Between the World Wars

Peace finally returned to the newly formed Irish Free State, but the path to the Elysian fields of prosperity was a long and rugged one. Freedom from foreign rule brought no solution for the unemployed. Britain was now at peace with the world, and this meant that the British Army and Royal Navy were no longer ready outlets to absorb the idle men. In Drogheda the dole queues were as long as ever, and the familiar sight of the corner-boys standing all day with their hands in their pockets at the Tholsel remained as before. Drogheda was stuck in a time warp.

The town was glad to have its wide diversity of industries, most of which had been in existence in one form or another for a century or more – a legacy from the Ascendancy times. The textile factories in particular were always busy, and the produce were exported throughout the world. The Boyne Mills 'made all the sheets and pillowcases for the army. Big white suits of heavy linen went to Cuba, and white linen also went to New York. Thousands and thousands of bales of canvas [stiff lining for suits] went to Bombay; we also sent out *dhooties* – they were long white loincloths used by the men in India. Now it is the other way round – they are sending stuff here! (TM) (The clattering looms finally fell silent in 1976 with the closure of Greenmount and Boyne Mills). Those workers who had been fortunate enough to find employment in these factories were assured of a job for life provided they were diligent at the workbench.

The scars left by the discriminatory legislation of earlier centuries were still very much in evidence. The political supremacy of the privileged class had gradually faded through the operation of the democratic process, but their long-standing economic muscle in terms of wealth and working capital still remained. This characteristic was conspicuous among the industrialists, merchants and professionals of the town, such as bakers, builders' providers, contractors, drapers, hardware merchants, auctioneers, accountants, etc., the major ones almost in entirety being Protestant.

As for the factories, a glance at the list of the town's main industries during the first twenty/thirty years of the twentieth century reveals this preponderance:- the Boyne Linen Mills, Cairnes Brewery, the Drogheda Ironworks, Drogheda Chemical Manures, Drogheda Oatmeal Milling Company, Eagle Sparking Plug factory, McCann and Hill (millers), Robert Usher (textiles), – these were the industrial giants at local level; all of them were eminent, thriving concerns, and some were important exporters. Together they constituted the town's commercial heart, pumping life-blood in the form of pay-packets into the humble homes of Drogheda and putting stirabout on the tables. At cockcrow the factory hooters sounded as the mill girls stepped nimbly toward Greenhills, the dusty millers and the brewerymen streamed each morning towards their places of work on the Quays and the Marsh Road. The town's labour force in turn was grateful to have such secure industries to keep them in constant employment. *Not one of these enterprises was in Catholic hands* when the Irish Free State was formed in 1922.

The working class element of the town, which totalled about 12,000/15,000 during the first thirty years of the century, was dependent on these firms for employment. They did not experience discrimination on the factory floor – Protestants were not in competition at that level of society. Deference was shown as the occasions arose. "My father, who worked for Henlys [Protestant building contractors], often related how Fred Henly would go about the men at five minutes to twelve on a church holiday to ensure that they had attended Mass, and he let off those who had not already been to Mass – this would not be deducted from their wages"(JW). Discrimination was still prevalent at management and executive level, and this was most noticeable in institutions such as insurance companies, banks, etc. In one of them (about 1950), a manager was reprimanded and was threatened with dismissal because he became engaged to a girl who happened to be a Catholic.

"A family that had someone working in the Boyne Mills or Ushers was well off. For the others there were no jobs to be got, so you just took the boat to England. The Protestants were the people with the money and you never saw a poor one."(JM).

"There was total acceptance of the conditions as they then existed. It was just taken for granted, and nobody questioned it. It was the same in the banks. – there wasn't one Catholic among the staff of the Bank of Ireland"(EC).

"Housing was very bad. From the railway station onwards up the Dublin Road every house was owned by a Protestant on both sides of the road, the only exceptions being Jack Kealy the solicitor and Crilly's pub, right up to and including Colonel Cairnes at Stameen. Our row [seven labourers' cottages opposite Glanbia, built by the Cairnes Trust for their employees] was nicknamed 'Sandy Row' because of Sandy Row in Belfast"(JM).

There had been a boost for both male and female employment when a new factory went into production in 1920. This was the Irish Packing Company. There had always been a cry to process beef locally, instead of exporting it 'on the hoof'. The premises were located on the Marsh Road, and it utilised the latest techniques in handling cattle for slaughter, in butchering, dressing, freezing and packing the meat for export. The animals were herded into lairs in a central yard. A sloping gangway had been constructed along the outer side of the building, leading upwards from the yard to the top storey. The cattle were driven to the top of the gangway or ramp where, one by one, they entered a chamber and were humanely slaughtered. Each carcass was then hoisted by its hind legs with a chain and pulley and conveyed to the butchering department where three gangs of four butchers set to work. They were geared to handle 120 carcasses per day. Lower floors of the building dealt with dressing, chilling, weighing, freezing and packing. Ancillary departments handled hides, gore, tongues, kidneys and offal. The blood was utilised by being collected in barrels. Two ships, the *'Louthside'* and the *'Meathside'* were at hand to transport the finished products to England.

All this sounded very well, but a disappointment was in store for people who expected an early upturn in the economy. Following independence, the Irish economy still remained securely tied to England's apron strings, with over 70% of all exports going to the UK. The prospect of a reduction in the dole queues was as remote as ever. The colour of the letterboxes had changed from red to green, but little else changed.

The Irish Packing Company, which began operation in such an aura of optimism, struggled for survival, and eventually fell flat on its face. Only a year after it went into production it suspended operations while the *'Louthside'* and the *'Meathside'* lay at anchor, one each side of the river, awaiting further cargoes which failed to materialise.

A Dáil Éireann. report dated 11th August 1921, in relation to the Dressed Meat Export Trade, referred in a truly baffling way to

*'... the danger involved in the establishment of a factory, such as that at Drogheda, which it was generally believed at the time **was meant to fail in the first instance and to fall eventually into the hands of the American Meat Trust".***

The issue surfaced again in 1929 when Frank Aiken (TD for Louth) asked the Minister for Industry and Commerce whether he had made inquiries into the failure of the Drogheda Meat Factory, and whether he was prepared to make a statement as to the cause of the failure. Mr. McGilligan replied: 'The failure of this undertaking was due mainly to uneconomic buying on the home market, to high oncosts in the factory, and to the inability of the selling organisation in Great Britain to obtain prices for the factory product equivalent to its quality". In other words, the project was doomed through ill-management at every stage of its operation – apart altogether from the unfathomable pronouncement that 'it was meant to fail in the first instance …'.

The Obelisk, a tall, 135m. (150ft.) tapering stone monument to commemorate King William's victory at the Boyne had been erected in 1736 on an outcrop of rock close to the water's edge and adjacent to King William's Glen. The inscription read:

Boyne Obelisk, Oldbridge, Drogheda.

'SACRED TO THE GLORIOUS MEMORY OF KING WILLIAM THE THIRD WHO ON THE JULY 1 1690, CROSSED THE BOYNE NEAR THIS PLACE, TO ATTACK JAMES THE SECOND AT THE HEAD OF A POPISH ARMY, ADVANTAGEOUSLY POSTED ON THE SOUTH SIDE OF IT, AND DID ON THAT DAY, BY A SUCCESSFUL BATTLE, SECURE TO US AND OUR POSTERITY, OUR LIBERTY, LAWS AND RELIGION.

IN CONSEQUENCE OF THIS ACTION, JAMES THE SECOND LEFT THIS KINGDOM AND FLED TO FRANCE.

THIS MEMORIAL OF OUR DELIVERANCE WAS ERECTED IN THE NINTH YEAR IN THE REIGN OF KING GEORGE THE SECOND, THE FIRST STONE BEING LAID BY LIONEL SACKVILLE, DUKE OF DORSET, LORD LIEUTENANT OF THE KINGDOM OF IRELAND. MDCCXXXVI.

His monument was erected by the grateful contributions of several Protestants of Great `Britain and Ireland.'

Having stood in place and the focal point of both artists and photographers for 187 years, it was inevitable that, under the newly formed Free State régime, it would not be countenanced for much longer. It was seen as incongruous among a people who had finally overthrown the yoke of foreign domination, and a symbol of injustices from an era now left behind. It was blown up on 15th August 1923.

The finger of suspicion for the demolition was pointed at the IRA. Rumours abounded, and a little bird hinted at a different cause. Recently a Drogheda veteran with close associations with republicanism informed this author in a most definitive way that "It was not the IRA who did it – it was the Irish Army that blew it up"(DF). An obituary notice in the Drogheda Independent many years later (October 1977) states that a certain captain in the army

'... travelled down from Monaghan on August 15th 1923, collected his comrades en route, blew up the monument, leaving only a stump to commemorate 'King Billy' and in James Bond fashion returned to his regiment to seek out the culprits the following day'. They were never caught.'[1]

"Kevin Fairclough, and the two Farrell brothers, Allie and Leo, were mitching from school that day, and they got the job of taking the pieces away. Allie Farrell later became Mayor of Drogheda"(DF).

Idleness Prevailed: Emigration was still the salvation for many. Most emigrants headed for England, and a few went to the United States. The scenes of parting with loved ones, often called 'Irish wakes', that are reminiscent of the 1800s still continued in Drogheda in the 1920s

376

and 1930s, although the numbers, by comparison, were much fewer. The vessels serving Drogheda port, the *'Mellifont'* and the *'Coleen Bawn'*, were familiarly known as the 'Melly' and the 'Colly', the latter carrying passengers in addition to livestock. They plied between Drogheda and Liverpool:

> *"The fare was 5/- steerage and 10/- saloon. There'd be singing and dancing on the quay, with people playing melodeons. You'd see boys and girls stuck here and there and they in tears saying goodbye to each other. Others would drink in Jemmy Kiernan's pub on the quay, opposite where the boat was berthed, and they'd come out before the boat sailed. There would be a crowd here singing, and another crowd there fighting, mostly men from Clogherhead; we used to come down to watch them. Some would go onwards from Liverpool to America"(JM).*

> *"There was no work at that time, no work. I started to work at 7/6 [€0.48] when Woodingtons boot factory started in 1934 [aged 19]. 'Dev' [de Valera] got the factories going. Before that I worked in the fields with farmers snagging turnips and that. [Since leaving school seven years earlier he had been idle, apart from casual farm work.] After that I joined the Royal Navy"(DMcE).*

> *"You couldn't get jobs. I was lucky, I got into the Brewery when I was only 14 and I was there all my life. I started in 1934 with eleven-and-nine a week [eleven shillings and nine pence = €0.73]"(KF).*

> *"I started work in McGee's Garage in West St. I got nothing, no pay, for the first six months, and for the next six months I got 2/6 (€0.16)"(PM).*

Incentives were offered for companies to set up factories in the Free State. Edward Donaghy's footwear factory in Lisburn had been set ablaze, as were several other Catholic premises, during the sectarian violence in the Ulster disturbances of 1920 – this set in motion an exodus of Catholics from Northern Ireland. Donaghy availed of the opportunity of acquiring one of the several redundant textile mills in Drogheda. He acquired the mill premises off Trinity St., and Woodingtons (also manufacturers of footwear) occupied the vacant mill property at the Marsh Road. Tariffs were imposed on imported footwear, so these home-based factories thrived, and they provided employment for about 500 workers. Newly formed joint stock companies enabled smaller capitalists engage in industrial production without the necessity of having hands-on expertise, and legislation was introduced which encouraged other newly established enterprises with tax incentives, e.g. the Irish Oil and Cake Mills Ltd. in 1935, and Irish Cement Ltd. shortly afterwards.

The IRA were lying low during the decade when de Valera's party had taken a decision not to participate in government, and accordingly they were out in the political wilderness. An isolated incident is recalled by a local:

> *"Superintendent Casserly was well known for chasing away the corner-boys who regularly hung about the Tholsel. A wave of his cane was enough to scatter them, and he was noted for being very officious. Whether that was the reason or not, I don't know, but anyway his life was threatened – this was about 1932. It seems that some IRA-men planned to do him in, and they got a machine gun for the job. He lived on the Dublin Road next to the Mercy Convent, and the plan was to hide behind the wall across the road and wait for him because they knew his movements; he was working in the barracks until midnight and he would always walk home.*
> *"However, the story goes that one of them thought they were going a bit too far, so he got to the place at 11 o'clock ahead of the others and began spraying the house with bullets, breaking the windows and all that. The front wall of the house was covered in ivy at that time and there is little or no trace of the bullet marks today. It is No. 12 St. Mary's Terrace, the terrace with the flights of steps leading up to the hall doors. I don't know if the men were ever caught and charged, but everyone knew who did it. Casserly left Drogheda shortly after that for a post in the Curragh, and the Courtney family then occupied it"(EC)*

Chapter Thirtyeight

World War Two

World War Two began on the 3rd of September 1939. Within nine months the invincible Nazi war machine had engulfed Poland, Denmark, Norway, Holland and Belgium, and finally France capitulated. Then Britain stood alone against Adolph Hitler and Nazism. The prospects looked very bleak for the free world, and Britain was in imminent danger of being invaded. It was at that time, June 1940, that Churchill made his stirring address in the House of Commons:

> " ... we shall defend our island, whatever the cost may be. We shall fight on the beaches, we shall fight on the landing grounds, we shall fight in the fields and in the streets, we shall fight in the hills; we shall **never** surrender ... "

... these were brave words indeed, especially as they were uttered during England's darkest hour. They galvanised the British nation.

It must be said that a sizeable minority of people in Drogheda favoured Germany at that time, and they gleefully absorbed the endless flow of news of German successes on the various battle fronts during the early war years. Setbacks to Britain, such as the sinking of great battleships and the fall of Singapore were greeted with satisfaction by many individuals, and Drogheda had a full share of these. This sprung, not from any particular affinity with Germany or Japan, but from an intense hatred of England and everything she stood for, a feeling that had become imbued in the Irish psyche caused by centuries of mistreatment.

> "I worked in an office where there were about thirty of a staff. They were all pro-German, and it was terrific reading in the paper that such-and-such a city had fallen, and the victories of generals like Rommel. Many people switched on their radios to hear the German propaganda emanating from Lord Haw Haw: 'Germany calling, Germany calling. This is the Reichcenter Hamburg, Station DJA on the 40 metre band...' But later when we heard of the concentration camps and the furnaces ...[slowly shaking his head] ...If only a fraction of that was true ...! "(DM).

> "My father had a radio, which was unusual at that time – it was a dry battery radio. The men used to come in to listen to Lord Haw Haw. They had no time for the British. When Britain was getting hammered they were quite happy"(JS).

Many others listened to the nightly news programmes being broadcast from Germany in English by William Joyce – dubbed 'Lord Haw Haw' by the defiant British people. Most listened simply for amusement and out of a sense of curiosity; it became a topic of conversation. Joyce's family originated in Galway, although he was born in New York. He spoke with a faint Irish accent, and in speech had the habit of eliding his r's, a peculiarity of many Drogheda people. Thus, the preliminary station announcement 'Germany calling' came across as 'Ge'many calling'. The author as a young boy recalls overhearing a neighbour telling his mother of one broadcast that revealed Lord Haw Haw at his vainglorious best. France had just capitulated, and a mere 30 kilometres of the English Channel then separated Britain from Nazism, and Lord Haw Haw could not contain himself. He gloated that Hitler was now poised for an invasion, and he detailed the consequences that lay ahead for the British people. He then added: "... and as for Ireland, haw-haw, we will make it our cabbage garden!" Whatever the sympathies the Irish nation held towards Germany, they needn't have expected mercy from the Nazis. Western democracy was hanging by a thread.

Hitler later had the temerity to declare war on the USA, thus setting in motion the vast industrial wheels of a hitherto dormant nation, the consequences of which gradually turned the tide in favour of the Allies. But for that, Ireland today would be speaking not

English or Irish, but German, and in Drogheda the Swastika would be flying from a flagpole at Millmount. A sobering thought!

At 4.00 am on the 9th April 1940 German troops swept across the Danish border unannounced. At the same time the Danish air force was destroyed on the ground by German dive-bombers, leaving the Danish government with no option but to surrender. A Danish merchant vessel, the 'Lilleaa' sailed up the Boyne that same day with a cargo of merchandise for Cement Ltd. The Irish authorities rendered its defensive guns, radio, etc. inoperable, and shortly afterwards it was moved upriver to be moored indefinitely opposite the Custom House (now the Employment Exchange). Not surprisingly, fraternising took place between some of the 13 crew members and the local lassies, resulting in at least one marriage. A year later the ship 'set out for Lisbon' which was another neutral port. The navigational equipment somehow malfunctioned, and the vessel took a wrong course – fortuitously or otherwise – and found itself in Belfast. This was at a time when ships in convoy crossing the Atlantic with essential supplies were sent to the bottom with appalling frequency by German U-boats, and replacements were sorely needed.

Drogheda was a strategically important town during "the Emergency", as the war years were called. It occupied an important position on the Belfast/Dublin corridor, and had two airports nearby, Gormanston and Collinstown, as well as a seaport. Precautions were soon taken to safeguard the town in the event of invasion:

* All road signposts were removed so as to inhibit an invading force. The presence today of road signs is taken for granted, but their removal during the war caused endless confusion to all who were unfamiliar with the locality, and travellers had to rely on locals for directions, and this often entailed knocking on doors in the countryside.

* A 'Black-out' was imposed, and this obliged every householder to replace all window blinds with black material to prevent light escaping outside at night time.

* Gas masks were issued to every individual in the State.

* Any factory or business premises that included 'Drogheda' in its title was obliged to expunge it from its fascia board; thus, names such as the Drogheda Gas Works, the Drogheda Chemical Manures and the Drogheda Independent had the first word of their names painted out. The efficacy of this step seems questionable in view of the town's very distinctive features such as the river, the viaduct, Millmount and the various church steeples; an invading force, whether by land or air, would find no difficulty in identifying the town by virtue of its unmistakable visage. Nevertheless, the regulation was enforced.

* The Mayoralty House was commandeered by the army, and a garrison occupied it throughout the war years. A wall of sandbags to a height of about two meters surrounded the building, extending along the edge of the footpath, and a sentry remained on duty night and day, with rifle at the ready.

* Sentries were also posted on the Viaduct. In one incident (unrelated to warfare) a local girl was tragically shot and killed.

* A string of 'pill boxes' were positioned at vantage points along the banks of the Boyne, and also at several strategic points within the town. As a child the author recalls seeing one of these being constructed by an army platoon at the bridge at Beaulieu where a small stream enters the Boyne. On enquiring what they were building, the answer given was 'a toilet'. Military secrecy was at the root of this excusable falsehood, but thankfully the finished object never served its intended defensive purpose, although its suitability as a toilet is another matter!

* The Local Defence Force (LDF) was brought into being, and advertisements were published inviting men of all ages to join. A stout pair of LDF boots and a waterproof ground sheet, issued free to recruits, were an inducement to many. "Churchill had said they were expecting an invasion, and we didn't know which way things were going to go. Roadblocks were put in place and some of us were detailed to man the Collon Road at weekends; we'd be there all night and we slept in the graveyard at Tullyallen with big heavy overcoats. We were issued with Lee Enfield rifles and .303 ammunition. We used to do target practice at the Gormanston Camp facility at Ben Head. We were paid on one weekend – we got 3s.2d. (€0.20)"(PB).

* To relieve the tedium of marching and drilling, a pseudo-battle was arranged one particular weekend for the LDF. It was given the rather vague appellation 'Manoeuvres'. But nobody need have worried. It entailed dividing the local force into two teams which were to engage in an adult game that was akin to a group of children playing Cowboys and Indians: 'Bang! – you're dead!' Some recruits were seen creeping furtively around corners or peddling hurriedly on their bikes with messages to their superior officers, while others climbed onto the roofs of local factories in efforts to outwit the other side. Needless to say, actual firearms were few. No casualties were reported, and that is not surprising because no live ammunition was used. Listening afterwards to the comments of non-participating adults, the general consensus was that Mother Ireland was indeed fortunate that neither Hitler nor Churchill violated her shores. Another incident is recalled:

"My father and Brian Bellew [from Barmeath Castle] were in the LDF. They were detailed to spike Annagassan beach because an invasion was expected. They were sent out with their men to hammer in wooden poles to impede an invading force. When they went out the next morning all the poles were gone – the locals had pulled them up and cut them up for firewood!" (PE).

Feverish preparations were in progress in Britain as D-Day approached. For the actual landings it was essential that the skies be cleared of German planes, and every RAF pilot was needed. It is a curious fact that interned RAF airmen in the POW camp in the Curragh were transferred at that time to a new camp at Gormanston. Officialdom came to the conclusion that the Curragh was becoming rather overcrowded, a circumstance that is explained more derisively by Tim Pat Coogan: 'There were so many of them that they were beginning to affect the health of the Germans'.[2] Someone must have forgotten to secure the locks on the camp doors, the result being that soon all of the internees were across the border where they were able to continue the fight against Hitler.

LIFE IN DROGHEDA DURING WORLD WAR TWO: The people of Drogheda were in a unique position in the matter of observing the religious duties concerning Lenten fast and abstinence. The Friday abstinence and other Lenten regulations, of course, continued to be strictly observed nationwide. But these rules were dispensed with for Catholics in Northern Ireland by virtue of the severe food rationing that applied throughout the UK, including the North. In Drogheda, some of the townspeople 'were more equal than others', the serene River Boyne being the determining factor. A Gilbertian situation had arisen. While the residents on the north side of the town (which forms part of the Armagh Diocese) could indulge in bacon and eggs *ad lib*, the dispensation did not apply to 'the Far Side' (which is in the Meath Diocese), and people living there were obliged to tighten their belts while the appetising aroma of bacon wafted across the river!

The Drogheda Corporation provided garden plots, or 'allotments' in which families could grow their own potatoes, cabbage and other vegetables. These were located in Hardman's Gardens and in the fields now occupied by the Bothar Brugha housing estate.

When Belfast received a severe bombing the fire brigades from neighbouring towns in Éire rushed up to help extinguish the flames. On arrival in Belfast the Drogheda unit received the public's attention by virtue of the fact that its colour was not the usual red associated with fire brigades – it was green.

Curiosity was aroused when a rumour circulated that a plane had crashed-landed in Termonfeckin:

"As soon as we heard the news we jumped on our bikes and peddled off as fast as we could to see it. Sure enough, there we saw a big plane on the strand – a German bomber. It was 'parked' a few hundred yards south of the small river called the Ballywater that passes through the village of Termonfeckin and enters the sea at Seapoint; it was right up against the grassy sand-banks or 'boroughs', intact and safely out of the sea's reach. Maybe the pilot had lost his way, but he could not have chosen a softer or more suitable landing spot, or perhaps he thought that things were getting too hot for him in the flak over Coventry and other such cities, and decided that discretion was the better part of valour. A few days later I went out

again to see it, and the Army were in the process of dismantling it to take it away. In those days all lorries were very small and light, so when a wing was secured onto the back of the lorry, nearly half of it was sticking out at the back. In that way they took away the entire plane, bit by bit"(TG).

On another occasion the town was shook by an exploding bomb that was dropped from a passing plane. Apparently, it was a German bomber that may have lost its way, and it was jettisoning its lethal load to conserve fuel in finding its way home. Fortunately, the bomb fell outside the town in a field at Mornington; the explosion caused every window in the town to rattle, resulting in an alarmed townspeople rushing into the streets or huddling into corners, but the only casualty was a rabbit!

Unemployment was still endemic up to the 1940s, and the tradition of joining the British armed forces had not fully died out. The option of serving 'the King' still remained for many idle men. "My brother Leo joined the British Army. He was too young himself – he was only 15, so he used my name when enlisting" (KF). Emigration was still the safety valve that relieved the pressure of unemployment – thousands took the boat to England and stepped into the places on the factory floor vacated by those who had joined the armed forces during World War II. Even those who were scornful of England were glad to eat humble pie and cross the water where there was work aplenty and pay packets were bulky. The once familiar faces that had disappeared were again seen on the streets of Drogheda at Christmas times, and the marked influx of English bank notes and coinage in circulation was very much in evidence, the English currency taking its place alongside its Irish equivalent in the shops. (Irish currency was on a par with Sterling, with English notes and coins being freely interchangeable).

The benefit to the local economy resulting from this inflow was very substantial, and by the end of World War II Ireland had built up a substantial external credit balance. Another reason for this healthy fiscal position was, of course, the inability to import foreign products throughout the entire war and for several years following the war's end.

LAURENCE J. WALSH (1883-1962)

– **A Pen-picture:** Few people have served Drogheda as well as Laurence J. Walsh, known universally as 'Larry'. He distinguished himself in the administrative affairs of the town during the middle years of the twentieth century, but prior to that he played a full part in the fight for Irish freedom. He had risked his life on many occasions in that cause, and served time in an English jail. When he died at the age of 79 his funeral was attended by the largest cortege ever witnessed in Drogheda, the mourners including such distinguished personages as Eamonn De Valera.

In the lean times of the turn of the century his first job was in the renowned milling firm of McCann and Hill on the Mall, the work, not very uplifting, consisting of attaching labels to sacks of oatmeal. The prospects of advancement at that operation did not look bright for this young lad who was brimming with energy, so at the age of 19 we find him on Ellis Island in the shadow the Statue of Liberty, queuing up with hordes of other emigrants seeking a new life in the New World.

His cousin Fr. Massey ministered in Florida, a hot, clammy, neglected State that was home to the Seminole Indians. There young Larry learned to grow and pack tomatoes for his employer. He also learned to admire the indomitable spirit of the Seminoles. Despite being hunted like wolves to near extinction, that tribe remained ever proud and defiant. They have the distinction of being the only tribe never to have submitted to the white man. Larry had a kindred spirit. He was in constant touch with them through Fr. Massey who was their pastor. Larry could correlate with their experiences – back home he had seen more that his share of similar marginalisation and deprivation.

He next moved north where he was a wine waiter in a superior hotel; he served at the Inaugural Dinner of the newly elected President William H. Taft. Many years later this president's son was to meet up with Larry in different circumstances.

In 'the land of opportunity' we next see him operating a steel press. He played a part, however small, in joining the waters of the Atlantic to those of the Pacific Ocean when the Panama Canal was finally completed. This vastly ambitious project, which between accidents and tropical fevers was responsible for 50,000 deaths, called for the provision of countless steel plates for use in shoring up the walls of the Canal, and Larry was engaged in producing these. His duties also included inspecting the individual plates and initialling them with 'LJW' if they conformed to the set standard.

He constantly yearned for the Oul' Sod, and eventually returned to Drogheda and set up in business in his new home at No. 100 Duleek Street, his letterhead reading 'Wholesale and Retail Provision Merchant'. He also operated a car hire business. His republican sentiments soon involved him in the Irish Republican Brotherhood, and it cannot be denied that, in servicing his various customers throughout East Meath and North Dublin (where there were many IRB/IRA sympathisers), his little van paid visits to homes where any connection with the grocery trade was tenuous at best.

In the immediate aftermath of the Easter Rising the Crown Forces swooped. On 13th May 1916 suspects numbering 273 were arrested overnight and, without trial, shipped over to Wakefield Prison. Ten of these were Droghedamen, and they included Larry Walsh. The peremptory manner in which the British Government had taken this action caused widespread indignation and much animosity, so that after fourteen months of agitation all of them were released.

The War of Independence soon followed, in which Larry Walsh played an active part, being appointed a Lieutenant. He relayed messages for General Frank Aiken (who later became Táiniste and a Minister of State); Government files released in later times reveal that he was in constant touch with Michael Collins. British rule in Ireland virtually collapsed at this period, with Sinn Féin having set up a quasi government that operated in parallel with, but in opposition to, the official administration. Larry was appointed a Justice in the (alternative) Court of Law. He was an associate both of the colourful Dan Breen and also Ben Briscoe who was later elected the first Jewish Lord Mayor of Dublin.

Anarchy prevailed throughout Ireland, and it was at this time that the British Government attempted to curb the activities of the subversives by introducing the Black and Tans. Larry accepted the challenge and was heavily involved in the escalating turmoil. Inevitably, his activities came to their attention, and they sought to impose on him their own notorious form of 'justice'. On occasions he was obliged to vacate his little delivery van in the course of his business trips and disappear across field to evade capture. His son Michael relates:

> "Sometimes he had to escape through the back of the house, climb into Sally Gibney's Lane and then cross into the Protestant graveyard in Mary Street where he would spend the night with a few sacks over him to keep himself warm. The Tans were really out for his blood and in the end he had to seek refuge in a safe house in Liverpool. He did this by dressing as a woman, and the dockers on the quay smuggled him on board the 'Coleen Bawn' – that's how he eluded them. The Tans were frustrated, so they broke into the shed where he kept all the stocks used in his business. They set the place on fire, burning everything – this meant that his livelihood was gone. When things had settled down afterwards some local businessmen helped him to get started again".

He sided with the anti-Treaty faction during the Civil War, which left him out in the cold during the early years of the newly formed Irish Free State. He married his sweetheart Mary Brigid Quatermas in 1924 – her unusual surname tells us of her Huguenot origins.

When De Valera took the decision to engage in administrative politics, Larry re-entered the political scene and stood in the local elections as a candidate in the newly formed Fianna Fail party in 1934. He headed the poll, and was elected on the first count, and was thereupon appointed Mayor. This meant that the first seat on which the Alderman sat during his career as a public representative was the Mayoral Chair of his native town.

This was truly remarkable, but more was to follow. He was re-elected Mayor in each of the following years spanning 1934 to 1942. This achievement of eight consecutive terms was without precedent in the long history of Drogheda's storied Corporation. Incredibly, he was to repeat that achievement in the years spanning 1948 to 1957 – a sincere endorsement of the people's faith in his ability as an administrator.

Furthermore, he entered national politics, and in the general elections he was returned to Dáil Éireann on four occasions, starting in 1937, and totalling 17 years in that role; he also served on the Louth County Council for approximately 20 years. He decided to step down as a TD in 1957 to make way for Pádraig Faulkner. The Taoiseach then appointed him to the Senate in recognition of his dedicated service.

A visitor to the town on one occasion was the American Ambassador. He was received by Mayor Walsh who was able to tell him that in an earlier year he had waited upon the Ambassador's father in an American hotel. The wheel had turned a full circle, because the Ambassador was none other than Mr. Taft, a son of the former President of the United States.

In all, Larry Walsh was Mayor of Drogheda for 16 terms, a record that may never be surpassed, and he was otherwise a member of the Corporation for a total of 28 years. "The attainment of records was never his objective – he was impelled more by the desire to serve the community", according to his son Michael.

Apart from the energies spent on Corporation affairs, he was mindful of the efforts made by those involved in the War of Independence, and he organised the collecting of 6d. per week to help those in need, and also arranged financial assistance for those who fought *on both sides* of the Civil War. He also had close involvement with other committees associated with the town's betterment, in particular the Vocational Education Committee, the Visiting Committee of the Ardee Mental Hospital, the Drogheda Harbour Board, the Louth County Council and the Municipal Committees of Ireland, all of which bodies benefited from the clear grasp he had of every matter coming up for discussion. His skills as chairman of countless such meetings enabled the business to be conducted with efficiency and impartiality. He was still in harness as chairman of the Drogheda Harbour Board in the year of his death.

THE POST WAR YEARS: The euphoria that accompanied the Armistice in the Great War was absent at the end of World War Two. On this occasion Ireland, as a sovereign state, had been a strictly neutral country. The war's end caused a general sense of relief nonetheless, and daily life gradually returned to normal, but it took several years before rationing finally ended. Returning to normal meant that those who had been working in England were now back in Drogheda, back to pursue the perennial quest for employment. Drogheda was in a better position than many other towns, being more industrialised. But factories such as the Irish Oil and Cake Mills, Cairnes Brewery, Irish Cement, two boot factories, the textile mills, etc. failed to fully absorb the available workforce, and the dole queues remained.

The infant Irish nation had got off to a disastrous start in 1922 through the Civil War. Two additional body blows which retarded an improvement in the economy during the 'Thirties were the Great Depression, which was a worldwide malaise, and the Economic War which was of concern to Ireland alone. Then came World War II, putting a brake on any plans for economic development. These factors were compounded by the conservative and idealistic dreams of An Taoiseach, Eamonn de Valera – his pipe-dream of young maidens dancing at the cross-roads, however admirable a concept this may seem, did not put food on the table.

His well-intentioned policies of protective tariffs and trade barriers were erected to promote budding industries at home, but were counter-productive in the long term. This has been well proved in today's economic climate, when tariff barriers have been swept away in favour of free trade allowing unrestricted commerce and setting the wheels of industry humming to the benefit of consumers and producers alike. Thus Drogheda continued to flounder in a state of stagnation, a situation that was to continue for another fifteen years and more, following the end of WW II.

The Saga of the Whitworth Monument: The increase in traffic at the Tholsel caused the Monument's removal in 1894 to the Mall. There it remained for a further 71 years until 1965 when, in an act of mindless barbarity, officialdom took the decision to demolish this unique structure, and the stonework was subsequently carted several times from place to place until finally dumped in a ditch at Newtownstalaban where rubble and soil was bulldozed over it. Such an act of crass insensibility by the authorities in Drogheda underlines the urgency for a more vigilant and enlightened populace to act as 'watchdogs' and to stay the hand of the philistines who may be intent on committing further acts of wanton destruction and sheer, gratuitous vandalism. When the Whitworth Monument was being *officially and permanently torn down*, some members of the Old Drogheda Society – to their eternal credit – made a valiant but vain protest by parading with placards at the site while the destruction was in progress, but an unheeding community otherwise failed to lend support.

A dereliction which is even more scandalous is the fate of the Whitworth Hall itself which had been given as a gift to the people of Drogheda by Benjamin Whitworth. It had been the venue for concerts, operas, film shows, roller skating, whist drives, trade displays, Chamber of Commerce meetings, public meetings and other such functions of public interest for more than a hundred years. Then it was allowed to fall into private hands, and at the time of writing it is the venue where drifters and depraved gamblers amuse themselves with an array of slot machines and one-armed bandits, a pursuit that uplifts neither the town nor a single member of its citizens.

THE RURAL ELECTRIFICATION SCHEME was introduced into Ireland in the early 1950s. It was a significant development that propelled rural Ireland from the darkness of the past into a brighter future. One of the first areas to receive attention was Clogherhead. The inhabitants of the village were as unsophisticated as those anywhere else in Ireland, but they had the advantage of a loosely-knit local organisation, a factor which influenced the E.S.B. in targeting Clogherhead with a supply of electricity because it eased their way in obtaining a consensus. The authorities approached Tom O'Reilly who operated a general store in the village; he supplied the local fishing fleet with everything from ropes to diesel oil, the farmers with seed and bran, and the housewife with the necessaries of the family.

> *"The E.S.B. approached me, asking me to influence the people to accept electricity, and they distributed forms for signing. They needed a 75% acceptance in order to proceed with the project, if not they would move to another destination. There was a lot of suspicion and scepticism – the people thought the electricity came out of the wall and would burn the thatch, so most people refused to sign. So we signed most of the forms ourselves and in that way we got a 90% acceptance. In the homes and the farms people were delighted. This was the first area in north Leinster to be supplied".[3](TO'R)*

Clogherhead, like every other rural area, was greatly isolated during the war, since there was virtually no petrol, and cars were off the road and public transport was virtually non-existent. The scene on the pier a few decades earlier is one of fishermen's wives sitting and chatting while waiting for the boats to return. "They were dressed in shawls and long skirts. My mother asked them what they were doing and they said they were crocheting. They

THE WHITWORTH MONUMENT

Top Left*: Erected in 1876 near the Tholsel with the pennies of a grateful Drogheda citizenry.*
Top Right: *Caringly transported and reconstructed at the Mall in 1894.*
Bottom Left: *Cromwell's successors doing their worst (1965)*
Bottom Right: *The Whitworth Monument today — bulldozed into a ditch at Newtown.*

asked her 'Would you like to learn, ma'am', and she said she would. After that she was able to make exquisite tablecloths and doilies. The fish carts used to come in from Clogherhead and line up in West Street, starting at the Tholsel. "You'd get a dozen herrings for a shilling [€0.06] and one for the baby."(GK)

Throughout the war Britain was gladly accepting all Ireland's surplus farm produce, and by war's end a substantial trade balance in Ireland's favour had accumulated. This was cushioning the overall weakness in the Irish economy, but it was gradually being exhausted in the course of subsequent years.

The Workhouse

Now demolished, it was a symbol of harrowing times, but the elegant stone façade should have been preserved.

Marshall Aid, in the form of many millions of USA dollars, was a godsend which was freely injected into a war-torn Europe. Its aim was to reconstruct Europe and put the prostrate nations back on their feet, and Ireland shared in this largesse. She was living off this and off the fat that had accumulated during the war years. This was a fool's paradise, and the seriousness of the situation was pointed out to Finance Minister Sweetman by a young civil servant of whom we shall hear more – T.K. Whitaker.

There remained the stark fact that in the 34 years leading up to 1960 the average annual national growth was at a dismal rate of 1.3%. After 1958 an improvement in the economy was detectable. Then a miracle occurred. The Annual Average Growth Rate suddenly shot up to 4.4% between 1960 and 1973. Multinational companies began to look to Ireland in their plans for expansion, and Drogheda was to the fore in this regard. Foreign investors recognised that the town had advantages that were superior to many other locations, not least of which was its proximity to Dublin Airport and its own sea port. Drogheda Corporation laid aside a site with facilities for the establishing of manufacturing enterprises – an industrial estate.

An Improving Economy: The wheels of industry had been set in motion and were now gathering speed, and the local workforce was developing a tradition of skills at the workbench. By this time unhealthy religious prejudices had all but vanished. The efforts of the teaching profession were also bearing fruit, and a phalanx of personnel with third level education and managerial ability was to hand.

These benefits underpinned another priceless element that was previously absent from the people's psychological make-up, especially among the working class, namely the qualities of self-esteem and human dignity. For several centuries many of the common people had laboured under the perception of being inferior.

This brings us back to the Battle of the Boyne and its consequences. A perusal of the Minute Book of the Drogheda Corporation covering past centuries clearly shows the steps taken to preclude the majority from sharing in the prosperity that was being generated – earlier chapters in this book have emphasised the exclusiveness of the preserve of these alien

386

masters, an arrangement that the 'new order' of that era had assumed to themselves. The Corporation had ordered:

> *"that they should, to the utmost of their power, preserve those laws inviolate, by which the Protestant Ascendancy has been preserved and supported in their Kingdom, and oppose any attempt to alter the same, or to destroy that repose and tranquillity under which we have so long lived and prospered".*

All efforts in the past to redress this situation had been repulsed, with the military garrison at Millmount always at the ready to enforce whatever legislation was being passed.. Even after Emancipation in 1829 it took a further hundred years to establish a degree of equilibrium in the matter of trade, commerce and employment, and to dispel the inferiority complex which had been ingrained in the Irish psyche – it had left a mark that was almost indelible. It is a compelling fact that it was the lack of manual skills that directed men and women towards blind alley occupations. This had left them without any worthwhile sense of purpose in life; they felt degraded, the consequence being that all too many had made friends with that deceiving arch-impostor – drink.

Irish history had now turned a page to a new chapter. No longer was 'Paddy' the stage Irishman to be lampooned in the music-halls of England. (Exclamations such as 'begorrah', begob' and 'bejapers' were still prevalent in Drogheda during the 1930s.) The era of the unskilled, uneducated labourer had ended at last. In its turn this helped in expurgating that stultifying sense of victimhood in which so many Irish minds were entrapped. Gone too was that deep-seated, visceral hatred of the neighbouring island that, whether real or imaginary, merited or otherwise, had been nurtured in so many Irish breasts. It was an attitude that was utterly sterile and served only to repress the people's progression towards better times. It now dawned on the underprivileged that the future offered more than the mere prospect of a life standing at a street corner or boarding the emigrant boat. *Personal advancement could be achieved by personal endeavour.*

What was the catalyst that brought about these elemental changes in the structure of Ireland's economy? De Valera's successor was Sean Lemass, who became Taoiseach in 1959. He had a more pragmatic turn of mind than his predecessor and he abandoned the protectionist economic policies of the past. He was guided by a new publication called *Economic Development* that was delivered to the government in May 1958. Lemass immediately saw the wisdom contained between its covers. It was published as a White Paper later that year under the title *'Programme for Economic Expansion'*. The work created quite a stir in the civil service, so much so that it was given the distinction of having the name of its author linked to it, a gesture that is without precedent among the hidebound procedures of the civil service. The author in question was T.K. Whitaker.

T.K. WHITAKER – A Pen-picture: The Whitaker family moved from Rostrevor to Drogheda shortly after the formation of the Irish Free State, and resided in Paradise Cottage, off William St. In later life Whitaker recalled: 'I shall never again be as happy this side of the real heaven'. His father was on the clerical staff of the Boyne Mills. Kenneth was educated by the Drogheda Christian Brothers who would have experienced little difficulty in providing him with the foundation that set him on the road to a brilliant career.

One classmate recalls that "He passed out all of us at deskwork. We could see he was in a category of his own"(DM). Another recollection of schoolhood days: "My brother Jack was in his class, and my father used to say: 'Why can't you bring prizes home like that chap Whitaker"(EC). Another school pal sums him up in one short, pithy sentence: 'He could teach the teachers'!(JM). Like every schoolboy of his day, his own memories are not so much of achievements in the classroom but of spinning a top or playing marbles all the way home; in his youth he was skilful both in the hand-ball alley and on the violin. One of his quaint recollections 'is of a man who sold fuel from a donkey and cart. His cry was 'Coal or Coke' but we got in first with 'What do you feed your ass on? (T.K.W)'.

Getting his BA and MScEcon came easy to him. He then took first place in four Civil Service exams, joining the service in 1934. He quickly rose in the ranks and, against all the creed-bound, ultra-orthodox rules as to seniority within the civil service, he found himself at the early age of 39 sitting in the chair of Secretary of the Department of Finance.

He recognised the futility of flogging the dead horse of de Valera's idealism. He identified Ireland's forte as being agriculture, and he advocated the policy of promoting free trade rather than protectionism and tariffs. This was a radical concept. In effect he was urging the adoption of the precepts of the European Union decades before that body was founded, thus easing Ireland's eventual entry into the world of the free economy. His overall policy was expounded in his resounding white paper '*Programme for Economic Expansion*'. Soon afterwards a few German factories arrived in Drogheda, introducing their capital, their traditional know-how and their managerial skills. These were followed a few years later by companies from USA, Sweden, Japan, France and Italy who set up factories in the new industrial estates of the town, and aided by grants. Not all of them stayed the course – the inducement of a tax benefit had been a major stimulant, and when the duration of the tax benefit expired, they packed their bags. But by then the break-through had been successfully made, and Drogheda was on its way. The overall benefits to the townspeople are manifest in the proliferation of private cars, new housing estates and in the smiles of well fed children. The dole queues dwindled and the corner boys were no more.

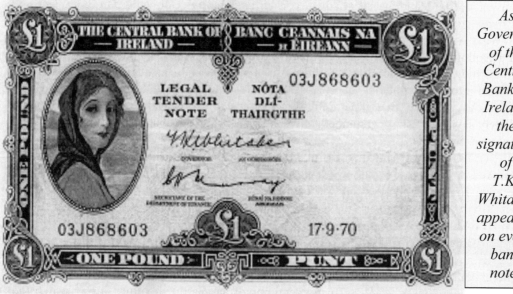

As Governor of the Central Bank of Ireland the signature of T.K. Whitaker appeared on every bank note.

An Taoiseach Sean Lemass shook hands and parleyed with the Prime Minister of Northern Ireland, Terence O'Neill, at Whitaker's prompting. This was a major break-through, a move that led to a thawing of the ice-cold and sterile relationship then existing. It was the first such public meeting between these two neighbouring governments since 1922, and ultimately led to the Good Friday Agreement.

He was Governor of the Central Bank for nine years, was appointed a senator, and in addition he held a host of other top posts with public bodies. He is a worthy recipient of the Freedom of Drogheda, and he still displays a keen interest in the town of his schoolhood days. He keeps abreast of the town's current affairs and attends the functions of the Old Drogheda Society.

Rounding The Corner to Prosperity: Whitaker's plans were put into practice and the result was a spate of industries springing up in many Irish towns that were hitherto dormant. Tax benefits and inducements from the IDA helped greatly. This was the great leap forward, with further enterprises of foreign origin arriving, the evidence of which exists in Drogheda's Industrial Estates. They came from the USA, Japan and numerous parts of Continental Europe.

A cautionary note is sounded for anyone who takes for granted the continuance of these halcyon times. Many of the investors who have been fuelling the Irish economy are of foreign origin, and have but little allegiance to Ireland. Sentiment occupies no place in the cut-throat world of the global economy, more particularly when tariff barriers have been removed. In the Far East alone there are literally *Billions* of hands prepared to snatch the bread from the plates of passive, nonchalant operatives in the West. Easy times induce self-indulgence and laziness. We are faced with the realisation, for example, that China's population stands at one thousand three hundred millions. (In this author's schooldays it was 'only' four hundred millions). A further one thousand millions are in India. Speedy and cost effective lines of communication are rendering all enterprises – from textile manufacturing to automobiles to electronics and call centres – subject to migrating to lower-priced labour sources. As unerringly as water seeking its own level, so does industry today in its impartial search of lower labour costs. It is a disquieting reality that eager hands in these distant regions are waiting in the wings, and their ambition is honed by hunger. We are thus obliged to accept that complacency must never be allowed to replace untiring, cost-effective endeavour.

Apart altogether from the trend for industries to migrate to the Far East, and the threat of being inundated with low-cost products of foreign manufacture, steps must be taken to accommodate the many refugees (political or otherwise) who began to arrive at our shores in great numbers during the early years on the New Millennium from the extended European Union and also from Asia and Africa. At Drogheda's doorstep is the former Mosney Holiday Camp; at the time of writing it is home to a plethora of alien tongues, colours, cultures and creeds – the year 2005 saw 85,000 of them arriving into Ireland. This scenario may not be the Ireland that John Boyle O'Reilly, Pearse and the other patriots fought for, but it must nonetheless be accepted that 'the law allows it and the court awards it'.

Having officially spread out the welcome mat for them, the challenge must now be faced of absorbing them and integrating them into the fabric of our nation, and at the same time accommodating their separate cultures and religions. This will not be easy, especially for the many who entertain private reservations on ethnic matters. What is certain is that if religious conflict is ever again to raise its ugly head, it will not be between Catholics and Protestants, but perhaps between Christians and those who aver so uncompromisingly that there is no god but Allah. Differences between the various Christian sects pale into insignificance compared with the fundamental ideologies of adherents to other religions who have reached our shores in recent decades. Future generations of minority cultures and religions will not be prepared to suffer in silence, as the underlings of the past have done.

Drogheda has changed utterly, and the days of leaning over the half-door and chatting to the neighbour have disappeared irretrievably like last year's snow. The Irish people have suffered the tragic consequences of many centuries of an apartheid culture during which the potential of a willing labour force was allowed to remain fallow, and the barrenness of the Ascendancy's policy of the past has already been covered in these pages. To repeat that policy today would be a double tragedy.

THE GREATER DROGHEDA AREA: The 2006 Census revealed that the town has 28,894 inhabitants. That figure relates to persons residing *within the designated boundary of the Drogheda Borough as presently constituted*. The Borough, restricted by this boundary, is bursting at the seams, and at the time of writing an extension of the boundary is under review. To the figure of 28,894 must be added the two sections of St. Peter's and St. Mary's Districts which lie outside the Borough boundary – this brings the total to 41,538 – by far the highest ever recorded.

To obtain a true picture of the town's growth and development we must also take into account the continuing migration of residents from within the actual boundary towards its satellite villages, e.g. Baltray, Duleek, Julianstown, etc. Some of these villages have shown phenomenal growth since the last census (2002), Stamullen's being an incredible 64% in the four years to 2006. Collectively, the population of these satellite villages has increased in four years by as much as 12,000 souls or 45%. Taking this into account, the population of the Greater Drogheda Area is in the region of 65,000, and is inexorably expanding further. It is clearly the largest town in Ireland, and its growth is accelerating.

The census of 1901 revealed that Drogheda's population was 12,760, and that the catastrophic decline that was a feature of the 1800s had at last been arrested. It had taken until 1971 – all of 170 years – to recover the figure attained at the time of the Act of Union. Famine and emigration had accounted for a decline of perhaps 8,000 persons in the intervening period. Subsequent censuses showed a slight but healthy increase. Thereafter the increase accelerated and at the treshhold of the New Millennium it had passed the 30,000 mark (31,020 in the year 2002). The projection for the first 30 years of the New Millennium sees the graph ascending into the blue yonder.

YEAR:	2002	2006	%
Clogher	1,814	2,491	+37.3
Collon	1,188	1,306	+ 9.9
Duleek	2,941	4,360	+48.2
Julianstown	5,806	8,281	+42.6
Slane	1,336	1,588	+18.9
Stamullen	2,329	3,822	+64.1
St.Mary's	5,457	8,707	+59.6
St. Peter's	2,641	3,937	+49.1
Termonfectin	2,033	2,579	+26.9
TOTAL:	**25,545**	**37,071**	**+45.1**

These figures of population from the Central Statistics Office reveal phenomenal growth in Drogheda's peripheral areas.

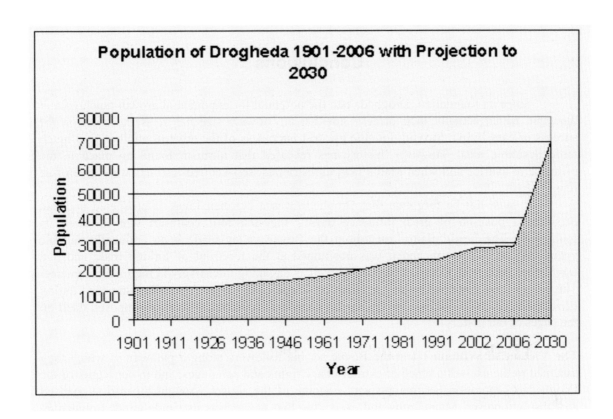

Population of Drogheda 1901-2006 with Projection to 2030

Is Big Beautiful? Is there an inherent danger in Drogheda's continuing growth? Much of the infrastructural development that has taken place during the era of the 'Celtic Tiger' has been in residential property, supermarkets and other extensive retail outlets – all geared towards appeasing the appetite of the indulgent consumer. This expansion must be counterbalanced *by enterprises that create wealth rather than dissipate it* by providing employment for the expanding population. Otherwise the town's growth is pointless, indeed counterproductive.

Logistically, central Drogheda is bursting at the seams, and its medieval streets are unable to accommodate the ever increasing vehicular traffic. Car parking is an unending nightmare. Meanwhile, newcomers continue to arrive from Dublin. The high price of housing in our capital city has directed many strangers towards Drogheda, and these commuters are facilitated with a rapid rail service linking them to their places of work in Dublin. To many people Drogheda is merely a convenient dormitory town. They have virtually no affinity or contact with the local populace – they may have little more than a nodding acquaintance with their next-door neighbours.

Who will these newly-arrived commuters vote for in a local election? The *Drogheda Leader* undertook an exercise in summer 2005 to ascertain the average voter's familiarity with the region's elected representatives and senior administrators.[4] The poll was a very limited one, but the results were nonetheless startling. The average score among the people interviewed was a deplorable 21%. Fewer than one in three identified the Mayor, and only 5% recognised the Town Clerk. Not one of the interviewees could identify the occupant of the County Manager's chair, the most influential post at local government level. These results point to an abysmal indifference and a dearth of solicitude towards civic affairs. It is difficult to envisage such persons making an informed selection of candidates on polling day – if in fact they would take the trouble to cast their votes. It is an axiom of the democratic process that we get the government we deserve. The sleaze perpetrated by public representatives in other areas, some of whom held high office, was exposed only when it was too late.

Conclusions

Since its foundation, Drogheda had the potential for exponential growth much greater than that which actually took place – not that any town's size *per se* is the criterion for success or easy living. Striving for 'the greatest happiness of the greatest number' is a much more desirable ideal. However, history has revealed that altruism found no place in the presence of avarice and when Man's raw, unrestrained, self-centred instincts were given free rein.

It must not be forgotten that Drogheda was a Norman town. It prospered and had occupied a position of great influence during the first four centuries that followed its foundation. The fertile plains that adjoin the Boyne valley made it an eminently suitable venue as a market town, and it was positioned at the forefront of foreign trade and had established links with Continental ports as well as engaging intensively in regional commerce. The commercial structure began to retract by virtue of the trade restrictions imposed during Elizabethen times, and thereafter the baleful spectre of religious differences imposed itself on the pages of our history.

The Victory of William III at the Boyne set his followers along a pathway in which they assumed to themselves a brace of extraordinary rights and privileges, and in consequence the Drogheda Corporation became the very epitome of the abuses wrought by institutionalised and absolute power. Maintaining and exercising that power was its single-minded objective, and this became a recurring theme that is well exemplified in the Corporation's records. The purposeful policy of exclusion created a two-tier system of citizenry in which the majority were side-lined from participation in the the fruits which human endeavour yield. This myopic policy was barren, and prevented the masses from acquiring wealth and of benefiting from the progression that an integrated society normally enjoys. Instead, it created a barrier which frustrated the workings upon which a normal, healthy community thrives, stifling the potential for economic development. This condemned many people to a state of beggary instead of justly enriching them through communal effort.

Had the opportunities to create wealth from the God-given bounties of the earth been apportioned with a modicum of even-handedness, prosperity would have replaced poverty for the multitudes, but the Ascendancy was blind to the travesty of misappropriating these bounties, and it failed to discharge its moral obligation to its fellow citizens.

It is a calamitous irony that the era of wretchedness to which so many were subjected was avoidable – it would have obviated the heart-rending centuries of misery, and the need for the workhouse and the emigrant ship. In the course of time the Ascendancy's policy of exclusion rebounded on itself.

Where Are They Now! : In the long term everyone suffered, not least the Ascendancy class itself. Where are they now! Their dynasty has vanished without trace. The decline first manifested itself in the wake of the Great Famine and it accelerated when legislation was (belatedly) directed towards tenants' rights. Later, during 'the Troubles' of 1919 to 1923 some 200 of the castles and 'big houses' (nationwide)[1] succumbed to the spleen of a resentful population. A knock late at night on a stately portal, a peremptory demand to leave at once and a can of petrol reduced many of these grand homes to gaunt, roofless hulks. One such victim (from Tipperary but who lived in Drogheda in his declining years) described to this author that he and his father sat out the night in the horse stable which was illuminated by the flames that were consuming their lovely mansion. Such losses were a national tragedy, for they represented a significant landmark in Irish history and formed a part of our heritage.

At local level there was no great destruction of Ascendancy property during the struggle for independence. Most of the landed gentry – those that still remained, such as the Osbornes of Dardistown Castle, the Smiths of Annesbrook, Duleek, the Peppers of Ballygarth

Castle, the Coddingtons of Oldbridge and the Cairnes's of Stameen – have nonetheless disappeared. And it must be said that not all of them were despots.

Gone, too, are the Balls, the Barlows, the Balfours, the Fortesques, the Hardmans, the Moores, the Ogles, the Singletons and the rest of the grand parade of gentry who ruled the roost with such culpable, self-advancing motivation. These were the grandees to whom the suppliant natives doffed their caps as they assembled for a foxhunt or trotted past in their carriages. Their names recur repeatedly throughout the pages of this book as the local property owners or members of the Assembly. Each and every one of them is gone. Nothing more innocuous than a few place-names remain today as evidence of their former superiority. Most of their stately homes have since reverted to the people at large and are represented by religious, charitable or State institutions; others are now occupied by the very people they distained. The rest have succumbed to the ravages of time and no longer dominate the skyline.

The disappearance of these families was caused neither by warfare nor by pestilence nor by acts of violence, but by virtue of the insidious canker that was inherent in the very policy that they themselves espoused. They administered their despotic régime through the Drogheda Corporation – this was the structure through which they held sway. But like Samson at the temple in Gaza, they themselves pulled down the edifice, however unwittingly, ultimately bringing about their own downfall. Not a solitary family name among the Ascendancy class who had governed Drogheda so autocratically remains today to render an account.

Even the prestigious Fosters of Collon have faded away – *the mortal remains of the all-powerful **John Foster**, Speaker of both Houses of Commons and later glorified as Lord Oriel, lie buried somewhere in a Dunleer churchyard in an unmarked grave.*

The central message which St. Patrick introduced in much earlier times somehow got lost on the way. It was supplanted by an uncompromisingly illiberal policy that revealed mankind's most base and ignoble qualities – though it was still being applied in the guise of religion. A chasm between Protestantism and Catholicism was thereby created. Inordinate efforts were taken by the power-wielding minority over a period of several hundred years to sustain themselves in a position of undisputed mastery and easy lifestyle at the expense of all others. In the long term there were no winners – everyone lost out, although the suppressed element survived and later bounced back in an emphatic way.

The conclusion presents us with the rueful paradox that there were too many Catholics and too many Protestants, and not enough Christians.

*　　　　*　　　　*　　　　*　　　　*　　　　*

Drogheda Takes the Lead Towards Reconciliation: The errors of the past are now being corrected, and Christians of all shades today live side by side in harmony. This is manifest in the election to the office of President of Drogheda's Chamber of Commerce. At the time of that body's foundation in 1894 the combined Anglican/Presbyterian/Methodist fraternity represented merely 7% of the town's population.[2] In deference to these minority sects, the office of the Chamber's Presidency, by an unwritten understanding, alternated from Catholic to Protestant and back again with the regularity of a clock's swinging pendulum, and this rhythmic harmony continued for the following 60 years and beyond, until there were no longer sufficient Protestant candidates to wear the presidential chains in strict rotation.

A bolder step towards reconciliation was made in Drogheda on Easter Sunday 2006 when the rector of St. Peter's Church of Ireland concelebrated mass with three Catholic priests in the Augustinian Church, affectionately known as 'the Low Lane'. His arrival on the altar was greeted with a spontaneous outburst of applause from the congregation, the vast majority of whom were Catholic'.[3]

'This is the first time since the Reformation that we in Drogheda have had a public celebration of the Eucharist by a catholic priest of the Anglican tradition in a Catholic church of the

Roman tradition ... the difference was minimal. We celebrate the same thing and we do it in the same way', said the Protestant minister, the Revd. Graham who also stated 'Here in Drogheda we have taken one small step in what, hopefully, will be a journey of a thousand miles'.[4]

The occasion was truly historic and it made headline news. The assemblage included members of the C of I community, as well as the Mayor and several Borough Councillors. It was their way of responding to a call made by Taoiseach Bertie Aherne to mark the 90th Anniversary of the Easter Rising. The gesture was symbolic and was an occasion of profound significance, for it demonstrated most emphatically the approval of the populace at large.

The public display of support was very heartening for the organisers, especially for Fr. O'Donovan who spear-headed the event. Whether he will be permitted to sustain this initiatve is another matter. At the time of writing it appears that Fr. O'Donovan has been suspended from his position as a teacher of Church History in Rome. It has also been announced that he will in the coming months face some kind of process or 'trial' before the congregation for the Doctrine of the Faith – a throw-back to the infamous Inquisition of a less enlightened era.

Indeed, if this ordeal is actually to take place, it will elevate Fr. O'Donovan into the exalted company of the brilliant astonomer Galileo (1564-1642), who affirmed the truth that the earth was not the centre of the universe but merely a planet that revolves around the Sun. That pronouncement was deemed blasphemous in the ecclesiastical circles of the time, and the unfortunate Galileo was hauled before the Inquisition. Under threat of torture, he was forced to recant 'before twelve bishps robed in scarlet', and he spent the rest of his life under house arrest. Thankfully, we now live in times of wider circumspection.

By the same token there are aspects of antique English/Protestant legislation that need updating. The statute book still contains some archaic gems of religious intolerance that ought properly to be expunged. Few persons in their proper senses today would volunteer to swim around in the goldfish bowl that is the Throne of England whose occupant (who ought to attract compassion rather than envy), is exposed to unceasing harassment and criticism from every conceivable angle; it is therefore a blessing that Catholics are forbidden by law from occupying it. Such laws – so patently discriminatory – are relics of an age long past, and arc unworthy of being countenanced in the 21st Century.

*   *   *   *

Taking one thing with another, we have compelling indications that the abyss of the religious divide is finally being bridged, and the discord experienced in past centuries that brought so much misery is being replaced by a general aura of benignity that allows communal harmony and equal opportunity to all. In today's more pragmatic world the differences of the past are becoming much less relevant, and the townspeople have recognised that a divided society breeds only fruitless confrontation and distress. Drogheda's ongoing success perfectly illustrates that it is immeasurably more rewarding to live in an atmosphere of accord. Moreover, this is a circumstance that is more in keeping with fundamental Christian ideals. 'Blessed are the peacemakers ...'

BETTER TIMES: By the time Ireland entered the new Millennium the GNP was routinely notching up an annual growth rate of seven to ten per cent, a rate that is phenomenal by any standard anywhere in the world. The labour shortage is being relieved by 184,000 workers of foreign nationality – they now represent 9% of the total labour force; this contribution to the overall economic growth is self evident. It was reported in 2006 that Ireland follows Japan as the second wealthiest country worldwide, and that it is home to 30,000 millionaires, more than a few of whom are Droghedeans

This wealth is being *shared among the populace at large* – in contrast to earlier centuries – and is evidenced by the fine, luxury housing estates that have sprung up beyond Stameen at Deepforde, Grange Rath and the many other townlands throughout suburbia, not to mention the 100,000 Irish families who own holiday homes along the sunny Mediterranean coast.

We see that Drogheda has stepped forward into the Third Millennium in an aura of continued optimism. The town is certainly prospering as never before, enabling it to take its place as a top-ranking, go-ahead, forward-looking city at the forefront of the nation's growing prosperity, leaving Cromwell's visit and the Battle of the Boyne and all their unpleasant connotations as nothing more than disturbing dreams. It is therefore fitting to conclude by echoing the sentiment so endearingly expressed by Peter Harbison in a recent publication:

'... the wounds ... will hopefully soon be forgotten so as to allow us all live peacefully together in this lovely little island of ours'.[5]

THE END

Woman Collecting Turf

by
Nano Reid

Bibliography – Sources Used

'An Observer' (1821)	*A Royal Visit*
Barnard, Toby	*The Kingdom of Ireland, 1641 – 1760 (Basingstoke 2004)*
Bassett, George Henry	*Louth County Guide and Directory (Dublin 1886)*
Barry, TP	*The Archaeology of Medieval Ireland (London 1998)*
Barry, Liam	*Selected Poems, etc. of John Boyle O'Reilly*
Bennett, Richard	*The Black and Tans (London 2001)*
Boyce, D. George	*Nineteenth-Century Ireland: The Search for Stability (Dublin 1990)*
Boran, Pat	*A Short History of Dublin (Cork 2000)*
Bottigheimer, Karl S.	*English Money and Irish Land*
Boylan, Henry	*A valley of Kings: The Boyne (Dublin 1998)*
Bradley; John	*The Topography and Layout of Medieval Drogheda (Drogheda 1997)*
Brennan, Martin	*The Stars and the Stones (London 1983)*
Broderick, David	*An Early Toll-Road (Dublin 1996)*
Byrne, Joseph	*Dictionary of Irish Local History (Dublin 2004)*
Geraldus Cambrensis	*The History and Topography of Ireland (London 1951)*
Cahill, Thomas	*How The Irish Saved Civilisation (New York 1996)*
Clarke, Aidan	*The Old English in Ireland (London 1996)*
Conlan, Patrick O.F.M.	*The Franciscans in Drogheda (Athlone 1987)*
Coogan, Tim Pat	*The I.R.A. (London 1987)*
Cusack, CF	*The Illustrated History of Ireland (London 1987)*
D'Alton, John	*History of Drogheda (Dublin 1863)*
Davies, Stevie	*A Century of Troubles (London 2001)*
de Breffny, Brian	*The Irish World (London 1977)*
de Courcy Ireland, John	*Ireland and the Irish in Maritime History (Dublin 1986)*
De Rossa, P	*Rebels (USA 1991)*
Dickson, etc.	*The United Irishmen (Dublin 1994)*
Downey, Margaret	*From the Nanny to the Boyne*
Drogheda, Lord	*Double Harness (London 1978)*
Duffner, Patrick O.S.A	*The Low Lane Church (Drogheda 1979)*
Dunn, Jane	*Elizabeth and Mary (London 2003)*
Ellis, Peter	*The Boyne Water (Belfast 1989)*
Forristal, Desmond	*The Siena Story (Dublin 1999)*
Foster, RF	*Modern Ireland (London 1988)*
Fraser, Antonia	*Cromwell Our Chief of Men (London 1989)*
Gallagher, Thomas	*Paddy's Lament – Prelude to Hatred (London 1982)*
Garry, Jim	*The Streets and Lanes of Drogheda (Drogheda 1996)*
Garvin, Tom	*Preventing the Future (Dublin 2005)*
Graham, BJ	*Anglo-Norman Settlements in County Meath*
Graham, Revd. M.	*St. Peter's Church of Ireland (Drogheda 2002)*
Hall, Brendan & Donal	*The Louth Rifles (Dun Laoghaire 2000)*
Harbison, Peter	*Irish High Crosses (Drogheda 1994)*
Harbison, Peter	*Treasures of the BoyneValley (Dublin 2003)*
Hall, Donal	*World War I and Nationalist Politics in County Louth 1914-1920*
Hay, Edward	*History of the Irish Insurrection (1803)*
Hughes, Anne	*Hughes History of Drogheda (Drogheda 1893)*
Hudson, M & M.Clark	*Crown of A Thousand Years (Essex 1947)*
Joyce, PW	*A Concise History of Ireland (Dublin 1916)*
Kissane, Noel	*The Irish Famine: A Documentary History (Dublin 1996)*
Knox, Oliver	*Rebels and Informers (London 1997)*
Lawlor, Brian (ed.)	*The Encyclopaedia of Ireland (Dublin 2003)*
de Tocqueville, Alex	*Journey in Ireland (translated by Emmet Larkin)*
Lenox-Conyngham, M. (ed.)	*Diaries of Ireland – an Anthology*
Litton, Helen	*The Irish Famine – An Illustrated History (Dublin 2003)*
Longford, Elizabeth	*Wellington – The Years of the Sword (London 1976)*
Lyons, FSL	*Charles Stewart Parnell (London 1977)*

Moody, TW & FX Martin	*The Course of Irish History (Cork 1967)*
MacKay, Donal	*Flight from Famine (Toronto 1990)*
MacLysaght, Edward	*Irish Life in The Seventeenth Century*
Malcomson, APW	*John Foster : the Politics of the Anglo-Irish Ascendancy (Oxford 1978)*
Marmion, Anthony	*Ancient & Modern History of Maritime Ports of Ireland (London 1858)*
Matthews, Brendan	*A History of Stamullen (Skerries 2003)*
McCarthy, Donal (ed.)	*Parnell – The Politics of Power -*
McConville, Michael	*Ascendancy to Oblivion (London 1986)*
McCormack, John	*A Story of Ireland(Dublin 2002)*
McEvoy, Michael	*Return to The Bull Ring (Drogheda 1997)*
McEnearney, E.(ed.)	*A History of Waterford and its Mayors (Waterford 1995)*
McNally, Michael	*The Battle of the Boyne 1690 (Oxford 2005)*
Mitchell, Frank	*Reading the Irish Landscape (Dublin 1998)*
Mitchell, Frank	*The Irish Countryside (Belfast 1987)*
Moroney, Anne-Marie	*Dowth – Winter Sunsets (Drogheda 1999)*
Munson, James	*Maria Fitzherbert (London 2001)*
Murphy, James	*Ireland: A Social, Cultural & Literary History 1791-1891 (Dublin 2003)*
O'Brien, George	*The Economic History of Ireland in the 17th Century (London 1919)*
O'Brien, George	*The Economic History of Ireland from the Union to the Famine*
O'Donnell, Stephen	*The RIC and the Black and Tans in County Louth 1919-1922*
O'Sullivan, Harold	*The House on the Ridge of the Weir (1998)*
O'Tuathaigh, Gearoid	*Ireland Before the Famine 1798 – 1848 (Malasia 1972)*
O'Malley, Ernie	*Raids and Rallies (Dublin 1983)*
Orpen, Goddard Henry	*Ireland Under the Normans (Oxford 1968)*
Pakenham, Thomas	*The Year of Liberty (London 1969)*
Parissien, Stephen	*George IV – The Grand Entertainment (London 2001)*
Power, Bill	*White Knights and Dark Earls (Cork 2001)*
Rice, Gerard P.P.	*Norman Kilcloon (Dublin 2001)*
Reilly, Tom	*Joe Stanley – Printer to the Rising (Dingle 2005)*
Roche, Richard	*The Norman Invasion of Ireland (1970)*
Ryan, Michael (ed.)	*The Illustrated Archaeology of Ireland (Dublin 1991)*
Skinner and Taylor	*Road Maps of Ireland*
Steen, L.J.	*The Battle of the Hill of Tara*
Story,-	*Wars of Ireland (1693)*
Stout, Geraldine	*Newgrange and The Bend of the Boyne (Cork 2002)*
Stalley, Roger	*The Cistercian Monasteries of Ireland (1987)*
Taylor, AJP	*The First World War and its Aftermath (London 1998)*
Thomas, Avril	*The Walled Towns of Ireland (Blackrock 1992)*
Tichbourne, Henry	*A Letter to His Lady of the Siege of Tredagh*
Tyrrell, John	*Weather and Warfare (Cork 2001)*
Wright, Thomas	*Louthiana (1763)*
Various	*Oxford Encyclopaedia of World History*
Various	*The Irish Sword Journals*
Various	*Drogheda and 1798*
Various	*A History of Julianstown*
Various	*Old Drogheda Society Journals*

Journals and Newspapers

The Drogheda Argus
The Drogheda Conservative Journal
The Drogheda Independent
The Drogheda Journal
The Drogheda Leader
The Irish Times
The Weekly Irish Times

Unpublished Material

Allen, W.P.	*Some Notes on the Old Fortifications of Drogheda*
Colmcille, OCSO, Rev.	*Mattock Rangers GFC*
Garry, Jim	*Townland Survey of County Louth –Mell*
ICA Gormanston Guild	*A History of Gormanston*
McAllister, Patricia	*The Cistercians at Mellifont (Thesis)*
Mountjoy School Magazine	*Special War Number – July 1919*
Murtagh, Harman (ed.)	*Irish Midland Studies*
O'Tierney, Una	*Fair St. and Drogheda (Thesis)*
Presentation Convent	*Historical Notes*
Quane, Michael	*Drogheda Grammar School*
Wright, Thomas	*Louthiana (second book)*

Contributions from Contemporaries

The names of the interviewees in Part 5 of the book are listed hereunder. Their recollections, as given to this author, are in most cases quoted *verbatim* throughout. Although they were given spontaneously and without any reservations, the author has deemed it politic to omit the contributor's name in a few isolated instances*. He has included a few experiences of his own childhood. K. Greene, some of whose recollections are also included, was his mother; her own mother was a member of the McCann family, building contractors, Fair St. – they also feature in several instances in the book.

In cases of persons born prior to 1925, the year of birth is given.

Continued

*Anon		PMcK	Patsy McKenna
PB	Paddy Buckley (1914-)	DM	Dermot Molloy (1913-)
TB	Dr. Tom Byrne (1913-2004)	PM	Paul Mohan (1914-)
EC	Eileen Courtney (1919-)	TM	Tom Munster (1915-)
MC	Maurice Collins (1907-2004)	PMy	Paddy Murray (1920-)
RD	Ray Dempsey	JO	Joe Owens (1890?- 1950?)
NE	Nuala Earley	TO'R	Tom O'Reilly (1913-)
PE	Peggy Emerson (1924-)	JQ	John Quinn (1910-2003)
DF	Dermot Fairtclough (1912-2005)	MR	Mary Reilly
HFJ	Harry Fairtclough Jnr	PlR	Paul Reilly
KF	Ken Fanning (1920-)	PR	Patrick Reilly (1914-)
PF	Pete Fay	MS	Mary Sherlock (1915-)
CF	Cepta Finnegan (1911-2006)	CS	Caroline Smith (1915-)
TG	Ted Greene	BT	Bridie Treacy (1913-)
GK	Gina Kearney (1903-2005)	RO	Religious Order
SK	Seamus Kelly (1917-2004)	JS	John Smith
CM	Carrie May (1922-)	JWh	Jim Walsh
TMcC	Ted McCormack (1913-2004)	MW	Michael Walsh
JM	Jack May (1913-)	KW	Ken Whitaker (1916-)
DMcE	Dan McEvoy (1915-2006)	JWs	Joe Winters (1925-)
MMcG	Marita McGuinness	TW	Tom Wiseman

Index

References/Sources

Chapter One

[1] Mitchell, F., *Reading the Irish Landscape,* Town House. (Dublin.1998)

[2] Stout, Dr. Geraldine *Newgrange and The Bend of the Boyne*, p. 26 Cork University Press (Cork 2002).

[3] ibid. p. 36.

[4] Moroney, Anne-Marie *Dowth: Winter Sunsets*, p. 11 Flax Mill Publications (Drogheda 1999).

[5] Brennan, Martin *The Stars and Stones*, p. 65 Thames & Hudson Ltd. (London 1983).

[6] Ryan, Michael (ed.) *The Illustrated Archaeology of Ireland,* p.112 Town House and Country House (Dublin 1991).

[7] Mitchell, F. *The Irish Countryside* p.223, The Blackstaff Press Ltd. (Belfast 1987)

[8] Gerald of Wales *The History and Topography of Ireland* p. 98, Penguin Group (London 1951).

[9] Pers. comm. Mr. L. Courtney

[10] *Drogheda Independent* (Jim Garry feature).

[11] Drogheda Corporation *Minute Book fol. 708*

[12] Duffner, OSA, Patrick *The Low Lane Church* p.33. Drogheda Printers Ltd. (Drogheda 1979).

Chapter Two

[1] Joyce, P.W. *A Concise History of Ireland* p.57, M.H. Gill and Son (Dublin 1916).

[2] Cahill, Thomas *How the Irish Saved Civilisation* p.192 Nan A. Talese (New York 1996).

[3] Joyce, P.W. *A Concise History Of Ireland* p.57 M.H. Gill and Son (Dublin 1916).

[4] D'Alton, John *History of Drogheda* p.11, McGlashan & Gill (Dublin 1863).

[5] Bradley, John *The Topography and Layout of Medieval Drogheda* p.8 Old Drogheda Society (Drogheda 1997).

[6] Harbison, Peter *Irish High Crosses* pp.43 & 61, The Boyne Valley Honey Company (1994).

Chapter Three

[1] Cahill, Thomas *How the Irish Saved Civilisation* p.211, Nan A. Talese (New York 1996).

[2] Harbison, Peter *Irish High Crosses* p.85, The Boyne Valley Honey Company (1994).

[3] Matthews, Brendan *A History of Stamullen* p.39, Morgan's Press (Skerries 2003)

[4] Boran, Pat *A Short History of Dublin* p.15, Mercier Press (Cork 2000).

[5] Gerald of Wales *The History and Topography of Ireland* p.119, Penguin Group (London 1951).

[6] Stout, Geraldine *Newgrange and the Bend of the Boyne* p. 81, Cork University Press (Cork 2002).

[7] Gerald of Wales *The History and Topography of Ireland* p.120/1, Penguin Group (London 1951).

Chapter Four

[1] Wright, Thomas *Louthiana* Thomas Payne (1763)

[2] Stalley, Roger *The Cistercian Monasteries of Ireland* p.13, Yale University Press (1987)

[3] Barry, T.P. *The Archaeology of Medieval Ireland,* Methuen (London 1988).

[4] McEneaney, Eamonn (ed.) *A History of Waterford and its Mayors,* Waterford Corporation (1995).

[5] Breffny, Brian de (ed.) *The Irish World* p.83, Thames and Hudson Ltd. (London 1977)

[6] Colmcille, Fr. *Mattock Rangers GFC* Journal pp 7, 9.

[7] ibid. p.9

[8] Barry, T.P. *The Archaeology of Medieval Ireland* p.26, Methuin (London 1988).

[9] Pers. Comm. Mr. M. McCullough.

[10] Breffny, Brian de & G. Mott *The Churches and Abbeys of Ireland* p.10, Thames and Hudson Ltd. (London 1976).

Chapter Five

[1] Roche, Richard *The Norman Invasion of Ireland* p.82, Anvil Books (1970).

[2] Orpen, G.H. *Ireland Under the Normans* Volume II

[3] Boran, Pat *A Short History of Dublin* p.25, Mercier Press (Cork 2000).

[4] D'Alton, John *History of Drogheda* pp 91,100, McGlashan & Gill (Dublin 1863).

[5] Drogheda Corporation *Minute Book* 11/11/1656

Chapter Six

[1] Gerald of Wales *The History and Topography of Ireland* p.33, Penguin (London 1951).

[2] ibid. p.35

[3] ibid. p.106-7

[4] Bradley John *The Topography and Layout of Medieval Drogheda* p.26, Old Drogheda Society (Drogheda 1997)

[5] ibid. p.28

[6] Hughes, A. *The History of Drogheda Up to Date* p.204/7 A. Hughes (Drogheda 1893).

[7] Bassett, George Henry *Louth County Guide and Directory* p.53/55 Sealy, Bryers & Walker (Dublin 1886).

[8] Drogheda Corporation *Minute Book.* fol. 20.

[9] Rice, F. Gerard *Norman Kilcloon 1171-1700* p.49 Kilcloon Jubilee Committee (Dublin 2001).

[10] O'Sullivan, Harold *The House on the Ridge of the Weir* p.22 Drumcar Park Enterprises (1998).

[11] Conlon, Patrick OFM *The Franciscans in Drogheda* (Athlone 1987).

[12] ibid. p.7

[13] Duffner, Patrick OSA *The Low Lane Church* p.12 Drogheda Printers (Drogheda 1979).

[14] Boylan, Henry *The Valley of the Kings: The Boyne* p.122

[15] Barry, T.P. *The Archaeology of Medieval Ireland* p.140 Methuin (London 1988).

[16] Colmcille, Rev. *Mattock Rangers GFC Journal*

[17] Moody, T.W. & F.X. Martin *The Course of Irish History* p.120 Mercier Press (Cork 1967).

[18] Barry, T.P. *The Archaeology of Medieval Ireland* p.179 Methuin (London 1988).

[19] Thomas, Avril *The Walled Towns of Ireland*

[20] Bassett, George Henry *Louth County Guide & Directory* p.59 Sealy, Bryers & Walker (Dublin 1886).

[21] Breffny, Brian de (ed.) *The Irish World* p.92 Thames & Hudson Ltd. (London 1977).

[22] D'Alton, John *History of Drogheda* p.170 McGlashan & Gill (Dublin 1863).

[23] *Dublin Penny Journal* 17/11/1832.

[24] *Drogheda and 1798* p.76 Old Drogheda Society (Drogheda 1998).

[25] *Drogheda Independent* (Supplement: Living in Drogheda) p.10.

[26] D'Alton, John *History of Drogheda* p.200 McGlashan & Gill (Dublin 1863).

[27] ibid. p.137

[28] ibid. p.137

Chapter Seven

[1] Breffny, Brian de & George Mott *The Churches and Abbeys of Ireland* p.105.

[2] Duffner, Patrick OSA *The Low Lane Church* p.26 Drogheda Printers (Drogheda 1979).

[3] Conlon, Patrick OFM. *The Franciscans in Drogheda* p.14 (Athlone 1987).

[4] McConville, Michael *Ascendancy to Oblivion* p. 53 Quartet Books (London 1986)

[5] Drogheda Corporation *Minute Book.* folio 808.

[6] O'Sullivan, Harold *The House on the Ridge of the Weir* p. 22 Drumcar Park Enterprises (1998).

[7] McConville, Michael *Ascendancy to Oblivion* p.23 Quartet Books (London 1986)

[8] ibid. p.30.

[9] O'Brien, George *The Economic History of Ireland in the Seventeenth Century* p.3 Maunsel & Company Ltd. (Dublin and London 1919)

[10] Joyce, P.W. *A Concise History of Ireland* p.115 M.H. Gill & Son (Dublin 1916).

[11] Graham, Michael *St. Peter's Church of Ireland* p.4 Drogheda Union of Parishes (Drogheda 2002).

[12] McConville, Michael *Ascendancy to Oblivion* p.64 Quartet Books (London 1986).

[13] Dunn, Jane *Elizabeth and Mary* p.25 Harpur Collins (London 2003).

Chapter Eight

[1] Drogheda Lord, *Double Harness* p.10 Weidenfeld & Nicholson. (London 1978).

[2] Stalley, Roger *The Cistercian Monasteries of Ireland* Yale University (*1987)*

[3] *Dublin Penny Journal* p.35

Chapter Nine

[1] Fraser, Antonia *Cromwell Our Chief of Men* p.73 Manderin Paperbacks (London 1989).

[2] Tichbourne, Sir Henry *A Letter to His Lady of the Siege of Tredagh* p.186

[3] D'Alton, John *History of Drogheda* p.227 McGlashan & Gill (Dublin 1863).

[4] Tichbourne, Sir Henry *A Letter to his Lady of the Siege of Tredagh* p.174

[5] *Rioct na Midhe* 1967

[6] Pers. comm. Mr. K. Allen.

[7] Downey, Margaret *From the Nanny to the Boyne* p.36 Meath East Co-operative Society Ltd.

[8] ibid. p.178

[9] ibid. p.179

[10] ibid. p. 179

[11] Tichbourne, *Sir Henry A Letter to his Lady of the Siege of Tredagh* p.176

[12] Downey, Margaret *From the Nanny to the Boyne* p.37

[13] Tichbourne, Sir Henry *A Letter to his Lady of the Siege of Tredagh.* p.176

[14] ibid. p.182

[15] ibid. p.177

[16] ibid. p.188

[17] ibid. p.190

[18] Borlace, *The History of the Execrable Irish Rebellion p.61*

[19] *ibid. p.62*

[20] Cusack, Mary Frances *Illustrated History of Ireland* p.483 Bracken Books (London 1987).

[21] Clarke, Aidan *The Old English in Ireland 1625-1642* Four Courts Press

[22] Conlon, Patrick OFM *The Franciscans in Drogheda* p.30 (Athlone 1987).

Chapter Ten

[1] *The Irish Sword* No.86

[2] Rice, F. Gerard *Norman Kilcloon 1171-1700* p.193 Kilcloon Jubilee Committee (Dublin 2001).

[3] Fraser, Antonia *Cromwell Our Chief of Men* p.24 Manderin Paperbacks (London 1989).

[4] Davies Stevie *A Century of Troubles* p.111 Channel 4 Books (London 2001)

[5] Pers. Comm. Mr. Tommy Lynch, (c. 85 years) Mornington

[6] *Dublin Penny Journal* 17/11/1832.

[7] Garry, James *The Streets and Lanes of Drogheda* p.104 North East Printers (Drogheda 1996).

[8] *The Irish Sword* No. 86

[9] Foster, R.F. *Modern Ireland 1600/1972* p.102 Penguin Books (London 1988).

Chapter Eleven

[1] Rice, F. Gerard *Norman Kilcloon 1171-1700* p.168 Kilcloon Jubilee Committee (Dublin 2001).

[2] Barnard, Toby The *Kingdom of Ireland 1641-1760* p.29 Palgrave Macmillan (China 2004).

[3] McConville, Michael *Ascendancy to Oblivion* p.93 Quartet Books (London 1986).

[4] Bottigheimer, Karl S. *English Money and Irish Land* p.140.

[5] ibid.

[6] Foster, R.F. *Modern Ireland 1600-1972* p. 111 Penguin Books (London 1988).

[7] ibid. p. 111

[8] D'Alton, John *History of Drogheda* p.188 McGlashan & Gill (Dublin 1886).

[9] Harbison Peter *"Treasures of the Boyne Valley"*

[10] D'Alton John *History of Drogheda p.91, 100*

[11] *ibid. p.227*

[12] *Irish Sword* No. 55 p.143

[13] Drogheda Corporation *Minute Book* 13/10/1665

[14] ibid. 14/10/1670

[15] ibid. 10/1/1700.

[16] ibid. 12/10/1683

[17] ibid. 16/1/1666

[18] Colmcille, Rev. *Mattock Rangers GFC Journal* p.11.

[19] Conlon, Patrick OFM *The Franciscans in Drogheda* p.24 (Athlone 1987).

[20] Duffner, Patrick OSA *The Low Lane Church* p.20 Drogheda Printers (Drogheda 1979).

[21] Drogheda Corporation *Minute Book* fol.. 22 (10/10/1656).

[22] ibid. fol. 25 (9/1/1656).

[23] ibid. fol. 25 (9/1/1656).

[24] ibid. (4/5/1660).

[25] Hughes, A. *History of Drogheda Up to Date* p. 23 A. Hughes (Drogheda 1893).

[26] Forristal, Desmond *The Siena Story* p. 23 The Monastery of St. Catherine of Siena (Dublin 1999).

Chapter Twelve

[1] Davies, Stevie *A Century of Troubles* Channel 4 Books, (London 2001)
[2] McNally, Michael *The Battle of the Boyne 1690* p.33 Osprey Publishing
[3] *The Conservative* 11/2/1860.
[4] Ellis, Peter Berresford *The Boyne Water* p.90 The Blackstaff Press Ltd.(Belfast 1989).
[5] Story's *Wars of Ireland* (1693)
[6] *Drogheda Advertiser* 29/4/1929.
[7] *The Irish Sword* No.95 p.31 et seq.
[8] *The Irish Sword* No 95 p 37.
[9] ibid. No 95 p. 42
[10] Drogheda Corporation *Minute Book* 15/1/1691
[11] ibid. 29/10/1691

Chapter Fourteen

[1] Foster, R.F. *Modern Ireland 1600-1972* p.14 Penguin Books. (London 1988)
[2] Reports from Commissioners on Municipal Corporations in Ireland pp. 811/2
[3] Drogheda Corporation *Minute Book* 12/1/1699.
[4] ibid. 11/10/1717.
[5] O'Brien, George *An Economic History of Ireland in the Seventeenth Century* p,214 Maunsel & Company Ltd. (Dublin & London 1919)
[6] CSO 1861 Census
[7] Byrne, Joseph *Byrne's Dictionary of Irish Local History* p.256 Mercier Press (Cork 2004)
[8] Drogheda Corporation *Minute Book.* 14/7/1669
[9] ibid. 6/10/1669.
[10] Barnard, Toby *The Kingdom of Ireland 1641-1760* p.4 Palgrave Macmillan (China 2004).
[11] O'Tierney, Una (Thesis)

Chapter Fifteen

[1] Allen W.P. *Some Notes on the Old Fortifications of Drogheda*
[2] *The Drogheda Journal* 12/2/1793
[3] Pers. comm. Mr. D. Molloy
[4] Conlon, Larry *The Heritage of Collon* p.37
[5] O'Brien, George *An Economic History of Ireland in the Seventeenth Century* pp140/1 Maunsel & Company Ltd. (Dublin & London 1919)
[6] Drogheda Corporation *Minute Book* 1767.

Chapter Sixteen

[7] Mitchell, Frank *Reading the Irish Landscape*
[8] Conlon, Larry *The Heritage of Collon* p.29
[9] Drogheda Corporation *Minute Book* 15/7/1715.
[10] ibid. 22/11/1814
[11] Wright, Thomas *Louthiana*
[12] ibid. 13/7/1770.
[13] Graham, Revd. Michael *St. Peter's Church of Ireland, Drogheda*
[14] Broderick, David *An Early Toll Road* p.12 Irish Academic Press Ltd. (Dublin 1996)
[15] ibid. p.53.

Chapter Seventeen

[1] *The Irish Sword* No. 42 p.33
[2] ibid. No. 64 p 169
[3] *The Drogheda Journal* 20/6/1793

Chapter Eighteen

[1] Paine, Thomas. *Rights of Man*
[2] McEneaney, Eamonn (ed.) *A History of Waterford and its Mayors* p.177 Waterford Corporation 1995.
[3] Foster, R.F. *Modern Ireland 1600-1972* p.164 Penguin Books (London 1988).
[4] Pers. comm. Mrs. M Sherlock
[5] Drogheda Corporation *Minute Book* fol. 816.

[6] Murphy, James H. *Ireland: A Social, Cultural and Literary History 1791-1891* p.21 Four Courts Press Ltd. (Dublin 2003).
[7] *Drogheda and 1798.*
[8] Steen, L.J. *The Battle of the Hill of Hara*
[9] *Drogheda Journal* 1794 .
[10] *Drogheda Journal* 15/4/1797.
[11] Drogheda Corporation *Minute Book* fol. 966.
[12] *Drogheda Journal* 25/2/1797.

Chapter Nineteen
[1] Pakenham, Thomas *The Year of Liberty* p.66 Panther Books Ltd. (London 1969)
[2] ibid. p.74
[3] Boyce, D. George *Nineteenth-Century Ireland: The Search for Stability* p.6 Gill & Macmillan Ltd. (Dublin 1990)
[4] ibid. p.339
[5] Pers. comm. Mr. J. Tallan
[6] Matthews, Brendan *A History of Stamullen* p.27 Morgan's Press (Skerries 2003)
[7] Pers. Comm. Ms. Christina Devaney
[8] Pakenham, Thomas *The Year of Liberty* p.209 Panther Books Ltd. (London 1969)
[9] Tyrrell, J., 2001 *Weather and Warfare* (p.86): The Collins Press. (Cork)
[10] Hay, Edward *History of Irish Insurrection* p.252 John Stockdale (1803)
[11] Pers. comm. Mr. J. Tallan
[12] Pakenham, Thomas *The Year of Liberty* p 292 Panther Books Ltd. (London 1969)
[13] Knox, Oliver *Rebels and Informers* p.61 John Murray (Publishers) Ltd. (London 1997)
[14] Pers. comm. Mr. T. Wiseman
[15] *The United Irishmen*; ed. David Dickson, Daire Keogh and Kevin Whelsn. The United Irishmen p.177. The Lilliput Press Ltd. (Dublin 1994)

Chapter Twenty
[1] McCormack, John *A Story of Ireland* Mentor Books (Dublin 2002)
[2] Drogheda Corporation *Minute Book* fol. 1031

Chapter Twentyone
[1] Pakenham, Thomas *The Year of Liberty* p.162 Panther Books Ltd. (London 1969).
[2] de Tocqueville, Alex *Journey in Ireland July-August 1835* p.79.
[3] Pers. Comm. Jack May
[4] Pers. Comm. Daughters of Charity
[5] ÓTuathaigh, Geaóid *Ireland before the Famine 1798-1848* p.p.119 Gill & Macmillan Ltd.(Malasia 1972).
[6] Power, Bill *White Knights, Dark Earls.* P.202 The Collins Press (Cork 2001)

Chapter Twentytwo
[1] Pakenham, Thomas *The Year of Liberty* p.184 Panther Books Ltd. (London 1969).
[2] Drogheda Corporation *Minute Book* 1/11/1832
[3] ibid. fol. 218.
[4] CSO
[5] Drogheda Corporation *Minute Book.* fol. 466.
[6] Author's Note: *The Drogheda Corporation's copy of the document was retrieved from a discarded sack of old papers by an observant historian. It was almost illegible, caused by neglect, with mildew having all but consumed it, and it has been deciphered only with the greatest difficulty. A follow-up enquiry made to the House of Lords Records Office elicited this response: '... I am very sorry but the originals of petitions were systematically destroyed between 1834-1951'.*
[7] D'Alton, John *History of Drogheda* p. 220 McGlashan & Gill (Dublin 1886).
[8] Drogheda Corporation *Minute Book* 14/11/1842
[9] ibid. 13/3/1843
[10] ibid. 3/4/1843
[11] ibid.11/11/1844
[12] ibid.16/11/1844
[13] ibid.1/2/1849
[14] Murphy, James H. *Ireland A Social, Cultural and Literary History 1791-1891* p.27 Four Courts Press (Dublin 2003).

Chapter Twentyfour

[1] *Drogheda Conservative Journal* 13/11/47.

[2] Pers. Comm .Patsy McKenna

[3] Pers. Comm. Paddy Buckley

[4] O'Brien George *The Economic History of Ireland before the Union.* p.14

[5] Pers. Comm. Sisters of Charity

[6] O'Brien, George *The Economic History of Ireland Before the Union* p.21

[7] *Drogheda Journal* 9/2/1830.

[8] O'Brien, George *The Economic History of Ireland Before the Union* p.330.

[9] Matthews, B. *A History of Stamullen* p.52

Chapter Twentyfive

[1] Drogheda Corporation *Minute Book* 4/3/1820

[2] Parissien, Stephen *George IV –The Grand Entertainment* p.309

[3] Drogheda Corporation *Minute Book* 4/5/1821

[4] Parissien, Stephen *The George IV - Grand Entertainment* p.309

[5] Hudson, M.E. and Mary Clark *The Heritage of Price Charles* p.126 Harper of Holloway (Essex 1947).

[6] *The Royal Visit* by An Observer (1820).

[7] *Maria Fitzherbert* pp336/7.

[8] Parissien, Stephen *George IV – The Grand Entertainment* p.92.

[9] Drogheda Corporation *Minute Book* fol. 236.

[10] Parsisien, Stephen *George IV - The Grand Entertainment p.317.*

Chapter Twentysix

[1] Ó'Tuathaigh, Gearóid *Ireland before the Famine* p.101 Gill & Macmillan Ltd. (Malasia 1972).

[2] Marmion, Anthony *Ancient and Modern History of the Maritime Ports of Ireland*

[3] Quane, Michael *Drogheda Grammar School* p.22.

[4] Forestal, Desmond *The Siena Story* The Monastery of St. Catherine of Siena.

[5] Pers. Comm. Jack May

[6] Presentation Convent, Drogheda. Notes.

[7] *History of the Diocese of Meath.*

Chapter Twentyseven

[1] Gallagher, Thomas *Paddy's Lament: Prelude to Hatred* p.86

[2] Kissane, Noel *The Irish Famine – A Documentary History* p.126 National Library of Ireland (1996).

[3] *Drogheda Conservative Journal* 12 Dec 1846

[4] ibid.19/12/1846

[5] McCarthy, Donal ed. *Parnell – The Politics of Power* p.40

[6] *Drogheda Conservative Journal* 17/11/1848.

[7] ibid. 8/1/47.

[8] MacKay, Donald *Flight from Famine* McClelland & Stewart Inc. (Toronto1990)

[9] ibid. p.266

[10] ibid. p.263

[11] Matthews, Brendan *The History of Stamullen* p.63.

[12] *Drogheda Conservative Journal* 21/2/1846

[13] Gallagher, Thomas *Paddy's Lament* p.69/70

[14] ibid. p.151

[15] Kissane, Noel *The Irish Famine – A Documentary History*; National Library of Ireland (1995)

[16] *Drogheda Conservative Journal* 18/4/1846.

[17] Pers. Comm. K.Greene

[18] Minute Book Drogheda Workhouse 11/2/1847

[19] *Drogheda Conservative Journal* 23/12/1848.

[20] ibid. 19/12/1846

[21] Litton, Helen *The Irish Famine - An Illustrated History* p.120 Wolfhound Press (Dublin 2003

[22] *Drogheda Argus* 19/1/1861.

Chapter Twentyeight

[1] O'Brien, George *Economic History of Ireland before the Union* p.381.

Chapter Twentynine

[1] De Courcy Ireland, John *Ireland and the Irish in Maritime History* p.197
[2] Longford, Elizabeth *Wellington: The Years of the Sword* p.582 Panther Books Ltd. (London 1976)
[3] *The Irish Sword* No. 88 p.160
[4] ibid No. 89
[5] ibid No. 89
[6] Pers. Comm.Dermot Fairclough
[7] *The Irish Sword* No. 88 p.160
[8] Pers. Comm. P. Murray
[9] Pers. Comm. P. Mohan
[10] *Dundalk Democrat*
[11] *The Irish Sword* No.91
[12] *Drogheda Argus* 7/8/1875
[13] McCarthy, Donal ed. *Parnell: The Politics of Power* p.22
[14] *Irish Sword No.* 84 p.179

Chapter Thirty

[1] John Boyle O'Reilly p.11
[2] Pers. Comm. Jack May
[3] Pers. Comm. Charles Greene
[4] Hughes, A. *The History of Drogheda Up to Date* pp 173/4 A. Hughes (Drogheda 1893)
[5] Barry, Liam *Selected Poems, Speeches, Dedications and Letters of JBOR*
[6] *The Conservative* 9/3/1867
[7] Hobart Library, Tasmania
[8] Port Arthur Penal Colony Records

Chapter Thirtyone

[1] Pers. Comm. K. Greene
[2] *Drogheda Independent* 5/6/1920
[3] Lyons, F.S.L. *Charles Stewart Parnell* p.51
[4] ibid. p.258
[5] Pers. Comm. B.Treacy
[6] Pers. Comm. Jack May
[7] CSO
[8] Pers. Comm. John Smith
[9] Pers. Comm. Jack May
[10] ibid.

Chapter Thirtytwo

[1] DF
[2] JQ
[3] DF
[4] BT
[5] PM
[6] BT
[7] D'Alton J. *History of Drogheda* p. 49

Chapter Thirtythree

[1] HFJ
[2] DeRossa, P. *Rebels* Doubleday (USA 1991)
[3] *A History of Gormanston* by Gormanston ICA Guild
[4] *Drogheda Independent* 4/1/1919

Chapter Thirtyfour

[1] *The Weekly Irish Times* 30th April 1916
[2] *Drogheda Independent.* 24/1/20
[3] Coogan, Tim Pat *The I.R.A.* p.4

Chapter Thirtyfive

[1] *Drogheda Independent* 22/3/19

[2] Reilly, T *'Joe Stanley – Printer to the Rising'*

[3] *Drogheda Independent* 11/1/19

[4] ibid.22/3/1919

[5] *Drogheda Independent* 24/1/20

[6] ibid. 24/1/20

[7] Bennett, Richard *The Black and Tans* p. 165 Spellman Ltd. London 2001

[8] ibid. p.37

[9] O'Malley, E. *Raids and Rallies* p.50

[10] O'Donnell, S. T*he Royal Irish Constabulary and the Black and Tans in County Louth 1919-1922* p44

[11] ibid. p.30

[12] Bennett, Richard *The Black and Tans* p.145 Spellman Ltd. (London 2001)

[13] Pers. Comm. Tom Munster

[14] Pers. Comm. Marita McGuinness

[15] Pers. Comm. Harry Fairclough Jnr

[16] Pers. Comm. Jim Glennon, Skerries. TD

[17] *Drogheda Independent* 25/9/20

[18] Bennett, Richard *The Black and Tans* p/97 Spellman Ltd. (London 2001)

[19] *Drogheda Indpendent* 2/10/20

[20] O.Malley, Ernie *Raids and Rallies*

[21] *Drogheda Independent* 31/1/1920

[22] Pers. Comm. Nuala Early

[23] *Drogheda Independent* 10/7/20

[24] Pers. Comm. Ml. McCullough

[25] Bennett, Richard *The Black and Tans* p.22 Spellman Ltd. (London 2001)

[26] Pers. Comm. Peggy Reilly

[27] *Drogheda Independent* 17/7/20

[28] ibid.1/1/21

[29] ibid. 5/3/21

[30] Taylor, AJP *The First World War and its Aftermath* p.323

[31] *Drogheda Independent* 4/1/19

Chapter Thirtysix

[1] Pers. Comm. Tom Munster

[2] Pers. Comm. Harry Fairclough Jnr.

Chapter Thirtyseven

[1] *Drogheda Independent:* Jim Garry feature.

Chapter Thirtyeight

[2] Coogan, Tim Pat *The IRA* p.208

[3] Pers. Comm. Tom O'Reilly

[4] *Drogheda Leader* 7/9/05

Conclusions

[1] Power, Bill. *White Knights, Dark Earls* p.233 The Collins Press (Cork 2001)

[2] Central Statistics Office

[3] *Drogheda Independent* 20/4/06

[4] *Drogheda Independent* 27/4/06

[5] Foreword to *The Battle of the Boyne 1690 – A Guide to the Battlefield* by Harman Murtagh, Boyne Valley Honey Co. (Drogheda 2006)